Hooked on Horror

Genreflecting Advisory Series

Diana Tixier Herald, Series Editor

Hooked on Horror

A Guide to Reading Interests in Horror Fiction
Second Edition

Anthony J. Fonseca
Our Lady of the Lake University
San Antonio, Texas

and

June Michele Pulliam
Louisiana State University

2002
Libraries Unlimited
Teacher Ideas Press
A Division of Greenwood Publishing Group, Inc.
Westport, Connecticut

For Agnes, who taught me how to curse. I hope that in the next world you have plenty of Pepsi-Cola® and bingo money, and that you find your teeth.

Libraries Unlimited, Inc.
A Division of Greenwood Publishing Group, Inc.
88 Post Road West
Westport, CT 06881
1-800-225-5800
www.lu.com

ISBN 1-56308-904-1

Contents

Acknowledgments

We would like to thank our friends and colleagues for their help and encouragement throughout this project, especially Gary Ferguson at the State Library of Louisiana and Robin Roberts at Louisiana State University. We are also most appreciative of those who actually made this publication possible: Barbara Ittner, our editor, and Diana Tixier Herald. Finally, we would like to thank Rosa for watching many horror films with us and enduring our neglect while we worked on "that stupid book."

Preface

The Appeal of Horror and the Genre's Popularity

Do people really read *that* stuff? If you are a horror fan, you may have heard that question more than once in your life, and if you are not, you may even have found yourself asking it. The answer in either case is a resounding "yes." From ancient oral narratives and retellings of dark and fantastic tales of supernatural, sometimes evil beings, to the inception of "The Gothic" as a literary genre in the late eighteenth century, to the more recent blockbuster sales of novels by Stephen King and Anne Rice, it is obvious that tales of terror captivate audiences of diverse ages and ethnicities. Even today, early in the new millennium, horror fiction is alive and well. Consider the following sampling of statistics taken from various sources over the past fifteen years:

1. *Publishers Weekly*, July 9, 2001, notes that Neil Gaiman's *American Gods* has sold 83,000 copies after three printings. The August 13 issue states that *Black House* by Stephen King and Peter Straub, published by Random, totaled 1.5 million copies in its first printing. Meanwhile, *Blood and Gold* by Anne Rice, published by Knopf, totaled 750,000 copies in its first printing, and Dean Koontz's *One Door Away from Heaven*, published by Bantam, totaled 525,000 copies in its first printing.

2. *Publishers Weekly*, April 2, 2001, chronicles the release of Stephen King's most recent novel, *Dreamcatcher*. The novel was launched by Scribner with a 1.25 million copy printing, and it debuted in the number 1 slot after a week or less in the stores. King's first week's sales at just the three national book chains totaled about 46,000 copies.

3. The following sales rankings are taken from the *Bowker Annual Library and Book Trade Almanac*, one of the best sources for sales information. These figures for the year 2000 bestsellers are from its 46th edition, published in 2001:

   Merick, by Anne Rice, ranked 25th, with 527,237 hardcover copies sold.

   The Green Mile (the reissue of the complete series), by Stephen King, sold 83,676 trade paperback copies.

   Hannibal, by Thomas Harris, sold 3,388,000,000 mass-market paperback copies, ranking third among paperbacks.

   The Green Mile, by Stephen King, boasted 2,400,000,000 copies sold in mass-market paperback, ranking fourth.

> *The Girl Who Loved Tom Gordon*, by Stephen King, sold 1,800,000,000 sales in mass market, ranking tenth.

4. According to *American Demographics Magazine*, July 1989, in 1987 there were approximately 1.2 million buyers of books about the supernatural and occult fiction. *American Demographics* predicted approximately the same number of buyers for the year 2010.

5. In *Publishers Weekly*, Sept. 20, 1993, Robert K. J. Killheffer, in "Rising from the Grave," notes that a 1988 Gallup organization study showed that there were at least two dominant segments in the horror audience: young males and older educated people, mostly females. Earlier, in *The New York Review of Science Fiction*, November 1991, David G. Hartwell, in "Notes on the Evolution of Horror Literature," wrote that this aforementioned Gallup poll indicated that the teenage readership for horror is almost exclusively male, but that much of the most popular horror is read by women. He noted that 60 percent of the adult audience is female, namely women in their thirties and forties. (*Note*: This information also appears in Hartwell's introduction to the anthology *Foundations of Fear*, published by Tor in 1992; the Gallup poll referred to can be found in the *Gallup Annual Report on Book Buying*, published out of Princeton, New Jersey, by the Gallup organization.)

These statistics may surprise readers who are unfamiliar with the genre or who simply eschew its authors, as they wonder why people read horror and watch horror films. They may ask themselves, what makes people enjoy being scared? One easy answer to that question is that life is scary and uncertain, and horror fiction allows us to experience the emotion of fear in a controlled setting and to defeat our fears by facing them vicariously. Although the world of horror fiction is peopled with the ranks of the undead, serial killers, ghosts, and mad scientists, the real world is populated by its own horrors, which are no less terrifying and unsettling: militant followers of terrorist organizations who think nothing of abruptly ending the lives of civilians who are just going about their everyday business; overly nationalistic citizens attacking innocent bystanders because of their appearance, out of a misplaced and misguided sense of justice; angry loners who think nothing of poisoning civilians randomly to protest government policy; drunk drivers who take away the lives of our loved ones so carelessly; child molesters who cruelly ruin young lives; and unscrupulous CEOs who, without compassion or any sense of fairness, downsize labor forces and release toxins on communities to increase the profits of billion dollar corporations. The list of real-life horrors could go on indefinitely.

In horror fiction, such evildoers are made into monsters, and fictional monsters—unlike their real-life counterparts listed in the previous paragraph—can usually be killed, or at least contained. There will always be more terrorists to take the place of those who die or are killed by military action. Nationalism rears its ugly head again and again whenever economies falter or entire groups of people are held responsible for the actions of a few in that group. There seems to be no end to the number of drunk drivers and child molesters who escape through the cracks in our justice system, only to ruin more lives of innocent people. Our belief in free enterprise at all costs will always make it possible for large corporations to "right size" as they call it, ruining the lives of loyal employees so that stockholders and executive boards can further line their pockets.

With fictional monsters, it is not only possible, but probable, that innocent people will triumph over evil. Even though Freddy Kreuger or Michael Myers may live to see another sequel, the pure hearted can ultimately stop them from wreaking havoc on the world. More important, the fans of horror fiction, in this case movie audience members, can leave the theater, safe in the knowledge that they are beyond the pursuit of invincible creatures that invade dreams and murder indiscriminately. In this sense, horror fiction allows us to face, fight, and defeat our fears safely.

So what types of people enjoy horror fiction? Do only people with fears they'd rather not face directly become fans of the genre? Do only people with a taste for blood read King, Koontz, Rice, and Straub? We ourselves were not entirely sure of this answer until we met our first group of students in our first-ever team-taught horror class at Louisiana State University in 1995. More than anything else, we found ourselves pleasantly surprised by the diversity of the students who were attracted to the opportunity to study vampires, werewolves, serial killers, ghosts, and indescribable masses of alien cells. Given the nature of the genre and its fans, we had expected a homogenous sea of "children of the night," eager to begin discussing the latest Koontz maniac, King monster, Rice bloodsucker, or Straub über-entity. In other words, we expected a group of mostly males who read horror and watched horror films because they enjoyed "the scare" or took perverse pleasure in witnessing the dismemberment of bodies. After all, this was the kind of reaction we always got after telling friends that we enjoyed the genre, and we had apparently bought into their rhetoric despite ourselves.

What we found was a class composed of honor students, athletes, older nontraditional students, black-clad goths, buzz-cut boys in baseball caps, body builders, girls with long wavy hair and blue finger nails, film buffs, Pagans, Catholics, Southern Baptists, a few miscellaneous weird people who sat in the back—and one student who looked a lot like Stephen King. The most remarkable feature was that the class was mostly female. All were eager to read writers we had at that time heard little of, and many of them were pleasantly surprised that they enjoyed Bram Stoker's *Dracula*, Mary Shelley's *Frankenstein*, and Kim Newman's *Anno Dracula*. Amazingly, not one of these students had ever committed a murder, tortured an animal, had an insatiable desire to drink blood, or (as far as we know) harbored thoughts of torturing his or her professors and classmates. These students were simply an eclectic collection of average people who had one thing in common: They all enjoyed reading and studying horror. Some liked the adrenaline rush associated with the production of fear; others emphasized the thematic concerns that could be read between the lines, taking a more intellectual approach; still others simply thought horror fiction was fun and exciting, suspenseful and entertaining. The point we are making here is that horror appeals to people in all walks of life, and for various reasons, not always associated with "the scare."

Of course, we are not the first to grapple with this question, as many cultural and literary critics have already attempted to describe the appeal of horror. William Patrick Day argues that people are simultaneously repulsed and attracted to horror, that it is a sort of fantastical manifestation of negative wish fulfillment (*In the Circles of Fear and Desire: A Study of Gothic Fantasy*, University of Chicago Press, 1985). In other words, a horror novel or film is like the accident that compels us to rubber-neck, even though we know in our hearts that we really don't want to see other humans broken and bloodied. Terry Heller takes a more physiological approach to the question of why we enjoy horror. He feels that horror gives people a safe adrenaline rush, like sky-diving with a parachute they know will always open, or riding a roller coaster (*The Delights of Terror: An Aesthetics of the Tale of Terror*, University of Illinois Press, 1987). People engage in these thrill-seeking activities because these death-defying acts allow them the chance to transcend the drudgery of daily life and, in a sense, to come face to face with mortality and walk away. One could say that according to this theory, horror allows us to face our fears and master them. Literary critic Carol J. Clover, on the other hand, looks at horror from a more psychological point of view. She notes that in slasher films, audience members are at various times encouraged to view the world from the perspective of both the monster and the victim (*Men, Women and Chain Saws: Gender in the Modern Horror Film*, Princeton University Press, 1992). This gives the horror fan a chance to vicariously experience fear from various points of view and to emerge unscathed from the theater.

We feel that horror does all of these, and also entertains and teaches. For example, Stephen King's modern classic *Carrie* gives a candid-camera view of a dysfunctional family who would be the quintessential guests on Jerry Springer (an episode entitled "My Mommy Is a Fundamentalist Freak Who Locks Me in the Closet" or "My Daughter Is the Spawn of Satan"). Carrie White's home life is painful, yet the reader cannot turn away from Margaret White's savage abuse of her child in the name of religion. The reader, like Sue Snell, the only character to survive Carrie's rampage on the night of the Black Prom, is able to walk among the exploding gas stations of Chamberlain, Maine, and watch people doing St. Vitus dances of pain while stepping on downed power lines. Yet the reader finishes the book having vicariously faced down the monster, no worse for the wear. Simultaneously, the reader is invited to see the world through Carrie's eyes, and any of us who have been the picked-on child in school can sympathize with Carrie's corrosive anger and know the literal meaning of the phrase "if looks could kill." Above all, the reader of *Carrie* experiences a good story told from multiple points of view by a talented young writer and perhaps learns a bit of a lesson at the end about how, if it takes a village to raise a child, it also takes a village to create a monster. This is a lesson learned all too well from the past decade's gun-toting children in Arkansas, Mississippi, Kentucky, Pennsylvania, Oregon, and Colorado, who have performed their own versions of Carrie's destroying the town of Chamberlain, Maine.

The important thing for readers' advisors to remember when dealing with patrons who are horror fans is that they are not all of one type, and therefore they do not read horror for the same reasons, which means that they will not all enjoy the same writers. Those who are goths (black clad, pale-skinned followers of musicians/bands such as Bauhaus, Nick Cave, Nine Inch Nails, TKK, and Nosferatu and authors such as Poppy Z. Brite, Christa Faust, and Caitlin R. Kiernan) may prefer the decadence of John Shirley and Kathe Koja, whereas those who enjoy action adventure will certainly want books by Dean Koontz or P. N. Elrod. And the more sophisticated horror fans (those who have read almost everything in the genre) will probably wish to find alternative literary works by the likes of Kim Newman, Bentley Little, or Ramsey Campbell. Librarians should also keep in mind that these readers are not disturbed individuals who need counseling, but are simply people who enjoy curling up with a scary or thought-provoking book. School librarians in particular should attempt to understand the reading tastes of their horror patrons, for it is in school libraries that horror works are often challenged and sometimes singled out for censorship. The bottom line they should keep in mind is that no child has ever murdered in the name of R. L. Stine or Christopher Pike. Children who go on rampages are products of dysfunctional homes and an aggressive society that exonerates its sports figures and politicians who break rules in the name of anger or financial gain.

Rule number one of readers' advisory is one of Raganatham's Five Laws: every reader his or her book. Understanding that horror appeals to more than simply the baser human emotions will help librarians to realize that every horror patron deserves his or her book of choice, and that no one individual or group has the right, especially given our constitutional freedom of expression, to prevent the match of that reader with that book of choice, even if the book is the latest by Stephen King or Anne Rice. In short, horror fans are not second-class readers simply because they are genre readers and enjoy scary books. They are potential library patrons with the same rights and privileges as the patron who seeks novels by Jane Austen, Zora Neale Hurston, William Faulkner, or Gabriel Garcia Marquez. *Hooked on Horror* is a tool that will aid librarians in granting horror patrons those rights.

Introduction

The Goals of This Book

General Information

Hooked on Horror is an in-depth guide to the horror genre, a genre that has often been overlooked by literary critics, readers, and librarians. The consensus seems to be that "scary stories" are best left for children, to be told around camp fires and published by presses that cater to young adults, and that adults who enjoy horror are at best, childish, and at worst, ghouls who secretly admire the likes of Jeffrey Dahlmer. Cutting our teeth in the academic world of English departments, we grew accustomed to the ivory tower view that Stephen King, Ramsey Campbell, and Anne Rice were simply not acceptable reading material, that the fiction of these writers was somehow inferior to that of authors who published Literature (with a capital L). Imagine our shared surprise when we discovered that some library directors and librarians also viewed horror fans as nothing more than a subclass of "genre" readers (and disturbed ones at that), and therefore as less serious than patrons who read classics or works by Joyce Carol Oates or Toni Morrison, or the latest book on Oprah Winfrey's list. It is perhaps because of this attitude that very few readers' advisory tools exist for the horror genre. In fact, horror almost always gets grouped with the ghettoized genres science fiction and fantasy, which robs readers of even the possibility of comprehensive bibliographies and readers' advisory tools devoted solely to the genre. In other words, horror fiction is mistakenly treated as a subgenre of what for want of a better term would be called fantastical literature or speculative fiction, and therefore usually gets less than one-third of the length of a book-length bibliography, when it gets any recognition whatsoever. It is this need for an in-depth, book-length source on horror fiction that this text addresses.

Hooked on Horror differs from dark fantasy bibliographies in that it is primarily intended as a readers' advisory resource and therefore reflects popular reading interests. It is not a critical or historical guide and review source. For this reason, its annotations usually contain descriptive, rather than evaluative, terms. Unlike earlier readers' guides, *Hooked on Horror*, as its title suggests, deals *only* with horror fiction, without treating it as the red-headed stepchild of the fantastic. Because it deals solely with the horror genre, it provides the reader with a more complete list of *annotated* novels, collections by single authors, and anthologies by diverse hands than currently exists anywhere. In addition, it is written by two experts in the horror field who thoroughly enjoy their work, so the essays that begin each subgenre listing are enthusiastic and informative, and each annotation shows the care and seriousness used to emphasize the appeal of each work, based on its own merits.

Of course, the main function of a readers' advisory tool is to enable librarians to be conversant in an area of literature where they may have little or no experience, and this book attempts to fill that need by grouping titles according to reading interests and by suggesting similar titles for reader favorites. *Hooked on Horror* also leads readers' advisors to similar titles by identifying important subject headings for each work, subject headings based not on LOC or Sears headings but rather on keyword identifiers indicative of themes and issues central to the genre itself, and then by matching—using these subject keywords—fictional texts with similar reads. In this way, reads that may not be completely similar but that contain the same thematic concerns as the original book under consideration can be identified. More important, this book goes beyond the generalizations used in older readers' advisory texts for the genre, which group items under umbrella-term headings such as *monsters.* Rather, we have attempted to deconstruct readers' tastes as specifically as possible, grouping items under specific terms such as *Frankenstein's monster (character), subterranean monsters, serial killers, werewolves,* and *zombies.* In other words, what we hope to accomplish with this text is to fill the need for a readers' advisory guide geared specifically toward horror fans, using their terminology and keeping in mind their preferences.

We must reiterate that *Hooked on Horror,* however, is *not* a critical guide to horror fiction. We of course acknowledge that one of the most daunting problems with selecting genre fiction of any type, horror fiction included, is that generally it is not reviewed in mainstream review sources. Although *The New York Times Book Review* may condescend to review the latest bestsellers by Koontz or Rice, it does so only because readers would demand the blood of the reviewers if they failed to acknowledge these works. Library trade journals such as *Kirkus Reviews, Booklist,* and *Library Journal* consistently provide brief annotations with some evaluative content, but these summaries may prove inadequate for readers' advisory purposes because these journals typically evaluate based on the literary merit or circulation potential of works, not on their appeal to fans of the genre. Despite the obvious need for such review sources, we must remain emphatic in our belief that a readers' advisory guide cannot, by its very nature, also serve as a critical guide or source for reviews. To that end, librarians and readers are best served by examining genre-oriented periodicals such as *Horror: The Newsmagazine of the Horror and Dark Fantasy Field, Aberrations,* and *Cemetery Dance* (briefly annotated in chapter 18). These are the best sources for horror reviews readily available to librarians. Another excellent source for horror reviews is the World Wide Web, with individually run sites such as Dark Echo's Page (www.darkecho.com), HorrorNet (www.horrornet.com), and *Necropsy: The Review of Horror Fiction* (www.lsu.edu/necrofile). In addition, librarians can use Web directories, such as the horror area of about.com (http://horror.about.com). Finally, the publishing mega-site Amazon.com often provides substantive guest reviews, sometimes by published reviewers.

Scope of This Guide

Writing a selective bibliography of genre fiction is a daunting task. Many of the novels, short story collections, and anthologies published in any given year are pulp and therefore are cursed with an ephemeral existence. Often first editions of horror texts are released in paperback, and sometimes second printings are not forthcoming. Only works by best-selling writers tend to enjoy what would be the publishing world's version of immortality. For this reason, while attempting to demonstrate the broad spectrum of titles available to readers of the horror genre, we were selective in what we chose to include and annotate in this guide.

Novels, Anthologies, and Collections

As we did the first edition, we consider this readers' guide to be as "comprehensive" a bibliography of horror in print and currently available as possible. The first edition of *Hooked on Horror* included horror in print up to 1998. This edition is a continuation of the first, a second volume if you will, focusing on titles from 1998 to the present (January 2002). This is not an arbitrary decision, but rather one that is practical. The purpose of a readers' guide is to inform readers and librarians of titles they can actually get their hands on; hence we have attempted to thoroughly cover the most recent titles.

We began with a list of books in print in the year 2001. In short, if a work of horror was in print at the time we began writing this edition, we attempted to procure and examine a copy of the text, so that we might fully annotate it. We attempted to do this with all three formats: novels, anthologies, and collections by single writers. For reference works and books of criticism, we were just as selective, choosing mainly those books we felt would appeal to our primary target audience of horror fans, with secondary concern for what we consider to be our secondary audience, horror scholars.

Because many books are available via interlibrary loan (ILL) (or other resource sharing) and publishers' backlists, and therefore might be requested by patrons, we consulted union catalogs of various state library systems, public library online catalogs, and online booksellers for a core list. Although we attempted to be inclusive, we found that some works published since 1998 were unavailable, even through the publishers, forcing us to eliminate those titles. In essence, our philosophy for books published between 1998 and 2001 was that if they are available through any means, they are included in this guide. We added to this list titles in horror series, such as Anne Rice's Vampire Chronicles or Laurell K. Hamilton's Anita Blake Series, as long as the most recent work in that series was published in 1998 or later. Our reasoning was that it was possible, perhaps even likely, that the author could once again take up the series, and readers would begin requesting older titles in that series. The only exceptions to this rule are series that are considered classics and those in which one book was a major award winner (as we include all Bram Stoker and International Horror Guild award titles in this edition). These were included no matter what the date of the most recently published title happened to be.

In the case where a series had no official or designated name, located in either the Library of Congress cataloging information on the title page of the books, or in OCLC, we simply named it after the first novel in the series.

Individual works that have achieved the status of "classic" and *all* works by those writers considered benchmark authors are included in this guide. For the sake of inclusion, we tried to identify all classics in the genre, such as Bram Stoker's *Dracula*, Mary Shelley's *Frankenstein*, and Richard Matheson's *I Am Legend*, even if some of these classics were currently out of print or temporarily between editions. Most libraries own these classics, and readers are often acquainted with these tales, so their placement in this work serves as an entry point for readers' advisors, helping users of this guide to identify specific subgenres and themes that readers of classics enjoy. In addition, we identified eight popular authors in the genre, namely Robert Bloch, Ramsey Campbell, Stephen King, Dean Koontz, Richard Matheson, Anne Rice, Peter Straub, and Chelsea Quinn Yarbro, and included all of their work. Readers often request texts by those particular authors because of their popularity and reputation. We assumed that as more university curricula included horror classics, which is a trend sweeping the nation's universities, these works would likely be reissued by publishers. By necessity, we calculated which texts may become "modern classics," either because they were award winners or because they received consistent rave reviews, and we included all of those in this edition.

We have included a full range of horror fiction—everything from atmospheric, gothic texts, such as those by Ramsey Campbell and Thomas Tessier; to characterization novels like those of Tananarive Due; to erotic horror such as works by Anne Rice—with no exclusions being made based on a work's subtlety, its level of sensuality, its inclusion of overt sexuality, or its reliance on graphic violence. We did, however, exclude works of Christian fiction, science fiction, and fantasy if those works did not exhibit what we consider the main characteristic of horror: an *emphasis* on some type of monster or threatening entity that had the potential, and realized the potential, of causing great harm to humanity. In other words, the inclusion of an angel, an alien, or a dragon in a text did not merit its inclusion in this guide. That angel, alien, or dragon had to be menacing rather than helpful; it had to show its ability to bring death and destruction to innocent human beings. In Christian fiction, science fiction, and fantasy, these types of supernatural beings often are not monstrous. For a text including one of these beings to be called horror, that being *must* be monstrous, perhaps even evil, and *must* be the emphasis of the dread in the text. *The Lord of the Rings* contains many a threatening mutant, troll, and dragon, but these monsters are not the raison d'être of the text. They simply exist in the world inhabited by the characters. By contrast, in Graham Joyce's *The Tooth Fairy* and Martin M. Hunt's *Dark Soul*, fairies and angels or demons are the central antagonists, and they are extremely menacing and destructive.

History, Criticism, and Reference

To direct readers' advisors and readers to other sources of useful information, we have listed horror's most prominent reference and critical works, as well as some of its more informative periodicals. In these cases, we were selective, yet more flexible about publication date, because many of these works are published by academic presses and therefore have a short publication run but are readily available through university ILL departments. These critical and biographical works are still consulted by fans and scholars for their ground-breaking ideas, so we chose to include the "classics" by scholars such as Montague Summers, Mike Ashley, Julia Briggs, William Patrick Day, and David Punter, among others. Works that are still in print or are readily available were also included, albeit selectively. In short, we did not attempt to be comprehensive in our selection of critical and reference texts, as they are not the primary focus of this guide.

Young Adult Titles

Young adult horror (YA titles) is *not* covered, because the inclusion of such writers as R. L. Stine, Christopher Pike, and Annette Curtis Klaus would triple the number of titles in this guide. Instead we leave the compilation of a YA readers' advisory guide to horror to other bibliographers; it would take a book-length study, rather than the inadequate chapter listing that we could at best manage, to do the subgenre of YA horror justice. The only YA titles found in this guide are those commonly read by adults, such as Brandon Massey's *Thunderland*.

The Inclusion of Film

Horror fiction has been greatly influenced by the film industry. What would have become of Mary Shelley's *Frankenstein* had not Boris Karloff popularized the creature and the work with his movie performance? Would Bram Stoker's count have become a pop culture icon had not Bela Lugosi, and later Frank Langella and Gary Oldman, brought him to life on the big screen? Because of this interplay between literary and film horror, and because an increasing number of libraries include videotapes in their collections, we decided to offer information about horror on film in this guide. However, because the sheer number of horror films still available for purchase is immense, and because of space limitations, we chose not to be all-inclusive in this category. This guide is, after all, *primarily* a bibliography of *written* horror. Only horror films on VHS or DVD that we consider important in forming the genre, films that no public library with a large horror readership should be without, were chosen for inclusion.

Of course, virtually all horror fans and most librarians are familiar with the classics of the genre, beginning with Fritz Marnau's *Nosferatu* (1922), Tod Browning's *Dracula* (1931), James Whale's *Frankenstein* (1931), and Lambert Hillyer's *Dracula's Daughter* (1936). These are titles that all libraries with a large horror fan patronage should include in their collections, not only for the quality of film making that each represents, but also for the important role each has played in changing the very landscape of the genre itself, by completely reinterpreting Bram Stoker's, Mary Shelley's, and Joseph Sheridan Le Fanu's works. Bela Lugosi's portrayal of the suave, sophisticated, international jet setter in *Dracula* allowed the Count to evolve into the sympathetic creature he became in 1992, when Gary Oldman presented audiences with a Dracula who was more a victim of love than a creature of the night, and these films in turn have influenced literature, resulting in the sophisticated vampires of Anne Rice and Chelsea Quinn Yarbro.

Horror films often take the pulse of a society at a given moment in its cultural history, and the films we have included from the 1950s through the 1980s captured the prevalent fears of those eras. Pop culture icons such as Jack Arnold's *The Incredible Shrinking Man* (1957), Dan Siegel's *Invasion of the Body Snatchers* (1956), Alfred Hitchcock's *Psycho* (1960) and *The Birds* (1963), Brian De Palma's *Carrie* (1976), and Ridley Scott's *Alien* (1979), can also be found in this guide. In addition, we recognized the value of some of the B-movie counterparts of these classics, such as Nathan Juran's *Attack of the 50 Foot Woman* (1958), Herk Harvey's *Carnival of Souls* (1962), and George Romero's *Night of the Living Dead* (1968). These films bring to light Americans' preoccupation with changing gender roles (often viewed as emasculation), female sexuality, and women's rights, as well as their fears of McCarthyism, Communism, nature, the Cold War and its nuclear buildup, minority empowerment, and space exploration.

We were even more selective in choosing contemporary films, including mainly those works that received critical acclaim and those that tested the boundaries of the horror movie—sometimes making it art. Therefore, we included films such as Jonathan Demme's Oscar-winning *The Silence of the Lambs* (1992), Francis Ford Coppola's lush and stylized operatic *Bram Stoker's Dracula* (1992), Bernard Rose's ingenious metageneric *Candyman* (1992), Guillermo Del Toro's Cannes Film Festival winner *Cronos* (1992), Rusty Cundieff's extremely clever horror/comedy *Tales from the Hood* (1995), M. Night Shayamalan's Hitchcock-esque *The Sixth Sense* (1999), Alejandro Amenabar's shocker

The Others (2001), Tarsem Singh's truly psychologically disturbing *The Cell* (2000), and E. Elias Merhing's metatextual *Shadow of the Vampire* (2001).

New to This Edition

Of the more than 825 fiction titles in this edition, approximately 70 percent are new. In addition, approximately 50 percent of the 230 plus nonfiction titles listed in this guide are new. Although we consistently refer to this guide as a second edition, librarians and readers should keep in mind that it is, for all practical purposes, volume 2 of *Hooked on Horror*. This is because space constraints make it impossible for us to list most of the titles that are found in the first edition. Therefore, readers' advisors and collection development officers who own the first edition are advised to use this guide as a supplement rather than as a stand-alone product. We do repeat some 275 titles from the first edition because these particular titles are parts of series or are written by benchmark authors. However, we make no claim to repeating some 530 titles from the first edition. Therefore, librarians and readers will need to consult the first edition for writers like Clive Barker, Suzy McKee Charnas, Robin Cook, P. N. Elrod, Jeanne Kalogridis, Ira Levin, Bentley Little, Brian Lumley, Kim Newman, Michael Palmer, Fred Saberhagen, John Saul, and Dan Simmons. Granted, repeating more titles would have been useful to librarians and readers alike, but it would have made this edition unwieldy.

The first edition of *Hooked on Horror* received many reviews, both positive and negative. Before beginning this edition, we carefully reviewed the criticism and comments. In light of the feedback we received from reviewers and input from practicing readers' advisors, we made various changes to this edition, as follows:

1. We added "similar reads" for the films that conclude each chapter. By adding this feature we hoped to encourage horror movie buffs to pick up a novel or collection of stories that had a similar "feel" or thematic concern to a favorite film. The ultimate goal here is to increase library circulation by adding new readers to its patronage.

2. Whenever possible, we noted fictional texts that are available in formats other than print, particularly on audiocassette or via e-book.

3. Whereas the first edition of *Hooked on Horror* had a similar titles listing at the end of only some of the annotated texts, this edition has a "similar titles" listing at the end of *every* annotated entry. Our hope here is to facilitate the ease with which users of this guide can locate "read alikes." We admit to a measure of subjectivity in identifying similar titles; however, we relied on our combined experience and expertise to identify the most likely candidates for readers.

4. In this edition, we added more classic texts by writers such as M. G. Lewis, Charles Brockden Brown, H. P. Lovecraft, E. F. Benson, Bram Stoker, and others. In addition, we added more classic film.

5. We added a collection development core list in appendix B. This appendix lists what we consider to be the texts that any library with a high horror readership should possess. It is also subjective, of course, and should be interpreted that way.

6. We included a select group of graphic novels, as readers are being drawn to this alternative format. We are aware that our listing of graphic novels is in no way inclusive; we included about a dozen or so titles merely to whet readers' appetites for the format and to demonstrate the range of the genre.

7. We expanded the cross-genre listings that made up chapter 20 of the first edition and moved them to a more easily accessed location (see appendix A). We have added special interest areas such as romance, gentle reads, classics, and detective fiction to better assist readers and readers' advisors in isolating those types of works.

8. We omitted the list of benchmark authors and their bibliographies that was included in our first edition. We did, however, keep nearly every publication by those authors who are extremely popular in the genre, such as King, Koontz, Rice, and Straub. Readers who wish to consult such a list should refer to the first edition of the book.

9. Unlike in the first edition, we did not list the pseudonyms of selected writers. Rather, we identified each text by a given author's most common publishing name (usually the name that author is listed by in authority headings). In addition, pseudonyms are cross-referenced in the author/title index. Thus, Richard Bachman's books are found under King, Stephen; and works by Leigh Nichols can be found under Koontz, Dean. Readers can always find pseudonyms for writers by consulting bio-bibliographical sources such as *Contemporary Authors*. However, in virtually all cases, they will find the identification of pseudonyms unnecessary because we have identified published works under the author's authoritative name.

Final Note

From the outset, we understood the impossibility of creating a comprehensive bibliography of this rich and varied genre, so we instead set out to create what we considered a useful guide for librarians in readers' advisory and collection development officer capacities. Therefore, when considering content, we included all novels that are generally classified as horror, as well as some that straddle genres but obviously fit the definitions we set forth for each subgenre. We hope that as readers' advisors or horror fans, you find this volume helpful. We are always seeking ways to make our work more useful, and to that end, we invite your comments and suggestions, which can be sent to us via our publisher, Libraries Unlimited, at lu-books@lu.com.

Part 1

Introduction to
Horror Fiction

Chapter 1

A Definition of Horror

The Definition of Horror as Used in This Book

> Horror is not a genre, like the mystery or science fiction or the western. It is not a kind of fiction meant to be confined to the ghetto of a special shelf in the ghetto of libraries or bookstores . . . horror is an emotion.
>
> —Douglas E. Winter in the introduction to *Prime Evil* (New York: New American Library, 1988)

> Tragedy is when I cut my finger. Comedy is when you fall down the sewer and die. Horror is when you return from the dead and haunt me for laughing at your nasty trip down that sewer.
>
> —June Pulliam's embellishment upon an old saw

> What we fear in the night in the day comes to call anyway.
>
> —Counting Crows, "Einstein on the Beach"

On the most basic level, horror fiction contains a monster, whether it be supernatural, human, or a metaphor for the psychological torment of a guilt-ridden human. This monster can take on various forms: It can be one of the walking dead, the living impaired who stumble around aimlessly chanting "Brains! Brains!" and snacking on anyone in heels who has the misfortune to trip on the terrain. It can be a vengeful ghost of a child molester, horribly disfigured through the vigilante justice of outraged parents and fully equipped with twelve-inch razors for finger nails and the ability to invade victims' dreams, cracking jokes as it slaughters the innocent. It can be an angry stripper, a once abused wife or mother, who will now rid the world of men who would batter those they should protect. It can be the hideous and therefore unlovable creation of a mad scientist who fancies himself greater than God but is nothing more than a dead-beat dad creating illegitimate offspring that he refuses to love and parent. Or it can be a preternaturally beautiful immortal who is physically, emotionally, and intellectually superior to the humans who envy his every move, but an immortal who must nevertheless drink the blood of his admirers for survival.

Although we begin this definition very simply and straightforwardly, by defining a horror text as a work of fiction that must contain a monster of some type and one that often has the effect of scaring the reader, for the purposes of creating a broader and more accurate definition and determining inclusion in this guide, we also recognize that a work of horror fiction does not necessarily have to have as its raison d'être the intention of producing fear in the reader. Of course, most works in the genre do, and readers' advisors will find that this type of horror fiction predominates in the listings in this guide. However, there are many excellent and well-respected works in the genre that do not intend to induce fear. Anne Rice's Vampire Chronicles, for example, emphasize the philosophical dilemma of outliving friends and family while never growing old and questions the uncertainty of an amoral universe. Although these realizations about the nature of life, humanity, and divinity may be horrific to some, *The Vampire Lestat* has little in common with a novel like *'Salem's Lot*, which has the loftiest of all horror fiction goals: to scare readers (in this case into remembering to keep their feet covered with the blanket at night). Despite the obvious differences in authorial intent, both *The Vampire Lestat* and *'Salem's Lot* are considered horror works by publishers, booksellers, bookstores, libraries, fans, professors who teach horror literature, and the authors themselves. By the same token, Laurell K. Hamilton's Anita Blake Series and P. N. Elrod's Vampire Files both have more in common with the hard-boiled detective novels of Raymond Chandler than they do with the latest vampire tale by Whitley Strieber or T. M. Wright, yet both center around vampires, werewolves, and vampire hunters, thus placing them solidly in the genre.

But what of novels like Mitch Cullen's *Tideland*, a grotesque version of *Alice in Wonderland*, or Joe R. Lansdale's Southern gothic detective novel *The Bottoms*, not to mention various works by the most universally acknowledged modern master in the genre, Ramsey Campbell? Although stories of psychological horror are for the most part devoid of both supernatural monsters like vampires and ghosts and bloodthirsty psychopaths and vengeful strippers, they are no less frightening. They explore the mental torment stemming from mental illness, child abuse, guilt, or countless other types of human suffering and emotional instability. These fictional works are indeed horrific because these are the novels that question the very nature of our world, as do most horror texts in general, taking that inquiry one step further. They challenge both the readers' reality and the fictional reality created by the author. Perhaps the best way to define psychological horror is by examining two of the better examples of the subgenre, Cullen's *Tideland* and Campbell's *Obsession*. Cullen creates a world in which an eleven-year-old girl with the understanding of a five-year-old is left completely alone and friendless. Only the four Barbie heads she keeps on her fingers give her someone to talk to. In *Tideland*, the living and the dead share the same abodes, unable to distinguish one from the other. Campbell's novel about being haunted by our childhoods suggests that the characters' obsession with their own guilt due to youthful indiscretions, to which they attribute their adult fears, are more horrific than any ghost or phantom sent from a supernatural realm. In the gothic worlds of Campbell or of cult favorite Caitlin R. Kiernan, adults suffer not only because they are un*able* to break away from a harmful situation, but because they are un*willing* to challenge cultural expectations that created the harmful situation, and thus they are willing participants in their own victimization. This behavioral pattern is evident in one of the classic works of the subgenre, Daphne DuMaurier's *Rebecca*. The nameless, cringing second Mrs. Maxim de Winter will forever be commanded by her husband, and the far more interesting but dead Rebecca will always cast a shadow over her.

Our development of this inclusive definition has far-reaching consequences in that it helped determine how we categorized the world of horror literature into its subgenres. In the past various readers' advisory tools and guides to the literature have used either style-based categories (i.e., gothic horror, comic horror, splatterpunk, gentle reads, etc.) or a combination of style-based and monster-based (for want of a better term) categories, whereas our categorization emphasizes a type of monster or horror that predominated in the fictional text. Our reasoning for this decision is simple: Most readers who like a vampire novel like it because it has vampires, or those who enjoy a psychological thriller starring a maniacal sociopath enjoy slasher narratives with human monsters. Therefore, when these readers seek a similar read, they are literally looking for, in most cases, another work with the same type of monster. In three instances, however, we veered from this classification schema: comic horror, splatterpunk, and psychological horror. Because these first two subgenres are defined mainly by their *approach* to telling the story, not individual elements in the story itself, we felt obliged to treat them differently. So although comic horror and splatterpunk are not, according to our scheme of categorization, actual subgenres, they are treated as such for the purposes of practicality, to enhance the usefulness of this guide. As for psychological horror, we simply felt that we would be remiss if we excluded those texts that seemed to argue, "we have met the monsters, and they are us," because these make up a reasonably large portion of the texts in the genre.

Without a doubt, defining horror fiction is difficult since it is not all of one type. It would be easy if we could state that horror is solely fiction that contains threatening monsters, but that definition would preclude works of psychological horror, where the threat is only perceived but is no less real than had it been tangible. Or it would be easy if we could state that horror is fiction that intends to horrify, or that has the effect of scaring the reader, but this would not account for comic horror or the psychological Vampire Chronicles of Anne Rice, which definitely belong to the genre. In addition, we could point out that horror fiction is the story of monsters, and that the word *monster* stems from the Latin word *monstere*, which means portent or omen, often a divine warning; therefore, horror fiction is arguably fiction that attempts to warn its readers of a certain danger, of an action or belief that can have negative results. Yet not all fiction that attempts to instruct, even metaphorically, is horror fiction, not even that which uses the supernatural as metaphor, as do fantasy and magical realism. Horror may have elements in common with fantasy and magical realism, but fans of either will be quick to note that the two are in no way interchangeable. After some careful thought, we decided that the best way to describe horror as a genre is through its various subgenres, to allow the reader to put the horror puzzle together by supplying the pieces and a general framework for their interrelationships. Of course, these subgenres are often insufficient in and of themselves to accurately describe a work of horror, but put together, these pieces help create a whole picture. In short, they help describe what horror is.

Ghosts and Haunted Houses: Dealing with Presences and Absences

Ghost and haunted house stories are tales of guilt thought to be long buried in the unconscious mind. The ghost or the haunted house serves as a portent to the person guilty of repressing knowledge of wrongdoing, as well as to others who know nothing of his or her sin, often reminding the haunted individual of the inadvisability of burying this knowledge in the unconscious mind. Contrary to popular belief, ghosts don't necessarily reside in haunted houses. Ghosts more often exist to seek justice for a wrong they suffered in life or to protect one of the living from harm. The haunted house, on the other hand, can be likened to an abused child. It is a victim of events that either happened in the house itself or on the site of the house prior to its erection, and it now lashes out at its occupants or sometimes cries for love.

Examples of the genre: Emily Brontë, *Wuthering Heights*; Ramsey Campbell, *Nazareth Hill*; Shirley Jackson, *The Haunting of Hill House*; Stephen King, *Bag of Bones*; Toni Morrison, *Beloved*; Peter Straub, *Ghost Story*.

Golem, Mummies, and Reanimated Stalkers: Wake the Dead and They'll Be Cranky

The dead can be purposefully reanimated, as is the case with zombies, or reanimated by accident, as is the case in George Romero's film *Night of the Living Dead,* in which the newly dead rise from their graves due to radiation released by a recent space probe. Or the dead can be raised by the living who simply can't accept the finality of death, as is the case in Stephen King's *Pet Sematary*. The golem, another form of reanimated dead, can be seen in Mary Shelley's novel *Frankenstein*, and later in countless other works of fiction and films. But unlike other reanimated dead, golem are soulless and angry beings fashioned from human parts. They are not reanimated bodies, but rather crazy quilts of body parts, genes, souls, etc.

Examples of the genre: Stephen King, *The Dark Half*; Dean Koontz, *Mr. Murder*; Anne Rice, *The Mummy, or Ramses the Damned*; Mary Shelley, *Frankenstein*.

Vampires and Werewolves: Children of the Night

Vampires are creatures of the night who must often enter into parasitic relationships with others. Thus, vampirism has frequently been used as a metaphor for love, the parent/child bond, sexual relationships, and power structures in general. Yet vampires are easily the most identifiable and often the most sympathetic—in short, the most appealing—of all monsters, mainly because vampires must, in some way, resemble the humans on which they prey. In fact, vampirism is often represented as nothing more than superhuman immortality, with a little bloodlust thrown in for a good scare. Vampires often possess extraordinary powers, whether they are the ability to hypnotize victims, control the weather, shapeshift, control people's minds and bodies, or super strength and speed as well as the ability to fly.

Vampires can be sort of an evil version of Superman. Finally, vampires are almost always erotic or sensual in some way, which is one of their greatest appeals.

Werewolves are related to vampires, and hence are included in this subgenre. The werewolf derives from vampire folklore that specified that the undead could usually turn into bats and wolves. According to the same folklore, wolves are a vampire's best friend and do their bidding. In fact, in *Dracula* the Count refers to wolves as "the children of the night" when he praises their musical howling. This association with the vampire is what caused the werewolf to grow into a separate beast with its own literature.

> Examples of the genre: David Holland, *Murcheston, The Wolf's Tale*; Tom Holland, The Lord of the Dead Series; Anne Rice, The Vampire Chronicles; Bram Stoker, *Dracula*; Chelsea Quinn Yarbro, The Saint-Germain Series.

Demonic Possession, Satanism, Black Magic, and Witches and Warlocks: The Devil Made Me Do It

Tales of black magic and demonic possession predate the Judeo-Christian *Bible*, and this subgenre of horror is arguably one of the oldest. Tales of demonic possession involve innocents possessed by demons or by the devil himself. Tales of Satanism and black magic can also be about witches, warlocks (note that not *all* witches and warlocks practice black magic), and others who willingly become involved with dark forces. Many stories in this subgenre feature Catholics who have either lost their faith or see their brand of black magic as an extension of their faith. However, a few narratives feature Protestants.

> Examples of the genre: William Peter Blatty, *The Exorcist*; Walter de la Mare, *The Return*; Nancy Holder, *Dead in the Water*; Stephen King, *The Shining*; Ira Levin, *Rosemary's Baby*; Richard Lortz, *Lovers Living, Lovers Dead*; Graham Masterton, *The Manitou*; Anne Rice The Mayfair Witches Series.

Mythological Monsters and "The Old Ones": Invoking the Gods

Every mythology has its monsters. From Kali the Destroyer in India, to the destructive one-eyed giant Cyclops in ancient Greece, to the Anglo-Saxon human-eater Grendel, to Lucifer in Christianity, all cultures incorporate some being into their belief systems that, although human-like, is nonetheless monstrous and destructive, often threatening entire populations. Narratives from this subgenre either represent the non-Christian gods as unadulterated, monstrous Other, or angry deities supplanted by Christianity who want back their devoted followers. Narratives in this subgenre also deal with individuals who rediscover the old gods and tap into their power, much to the horror of their hapless victims.

Examples of the genre: Tananarive Due, *My Soul to Keep*; H. P. Lovecraft (and others), The Cthulhu Mythos Stories; Anne Rice, *The Servant of the Bones.*

Telekinesis and Hypnosis: Chaos from Control

In the nineteenth century, Dr. Anton Mesmer popularized the idea of mesmerism (later known as hypnotism), whereby an individual could get others to do his or her bidding through mind control. This pseudo-science, compounded with the reality that some charismatic individuals are able to exert an almost superhuman influence over others, gave rise to stories about evil individuals using the powers of their minds to control others. Telekinesis is another mind power. But where hypnotism requires the use of another person to accomplish the hypnotist's desires, telekinesis is more direct. The individual with telekinetic abilities can move objects with his or her mind. Furthermore, the person with telekinetic abilities is generally an angry outcast who, pushed beyond the limits of endurance, goes "postal," wreaking havoc with his or her telekinetic abilities, rather than with an AK-47.

Examples of the genre: Charles Grant, *The Pet*; John Farris, *The Fury*; Stephen King, *Carrie*; Dean Koontz, *Dragon Tears.*

Small Town Horror: Villages of the Damned

Small town horror is the dark side of *The Andy Griffith Show*. Mayberry is an appealing place because its diminutive size permits a sort of neighborly intimacy just not possible in the big city. But this small size makes small towns equally dangerous. Their remote location removes them from the laws governing civilization as a whole. Many small towns are havens of the Klan, or of money-hungry sheriffs who give speeding tickets to hapless out-of-towners who have no recourse since the judge will inevitably treat an outsider with suspicion. Or these villages outside of the mainstream may be governed by customs different from our own, such as laws requiring human sacrifices to pagan gods or demons. This type of horror, often referred to as small town horror, scares the reader with the realization that once he or she is away from the sanctity and security of home and civilization that plays by a known set of rules, anything is possible. Although monsters may reside in these small towns and prey on residents, the location itself facilitates the evil in that it is possible for something outside of the norm (for example, men turning their wives into robots or children being kept out of school because they are destined to be the next sin eater) to go unchallenged.

Examples of the genre: Robin Hardy and Anthony Shaffer, *The Wicker Man*; Ira Levin, *The Stepford Wives*; Elizabeth Massie, *Sineater*; Bentley Little, *The Store.*

Maniacs and Sociopaths, or the Nuclear Family Explodes: Monstrous Malcontents Bury the Hatchet

This is a relatively new subgenre of horror, as the nuclear family is a relatively new phenomenon, seeing its halcyon days in the post-World War II 1940s and 1950s. The nuclear, nonextended family was touted by psychologists as the norm and celebrated in situation comedies through the new medium of television. But Father doesn't always know best, and Mom isn't always content to stay home and clean the house while wearing pearls and her best Sunday dress, and there's no one to turn to in this supposedly self-sufficient family when the stress of everyday life becomes too much; seriously disturbed children, and sometimes parents, are the result. Works in this subgenre play on the all-too-American fear that every family unit has a dark side that surfaces only behind closed doors, and that children from these types of families will grow up to turn order into chaos.

> Examples of the genre: Robert Bloch, *Psycho*; Ramsey Campbell, *The Face That Must Die*; Susan Kay, Stephen King, and Peter Straub, The Talisman Series; Gaston LeRoux, *Phantom of the Opera*; Joyce Carol Oates, *Zombie*; Robert Louis Stevenson, *Dr. Jekyll and Mr. Hyde*; Peter Straub, The Blue Rose Series.

Technohorror: Evil Hospitals, Military Screw-Ups, Scientific Goofs, and Alien Invasions

With experiments in genetic cloning and anthrax scares and germ warfare, technohorror once again takes its place among the most popular subgenres of horror fiction. People are naturally afraid of the unknown. Technohorror exploits that fear, especially when it results from scientific experimentation gone awry or knowledge being misused. More than any horror subgenre, technohorror taps into Americans' (and others') fears when faced with the modern age's realization that any seemingly benevolent discovery, such as Einstein's Theory of Relativity, can easily find itself being transformed, Jekyll and Hyde fashion, into an element of destruction. Sometimes scientific principles take on nearly supernatural qualities. In horror of the 1950s, radiation precipitated male shrinkage and female growth. In medical horror, all that is necessary for the reader to suspend disbelief is the presence of giant corporations or HMOs in order for science to be misused and the results to achieve monstrous proportions.

> Examples of the genre: Dean Koontz, *Demon Seed*; Richard Matheson, *The Incredible Shrinking Man;* Kurt Siodmak, *Donovan's Brain*; James Whale, *Frankenstein* (film version).

Ecological Horror: Rampant Animals and Mother Nature's Revenge

The Judeo-Christian *Bible* says, "And man shall have dominion over all Earth's creatures." But what happens when those creatures, or even nature itself, strikes back? Horror fiction in this category shows the frightening result of humanity's tinkering with the forces of nature. And sometimes natural monstrosities aren't even the fault of humans; nature itself can be completely unpredictable and chaotic, and thus scary. Or if humans are to blame, it is because of their androcentric view of the universe, which makes them heedless in dealing with a world that doesn't necessarily put them at the top of the food chain. The horror of

Mother Nature's revenge serves as a reminder that we must face the repercussions of our actions when we mine the land and pollute the air and waterways or violate laws that are at least perceived as being "natural laws." Mother Nature's revenge also restores humans to their rightful place as *part* of the universe, rather than as creatures who are separate from the natural world.

Examples of the genre: Steve Alten, The Meg Series; Stephen King, *Cujo*; David Searcy, *Ordinary Horror*.

Psychological Horror: It's All In Your Head

You'll find no supernatural beings in this type of horror and no flesh-and-blood psychopath stalking an innocent. Instead, narratives in this subgenre expand upon the proposition that what happens in someone's mind can be just as real, and often just as terrifying, as being menaced by a vampire or hunted by Hannibal Lecter. The source of terror can be guilt over one's actions, living in proximity to one's tormentor, or sometimes just having to deal with events so extraordinarily awful that the protagonist has no previous frame of reference for guidance, as is the case in Mitch Cullen's *Tideland*, in which an eleven-year-old girl alone in rural Texas must learn to survive after the death of her father. The lack of a supernatural element in this type of horror often makes it seem more erudite than its more fantastical counterparts, and thus it is more likely to be accepted as mainstream literature rather than to be dismissed as trite genre fiction.

Examples of the genre: Ramsey Campbell, *Obsession*; Mitch Cullen, *Tideland*; Daphine DuMaurier, *Rebecca*; Nathaniel Hawthorne, *The House of the Seven Gables*; Stephen King, *Gerald's Game*; John Wooley and Ron Wolfe, *Old Fears*.

Splatterpunk: The Gross Out

The most recent subgenre of horror (emerging sometime in the late 1980s), splatterpunk is a *style* of writing more than it is a theme with any particular type of monster. It is also known by the name "extreme horror." In the typical splatterpunk story, graphic sex and violence abound as a result of the decadent indulgences of bored mortals and immortals rather than as shocking excesses of monsters that must be stopped. Punk, alternative, and heavy metal music are often part of the backdrop of a splatterpunk story. There are no reluctant vampires or antiheroes here; splatterpunk monsters revel in their monstrosity.

Examples of the genre: Simon Clark, *Blood Crazy*; Robert Devereaux, *Santa Steps Out*; Michael Slade, The Headhunter Series.

Comic Horror: Laughing at Our Fears

Many people do not realize that horror has almost always had an element of the comic in it. Although Freddy Kreuger may have been the first monster to crack jokes before disposing of his victims (many might argue that lines such as "she has a nice neck" in *Nosferatu* can be seen as comic threats that predate Freddy's by more than 50 years), humor in horror can be found in the understated reactions of Hrothgar's warriors to the monster

Grendel in *Beowulf*, in the melodrama and irony of a good Poe tale, or in the stock stooge character that played a minor role in early Universal Studios horror films such as *Dracula, Frankenstein*, and *Bride of Frankenstein*. Humor and horror also go hand in hand in the reactions of both the characters in horror texts and the readers or viewers of horror texts. The former, in their hurry to escape the monster, run into things, trip over themselves, and often make highly ironic comments foreshadowing their own deaths; the latter laugh nervously when their expectations are built up—and the mysterious noise turns out to be only a cat rummaging in a trash can. Despite this relationship between fear and laughter, true comic horror is a new and seldom visited subgenre, by writers and readers alike.

> Examples of the genre: Kingsley Amis, *The Green Man*; Laurell
> K. Hamilton, The Anita Blake Series; Greg Kihn, *Big
> Rock Beat*; Dean Koontz, *Ticktock*; Oscar Wilde, *The
> Canterville Ghost*.

Chapter 2

How to Use This Book

Most librarians would agree that the purpose of a good readers' advisory program is to encourage reading and improve circulation by matching readers with books that they will love. The job of the readers' advisor is often to interview the reader and determine his or her reading tastes based on limited information concerning the types of books the reader usually reads, the topics and thematic concerns that the reader is drawn to, the writing styles that the reader enjoys and those he or she does not particularly like, the settings (geographic locations, periods in history, etc.) that the reader most enjoys reading about, and the individual writers whom the reader likes or hates. Based on this interview, a readers' advisor must be able to create a list of books that the reader will probably enjoy. This is a daunting task in and of itself for general fiction, but the task becomes nearly impossible when that particular reader is one like those identified in our preface, a patron who reads almost exclusively in the horror genre. If the librarian who is serving as readers' advisor happens to be a horror fan himself or herself and happens to have read nearly everything written in the past five years in the genre, or at least all books in print and available through ILL, then that librarian will be able to easily identify five to ten books that the reader might enjoy.

Unfortunately, it is unrealistic to expect any librarian to keep abreast of so many published works. For this reason, several publications exist for the sole purpose of aiding readers' advisors in their efforts to identify similar titles and authors to suit any given patron's reading tastes. These text-based and CD-ROM publications alert readers' advisors to the existence of readily available genre fiction that may be of interest to the reader at hand. By using Libraries Unlimited's Genreflecting series, Gale's What Do I Read Next series of bibliographies, or the CD-ROM products *Novelist* and *What Do I Read Next?*, a readers' advisor can match a popular title, such as the latest bestseller by Stephen King, with other titles that possess the same general appeal and will therefore more than likely appeal to the reader. Before 1999, there was only one genreflecting guide, and it covered all genres—horror, fantasy, romance, Western, Christian, science fiction, and detective fiction—in a single volume and was therefore unable to extensively cover works in any particular genre. This

13

limited its usefulness for hardcore fans of a single genre, those who chose to read almost exclusively in one genre or the other (as most of us who read genre fiction do).

As one of the pioneer works in the Genreflecting advisory series to address the need for individualized readers' guides, *Hooked on Horror* focuses solely on the horror genre. It attempts to list, annotate briefly, and match with similar titles virtually every readily available horror title, thereby giving readers' advisors and readers an in-depth look at the possibilities of the genre. Although it treats each of the subgenres of horror (such as vampire fiction, technohorror, small town horror, and maniac horror) separately, identifying similar titles by grouping them under one umbrella term, it also links titles within one subgenre with similar ones in other subgenres. Also, *Hooked on Horror* attempts to go beyond the vague or selective coverage seen in generalized readers' guides; because approximately 75 percent of the titles listed in this bibliography were actually obtained from publishers and local libraries, they were annotated based on firsthand experience with the text, which resulted in annotations that go beyond the general "blurb." The annotations in each chapter note or hint at the writing style and appeal of the majority of the works listed in this guide. The entries also indicate when a book has received an award and when it is available in other formats.

On the title line:

 Bram Stoker award winners   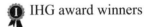 IHG award winners

 Pulitzer Prize winning titles    American Book Award

At the end of the annotation:

🖉 audiotape, audio download, compact disc

🖰 CD rom, e-book

👓 large print

✎ graphic novels

Having the texts in hand also proved helpful in assigning subject headings for each entry. These headings serve two purposes: (1) to act as access points for titles and (2) to allow readers to isolate thematic concerns, characters, settings, etc.—whatever most appealed to them about a work—and based on that, locate similar texts.

In short, *Hooked on Horror* identifies many appeal features to match texts. The most obvious is the subgenre designation itself. In other words, all works that deal mainly with vampires are grouped in the vampire fiction chapter; all novels and collections of stories about serial murderers and stalkers can be found in the chapter on maniacs; and all works dealing with technohorror (horror stemming from technology or scientific experimentation) are grouped together in that chapter. This makes it easy for fans of "Vampire's Point of View" narratives, Hannibal Lector type villains, and medical thrillers to, at a glance, find similar titles. The reader, or his or her readers' advisor, need only turn to the annotated lists in the vampire, maniac, or technohorror chapters and skim the descriptions to create a bibliography of similar reads.

The second layer of matching can be found at the end of virtually all annotations in this guide, where a few titles that are most similar to the work under consideration are identified. For the purpose of matching similar titles this way, we asked ourselves, "What title does this most read like?" We based our answers—the brief lists of similar titles—on thematic concerns, plot structures, or writing style. We realize that the problem here, of course, is that these matches are highly subjective. Also, since some books are entirely too unique for accurate matching, we were unable to assign obvious similar titles to all texts, and in some cases, we simply had to use our own best judgment.

Finally, we assigned subject headings to each entry; these headings serve as keyword identifiers that are indexed, so that the entries that are assigned the same subject heading (keyword) end up being grouped together in the index, under that subject/keyword term. In this respect, *Hooked on Horror* acts as a database, in print form, linking similar items based on specific literary elements such as setting, character types, or thematic issues. Therefore, a fan of *Rosemary's Baby* may realize that the aspect of the novel that he or she most enjoyed or identified with was its setting, New York City, or that one of the main characters was an actor, or that the main thrust of the story concerns demons and impregnation. Each of these themes is standardized in a subject term, which is then assigned to the novel. Once indexed, these subject terms act as an access point to *Rosemary's Baby*. All the reader or readers' advisor need do is find *Actor as Character, New York City, Demons,* or *Pregnancy* in the subject index, and he or she will find not only a reference to Levin's novel of demonic possession but also a list of all works that were assigned one of those subject terms, as indicated by the page numbers listed after the term. The reader then need only turn to one of those pages, and he or she will find other titles that were assigned the subject term in question, which denotes that these titles are reasonably similar reads in that they are concerned with at least one of the major themes of the original fictional text under consideration.

We recommend that, as a first step in using this readers' guide, the readers' advisor (and the reader, if he or she is interested) become familiar with the parameters of each of the subgenre chapters by reading the overview of subgenres in chapter 1 and the essays that begin each chapter. We also suggest that users of this selective bibliography familiarize themselves with the methods for standardization of terms in the subject index by scanning through some of its pages. This will help users get a feel for what types of match points for similar titles are possible and will save those users time in the long run by preventing them from searching for terms that are not indexed because they are too specific or too broad, although we did attempt to handle some of those possibilities with extensive *see* and *see also* listings. Readers can then familiarize themselves with how these subject headings, aside from being match points for finding similar titles, also serve as access points for those who are not looking for a similar title but rather need to find a work based on limited information. For example, a reader who has heard about the "Anita Blake" novels but knows nothing besides the recurring character's name will find in the subject index that Blake, Anita (character) is a subject keyword that refers back to various Laurell K. Hamilton books, each of which is indicated by a list of relevant page numbers in *Hooked on Horror* where works with *Blake, Anita (character)* as a subject keyword assigned to certain texts can be located.

We attempted to keep the overall searching and matching mechanisms of *Hooked on Horror* as simple as possible by generalizing and standardizing subject headings, by using extensive *see* and *see also* cross-referencing in the subject keyword index, and by alphabetizing all entries, whether they be in the subgenre chapters or in the indexes, in the most literal and consistent method possible. Our hope is that we have put enough care and hard work into the making of this bibliographic reference tool that the readers' advisor and reader will be saved valuable time in searching and creating bibliographies of similar horror titles.

Chapter 3

A Brief History of the Horror Genre and Its Current Trends

Historically speaking, the first horror novel was published in 1764, when Horace Walpole penned the tale of a family curse, a damsel in distress, and a giant helmet that crushes humans. The popularity of *The Castle of Otranto* encouraged the publication of other gothic novels, such as Anne Radcliffe's *The Mysteries of Udolpho* and M. G. Lewis's *The Monk*, the latter becoming the prototype for the erotic horror novel. At about the same time, the first gothic satire, Jane Austen's *Northanger Abbey*, became popular among the middle classes. On this side of the pond, there were some early American gothic texts, such as those by Charles Brockden Brown and Washington Irving, but these in general bear little resemblance to what we now recognize as the horror tale. Brown's *Wieland* bordered on being what we now recognize to be psychological horror, and Washington Irving came very close to writing comic horror in "The Legend of Sleepy Hollow," but neither writer seems to capture the atmosphere, the gothicism, or the emotion of horror. It wasn't until the mid-1800s that two American writers, Edgar Allan Poe and Nathaniel Hawthorne, began publishing short fiction that for all practical purposes could be considered the literary ancestor of what we now call horror. Poe wrote often through the eyes and consciousness of a maniacal killer or a madman (the maniac subgenre), and Hawthorne examined, in more reasoned and detached prose, the darkest recesses of the disturbed mind (the psychological horror subgenre). Another American, Ambrose Bierce, known more for his fanciful weird fiction than for his horror fiction, later added the themes of aliens, demons, shapeshifters, and monsters in his explorations into cosmic horror (a term later coined by H. P. Lovecraft to describe his own fiction) and the supernatural.

Although a few canonical authors (namely Edith Wharton and Henry James) dabbled in the horror genre near the turn of the century, monsters basically lay dormant until the 1930s, when Americans saw the resurgence of horror fiction in the form of pulp magazine publications. This was the era of Lovecraftian horror and the weird tales of *Blackwood's*. Masters like H. P. Lovecraft and Arthur Machen introduced a generation of Americans to fears of the Old Ones, darker gods who reigned before humans inhabited the Earth, who desired to regain their stronghold on the planet by bringing about either the subjugation of humanity or the apocalypse. The benchmark texts of this decade were Lovecraft's Cthulhu tales and Machen's story of subterranean gods, *The White People*. The 1950s saw some resurgence in the genre; however, the benchmark texts of that era were those adapted for the screen, such as Richard Matheson's *The Incredible Shrinking Man* (1957).

The most recent wave of popular horror began in 1968 when Ira Levin published *Rosemary's Baby*, and thanks to the perennial bestsellers of Levin, Stephen King, Anne Rice, Dean Koontz, and Peter Straub, the 1970s and 1980s saw no break in the popularity of horror. Benchmark texts of this period include King's *Carrie* and *The Shining*, Straub's *Shadowland* and *Ghost Story*, Rice's *Interview with the Vampire*, Richard Lortz's *Lovers Living, Lovers Dead*, Levin's *The Stepford Wives*, Koontz's *Demon Seed*, and various titles by Graham Masterton. Today's up and coming writers promise to keep the horror genre viable and exciting. Despite the fact that the number of horror titles published in the past few years shows a slow decline in popularity, the emergence of Poppy Z. Brite and Christa Faust has produced legions of new fans who have awarded them cult status. In addition, Charles Grant and Robert R. McCammon, both of whom have been around a while, seem to be hitting their stride when it comes to creating new stories based on familiar mythologies. Bentley Little, Scott Nicholson, and Robert Weinberg are reintroducing the weird tale usually concerned with everyday life. Elizabeth Hand, Phil Rickman, Tananarive Due, and Jemiah Jefferson are giving horror a multicultural voice, and Ramsey Campbell continues to awe the literary world by showing it that works of horror can be erudite as well as entertaining.

In the meantime, horror film continues to be a big draw at the box office, with the *Scream* and *I Know What You Did Last Summer* series; numerous *Dracula* remakes and related biographical flicks; and new films such as *The Sixth Sense*, *The Cell*, and *The Mummy* promising to do well among teenagers and young adults. The release of a handful of extremely well-made horror films that threaten to be serious Oscar and Golden Globe material began in 2001. Films such as *The Others*, *Hannibal*, *From Hell*, and *With a Friend Like Harry . . .* are redefining horror movies for both directors and audiences. As is typical of the relationship between horror film and horror literature, the popularity of one aids in increasing the popularity of the other (for a more detailed discussion of the relationship of horror film to horror literature, see the introduction), as well as in determining the trends that change the genre.

Rather than discuss these trends in essay format, we have decided that it makes more sense to look at each trend individually for reasons of practicality and brevity, with the caveat that we ask readers to remember that these trends are interrelated, that none of them exists within a vacuum. To that end, we present the following list of some of the current trends that we have noticed in our readings for this edition:

Alternative literature: The literary term "alternative literature" refers to the rewriting or retelling of classic works in the genre, which involves shifting the point of view, adding details omitted by the earlier work, or changing the story completely. This trend can be seen in the various rewritings of Bram Stoker's *Dracula*, such as Kim Newman's Anno Dracula Series, which examines the world had the Count defeated Van Helsing's party of vampire hunters. Other examples are Tom Holland's *Lord of the Dead* (a retelling of John Polidori's *The Vampyre*) and Kyle Marffin's *Carmilla: The Return* (a retelling of Joseph Sheridan Le Fanu's *Carmilla*).

Divine warnings: Monsters still serve their original function, as warnings to humans about the negative consequences of their actions. The word *monster* derives from the Latin *monstere*, which means to show. Here, the monster may be frightening but is not evil per se. For example, in *Tales from the Hood*, those creatures we'd commonly identify as monsters (zombies, flesh-eating dolls, and other creatures with supernatural powers) may be terrible to look at, but they aren't the true monsters, the ones whose actions bring suffering to all. Instead, these creatures have come to expose evil-doers (abusive police officers, white supremacists masquerading as moderates, drug dealers) who by the light of day do not appear as bad. This trend is most notably demonstrated in ecological horror, in fiction by Native American writers, and in horror fiction that borrows from Christian mythology.

The horror of everyday life: Life itself, in its everyday ugliness and frightening lack of order and justice, is sufficiently terrifying. This type of horror is most often seen in psychological horror. Examples of this trend are Bentley Little's *The Association* and Andrew Neiderman's *Neighborhood Watch,* both about the horrors of over-zealous neighborhood associations whose demands for conformity are so extreme that they can punish individuals for painting their houses the wrong color. Other titles are *The One Safe Place*, by Ramsey Campbell; *Gift Giver*, by Jean Sapin; and *The Dress Lodger*, by Sheri Holman.

Genre-crossing: Horror texts cross over into other well-established genres such as action adventure, police procedurals, detective fiction, and romances. For titles associated with this trend, see the list of cross-genre horror novels in appendix A.

Historical horror: Historical figures can be represented as monsters or monster-killers, adding a new dimension to their actions and often to the myths that surround them. In some cases, the historical figures are simply used as characters that inform the novel. Examples of novels that use historical characters are Kim Newman's Anno Dracula Series and Tom Holland's Lord of the Dead Series, Rose Earhart's *Dorcas Good* and *Salem's Ghosts*, and Thomas M. Sipos's *Vampire Nation*. One anthology of note that makes use of this trend is *Historical Hauntings*, by Jean Rabe and Martin H. Greenberg (editors).

Intertextual horror: Writers populate their fiction with characters from other well-known writers, with characters from their own previous creations, and with characters from popular culture, creating a continuity of the horror universe. Examples of this trend are Kim Newman's Anno Dracula Series; Anne Rice's Vampire Chronicles, New Tales of the Vampire and Mayfair Witch Series, and the Universal Monsters Series; and various Stephen King novels set in Castle Rock, Maine.

The Reemergence of the small press and chapbooks: In the first edition of *Hooked on Horror*, we noted that large presses had been curbing their horror offerings. While working on this edition, we found that approximately 35 to 40 percent of available horror titles between 1998 and 2001 came from small presses, some of these titles in the form of chapbooks. These small presses include Dark Tales Publications (Kansas City, Missouri), Yard Dog Press

(Alma, Arkansas), The Stealth Press (Lancaster, Pennsylvania) and Second Chance Press (Sagaponak, New York) (Stealth and Second Chance re-issue previously published novels that were underappreciated when first issued.), Crazy Wolf Publishing (New Hyde Park, New York), Cumberland Press (Nashville, Tennessee), Erica House (Baltimore, Maryland), Gray Wolf Press (St. Paul, MN), IFD Publishing (Eugene, Oregon), ImaJinn Books (Hickory Corners, Michigan), The Permanent Press (New York, NY), and various university presses.

The return of the strange story: The phrase "strange story" was coined by Peter Straub to describe the fiction of Robert Aickman. Aickman's fiction was a mixture of horror, dark fantasy, and magical realism. Perhaps the best way to describe this type of fiction, as readers will note we have done throughout this edition, is by comparing it to the stories and screenplays of Rod Serling. In these types of stories, monsters aren't always necessary, and the horror isn't always terrifying as much as it is unsettling. The return of the strange story is especially prominent in recent horror films, such as M. Night Shyamalan's *The Sixth Sense*, Tarsem Singh's *The Cell*, and Alejendro Amenabar's *The Others*. Literary examples include Scott Nicholson's *Thank You for the Flowers* and Robert Weinberg's *Dial Your Dreams*, as well as novels by John Wooley and Ron Wolfe.

Splatterpunk: Splatterpunk involves an over-the-top usage of violence, gore, sex, and cruelty. The typical splatterpunk anti-heroes relish their careers as a monster. Their exploits would shame Caligula. The most extreme writers in this subgenre are Poppy Z. Brite, John Shirley, and Michael Slade.

Part 2

An Annotated Bibliography of Horror Novels and Films

Chapter 4

Ghosts and Haunted Houses: Dealing with Presences and Absences

Ambrose Bierce, in *The Devil's Dictionary*, defines the word *ghost* as "the outward manifestation of an inward fear." Though humorous, Bierce's commentary on spirits implies what writers of traditional ghost tales have known for a long time: Most sightings are more a result of an individual's overactive imagination fed by guilt, remorse, grief, or paranoia, than they are the result of actual visitations of otherworldly beings. On one level, ghost and haunted house stories can be viewed as tales of guilt—guilt thought to be long buried in the unconscious mind. The ghost or the haunted house serves as a portent, or warning, to the haunted person, who is often guilty of repressing knowledge of a wrongdoing. In Stephen King's *The Shining*, for example, Jack Torrance knows of the murders associated with the Overlook Inn, but he represses the implication of that knowledge: that he himself has a history of violence and substance abuse and is capable of going over the edge. He also refuses to acknowledge the problem that his alcoholism has become. The poltergeist and possessed abode can also serve as a signal to others who know nothing of the past sin, often reminding the unwitting haunted individual of the inadvisability of burying this newly acquired knowledge in the unconscious mind. Haunted houses of this type are often those built on Native American burial grounds, which disrespect the religious customs of a minority culture (and the houses thus remind Europeans that they are responsible for these Native American dead), or those built on sites where great social wrongs occurred. In King's *Bag of Bones*, a racially motivated rape and murder is the cause not only of a house being haunted but of an entire town being supernaturally besieged. Taken in this context, haunted houses can be interpreted as symbols of the psyche.

Although ghosts and haunted houses often go hand in hand, in this chapter we include works concerned with both phenomena and with either one type of supernatural visitation or the other. We argue that, contrary to popular belief, ghosts don't necessarily reside in haunted houses, and haunted houses do not necessarily have individuated ghosts in them. A metaphorical comparison may better help explain the difference between the two: Haunted houses are a sort of architectural version of abused children who lash out at the world, as in

Shirley Jackson's *The Haunting of Hill House.* In this novel, Hill House is simply "evil" because of the way it was built. In essence, it was born bad. On the other hand, the ghost's function is to educate the wrongdoer, as in mainstream literature: The three ghosts in Dickens's "A Christmas Carol" teach Scrooge the meaning of Christmas, and Hamlet's father's ghost warns him of a murder most foul. Often in horror, as in the Dickens example, ghosts are created or summoned by the wrongdoer's transgression. Other ghosts may appear to help people adjust to new phases in their lives, such as the child ghosts in the film *The Sixth Sense* and the otherworldly servants in the film *The Others.*

The haunted house, however, is a victim of events that either happened in the house itself or on the site of the house, prior to its erection. Hill House, in Shirley Jackson's novel, is haunted because its creator and original inhabitant, Hugh Crane, was a twisted New England Puritan incapable of love. The brand new prefabricated suburban homes in the 1980s film *Poltergeist* are haunted because the builder located his development on top of an old cemetery without bothering to first remove the bodies. Unlike ghosts, haunted houses don't try to educate later occupants about the wages of sin or repressed guilt; instead, they lash out and frighten anyone unfortunate enough to come under their roofs, sometimes with fatal consequences. Sometimes these houses are in need of love themselves. Hill House repeatedly urges Eleanor Vance to "come home," presumably to care for the decaying and awkwardly framed manse.

Finally, more than any other subgenre, ghost and haunted house tales lend themselves to the short story format. Many cross-referenced entries in this chapter include entire anthologies and single author collections of ghost and haunted house stories. Perhaps this is because the conventions of this genre are so ingrained in our consciousness that not much is needed to establish the details of a given tale. Thus, it is quite easy to write a ghost or haunted house story in such a diminutive format.

This chapter includes works that trace the ghost story from its literary beginnings with Robert Louis Stevenson, to its development, by late nineteenth- and early twentieth-century writers like Henry James, Edith Wharton, M. R. James, and Oliver Onions, into the form we recognize today in the works of Shirley Jackson, Stephen King, and Peter Straub. Representative titles in this chapter include not only scary, but also emotive, tragic tales like Toni Morrison's *Beloved*, Graham Masterton's *Spirit*, and Anne Rice's *Violin*. In addition, we cover works that trace the beginnings of the literary haunted house in Britain, with the prototypes seen in *Wuthering Heights*, *The Castle of Otranto,* and *Northanger Abbey.* We also annotate novels that demonstrate how the Americanization of the haunted house led to the development of the haunted forest/landscape and the haunted mind, as seen in the fiction of Nathaniel Hawthorne, Edgar Allan Poe, and Henry James. Benchmark titles in this chapter include Shirley Jackson's *The Haunting of Hill House*, Stephen King's *The Shining*, and Peter Straub's *Ghost Story.*

Note: Many collections and anthologies of ghost stories can be found in chapter 17. Individual collection titles can be accessed through the subject/keyword index under "ghost" and "haunted houses" as well. In addition, users are advised to check chapter 7, on demonic possession, which contains many titles of interest to readers who enjoy ghost stories. Again, check the keyword index for specific titles.

Appeals: Universal Fear of the Returning Dead; Simulation of "Campfire" Stories; Affirms Human Beliefs of Life After Death; Universal Fear of "Bumps in the Night" When Nothing Is There; Works Well for "Guilt" Stories; More Psychological Than Other Supernatural Tales

Amis, Kingsley.

The Green Man. *New York: Harcourt Brace, 1969. 252p.* (See chapter 16, "Comic Horror: Laughing at Our Fears.")

Aycliffe, Jonathan.

A Shadow on the Wall. *Sutton, England: Severn House, 2000. 217p.* Atherton, Rector of Thornham St. Stephen, should never have meddled with the tomb of the fourteenth-century Abbot of Thornham, even in the interests of restoration. For when the workmen raised the lid of the tomb, he saw a black shadow emerging. Now he needs the help of antiquarian Richard Asquith, a Cambridge professor. But Richard begins seeing visions, and a mysterious plague threatens to wipe out an entire town. **Similar titles:** *Riverwatch*, Joseph M. Nassie; *The Talisman*, Jonathan Aycliffe; *The Rag Bone Man*, Charlotte Lawrence; *The Book of the Dark*, William Meikle.

> *Academia • Clergy as Character • Cursed Objects • Dreams • England • Revenging Revenant*

Barker, Clive.

Coldheart Canyon. *New York.: HarperCollins, 2001. 676p.* Barker's new novel is a ferocious indictment of Hollywood, depicted as a nexus of human and inhuman evil, a place where fleshly pursuits corrupt the spirit. In 1920, a glamorous movie vamp and her manager go shopping in her homeland, Romania. They purchase the panorama on the walls of a subterranean room in an ancient fortress-turned-monastery. The tiles, which are cursed, are remounted in the star's mansion in Coldheart Canyon, a Hollywood residential area. Many ghosts haunt the canyon, and they are imprisoned in the mansion. **Similar titles:** *The Picture of Dorian Gray*, Oscar Wilde; *Elixir*, Gary Goshgarian; *Wetbones*, John Shirley.

> *Actor as Character • Cursed Objects • Eroticism • Haunted Houses • History, Use of • Hollywood, California • Immortality • Sado-Masochism*

Barlog, J. M.

Dark Side: The Haunting. *Chicago: BAK Books, 1999. 293p.* A talented surgeon makes Jenny Garrett almost as good as new after a horrendous accident. But someone wanted Jenny dead, and now Detective Rick Walker has to find out who and why. Jenny can't help with the investigation though, for her memory of the accident, and the weeks preceding it, has been wiped out, and she has recently been seeing her doppelgänger and questioning her sanity. **Similar titles:** *Psyclone*, Roger Sharp; *Hideaway*, Dean Koontz; *Fight Club* (film); *Amnesia*, Andrew Neiderman; *The Bad Place*, Dean Koontz.

> *Alter Ego • Amnesia • Police Officer as Character • Replicants • Stalkers*

Barron, Diana.

Phantom Feast. *St. Petersburg, Fla.: Barclay Books, 2001. 269p.* (See chapter 13, "Ecological Horror: Rampant Animals and Mother Nature's Revenge.")

Beman, Donald.

Dead Love. *New York: Leisure, 2001. 346p.* Thirty years ago, a teenaged Sean MacDonald promised to love Judith forever, but her life was cut short before they could take their relationship any further. Now Sean has returned to his hometown with his new love, Pamela. But Judith won't let a small matter such as her own death stand in the way of her relationship with Sean. Judith attacks Pamela and puts her into a coma, then possesses the body of someone else to make sure Pamela is never a threat to her relationship with Sean. And Judith doesn't stop there. She's willing to kill anyone who might come between her and her sweetheart. **Similar titles:** *What Lies Beneath* (film); *The Tides*, Melanie Tem; *Thunderland*, Brandon Massey; *The Tormentor*, Bill Pronzini.

New York State • Revenging Revenant • Writer as Character

Bischoff, David.

The Crow: Quoth the Crow. *New York: HarperPrism, 1998. 256p.* Based on The Crow series and "The Raven" by Edgar Allen Poe, this novel tells a tale of blackmail and black magic. Bischoff's emphasis is on characterization and action. **Similar titles:** *The Crow: Clash by Night*, Chet Williamson; *The Crow: Lazarus Heart*, Poppy Z. Brite; *Gothique*, Kyle Marffin; *Silk*, Caitlin R. Kiernan .

Academia • Alternative Literature • The Crow (character) • Gothicism

Bradley, Marion Zimmer.

Gravelight. *New York: Tor, 1998, ©1997. 350p.* In the small town of Morton's Fork, researchers from a local institute discover the cause of various visions, poltergeists, and vanishings: a gate that opens to the underworld. Four people are then thrown together, and they must fight off their own inner demons and self-doubts to triumph over the dark power of the Gate. **Similar titles:** *The House*, Bentley Little; *Isle of the Whisperers*, Hugh B. Cave; *The Book of the Dark*, William Meikle; *Dark Soul*, M. Martin Hunt.

Actor as Character • Alcoholism • Appalachia • Blackburn, Truth (character) • Parapsychology • Virginia

Brite, Poppy Z.

The Crow: The Lazarus Heart. *New York: HarperPrism, 1998. 256p.* (See chapter 11, "Maniacs and Sociopaths, or the Nuclear Family Explodes: Monstrous Malcontents Bury the Hatchet.")

Brontë, Emily.

Wuthering Heights. *New York: Cambridge University Press, 1997, ©1847. 416p.* Catherine Earnshaw has loved Heathcliff ever since her father brought him home as a stray waif. But Catherine's father passes away, and when she comes of age, her brother refuses to countenance her relationship with the gypsy foundling, instead encouraging his sister to marry the more gently bred Edgar Linton. Heathcliff is driven mad by his thwarted love, and after Catherine's death, seeks to destroy the Linton and Earnshaw families. But revenge cannot calm Heathcliff, and Catherine's ghost at Wuthering Heights forever haunts him. This classic has inspired several films, including one directed by Luis Bunuel in 1954. **Similar titles:** *The Phantom of the Opera*, Gaston LeRoux; *Northanger Abbey*, Jane Austen; *Frankenstein*, Mary Shelley; *Weiland*, Charles Brockden Brown.

England • Gothic Romance • Revenge • Sibling Rivalry

Cady, Jack.

The Haunting of Hood Canal. *New York: St. Martin's Press, 2001. 306p.* Hood Canal has always been a sleepy backwater, until Sugar Bear Smith, a moody blacksmith, dumps the corpse and car of a suspected child molester in the local waterway. Unfortunately, his action awakens a water spirit with a suddenly voracious appetite for other vehicles and their drivers. Thereafter, the town is besieged by an assortment of hustlers, con artists, and well-heeled entrepreneurs who smell exploitable business prospects in its atmosphere. **Similar titles:** The Bewdley Series, Tony Burgess; *The Cleanup*, John Skipp and Craig Spector; *The Peddler and the Cloud*, Scott Badger (editor); *The Apostate*, Paul Lonardo.

Demons • Revenge • Vigilantism • Washington State

Campbell, Ramsey.

Nazareth Hill. *New York: Doherty, 1997. 383p.* When her father holds up eight-year-old Amy so she can see inside one of the windows of Nazarill, an old decrepit building in Partington, England, she sees something move, something spidery and ghost-like. Eight years later, her father is the caretaker of Nazarill, now a renovated hostelry. When one of Nazarill's tenants dies of heart failure, Amy suspects the ghost she saw as a child is seeking revenge. But can she get anyone, even her own father, to believe her? This is a truly spellbinding book that was a recipient of an International Literary Guild Award for Best Novel. **Similar titles:** *The Shining*, Stephen King; *Midwinter of the Spirit*, Phil Rickman; *The Mammoth Book of Haunted House Stories*, Peter Haining (editor); *Bag of Bones*, Stephen King.

Haunted Houses • Parenting • Photographer as Character

Clegg, Douglas.

The Infinite. *New York: Leisure Books, 2001. 377p.* This tale revolves around the formally engineered meeting of Chet Dillinger, Cali Nytbird, and Frost Crane, all of whom are endowed with psychic proclivities that have been more curse than gift in their lives. The three are invited to a haunted mansion by a psychic researcher. Each is a spiritually scarred survivor who hopes his or her experiment will exorcise personal demons as well as those associated with Harrow House. **Similar titles:** *The Haunting of Hill House*, Shirley Jackson; *Mischief*, Douglas Clegg; *Death's Door*, John Wooley and Ron Wolfe; *Five Mile House*, Karen Novack.

Afterlife, The • Clairvoyant as Character • Grieving • Haunted Houses • New York State • Parapsychology

Costello, Matthew J.

Poltergeist, the Legacy: Maelstrom. *New York: Ace Books, 2000. 229p.* Based on the television series of the same name, this action-oriented novel is a good versus evil tale, with the Ancient Egyptian Deities represented as evil Demons, and the Christian God as the Savior. The Legacy is confronted by an evil conspiracy and tries to recover a lost manuscript from the bottom of the sea. Fans of the TV series will enjoy this adaptation. **Similar titles:** *Poltergeist* (film); The Buffy the Vampire Slayer Series, various authors; *Dark Soul*, M. Martin Hunt; *Twilight Dynasty: Courting Evil*, Barry H. Smith.

Religion—Ancient Egyptian • Religion—Christianity

Danielewski, Mark Z.

House of Leaves. *2d ed. London, England: Anchor, 2000. 709p.* (See chapter 14, "Psychological Horror: It's All in Your Head.")

Desmond, Sean.

Adam's Fall. *New York: Thomas Dunne Books, 2000. 245p.* The unnamed occupant of B-46 in Adam's House is a Harvard senior, working on his English honors thesis so he can obtain a fellowship to study in England. But things change when his roommate catches him with his girlfriend and commits suicide due to her perfidy. Now the occupant begins to hear strange noises that no one could be causing. Then a shadow man emerges from the fog and begins to communicate with him, demonstrating knowledge of his deepest, darkest desires. Is the occupant of B-46 imagining things, or is he truly being visited by beings from another dimension? **Similar titles:** *Bag of Bones*, Stephen King; *Midwinter of the Spirit*, Phil Rickman; *The White Room*, Rick Hautala.

> *Cambridge, Massachusetts • Secret Sin*

Durchholz, Eric.

The Promise of Eden. *Antioch, Tenn.: Concrete Books, 1999. 204p.* A spirit named Anna, a ghost who claims that she needs help getting into heaven, visits Gregory Coleman when he is five. She tells Gregory that he must be her advocate in order for her to achieve the Eden that was promised in the afterlife, but as he grows older he comes to realize that Anna is not solely a benevolent spirit, that her plans for him are more insidious than she let on. The emergence of a 200-year-old spirit named Slyvie further complicates Gregory's life, as he becomes unwittingly involved with the netherworld's plans to alter reality. This Christian crossover is well written and thought provoking, at times poetic. **Similar titles:** *Blood Covenant*, Marilyn Lamb; *Soul Temple*, Steven Lee Climer; *Project Resurrection*, Karen Duval; *Bag of Bones*, Stephen King; *Salem's Ghosts*, Rose Earhart.

> *Afterlife, The • Childhood • Cults • Dramatic Monologue • Eroticism • Homoeroticism • Indiana • Religion—Christianity*

Gonzalez, Gregg.

The Fifth Horseman: A Sleepy Hollow Legend. *Pleasantville, N.Y.: Milagro Publishing, 1999. 417p.* (See chapter 11, "Maniacs and Sociopaths, or the Nuclear Family Explodes: Monstrous Malcontents Bury the Hatchet.")

Grant, Charles. The Black Oak Series.

Black Oak 3: Winter Knight. *New York: Penguin-ROC, 1999. 224p.* Ethan Proctor, while continuing to search for a powerful multi-millionaire's missing daughter, is called to a small town in England. There he meets the ghost of Sir Jared Battle, a nobleman of the House of Lancaster who needs souls so he can cease living among the undead. In the battle between the ghost hunter and the vengeful revenant, who will win? **Similar titles:** *Alymer Vance: Ghost Seer*, Alice Askew and Claude Askew; *The Complete John Silence Stories*, Algernon Blackwood; *Full Moon, Bloody Moon*, Lee Driver; The Anita Blake, Vampire Hunter Series, Laurell K. Hamilton.

> *Black Oak Security • England • History, Use of • Proctor, Ethan (character) • Revenging Revenant*

Halsey, W[inifred] F.

To Kill an Eidolon. *Dekalb, Ill.: Speculation Press, 1999. 243p.* (See chapter 9, "Telekinesis and Hypnosis: Chaos from Control.")

Hautala, Rick.

Poltergeist, the Legacy: The Hidden Saint. (See the Poltergeist, the Legacy Series in this chapter.)

Hautala, Rick. [as A. J. Matthews]

The White Room. *New York: Berkley, 2001. 359p.* Four years after a miscarriage, Polly Harris is trying to get back to a semblance of normal life, so she volunteers at a local hospital. During her first day in the emergency room, Heather, a young girl, dies while holding Polly's hand. Now Polly is hearing Heather's voice, expressing fear at being in a white room and seeing terrifying visions outside of her "window." In an attempt to help Polly get over her present state of mind, her husband takes the family to stay in his brother's cabin in rural Maine, but this change of scenery isn't much better. The bones of a child are unearthed near the cabin, and Polly begins to make grisly discoveries inside the house.

Similar titles: *House of Pain*, Sephera Giron; *Spirit*, Graham Masterton; *What Lies Beneath* (film).

Afterlife, The • Maine • Revenging Revenant • Secret Sin

Hawthorne, Nathaniel.

The House of the Seven Gables. *New York: Oxford University Press, 1991,* ©*1851. 328p.* (See chapter 14, "Psychological Horror: It's All in Your Head.")

Hill, William.

California Ghosting. *Middleburg, Fla.: Otter Creek Press, 1998. 523p.* (See chapter 16, "Comic Horror: Laughing at Our Fears.")

Hynd, Noel.

The Prodigy. *New York: Kensington, 1999. 352p.* (See chapter 14, "Psychological Horror: It's All in Your Head.")

Jackson, Shirley.

The Haunting of Hill House. *Cutchogue, N.Y.: Buccaneer Books-Lightyear, 1993,* ©*1949. 306p.* Four people spending a weekend at Hill House to study the paranormal find themselves haunted by a sinister spirit. To make matters worse, one of the guests, Eleanor, a shy young woman in her thirties, seems to be singled out by the "house." Jackson shows her mastery of storytelling and characterization in this classic of the genre, which was later made into an effective film by Robert Wise (*The Haunting*). *Hill House* is written in her characteristic third person objective style, but is very effective. **Similar titles:** *The Haunting* (film); *Hell House*, Richard Matheson.

Haunted Houses • New England • Parapsychology • Religion—Christianity—Protestantism • Suicide

Johnstone, William W.

The Devil's Heart. *New York: Kensington-Pinnacle, 1999. 400p.* (See chapter 8, "Mythological Monsters and 'The Old Ones': Invoking the Dark Gods.")

Kearsley, Susanna.

The Shadowy Horses. *London: Vista, 1998. 316p.* Archeologist Verity Grey joins an expedition launched by a wealthy eccentric who, for the past forty years, has searched for the Ninth Legion of the Roman army, which mysteriously disappeared from Scotland about 115 a.d. The only evidence that the famed lost legion lies buried on the site comes from an eight-year-old boy, who regularly communes with a ghostly Roman sentinel who speaks to him in Latin. Kearsley is strong on atmosphere. **Similar titles:** *Dark Sister*, Graham Joyce; *The Sleeper in the Sands*, Tom Holland; *The Shadow Out of Time*, H. P. Lovecraft.

Archeology • Precognition • Romans—Ancient • Scholars • Scotland

King, Stephen.

Bag of Bones. *New York: Scribner, 1998. 560p.* A writer of thriller novels returns to his lake home in Maine to investigate his wife's death. In the process, he leaves himself open to visitations from various ghosts, one of which desires to destroy him and the entire town for a past evil committed by their ancestors. This vintage King story is truly remarkable in its ability to frighten with subtlety. **Similar titles:** *Salem's Ghosts*, Rose Earhart; *Violin*, Anne Rice; *The Haunting of Hip Hop*, Bertice Berry.

🎧 audiotape, audio download, compact disc   🖱 e-book   🔎 large print

Haunted Houses • Maine • Racism • Rape • Secret Sin • Writer as Character

Klavan, Andrew.

The Uncanny. *New York: Crown, 1998. 343p.* (See chapter 16, "Comic Horror: Laughing at Our Fears.")

Koontz, Dean.

The House of Thunder. *New York: Berkley, 1992. 253p.* (See chapter 14, "Psychological Horror: It's All in Your Head.")

Kosciolek, David.

Green Light Cemetery. *Hazlet, N.J.: Green Light Ventures, 1999, ©1993. 183p.* (See chapter 14, "Psychological Horror: It's All in Your Head.")

Laymon, Richard.

Friday Night in Beast House. *Baltimore: Cemetery Dance, 2001, ©1979. 161p.* This novella features all the trademark Laymon touches: Mark accepts a dare from Alison, the girl of his wet dreams, so he helps to sneak her into Beast House, the scene of several horrific murders during past decades and now a major tourist attraction in the small West Coast town where it stands. **Similar titles:** *Haunted Houses*, Nancy Roberts; *Blair Witch 2* (film); *California Ghosting*, William Hill.

High School • Haunted Houses • Psychosexual Horror • Revenging Revenant

The Midnight Tour. *Baltimore: Cemetery Dance Publications, 1998, ©1994. 596p.* (See chapter 14, "Psychological Horror: It's All in Your Head.")

Lee, Edward.

The Chosen. *New York: Kensington-Pinnacle, 2001, ©1993. 379p.* Vera Abbot's new position as the boss of Wroxton Hall seems like every restaurant manager's dream. She is paid a high salary, has an unlimited budget, and entertains an exclusive clientele. It is the perfect escape from her dead-end job in town and from a cheating, drug-addicted fiancé. But pretty soon too many things at the bizarre country inn don't add up: footsteps and voices when the inn is empty, strange mute servants, and nightmares of demented sex with a faceless stranger. **Similar titles:** *The Dead Inn*, Shane Ryan Staley (editor); *Six Inch Spikes*, Edo Van Belkom; *Black Butterflies*, John Shirley; *Embraces*, Paula Guran (editor).

Demons • Dreams • Haunted Houses • Psychosexual Horror • Torture

Little, Bentley.

The House. *New York: Signet, 1999. 360p.* A postmodern haunted house tale in which the haunted dwelling isn't so much one specific building but rather an archetypal childhood home that each of us carries in our minds. Five characters are simultaneously plunged back to this archetypal home to confront their own deeply repressed guilt. **Similar titles:** *The Haunting of Hill House*, Shirley Jackson; *Night Terrors*, Drew Williams; *Gravelight*, Marion Zimmer Bradley; *Beloved*, Toni Morrison.

Childhood • Demons • Fantasy • Haunted Houses • Parallel Universe • Secret Sin • Shapeshifters

Masterton, Graham.

Prey. *New York: Leisure, 1999, ©1992. 352p.* (See chapter 8, "Mythological Monsters and 'The Old Ones': Invoking the Dark Gods.")

Spirit. *New York: Leisure, 2001. 424p.* Five-year-old Peggy Buchanan was very close to her sisters Laura and Elisabeth, so close, in fact, that even after she dies from a fall into the family swimming pool in winter, she returns again and again, at various ages, often to avenge a wrongdoing committed against one of her sisters. But when Peggy's spirit becomes overprotective and overzealous, people begin to mysteriously die agonizing deaths caused by severe frostbite and its complications. Masterton has succeeded in producing yet another atmospheric and truly eerie novel. **Similar titles:** *Thunderland*, Brandon Massey; *Wither*, J. G. Passarella; *Lasher*, Anne Rice; *The Tides*, Melanie Tem.

Actor as Character • California • Childhood • Child Molesters • Grieving • New England • Parenting • Revenging Revenant • Sibling Rivalry

Matheson, Richard.

Hell House. *New York: Tor, 1999, ©1971. 301p.* A scholar and his students come to study the Belasco House, also known as Hell House, the most haunted place on Earth. Hell House, site of unimaginable decadence and cruelty during its original owner's lifetime, has driven its inhabitants to madness, suicide, and murder. Can the professor and his helpers survive their stay in a dwelling no one has attempted to inhabit in twenty years? **Similar titles:** *The Haunting of Hill House*, Shirley Jackson; *The Haunting* (film); *Darker than Night*, Owl Goingback.

Haunted House • Parapsychology • Revenging Revenant • Scholars • Secret Sin

Stir of Echoes. *New York: Tor, 1999, ©1958. 211p.* After being hypnotized at a party, the doors of perception are permanently opened for Tom Wallace. Now he can read minds, see into the future, and even communicate with the dead. He can no longer have the privacy he craves. Instead, he is held captive by a sort of perverse idea of 1950s family and neighborhood togetherness when he is privy to the neighbors' most intimate secrets. And now, a revenant insists he dig into his landlord's past. Matheson's novel was made into a film of the same name in 2000. **Similar titles:** *Lost Boys*, Orson Scott Card; *The Sixth Sense* (film); *Thank You for the Flowers*, Scott Nicholson; *Don't Dream*, Donald Wandrei.

California • Dreams • Haunted Houses • Hypnotism • Marriage • Secret Sin

Matthews, A. J.

The White Room. (See **Hautala, Rick,** *The White Room.*)

McFarland, Dennis.

A Face at the Window. *New York: Bantam, 1998. 309p.* Ex-alcoholic and addict Cookson Selway travels to England with his wife Ellen, a mystery writer. While staying at the Willerton Hotel, Selway meets three ghosts, leading to a relationship that strains his hold on reality. McFarland's emphasis is on characterization and psychology. **Similar titles:** *Nazareth Hill*, Ramsey Campbell; *The Shining*, Stephen King; "The Beckoning Fair One," Oliver Onions; *Violin*, Anne Rice; *The Green Man*, Kingsley Amis.

Alcoholism • Haunted Houses • London, England • Marriage • Writer as Character

Morrison, Toni.

Ⓟ **Beloved.** *New York: Plume, 1987. 275p.* Sethe and her children cross the Ohio River to freedom in the 1840s but are soon tracked by a bounty hunter. Sethe, determined that she and her children will never be slaves again, does the unthinkable: She attempts to help her entire family escape slavery through death. She succeeds in freeing her infant daughter Beloved in this manner, but ultimately she cannot be free from the curse of slavery or from Beloved's ghost, who returns to destroy her entire family. This amazing novel was the winner of a Pulitzer Prize for Fiction in 1988. It is a highly literate masterpiece that tells a story of slavery through the all too often dismissed genre of horror. Jonathan Demme made *Beloved* into a film of the same name in 1998. **Similar titles:** *Bag of Bones*, Stephen King; *Nazareth Hill*, Ramsey Campbell; *Spirit*, Graham Masterton; *Beloved* (film).

> *African-American Characters • Grieving • Haunted Houses • Ohio • Parenting • Revenging Revenant • Slavery • United States—19th Century*

Mullen, Laura.

The Tales of Horror: [A Flip Book]. *Berkeley, CA: Kelsey St. Press, 1999. 107p.* (See chapter 14, "Psychological Horror: It's All in Your Head.")

Novack, Karen.

Five Mile House. *New York: Bloomsbury, 2000. 228p.* A police detective is driven to her limits by a serial murderer of children. After she commits an act of vigilantism, one that leads to murder, she is given time off to get psychiatric help and to relax. Unfortunately, she, her husband, and her two children chose to retire to the Five Mile House, a house haunted by the ghost of a young woman who once murdered her children. This novel is narrated in two voices, of the detective and of the ghost. **Similar titles:** *The Shining*, Stephen King; *House of Pain*, Sephera Giron; *The House That Jack Built*, Graham Masterton; *Beloved*, Toni Morrison.

> *Haunted Houses • New England • Police Officer as Character • Religion—Paganism • Serial Killers • Witchcraft*

Patrick, Erin.

Moontide. *Holicong, Pa.: Wildside Press, 2001. 260p.* Set amid the breathtaking scenery of coastal Maine, this novel tells the tale of how Melanie Gierek hit bottom after her family died in a car accident in Chicago. After the funeral, she drives to Maine, where she spent calm summers as a child. Melanie takes a job on a ninteeenth-century schooner, the *Louisa Lee.* The job should be the answer to her prayers, but Melanie finds the ship possessed by a sentient malevolence. To solve the mystery of the ship and save her own life, Melanie must hunt down the past. **Similar titles:** *Clickers*, J. F. Gonzales and Mark Williams; *Ghostly Lights* and *Ghostly Lights Return*, Annick Hivert-Carthew; *Bag of Bones*, Stephen King.

> *Grieving • Maine • Maritime Horror • Revenging Revenant*

Piccirilli, Tom.

The Deceased. *New York: Leisure, 2000. 342p.* When he was a young boy, Jacob Maelstrom watched as his sister slaughtered his brother, father, and mother. Now his dreams are forcing him to return to the Maelstrom Mansion, where he must face and defeat the ghosts that haunt him daily—before they destroy him and his living loved ones. Piccirilli's emphasis is on atmosphere and suspense. **Similar titles:** *Spirit*, Graham Masterton; *Mischief*, Douglas Clegg; *The Haunt*, J. N. Williamson; *Riverwatch*, Joseph N. Nassie.

> *Dreams • Family Curse • Haunted Houses • Scholars • Sibling Rivalry • Writer as Character*

The Night Class. *Centerville, Va.: Shadowlands Press, 2001. 247p.* When Cal Prentiss returns to college after winter break, he discovers that a girl was murdered in his dorm room. He decides to write his senior thesis about his fantasies concerning the victim, when he believes he's haunted by her ghost (or perhaps just coming apart due to the stress of having to enter the "real world" soon). Cal attempts to unearth details about the girl's murder, only to run afoul of friends and a university administration gone mad. And to make things even more strange, Cal suffers from stigmata whenever someone close to him dies. **Similar titles:** *Beasts*, Joyce Carol Oates; *Naomi*, Douglas Clegg; *Bag of Bones*, Stephen King.

> *Academia • Obsession • Stigmata*

Poltergeist, the Legacy Series. Various Authors.

Hautala, Rick.

Poltergeist, the Legacy: The Hidden Saint. *New York: Ace Books, 1999. 230p.* Legacy member Alexandra Moreau and her friend Holly Brown, accompanied by her son Evan, visit Plymouth Rock on Thanksgiving. They see an enjoyable tourist attraction turn into a terrorist attack leading to the death of almost twenty innocent people. Evan is part of the body count. While Holly is recuperating in the hospital, the ghost of Evan visits her. He demands that she kill the evil Mr. Hunter, the militia leader who masterminded the assault. **Similar titles:** *Poltergeist* (film); The Buffy the Vampire Slayer Series, various authors; *Twilight Dynasty: Courting Evil*, Barry H. Smith.

> *Domestic Terrorism • Grieving • Moreau, Alexandra (character) • New England • Parenting • Revenging Revenant*

Rice, Anne.

Violin. *New York: Alfred A. Knopf, 1997. 289p.* Following the death of her current lover Karl, Triana Becker seems to be losing her mind. A mysterious violinist on the streets of New Orleans forces her back into her painful past through his music, and his playing is relentless. As it turns out, violinist Stefan Stefanovsky is a ghost, damned by his hatred and guilt to wander aimlessly, and he wants Triana. One of the masters of the gothic and horror tale weaves a new version of the classic ghost story. Rice is subtle in her approach. **Similar titles:** *Bag of Bones*, Stephen King; *Magic Terror*, Peter Straub; *Escaping Purgatory*, Gary A. Braunbeck and Alan Clark.

> 🎧 audiotape

> *Grieving • Music—Classical • New Orleans, Louisiana • Sibling Rivalry*

Rickman, Phil.

The Chalice. *London: Pan Books, 1998, ©1997. 646p.* (See chapter 10, "Small Town Horror: Villages of the Damned.")

Rummel, Keith.

Spirit of Independence. *St. Petersburg, Fla.: Barclay Books, 2001. 276p.* (See chapter 8, "Mythological Monsters and 'The Old Ones': Invoking the Dark Gods.")

Straub, Peter.

Ghost Story. *New York: Simon & Schuster, 1979. 567p.* Five septuagenarians in New England share a terrible secret, one that has them all consumed by guilt. When satanic slayings of animals begin to occur, and the old men begin dying of mysterious causes, the survivors suspect an evil presence is haunting them. Can a young Hawthorne scholar save them? Can anything save the town against an evil older than humanity itself? Straub is highly literate and complex. **Similar titles:** *Old Fears*, John Wooley and Ron Wolfe; *Phantoms*, Dean Koontz; *The Apostate*, Paul Lonardo; *One Rainy Night*, Richard Laymon.

🎧 audiotape

New England • Reincarnation • Revenging Revenant • Secret Sin • Senior Citizen as Character • Shapeshifters

Tem, Melanie.

The Tides. *New York: Leisure, 1999. 308p.* A young nursing home administrator finds herself faced with the unenviable task of admitting her own father. But circumstances become even more complicated when he begins to see a mysterious woman from his past, a ghost who will stop at nothing to get his daughter—even if that means hurting a few of the home's residents in the process. **Similar titles:** *Black House*, Stephen King and Peter Straub; *Darkness Demands*, Simon Clark; *Spirit*, Graham Masterton; *Lasher*, Anne Rice.

Alzheimer's Disease • Nurse as Character • Nursing Homes • Revenging Revenant • Senior Citizen as Character

Tessier, Thomas.

Fog Heart. *New York: St. Martin's Press, 1998. 320p.* (See chapter 14, "Psychological Horror: It's All in Your Head.")

Truong, Chau Van.

Secrets Kept (novella). In *For the Love of the Kill. Miami: Minerva Publishing, 2001. 49p.* A middle-aged couple move into their dream house in Miami, but during their first night out on the town, their teenaged daughter allegedly murders a schoolmate turned would-be rapist in a bizarre fashion: by pinning him to the wall of the living room with a butter knife. Soon the couple discover that the murder, and other strange occurrences in the house, is the product of a young woman's ghost. The ghost enlists them to help find her murderer, who just happens to be one of their neighbors. This is an easy read, but very well written. **Similar titles:** *Bag of Bones*, Stephen King; *What Lies Beneath* (film); *Bones* (film).

Asian-American Characters • Grieving • Haunted Houses • Miami, Florida • Revenging Revenant

Wilde, Oscar.

The Canterville Ghost. *Cambridge, MA: Candlewick Press, 1996. ©1891. 128p.* (See chapter 16, "Comic Horror: Laughing at Our Fears.")

Williamson, Chet.

The Crow: Clash by Night. *New York: HarperPrism, 1998. 256p.* This is Williamson's contribution to the Crow mythology, with the ghost/hero facing off against terrorists. **Similar titles:** *The Crow: Quoth the Crow*, David Bischoff; *The Crow: Lazarus Heart*, Poppy Z. Brite; *Silk*, Caitlin R. Kiernan.

The Crow (character) • Gothicism • Terrorism

Williamson, J. N.

The Haunt. *New York: Leisure, 1999. 363p.* A family haunt protects Ray and Jack Kidd. Like their parents before them, they never get sick, are relatively immune from speeding tickets, and don't have to work to keep a roof over their heads. But the haunt is like an overprotective parent, punishing them, sometimes with deadly force, for what it perceives as any deviation from its ideas of morality. Neither brother can bring anyone in the house or even marry without the haunt's permission. Now the haunt is lonely and believes it will be happier if one of its charges reproduces, making more Kidds for it to control. This novel is compelling and original. **Similar titles:** *Spirit*, Graham Masterton; *The House*, Bentley Little; *The Bell Witch*, Brent Monahan; *Bag of Bones*, Stephen King.

> *Haunted Houses • Indiana • Marriage • Parapsychology • Poltergeists • Secret Sin*

Wright, T. M.

Sleepeasy. *New York: Leisure, 2001. ©1993. 310p.* Harry Briggs and his wife drown in a freakish pool accident and "cross over" into the afterlife, a place where an individual creates his or her own reality through subconscious thought. Unfortunately, one of those thoughts, a serial killer, escapes back into the world of the living. Now Harry must stop his creation before it continues to kill. **Similar titles:** *The Dark Half*, Stephen King; *Mr. X*, Peter Straub; *Thunderland*, Brandon Massie; *Strangewood*, Christopher Golden.

> *Afterlife, The • Greenstreet, Sydney (character) • New York City • Police Officer as Character • Serial Killers*

Film

Beloved. *Jonathan Demme, dir. 1998. 187 minutes.* In Demme's eerie and atmospheric interpretation of Morrison's Pulitzer Prize-winning novel of the same name, escaped slave Sethe (Oprah Winfrey) does the unthinkable to keep her children from being put back into bondage: She tries to kill them all. She succeeds in freeing only her infant daughter Beloved in this manner, but Beloved will not lie quietly, and instead returns twenty years later to destroy her entire family. Danny Glover also stars. **Similar reads:** *Beloved*, Toni Morrison.

> *African-American Characters • Grieving • Haunted Houses • Ohio • Parenting • Revenging Revenant • Slavery • United States—19th Century*

Candyman. *Bernard Rose, dir. 1992. 98 minutes.* Candyman is the embodiment of the urban legend about the Hook, an escaped lunatic with a hook for a hand who menaces young lovers in compromising positions. And when two graduate students attempt to unearth the legend of Candyman, they find the real revenant, a black man who, in the 1890s, was lynched for miscegenation and now exacts revenge on those who would doubt his existence. This artistic movie is based on "The Forbidden" by Clive Barker, and stars Virginia Masden and Tony Todd, with a soundtrack scored by Philip Glass. **Similar reads:** *One Rainy Night*, Richard Laymon; *The Bell Witch Haunting*, Pat Fitzhugh.

> *African-American Characters • Chicago, Illinois • Racism • Reincarnation • Revenging Revenant • Urban Legend*

Ghost Story. *John Irvin, dir. 1981. 110 minutes.* Fred Astaire, Melvyn Douglas, Douglas Fairbanks Jr., and John Houseman star in this adaptation of Peter Straub's novel about a vengeful ghost. The four elderly men harbor a secret from their youth: their involvement in the accidental death of Eva Galli, a beautiful young secretary. Now their pasts have come back to haunt them, as the ghost of Galli is out for revenge. Irvin's film includes some truly scary moments, even though it is subtle in its entirety. Patricia Neal and a young Alice Krige also star. **Similar reads:** *Bag of Bones*, Stephen King; *Spirit*, Graham Masterton.

New England • Revenging Revenant • Secret Sin • Senior Citizen as Character

The Haunting. *Richard Wise, dir. 1963. (Black-and-white.) 112 minutes. .* This classic is an eerie and faithful version of Shirley Jackson's *The Haunting of Hill House*. Although this film lacks the special effects found in most of today's blockbusters, fine acting and good direction make a very chilling and atmospheric film. Julie Harris and Claire Bloom star. **Similar reads:** *The Haunting of Hill House*, Shirley Jackson; *Hell House*, Richard Matheson.

Haunted Houses • New England • Parapsychology • Religion— Christianity— Protestantism • Suicide

Nightmare on Elm Street. *Wes Craven, dir. 1984. 92 minutes.* Freddy Krueger, a school janitor who molested children, is released from prison, and a posse of enraged parents burn him to death. But the ghost of Freddy returns, entering their children's dreams and causing them to die hideous deaths. Robert Englund and a very young Johnny Depp star. **Similar reads:** *Old Fears*, John Wooley and Ron Wolfe; *Night Terrors*, Drew Williams.

Child Molester • Dreams • Revenging Revenant • Secret Sin

The Others. *Alejandro Amenabar, dir. 2001. 101 minutes.* After World War II, Grace (Nicole Kidman) and her photo-allergic children live in isolation in a sprawling mansion on the isle of Jersey, waiting for her husband to return from the war. Cut off from civilization, and even from electricity, the small family lives with only the help of three mysterious servants, who appeared a week after the previous help left in the middle of the night with no explanation. Then the children claim to see strange people in the house, and Grace herself finds furniture disturbed and locked doors left open. This fine film is gothic and atmospheric. **Similar reads:** *Thank You for the Flowers*, Scott Nicholson; *The Haunting of Hill House*, Shirley Jackson.

Afterlife, The • England • Ghost's Point of View • Gothicism • Grieving • Haunted Houses • Parapsychology • Secret Sin

Poltergeist. *Tobe Hooper, dir. 1982. 114 minutes.* A developer and his wife discover that their brand new suburban home is haunted when their daughter is snatched by one of the poltergeists she communicates with through the television. It's not enough to hire a medium to journey to the spirit world to retrieve their daughter; the family must discover the *reason* for the haunting in the first place. **Similar reads:** Poltergeist, the Legacy Series, various authors; *The House That Jack Built*, Graham Masterton.

California • Clairvoyant as Character • Haunted House • Poltergeists • Revenging Revenant • Suburbia

Shining, The. *Stanley Kubrick, dir. 1980. 142 minutes.* (See chapter 7, "Demonic Possession, Satanism, Black Magic, and Witches and Warlocks.")

The Sixth Sense. *M. Night Shyamalan, dir. 1999. 106 minutes.* Bruce Willis stars as a child psychologist who must help a little boy come to terms with his special gift: He sees dead people. During the course of the child's therapy, Willis's character learns about his own true nature. This fine film is chilling and original. **Similar reads:** *Darkness Divided*, John Shirley; *Thank You for the Flowers*, Scott Nicholson.

Afterlife, The • Childhood • Ghost's Point of View • Gothicism • Haunted Houses • Parallel Universe • Philadelphia, Pennsylvania • Psychiatrist as Character

What Lies Beneath. *Robert Zemeckis, dir. 2000. 129 minutes.* When Claire Spenser begins hearing voices and seeing strange faces in her lakeside home, at first she believes that it is haunted by the ghost of her neighbor. But her neighbor isn't dead; she is just absent after a blow-up with her spouse. Now Claire's husband believes that she's suffering a mental breakdown brought about by their only daughter's leaving for college or her going through "the change." Claire perseveres, and with the help of the ghost, discovers the truth about her husband. This is a sort of feminist rewriting of *Fatal Attraction*, with supernatural elements. Harrison Ford and Michelle Pfeiffer star. **Similar reads:** *Bag of Bones*, Stephen King; *Dead Love*, Donald Beman.

Haunted Houses • Marriage • Musician as Character • Revenging Revenant • Scholar as Character • Secret Sin • Vermont

Our Picks

June's Picks: *Beloved,* Toni Morrison (Plume); *Wuthering Heights*, Emily Brontë (Cambridge University Press); *The Others* (film); *The Sixth Sense* (film); *What Lies Beneath* (film).

Tony's Picks: *Bag of Bones*, Stephen King (Scribner); *Beloved*, Toni Morrison (Plume); *Nazareth Hill*, Ramsey Campbell (Doherty); *Secrets Kept*, Chau Van Truong (Minerva Publishing); *Violin*, Anne Rice (Alfred A. Knopf); *Beloved* (film); *Candyman* (film); *The Haunting* (film); *The Others* (film).

Chapter 5

Golem, Mummies, and Reanimated Stalkers: Wake the Dead and They'll Be Cranky

Burial customs are more than just accepted methods of dealing with the remains of our loved ones; they're also methods of keeping the dead, both in body and spirit, from walking once more among the living. Ancient Egyptians took great care in making sure that their dead rulers, who were thought to be divine, could successfully make the journey from this world to the next. Not only were the bodies carefully preserved through mummification, but also the tomb was stocked with everything the dead would need in the next world, such as food and slaves. Furthermore, precautions were taken against invaders who might derail this journey. The various curses cast to protect the gravesites of the pharaohs were so well known and so well ingrained in popular culture that they inform most of the stories surrounding Howard Carter's discovery of King Tut's tomb.

When these precautions are not taken in the modern funeral process, the results can be disastrous: Grave robbers can steal the loved one's body or even appropriate any jewelry or riches buried with the body. In the world of horror, which metaphorically reflects societal fears with its dark atmosphere and grotesque imagery, even more terrifying outcomes are possible. In these fictional worlds, the dead can rise, not as ghosts but in corporeal form, and they will usually seek revenge on the living who disappointed or angered them. In some instances, the dead rise from their graves in the form of zombies, or soulless bodies, to walk about and indiscriminately murder the living.

Modern stories about mummies involve the dead for whom all precautions weren't taken, and who, when unearthed by naive archeologists centuries later, roam the earth in search of what they need to rest. This is the case with Boris Karloff's character in the Universal Studios picture *The Mummy* and with Ramses the Damned in Anne Rice's novel *The Mummy*. To make matters worse, it isn't just dead nobles who can be roused from their eternal slumbers, for even the average Joe or Jane Doe may become a reanimated corpse, if circumstances are favorable for the creation of zombies. Whether the dead are purposefully reanimated, as is the case with Haitian Voodoo in novels like Michael Reeves's *Voodoo Child*, or reanimated by accident, as is the case in George Romero's film *Night of the Living Dead* (in which the newly dead rise from their graves due to radiation released by a recent space probe), they are always dangerous to the living. Psychologically speaking, the dead are raised by the living who simply can't accept the finality of death, as is the case in Stephen King's *Pet Sematary*.

The golem, or human made out of clay, is another manifestation of the reanimated dead. Unlike mummies or zombies, the golem was never a human being with a soul. Instead, its creator bypassed the natural process of reproduction and artificially created something monstrous that will ultimately attempt to destroy its maker. The original golem comes from a medieval Jewish folktale in which a rabbi creates a large man of clay to protect his congregation from gentiles bent on making their lives miserable. But the golem, who has no soul, must be returned to the dust when he insists on being treated like a human. The most famous golem can be found in Mary Shelley's novel *Frankenstein*, in which Victor Frankenstein's creature is assembled from parts stolen from the local charnel house. Instead of making a god among men, Dr. Frankenstein makes a creature so hideous that all run from it. The tormented and lonely creature finally seeks to destroy his maker out of anger.

Contemporary golem stories range from murderous fictional characters (created by the fictional writers in the tales) who take corporeal form, as in Stephen King's *The Dark Half,* to an assassin cloned from stolen DNA and who is drawn to his genetic "twin," believing this person has stolen his life, as is the case in Dean R. Koontz's *Mr. Murder.*

The bottom line is, when the dead are raised, they're cranky; and soulless creatures will always be rebellious and angry children, bent on self-destruction and the destruction of their makers. Zombies almost always have a taste for human flesh, and the dead raised by grief, as in *Pet Sematary*, are ungrateful for their second chance at life and attempt to kill those who raised them. Golem are similarly ungrateful for their first chance at life and will attempt to erase their creators and the very act of their (the creatures') creations through murder, as is the case in Shelley's novel, or just kill indiscriminately, as in James Whale's 1931 film version of Shelley's novel.

Representative works in this section include Mary Shelley's *Frankenstein* and Stephen King's *Pet Sematary*. Readers should note that many of the more popular and influential of these fictions include film, such as *Frankenstein*, *Bride of Frankenstein*, *The Mummy* (and various versions of the same), *Night of the Living Dead*, *The Evil Dead*, and *Re-Animator*. These texts all teach us what Johnny learns the hard way early on in George Romero's *Night of the Living Dead* and what Victor Frankenstein discovers eventually in Mary Shelley's *Frankenstein*: Lack of respect for the ancestral dead and for our living creations can produce disastrous results.

Note: Readers who enjoy titles in this chapter can also find stories about golem, mummies, and other reanimated stalkers in chapter 17, "Collections and Anthologies." The keyword/subject index contains references to specific titles under the keywords "golem" and "mummies."

Appeals: Universal Fear of the Returning Dead; Universal Fear of Graveyards and Zombies; Emphasis on Creation, on "Playing God"

Anderson, Kevin J.

Resurrection, Inc. *Woodstock, Ga.: Overlook Connection Press, 1999. 263p.* (See chapter 12, "Technohorror: Evil Hospitals, Military Screw-Ups, Scientific Goofs, and Alien Invasions.")

Brandner, Gary.

Carrion. *Lincoln, Neb.: iUniverse.com, 2000. 265p.* McAllister Fain is a likable charlatan. He makes his living telling phony fortunes. Then he discovers an awesome power, the ability to revive the dead. But there is a terrible catch: The soulless creatures he resurrects are nothing more than meat. As their bodies decay these creatures have only one purpose, to find and destroy the man who brought them back. **Similar titles:** *Frankenstein* (film); *Resurrection, Inc.*, Kevin J. Anderson; *The Walking*, Bentley Little; *Awash in the Blood*, John Wooley.

Clairvoyant as Character • Grieving • Zombies

Clark, Simon.

Darker. *New York: Leisure, 2002. 410p.* Richard Young is a starving nebbish languishing in Greece after attempting to start his own business conducting tours. So when a disembodied voice offers him absolute power over people, the power to command others so absolutely that they would willingly die for him, Richard jumps at the opportunity before acquainting himself with the details of this arrangement. Absolute power is intoxicating, but it comes at a price. The force that gives Richard this charisma must also be fed, and if Richard can't arrange the occasional human sacrifice, he himself will fall victim to this mysterious entity that has changed his life. **Similar titles:** *Nailed by the Heart*, Simon Clark; *Darkness Demands*, Simon Clark; *Something Dangerous*, Patrick Redmond.

5

England • Human Sacrifice • Magic • Mind Control

Nailed by the Heart. *New York: Leisure, 2000. 392p.* The Stanforth family moves to a quaint island village to convert an old fort into a profitable resort and begin a new life. But the old fort is deserted for a reason: It was once a site of old beliefs and sacrifice connected to a crew of ancient warriors, sunk just off the coast. The Stanforths' presence in this sacred site has awakened the slumbering crew, who will not be appeased until they have tasted more blood. Clark's story is original and frightening. **Similar titles:** *Darkness Demands*, Simon Clark; *Brass*, Robert J. Conley; *Night of the Living Dead* (film).

England • Islands • Human Sacrifice • Maritime Horror

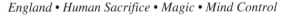

Collins, Max Allan.

The Mummy Returns. *New York: Berkley Boulevard, 2001. 290p.* Collins penned this novelization of the popular film, which begins ten years after Rick O'Connell and Evelyn Carnahan (now O'Connell's wife) sent Imhotep back to the underworld. He is raised from the dead once more and bent on destroying the world as we know it. Now Rick and Evelyn must remember their own past lives and relationships with Imhotep to thwart his plan and must protect their only son from the mummy and the Scorpion King. Collins's emphasis is on action adventure. **Similar titles:** *Into the Mummy's Tomb*, John Richard Stevens (editor); *The Sleeper in the Sands*, Tom Holland; *The Jewel of Seven Stars*, Bram Stoker; *The Mummy, or Ramses the Damned*, Anne Rice; *The Mummy* and *The Mummy Returns* (film).

Archeology • Carnahan, Evelyn (character) • Cursed Objects • Egypt • Imhotep (character) • Immortality • Mummies • O'Connell, Rick (character) • Revenging Revenant

Duval, Karen.

Project Resurrection. *Dekalb, Ill.: Speculation Press, 2000. 288p.* (See chapter 12, "Technohorror: Evil Hospitals, Military Screw-Ups, Scientific Goofs, and Alien Invasions.")

Golden, Christopher.

Strangewood. *New York: Signet, 1999. 304p.* (See chapter 8, "Mythological Monsters and 'The Old Ones': Invoking the Dark Gods.")

Jacobs, David. The Devil's Brood Series.

(See chapter 6, "Vampires and Werewolves: Children of the Night.")

Johnstone, William W.

The Devil's Touch. *Kensington-Pinnacle, 1999. 400 p.* (See chapter 8, "Mythological Monsters and 'The Old Ones': Invoking the Dark Gods.")

Karr, John.

Dark Resurrection. *St. Petersburg, Fla.: Barclay Books, 2001. 320p.* (See chapter 15, "Splatterpunk: The Gross-Out.")

King, Stephen.

The Dark Half. *New York: Signet, 1989. 484p.* Thad Beaumont, best-selling author of slasher novels, would like to say he has nothing to do with the series of monstrous murders that keep coming closer to his home. But how can Thad disown the ultimate embodiment of evil that goes by the name of one of his characters and signs its crimes with Thad's bloody fingerprints? **Similar titles:** *Mr. Murder*, Dean Koontz; *Dr. Jekyll and Mr. Hyde*, Robert Louis Stevenson; *Mr. X*, Peter Straub; *Fight Club* (film); *Strangewood*, Christopher Golden.

Castle Rock, Maine • Pangborn, Alan (character) • Police Officer as Character • Slasher • Writer as Character

Pet Semetary. *New York: Pocket Books, 2001, ©1984. 417p.* When Dr. Louis Creed's son's pet cat is hit by a car, he doesn't want to expose his son to the grim reality of death at his tender age. Over a few beers, a helpful neighbor tells him about the Micmac burying ground, which has the power to reanimate the dead. When Louis inters the cat in this profaned space, the animal returns, but it isn't the old feline his family knows and loves. Instead, it's a frightening shell of the old cat. Louis, however, doesn't learn from his mistakes. When his son is killed by a speeding truck, he can't accept that this is the end, and he takes his child to the Micmac burying ground to rejuvenate him. Like the reanimated family cat, the boy becomes a zombie bent on destroying the family. **Similar titles:** *Project Resurrection*, Karen Duval; *Bereavements*, Richard Lortz; *Beloved*, Toni Morrison; *Magic Terror*, Peter Straub.

🎧 audiotape, compact disc

Grieving • Maine • Physician as Character • Religion—Native American • Zombies

Koontz, Dean.

Mr. Murder. *New York: Berkley Books, 1993. 376p.* Marty Stillwater, well-known writer of murder mysteries, is being stalked by Alfie, his double, a genetically engineered hit man who, unknown to Marty, was cloned from his DNA. Alfie is psychically drawn to Stillwater, believing that he has stolen his life and memories, and Alfie aims to get them back. **Similar titles:** *The Dark Half*, Stephen King; *Frankenstein*, Mary Shelley; *Dr. Jekyll and Mr. Hyde*, Robert Louis Stevenson.

𝔇 audiotape, audio download

California • Cloning • Organized Crime

Perry, S. D.

Virus. *New York: Tor, 1998. 224p.* The *Electra* runs across the *Wan Xuan*, an abandoned Chinese ship adrift in the Pacific, and crew members are eager to board it and lay claim to the millions of dollars' worth of top-secret electronics aboard. But the *Wan Xuan* is far from deserted—something is alive in the ship's computers, and it's assembling physical form from the pieces of machinery and bodies of the hapless Chinese crew. **Similar titles:** *Alien* (film); *Resurrection, Inc.*, Kevin J. Anderson; *Geometries of the Mind*, Norman Eric Keller; *Demon Seed*, Dean Koontz.

Artificial Intelligence • Computers • Sailor as Character • Maritime Horror

Rice, Anne.

The Mummy, or Ramses the Damned. *New York: Ballantine Books, 1989. 436p.* As a mortal, King Ramses sought the elixir of life to bring eternal prosperity upon his people. But humans aren't meant to be immortal, so his experiment failed, and Ramses himself was "doomed forever to wander the earth, desperate to quell hungers that can never be satisfied." Ramses is reawakened in Edwardian London, where he becomes Dr. Ramsey, expert in Egyptology and close friend of the heiress Julie Stratford. However, the pleasures he enjoys with his new companion cannot soothe him. **Similar titles:** *Elixir*, Gary Goshgarian [as Gary Braver]; *The Vampire Lestat* and *Servant of the Bones*, Anne Rice; *The Jewel of Seven Stars*, Bram Stoker; *Cronos* (film).

𝔇 audiotape, audio download

Egypt • London, England • Mummies • Religion—Ancient Egyptian

Rovin, Jeff.

Return of the Wolf Man. *New York: Penguin-Putnam, 1998. 339p.* (See chapter 6, "Vampires and Werewolves: Children of the Night.")

Shelley, Mary.

Frankenstein. *Oxford: Oxford University Press, 1998, ©1818. 322p.* Dr. Victor Frankenstein thirsts for knowledge that humans aren't meant to know when he builds a creature out of spare parts from charnel houses. The result is a hideous being whose appearance terrifies humans, dooming him to loneliness. The creature's solitary condition causes him to destroy his maker and his family. This is a classic that has inspired various films and alternative retellings. **Similar titles:** *Dracula*, Bram Stoker; *Mr. Murder*, Dean Koontz; *Donovan's Brain*, Curt Siodmak; *The Invisible Man*, H. G. Wells.

𝔇 audiotape   🖫 CD rom   👓 large print

> *Diary Format • Frankenstein's monster (character) • Frankenstein, Caroline (character) • Frankenstein, Dr. (character) • Lavenza, Elizabeth (character) • Mad Scientist • Revenge • Science Fiction • Switzerland*

Siebert, Steven.

Cleopatra's Needle. *New York: Tor, 1999. 426p.* Dan Rawlins, a renowned Egyptologist, becomes unwittingly involved with the Mossad and with an international terrorist who is the reincarnation of a 3,000-year-old Egyptian general skilled in ancient Egyptian magic. Rawlins and the Mossad must prevent this terrorist from finding the missing half of a powerful ankh that permits him to raise the dead and will make it possible to unleash an ancient evil during the first solar eclipse of the new millennium. **Similar titles:** *The Sand Dwellers*, Adam Niswander; *The Queen of the Damned*, Anne Rice; *Twilight Dynasty: Courting Evil*, Barry H. Smith.

> *Afterlife, The • Archeologist as Character • Egypt • Espionage • History, Use of • Immortality • Mossad, The • Mummies • Reincarnation • Religion—Ancient Egyptian • Shapeshifters*

Stoker, Bram.

The Jewel of Seven Stars. *Oxford; New York: Oxford University Press, 1996, ©1903. 214p.* An Egyptologist accidentally awakens the soul of the mummy, which then possesses his daughter. He can save her only by bringing the body of the mummy back to life. **Similar titles:** *The Mummy, or Ramses the Damned*, Anne Rice; *The Mummy* (film); *Into the Mummy's Tomb*, John Richard Stephens (editor); *The Mummy Returns*, Max Allan Collins.

> *Archeology • Cursed Objects • Lawyer as Character • Mummies • Police Officer as Character • Religion—Ancient Egyptian*

Whitman, David.

Deadfellas. *Kansas City, Mo.: Dark Tales, 2001. 54p.* (See chapter 16, "Comic Horror: Laughing at Our Fears.")

Willis, Brian (editor).

Hideous Progeny. *Cardiff, Scotland: RazorBlade Press, 2000. 293p.* (See chapter 17, "Collections and Anthologies.")

Wright, T. M.

Sleepeasy. *New York: Leisure, 2001, ©1993. 310p.* (See chapter 4, "Ghosts and Haunted Houses: Dealing with Presences and Absences.")

Film

Bride of Frankenstein. *James Whale, dir. 1935. (Black-and-white.) 75 minutes.* Boris Karloff reprises his role as Frankenstein's monster in this rendition of the second half of Mary Shelley's novel. The lonely and somewhat inarticulate creature that evaded destruction in *Frankenstein* now demands that his creator make him a mate. This classic stars Boris Karloff, Elsa Lancaster, and Colin Clive. **Similar reads:** The Universal Monsters Series, various authors; *Frankenstein*, Mary Shelley.

> *Frankenstein, Dr. (character) • Frankenstein's monster (character) • Germany • Mad Scientist*

Frankenstein. *James Whale, dir. 1931. (Black-and-white.) 71 minutes.* James Whale's rendition of the first half of Mary Shelley's novel is set in the twentieth century. But in this film, Dr. Frankenstein's creation isn't a monster because of the arrogance of his creator in usurping the powers of God or because of the intolerance of society at large. Instead, this creature is monstrous because he is made with inferior parts. If Dr. Frankenstein's bumbling assistant hadn't procured an abnormal brain, then presumably the creature would have truly been the new Adam. This classic stars Boris Karloff as the monster. **Similar reads:** *Frankenstein*, Mary Shelley; *Donovan's Brain*, Curt Siodmak.

> *Frankenstein, Dr. (character)* • *Frankenstein's monster (character)* •
> *Germany* • *Mad Scientist*

The Mummy. *Karl Freund, dir. 1932. (Black-and-white.) 72 minutes.* When the mummy's tomb is desecrated by archeologists, he is reanimated and kills those responsible for disturbing his rest. He then discovers that the reincarnation of his mate is among the band of archeologists. Boris Karloff stars as the mummy. Be sure to look for the zipper in the back of his mummy costume. **Similar reads:** *The Mummy Returns*, Max Allan Collins; *The Jewel of Seven Stars*, Bram Stoker.

> *Archeology* • *Curse* • *Egypt* • *Imhotep (character)* • *Immortality* •
> *Mummies* • *Reincarnation* • *Revenging Revenant*

The Mummy. *Stephen Sommers, dir. 1999. 124 minutes.* (See chapter 16, "Comic Horror: Laughing at Our Fears.")

Son of Frankenstein. *Rowland V. Lee, dir. 1939. (Black-and-white.) 99 minutes.* The son of Dr. Frankenstein, played by Basil Rathbone, returns to his ancestral castle approximately twenty-five years after the monster's presumed death. But the creature isn't dead—he's only disabled and guarded by Igor (Bela Lugosi), the last of his father's misshapen attendants. The doctor's scientific curiosity gets the better of him, and he reanimates the creature, believing that this time he can prevent it from going on yet another fatal rampage. Boris Karloff stars again as the creature in the third of the Universal Studios Frankenstein films. **Similar reads:** The Universal Monsters Series, various authors; *Frankenstein*, Mary Shelley.

> *Frankenstein's monster (character)* • *Germany* • *Immortality* • *Mad Scientist* • *Revenge*

Films Related to the Horror Industry

Gods and Monsters. *Bill Condon, dir. 1998. 105 minutes.* Aging horror film director James Whale (Ian McKellen) reviews his life and career during his last days. Meanwhile, he continues to use his celebrity to lure beautiful young men into his bed, including his dangerously homophobic grounds keeper, Clayton Boone (Brendan Fraser). His deeply religious and devoted housekeeper Hanna (Lynn Redgrave) fears that Mr. Jimmy will spend eternity in hell because of his homosexuality. Lolita Davidovich also stars. Based on Christopher Bram's novel, *Father of Frankenstein*.

> *Gay/Lesbian/Bisexual Characters* • *Hollywood, California* •
> *Homoeroticism* • *Horror Movie Industry* • *Popular Culture* • *Whale, James (character)*

Our Picks

June's Picks: *The Dark Half* and *Pet Semetary,* Stephen King (Signet and Pocket Books); *Frankenstein*, Mary Shelley (Oxford University Press); *Bride of Frankenstein* (film); *Gods and Monsters* (film).

Tony's Picks: *Darker*, Simon Clark (Leisure); *The Dark Half*, Stephen King (Signet); *Mr. Murder*, Dean Koontz (Berkley); *Frankenstein* (film).

Chapter 6

Vampires and Werewolves: Children of the Night

The most popular of all monsters, vampires have evolved considerably since their introduction into literature and popular culture with the nineteenth-century publication of the serial adventure *Varney the Vampyre* and Bram Stoker's classic *Dracula*. Count Dracula, prototype of virtually all vampires as we know them today, was originally a monstrous, megalomaniacal foreigner who represented British xenophobia and the Western European fear of The Other (vampires are derived from an Irishman's interpretation of the mythology of Transylvania, or what is today known as Romania). This saber-toothed, bloodsucking creature, originally cousin to the werewolf, evolved into a suave, sophisticated, intelligent superhuman—and then de-evolved into a bloodthirsty superpunk who, like the werewolf, rips victims to shreds. There are only a few famous werewolves in fiction, but notable vampires are plentiful, ranging from the monstrous nosferatu of *Varney* and of Stoker's *Dracula* to the sophisticated aristocrat of Anne Rice's Vampire Chronicles. Vampires have since evolved into other forms, including the mind-controlling, war-mongering mutant humans in Dan Simmons's *Carrion Comfort* and members of an ancient alien race that has always fed on humans through sexual intercourse, as in Gloria Evans's *Meh'Yam*. Despite these differences, all vampires and werewolves are monsters because they must somehow feed on their victims' vital essences: flesh, blood, emotion, love, even tendencies toward violence.

Vampirism involves a creature of the night and his or her parasitic relationship with another, and this relationship has been used as a metaphor for love, the parent/child bond, sexual relationships, and power structures in general. Yet vampires are easily the most identifiable and often the most sympathetic, the most appealing of all the genre's monsters, mainly because vampires must, in some way, resemble the humans on which they prey. Moreover, vampirism is often represented as a sort of dark god-hood, as a variant of immortality, with a little bloodlust thrown in for a good scare. The classical vampire was once human (like the mummy, ghost, or werewolf), but only the vampire can retain—and often eclipse—human beauty. Also, vampires often possess some sort of extraordinary powers:

super strength, hypersexuality, and the abilities to hypnotize victims, control the weather, shapeshift, or compel animals to do their bidding; they also often possess the ability to fly. In general, vampires can range from superhuman predators to subhuman beasts, states appealing to both sides of the human experience, ranging from when we need to feel strong and invulnerable to those times when we feel powerless and vulnerable and seek to deal vicariously with this shortcoming. Finally, vampires are almost always erotic or sensual in some way, which is one of their greatest appeals.

Some vampires embrace their undead existence as a superior form of being. In Jemiah Jefferson's *Voice of the Blood* and Whitley Streiber's The Hunger Series, the children of the night are forever young and can spend their existence going to nightclubs and indulging in the pleasures of the flesh. In *Blade* and The Anno Dracula Series, many vampires see humans as nothing more than cattle. Other vampires experience their undeath as a curse rather than a blessing, and would like to be human again. Anne Rice's Vampire Chronicles is populated with nosferatu who are unable to lose their aversion to shedding human blood. In Rice's *Interview with the Vampire*, a bitter Louis loathes his maker, who has transformed him into a creature that must do what he finds morally repugnant to survive. And while Rice's Lestat de Lioncourt revels in his undead state, he too often pities and envies the mortals who must slake his thirst. In *Tale of the Body Thief*, Lestat is granted his wish to be human once again, only to find that he's been tricked into switching bodies with a human who, among other things, has the flu at the time of the change. Billie Sue Mosiman's novel *Red Moon Rising* concerns a neophyte vampire who must make a choice about where she'll fit in this philosophical continuum. Will she be a Predator, killing her victims without remorse; a Craven, so appalled at the whole idea of shedding human blood that she must depend on the kindness of Predators to survive; or a Normal, someone who exists between these two extremes?

Of all vampire texts, Bram Stoker's narrative is the most widely known, and arguably the most influential in the genre. All later vampire narratives must pay some sort of homage to *Dracula*, with its skillful combination of traditional Eastern European vampire folklore and nineteenth-century British xenophobia. Later vampire narratives sometimes add to the Dracula mythology established by Stoker, sometimes refute it, and often do a little of both. Anne Rice's Vampire Chronicles feature both aristocratic and bourgeois nosferatu, but vampires who held titles while "warm" have less difficulty adapting to the undead lifestyle, which is really just an extension of aristocratic privilege. Stoker's vampires are frequently repulsive and incapable of loving; Rice's vampires are almost always preternaturally beautiful and capable of passionate, platonic relationships. Kim Newman's Anno Dracula Series returns the legend to its beginnings, as it is an alternative history speculating about what Victorian England would be like if Dracula had defeated Van Helsing and his party of vampire hunters. Newman incorporates facts about the "real" Dracula (as identified by Raymond McNally and Radu Florescu), Romanian Prince Vlad Tepes, into his representation of Dracula. Newman's series also incorporates into the narrative every well-known literary vampire as well as vampire folklore from every culture. Vampires have indeed come a long way, and writers in the subgenre are constantly rewriting the vampire myth anew, with the possibilities being endless.

And then there are werewolves, cousins to the vampires. The werewolf comes from traditional vampire folklore, in which the undead frequently assume the form of a wolf to facilitate their nocturnal feedings. The werewolf is the alter ego of the suave, sophisticated vampire: if the vampire is a sort of monstrous Superego, the werewolf is the raging Id. The werewolf represents our most essential desires—for food, sex, comfort, even violence—in their most bestial form. Famous werewolves include Lawrence Talbot of Universal Film Studios fame, as well as Wilfred Glendon III, recently resurrected by David Jacobs in the Universal Monsters Series "devil's brood" books. The past decade has seen the creation of some memorable literary werewolves, including a couple of series that may some day popularize the lycanthrope in the same way that Anne Rice's Vampire Chronicles and Chelsea Quinn Yarbro's Saint-Germain Chronicles popularized the vampire. David Holland's *Murcheston: The Wolf's Tale* features an aristocratic werewolf who embraces his lycanthropy with abandon. Donna Boyd and Alice Borchardt are just beginning their extremely popular werewolf series. In Boyd's The Devoncroix Dynasty Series, werewolves take on a romantic quality, as they become rich, powerful, and beautiful when in their human forms. Borchardt, on the other hand, in The Silver Wolf Series, pens tales of historical werewolves (one of which is a female, a new twist), reminiscent of Rice's Vampire Chronicles in their breadth and epic quality.

Note: Stories about vampires and werewolves can also be found in the collections and anthologies described in chapter 17. Refer to the subject/keyword index for specific titles under the various keywords that include the word "vampire."

Appeals: Sympathetic, Sometimes Enviable "Monsters"; Ongoing Dialogue of Immortality Versus Humanity; Sex Appeal; Eroticism; Homoeroticism; Identification with the Bestial Side of Human Nature; Memorable Recurring Characters; More Series Than Other Subgenres; Lots of Historical Romance Tossed in; Excellent Monster for Metaphor (Vampire Can Symbolize Almost Anything)

Adams, Scott Charles.

> **Never Dream.** *Maple Shade, N.J.: S. C. Adams, 1999. 239p. Never Dream* is a masculine, action-oriented novel about warring vampire clans in modern America. Readers have found it to be original, clever, and captivating, an attention grabber from beginning to end. **Similar titles:** Mick Farren's The Time of Feasting Series; *Gothique*, Kyle Marffin; *Vampire's Waltz*, Thomas Staab; *Blade* (film).
>
> > *Vampire as New Species • Vampire Clans • Vampire's Point of View*

Africa, Chris N.

> **When Wolves Cry.** *Edmonton, Alb.: Commonwealth, 1998. 312p.* (See chapter 13, "Ecological Horror: Rampant Animals and Mother Nature's Revenge.")

Amsbary, Jonathan H. The Cyber Blood Chronicles.

> **Cyber Blood.** *Philadelphia: Xlibris, 2000. 232p.* David meets the woman of his dreams in an Internet chat room. His online encounters become more intense, and his dreams become more horrific. Can even the combined efforts of his real life and online friends, and a mysterious vampire hunter named Kit, who has recently joined an organization known as The Committee, save David? **Similar titles:** The Buffy the Vampire Slayer Series, various authors; The Anita Blake Series, Laurell K. Hamilton; The Host Series, Selena Rosen; *The Licking Valley Coon Hunters Club*, Brian A. Hopkins.
>
> > *Academia • Computers • The Internet • Vampire as New Species • Vampire Hunters*

KIT: The Cyber Blood Chronicles Part II. *Philadelphia: Xlibris, 2001. 245p.* The sequel to *Cyber Blood* follows the adventures of the vampire hunter Kit and her troupe of vampire killers in The Committee. Amsbary has a strong sense of action-adventure and interesting characters. **Similar titles:** The Buffy the Vampire Slayer Series, various authors; The Anita Blake Series, Laurell K. Hamilton; The Host Series, Selena Rosen; *The Licking Valley Coon Hunters Club*, Brian A. Hopkins.

Academia • Eroticism • Vampire Hunters

Andrews, Christopher.

Pandora's Game. Philadelphia: Xlibris, 1999. 248p. (See chapter 14, "Psychological Horror: It's All in Your Head.")

Anscombe, Roderick.

The Secret Life of Laszlo, Count Dracula. *Collingdale, Pa.: DIANE Publishing Company, 2000, ©1994. 409p.* A young medical student, Laszlo Dracula, accidentally murders a prostitute. Twenty years later and in a new location, Laszlo again acts out his bloodlust and becomes a serial murderer. Emphasis is on psychology and characterization. This novel is one of the few non-supernatural versions of the Dracula tale. **Similar titles:** The Anno Dracula Series, Kim Newman; *Voice of the Blood*, Jemiah Jefferson; *Dracula*, Bram Stoker; The I, Vampire Series, Michael Romkey.

Diary Format • Mad Scientist • Medical Horror • Paris, France • Serial Killers • Sex Crimes

Armstrong, Kelley.

Bitten. *Toronto: Random House Canada, 2001. 342p.* Growing up as an orphan left Elena Michaels vulnerable to the charm of Clayton. However, instead of marriage, two kids, and a picket fence, Clayton gives Elena a dark gift, turning her into the world's only known female werewolf. Elena joins Clayton's pack in remote Stonehaven, New York, for awhile, but soon leaves to return to her Toronto home to try to live a human life. An enemy pack of werewolves captures Clayton and demands they be given Elena so she can be enslaved on a breeding farm of purebred lycanthropes. **Similar titles:** The Midnight Series, Nancy Gideon; *Bound in Blood*, David Thomas Lord; *De Lore's Confession*, Paulette Crain; The Devoncroix Dynasty Series, Donna Boyd.

New York State • Shapeshifters • Toronto, Ontario • Werewolf Clans • Werewolves

Arthur, Keri.

Dancing with the Devil. *Hickory Corners, Mich.: ImaJinn Books, 2001. 248p.* Private Investigator Nikki James grew up on the tough streets of Lyndhurst and believes that nothing can surprise her. Michael Kelly has come to Lyndhurst determined to end the war between himself and a fellow creature of the night. Nikki breaches his formidable barriers with her psychic abilities and makes Michael believe he may finally have found a woman strong enough to walk by his side and ease the loneliness in his heart. But will his love be enough to protect her from a madman hell-bent on revenge? **Similar titles:** The Host Series, Selena Rosen; The Anita Blake Series, Laurell K. Hamilton; The Silver Wolf Series, Alice Borchardt; The Saint-Germain Series, Chelsea Quinn Yarbro.

Private Investigator as Character • Revenge • Vampire Clans • Vampire's Point of View

Atkins, Peter.

Morningstar. *Lancaster, Pa.: Stealth Press, 2000, ©1992. 244p.* (See chapter 11, "Maniacs and Sociopaths, or the Nuclear Family Explodes: Monstrous Malcontents Bury the Hatchet.")

Baker, Trisha.

Crimson Kiss. *New York: Pinnacle, 2001. 432p.* (See chapter 15, "Splatterpunk: The Gross-Out.")

Baugh, Bruce, and Richard E. Dansky.

Darkness Revealed: Descent into Darkness. *Clarkston, Ga.: White Wolf, 1998. 118p.* A collection of three adventure stories centering on the Huang-Marr Project and experiments in biotechnology. These tales are billed as an Adventure Series Sourcebook for Trinity. **Similar titles:** *Never Dream*, Scott Charles Adams; The Universal Monster Series, various authors; *Gothique*, Kyle Marffin; *Vampire Nation*, Thomas M. Sipos.

> *Genetics • Huang-Marr Project, The • Role Playing Games • Terrorism*

Bergstrom, Elaine.

Blood to Blood: The Dracula Story Continues. *New York: Ace, 2000. 309p.* After having been given power and money by Dracula, who's now dead, Mina decides to challenge the patriarchal relationship that Jonathan Harker desires. Enter into the equation another powerful woman, Joanna Tepes, come to avenge the death of her brother Vlad. This is a clever and well-conceived footnote to Stoker's fictional creation. **Similar titles:** *The Secret Life of Laszlo, Count Dracula*, Roderick Anscombe; *Anno Dracula*, Kim Newman; *Dracula in London*, P. N. Elrod (editor).

> *Feminism • Harker, Jonathan (character) • Harker, Mina (character) • History, Use of • Jack the Ripper Murders • Revenge • VanHelsing, Abraham (character) • Victorian England*

Blake, Dan L.

Killing Frost. *Catskill, N.Y: Press-Tige, 1998. 300p.* (See chapter 15, "Splatterpunk: The Gross-Out.")

6

Borchardt, Alice. The Silver Wolf Series.

The Silver Wolf. *New York: Ballantine, 1998. 451p.* A young female werewolf named Regeane is held captive in 30 b.c. Rome, where she witnesses the decadent tastes of the emperors and their courts. Can she escape the arranged marriage to a Roman nobleman for whom she is being held; can a fellow werewolf who lurks outside the city help her? And what plans does this loner, the Silver Wolf, have for Regeane? Borchardt is heavy on description and characterization. **Similar titles:** *Pandora: New Tales of the Vampire*, Anne Rice; *Murcheston: The Wolf's Tale*, David Holland; The Anita Blake Series, Laurell K. Hamilton.

> *Fantasy • Gothic Romance • History, Use of • Immortality • Marriage • Rome, Italy • Torture • Werewolf's Point of View • Werewolves • Witchcraft*

Night of the Wolf. *New York: Ballantine, 1999. 454p.* This is the sequel to *The Silver Wolf*, in which Gaul assassin Dryas teams up with the werewolf Maeniel to avenge the brutalization of the Celts by the Romans. An interesting hybrid of dark fantasy and historical fiction, the novel also contains a tinge of romance. It is action-oriented but also deals with the psychological nature of Maeniel's condition. **Similar titles:** The Vampire Chronicles, Anne Rice; *Dracula's Children*, Richard Lortz; The Universal Monsters Series, David Jacobs and Jeff Rovin; The Devoncroix Dynasty Series, Donna Boyd.

Fantasy • Feminism • History, Use of • Julius Caeser (character) • Maeniel (character) • Religion—Druidism • Revenge • Rome, Italy • Werewolf's Point of View • Werewolves

The Wolf King. *New York: Ballantine, 2001. 384p.* The Wolf King, the third in Borchardt's series of alternate history novels with shapeshifting protagonists, is one in which she mixes fantasy, horror, romance, suspense, action-adventure, political intrigue, and a realistic portrait of Italy in the late eighth century. In it, werewolves join with a runaway Saxon slave to head for Geneva to pledge allegiance to Charlemagne, who's about to cross the Alps. However, Maeniel ends up in enemy territory and in danger. Regeane follows him, despite his prohibition. Together, they face Regeane's vengeful cousin Hugo. **Similar titles:** New Tales of the Vampire Series, Anne Rice; The Devoncroix Dynasty Series, Donna Boyd; The Vampire Chronicles, Anne Rice; The I, Vampire Series, Michael Romkey.

Charlemagne (character) • Dark Ages • History, Use of • Italy • Maeniel (character) • Regeane (character) • Werewolves

Boyd, Donna. The Devoncroix Dynasty Series.

The Passion. *New York: Avon Books, 1998. 387p.* The murder of three "distinguished" humans/werewolves leads to this tale within a tale told by multi-millionaire werewolf pack leader Alexander Devoncroix. Devoncroix relates how werewolves have always capitalized on the United States's market-driven economy and have run billion dollar companies throughout history. Now he must come to terms with the fact that he is directly responsible for the murders of three fellow werewolves. The story traces his complicity in the family secret as it follows his tale of lust and passion though nineteenth-century France and Siberia. Does for werewolves what Anne Rice does for vampires. This is an unusual and clever novel. **Similar titles:** The Mayfair Witches Series, Anne Rice; The Time of Feasting Series, Mick Farren; *DeLore's Confession*, Paulette Crain.

Devoncroix, Alexander (character) • Eroticism • Family Curse • History, Use of • New York City • Paris, France • Revenge • Siberia • Werewolf Clans • Werewolves

The Promise. *New York: Avon, 1999. 340p.* In this novel, the sequel to *The Passion*, the Devoncroix family diary is found and read, creating a flashback to the births of Matise and Brianna Devoncroix, and their eventual separation. The modern-day part of the plot involves the conflict between Alexander Devoncroix and his son over the ongoing "agreement" between werewolves and humans. **Similar titles:** The Mayfair Witches Series, Anne Rice; The Time of Feasting Series, Mick Farren; The Midnight Series, Nancy Gideon.

Alaska • Devoncroix, Alexander (character) • Devoncroix, Matise (character) • Incest • Werewolves • Werewolf's Point of View • Werewolf Clans

Brand, Rebecca.

The Ruby Tear. (See **Suzy McKee Charnas [as Rebecca Brand].**)

Brooker, Alan M.

The Battle for Barnstable. *Princeton, N.J.: Xlibris Corp., 1998. 174p.* Barnstable Manor has existed for many centuries. It is a historic monument to the Barnstable family, which had migrated from Europe and founded the dynasty that is responsible for the peace and prosperity of the surrounding villages. They are also responsible for the problems that plague the villages, after the dynasty crumbles with the death of the last Lord, for there have been strange and unaccountable events following the sale of the manor and the arrival of the new Lord, events that had driven several families from the valley in fear of their sanity and their lives. **Similar titles:** *Blood Covenant*, Marilyn Lamb; *De Lore's Confession*, Paulette Crain; *Darklost*, Mick Farren; *Gothique*, Kyle Marffin.

> *Family Curse • Religion—Satanism • Satan (character) • Vampire's Point of View • Writer as Character*

The Buffy the Vampire Slayer Series. Various Authors.

Golden, Christopher.

Buffy the Vampire Slayer: Angel, the Hollower. *Milwaukie, Oreg.: Dark Horse Comics, 2000. 88p.* Following an encounter with Catherine, a figure from his past, Angel must now face a horror that he had thought long destroyed: the Hollower. The Hollower is a demon that is the only natural predator of the vampire, and this hideous tentacled abomination could hold the key to Angel's salvation or his destruction. **Similar titles:** The Buffy the Vampire Slayer Series, Various Authors; The Witchblade Series, Christina Z. and David Wohl; *Spawn 8*, Todd McFarland, Alan Moore, and Greg Capullo; *The Sandman*, Neil Gaiman.

> *Angel, the Vampire (character) • Demons • Graphic Novel • Summers, Buffy (character) • Vampire's Point of View*

Spike and Dru: Pretty Maids All in a Row. *New York: Pocket Books, 2000. 305p.* For his vampire lover Drusilla's birthday, the vampire Spike decides to go to Norway to look for a necklace that gives its wearer the ability to shapeshift. Together, he and Dru tour World War II torn Europe with a special plan in mind: murder all the chosen vampire "slayers" in exchange for the necklace. Now, only Sophie the Vampire Slayer can stop them. **Similar titles:** *Blade* (film); *Lifeblood*, P. N. Elrod; The Host Series, Selena Rosen.

> *Demons • Magic • Norway • Paris, France • Summers, Buffy (character) • War—World War II • Vampire Hunters • Vampire's Point of View*

Passarella, Jack.

Buffy the Vampire Slayer: Ghoul Trouble. *New York: Pocket, 2000. 239p.* All is not right in Sunnydale when an all-female rock band comes to town and spellbinds the male portion of its audience. And now Buffy must figure out who has sucked dry some human bones. **Similar titles:** Poltergeist, the Legacy Series, various authors; The Vampire Files, P. N. Elrod; The Anita Blake, Vampire Hunter Series, Laurell K. Hamilton.

> *Mind Control • Music—Rock Music • Summers, Buffy (character) • Vampire Hunters*

Holder, Nancy.

The Book of Fours. *New York; London: Pocket, 2001. 352p.* The ghosts of slayers past come to Sunnydale in this novel based on the hit television show. Hurricanes, flash floods, and fires plague the town. The slayers, Buffy and Faith, as well as their friends, realize something supernatural is behind the natural disasters when mysterious ax-wielding figures appear amid the chaos. The spirits have been summoned by a powerful sorceress to kill the slayers and feed their essence to the Gatherer, a being made up of pure evil. **Similar titles:** *Angel: The Hollower*, Christopher Golden; Poltergeist, the Legacy Series, Various Authors; The Anita Blake, Vampire Hunter Series, Laurell K. Hamilton; The Host Series, Selena Rosen.

Apocalypse • Demons • High School • Natural Disasters • Summers, Buffy (character) • Vampire Hunters

Cacek, P. D.

Canyons. *New York: Tor, 2000. 302p.* Lucas, a refined werewolf in Denver who lives peaceably among humans, saves the life of a tabloid reporter. She repays him, however, by publishing an article claiming that dangerous werewolves haunt the streets of the city. Lucas must keep a low profile to avoid being hunted, but how can he do so when a rival werewolf gang enters Denver and begins hunting humans? **Similar titles:** The Time of Feasting Series, Mick Farren; The Devoncroix Dynasty Series, Donna Boyd; *Murcheston: The Wolf's Tale*, David Holland.

Denver, Colorado • Gang Violence • Journalist as Character • Werewolf Clans • Werewolf's Point of View • Werewolves

Night Prayers. *Darien, Ill.: Design Image, 1998. 219p.* After a three-day binge, Allison Garrett finds herself turned into a vampire, and she has no idea how to survive as one. This satire set in Los Angeles exposes the underworld of Southern California life, in a quirky and clever way. **Similar titles:** *The Voice of the Blood*, Jemiah Jefferson; *Interview with the Vampire*, Anne Rice; *Red Moon Rising*, Billie Sue Mosiman; *Awash in the Blood*, John Wooley.

Clergy as Character • Los Angeles, California • Vampire Clans • Vampire Hunters • Vampire's Point of View

Carter, Margaret L.

Shadow of the Beast: A Werewolf Novel. *Darien, Ill.: Design Image Group, Inc., 1998. 241p.* A nightmare legacy arises from Jenny Cameron's past, destroying her family, threatening everyone she loves. Now her past has come to claim her in an orgy of violence and death. A beast roams the dark streets of Annapolis, Maryland, and the only way Jenny can combat the evil from her past is to surrender to the dark and violent power lurking within herself. Her humanity is at stake, and much more than death may await her under the shadow of the beast. **Similar titles:** *Murcheston, the Wolf's tale*, David Holland; The Silver Wolf Series, Alice Borchardt; *Ginger Snaps* (film).

Annapolis, Maryland • Family Curse • Shapeshifters • Werewolves

Charnas, Suzy McKee [as Rebecca Brand].

The Ruby Tear. *New York: Tor, 1998. 247p.* The Ruby Tear, a jewel on a par with the Hope Diamond, is the source of playwright/playboy Nic Griffin's family wealth and has brought both financial success and untimely death to the Griffin men. Nic must have the final showdown with the vampire von Cragga, who holds the key to the mystery of the Griffin family curse. Written by Suzy McKee Charnas under a pen name, this novel is strong on portrayal of the New York City theater world. **Similar titles:** *De Lore's Confession*, Paulette Crain; *The Red Witch*, Serena Devlin; *The Blood Covenant*, Marilyn Lamb; The Midnight Series, Nancy Gideon.

Actor as Character • Cursed Objects • Gothic Romance • New York City • Vampire's Point of View

The Clan Novel Series. Various Authors.

Fleming, Gherbod.

Clan Novel: Ventrue. *Clarkston, Ga.: White Wolf, 1999. 269p.* This novel deals with the Camarilla trying to regroup and manage the refugee situation in Baltimore after the successful Sabbat sieges in Atlanta and Washington, D.C. It emphasizes Fleming's ability to develop his Ventrue characters and the intrigues involving them, much of it involving the seductive Victoria Ash and the Nosferatu who play all sides against each other. **Similar titles:** The Time of Feasting Series, Mick Farren; Buffy the Vampire Slayer Series, various authors; *Vampire's Waltz*, Thomas Staab; *Gothique*, Kyle Marffin.

Baltimore, Maryland • Camarmilla, The • Role Playing Games •
Vampire as New Species • Vampire Clans • Vampire's Point of View

Griffin, Eric.

Tremere. *Clarkston, Ga.: White Wolf, 2000. 283p.* This is a novel of magic, manipulation, and murder. Aisling Sturbridge is the Regent of the besieged Chantry of Five Boroughs. With one foot firmly planted in the mythic and the other rooted in the unforgiving streets of New York, Sturbridge serves as a leader, a teacher, and a guardian to the novices entrusted to her care. She must struggle to unravel a murder in the very heart of her chantry and to survive the unwelcome attention from the fatherhouse in Vienna. **Similar titles:** The Time of Feasting Series, Mick Farren; The Buffy the Vampire Slayer Series, Various Authors; *Vampire's Waltz*, Thomas Staab; *Gothique*, Kyle Marffin.

Fantasy • New York City • Role Playing Games • Sturbridge, Aisling
(character) • Vampire Clans

Widow's Walk. *Clarkston, Ga.: White Wolf, 2000. 284p.* This sequel begins where *Tremere* left off. New York is a city teetering on the brink. A fledgling prince is restlessly pacing the battlements. In the wake of the Camarilla liberation of New York, the real battle is just beginning. A floodtide of refugees, immigrants, opportunists, prospectors, pariahs, carpetbaggers, anarchs, pioneers, and outlaws washes over the city, each of the newcomers intent on carving out his or her own piece of the Blood-Red Apple. **Similar titles:** The Time of Feasting Series, Mick Farren; Buffy the Vampire Slayer Series, various authors; *Vampire's Waltz*, Thomas Staab; *Gothique*, Kyle Marffin.

 6

Fantasy • New York City • Role Playing Games • Sturbridge, Aisling
(character) • Vampire Clans

Widow's Weeds. *Clarkston, Ga.: White Wolf, 2001. 288p.* In the follow-up to *Widow's Walk*, Antigone Baines, exiled from the communion of the Tremere, sheds the robes of her novitiate and in their place dons the Widow's Weeds: the formal mourning clothes, symbol of her solitary vigil over the restless dead. Alone she must unravel the riddle of the Conventicle, discover the identity of the prince's would-be-assassin, and carve out her own place along the treacherous precipice between the worlds of the quick and the dead. **Similar titles:** The Time of Feasting Series, Mick Farren; The Buffy the Vampire Slayer Series, various authors; *Vampire's Waltz*, Thomas Staab; *Gothique*, Kyle Marffin.

Fantasy • New York City • Role Playing Games • Sturbridge, Aisling
(character) • Vampire Clans

Wieck, Stewart.

Clan Novel: Malkavian. *Clarkston, Ga.: White Wolf, 2000. 287p.* This clan novel reflects the madness of the Malkavian mind, a subtle clan to comprehend. It is unique in the series in that it is a first person narrative, and the teller is a madman. **Similar titles:** The Buffy the Vampire Slayer Series, various authors; *Gothique*, Kyle Marffin; *Vampire's Waltz*, Thomas Staab; The Time of Feasting Series, Mick Farren.

Dramatic Monologue • Role Playing Games • Vampire Clans •
Vampire's Point of View

Clark, Simon.

Vampyrrhic. *London: Hoddard and Stoughton, 1998. 441p.* David Leppington returns to his ancestral home to discover a dark family secret: The Leppingtons originated from a vampire clan created by the Norse god Thor. Will he give in to his genetics and become a bloodsucker? **Similar titles:** *Nailed by the Heart*, Simon Clark; The Lord of the Dead Series, Tom Holland; The Vampire Chronicles, Anne Rice; *Dracula 2000* (film).

> *England • Family Curse • Religion—Christianity • Religion—Paganism • Vampire Clans*

Clegg, Douglas.

You Come When I Call You. *New York: Leisure, 2000. 393p.* (See chapter 7, "Demonic Possession, Satanism, Black Magic, and Witches and Warlocks: The Devil Made Me Do It.")

Collins, Nancy A.

Sunglasses After Dark. *Clarkston, GA: White Wolf, 2000, ©1989. 253p.* Denise Thorne, heiress, is raped by a vampire, and after nine months in a coma, she is reborn as Sonja Blue, a vampire who can inhabit dream worlds, who violently kills cruel humans, and who terminates ghosts and other revenants. Considered by critics and vampire fans to be one of the finest original vampire tales of the past decade, this novel is unique and erudite. It is the recipient of a Bram Stoker Award. **Similar titles:** The Anita Blake Series, Laurell K. Hamilton; The Host Series, Selina Rosen; *Full Moon, Bloody Moon*, Lee Driver; The Black Oak Series, Charles Grant.

> *Blue, Sonja (character) • Dreams • Rape • Telepathy • Vampire's Point of View*

Conner, Miguel.

The Queen of Darkness. *New York: Warner, 1998. 276p.* Vampires arrange a nuclear holocaust on Earth to create artificial darkness and thin out their human opposition. Now that they rule, their greatest enemy is one of their own. **Similar titles:** *I Am Legend*, Richard Matheson; *The Vampire's Waltz*, Thomas Staab; *Queen of the Damned*, Anne Rice.

> *Byron, George Gordon, Lord (character) • Nuclear Holocaust • Vampire's Point of View*

Dietz, Ulysses G.

Desmond: A Novel of Love and the Modern Vampire. *Los Angeles: Alyson Books, 1998. 331p.* Desmond, an openly gay vampire living the high life in the Bowery section of Brooklyn, has found a cure for his loneliness: a young student of antiques. But to have him as a lover, Desmond will first have to reveal his dark secret and save the young man's life. **Similar titles:** *Interview with the Vampire* and *The Vampire Lestat*, Anne Rice; *Bound in Blood*, David Thomas Lord; The Hunger Series, Whitley Streiber; *Mother Julian and the Gentle Vampire*, Jack Pantaleo.

> *Gay/Lesbian/Bisexual Characters • Gothic Romance • History, Use of • Homoeroticism • New York City • Vampire's Point of View*

Ellis, Jack.

Nightlife. *New York: Pinnacle Books, 2000, ©1996. 379p.* Richard Carnitch is a 200-year-old vampire who hunts the homeless. He has nothing but contempt for his prey and enjoys inflicting as much pain as possible on his victims, delighting at the ease with which he can control them. But one night Simon Babych spies Carnitch dispatching a friend of his. Carnitch pursues Babych, who escapes, realizing that there is a vampire in Minneapolis who's been killing off the homeless for the past thirty years, and he must be stopped. **Similar titles:** '*Salem's Lot*, Stephen King; The Buffy the Vampire Slayer Series, various authors; *Vampire Slayers*, Martin H. Greenberg and Elizabeth Ann Scarborough.

> *Homeless People as Character • Minneapolis, Minnesota • Vampire Hunters*

Elrod, P. N. The Vampire Files.

Bloodlist. *New York: Ace Books, 1990. 200p.* This is the first novel in this series, in which Jack Flemming initially suspects he may become a vampire and finds out for sure when he is killed in a gangland hit. Now, as a vampire, he is out for revenge. **Similar titles:** The Anita Blake Series, Laurell K. Hamilton; The Black Oak Series, Charles Grant; *Full Moon, Bloody Moon*, Lee Driver; *Sunglasses After Dark*, Nancy Collins.

> *Flemming, Jack (character) • Organized Crime • Private Investigator as Character • Vampire's Point of View*

Lifeblood. *New York: Ace Books, 1990. 208p.* In this second in the series, Jack Fleming, journalist vampire, must deal with a group of vampire hunters. **Similar titles:** The Host Series, Selina Rosen; The Anita Blake Series, Laurell K. Hamilton; *Sunglasses After Dark*, Nancy Collins.

> *Flemming, Jack (character) • Journalist as Character • Private Investigator as Character • Vampire Hunters • Vampire's Point of View*

Bloodcircle. *New York: Ace Books, 1990. 202p.* This is a reissue of the third book in the series. Jack Flemming continues searching for the vampire who made him. **Similar titles:** *The Vampire Lestat*, Anne Rice; The Anita Blake Series, Laurell K. Hamilton; *Full Moon, Bloody Moon*, Lee Driver; The Black Oak Series, Charles Grant;

> *Flemming, Jack (character) • Private Investigator as Character • Vampire's Point of View*

Art in the Blood. *New York: Ace Books, 1991. 208p.* Fourth in the series, this book follows the exploits of vampire private investigator Jack Flemming, in a case where he must help find the killer of a young artist. As is the entire series, this novel is humorous and fun, an easy read. **Similar titles:** The Saint-Germain Chronicles, Chelsea Quinn Yarbro; The Black Oak Series, Charles Grant; *Sunglasses After Dark*, Nancy Collins.

> *Flemming, Jack (character) • Private Investigator as Character • Vampire's Point of View*

Fire in the Blood. *New York: Ace Books, 1991. 198p.* This is the fifth book in the series starring vampire private eye Jack Flemming. **Similar titles:** The Anita Blake Vampire Hunter Series, Laurell K. Hamilton; The Saint Germain Chronicles, Chelsea Quinn Yarbro; *Full Moon, Bloody Moon*, Lee Driver.

> *Flemming, Jack (character) • Private Investigator as Character • Vampire's Point of View*

Blood on the Water. *New York: Ace Books, 1992. 199p.* Vampire private eye Jack Flemming runs afoul of the Mafia in Chicago. Will his thirst for blood lead to a Mafia hit—on him? Part six of the series. **Similar titles:** The Black Oak Series, Charles Grant; The Host Series, Selina Rosen; The Anita Blake Series, Laurell K. Hamilton.

> *Chicago, Illinois • Flemming, Jack (character) • Organized Crime • Private Investigator as Character • Vampire's Point of View*

Chill in the Blood. *New York: Ace Books, 1998. 327p.* The seventh addition to the series, this is the tale of the world's first undead private investigator. It is a mixture of comedy and hard-boiled detection, with the emphasis on Jack Flemming's character development. **Similar titles:** The Anita Blake Series, Laurell K. Hamilton; The Saint-Germain Chronicles, Chelsea Quinn Yarbro; *Full Moon, Bloody Moon*, Lee Driver.

> *Chicago, Illinois • Fleming, Jack (character) • History, Use of • Organized Crime • Private Investigator as Character • Vampire's Point of View*

The Dark Sleep. *New York: Ace Books, 1999. 359p.* In this, the eighth book in the series, hard-boiled private investigator Jack Flemming is up to his fangs in relationship problems: His girlfriend is being pursued by a radio producer who is interested in more than her talents, and the ex-lover of a rich client possesses letters that Jack must procure before they can be used for blackmail. The novel is narrated in Chandler-esque first person. **Similar titles:** The Anita Blake Series, Laurell K. Hamilton; The Saint-Germain Chronicles, Chelsea Quinn Yarbro; The Black Oak Series, Charles Grant.

> *Chicago, Illinois • Flemming, Jack (character) • Private Investigator as Character • Vampire's Point of View*

Evans, Gloria.

Meh'Yam. *Gainesville, Fla.: T. Bo Publishing, 2000. 257p.* The Meh'Yam, a race of beings who need melanin to survive, travel the galaxy in search of their sustenance. One of their kind, Pomoda, has discovered Earth, with its dark-skinned inhabitants who slake his thirst. Can his plan to conquer the planet be thwarted before all Africans are enslaved as the Meh'Yam's cattle, and all other humans are wiped out? Original. **Similar titles:** *I Am Legend*, Richard Matheson; The Living Blood Series, Tananarive Due; *Blade* (film); *Carrion Comfort*, Dan Simmons.

> *African-American Characters • Center for Disease Control • Federal Bureau of Investigation • Orlando, Florida • Racism • Vampire Hunters • Vampire's Point of View • Vampire as New Species*

Farren, Mick. The Time of Feasting Series.

The Time of Feasting. *New York: Tor, 1996. 394p.* In this action-oriented tale, vampire clan leader Victor Renquist has a few problems: His clan is getting restless during "The Time of Feasting," which occurs every seven years, and a young upstart vampire named Kurt wants to oust him as leader. When bodies start turning up all over New York City, Renquist realizes that Kurt and his followers are behind the slayings that threaten to expose the clan, and that something must be done before the humans catch on. **Similar titles:** *The Vampire's Waltz*, Thomas Staab; *Blade* (film); *Red Moon Rising*, Billie Sue Mosiman.

> *Gay/Lesbian/Bisexual Characters • New York City • Renquist, Victor (character) • Vampire as New Species • Vampire Clans • Vampire's Point of View*

Dark Lost. *New York: Tom Doherty, 2000. 470p.* In this sequel to *The Time of Feasting*, Victor Renquist and his vampire clan leave New York for Los Angeles, where they discover an ex-clan member who wants to challenge Renquist's power, as well as "The Nine," a group of Cthulhu worshippers who threaten to lure the old gods back into modern society. Renquist must meet both the threat to his power and the threat of annihilation of the human race. Can Victor, Lupo, Julia, and company save humanity? **Similar titles:** *The Vampire's Waltz*, Thomas Staab; *The Vampire World Trilogy*, Brian Lumley; *Blade* (film); *Red Moon Rising*, Billie Sue Mosiman.

> *Cthulhu (character) • Gay/Lesbian/Bisexual Characters • Los Angeles, California • Police Officer as Character • Renquist, Victor (character) • Religion—Satanism • Vampire as New Species • Vampire Clans • Vampire's Point of View*

More Than Mortal. *New York: Tor, 2001. 383p.* Nosferatu Victor Renquist struggles to rebuild his American-based vampire colony when he receives the summons from three females of his species, including a former love. Knowing this is not a friendly visit between old friends, Victor drops everything to go to Ravenskeep Priory, England, where he learns that Homo sapiens archeologists disturbed the gravesite of Taliesin, better known as Merlin. The question facing Victor and his vampire allies is whether to kill Taliesin before he becomes a powerful wizard who could destroy the current balance of power. **Similar titles:** The Vampire Chronicles and New Tales of the Vampire, Anne Rice; The Universal Monsters Series, various authors.

> *Archeology • England • Magic • Merlin (character) • Renquist, Victor (character) • Vampire Clans • Vampire's Point of View*

Fleming, Gherbod. (*See The Clan Novel Series* in this chapter.)

Gideon, Nancy. The Midnight Series.

Midnight Enchantment. *Hickory Corners, Mich.: ImaJinn Books, 1999. 264p.* When 400-year-old vampire Gerard Pasquale is approached by a lawyer named Percy in New Orleans, he is offered a strange deal: The solicitor will not tell the world Pasquale is a vampire, if the vampire marries Percy's sister and leaves her and him one-quarter of his riches. Pasquale goes through with the deal despite the risks of discovery and falling in love. Gideon's series follows the basic "beauty and the beast" romance formula. **Similar titles:** *De Lore's Confession*, Paulette Crain; *Bound in Blood*, David Thomas Lord; The Saint-Germain Chronicles, Chelsea Quinn Yarbro; *The Ruby Tear*, Suzy McKee Charnas [as Rebecca Brand].

> *Lawyer as Character • Marriage • New Orleans, Louisiana •*
> *Religion—Voodoo • Vampire's Point of View • Witchcraft*

Midnight Gamble. *Hickory Corners, Mich.: ImaJinn Books, 2000. 278p.* Rica LaValois is a vampire's worst nightmare: a fellow member of the undead who hunts down and destroys vampires who have gotten out of line and therefore threaten the race. Her next target is Eduard D'Arcy, an immortal who masquerades as a crime boss in New York's seedy underground. She tracks down D'Arcy and cozies up to him, only to find herself falling in love. **Similar titles:** *De Lore's Confession*, Paulette Crain; *Bound in Blood*, David Thomas Lord; The Saint-Germain Chronicles, Chelsea Quinn Yarbro; *The Ruby Tear*, Suzy McKee Charnas [as Rebecca Brand].

6

> *Feminism • New York City • Organized Crime • Roaring Twenties, The •*
> *Vampire's Point of View • Vampire Clans • Vampire Hunters*

Midnight Redeemer. *Hickory Corners, Mich.: ImaJinn Books, 2000. 283p.* Geneticist Stacy Kimball is onto something big—perhaps a cure for AIDS or any other disease known to humanity. The problem at the center of her theory is a vampire, billionaire Louis Redman, who is also contracting Stacy Kimball so she may find a "cure" for his curse. In the meantime, a serial killer is draining blood from his victims and is sending Mr. Kimball clues in the mail. Is the killer Redman? Is he simply using Stacy, or is the vampire falling in love? **Similar titles:** *De Lore's Confession*, Paulette Crain; *Bound in Blood*, David Thomas Lord; The Saint-Germain Chronicles, Chelsea Quinn Yarbro; *The Ruby Tear*, Suzy McKee Charnas [as Rebecca Brand].

> *Genetics • Seattle, Washington • Serial Killers • Vampire's Point of View •*
> *Weird Science*

Gioia, Dana.

Nosferatu: An Opera Libretto. *St. Paul, Minn.: Graywolf Press, 2001. 85p.* Gioia produces a poetic/operatic script in this interpretation of F. W. Murnau's 1922 film *Nosferatu*. Erik Hutler, a young clerk, is convinced by his employer to sell a questionable piece of real estate to an unsuspecting Hungarian nobleman. Hutler unwittingly brings to Germany the vampire who will threaten the life of his only love, his wife Ellen. **Similar titles:** *Nosferatu* (film); *Dracul: An Eternal Love Story*, Nancy Kilpatrick; *The Tales of Horror*, Laura Mullen.

Count Orlock (character) • Germany • Vampire's Point of View

Golden, Christopher.

Buffy the Vampire Slayer: Angel, the Hollower. (See The Buffy the Vampire Slayer Series in this chapter.)

Spike and Dru: Pretty Maids All in a Row. (See The Buffy the Vampire Slayer Series in this chapter.)

Gottlieb, Sherry Gershon. The Love Bite Series.

Love Bite. *New York: Warner Books, 1994. 277p.* A police detective with a terminal disease stumbles across a case that may offer a way to avoid death; victims are found completely drained of blood, the sign of a vampire/killer. The emphasis in this story is on the romantic angle as much as it is on horror. **Similar titles:** The Anita Blake Series, Laurell K. Hamilton; The Cyber Blood Chronicles, Jonathan Amsbary; *Voice of the Blood*, Jemiah Jefferson; *Quenched* and *Sips of Blood*, Mary Ann Mitchell.

Cadigan, Risha (character) • Immortality • Levy, Jace (character) • Police Officer as Character • Serial Killers

Worse Than Death. *New York: Tor, 2001. 245p.* Gottlieb's *Love Bite* introduced Los Angeles homicide detective Jace Levy, who falls under the spell of the damnably attractive vampire Risha Cadigan. This sequel plunges Jace still deeper into vampire country in another tale uniting horror, suspense, and eroticism. Retired from the force, Jace still does private investigations, and he takes on a Hollywood extortion case. **Similar titles:** The Anita Blake Series, Laurell K. Hamilton; The Cyber Blood Chronicles, Jonathan Amsbary; *Voice of the Blood*, Jemiah Jefferson; *Quenched* and *Sips of Blood*, Mary Ann Mitchell.

Cadigan, Risha (character) • Eroticism • Immortality • Levy, Jace (character) • Los Angeles, California • Private Investigator as Character • Vampire's Point of View

Grant, Charles. The Black Oak Series.

Genesis [Black Oak I]. *New York: ROC, 1998. 271p.* Black Oak Security is an investigative firm that handles office fraud, missing persons, and a variety of white-collar crime. Black Oak also investigates situations that are paranormal, as private investigator Ethan Proctor discovers when one of his operatives turns up dead in a town besieged by something roaming the hills, leaving dead bodies in its wake. Charles Grant is a brilliant storyteller who never lets his audience know if they are on the mortal or supernatural plane. **Similar titles:** *Aylmer Vance: Ghost-Seer*, Alice Askew and Claude Askew; *Full Moon, Bloody Moon*, Lee Driver; The Anita Blake Series, Laurell K. Hamilton; *The Complete John Silence Stories*, Algernon Blackwood.

Black Oak Security • Cumberland Mountains • Kentucky • Proctor, Ethan (character)

Black Oak 2: The Hush of Dark Wings. *New York: Penguin—ROC, 1999. 236p.* (See chapter 10, "Small Town Horror: Villages of the Damned.")

Black Oak 4: Hunting Ground. *New York: Penguin, ROC, 2000. 246p.* (See chapter 11, "Maniacs and Sociopaths, or the Nuclear Family Explodes: Monstrous Malcontents Bury the Hatchet.")

Black Oak 5: When the Cold Wind Blows. *New York: Penguin, 2001. 241p.* Ethan Proctor and the Black Oak Security Team are called to the swamplands of Georgia to investigate a series of murders in which the victims were all partially eaten. Proctor suspects that there is a loup-garou or shapeshifter loose near Atlanta, and that an old hermit who lives in the swamps holds the secret to its existence and power. But even Proctor is no match for the monster. Written with the same flair and sense of humor that defines the other novels in the series, and is excellent for fans of gentle reads and traditional horror. **Similar titles:** *Full Moon, Bloody Moon*, Lee Driver; *Murcheston: The Wolf's Tale*, David Holland; *Southern Blood*, Lawrence Schimel and Martin H. Greenberg; *Whispers in the Night*, Basil Copper.

Atlanta, Georgia • Black Oak Security • Blaine, Taylor (character) • Proctor, Ethan (character) • Shapeshifters • Werewolves

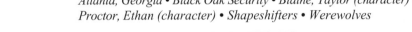

Gresham, Stephen.

In the Blood. *New York: Kensington, 2001. 381p.* Soldiers' Crossing, Alabama, is home to the Trackers, a dysfunctional extended family bound by blood and family ties. Some say the Trackers are cursed, that their blood is tainted because in the antebellum South, their ancestors were cruel to their slaves, that there were even Trackers who would return runaway slaves to their masters. Now every Tracker who is a descendant of those at the Sweet Gum Plantation has been infected with something that turns him or her into a monster, a vampire who can only drink the blood of his or her kin. Franklin Tracker intends to turn every Tracker into a vampire, but Jacob Tracker is just as determined to stop him. **Similar titles:** *Blood Covenant*, Marilyn Lamb; *De Lore's Confession*, Paulette Crain; *A Darkness Inbred*, Victor Heck; The Time of Feasting Series, Mick Farren.

6

Family Curse • Slavery • South, The • Vampire as New Species • Vampire Hunters

Griffin, Eric.

Tremere; Widow's Walk; Widow's Weeds. (See The Clan Novel Series in this chapter.)

Hamilton, Laurell K. The Anita Blake, Vampire Hunter Series.

(See chapter 16, "Comic Horror: Laughing at Our Fears.")

Hays, Clark, and Kathleen McFall.

The Cowboy and the Vampire. *St. Paul, Minn.: Llewellyn, 1999. 318p.* (See chapter 16, "Comic Horror: Laughing at Our Fears.")

Haytko, Carol.

After Dark. *San Jose, Calif.: Writers Club Press, 2001. 131p.* Kae Jude is a tough-as-nails U.S. Marshall, specializing in paranormal activity. In Spring Lake, New Jersey, blood-sucking vampires have made their mark on the world, running exclusive nightclubs where the main attraction is the undead. When the two worlds collide after dark, no one is safe. **Similar titles:** *Blade* (film); The Anita Blake, Vampire Hunter Series, Laurell K. Hamilton; The Host Series, Selena Rosen; *Gothique*, Kyle Marffin.

Government Officials • Jude, Kae (character) • New Jersey • Vampire Hunters

Hendee, Barb.

Blood Memories. *Flushing, N.Y.: Vision Novels, 1998. 171p.* Vampires have lived among humans for countless years, hiding in the darkness, from where they hunt, feed on, and kill innocent mortals. They live lives of utter secrecy, scattered far apart, always aware that the surging tide of humanity could crush them if they became truly aware of their presence. For Eleisha, a young vampire who has remained hidden since the nineteenth century, things are about to change. **Similar titles:** The Time of Feasting Series, Mick Farren; The Vampire Chronicles, Anne Rice; *Voice of the Blood*, Jemiah Jefferson.

Vampire Hunters • Vampire's Point of View

Hill, William.

Dawn of the Vampire. *New York: Kensington-Pinnacle, 2001, ©1991. 480p.* Wreythville's cemetery had rested quietly under South Holston Lake, but now the receding waters expose an island of graves. As the tombstones emerge, so do the unstaked dead who had been buried beneath them. Freed, the ancient breed seeks vengeance on humanity. **Similar titles:** *Riverwatch*, Joseph M. Nassise; *A Darkness Inbred*, Victor Heck; *The Light at the End*, John Skipp and Craig Spector; *'Salem's Lot*, Stephen King.

Cemeteries • Maritime Horror • Shapeshifters • Vampire as New Species • Vampire Clans

The Vampire Hunters. *Doctors Inlet, Fla.: Otter Creek Press, 1998. 286p.* (See chapter 10, "Small Town Horror: Villages of the Damned.")

Holder, Nancy.

The Book of Fours. (See The Buffy the Vampire Slayer Series in this chapter.)

Holland, David.

Murcheston: The Wolf's Tale. *New York: Tor, 2000. 349p.* This novel is an erudite frame tale of the Duke of Darnley, a Victorian lycanthrope. Darnley documents in his journal how his transformation from gentleman to beast gives him a refreshing perspective on the conventions of civilization. Holland's neo-Victorian writing style, reminiscent of Stoker's *Dracula* and Stevenson's *Dr. Jekyll and Mr. Hyde*, makes this a particularly enjoyable read. **Similar titles:** The Lord of the Dead Series, Tom Holland; *The Vampire Lestat*, Anne Rice; The Silver Wolf Series, Alice Borchart; *Canyons*, P. D. Cacek.

Alter Ego • Animals Run Rampant • Class System • Diary Format • England • Secret Sin • Shapeshifters • Victorian England • Werewolf's Point of View • Werewolves

Holland, Tom. The Lord of the Dead Series.

Lord of the Dead. *New York: Simon& Schuster, 1995. 342p.* Lord Byron, the real-life model for Dr. Poldori's nosferatu Lord Ruthven from his story *The Vampyre*, really *is* a vampire himself. He narrates the story of his undead existence to a "real life" descendant of the fictional Ruthven. Being a vampire has only exacerbated his rakishness and is the ultimate ruin of his friendship with Poldori and Shelley. Holland, a Byron scholar, cleverly blends facts about Byron and his friends, Dr. Poldori and Mary Shelley, with fiction. **Similar titles:** The Anno Dracula Series, Kim Newman; *Murcheston: The Wolf's Tale*, David Holland; *The London Vampire Panic*, Michael Romkey.

🎧 audiotape

Alternative Literature • al-Vakhel, Haroun (character) • Byron, George Gordon Lord (character) • Epic Structure • Eroticism • Greece • Haidee (character) • Incest • Polidori, John (character) • Shelley, Percy B. (character) • Vampire's Point of View

Slave of My Thirst. *New York: Simon & Schuster, 1996. 421p.* The "real" story behind Bram Stoker's novel *Dracula* casts Stoker as Abraham Van Helsing, intent on saving England from the peril of vampires. But in this narrative, England isn't threatened by a predatory Transylvanian count with a penchant for London real estate. Instead, the threat is unknowingly "imported" from colonial soldiers in India who awaken the goddess Kali. Holland's novel is a literate piece of alternative literature told from multiple points of view. **Similar titles:** The Anno Dracula Series, Kim Newman; *Murcheston: The Wolf's Tale*, David Holland; *The London Vampire Panic*, Michael Romkey.

> *Alternative Literature • Epic Structure • Epistolary Format • Eroticism • Jack the Ripper Murders • Kali (character) • Lillith (character) • Polidori, John (character) • Shapeshifters • Stoker, Bram (character) • Victorian England*

Deliver Us from Evil. *New York: Warner, 1998. 578p.* (See chapter 8, "Mythological Monsters and 'The Old Ones': Invoking the Dark Gods.")

The Sleeper in the Sands. *London: Little, Brown, 1999, ©1998. 428p.* (See chapter 8, "Mythological Monsters and 'The Old Ones': Invoking the Dark Gods.")

Hopkins, Brian A.

The Licking Valley Coon Hunters Club. *Alma, Ark.: Yard Dog Press, 2000. 173p.* (See chapter 16, "Comic Horror: Laughing at Our Fears.")

Jacobs, David.

The Devil's Brood. (See The Universal Monsters Series in this chapter.)

The Devil's Night. (See The Universal Monsters Series in this chapter.)

Jefferson, Jemiah.

Voice of the Blood. *New York: Leisure, 2001. 283p.* A graduate student in biology accidentally confronts a vampire who, out of hunger, has trashed her laboratory and killed her mice. Thus begins Ariane's fascination with the undead—and her trek from humanity to vampirism. Jefferson's emphasis is on characterization in this well-written novel that is as highly erotic and philosophical as the early novels of Anne Rice. **Similar titles:** *Bound in Blood*, David Thomas Lord; *The Last Vampire*, T. M. Wright; The Hunger Series, Whitley Streiber.

6

> *Academia • Eroticism • Immortality • Los Angeles, California • San Francisco, California • Vampire's Point of View*

Kelly, Ronald.

Blood Kin. *New York: Pinnacle, 2001. 384p.* In Green Hollow, Tennessee, a bride turns on her husband, a pet rat develops a murderous streak, and an insane preacher slaughters his congregation. The Craven family vampire curse is upon the town once again. **Similar titles:** *Blood Crazy*, Simon Clark; *Shadow Child*, Joseph Citro; *Hexes*, Tom Piccirilli; *'Salem's Lot*, Stephen King.

> *Shapeshifters • Tennessee • Vampire Hunters*

Kemske, Floyd. The Corporate Nightmare Series.

Human Resources. *North Haven, Conn.: Catbird Press, 1995. 223p.* In this novel in the series, a failing biotech company hires a turnaround specialist whose special talent is draining valuable resources from employees for the benefit of both himself and his bosses. Since the specialist is a vampire, he's had lots of experience draining things. Flashbacks of the vampire's early life as an eighteenth-century efficiency expert learning at the feet of Talleyrand provide interesting historical satire in this witty and original send-up of corporate mentality. **Similar titles:** The Devoncroix Dynasty Series, Donna Boyd; *Resume with Monsters*, William Browning Spencer; *The Store*, Bentley Little.

> *Corporations • Economic Violence • Fantasy • France • History, Use of • Vampire's Point of View*

Labor Day. *North Haven, Conn.: Catbird Press, 2000. 203p.* (See chapter 14, "Psychological Horror: It's All in Your Head.")

Kilpatrick, Nancy.

Child of the Night: Power of the Blood 1. *Nottingham, England: Pumpkin Books, 1998, ©1996. 276p.* While vacationing in France, Carol Robins meets a stranger who attacks her. When she realizes he's a vampire, she bargains for her life, using the only advantage she has: sex. Now pregnant, she is forced to come to grips with her ambivalent feelings of love and hate for her attacker. This is a bodice ripper with vampires. **Similar titles:** *Bound in Blood*, David Thomas Lord; *The Voice of the Blood*, Jemiah Jefferson; *Awash in the Blood*, John Wooley; The Midnight Series, Nancy Gideon.

> *AIDS • Eroticism • France • Hypnotism • Parenting • Pregnancy • Torture • Vampire Clans*

Dracul: An Eternal Love Story. *San Diego: Lucard Publishing, 1998. 217p. + one music CD.* The first of twenty planned musical novels by Lucard Publishing, *Dracul* reads like a stage play of Stoker's tale, with the twist of a love story intertwined with the horror. Vlad Dracul must recapture the woman who is the reincarnation of his long lost love, but to do so he risks death. The novel is accompanied by a music CD and song lyrics. **Similar titles:** *Nosferatu: An Opera Libretto*, Dana Gioia; *Emerald Germs of Ireland*, Patrick McCabe; *Dracula*, Bram Stoker; *Bram Stoker's Dracula* (film).

> *Dracula (character) • Harker, Jonathan (character) • Harker, Mina Murray (character) • Music—Broadway • Van Helsing, Abraham (character) • Seward, John (character) • Vampire's Point of View*

King, Stephen.

Cycle of the Werewolf. *Illustrated by Berni Wrightson. New York: Signet, 1985. 128p.* In this graphic novel, Stephen King traces the effect of the moon's monthly phases on a small town called Tarker's Mills, where a werewolf is victimizing townfolk on a regular basis. Only a wheelchair-bound boy knows the identity of the monster and can stop it before it claims another victim. King's graphic novel is good for fans of traditional horror and young adult readers as well, and was the basis for the movie *Silver Bullet.* **Similar titles:** The Buffy the Vampire Slayer Series, Various Authors; The Universal Monsters Series, various authors; *The Wolf Man* (film); *Black Oak 5: When the Cold Wind Blows*, Charles Grant.

🗩 graphic novels

> *Clergy as Character • Graphic Novel • New England • Quadriplegic/Paraplegics as Character • Werewolves*

'Salem's Lot. *Garden City, N.J.: Doubleday, 1975. 439p.* Jerusalem's Lot is a town that is well acquainted with darkness and evil. After all, the sins of the town legend, Hubie Marsten, were kept alive in rumor and gossip. But there is a new evil in the Marsten house, in the form of Richard Throckett Straker, an antique furniture dealer who is also a vampire. King's work is good on scares and suspense. **Similar titles:** *Needful Things*, Stephen

King; *The Light at the End*, John Skipp and Craig Spector; *The London Vampire Panic*, Michael Romkey.

⚭ large print

> *Clergy as Character • Haunted Houses • Maine • Physician as Character • Secret Sin • Teacher as Character • Vampire Hunters • Writer as Character*

Lamb, Marilyn.

Blood Covenant. *Barrie, Ontario: Free Spirit Press, 1999. 381p.* In this Christian fiction crossover, Adrian Kristan is forced to sign a blood pact with a demonic vampire to fulfill his part of a family bargain made centuries before his birth. Now he owes his life and soul, as well as those of his wife and her unborn, to the evil Jonathan Cravers. Even with angels watching over them constantly, can the Kristans defeat the demons that are constantly buzzing around them, aiding Cravers in his pursuit of their souls? **Similar titles:** The Spirit Chronicles, Keith Rummel; *Soul Temple*, Steven Lee Climer; *Project Resurrection*, Karen Duval; *De Lore's Confession*, Paulette Crain.

> *Angels • Demons • Family Curse • New England • Ohio • Religion—Christianity*

Lauria, Frank.

Raga Six. *Berkeley, Calif.: North Atlantic Books, 2001. 275p.* Dr. Owen Orient, a psychic detective, meets Raga Six, a vampire who has been undead for hundreds of years. He falls in love with her and tries to protect her from evil forces. But after discerning her real identity and witnessing the destruction she causes, he sets out to defeat her magically. **Similar titles:** *Full Moon, Bloody Moon*, Lee Driver; *The Licking Valley Coon Hunters Club*, Brian A. Hopkins; The Black Oak Series, Charles Grant; The Repairman Jack Series, F. Paul Wilson.

 6

> *Clairvoyant as Character • Orient, Dr. Owen (character) • Parapsychology • Science Fiction • Vampire Hunters*

Laymon, Richard.

Bite. *New York: Leisure, 1999, ©1996. 378p.* When Sam's ex-girlfriend Cat Lorimer shows up at his apartment out of the blue after ten years, he is ecstatic to see her—until he finds out that she needs him to stake a vampire stalker. *Bite* is a darkly comic first person narrative of the problems about disposing of a vampire's body. **Similar titles:** *The Traveling Vampire Show*, Richard Laymon; The Anita Blake Vampire Hunter Series, Laurell K. Hamilton; *Dead Heat*, Del Stone, Jr.; *Deadfellas*, David Whitman.

> *Biker as Character • Domestic Violence • Los Angeles, California • Vampire Hunters*

Ⓑ **The Traveling Vampire Show.** *New York: Leisure, 2001. 391p.* (See chapter 14, "Psychological Horror: It's All in Your Head.")

Le Fanu, Sheridan.

Carmilla. *In In a Glass Darkly. New York: Oxford University Press, 1999. ©1872. 347p.* In this novella, a young girl, Laura, befriends the temptress Carmilla, a young aristocratic girl who is actually a vampire. This influential nineteenth-century tale is characterized by its highly descriptive prose and indirect style, as well as by its use of first person narration in journal form, included in a frame tale format. **Similar titles:** *Carmilla*, Kyle Marffin; *Dracula's Daughter* (film); *The Hunger*, Whitley Streiber.

🎧 audiotape

> *Diary Format • Homoeroticism • Karnstein, Carmilla (character) • Vampire Hunters*

Longstreet, Roxanne.

Cold Kiss. *New York: Pinnacle, 2001, ©1994. 256p.* Surgeon Michael Bowman became a vampire, and his mentor and friend, Adam Radburn, also a vampire, was captured by a powerful and sadistic über-vampire named William. In this sequel, Michael has to put a great deal of effort into adapting to his new state of existence and just surviving. Nonetheless, he is determined to free Adam—if he can just figure out whom he can trust for help. **Similar titles:** *Vampire Nation*, Thomas M. Sipos; The I, Vampire Series, Michael Romkey; *Interview With the Vampire*, Anne Rice.

> *Surgeon as Character • Torture • Vampire Clans • Vampire's Point of View*

Lord, David Thomas.

Bound in Blood. *New York: Kensington, 2001. 346p.* New York's finest think they have a serial killer on their hands when bodies of young men start turning up every few days. What they don't know is that killer Jean-Luc Courbet is a vampire, one who hunts the streets by night, using his sexual prowess as a weapon to lure would-be victims from nightclubs. Actor Claude Halloran is unfortunate enough to hook up with Courbet; however, Courbet's emotions get in the way of his next kill, and he falls for Halloran. Will this be the end of the predator life for Courbet? Narrated in third person objective viewpoint, with news reports interspersed for a documentary feel. **Similar titles:** *Voice of the Blood*, Jemiah Jefferson; *Bending the Landscape*, Stephen Pagel and Nicola Griffith (editors); *Meh'Yam*, Gloria Evans; The Midnight Series, Nancy Gideon.

> *Actor as Character • Gay/Lesbian/Bisexual Characters • Journalist as Character • London, England • Matricide/Patricide • New York City • Paris, France • Serial Killers • Vampire's Point of View*

Lortz, Richard.

Dracula's Children. *New York: Permanent Press, 1981, ©1974. 202p.* Lortz's classic is a character study narrative about impoverished Latino children in New York City who take to attacking and devouring Gothamites in and around Central Park. The emphasis here is on characterization and motivation rather than a linear narrative plot line. Lortz's prose, which borders on poetry, is unique and fascinating. **Similar titles:** *Murcheston: The Wolf's Tale*, David Holland; *Carrie*, Stephen King; *Emerald Germs of Ireland*, Patrick McCabe; *Dorcas Good: Diary of a Salem Witch*, Rose Earhart.

> *Childhood • Economic Violence • Hispanic-American Characters • New York City • Vampire as New Species • Werewolves*

Marffin, Kyle.

Carmilla: The Return. *Darien, Ill.: Design Image Group, 1998. 296p.* Marffin's tale is a retelling of the Joseph Sheridan Le Fanu classic about a female vampire who stalks a young girl, updated to occur in the twentieth century. Carmilla herself narrates this darkly erotic tale. **Similar titles:** *Carmilla*, Joseph Sheridan Le Fanu; The Hunger Series, Whitley Streiber; The Anno Dracula Series, Kim Newman; *Nadja* (film); *Sisters of the Night: The Angry Angel*, Chelsea Quinn Yarbro.

> *Alternative Literature • Homoeroticism • Karnstein, Carmilla (character)*

Gothique: A Vampire Novel. *Darien, Ill.: The Design Image Group, 2000. 431p.* A young journalist is thrown off the Hancock Tower because of an assignment she is working on dealing with a new Chicago nightclub, and her assistant, her younger sister, and her sister's roommate suddenly find themselves involved in the shady Chicago underworld. To make matters worse, the leader of this new "mafia" group is a heartless vampire. Marffin's emphasis is on action and character, with complex plot lines. **Similar titles:** The Time of Feasting Series, Mick Farren; The Vampire Files, P. N. Elrod; The Midnight Series, Nancy Gideon.

> *Chicago, Illinois • Gay/Lesbian/Bisexual Characters • Gothicism • Journalist as Character • Organized Crime • Role Playing Games • Vampire Clans*

Matheson, Richard.

I Am Legend *(novella). In Matheson, Richard. I Am Legend. New York: Tor, 1995, ©1954. 312p.* Radiation has turned all but one man into a vampire, and he is determined to survive rather than join the ranks of undead ghouls who wait for him outside his door on a nightly basis. Matheson's frightening and original novella was the basis for the movie *The Omega Man.* **Similar titles:** "The Incredible Shrinking Man," Richard Matheson; *Blade* (film); *Blood Crazy*, Simon Clark; *Never Dream*, Scott Charles Adams.

> *Isolation • Radiation • Science Fiction • Weird Science • Vampire as New Species*

Meikle, William.

The Book of the Dark. *greatunpublished.com, 2001. 273 p. Published on Demand.* Two young boys in Scotland find an underground cavern that has been boarded up for decades. Unfortunately for them and for their neighbors and friends, their intrusion has awakened a powerful vampire, one of the descendants of the fallen angels. Now only a small town clergyman armed with one book, *The Book of the Dark*, a text that chronicles the creation of "the Eldren," knows the secret to stopping the evil from draining all the citizens of a sleepy Western Scottish town. **Similar titles:** *Cold Print*, Ramsey Campbell; *The Light at the End*, John Skipp and Craig Spector; *The Traveling Vampire Show*, Richard Laymon; *The Lost Boys* (film).

 6

> *Angels • Bible, The • Clergy as Character • High School • Religion—Christianity • Scotland • Vampire's Point of View*

Mitchell, Mary Ann. The Sips of Blood Series.

Sips of Blood. *New York: Leisure, 1999. 358p.* The Marquis de Sade is alive and well as a member of the undead, and now he's introducing fourteen-year-old girls to his vices. And he and his dominatrix mother-in-law accidentally turn others into vampires while indulging their carnal desires. Mitchell's emphasis is on action. **Similar titles:** The Lord of the Dead Series, Tom Holland; The Anno Dracula Series, Kim Newman; *Historical Hauntings*, Jean Rabe and Martin H. Greenberg.

> *Eroticism • Marquis de Sade (character) • Sado-Masochism • Vampire's Point of View*

Quenched. *New York: Leisure, 2000. 363p.* Will and his bitter and crippled father Keith are adjusting to their new lives as vampires after the Marquis de Sade and his mother-in-law accidentally turned them. With no money and no one to tutor them in the ways of the undead, they must learn how to obtain victims without attracting too much attention. Their only hope for survival is to find their maker.

> **Similar titles:** The Lord of the Dead Series, Tom Holland; The Anno Dracula Series, Kim Newman; *Historical Hauntings*, Jean Rabe and Martin H. Greenberg.
>
> *Eroticism • Marquis de Sade (character) • Reincarnation • San Francisco, California • Vampire's Point of View*

Moore, Elaine.

Madonna of the Dark. *Irving, Tex.: Authorlink Press, 1999. 267p.* Across distance and time, Victoria MacKay is compelled to love a vampire, Johann Nikolai Valfrey. However, the clash between Victoria's vampire nature and the "gifts" resulting from her Celtic bloodline make Victoria not only more than human but also more intimately bound to the living than the undead. This is the 300-year tale of how she is pursued by the dark forces she cannot join. **Similar titles:** *De Lore's Confession*, Paulette Crain; The Midnight Series, Nancy Gideon; The Silver Wolf Series, Alice Borchardt; *Queen of the Damned*, Anne Rice.

> *Religion—Paganism • Vampire's Point of View*

Mosiman, Billie Sue.

Red Moon Rising. *New York: DAW, 2001. 320p.* Dell is a normal teenaged girl worried about dating and grades until the day she develops lesions on her body. Then she discovers that she too, like her parents and her brother, is a vampire. Now, with the help of Mentor, the creature who has helped her species for generations, she must discover what sort of vampire she'll be: a Predator, who kills without remorse; a Craven, who is utterly incapable of taking blood and so must depend on the kindness of Predators to survive; or a Normal, something in between a Craven and a Predator. **Similar titles:** *The Traveling Vampire Show*, Richard Laymon; The American Vampire Series, Martin H. Greenberg; The Buffy the Vampire Slayer Series, Richard Laymon; *Ginger Snaps* (film).

> *Adolescence • Dallas, Texas • Immortality • Physician as Character • Porphyria • Shapeshifters • Telepathy • Vampire Clans • Vampire's Point of View*

Newman, Kim. The Anno Dracula Series.

Anno Dracula. *New York: Avon, 1992. 409p.* What would've happened if Dracula had actually defeated Van Helsing? Kim Newman rewrites Stoker's narrative using historical, literary, and popular cultural figures to create an intricate rewriting of the *Dracula* story while including every known vampire myth. This astounding work is the recipient of an International Literary Guild Award for Best Novel. **Similar titles:** The Lord of the Dead Series, Tom Holland; *The London Vampire Panic*, Michael Romkey; *From Hell* (film).

> *Alternative History • Alternative Literature • Beauregard, Charles (character) • Holmwood, Arthur (character) • Jack the Ripper Murders • London, England • Seward, John (character) • Tepes, Vlad (character) • Vampire's Point of View • Victorian England*

Bloody Red Baron. *New York: Avon, 1995. 370p.* This novel continues twenty years after *Anno Dracula* ends. Previously, the evil Prince Vlad had been chased from England, and all think he has been defeated. However, Vlad Tepes has been regrouping his forces in Germany and has got one of his own vampires to assassinate Archduke Ferdinand to start World War I. Newman writes highly literate prose and possesses a knowledge of history. **Similar titles:** *The Last Vampire*, T. M. Wright; The Lord of the Dead Series, Tom Holland; *The London Vampire Panic*, Michael Romkey; *From Hell* (film).

> *Alternative History • Alternative Literature • Beauregard, Charles (character) • Holmwood, Arthur (character) • London, England • Tepes, Vlad (character) • Vampire's Point of View • War—World War I*

Judgment of Tears: Anno Dracula 1959. *New York: Carroll & Graf, 1998. 240p.* In the third novel of this series, Vlad Tepes is set to marry yet again for political gain, this time in Rome, the Eternal City. But someone is murdering vampire elders, some born to darkness as long ago as the Middle Ages. Newman demonstrates a thorough command of place and time and peppers his narrative with walk-on appearances by well-known historical figures and fictional characters. Featured in this novel are John and Morticia Addams, James Bond, Father Merrin from *The Exorcist*, an enormous Orson Wells, and a gloomy Edgar Allan Poe who, after becoming a vampire, is now a hack screen writer. **Similar titles:** The Madagascar Manifesto, Janet Berliner and George Guthridge; The Lord of the Dead Series, Tom Holland; *The London Vampire Panic*, Michael Romkey; *From Hell* (film).

> *Alternative History • Alternative Literature • Rome, Italy • Tepes, Vlad (character) • Vampire's Point of View*

Odom, Mel, and David S. Goyer.

Blade. *New York: Harper Mass Market Paperbacks, 1998. 343p.* This is a novelization of the 1998 film of the same name. Blade is a half-human, half-vampire who struggles against his nosferatu half and protects humanity from those who see the human race as nothing more than cattle. His mixed heritage gives him an advantage over the "children of the night" in that he can walk in the sunlight. **Similar titles:** *Blade* (film); *Morningstar*, Peter Atkins; *Vampire Slayers*, Martin H. Greenberg and Elizabeth Ann Scarborough; The Anita Blake Vampire Hunter *Series*, Laurell K. Hamilton.

> *African-American Characters • Blade (character) • Fantasy • New York City • Physician as Character • Revenge • Vampire Clans • Vampire Hunters*

Pantaleo, Jack.

Mother Julian and the Gentle Vampire. *Roseville, Calif.: Dry Bones Press, 1999. 268p.* In fourteenth-century England, a mystic nun, Julian of Norwich, allows Lesbiana, a vampire, to drink of her own sacred blood. As a result, Lesbiana becomes a sort of reverse vampire: Instead of having to slake her thirst with human blood, she must now give her own blood to humans to survive. Now, in the twentieth century, Lesbiana is giving her healing blood to humans in need, restoring their self-esteem to the point that they no longer allow themselves to be victimized. But there are those who would stop Lesbiana's work, even if it means taking her life to do so. **Similar titles:** *The Vampire Lestat*, Anne Rice; *Awash in the Blood*, John Wooley; *My Soul to Keep*, Tananarive Due; The Saint-Germain Chronicles, Chelsea Quinn Yarbro.

> *Clergy as Character • England • Eroticism • Feminism • Gay/Lesbian/Bisexual characters • Immortality • Julian of Norwich (character) • Physician as Character • Religion—Christianity—Catholicism • San Francisco, California • Vampire Clans • Vampire's Point of View*

Parker, Lara.

Dark Shadows: Angélique's Descent. *New York: Harper Mass Market, 1998. 515p.* This novel is a prequel to the *Dark Shadows* television series of the 1970s, explaining how the love affair between Barnabas Collins and Angelique began. Barnabas, heir of a New England shipping magnate, toys with the affections of young Angelique when he meets her in Martinique, but soon deserts her, becoming engaged to another. But Angelique is skilled in the black arts and casts a spell on her deceitful lover that will turn him into a vampire and bind him to her for eternity. The author of this novel played Angelique in *Dark Shadows*. **Similar titles:** The Vampire Chronicles, Anne Rice; The Saint-Germain Chronicles, Chelsea Quinn Yarbro; The Devoncroix Dynasty Series, Donna Boyd; *Wuthering Heights*, Emily Brontë.

> *Collins, Barnabas (character) • Eroticism • Immortality • Magic • Martinique • Revenge • Witchcraft*

Passarella, Jack.

Buffy the Vampire Slayer: Ghoul Trouble. (See The Buffy the Vampire Series in this chapter.)

Polidori, John.

The Vampyre. *In The Vampyre and Other Tales of the Macabre, Robert Morrison and Chris Baldick, editors. New York, Oxford: Oxford University Press, 1997. 23p.* John Polidori, traveling companion to Lord Byron, wrote this story in response to the famous contest to write a chilling tale while at Lake Geneva with Mary Shelley and Percy B. Shelley. Mary Shelley's *Frankenstein* is probably the best-known fruit of this contest, but the influence of Polidori's story persists. In this tale, Lord Ruthven preys on men and women of good fortune, gleefully seeking their ruin. Aubrey, his traveling companion, is eventually appalled by the lord's behavior and quits his company, only to be later nursed back from the brink of death by the noble. Later, Lord Ruthven appears to be fatally wounded and elicits a promise from Aubrey not to reveal his death or his evil deeds for a year and a day after his passing. Aubrey agrees, only for Ruthven to appear later and ruin his own family. Ruthven and Aubrey's relationship is loosely modeled on Byron and Polidori's own ill-fated friendship. Polidori is credited with transforming the vampire figure from a laughable blood-sucking peasant into a suave, seductive nobleman. **Similar titles:** *Lord of the Dead*, Tom Holland; *Frankenstein*, Mary Shelley; *Dracula*, Bram Stoker.

> *England • Greece • Lord Ruthven (character) • Secret Sin*

Rice, Anne.

Merrick. *New York: Alfred A. Knopf, 2000. 307p.* (See chapter 7, "Demonic Possession, Satanism, Black Magic, and Witches and Warlocks: The Devil Made Me Do It.")

Rice, Anne. The New Tales of the Vampire Series.

Pandora: New Tales of the Vampire. *New York: Alfred E. Knopf, 1998. 288p.* This first person narrative is a pseudo-historical romp through the Rome of Augustus Caesar and through modern-day Paris, starring Pandora, an innocent Roman girl made into a vampire by Marius. Rice's emphasis is on historical accuracy rather than vampirism per se, with the main character being one of the few strong Rice-created females. **Similar titles:** The Devoncroix Dynasty Series, Donna Boyd; The Saint-Germain Chronicles, Chelsea Quinn Yarbro; The Silver Wolf Series, Alice Borchart.

> ♪ audiotape, audio download, compact disc   ᴼᴼ large print

> *Akasha and Enkil (characters) • History, Use of • Homoeroticism • Marius (character) • Religion—Christianity • Rome, Italy • Vampire's Point of View*

Vittorio, the Vampire. *New York: Alfred A. Knopf, 1999. 292p.* Set in Renaissance Italy, this is a first person narrative by the 500-year-old vampire who was educated in the Medici court. The story chronicles his transformation from human to immortal at the hands of Ursula, the vampire who haunts his family. **Similar titles:** The Devoncroix Dynasty Series, Donna Boyd; The Saint-Germain Chronicles, Chelsea Quinn Yarbro; The Silver Wolf Series, Alice Borchart.

> ♪ audiotape, audio download, compact disc   ᴼᴼ large print

Artist as Character • Clergy as Character • diRaniari, Vittorio (character) • Eroticism • Florence, Italy • History, Use of • Religion—Christianity—Catholicism • Ursula (character) • Vampire's Point of View

---

Rice, Anne. The Vampire Chronicles.

Interview with the Vampire. *New York: Ballantine, 1977. 346p.* This first novel in Rice's series contains the first person confessions of reluctant vampire Louis, who during a time of overwhelming grief was seduced into the undead life by Lestat de Lioncourt. Rice transports readers into the world of the undead in the New Orleans of 200 years ago. An immensely popular best-seller that led to Rice's own "immortality" on the best-seller list. The novel was made into a film in 1995. **Similar titles:** The Saint-Germain Chronicles, Chelsea Quinn Yarbro; The Lord of the Dead Series, Tom Holland; *Voice of the Blood*, Jemiah Jefferson.

🎧 audiotape, audio download, compact disc

Armand (character) • Claudia (character) • Homoeroticism • Lestat de Lioncourt (character) • Louis (character) • New Orleans, Louisiana • Vampire's Point of View

The Vampire Lestat. *New York: Ballantine, 1985. 550p.* This novel, the second in Rice's series, details the Vampire Lestat's undead, and pre-undead, existence, and his search for the meaning of life. Written in the first person from Lestat's point of view, this novel is a reaction to *Interview with the Vampire*, a tell-all book published by Lestat's former lover Louis, which represents Lestat as a thoughtless bloodsucker. **Similar titles:** The Saint-Germain Chronicles, Chelsea Quinn Yarbro; The Lord of the Dead Series, Tom Holland; *Voice of the Blood*, Jemiah Jefferson.

🎧 audiotape, audio download

Akasha and Enkel (characters) • Armand (character) • Claudia (character) • History, Use of • Homoeroticism • Lestat de Lioncourt(character) • Louis (character) • Marius (character) • Music—Rock Music • Vampire's Point of View

The Queen of the Damned. *New York: Ballantine, 1989. 491p.* The third book in the Vampire Chronicles, this novel picks up where *The Vampire Lestat* stopped with Akasha and Lestat. The mother of all vampire-kind, Akasha, has freed herself from Enkil, her husband and jailer for the past 2,000 years, and has taken Lestat as an unwilling personal assistant to help carry out her plan to kill nine out of every ten men on Earth. **Similar titles:** The Saint-Germain Chronicles, Chelsea Quinn Yarbro; The Lord of the Dead Series, Tom Holland; *Voice of the Blood*, Jemiah Jefferson; *Anno Dracula*, Kim Newman.

🎧 audiotape, audio download

Akasha and Enkil (characters) • Babylon • History, Use of • Homoeroticism • Lestat de Lioncourt (character) • Lightner, Aaron (character) • Louis (character) • Maharet and Mekare (characters) • Marius (character) • Religion—Ancient Egyptian • Talamasca • Vampire's Point of View

The Tale of the Body Thief. *New York: Ballantine, 1992. 435p.* Rice's fourth book in the Vampire Chronicles, and the third book "written" by Lestat, *The Tale of the Body Thief* concerns Lestat's adventures as a mortal. Bored with the undead life, Lestat longs to experience mortal pleasures once more such as eating and making love, but he also rediscovers the mortification of being encased in human flesh. **Similar titles:** The Saint-Germain Chronicles, Chelsea Quinn Yarbro; The Lord of the Dead Series, Tom Holland; *Voice of the Blood*, Jemiah Jefferson.

👂 audiotape, audio download

Homoeroticism • Lestat de Lioncourt (character) • Louis (character) • New York City • Talamasca • Talbot, David (character) • Vampire's Point of View

Memnoch the Devil. *New York: Alfred A. Knopf, 1995. 354p.* This was to be the last of the five novels in the series. For centuries Lestat has doubted the existence of God and Satan, until Satan comes to him, shows him the world of the living and the dead, and asks him to be his Second in Command. **Similar titles:** The Saint-Germain Chronicles, Chelsea Quinn Yarbro; The Lord of the Dead Series, Tom Holland; *Voice of the Blood*, Jemiah Jefferson.

👂 audiotape, audio download

Armand (character) • Claudia (character) • Homoeroticism • Lestat de Lioncourt (character) • Louis (character) • Maharet and Mekare (characters) • New Age • New York City • Religion—Christianity • Satan (character) • Vampire's Point of View

The Vampire Armand: The Vampire Chronicles. *New York: Alfred A. Knopf, 1998. 384p.* This sixth novel in Rice's Vampire Chronicles begins at the end of *Memnoch the Devil*, the fifth novel in the series. Lestat lies unconscious on the floor of a cathedral after his encounter with Satan, and all the vampires of the world have gathered at his side. It is during this occasion that David Talbot bids Armand to take the opportunity to tell about his human life with Marius in Renaissance Italy, and later as leader of a coven of vampires in Paris. **Similar titles:** The Saint-Germain Chronicles, Chelsea Quinn Yarbro; The Lord of the Dead Series, Tom Holland; *Voice of the Blood*, Jemiah Jefferson.

👂 audiotape, audio download, compact disc ℞ large print

Armand (character) • History, Use of • Homoeroticism • Marius (character) • Religion—Christianity • The Renaissance • Santino (character) • Talbot, David (character) • Vampire's Point of View • Venice, Italy

Blood and Gold. *New York: Alfred A. Knopf, 2001. 470p.* In this latest installment of the Vampire Chronicles, Rice follows the lonely life of Marius, caretaker of Akasha and Enkil, Those Who Must Be Kept. Plucked from his life as a Roman patrician 2,000 years ago, Marius finds immortality to be both a blessing and a curse, allowing the scholar and artist sufficient time to achieve all of his life's goals yet preventing him from engaging in relationships with others for fear of revealing his burden. **Similar titles:** The Lord of the Dead Series, Tom Holland; The New Tales of the Vampire Series, Anne Rice; The Silver Wolf Series, Alice Borchadt; The Saint-Germain Chronicles, Chelsea Quinn Yarbro.

👂 audiotape, compact disc ℞ large print

Akasha and Enkil (characters) • Homoeroticism • Immortality • Marius (character) • Religion—Druidism • Rome, Italy • Scholar as Character • Vampire's Point of View

---

Romkey, Michael. The I, Vampire Series.

I, Vampire. *New York: Fawcett Books, 1990. 360p.* Good and evil vampire clans led by famous historical figures such as Julius Caesar and Lucretia Borgia highlight this action-oriented exploration of immortality. Romkey is plot driven, and many vampire enthusiasts consider the book a benchmark text. **Similar titles:** The Anno Dracula Series,

Kim Newman; *The Book of the Dark*, William Meikle; The Silver Wolf Series, Alice Borchardt.

> *History, Use of • Parker, David (character) • Vampire Clans • Vampire's Point of View*

The Vampire Papers. *New York: Fawcett Books, 1994. 433p.* In this much-awaited sequel to *I, Vampire,* vampire clans led by David Parker and John Wilkes Booth clash in the colonial South. **Similar titles:** The Anno Dracula Series, Kim Newman; *The Book of the Dark*, William Meikle; The Silver Wolf Series, Alice Borchardt.

> *History, Use of • Parker, David (character) • The South • Vampire Clans • Vampire's Point of View*

The Vampire Princess. *New York: Fawcett Books, 1996. 339p.* This is the third book of the *I, Vampire* series, dealing with David Parker's vampire lover, Princess Nicoletta Vittorini di Medusa. The two undead lovers take a cruise aboard the *Atlantic Princess*, and David once again finds himself pitted against evil. **Similar titles:** The Anno Dracula Series, Kim Newman; *The Book of the Dark*, William Meikle; The Silver Wolf Series, Alice Borchardt.

> *Gothic Romance • Parker, David (character) • Vampire's Point of View*

The Vampire Virus. *New York: Ballantine, 1997. 295p.* In the jungles of Costa Rica, an unknown virus is introduced to the world—with lethal results. Doctor Bailey Herrison of the Centers for Disease Control travels there to investigate, and she also finds a centuries-old ruler who is slave to a centuries-old thirst. **Similar titles:** The Anno Dracula Series, Kim Newman; *The Book of the Dark*, William Meikle; The Silver Wolf Series, Alice Borchardt.

> *Archeology • Costa Rica • Epidemic • Vampire as New Species*

The London Vampire Panic. *New York: Ballantine, 2001. 295p.* A scholar uncovers the documents of a London physician that chronicle the chaos created in the late nineteenth century by a murderous vampire. Romkey's newest thriller pits historical and literary characters against the undead. Can the team of eight vampire hunters led by Abraham Van Helsing defeat the undead? **Similar titles:** *Anno Dracula*, Kim Newman; The I, Vampire Series, Michael Romkey; *From Hell* (film).

> *Alternative Literature • Epistolary Format • History, Use of • London, England • Vampire Hunters • Van Helsing, Abraham (character) • Victorian England*

Rosen, Selina. The Host Series.

The Host. *Alma, Ark.: Yard Dog Press, 1997. 164p.* In the opening book of this series, vampire hunter Rabbi Tracy Cohen is pitted, along with her friends, against the undead, who have invaded her home of Jones Port, Arkansas. During the battle, she meets reporter Jane Weston, who seems to be the center of attention for the undead. Can Tracy save her new romantic interest from their clutches? **Similar titles:** The Anita Blake Vampire Hunter Series, Laurell K. Hamilton; *Full Moon, Bloody Moon*, Lee Driver; The Black Oak Series, Charles Grant; *Bubbas of the Apocalypse*, Selina Rosen (editor).

> *Clairvoyant as Character • Clergy as Character • Cohen, Tracy (character) • Gay/Lesbian/Bisexual Characters • Jewish-American Characters • Journalist as Character • Vampire as New Species • Vampire Hunters*

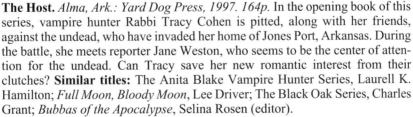

Fright Eater. *Alma, Ark.: Yard Dog Press, 1998. 175p.* In the second book of the series, clairvoyant vampire hunter Tracy Cohen is sent to Wako City to investigate a series of serial killings. But away from her the love of her life, she lacks much of the psychic energy that allows her to see into the hearts and souls of killers. Can she muster enough power to defeat a Nazi cult and the vampiric "fright eaters?" **Similar titles:** The Anita Blake Vampire Hunter Series, Laurell K. Hamilton; *Full Moon, Bloody Moon*, Lee Driver; The Black Oak Series, Charles Grant; *Bubbas of the Apocalypse*, Selina Rosen (editor).

> *Arkansas • Clairvoyant as Character • Clergy as Character • Cohen, Tracy (character) • Gay/Lesbian/Bisexual Characters • Jewish- American Characters • Nazism • Police Officer as Character • Serial Killers • Vampire as New Species • Vampire Hunters*

Gang Approval. *Alma, Ark.: Yard Dog Press, 1999. 195p.* In the third book of the series, rival gangs of vampires are turning the inner city into rubble with their gang wars. In steps vampire hunter Rabbi Tracy Cohen, the IDL's best agent for fighting the undead. Tracy, her wife Jane, and her motley crew of vampire hunters face their biggest challenge yet in this action-oriented novel. **Similar titles:** The Anita Blake Vampire Hunter Series, Laurell K. Hamilton; *Full Moon, Bloody Moon*, Lee Driver; The Black Oak Series, Charles Grant; *Bubbas of the Apocalypse*, Selina Rosen (editor).

> *Clairvoyant as Character • Clergy as Character • Cohen, Tracy (character) • Gang Violence • Gay/Lesbian/Bisexual Characters • Jewish-American Characters • Vampire as New Species • Vampire Hunters*

Rovin, Jeff.

Return of the Wolf Man. (See The Universal Monsters Series in this chapter.)

Roycraft, Jaye.

Double Image. *Hickory Corners, Minn.: ImaJinn, 2001, 294p.* Photographer Tia Martell's latest assignment is to take pictures of the stately homes in Natchez, Mississippi. It is here she meets Dallas Aldgate, vampire. Tia becomes involved with Dallas when she inadvertently photographs a hit and run accident somehow connected with him. And now Dallas wants to bring Tia into his own world to protect her from a powerful enemy of his own kind who wishes to destroy all he cares about. **Similar titles:** *Lords of the Night*, Monique Ellis et. al. (editor); *Voice of the Blood*, Jemiah Jefferson; The Midnight Series, Nancy Gideon; The Saint-Germain Chronicles, Chelsea Quinn Yarbro; *Red Moon Rising*, Billie Sue Mosiman.

> *Natchez, Mississippi • Photographer as Character • Vampire's Point of View*

Schildt, Christopher.

Night of Dracula. (See The Universal Monster Series in this chapter.)

Skipp, John, and Craig Spector.

The Light at the End. *Lancaster, Pa.: Stealth Press, 2000, ©1986. 370p.* A subway train in New York City is attacked late at night by a centuries-old vampire. Now the only survivor of the massacre, a young ne'er-do-well named Rudy, finds himself craving human blood and flesh, and he must hide in the subway to satisfy his bloodlust. But when Rudy's best friend, his ex-girlfriend, and a handful of other makeshift "vampire hunters" start combing the subways to look for him, they risk running into "The Dark One." This novel is suspenseful and atmospheric; the authors produce a nicely crafted, truly frightening tale. **Similar titles:** *The Book of the Dark*, William Meikle; *The Traveling Vampire Show*, Richard Laymon; *The Cleanup*, John Skipp and Craig Spector; *The Hunger*, Whitley Streiber.

Dreams • Grieving • Horror Movie Industry • New York City • Subterranean Horror • Writer as Character • Zombies

Simmons, Dan.

B Carrion Comfort. *New York: Warner, 1989. 883p.* In this extremely complex and lengthy narrative, mind-controlling vampires dictate human history by feeding off of and magnifying the violence inherent in humans. Simmons's prose is multilayered, suspense-oriented, and erudite, and the story takes unexpected twists and turns at every juncture. This novel, which contains believable, multidimensional characters, is told through multiple points of view, and is a recipient of a Bram Stoker Award. **Similar titles:** The Devoncroix Dynasty Series, Donna Boyd; *The Evil Returns*, Hugh B. Cave; *The Flesh, the Blood, and the Fire*, S. A. Swiniarski.

> *Charleston, South Carolina • Holocaust, The • Mind Control • Nazism • Philadelphia, Pennsylvania • Televangelism • Vampire Hunters • Vampire as New Species • Vampire's Point of View • Violence—Theories of*

Sipos, Thomas M.

Vampire Nation. *Philadelphia: Xlibris, 1998. 256p.* A Hollywood screenwriter is sent to Romania to scout a location for an upcoming vampire film and to meet with a Romanian dignitary who is acting as the production company's local liaison. Once there, however, he finds himself involved in an assassination plot—the target, Nicolae Ceaucescu. Sipos is lots of fun to read. **Similar titles:** *Anno Dracula*, Kim Newman; The Saint-Germain Chronicles, Chelsea Quinn Yarbro; *Awash in the Blood*, John Wooley.

> *Ceaucescu, Nicolae (character) • Caeucescu, Elena (character) • Central Intelligence Agency • Espionage • History, Use of • KGB • Romania • Vampire Hunters*

Smith, Beecher.

The Guardian. *Memphis, Tenn.: Hot Biscuit Productions, 1999. 349p.* In this modernization of *Dracula*, the Count and a real estate agent named Reynolds Fields do battle with the surviving descendant of Elizabeth de Bathory in modern-day Memphis. Informed with literary and historical characters, this novel emphasizes story-telling technique and is clever and enjoyable. **Similar titles:** *Vampire's Waltz*, Thomas Staab; *Dracula*, Bram Stoker; *More Monsters from Memphis*, Beecher Smith.

> *AIDS • Alternative Literature • Bathory, Elizabeth de (character) • Dracula (character) • History, Use of • Lawyer as Character • Memphis, Tennessee • Police Officer as Character • Reincarnation • Renfield (character) • Transylvania • Vampire Hunters*

6

Staab, Thomas.

Vampire's Waltz. *New Hyde Park, N.Y.: Crazy Wolf Publishing, 1999. 495p.* Christine Ferranti's unborn child holds the key to the destruction of the human race, especially if a race of hybrid vampires can find her and snatch the unborn in time. Pitted against the vampires are an immortal and a shapeshifting guardian, each the last of their races. With the help of two young male humans who survived an attack on New York City by the vampires, the Immortal and the Guardian attempt to stop the destruction of the human race. Staab's emphasis is on atmosphere and characterization. **Similar titles:** *Blade* (film); *The Millennium Quartet,* Charles Grant; *I Am Legend,* Richard Matheson; *Riverwatch,* Joseph M. Nassie.

> *African-American Characters • Apocalypse • Immortality • Mind Control • New York City • Shapeshifters • Vampire Clans • Vampire Hunters • Vampire's Point of View • Werewolves*

Stoker, Bram.

Dracula. *New York: Viking Penguin, 1998, ©1897. 560p.* The mother of all vampire texts, Stoker's classic tale is one of the few horror novels that has stood the test of time. Count Dracula comes to England, feeds from, and subsequently infects with vampirism the wives and girlfriends of his enemies, and plans to take over the country. The story unfolds through journal entries, phonograph recordings, and letters of the vampire hunters, as well as a few newspaper articles. The novel is unique in that the vampire never speaks for himself. It has inspired countless films and rewritings of Stoker's original tale. **Similar titles:** *Carmilla,* Joseph Sheridan Le Fanu; *Midnight Tales,* Bram Stoker; *Bram Stoker's Dracula Unearthed,* Clive Leatherdale (editor); *Bram Stoker's Dracula* (film).

> ⑨ audiotape, audio download, compact disc   ᵔ⏱ e-book   ᏇᏒ large print
>
> *Diary Format • Documentary Techniques • Dracula (character) • Eroticism • Harker, Jonathan (character) • Harker, Mina Murray (character) • Holmwood, Arthur (character) • London, England • Renfield (character) • Seward, John (character) • Transylvania • Vampire Hunters • Van Helsing, Abraham (character) • Victorian England • Westenra, Lucy (character)*

Bram Stoker's *Dracula* Unearthed [Annotated Edition of Dracula]. *Clive Leatherdale (editor). Westcliff-on-Sea, Esssex: Desert Island Books, 1998, ©1897. 512p.* (See Leatherdale, Clive [editor] in chapter 18, "Resources.")

Streiber, Whitley. The Hunger Series.

The Hunger. *New York: Avon, 1981. 307p.* For thousands of years, Miriam has been forever young and has enjoyed the love of numerous companions in darkness. But while Miriam is forever young, she cannot promise the same for her lovers. She can merely bestow eternal life trapped in a rotting husk of a body. Tony Scott, brother of famous director Ridley Scott, made this novel into a film in 1983. **Similar titles:** *The Guardian,* Beecher Smith; *The Last Vampire,* T. M. Wright; *Carmilla,* Joseph Sheridan Le Fanu; *The Hunger* (film).

> *Aging • Blaylock, Miriam (character) • Gay/Lesbian/Bisexual Characters • Homoeroticism • New York City • Religion—Ancient Egyptian • Roberts, Sarah (character) • Vampire's Point of View*

The Last Vampire. *New York: Pocket, 2001. 303p.* In the long-awaited sequel to *The Hunger,* Interpol agent Paul Ward travels throughout the world, exterminating those vampires known as The Keepers as he finds them. After one of his assassinations, he discovers the book that lists the names and locations of all The Keepers throughout the world. In no time, he and his accomplices have eliminated all but one vampire, Miriam Blaylock, and now Paul Ward has traced her to New York City. The hunt is on; will the last vampire survive? **Similar titles:** *The Guardian,* Beecher Smith; *The Last Vampire,* T. M. Wright; *Carmilla,* Joseph Sheridan Le Fanu.

> *Blaylock, Miriam (character) • Paris, France • New York City • Roberts, Sarah (character) • Vampire as New Species • Vampire Hunters • Vampire's Point of View*

Swiniarski, S. A.

The Flesh, the Blood, and the Fire. *New York: DAW Books, 1998. 361p.* Headless bodies, mysteriously preserved from the ravages of death, begin turning up in Depression-era Cleveland, but the killer eludes the police. Soon Eliot Ness is hired as part of the new mayor's crime-fighting taskforce, and he handpicks some of Cleveland's finest to quietly investigate the gruesome crimes. But when these officers unearth compelling evidence that the murders are the work of an ancient supernatural entity, Ness refuses to listen and kicks them off the case. Now officers Ryzard and Lapidos must conduct their own investigation before this creature takes over the city with his ever-growing army of undead tramps and prostitutes. Swiniarski has a feel for this city and time period, and his vampire tale rises above the usual one-dimensional clichéd contest between good and evil. **Similar titles:** *The Devil's Brood*, David Jacobs; *The Vampire Files*, P. N. Elrod; *Gothique*, Kyle Marffin; *Carrion Comfort*, Dan Simmons.

> *Cleveland, Ohio • Great Depression, The • Mind Control • Ness, Eliot (character) • Serial Killers • Police Officer as Character • Police Procedural • Vampire Clans • Vampire Hunters • Vampire's Point of View • Zombies*

Taylor, Karen E. The Vampire Legacy Series.

Blood Ties. *New York: Pinnacle, 1995. 352p.* Deirdre and Mitch must track down a vampire who is killing off New York's undead. **Similar titles:** The Devoncroix Dynasty Series, Donna Boyd; The Blood Series, Tanya Huff; The Vampire Files, P. N. Elrod; The Anita Blake, Vampire Hunter Series, Laurell K. Hamilton.

> *Greer, Mitch (character) • Griffin, Deirdre (character) • New York City • Police Officer as Character • Vampire Clans • Vampire Hunters • Vampire's Point of View*

6

Bitter Blood. *New York: Pinnacle, 2000. 352p.* When Deirdre hears that Mitch is in a mental institution, she hops the next flight back to the states to help him. But Mitch is being used as bait to lure Deirdre into a trap so that the clan of a vampire whose master she killed can exact their revenge. **Similar titles:** The Devoncroix Dynasty Series, Donna Boyd; The Blood Series, Tanya Huff; The Vampire Files, P. N. Elrod; The Anita Blake, Vampire Hunter Series, Laurell K. Hamilton.

> *Greer, Mitch (character) • Griffin, Deirdre (character) • New York City • Police Officer as Character • Revenge • Vampire Clans • Vampire Hunters • Vampire's Point of View*

Blood of My Blood. *New York: Pinnacle, 2000. 352p.* When Deirdre was first made a vampire, she was pregnant, and the resulting transformation caused her to give birth to a child she believed to be stillborn. But the tiny undead Lily clawed her way out of her grave and has since been raised in New Orleans by a succession of practitioners of voodoo. Now, when her current "maman" and her dearest friend are viciously murdered, Lily decides to take revenge on the woman who "abandoned" her 150 years ago. **Similar titles:** The Devoncroix Dynasty Series, Donna Boyd; The Blood Series, Tanya Huff; The Vampire Files, P. N. Elrod; The Anita Blake, Vampire Hunter Series, Laurell K. Hamilton.

> *Greer, Mitch (character) • Griffin, Deirdre (character) • Maine • New Orleans, Louisiana • Parenting • Revenge • Vampire's Point of View*

Blood Secrets. *New York: Pinnacle, 2000. 352p.* A renegade vampire is killing innocent people and trying to frame Deirdre for the murder. Meanwhile, Deirdre is falling in love with Detective Mitch Greer, who is heading the investigation of the murders. **Similar titles:** The Devoncroix Dynasty Series, Donna Boyd; The Blood Series, Tanya Huff; The Vampire Files, P. N. Elrod; The Anita Blake, Vampire Hunter Series, Laurell K. Hamilton.

> *Greer, Mitch (character) • Griffin, Deirdre (character) • New York City • Police Officer as Character • Vampire Clans • Vampire Hunters • Vampire's Point of View*

The Vampire Vivienne. *New York: Pinnacle, 2001. 303p.* This latest installment in The Vampire Legacy Series follows the lengthy career of Vivienne the Vampire, a minor character in other books in the series. **Similar titles:** The Devoncroix Dynasty Series, Donna Boyd; The Blood Series, Tanya Huff; The Vampire Files, P. N. Elrod; The Anita Blake, Vampire Hunter Series, Laurell K. Hamilton.

> *New Orleans, Louisiana • New York City • Paris, France • Vampire Clans • Vampire's Point of View*

Thompson, James M.

Night Blood. *New York: Pinnacle, 2001. 400p.* A team trying to catch a serial killer come to believe they're dealing with something not quite human after thoroughly examining some of his victims. Meanwhile, the killer on the loose is a vampire, turned over 200 years ago when he was infected with a mutation of Erythropoietic Uroporphyria mixed with a virus. And although the vampire would like to find a cure for his condition, still, he must eat, and finds himself enslaved to his violent hunger. **Similar titles:** *Red Moon Rising*, Billie Sue Mosiman; *Human Resources*, Floyd Kemske, *Voice of the Blood*, Jemiah Jefferson.

> *Houston, Texas • Medical Horror • Serial Killers • Vampire Hunters • Vampire as New Species • Vampire's Point of View*

Thorne, Tamara.

Candle Bay. *New York: Pinnacle, 2001. 400p.* The once-opulent Candle Bay Hotel and Spa was neglected for decades before Steven Darling restored it to its former glory and filled it with wealthy guests. Assistant concierge Amanda Pearce is awed by her surroundings, but also filled with dread by the odd behavior of her employers and the mysterious splatters of blood. Little does she know that her new employers are vampires who nearly exterminated a rival clan of undead over a century ago, and the surviving members of this clan are about to return for revenge. Meanwhile, Amanda's feelings for Steven are growing, and soon she must decide if she will die as a human or join the ranks of the undead.

> *California • Revenge • Vampire Clans*

Tilton, Lois.

Darkspawn. *Tulsa, Okla.: Hawk Publishing, 2000. 513p.* In this dark fantasy epic, a vampire prince, leader of the land of Kharithyna, is betrayed by one of his generals and is imprisoned for 300 years. Lord Erme Bukhany, vampire prince and practitioner of the Moon Religion, is then set free, only to find that during his incarceration, Sun Worshippers have taken over his homeland. With a small band of followers, Lord Emre must now battle to take back his kingdom. This is a gentle read that will appeal to fans of fantasy fiction. **Similar titles:** *Dark Soul*, M. Martin Hunt; The Talisman Series, Stephen King and Peter Straub; *The Stand*, Stephen King.

> *Bakhany, Lord Emre (character) • Epic Structure • Fantasy • Magic • Vampire's Point of View*

The Universal Monsters Series. Various Authors.

Rovin, Jeff.

Return of the Wolf Man. *New York: Penguin-Putnam, 1998. 339p.* The small Florida town of LaMirada is placed on the map because of the number of murdered and mutilated bodies that are found in the 1930s. While the police suspect a serial killer, no one realizes that a scientist and her lab assistant, the two people who were the first victims of the killer, are responsible for the supernatural evil. Some sixty years later, the reappearance of a hairy killer has police worried that bodies may start piling up again. Little do they know that the wolfman, and two other horrific creatures, are once again preying on the locals of LaMirada. **Similar titles:** *The Wolf Man* (film); *Murcheston: the Wolf's Tale*, David Holland; *Ghosts, Werewolves, Witches, and Vampires*, Jo-Anne Christensen.

> *Dracula (character)* • *Florida* • *Frankenstein's Monster (character)* •
> *Shapeshifters* • *Talbot, Lawrence (character)* • *Weird Science* •
> *Werewolves*

Jacobs, David.

The Devil's Brood. *New York: Berkley Boulevard, 2000. 316p.* Dracula's daughter, the Countess Marya Zalenska, has plans to resurrect the bride of Frankenstein's monster. But to do so, she will need the help of various Universal Studios monsters, including the wolfman and Dracula himself. In the meantime, a two-bit gangster who acts as a loan shark finds himself with the unenviable task of grappling with the grotesque creatures that Zalenska has already resurrected. Suddenly, he finds himself, and the organized crime industry, on the side of good in the ultimate battle of good versus evil. This clever, gentle read is excellent for fans of traditional horror. **Similar titles:** *Dracula's Daughter* (film); The Anno Dracula Series, Kim Newman; The Buffy the Vampire Slayer Series, various authors.

 6

> *Dracula (character)* • *Frankenstein's Monster (character)* • *Glendon,*
> *Wilfred III (character)* • *Horror Movie Industry* • *Organized Crime* •
> *Universal Studios* • *Vampire's Point of View* • *Werewolves* • *Zalenska,*
> *Marya (character)* • *Zombies*

The Devil's Night. *New York: Berkley Boulevard, 2001. 252p.* Werewolf Wilfred Glendon III has been kidnapped, and he is being used in an evil experiment by a group of scientists who belong to a Satanic cult led by Countess Marya Zalenska, the daughter of Count Dracula. As more of the Universal Studios horror monsters are similarly rounded up, a fiendish plan for world domination begins to take shape. This gentle read is excellent for fans of traditional horror. **Similar titles:** *Murcheston: The Wolf's Tale*, David Holland; The Anno Dracula Series, Kim Newman; The Buffy the Vampire Slayer Series, various authors.

> *Dracula (character)* • *Frankenstein's Monster (character)* • *Glendon,*
> *Wilfred III (character)* • *Horror Movie Industry* •
> *Religion—Satanism* • *Universal Studios* • *Vampire's Point of*
> *View* • *Werewolves* • *Weird Science* • *Zalenska, Marya (character)*

Schildt, Christopher.

Night of Dracula. *New York: Pocket, 2001. 272p.* The Count Dracula we know and love from the Universal Studios horror films returns for another adventure in the twenty-first century. **Similar titles:** *Frankenstein:The Legacy*, Christopher

Schildt; Dracula (film); *The Return of the Wolfman*, Jeff Rovin; *Dracula in London*, P. N. Elrod (editor).

> *Dracula (character)* • *Vampire's Point of View*

Wieck, Stewart.

Clan Novel: Malkavian. (See The Clan Novel Series in this chapter.)

Williamson, J. N.

Bloodlines. *New York: Leisure, 1999. 320p.* Suspecting that he has been abusing her son, Marshall Madison's wife commits suicide. In reality Marshall had been converting his son into a vampire, like himself, and although forced to leave, he promises to return for his son. **Similar titles:** *In the Blood*, Stephen Gresham; *Blood Covenant*, Marilyn Lamb; *My Soul to Keep*, Tananarive Due.

> *Childhood* • *Family Curse* • *Parenting* • *Vampire's Point of View*

Wilson, David Niall.

This Is My Blood. *Black River, N.Y.: Terminal Fright Press, 1999. 251p.* This novel of alternate literature/history and dark fantasy follows the journey of Mary Magdalen, here a fallen angel, one cursed as a vampire. This is a clever, subtle, deftly conceived novel in which the vampire is both a metaphorical device and a supernatural character. **Similar titles:** *Cronos* (film); *My Soul to Keep* and *The Living Blood*, Tananarive Due; *Mother Julian and the Gentle Vampire*, Jack Pantaleo.

> *Alternative Literature* • *Bible, The* • *History, Use of* • *Immortality* • *Iscariot, Judas (character)* • *Magdalen, Mary (character)* • *Religion—Christianity* • *Vampire's Point of View*

Wooley, John.

Awash in the Blood. *Tulsa, Okla.: Hawk Publishing, 2001. 246p.* The Reverend Mo Johnston, televangelist extraordinaire, travels to Romania to minister to the locals, but he finds himself being converted instead, by a Transylvanian vampire. However, he goes into a state of deep denial about his newfound dark powers and returns to America with a story of how he faced and defeated Satan himself. Once his vampiric powers develop, he must wrestle with himself, his ability to grant immortality, and his rising popularity. Wooley's text is extremely intelligent and clever, a new twist on an old theme. **Similar titles:** *Carrion Comfort*, Dan Simmons; *Interview with the Vampire*, Anne Rice; *The Last Vampire*, T. M. Wright.

> *Clergy as Character* • *Immortality* • *Religion—Christianity* • *Televangelism* • *Transylvania* • *Vampire's Point of View*

Wright, T. M.

The Last Vampire. *New York: Leisure, 2001. 275p.* Reading like an update of the philosophical issues in Anne Rice's *Interview with the Vampire*, this novel is the story of Elmo Land, a young man who in 1907 met the woman who ended his life as a human but began it as a vampire. *The Last Vampire* takes place in the year 2047, when Land meets a stranger at a party for online chat friends and proceeds to tell his history, beginning with his escapades as a rodeo hand, a job that taught him about the ugliness of life and death. Land also relates his history through World War I, where he honed his philosophical and existential temperament. This futuristic tome is a wonderful character study that reexamines the human condition as seen through the eyes of immortality. **Similar titles:** *Voice in the Blood*, Jemiah Jefferson; *Meh'Yam*, Gloria Evans; The Saint-Germain Chronicles, Chelsea Quinn Yarbro; *The Cowboy and the Vampire*, Clark Hayes and Kathleen McFall.

Academia • Cowboy as Character• The Internet • New York City •
Teacher as Character • Vampire's Point of View • War—World War I

Yarbro, Chelsea Quinn. The Atta Olivia Clemens Series.

A Flame in Byzantium. *New York: Tor, 1987. 470p.* Atta Olivia Clemens flees sixth-Century Rome because of war. In Constantinople, she is accused of sorcery, and her existence depends on being able to keep her identity as a vampire a secret while her private life is being probed in an investigation. **Similar titles:** The Angry Angel Series, Chelsea Quinn Yarbro; The Hunger Series, Whitley Streiber; New Tales of the Vampire, Anne Rice.

> *Clemens, Atta Olivia (character) • Espionage • History—Use of •*
> *Rome—Ancient Rome • Vampire's Point of View*

Crusader's Torch. *New York: Tom Doherty, 1988. 459p.* This is the second of the Atta Olivia Clemens novels, in which Olivia returns to Rome from Tyre, traveling across deserts filled with crusaders and seas besieged by pirates. Her only companion on the journey is a crazed knight who grows more mentally unstable with each day. **Similar titles:** The Angry Angel Series, Chelsea Quinn Yarbro; The Hunger Series, Whitley Streiber; New Tales of the Vampire, Anne Rice.

> *Clemens, Atta Olivia (character) • Crusades, The • History—Use of •*
> *Rome—Ancient Rome • Vampire's Point of View*

A Candle for D'Artagnan: An Historical Horror. *New York: Tor, 1989. 485p.* This, the third novel in the Atta Olivia Clements Series, takes readers to France during the reigns of Louis XIII and XIV. There, Olivia begins a romance with the Musketeer D'Artagnan. As usual with Yarbro, the strengths of this novel lie in its historical description. **Similar titles:** The Angry Angel Series, Chelsea Quinn Yarbro; The Hunger Series, Whitley Streiber; New Tales of the Vampire, Anne Rice.

> *Alternative Literature • Espionage • Gothic Romance • History, Use of •*
> *Paris, France • Three Musketeers (characters)*

Yarbro, Chelsea Quinn. The Angry Angel Series.

Sisters of the Night: The Angry Angel. *New York: Avon, 1998. 359p.* Yarbro begins her *Sisters of the Night* trilogy (about Dracula's three vampire concubines) with this novel about Kalene of Salonica. Dracula visits her, and he wants her as one of his entourage. Yarbro's emphasis is on description, history, and characterization. **Similar titles:** *Dracula*, Bram Stoker; The Silver Wolf Series, Alice Borchardt; The Covenant with the Vampire Series, Jeanne Kalogridis.

> *Alternative Literature • Angels • Dracula (character) • Gothic Romance •*
> *History, Use of*

The Soul of an Angel. *New York: Avon, 1999. 384p.* The follow-up to Yarbro's *The Angry Angel*, this traces the seduction of a wealthy sixteenth-century Venetian noblewoman by Count Dracula. **Similar titles:** *Dracula*, Bram Stoker; The Silver Wolf Series, Alice Borchardt; The Covenant with the Vampire Series, Jeanne Kalogridis.

> *Alternative Literature • Dracula (character) • Gothic Romance •*
> *History—Use of • Italy*

Yarbro, Chelsea Quinn. The Saint-Germain Chronicles.

Blood Games: A Novel of Historical Horror. *New York: St. Martin's Press, 1979. 458p.* Saint-Germain shows up in ancient Rome, where he must come to terms with the cruelties and casual disregard of human life he encounters among his new countrymen. **Similar titles:** The Vampire Chronicles, Anne Rice; The Devoncroix Dynasty Series, Donna Boyd; *The Last Vampire*, T. M. Wright; The Silver Wolf Series, Alice Borchart.

> *History—Use of • Rome, Italy • Saint-Germain, Count Ragoczy de (character) • Vampire's Point of View*

Path of the Eclipse. *New York: St. Martin's Press, 1981. 433p.* The fourth in Yarbro's Count de Saint-Germain novels finds the alchemist vampire in medieval China with Buddhists, Muslims, and Hindus, all attempting to flee the wrath of the Mongols. Yarbro's gentle vampire protagonist is more human than superhuman; he eschews violence, and can only receive sexual gratification through completely satisfying his partner. And Yarbro's erudite style demonstrates a thorough knowledge of world history. **Similar titles:** The Vampire Chronicles, Anne Rice; The Devoncroix Dynasty Series, Donna Boyd; *The Last Vampire*, T. M. Wright.

> *China • Epistolary Format • History, Use of • Religion—Buddhism • Religion—Christianity • Religion—Hindu • Religion—Islam • Saint-Germain, Count Ragoczy de (character) • Vampire's Point of View*

Better in the Dark: An Historical Horror. *New York: Tor, 1993. 412p.* Saint-Germain is captured and taken to Saxony during the Dark Ages. There he begins a romance with a beautiful lady of King Otto's court, but once more is doomed to be hunted, this time as a witch. **Similar titles:** The Vampire Chronicles, Anne Rice; The Devoncroix Dynasty Series, Donna Boyd; *The Last Vampire*, T. M. Wright; *The Red Witch*, Rose Earhart.

> *Epistolary Format • Gothic Romance • History, Use of • Saint Germain, Count Ragcozy de (character)*

Darker Jewels. *New York: Orb, 1995. 398p.* Saint-Germain is assigned to help Istaven Bathory, Transylvanian king of Poland, ward off the Ottoman Turks. En route, he runs into problems with suspicious clergymen, arranged marriages, and feuding nobles. This book is dense with period and place description. **Similar titles:** The Vampire Chronicles, Anne Rice; The Devoncroix Dynasty Series, Donna Boyd; *The Last Vampire*, T. M. Wright; *Bram Stoker's Dracula* (film).

> *Clergy as Character • Espionage • Gothic Romance • History, Use of • Poland—16th Century • Religion—Christianity—Catholicism • Saint Germain, Count Ragcozy de (character) • Vampire's Point of View*

Mansions of Darkness: A Novel of Saint-Germain. *New York: Tor, 1997. 432p.* Saint-Germain travels to seventeenth-century Spanish America, where he runs into the forces of the Spanish Inquisition, as well as the usual vampire hunters. Yarbro weaves a tapestry of historical romance, vampire fiction, and anthropology. **Similar titles:** The Vampire Chronicles, Anne Rice; The Devoncroix Dynasty Series, Donna Boyd; *The Last Vampire*, T. M. Wright.

> *Gothic Romance • History, Use of • Inquisition, The • Native American Characters • Peru—17th Century • Saint Germain, Count Ragcozy de (character) • Vampire's Point of View*

Writ in Blood: A Novel of Saint-Germain. *New York: Tor, 1997. 543p.* Czar Nicholas sends Saint-Germain, who is residing in St. Petersburg, to deliver a top-secret peace proposal to Edward VI of England and Germany's Kaiser Wilhelm. Saint-Germain must contend with the political ambitions of the Czar's kinsmen, as well as the machinations of an ambitious arms manufacturer, Von Wolgast. This is a thoughtfully written historical novel in a series that rivals Rice's Vampire Chronicles. **Similar titles:** The Vampire Chronicles, Anne Rice; The Devoncroix Dynasty Series, Donna Boyd; *The Last Vampire*, T. M. Wright; The Anno Dracula Series, Kim Newman.

> *Epistolary Format • Espionage • History, Use of • London, England •*
> *Saint-Germain, Count Ragoczy de (character) • Vampire's Point of View •*
> *War—World War I*

Blood Roses. *New York: Tor, 1998. 384p.* Saint-Germain settles in a small French town in the fourteenth century, during the time of the Black Death. Can he use his knowledge of healing without drawing suspicion of his true nature? **Similar titles:** The Vampire Chronicles, Anne Rice; The Devoncroix Dynasty Series, Donna Boyd; *The Last Vampire*, T. M. Wright; *My Soul to Keep*, Tananarive Due.

> *Epidemics • France—14th Century • History—Use of • Saint-Germain,*
> *Count Ragoczy de (character) • Vampire's Point of View*

Come Twilight: A Novel of Saint-Germain. *New York: Tor, 2000. 479p.* Saint-Germain and Rogerian, his servant, flee to the seventh-century village of Mont Calcius, where the sole inhabitant is a young pregnant woman. Forced to save her life by giving her immortality, Yarbro's vampiric hero unwittingly creates the leader of a rival group of vampires who threaten to disturb the peaceful coexistence between vampires and humans. **Similar titles:** The Vampire Chronicles, Anne Rice; The Devoncroix Dynasty Series, Donna Boyd; *The Last Vampire*, T. M. Wright; *My Soul to Keep*, Tananarive Due.

6

> *Epistolary Format • History, Use of • Religion—Christianity •*
> *Saint-Germain, Count Ragoczy de (character) • Spain •*
> *Vampire Clans • Vampire Hunters • Vampire's Point of View*

A Feast in Exile. *New York: Tor, 2001. 480p.* In the latest Saint-Germain romance, the vampire-hero, alias Sanat Ji Mani, lives in Delhi at the end of the fourteenth century. With him are his faithful servant Rojire and Avasa Dani, a young Indian woman abandoned by her husband. Enemies surround them, namely the relatives of the corrupt sultan who is constantly demanding more in taxes. And the brutal warlord Timur-i is approaching Delhi, intent on sacking the city. Saint-Germain is captured by Timur-i, who has heard of his talent as a healer. Will he be able to escape the clutches of the evil warlord? **Similar titles:** The Midnight Series, Nancy Gideon; The Devoncroix Dynasty Series, Donna Boyd; The Silver Wolf Series, Alice Borchardt; The Vampire Chronicles and New Tales of the Vampire, Anne Rice.

> *History, Use of • India • Saint-Germain, Count Ragoczy de (character) •*
> *Vampire's Point of View • Torture*

Hotel Transylvania. *Lancaster, Pa.: Stealth Press, 2001, ©1978. 277p.* Saint-Germain must save Madeleine de Montalia, an independent young woman with whom he has fallen in love, from the clutches of an evil cult. This sequel is set in eighteenth-century France. **Similar titles:** The Vampire Chronicles, Anne Rice; The Devoncroix Dynasty Series, Donna Boyd; *The Last Vampire*, T. M. Wright.

> *Cults • Gothic Romance • History—Use of • Paris, France • Religion—Satanism •*
> *Saint-Germain, Count Ragoczy de (character) • Vampire's Point of View*

The Palace. *Lancaster, Pa.: Stealth Press, 2001. ©1978. 390p.* In fifteenth-century Florence, Franceco Ragoczy da San Germano builds himself a home that rivals the most sumptuous in the city, and people suspect many things. The stranger never eats in public, has no mirrors in his home, and even his manner of lovemaking is strange. **Similar titles:** The Vampire Chronicles and New Tales of the Vampire, Anne Rice; The Devoncroix Dynasty Series, Donna Boyd; *The Last Vampire*, T. M. Wright.

> *Epistolary Format • Florence, Italy • History, Use of • Inquisition, The •*
> *Saint-Germain, Count Ragoczy de (character) • Vampire's Point of View*

Tempting Fate. *Lancaster, Pa.: Stealth Press, 2001, ©1982. 659p.* In a series of letters intermixed with narration, Yarbro places Saint-Germain during the Russian Revolution, where he must help a Russian countess escape revolutionary forces, as well as help a young war orphan. The novel is rich in description and history. **Similar titles:** The Vampire Chronicles, Anne Rice; The Devoncroix Dynasty Series, Donna Boyd; *The Last Vampire*, T. M. Wright.

> *Epistolary Format • History, Use of • Saint-Germain, Count Ragoczy de*
> *(character) • Vampire's Point of View • War—Russian Revolution*

Film

Blackula. *William Crain, dir. 1972. 92 minutes.* Manuwalde, Ambassador of Ebonia, meets with Dracula to persuade him to stop supporting slave trading. Instead, Dracula makes Manuwalde one of the undead, imprisoning him in a coffin to thirst eternally. Manuwalde awakens 150 years later in 1970s Los Angeles, hungering for blood and the reincarnation of his long-deceased wife, who is now an Angelino. William Marshall stars as the first African-American vampire in horror cinema history. **Similar reads:** *Meh'Yam*, Gloria Evans; *Voice of the Blood*, Jemiah Jefferson.

> *African-American Characters • Blacksploitation • Los Angeles, California •*
> *Reincarnation • Vampire Hunters*

Blade. *Stephen Norrington, dir. 1998. 120 minutes.* Blade (Wesley Snipes) is half human, half vampire, cursed to crave human blood when his pregnant mother was attacked by one of the undead. Now, with the combined strengths of vampires and humans, Blade seeks to eliminate all blood-sucking fiends from the earth before they turn all humans into cattle. This futuristic film is gory and action oriented with excellent special effects, and is based on the DC Comics series of the same name. **Similar reads:** The Anita Blake, Vampire Hunter Series, Laurell K. Hamilton; The Host Series, Selina Rosen.

> *African-American Characters • Blade (character) • Fantasy • New York City •*
> *Physician as Character • Revenge • Vampire Clans • Vampire Hunters*

Bram Stoker's Dracula. *Francis Ford Coppola, dir. 1992. 130 minutes.* Coppola returns to the original source of the Dracula myth, drawing on Stoker's novel, as well as the historical Vlad Tepes. The result is not so much an immortal monster who must be destroyed at all costs as a man who has defied death because his church and country have betrayed him. Gary Oldman, Winona Ryder, Anthony Hopkins, and Keanu Reeves star in this operatic film. **Similar reads:** *Dracula*, Bram Stoker; *Anno Dracula*, Kim Newman.

> *Dracula (character) • Harker, Jonathan (character) • Harker, Mina Murray*
> *(character) • Holmwood, Arthur (character) • London, England • Reincarnation •*

Seward, Jack (character) • Vampire Hunters • Vampire's Point of View • Van Helsing, Abraham (character) • Westenra, Lucy (character)

Cronos. *Guillermo Del Toro, dir. 1992. 92 minutes.* This is an award- winning Mexican film in which an elderly antiques dealer, Jesus Gris, stumbles upon the Cronos device, an invention of a fourteenth-century alchemist, which makes the bearer immortal. In spite of several serious accidents and an attempt to embalm him, Jesus cannot die, and his discovery of the device has alerted the attention of an Anglo corporate mogul who will stop at nothing to steal it from Gris. Ron Perlman stars. **Similar reads:** *Awash in the Blood*, John Wooley; *Murcheston: A Wolf's Tale,* David Holland.

Immortality • Mexico • Weird Science

Dracula. *Tod Browning, dir. 1931. (Black-and-white.) 75 minutes.* This film is an adaptation of both Bram Stoker's novel and Hamilton Deane and John Balderston's stage play of Stoker's novel. It gave Bela Lugosi his first film role. As in Stoker's novel, Count Dracula comes to London via Transylvania, purchases a ruined abbey, and hopes to search for victims by night. But Bela Lugosi's interpretation of Dracula is the suave cape- and tuxedo-wearing creature of the night first seen in Deane and Balderston's stage play, rather than the hooked nosed and halitosis plagued nosferatu of Stoker's tale. **Similar reads:** *Dracula*, Bram Stoker; *The Guardian*, Beecher Smith.

Dracula (character) • London, England • Renfield (character) • Vampire Hunters • Van Helsing, Abraham (character)

Dracula 2000. *Patrick Lussier, dir. 2000. 127 minutes.* Christopher Plummer stars as Abraham Van Helsing, wealthy and eccentric owner of Carfax antiques and now immortal keeper of the vanquished Dracula. When thieves attempt to steal what he has hidden in the vault, they unwittingly unleash the undead count. Dracula flees to New Orleans to exact his vengeance on Van Helsing's daughter and create a new army of the undead. **Similar reads:** *The Last Vampire*, T. M. Wright; *Meh'Yam*, Gloria Evans.

 6

Dracula (character) • Immortality • Iscariot, Judas (character) • London, England • New Orleans, Louisiana • Religion—Christianity • Westenra, Lucy (character) • VanHelsing, Abraham (character)

Dracula's Daughter. *Lambert Hillyer, dir. 1936. (Black-and-white.) 71 minutes.* This film picks up where the 1931 version of *Dracula* left off, with Dr. Van Helsing having killed Count Dracula and believing he has rid the world of vampires. But Dracula's daughter, Countess Marya Zaleska, claims her father's body, and soon several people are found mysteriously killed. Otto Kruger, Gloria Holden, and Marguerite Churchill star. **Similar reads:** *Camilla*, Joseph Sheridan Le Fanu; The Hunger Series, Whitley Streiber.

Family Curse • Homoeroticism • London, England • Psychiatrist/Psychologist as Character • Zalenska, Marya (character)

Ginger Snaps. *John Fawcett, dir. 2000. 108 minutes.* At the ages of sixteen and fifteen, Ginger and Bridget Fitzgerald are unusual in that neither has entered menarche, but all of that changes for Ginger when one night "the curse" comes cascading down her legs. Unfortunately for Ginger, a werewolf has been worrying their quiet, suburban town, mutilating dogs unfortunate enough to be left outside. Now the scent of Ginger's menses attracts the wolf, who manages to scratch her and chase the sisters through the woods before being killed. But werewolf bites are more severe than dog bites. They have the power to transform the recipient into a lycanthrope. Now Bridget must save her sister before she completely transforms and ravages the town. Emily Perkins and Katherine Isabell star as the Fitzgerald sisters. Also starring Mimi Rodgers as Mrs. Fitzgerald. **Similar reads:** *Carrie*, Stephen King; *Murcheston: The Wolf's Tale*, David Holland.

> *Adolescence • Animals Run Rampant • Canada • High School • Menstruation • Werewolves*

Hellraiser. *Clive Barker, dir. 1987. 94 minutes.* (See chapter 8, "Mythological Monsters and 'The Old Ones': Invoking the Dark Gods.")

The Hunger. *Tony Scott, dir. 1983. 100 minutes.* Miriam and John Blaylock are forever young and beautiful because they're vampires. When John begins to age at an accelerated pace, Miriam must seek the help of an outsider, a scientist who studies aging and who will be seduced by Miriam's promise of eternal youth. Catherine Deneuve, David Bowie, and Susan Sarandon star in this classic. **Similar reads:** The Hunger Series, Whitley Streiber; The Vampire Chronicles, Anne Rice.

> *Aging • Blaylock, Miriam (character) • Gay/Lesbian Bisexual Characters • Homoeroticism • New York City • Physician as Character • Roberts, Sarah (character)*

Interview with the Vampire. *Neil Jordan, dir. 1994. 123 minutes.* The film version of Anne Rice's novel of the same name, this movie sports an all-star cast including Tom Cruise, Brad Pitt, Christian Slater, Antonio Banderas and Kirsten Dunst. **Similar reads:** The Vampire Chronicles, Anne Rice; *The Last Vampire*, T. M. Wright.

> *Claudia (character) • Homoeroticism • Lestat de Lioncourt (character) • Louis (character) • New Orleans, Louisiana • Vampire's Point of View*

The Lost Boys. *Joel Schumacher, dir. 1987. 97 minutes.* A family moves to what they believe will be a peaceful town, Santa Carla, California, only to discover that they reside in the murder capital of the world and the local gang is a pack of teenaged vampires who, like Peter Pan, never want to grow up. Kiefer Sutherland and Dianne Wiest star. **Similar reads:** *Red Moon Rising*, Billie Sue Mosiman; *The Book of the Dark*, William Meikle.

> *California • Gang Violence • Vampire Clans*

Nadja. *Michael Almereyda, dir. 1996. (Black-and-white.) 92 minutes.* Twin brother and sister vampires, children of Count Dracula, struggle against each other and against their own dual desires to be mortal and immortal. Set in modern-day New York City, this stylish parody of art films is also a remake of the 1936 version of *Dracula's Daughter*. It stars Peter Fonda and Elina Lowensohn. **Similar reads:** *Carmilla*, Joseph Sheridan Le Fanu; The Time of Feasting Series, Mick Farren.

> *Gay/Lesbian/Bisexual Characters • Homoeroticism • New York City • Renfield (character) • Twins • Vampire Hunters • Vampire's Point of View • VanHelsing, Abraham (character)*

Nosferatu. *F. W. Murnau, dir. 1922. (Black-and-white.) 63 minutes.* This silent classic is an adaptation of Stoker's *Dracula*. Because of the complexities of German copyright law, Murnau's film had to change the names of the principals, but Count Orlock, his version of Count Dracula, is much closer to Stoker's idea of Dracula than the celluloid Dracula made famous by Bela Lugosi in 1931. This classic stars Max Schreck. **Similar reads:** *Dracula*, Bram Stoker; *The Vampyre*, John Polidori.

> *Count Orlock (character) • Germany • Harker, Jonathan (character) • Renfield (character)*

Queen of the Damned. *Michael Rymer, dir. 2002. 110 minutes.* In this second film based on Anne Rice's Vampire Chronicles, Lestat (Stuart Townsend) becomes a rock star and challenges all the other vampires who hide from the human race to make themselves known. Now he has incurred the wrath of all other vampires, whose survival depends on keeping their ways secret. And he has also awakened Akasha (Aaliyah), the bloodthirsty mother of all vampires who, in Ancient Times, nearly drank the human race dry before experiencing a terrible sense of ennui and going dormant. **Similar reads:** The Vampire Chronicles, Anne Rice; *Anno Dracula*, Kim Newman.

> *Akasha and Enkil (characters) • Immortality • Lestat de Lioncourt (character) • Los Angeles, California • Maharet and Mekare (characters) • Marius (character) • Music, Rock Music • Vampire's Point of View*

Shadow of the Vampire. *E. Elias Merhing, dir. 2001. 92 minutes.* In 1922, F. W. Murnau finds an actual vampire to play the role of Count Orlock and add realism to his film, *Nosferatu*. But vampires aren't as easily controlled as actors and can't be prevented from snacking on the occasional camera operator. Willem Dafoe and John Malcovich star as Max Schreck and F. W. Murnau. **Similar reads:** *Awash in the Blood*, John Wooley; *Carrion Comfort*, Dan Simmons.

> *Actor as Character • Alternative Literature • Czechoslovakia • Director as Character • Germany • History, Use of • Immortality • Vampire's Point of View*

The Wolf Man. *George Waggner, dir. 1941. (Black-and-white.) 70 minutes.* A Universal Studios classic starring Lon Cheney Jr., who is bitten by a vampire in wolf form (Bela Lugosi) and turned into a werewolf. Claude Rains also stars. **Similar reads:** The Universal Monsters Series, various authors; *Murcheston: The Wolf's Tale*, David Holland.

> *Animals Run Rampant • Werewolves*

 6

Our Picks

June's Picks: The Anno Dracula Series, Kim Newman (Avon); *Carmilla*, Joseph Sheridan Le Fanu (Oxford University Press); *Carrion Comfort*, Dan Simmons (Warner); *Dracula*, Bram Stoker (Oxford University Press); *The Flesh, the Blood and the Fire*, S. A. Swiniarski (DAW Books); The Lord of the Dead Series, Tom Holland (various publishers); *Murcheston: The Wolf's Tale*, David Holland (Tor); *The Traveling Vampire* Show, Richard Laymon (Leisure); The Vampire Chronicles and New Tales of the Vampire, Anne Rice (Ballantine and Knopf); *Voice of the Blood*, Jemiah Jefferson (Leisure); *Blackula* (film); *Blade* (film); *Bram Stoker's Dracula* (film); *Dracula's Daughter* (film); *The Hunger* (film); *Ginger Snaps* (film); *Nadja* (film); *Queen of the Damned* (film); *Shadow of the Vampire* (film).

Tony's Picks: *Anno Dracula*, Kim Newman (Avon); *Awash in the Blood*, John Wooley (Hawk); *Carrion Comfort*, Dan Simmons (Warner); *Dracula*, Bram Stoker (Oxford University Press); *The Queen of the Damned*, Anne Rice (Ballantine); *Voice of the Blood*, Jemiah Jefferson (Leisure); *Cronos* (film); *Queen of the Damned* (film); *Shadow of the Vampire* (film).

Chapter 7

Demonic Possession, Satanism, Black Magic, and Witches and Warlocks: The Devil Made Me Do It

Tales of black magic and demonic possession predate the Judeo-Christian *Bible,* so this subgenre of horror is arguably one of the oldest. Students of literature know that demons abound in the poetry of Milton and Blake, but it was not until the late 1700s that the earliest novel featuring demons was published. Matthew "Monk" Lewis's *The Monk* is a study in necrophilia, which set the stage early for the "beautiful young woman as demon in disguise" theme. Nonetheless, the quintessential possession novel is a very recent one: William Peter Blatty's *The Exorcist*, the tale of a young girl possessed by Satan after ancient artifacts are unearthed in Iraq and later unleash the devil's power. Whether these stories are about misled monks or innocent-but-soon-to-be-demonic teenaged girls, what makes tales of possession particularly frightening is that more often than not, innocent humans are possessed by demons, or even by the devil himself.

Tales of Satanism and black magic can also take the form of stories about witches, warlocks, and other people who *willingly* become involved with dark forces. In Ira Levin's *Rosemary's Baby*, Guy Woodhouse sells his soul, and his wife's womb, to Satan, in exchange for worldly success as an actor. More contemporary possession/witchcraft tales include Anne Rice's The Mayfair Witches Series, which concerns itself with thirteen generations of Mayfair witches and their profitable connection to the demon Lasher.

Interestingly, most stories in this subgenre generally feature Catholics who have either lost their faith or see their brand of black magic as an extension of their faith. Indeed, Satanism is more often than not represented as the polar opposite not of Christianity, but of Roman Catholicism, as in David Seltzer's *The Omen*, or in Levin's *Rosemary's Baby*. Perhaps this is because Catholicism was at one point considered the "universal" version of Christianity and is therefore a good "default" religion for horror; or because Catholicism is more ritual-oriented than other Christian sects, making it the perfect foil of Satanism, which also values ritual; or because the original possession narratives were produced by a culture that demonized Catholicism, and the tradition or formula was simply continued by later writers.

Despite the prevalence of Catholicism in possession stories, other Christian sects have played an important role in the evolution of the subgenre. For example, many narratives feature Protestantism as the religion that ushers in evil. Nathaniel Hawthorne's tales often feature upright, New England Puritans and their connections with the Evil One. In Stephen King's *Needful Things*, town members unwittingly sell their souls to the devil, and Satan gains a toehold by first setting the Catholics and Protestants against one another. But no matter which sect is responsible for raising the devil, the bottom line of the possession tale is that the possessed character is forgivable because he or she was not responsible for his or her actions while in that state.

Works in this section are also about witches and witchcraft. Unlike narratives about possession and Satanism, witches and warlocks *aren't* necessarily evil. Many tales of witches and witchcraft are about women either practicing Wicca or adhering to an alternative spirituality. Judith Hawkes's *The Heart of a Witch* and J. G. Passarella's *Wither* pursue this theme. In both novels, the protagonists *choose* to become witches, or adherents of Wicca, practicing a religion that encourages adherents to experience themselves as part of the natural world. Unlike monotheistic traditions, these neopagan belief systems empower women by validating their ways of knowing the world and their sexuality. In Graham Joyce's *Dark Sister*, Maggie, an underappreciated stay-at-home mother, finds empowerment in the witch's diary she finds concealed behind her chimney bricks. Not surprisingly, adherents of these beliefs are frequently persecuted. Thus, the intolerant individuals who are the witches' persecutors are the evil ones in these novels.

Novels such as Rose Earhart's *Dorcas Good: The Diary of a Salem Witch* and *Salem's Ghosts* are fictionalized accounts of individuals who didn't practice witchcraft by any modern understanding of the term but were accused nevertheless, and were murdered by the Puritan fathers of Salem village because they were seen as suspicious.

Other stories in this segment include those of practitioners of another maligned belief system, Voodoo. In the film *Angel Heart*, New Yorker Harold Angel is shocked by his first encounter with Voodoo as practiced in the bayous of South Louisiana, to which one of the participants comments that "we're not all Baptists down here." Michael Reaves's novel *Voodoo Child* is about a battle between two Voodoo priests, one good and one evil. The good priest is content to conjure the loas (roughly, the Voodoo equivalent of helpful spirits) to help his followers, whereas the evil one makes human sacrifices to his dark gods.

Representative works in this chapter include Ramsey Campbell's *Obsession*, Fritz Leiber's *The Conjure Wife*, Peter Straub's *Shadowland*, and Straub's *Floating Dragon*, as well as various works by Anne Rice. Benchmark works in this chapter include Blatty's *The Exorcist* and Levin's *Rosemary's Baby*.

Note: Tales about demonic possession, Satanism, black magic, witches, and warlocks can also be found in the collections and anthologies described in chapter 17. Refer to the subject/keyword index for specific titles, using the keywords "possession," "witches," "witchcraft," "magic," "warlocks," and "religion—Satanism."

Appeals: Identification with Innocent but Possessed Characters; Familiarity with Satan/ the Devil as Ultimate Monster; Curiosity Concerning the Occult; Reaffirmation of the Universal Fear of Demons; Believability (for the Religious); Affirmation of Religious Beliefs

Allen, Bill.

Shadow Heart. *Alma, Ark.: Yard Dog Press, 1998. 210p.* Body-snatching demons are possessing the corpses of humans and turning them into vicious serial killers to usher in the age of ultimate evil. Three men—a husband and father whose family was murdered, a police detective, and a well-meaning televangelist—find themselves caught up in a chess game of good versus evil. But this is a game where the enemy can take any form, and one never knows whom he is working for. This is a suspenseful and original tale told from multiple points of view. **Similar titles:** *Phantoms,* Dean Koontz, *Voodoo Child,* Michael Reaves; *Fallen* (film); *Lifetimes of Blood,* Adam Johnson; *Carrion Comfort,* Dan Simmons; *Invasion of the Body Snatchers* (film).

> *Demons • Grieving • Mind Control • Police Officer as Character • Religion—Christianity • Serial Killers • Shapeshifters • Televangelism • Zombies*

Allred, Sam.

If Witches We Be. *San Jose, Calif.: Writer's Showcase, 2000. 218p.* (See chapter 16, "Comic Horror: Laughing at Our Fears.")

Arensberg, Ann.

Incubus. *New York: Alfred A. Knopf, 1999. 322p.* The wife of the pastor of Dry Falls, Maine, narrates a tale of disturbances during an atypical summer when the crops all die, animals give birth to monstrosities, the sex lives of all married couples dry up, and six young girls are found naked, asleep, and in a heightened state of sexual arousal. Arensberg's emphasis is on atmosphere and characterization. **Similar titles:** *Ordinary Horror,* David Searcy; *The Apostate,* Paul Lonardo; *Dark Within,* John Wooley.

> *Clergy as Character • Demons • Dreams • Maine • Marriage • Psychosexual Horror • Religion—Christianity*

Bachman, Richard.

Thinner. (See King, Stephen. *Thinner.* New York: New American Library, 1984. 282p.)

Bacon-Smith, Camille. The Eye of the Daemon Series.

Eye of the Daemon. *New York: DAW Books, 1996. 332p.* This is Bacon-Smith's first Kevin Bradley novel, in which the superhuman sleuth matches wits with equally unnatural kidnappers. **Similar titles:** The Anita Blake: Vampire Hunter Series, Laurell K. Hamilton; The Vampire Files Series, P. N. Elrod; *Full Moon, Bloody Moon,* Lee Driver; The Black Oak Series, Charles Grant; *Dark Detectives,* Stephen Jones (editor).

> *Bradley, Kevin (character) • Fantasy*

Eyes of the Empress. *New York: DAW Books, 1998. 304p.* The crystals of the Dowager Empress of China are disappearing, and a group of American detectives is called in to solve the case. However, they discover that the thief has ties beyond the natural world. **Similar titles:** The Anita Blake: Vampire Hunter Series, Laurell K. Hamilton; The Vampire Files Series, P. N. Elrod; *Full Moon, Bloody Moon,* Lee Driver; The Black Oak Series, Charles Grant; *Dark Detectives,* Stephen Jones (editor).

> *Bradley, Kevin (character) • Demons • Fantasy*

Beman, Donald.

Dead Love. *New York: Leisure, 2001. 346p.* (See chapter 4, "Ghosts and Haunted Houses: Dealing with Presences and Absences.")

Blatty, William Peter.

The Exorcist. *New York: Bantam, 1971. 403p.* When twelve-year-old Regan McNeil begins acting strangely, her mother suspects that she may be possessed by demons. Could Regan's possession have something to do with Fr. Lankaster Merrin's archaeological dig in Northern Iraq? And will Merrin and Fr. Damien Karras, a young priest questioning his own faith, be able to stop the demon? This novel was made into one of the benchmark horror films of the 1970s, by director William Friedkin. **Similar titles:** *The Blood of the Lamb*, Thomas Monteleone*; Midwinter of the Spirit*, Phil Rickman; *Rosemary's Baby* and *Son of Rosemary*, Ira Levin; *The Manitou*, Graham Masterton; The Millennium Quartet, Charles Grant.

     ℭ audiotape, audio download

> *Clergy as Character • Demons • Exorcism •*
> *Religion—Christianity—Catholicism*

Brass, Perry.

Warlock: A Novel of Possession. *Bronx, N.Y.: Belhue Press, 2001. 219p.* Allen Barrow is nothing special; he is a thirty-something gay bank clerk with no remarkable physical attributes. So it comes as quite a surprise to him that the wealthy, handsome Destry Powars wants Barrow as his soul mate. Powars is full of secrets—about the source of his wealth, about what's kept behind locked doors in his spectacular apartment, about what he's done to Barrow's genitals during their lovemaking, and about his strange "friends." Brass's novel is subtle, with an emphasis on characterization. **Similar titles:** *Interview with the Vampire*, Anne Rice; *Desmond: A Novel of Love and the Modern Vampire*, Ulysses G. Dietz; *The Hunger*, Whitley Streiber; *Bending the Landscape*, Nicola Griffith and Stephen Pagel.

> *Corporate Horror • Eroticism • Gay/Lesbian/Bisexual Characters • Gothicism •*
> *Homoeroticism • New York City*

Brown, Charles Brockden.

Wieland, or the Transformation. *New York: Modern Library, 2002, ©1798. 274p.* A stranger pays a visit in this tale of one family's slide down the slippery slope of reality. Theodore Wieland hears mysterious voices. Are these the result of delusions, ventriloquism, or divine forces? In this gothic thriller, Brown portrays a man beset by religious guilt that erupts into mania, making him an extreme danger to others. **Similar titles:** *Thirty-Two Stories*, Edgar Allan Poe; *The Ghost Stories of Edith Wharton*, Edith Wharton; *The Monk*, M. G. Lewis; *The Ghost Stories of Henry James*, Henry James.

> *Epistolary Format • Family Curse • New England • United States—19th Century*

Campbell, Ramsey.

Ancient Images. *New York: Tor, 1989. 311p.* Film editor Sandy Allan has a chance to work on a rare Lugosi/Karloff movie that one of her colleagues has just located. But then, when her colleague mysteriously dies, strange things begin to happen to those who are associated with the movie or the rare British short story on which it was based. **Similar titles:** *The Light at the End*, John Skipp and Craig Spector; *The Talisman*, Jonathan Aycliffe; *Deathwindow*, Grace Chetwin; *Darker than Night*, Owl Goingback.

> *Cursed Objects • Horror Movie Industry*

The Claw. *London: Little, Brown, 1992. 380p.* Alan Knight, a writer from Norwich, agrees to take a talisman, a beautifully crafted metal claw, from Nigeria back to his hometown in England, to present it to one of the African Studies Museums there. However, he is unaware of the curse that has been passed on to him, as it is to all who have the claw in their possession. After a local youth who accidentally scratched himself on the claw becomes extremely violent, and members of his own family begin to feel its influence, Knight realizes that he must return the talisman to the man who gave it to him, even if it means killing that man. **Similar titles:** *The Mummy Returns*, Max Allan Collins; *The Chalice*, Phil Rickman; *Into the Mummy's Tomb*, John Richard Stephens; *The Rag Bone Man*, Charlotte Lawrence.

> *Africa • Childhood • Cursed Objects • England • Religion—African • Writer as Character*

The Influence. *New York: Macmillan, 1988. 260p.* After Hermione's Aunt Queenie dies, she begins to suspect that her niece Rowan's new friend Vichy is somehow Queenie's ghost, and that Queenie's spirit is ultimately trying to possess Rowan's body. To stop this, Hermione must go out to her Aunt's grave. But is Aunt Queenie fully dead? **Similar titles:** *Affinity*, J. N. Williamson; *Midwinter of the Spirit*, Phil Rickman; *What Lies Beneath* (film); *Dark Sister*, Graham Joyce.

> *Family Curse • Reincarnation • Wales*

The Nameless. *London: Little, Brown, 1992, ©1985. 278p.* (See chapter 11, "Maniacs and Sociopaths, or the Nuclear Family Explodes: Monstrous Malcontents Bury the Hatchet.")

Nazareth Hill. *New York: Doherty, 1997. 383p.* (See chapter 4, "Ghosts and Haunted Houses: Dealing with Presences and Absences.")

The Parasite. *New York: Tom Doherty, 1989, ©1980. 337p.* As a ten-year-old, Rose Tierney participates in a séance held in a house where a murder had once occurred, unwittingly leaving herself open to the spirit of an occultist named Peter Grace, who spent his life working on methods of transferring souls into the bodies of the living after death. Now, as an adult, Rose finds herself being stalked by a strange man and begins to suspect that the soul of Peter Grace may have been passed into her body, and perhaps into that of her unborn child. **Similar titles:** *The Haunt*, J. N. Williamson; *Soul Temple*, Steven Lee Climer; *The Revelation*, Bentley Little.

> *Childhood • Cults • Liverpool, England • Nazism • Parapsychology • Pregnancy • Stalkers • Writer as Character*

Cave, Hugh B.

The Evil Returns. *New York: Leisure, 2001. 359p.* Margal the Sorcerer, a Haitian Voodoo practitioner thought to have been killed in a fiery blaze, returns in an attempt to take over the world by influencing its biggest political power. When the wife of a presidential advisor's son wakes one morning to find her daughter has been kidnapped, little does she know that the young girl is being used as bait to lure her husband into Margal's control. Now she and her college sweetheart must rescue both the husband and child. In this novel, Cave does an excellent job of reproducing local Haitian color and adventure. **Similar titles:** The Black Oak Series, Charles Grant; *Voodoo Child*, Michael Reaves; *Angel Heart* (film); *Carrion Comfort*, Dan Simmons.

> *Government Officials • Haiti • Handicapped Characters • Miami, Florida • Mind Control • Religion—Voodoo*

Isle of the Whisperers. *Nottingham, England: Pumpkin Books, 1999. 265p.* Dr. Martha Rowe is a most experienced archeologist surveying a cave system on an island. But she is human, and she can make a mistake. This time her mistake is finding what she is looking for: a passage to what may be another dimension. Once the doorway is accidentally opened, everyone on the island suddenly becomes prey to demons, both inner and outer. **Similar titles:** *The Book of the Dark*, William Meikle; *Old Fears*, John Wooley and Ron Wolfe; *The Mummy Returns*, Max Allan Collins.

>*Archeologist as Character • Demons • Maritime Horror • Subterranean Horror*

Chetwin, Grace.

Deathwindow. *New York: Feral Press, 1999. 216p.* Writer Helen Clayton moves to an isolated town in England to be with her dying father-in-law and finds herself at odds with the local spinster—who just happens to practice witchcraft to get rid of her enemies. Narrated through letters, dreams, and objective point of view, this is an easy read, yet one filled with atmosphere and suspense. **Similar titles:** *Bag of Bones*, Stephen King; *A Game of Colors*, John Urbancik; *The Man in the Moss*, Phil Rickman; *Dark Sister*, Graham Joyce, *Rosemary's Baby*, Ira Levin.

>*Cursed Objects • England • Epistolary Format • Nurse as Character • Senior Citizen as Character • Witchcraft • Writer as Character*

Citro, Joseph.

Shadow Child. *Hanover, NH: University Press of New England, 1998, ©1987. 283p.* (See chapter 10, "Small Town Horror: Villages of the Damned.")

Clegg, Douglas.

The Halloween Man. *New York: Leisure, 1998. 360p.* (See chapter 10, "Small-Town Horror: Villages of the Damned.")

Naomi. *New York: Leisure, 2001. 344p.* Newly divorced Jake Richmond goes in search of his childhood sweetheart, a woman named Naomi who mysteriously disappeared into the New York subway system—but who comes to him in prophetic dreams. His search leads him into The Below, where a centuries-old creature is waiting its chance to return to the world of humans. This novel is written with a flair for imagery and intricacy of plot structure. **Similar titles:** *Paperhouse* (film); *Affinity*, J. N. Williamson; *Ambrosial Flesh*, Mary Ann Mitchell; *Strangewood*, Christopher Golden; *Thunderland*, Brandon Massey.

>*Dreams • Epistolary Format • History, Use of • New York City • Obsession • Satan (character) • Subterranean Monsters • Witchcraft • Writer as Character*

You Come When I Call You. *New York: Leisure, 2000. 393p.* Four young adults are interviewed following a wave of mutilations in the desert town of Palmetto, California. In tapes and diary entries, they tell of a deal they unwittingly struck with a female demon, and of the events that led to the killings. Clegg's novel is heavy on atmosphere and is told from various points of view. **Similar titles:** *Riverwatch*, Joseph M. Nassie; *The Cleanup*, John Skipp and Craig Spector; *Spanky*, Christopher Fowler; *Hexes*, Tom Piccirilli; *The Town*, Bentley Little, *The Halloween Man*, Douglas Clegg.

>*California • Demons • Diary Format • Eroticism • Human Sacrifice • Matricide/Patricide • Secret Sin • Shapeshifters • Werewolves*

Crain, Paulette.

De Lore's Confession. *New Orleans: Oak Tree Press, 1999. 337p.* Forty-year-old interior designer Ashley Winthrop has been given the assignment of a lifetime, to restore the eerie yet beautiful De Lore Mansion now that its owner, Tryn De Lore, has moved in. What Ashley does not know is that Tryn De Lore possesses a power over both her and her brother Michael, and that he harbors a dark secret that will unlock the closed doors to her true past. When Tryn offers Ashley and Michael the family gift of eternal youth, will they be able to refuse, or can they go against family tradition, and their own natures, to save their souls? **Similar titles:** *The Red Witch*, Serena Devlin; *The Door Through Washington Square*, Elaine Bergstrom; *My Soul to Keep*, Tananarive Due; *Mother Julian and the Gentle Vampire*, Jack Pantaleo.

> *Dreams • Family Curse • Gay/Lesbian/Bisexual Characters • Haunted Houses • Immortality • Interior Designer as Character • Mind Control • New Orleans, Louisiana • San Francisco, California*

Cross, Quentin.

The Witch Rising. *Philadelphia: Xlibris, 2000. 209p.* In a small town in the wooded hills of present-day Connecticut, children are turning up dead. Could it be the work of a witch put to death over 200 years ago, or has a man who moved to the town for peace and quiet become involved with a murderer? **Similar titles:** *Seize the Night*, Dean Koontz; *The Blair Witch Project: A Dossier*, D. A. Stern; *Death From the Woods*, Brigitte Aubert; *Brotherly Love*, David Case.

> *Child Molesters • Connecticut • Revenging Revenant • Witches*

de la Mare, Walter.

The Return. *Mineola, N.Y.: Dover, 1997, ©1922. 224p.* Arthur Lawford falls asleep on the grave of an eighteenth-century pirate, only to wake up and discover that his face is no longer his own. And while he believes himself to be essentially unchanged psychologically, he notices that another personality is insinuating itself into his consciousness. **Similar titles:** *Dr. Jekyll and Mr. Hyde*, Robert Louis Stevenson; *Rebecca*, Daphine DuMaurier; *Affinity*, J. N. Williamson; *The Door Through Washington Square*, Elaine Bergstrom.

> *Alter Ego • England • Mind Control*

Devlin, Serena.

The Red Witch. *New York: Pendleton Books, 2000. 415p.* In Salem, Massachusetts, in 1995, white witch Rebecca Love meets the ghost of a pirate named Jamie O'Rourke, toward whom she feels an instant attraction. She then gets a friend to perform a magic ceremony that transports her back to the Salem of 1695, where she is captured by O'Rourke's band of renegades. Circumstances lead to her being imprisoned by authorities as a witch, and she is faced with the reality that she must manage her escape so that she can help O'Rourke lift a family curse, and so that she can return to 1995, where she hopes she will discover O'Rourke's hidden treasure. **Similar titles:** *Dorcas Good: Diary of a Salem Witch*, Rose Earhart; *The Door Through Washington Square*, Elaine Bergstrom; *Midnight Enchantment*, Nancy Gideon; *The Silver Wolf*, Alice Borchardt; *DeLores' Confession*, Paulette Crain.

 7

> *Colonial New England • Family Curse • Ghosts • History, Use of • Magic • Pirates • Salem, Massachusetts • Time Travel • Witches*

Driver, Lee.

Full Moon, Bloody Moon: A Chase Dagger Mystery. *Schereville, Ind.: Full Moon Publishing, 2000. 280p.* (See chapter 11, "Maniacs and Sociopaths, or the Nuclear Family Explodes: Monstrous Malcontents Bury the Hatchet.")

Durchholz, Eric.

The Promise of Eden. *Antioch, Tenn.: Concrete Books, 1999. 204p.* (See chapter 4, "Ghosts and Haunted Houses: Dealing with Presences and Absences.")

Duval, Karen.

Project Resurrection. *Dekalb, Ill.: Speculation Press, 2000. 288p.* (See chapter 12, "Technohorror: Evil Hospitals, Military Screw-Ups, Scientific Goofs, and Alien Invasions.")

Earhart, Rose.

Dorcas Good: The Diary of a Salem Witch. *New York: Pendleton Books, 2000. 375p.* Before she was five years old, Dorcas Good shared a prison cell with her mother Sarah, one of the infamous women executed for witchcraft in Salem, Massachusetts. Dorcas survives the ordeal, only to be cruelly used by her alcoholic father, who supports his dipsomania by pimping his only daughter. All who love Dorcas and attempt to save her have their attempts thwarted. Finally, only the ghost of Sarah can save Dorcas Good. Written in diary format, *Dorcas Good* is a compelling biographical novel of one of the women whose lives were blighted by the Salem Witch Trials. **Similar titles:** *The Bell Witch*, Brent Monahan; *Salem's Ghosts*, Rose Earhart; *Wither*, J. G. Passarella; The Mayfair Witch Series, Anne Rice.

> *Boston, Massachusetts • Child Abuse • Childhood • Clergy as Character • Diary Format • Domestic Violence • Ghosts • Good, Dorcas (character) • History, Use of • Incest • Rape • Religion— Christianity—Protestantism • Salem, Massachusetts • Salem Witch Trials • Schizophrenia/Multiple Personality Disorder • Telepathy*

Salem's Ghosts. *New York: Pendleton Books, 1998. 316p.* Mary English, accused of witchcraft during the Salem Witch Trials, tries to protect a distant ancestor of hers about to be raped and murdered in 1998. The spirit of one of Mary's tormentors, George Corwin, possesses the assailant. She and other ghosts from Salem's infamous past must join with Lillith March, a modern-day witch, and travel through time to protect those that George would destroy. Earhart's tale brings to life those who were killed or persecuted in the summer of 1692. **Similar titles:** *The Witching Time*, Jean Stubbs; *Dorcas Good: Child Witch of Salem*, Rose Earhart; *Wither*, J. G. Passarella; *The Red Witch*, Serena Devlin.

> *Afterlife, The • African-American Characters • Fantasy • Ghosts • History, Use of • Magic • Parenting • Rape • Religion—Christianity—Protestantism • Religion—Paganism • Revenging Revenant • Salem, Massachusetts • Salem Witch Trials • Satan (character) • Telepathy • Time Travel • Tituba (character) • Witches*

Fitzhugh, Pat.

The Bell Witch Haunting: An Historical and Modern-Day Account of the Most Terrifying Legend in American History. *Nashville: Armand Press, 1999. 124p.* In this half-fictional retelling, half-factual information text, Fitzhugh relates the classic folktale of Tennessee's infamous "Bell Witch" and provides the reader with in-depth information about the people who were involved, their lifestyles, and their religious convictions. He also provides a detailed "then and now" discussion of the area where the story took place, including its Native American roots and its evolution. **Similar titles:** *The Bell Witch*, Brent Monahan; *Other Worlds*, Barbara Michaels; *The Blair Witch Project: A Dossier*, D. A. Stern; *Dorcas Good*, Rose Earhart.

⌐🖰 e-book

> *Bell Witch Haunting, The • Family Curse • Folklore • Ghosts • Parapsychology • Tennessee*

Fowler, Christopher.

Spanky. *London: Little, Brown-Warner, 1998, ©1994. 338p.* Martyn Ross leads a mediocre life as a furniture salesman—until one day he meets his personal demon, a supernatural being who promises to help him change his life. Ross acquiesces, and gets everything he ever wanted. And then he learns that the demon's help comes with a price tag. Fowler's novel is a unique and erudite read. **Similar titles:** *Soul Temple*, Steven Lee Climer; *Dr. Jekyll and Mr. Hyde*, Robert Louis Stevenson; *Thunderland*, Brandon Massey; *Fight Club* (film); *The Cleanup*, John Skipp and Craig Spector; *Warlock*, Perry Brass; *Dreamside*, Graham Joyce.

Alter Ego • Angels • Demons • London, England • Psychosexual Horror • Wish Fulfillment

Gaiman, Neil.

The Sandman: The Dream Hunters. *New York: Vertigo-DC Comics, 1999. 126p.* (See chapter 14, "Psychological Horror: It's All in Your Head.")

Giron, Sephera.

House of Pain. *New York: Leisure, 2001. 360p.* Lydia thinks she's found security at last when she marries Tony, an up-and-coming executive who's just built their dream house in his hometown. But she can't bring herself to unpack in the strange house that gives her nightmares and frightens her and her dog Pilar when they go down to the basement. Unknown to Lydia, her new home's property has a bloody history: Twenty years before, a married pair of serial killers tortured their victims to death on this very spot. **Similar titles:** *Bag of Bones*, Stephen King; *Five Mile House*, Karen Novack; *The House that Jack Built* and *Prey,* Graham Masterton.

Childhood • Dogs • Dreams • Ghosts • Haunted Houses • Human Sacrifice • Magic • Sado-Masochism • Serial Killers • Shapeshifters • Torture

Goingback, Owl.

Evil Whispers. *New York: Signet, 2001. 340p.* Robert Patterson, his wife Janet, and their ten-year-old daughter Krissy go on vacation in the swamplands of Florida, staying for a few weeks at the Blackwater Fishing Camp. There, Robert and Krissy unknowingly awaken the spirit of an evil Bocor, or witch doctor, named Mansa Du Paul, and Du Paul's ghost needs a body so that it can use black magic to resurrect Du Paul whole. Unfortunately for the Pattersons, Krissy is in the wrong place at the wrong time, and Du Paul's spirit takes over her body. Can Robert and Janet reclaim their daughter, even with the help of a local Seminole medicine man? **Similar titles:** *Brass*, Robert J. Conley; *Crota*, Owl Goingback; *Ghost Dance*, Mark T. Sullivan; *Voodoo Child*, Michael Reaves.

African-American Characters • Childhood • Florida • Native American Characters • Parenting • Religion—Native American • Religion—Voodoo

Griffith, Kathryn Meyer.

Witches. *New York: Kensington-Pinnacle, 2000, ©1993. 383p.* When an evil coven filled with creatures from the depths of hell torments the residents of Canaan with unspeakable horrors, it threatens to unmask quiet Amanda Givens, a resident of Canaan, as one of its own. **Similar titles:** *Murder at Witches' Bluff*, Silver Ravenwolf; *A Game of Colors*, John Urbancik; *The Demon Circle*, Dan Schmidt.

Demons • Witches

Hardy, Earl.

Valley of the Shadow. *Sacramento, Calif.: ReGeJe Press, 1998. 247p.* Set in the Old West, this novel tells the tale of an unconventional minister who recruits three gunmen—a gunfighter, a bounty hunter, and a retired sheriff—to accompany him on a trip to a remote valley where they're to confront a malevolent force. Along the way, they must deal with the lesser minions of this evil, including a town full of zombies. These men have been called by God to fight the evil that has been loosed on Silver Valley, and each man must come face to face with his worst fear, his brightest hope, and his fate, whether it be a long-awaited redemption or everlasting Hell. **Similar titles:** The Millenium Quartet, Charles Grant; *The Stand*, Stephen King; *The Last Vampire*, T. M. Wright.

> *Clergy as Character • Demons • Gunfighter as Character • Police Officer as Character • United States—19th Century • West, The • Zombies*

Hawkes, Judith.

The Heart of a Witch. *New York: Signet, 1999. 418p.* Ever since they can remember, Kip and Shelley have been fascinated by the Lockley Arms, the sprawling Victorian inn across the street from their home, with its stream of mysterious and glamorous guests. As teenagers, the twins get jobs at the inn and soon wish to join the coven of witches who secretly practice their craft at the Lockley Arms. But as new initiates, Kip and Shelley don't know all of the coven's secrets. What's behind the mysteriously locked door on the third floor of the inn? What really happened to the original founders of the coven? And is the coven somehow connected to the disappearance of two local boys? **Similar titles:** *The Witching Time*, Jean Stubbs; The Mayfair Witch Series, Anne Rice; *The People Under the Stairs* (film).

> *Childhood • Human Sacrifice • Incest • New York State • Obsession • Religion—Paganism • Revenge • Secret Sin • Twins • Witches • Witchcraft*

Hodgson, William Hope.

The House on the Borderland. *Halicong, Pa.: Wildside P. 2001, ©1908. 200p.* A reissue of a 1908 classic, *The House on the Borderland* is about a diary found in an ancient stone house that leads to a tale of subterranean monsters. Hodgson's novel is atmospheric. **Similar titles:** *Dark Sister*, Graham Joyce; *The Lurker at the Threshold*, H. P. Lovecraft; *Wuthering Heights*, Emily Brontë.

> ᡭᠵ large print

> *Diary Format • Ireland • Subterranean Monsters • Time Travel*

Holder, Nancy.

Ⓑ **Dead in the Water.** *New York: Bantam, 1994. 413p.* The cruise begins aboard the *Pandora* with a message from the ship's captain: "This is how it will be when you drown." The situation only gets eerier and more frightening, as crew members and passengers alike fall into and out of nightmarish, violent alternative realities. If only they can stop Captain Reade, the demonic puppeteer of their nightmares, they may survive. But no one, in any of Reade's previous lives, has stopped him before. This unique read is the winner of a Bram Stoker Award. Holder's novel is gory, but excellently written. **Similar titles:** *Dreamside*, Graham Joyce; *Green Light Cemetery*, David Kosciolek; *Thank You for the Flowers*, Scott Nicholson; *The Divinity Student*, Michael Cisco.

> *Demons • Dreams • Ghosts • Hispanic-American Characters • Maritime Horror • Psychosexual Horror*

Holleman, Gary.

Ungrateful Dead. *New York: Leisure, 1999. 395p.* Alana Magnus approaches a university professor of psychology and the paranormal with an interesting problem: She claims her dead mother is trying to possess her, body and soul. At first, he doubts her, but when she goes on a killing spree he realizes that Alana is indeed possessed, and he will have to fight a spirit from the netherworld to save himself. **Similar titles:** *What Lies Beneath* (film); *The Influence*, Ramsey Campbell; *The Shining*, Stephen King; *Drawn to the Grave*, Mary Ann Mitchell; *Hideaway*, Dean Koontz.

> *Ghosts • Parapsychology • Psychiatrist/Psychologist as Character • Religion—Druidism • Scholar as Character • Serial Killers*

Hollis, Claire.

The Light. *Tampa, Fla.: Warfare Publications, 1999. 176p.* (See chapter 8, "Mythological Monsters and 'The Old Ones': Invoking the Dark Gods.")

Houarner, Gerard.

The Beast That Was Max. *New York: Leisure, 2001. 392p.* (See chapter 15, "Splatterpunk: The Gross-Out.")

Jackson, Shirley.

The Haunting of Hill House. *Cutchogue, N.Y.: Buccaneer Books-Lightyear, 1993, ©1949. 306p.* (See chapter 4, "Ghosts and Haunted Houses: Dealing with Presences and Absences.")

Jak, Alister.

Tainted Lake: A Ghost Story for Grownups. *Greenfield, Ind.: Horror House Publishing, 1999. 331p.* (See chapter 14, "Psychological Horror: It's All in Your Head.")

Johnson, Adam.

Lifetimes of Blood. *Kansas City, Mo.: Dark Tales, 2000. 42p.* This novella about an immortal shapeshifter with the ability to possess human bodies relates the tale of his existence through various time periods, as he murders hapless humans and mutilates their bodies for sport. Only one entity can stop him—an immortal like himself—and humanity is not safe from either of them. This is a good gentle read that emphasizes character development. **Similar titles:** *My Soul to Keep*, Tananarive Due; The Time of Feasting Series, Mick Farren; *Deliver Us from Evil* and *The Sleeper in the Sands*, Tom Holland; *Dogma* (film).

> *History, Use of • Immortality • New York City • Serial Killers • Shapeshifters*

Joyce, Graham.

Dark Sister. *New York: Tor, 2000. 304p.* Maggie is an underappreciated stay-at-home mom whose husband is a selfish pig who won't even allow her to take a course at the local university for fear she'll find something better in life than cooking and cleaning. But then she finds a century old manuscript hidden in the chimney by a former occupant of their old Victorian brownstone. The diary, full of magical spells and herbalism, allows Maggie to find a sense of purpose in her life unconnected to her husband. But the manuscript's author, Maggie's dark sister, is also jealous of Maggie's time, and threatens her relationship with her family. **Similar titles:** *The Bell Witch*, Brent Monahan; *The Witching Time*, Jean

Stubbs; *The Conjure Wife*, Fritz Leiber; *Gift Giver*, Jean Sapin; *The Influence*, Ramsey Campbell; *What Lies Beneath* (film).

> *Alter Ego • Archeology • Dreams • England • Magic • Marriage • Parenting • Witches*

Kelly, Ronald.

Fear. *New York: Pinnacle, 2001,* ©*1994 480p.* (See chapter 10, "Small Town Horror: Villages of the Damned.")

King, Stephen.

Christine. *New York: Viking, 1983. 526p.* Dennis, the narrator of this first-person narrative, has a best friend named Arnie Cunningham, a high school loser whose only talent is his mechanical abilities. Enter Christine, a vintage Plymouth possessed by an angry spirit. This is one of King's more character-driven, psychological works. **Similar titles:** *One Rainy Night*, Richard Laymon; *Shadow Games*, Ed Gorman; *The Event*, Donald Silverman.

&⌢ large print

> *Cars • High School • Maine • Revenge*

Cujo. *New York: Signet, 1981. 304p.* (See chapter 13, "Ecological Horror: Rampant Animals and Mother Nature's Revenge.")

Desperation. *New York: Viking, 1996. 690p.* (See chapter 10, "Small Town Horror: Villages of the Damned.")

The Shining. *New York: Plume, 1977. 416p.* Alcoholic ex-teacher Jack Torrance has a second chance at life and at saving his relationship with his family. He has been hired as the innkeeper/overseer for The Overlook Hotel during the off-season winter months. The hotel itself has different ideas; it wants to add the psychic power that Jack's son Danny possesses to its own powers, and it will stop at nothing, not even at supplying Jack with liquor. Who will win Jack's soul, the Overlook or his family? A classic haunted house tale, this novel was made into a film of the same name directed by Stanley Kubrick. **Similar titles:** *Nazareth Hill*, Ramsey Campbell; *The Green Man*, Kingsley Amis, *The Face at the Window*, Dennis McFarland; *Boy in the Water*, Stephen Dobyns; *University*, Bentley Little.

> *Alcoholism • Colorado • Ghosts • Haunted Houses • Telepathy*

The Tommyknockers. *New York: Signet Books 1988. 747p.* Unknown to the residents of Haven, Maine, aliens have come to the small town and have given the residents extraordinary powers. After Bobbi Anderson stumbles across a metal object buried for millennia, the town becomes a very dangerous place for outsiders. **Similar titles:** *Invasion of the Body Snatchers* (Film); *Dreamcatcher*, Stephen King; *The Sand Dwellers*, Adam Niswander; *The Apostate*, Paul Lonardo.

> *Aliens • Maine • Mind Control • Police Officer as Character • Weird Science*

King, Stephen [as Richard Bachman].

Thinner. *New York: New American Library, 1984. 282p.* Billy Halleck, an attorney who is fifty pounds overweight and pushing a heart attack, sideswipes an old Gypsy woman as she crosses the street and uses his professional wiles to avoid compensating the woman's family for her death. One of the woman's clan curses Billy with the word "thinner," and Billy begins to lose weight uncontrollably. **Similar titles:** *The Walking*, Bentley Little; *Cronos* (film); *Bag of Bones*, Stephen King; *The Rag Bone Man*, Charlotte Lawrence.

𝔇 audiotape

> *Lawyer as Character • Maine • Revenge*

Klavan, Andrew.

The Uncanny. *New York: Crown, 1998. 343p.* (See chapter 16, "Comic Horror: Laughing at Our Fears.")

Koontz, Dean.

Cold Fire. *New York: Berkley, 1991. 421p.* Jim Ironheart has been suffering from visions that allow him to see when disaster will occur in time for him to prevent the tragedy. But can he and a young reporter who has taken a personal interest in him survive a showdown with evil? **Similar titles:** *Dead Zone*, Stephen King; *The Secret Life of Colors*, Steve Savile; *Tribulations*, J. Michael Straczynski; *The Cell* (film); The Host Series, Selina Rosen.

> *Dreams • Journalist as Character • Precognition*

Dark Fall. *New York: Berkley, 1984. 371p.* Two detectives, Jack Dawson and Rebecca Chandler, are called in to investigate brutal gangland slayings. Dawson soon realizes that a practitioner of black magic named Lavelle is summoning creatures from the depths of hell to exact revenge. And now Lavelle has threatened Dawson by promising to have his children brutally murdered if he does not back off the case. The final seventy pages are a masterpiece of suspense. **Similar titles:** *Voodoo Child*, Michael Reaves; *The Evil Returns*, Hugh B. Cave; *Shadow Heart*, Bill Allen; *Fallen* (film); *Carrion Comfort*, Dan Simmons.

> *Demons • New York City • Organized Crime • Police Officer as Character • Religion—Voodoo*

Hideaway. *New York: Putnam, 1992. 384p.* Hatch Harrison dies from a car accident but is revived by a brilliant doctor some seventy-five minutes later. Unfortunately, when he comes back from the afterlife, Hatch brings with him a demon that is using his body as a place to hide. Suffice it to say that no one should anger Hatch Harrison, or more specifically, his inner demon. The first hundred pages are incredible. **Similar titles:** *Dead Zone*, Stephen King; *Shadow Heart*, Bill Allen; *The Exorcist*, William Peter Blatty; *The 37th Mandala*, Mark Laidlaw; *Riverwatch*, Joseph M. Nassie.

> *Afterlife, The • Alter Ego • Artist as Character • Demons*

The Mask. *New York: Berkley Books, 1992, ©1981. 305p.* Paul and Carol want nothing more than to have beautiful, perfect children, and then one day an accident grants their wish. They now have Jane, a homeless teenaged girl who seems to be the perfect daughter. But Jane has a hidden agenda, which may involve murder. Koontz's emphasis on plot makes this a fast and easy read. **Similar titles:** *Bereavements*, Richard Lortz; *Wire Mesh Mothers*, Elizabeth Massie; *Spirit*, Graham Masterton.

> *Demons • Matricide/Patricide • Parenting*

Winter Moon. *New York: Random House, 1994. 472p.* When heroic LAPD officer Jack McGarvey and his family inherited the Quartermass Ranch in Montana from someone they'd never met, they considered themselves lucky. Little do they know what happened to its previous owner, Eduardo Fernandez, an old farmer who saw something in the moon. This builds up nicely to a gory, horrific climax. The writing is more subtle and traditional than Koontz's writing usually is. **Similar titles:** *The Tommyknockers*, Stephen King; *The Sand Dwellers*, Adam Niswander; *The Apostate*, Paul Lonardo; *The Boat Man*, Selina Rosen; *The Lost Boys* (film).

> *Aliens • Hispanic-American Characters • Montana • Police Officer as Character • Zombies*

Laidlaw, Marc.

The 37th Mandala. *New York: Leisure, 1999, ©1996. 352p.* Derek Crowe, a hack who wants to make money off New Age philosophy, unwittingly awakens an evil force when he converts followers using a mandala historically connected to Cambodia's killing fields. The mandalas, represented by Crowe in his best-selling book *The Mandala Rites* as comforting angels who can help any human who calls them, are actually otherworldly beings who feed off human suffering. And Crowe receives more than he bargained for when one of his fans follows the directions in his book and unwittingly becomes possessed by one of these beings. Literate and original, *The 37th Mandala* is a recipient of an International Horror Guild Award for Best Novel. **Similar titles:** *Twilight Dynasty: Courting Evil*, Barry H. Smith; *The Rag Bone Man*, Charlotte Lawrence; *Project Resurrection*, Karen Duval; *Wither*, J. G. Passarella.

> *Demons • Magic • New Age • Numerology • Religion—Paganism • San Francisco, California • War—Vietnam • Writer as Character*

Laymon, Richard.

One Rainy Night. *New York: Leisure, 2000. 410p.* (See chapter 11, "Maniacs and Sociopaths, or the Nuclear Family Explodes: Monstrous Malcontents Bury the Hatchet.")

Lee, Edward.

The Chosen. *New York: Kensington-Pinnacle, 2001, ©1993. 379p.* (See chapter 4, "Ghosts and Haunted Houses: Dealing with Presences and Absences.")

Leiber, Fritz.

The Conjure Wife. *New York: Tor, 1991, ©1978. 184p.* When sociology professor Norman Saylor rummages through his wife Tansy's closet one afternoon, he discovers that she has been using white magic to further his career. Determined to set her straight, he confronts her and then burns many of her protective charms. Suddenly, all hell breaks loose in Saylor's life, and his only hope is to try to save himself and his wife through the witchcraft he once eschewed. **Similar titles:** *Lovers Living, Lovers Dead*, Richard Lortz; *Dark Sister*, Graham Joyce; *My Soul to Keep*, Tananarive Due.

> *Academia • Magic • New England • Witchcraft*

Levin, Ira. The Rosemary's Baby Books.

Rosemary's Baby. *New York: Bantam Books, 1991, ©1968. 262p.* Young marrieds Guy and Rosemary Woodhouse move into their dream apartment in the Bramford, where they hope to start a family. They don't believe Rosemary's friend and mentor Hutch when he tells them about the Bramford's sinister past: proper Victorian spinsters who practiced cannibalism and a man who claimed to have conjured Satan. Rosemary isn't prepared to believe that the sweet old couple next door are practicing Satanists with designs on her womb. Levin's novel was made into a film of the same name directed by Roman Polanski. **Similar titles:** *The Demon Circle*, Dan Schmidt; *The Wicker Man*, Anthony Shaffer and Robin Hardy; *Third Ring*, Phillip Tomasso; *The Long Lost*, Ramsey Campbell.

> *Actor as Character • Marriage • New York City • Pregnancy • Religion—Christianity—Catholicism • Religion—Satanism • Woodhouse, Rosemary (character)*

Son of Rosemary. *New York: Dutton, 1997. 256p.* Rosemary Woodhouse awakens from a long coma to learn that her demonic son is now a charismatic religious leader preaching messages of peace and hope. Yet she also notes that demonic look he had in his eyes as an infant. *Son of Rosemary* is the sequel to *Rosemary's Baby.* **Similar titles:** *The Blood of the Lamb* and *The Reckoning,* Thomas F. Monteleone; *Dracula 2000* (film); *The Omen* (film); The Millennium Quartet Series, Charles Grant.

Antichrist, the (character) • Incest • New York City • Religion—Satanism • Televangelism • Woodhouse, Rosemary (character)

Lewis, Matthew.

The Monk. *New York: Oxford University Press, 1998, ©1796. 456p.* Satan tempts a well-respected clergyman in this novel that is one of the ancestors of erotic horror. *The Monk* is a chilling character study of the degeneration of a human being and his soul. **Similar titles:** *The Exorcist,* William Peter Blatty; *Gothic Readings: The First Wave,* Rictor Norton (editor); *The Castle of Otranto,* Horace Walpole.

Clergy as Character • Eroticism • Necrophilia • Satan (character) • Shapeshifters

Little, Bentley.

The Store. *New York: Signet, 1998. 431p.* (See chapter 10, "Small Town Horror: Villages of the Damned.")

The Walking. *New York: Signet, 2000. 373p.* Miles Hurdeen's father dies, but he is not at rest. Instead, his reanimated corpse gets up and walks from Los Angeles to the middle of the Arizona desert. Miles's father isn't the only dead man walking. Dozens of other dead have exhibited the same bizarre behavior. Now Miles must find out about his father's mysterious past life before a terrible vengeance is wreaked on the living. Eerie and original, this is a typical example of Little's horror, which incorporates magical realism with traditional elements of the genre. **Similar titles:** *Night of the Living Dead* (film); *Deadfellas,* David Whitman; *The Town,* Bentley Little; *Drawn to the Grave,* Mary Ann Mitchell.

 7

Arizona • California • Curse • Magic • Private Investigator as Character • Revenging Revenant • Secret Sin • United States—19th Century • Witches • Zombies

Lonardo, Paul.

The Apostate. *St. Petersburg, FL: Barclay Books, 2001. 254p.* (See chapter 10, "Small-Town Horror: Villages of the Damned.")

Lortz, Richard.

Lovers Living, Lovers Dead. *Sagaponak, N.Y.: Second Chance Press, 1981, ©1977. 222p.* A professor of comparative literature is beginning to suspect that his wife, Christine, an ex-student some twenty years his junior, is harboring dark secrets about her past. He teams up with Christine's psychologist, and the two begin a process of discovering the secrets of Christine's past—but what they find out may destroy them and two innocent children. Lortz's novel is unique and clever, with emphasis on characterization and atmosphere. **Similar titles:** *The Conjure Wife,* Fritz Leiber; *Son of Rosemary,* Ira Levin; *Naomi,* Douglas Clegg; *Travel Many Roads,* Robert E. Wheeler.

Academia • Childhood • Incest • Psychiatrist/Psychologist as Character • Religion—African • Teacher as Character

Lovecraft, H. P.

The Lurker at the Threshold. *New York: Carroll and Graf, 1999, ©1945. 186p.* (See chapter 8, "Mythological Monsters and 'The Old Ones': Invoking the Dark Gods.")

The Shadow Out of Time. *S. T. Joshi and David E. Schultz (editors). New York: Hippo-campus Press, 2001. 136p.* (See chapter 8, "Mythological Monsters and 'The Old Ones': Invoking the Dark Gods.")

Malvey, Cece.

The Blair Witch Project: An Illustrated History [Wood Witch Said]. *Southwold, Suffolk: ScreenPress Books, 1999. 63p.* Folklorist Jen Van Meter adapts a comic strip booklet written by a Johns Hopkins student who hanged himself after disappearing in the Burkittsville woods. This is yet another example of the clever marriage of fiction and documentary in the Blair Witch series. **Similar titles:** *The Blair Witch 2* (film); *The Bell Witch Haunting*, Brent Monahan; *Hellboy: The Chained Coffin and Others*, Mike Mignola; *The History of Witchcraft and Demonology*, Montague Sommers.

> *Blair Witch Haunting • Burkittsville, Maryland • Documentary Technique • Graphic Novel • History, Use of • Malvey, Cece (character) • Witchcraft*

Masterton, Graham.

The House That Jack Built. *New York: Leisure, 2000, ©1996. 384p.* High-powered attorney Craig Bellman and his wife Effie escape the harsh streets of New York City by moving into Valhalla, a centuries-old mansion erected by a legendary gambler and womanizer. Soon after they move in, ghostly voices make supernatural presences known to Effie. Can she convince Craig to leave before the evil spirit of the house's builder consumes him? **Similar titles:** *Lovers Living, Lovers Dead*, Richard Lortz; *Five Mile House*, Karen Novack; *Prey*, Graham Masterton; *Nazareth Hill*, Ramsey Campbell.

> *Ghosts • Haunted Houses • Lawyer as Character • New York State • Pregnancy • Revenging Revenant*

The Manitou. *Chicago: Olmstead Press, 2001, ©1975. 174p.* Karen Tandy goes to her doctor with what looks like a tumor on her neck, but x-rays reveal a fetus-like growth. Desperate, she turns to a well-known psychic, thus drawing him into the ultimate test of faith in himself and in the power of the spiritual world, when he must save her from the Manitou (ghost) of a powerful Native American medicine man. This classic is well-crafted and suspenseful, with emphasis on characterization and atmosphere. **Similar titles:** *Ghost Dance*, Mark T. Sullivan; *Brass*, Robert J. Conley; *Smoke Signals*, Octavio Ramos Jr.; *The 37th Mandala*, Mark Laidlaw; *The Exorcist*, William Peter Blatty.

 e-book

> *Demons • History, Use of • Medical Horror • Native American characters • New York City • Parapsychology • Police Officer as character • Pregnancy • Religion—Native American*

Prey. *New York: Leisure, 1999, ©1992. 352p.* (See chapter 8, "Mythological Monsters and 'The Old Ones': Invoking the Dark Gods.")

Maturin, Charles Robert.

Melmoth the Wanderer. *Victor Sage (editor). London, England; New York: Penguin, 2000, ©1820. 659p.* An Irish gentleman makes a deal with the devil that enables him to live for as long as he wishes. Eventually he wishes to dissolve his pact, but to do so he must travel the world over looking for someone who will take over his deal with the devil and volunteer for eternal life. Maturin's gothic novel is cumbersome at times but is an excellent example of early gothicism and the gothic atmosphere. **Similar titles:** *The Castle of Otranto*,

Horace Walpole; *The Monk*, Matthew Lewis; *Frankenstein*, Mary Shelley; *Wieland*, Charles Brockden Brown.

> *Gothicism • Immortality • Ireland • London, England • Satan (character)*

Michaels, Barbara.

Other Worlds. *New York: HarperCollins, 1999. 217p.* This tale of witchcraft set in nineteenth-century Robertson County, Tennessee, is based on the Bell Witch Haunting, a true case chronicled in American history. The novel follows the Bell family's first meeting with the witch and then changes pace to become a discussion of the case among Harry Houdini, Montague Summers, and Sir Arthur Conan Doyle. Philosophy rather than fright is emphasized. **Similar titles:** *The Bell Witch Haunting*, Brent Monahan; The Mayfair Witch Series, Anne Rice; *The Haunted Looking Glass: Ghost Stories Chosen by Edward Gorey*, Edward Gorey (editor).

> *Bell Witch Haunting • Doyle, Arthur Conan (character) • History, Use of • Houdini, Harry (character) • Tennessee • Summers, Montague (character) • Witchcraft*

Mitchell, Mary Ann.

Ambrosial Flesh. *New York: Leisure, 2001. 391p.* As a child, Jonathan discovered that consuming his own flesh was a far more satisfying alternative to taking holy communion. By adulthood, Jonathan's auto-cannibalism has become a full-blown fetish, which he yearns to share with his reluctant wife. But his love play goes too far, and his wife ends up dead. Then Yakut, a mysterious stranger, appears when Jonathan needs help most—to dispose of a decaying body and to continue indulging in his strange passion. Yakut demands that Jonathan sacrifice everyone he loves, and finally, his own soul, in exchange for this assistance. **Similar titles:** *Drawn to the Grave*, Mary Ann Mitchell; *Lovers Living, Lovers Dead*, Richard Lortz; *Rosemary's Baby*, Ira Levin; *House of Pain*, Sephera Giron.

> *Cannibalism • Eroticism • Human Sacrifice • Obsession • Psychosexual Horror • Religion—Christianity—Catholicism • Religion—Satanism • Satan (character) • Secret Sin • Shapeshifters • Subways • Torture • Wish Fulfillment • Yakut (character)*

 Drawn to the Grave. *New York: Leisure, 1997. 313p.* When Carl becomes terminally ill, he cannot face his own mortality, so he searches the world for a cure. In the Amazon rain forest, he finds a cure that necessitates his becoming intimately acquainted with his victim before stealing her life. But Carl's arrogance has made him overlook the desire of his latest victim to survive and wreak vengeance. As Beverly decays, she plots to take back what was stolen from her. This graphic and original tale was a recipient of an International Horror Guild Award for Best First Novel. **Similar titles:** *The Picture of Dorian Gray*, Oscar Wilde; *Ambrosial Flesh*, Mary Ann Mitchell; *My Soul to Keep*, Tananarive Due.

> *Aging • Eroticism • Immortality • Magic • Revenge*

Moore, James A., and Kevin Murphy.

Under the Overtree. *Decatur, Ga.: Meisha Merlin, 2000. 428p.* Fifteen-year-old Mark Howell is the odd man out when he first arrives in Summitville. Shy and overweight, he quickly becomes the target of the local bullies, who chase him through the woods. Here Mark falls on an ancient stone, his virgin blood awakening the forest's Fairy Folk, who make him their Chosen One and bestow upon him special powers. Soon Mark beings to lose weight and is dating the most desirable girl in school, and anyone who has ever been nasty to him disappears. **Similar titles:** *Carrie*, Stephen King; *One Rainy Night*, Richard Laymon; *Ginger Snaps* (film).

> *Adolesence • Colorado • Fairies • High School • Wish Fulfillment*

Neiderman, Andrew.

Curse: A Novel. *New York: Pocket, 2000. 357p.* (See chapter 14, "Psychological Horror: It's All in Your Head.")

Novack, Karen.

Five Mile House. *New York: Bloosmbury, 2000. 228p.* (See chapter 4, "Ghosts and Haunted Houses: Dealing with Presences and Absences.")

Passarella, J. G.

Wither. *New York: Simon & Schuster, 1999. 438p.* Windale, Massachusetts, is heir to a colorful colonial past, including women accused of witchcraft. Today, the town is home to many a new-age witch knowledgeable in occult lore and the use of herbs. But every 100 years, strange things seem to happen to the residents of Windale, and one of these witches is about to learn that the history of her town is more than just a quaint legend. **Similar titles:** *The Chalice*, Phil Rickman; *Bag of Bones*, Stephen King; *Ghost Story*, Peter Straub; *The Blair Witch Project* (film); *Blair Witch 2: Book of Shadows* (film).

> *Haunted Houses • Massachusetts • New Age • Revenging Revenant • Secret Sin • Witches • Witchcraft*

Piccirilli, Tom.

A Lower Deep. *New York: Leisure, 2001. 363p.* A mysterious drifter known as The Necromancer is being called back to his hometown to rejoin the coven that he is destined to lead. Although he refuses at first because this same coven was responsible for the death of his childhood love, he eventually returns to discover a nefarious plot to raise Christ himself from the dead, thus ushering in the Second Coming and Armageddon. Now The Necromancer must stop his old coven from bringing about the end of the world, and to do so, he must ally himself with some of the forces with which he has been at war throughout his life, including the ghost of his father. **Similar titles:** The Blood of the Lamb Series, Thomas F. Monteleone; The Millennium Quartet, Charles Grant; *The 37th Mandala*, Mark Laidlaw; *Dogma* (film).

> *Alter Ego • Apocalypse • Bible, The • Family Curse • Ghosts • Israel • Magic • Reincarnation • Religion—Christianity • Religion—Satanism • Witches*

Powers, Tim.

Declare. *New York: William Morrow, 2001. 517p.* Andrew Hale, an Oxford lecturer who first entered Her Majesty's Secret Service as an eighteen-year-old, is called back to finish a job begun after the end of World War II. It's now 1963, and Hale must bring down the Soviet government before it can harness powerful, otherworldly forces concentrated on the summit of Mount Ararat. **Similar titles:** *Cleopatra's Needle*, Steven Siebert; *Labor Day*, Floyd Kemske; *Vampire Nation*, Thomas M. Sipos; *Bloody Red Baron*, Kim Newman.

> *Cold War, The • England • Espionage • Fantasy • History, Use of • Middle East, The • Moscow, Russia • Mount Ararat • Parapsychology • Spy as Character*

Ramsey, J.

The Claw. (See Campbell, Ramsey. *The Claw.* London: Little, Brown, 1992. 380p.)

Ravenwolf, Silver.

Murder at the Witches' Bluff: A Novel of Suspense and Magick. *St. Paul, Minn.: Llewellyn, 2000. 449p.* When Siren McKay returns to her hometown of Cold Springs, Pennsylvania, after being acquitted of murder charges in New York, she receives a cold welcome from her friends and family and from the townspeople, who blame her relatives for the mysterious recurring fires that are destroying the town. As she attempts to learn the truth behind the fires, Siren discovers family secrets and vengeful plots. She will need all her magic to fight the dark powers that are destroying Cold Springs. **Similar titles:** *Twilight Dynasty: Courting Evil*, Barry H. Smith; *Smoke Signals*, Octavio Ramos Jr.; *The Rag Bone Man*, Charlotte Lawrence; *Mischief*, Douglas Clegg.

Appalachia • Family Curse • Fantasy • Magic • Pennsylvania • Religion—Paganism • Secret Sin • Witchcraft

Reaves, Michael.

Voodoo Child. *New York: Tor, 1998. 352p.* In 1988, Shane LaFitte returns to Haiti to discover his true calling as a Voodoo priest. While he is there, he meets Mal Sangre, practitioner of Voodoo, Santeria, and the dark arts. Mal Sangre isn't happy with his ability to conjure the loas to intercede on his behalf. Instead, he himself wishes to be a god. Thus, he leaves for New Orleans to embark on his sinister plot to use black magic to rule the world, and LaFitte must stop him. Reaves accurately represents the religion of Voodoo, rather than falling back on the silly parodies favored by so many writers. **Similar titles:** *The Evil Returns*, Hugh B. Cave; *The 37th Mandala*, Mark Laidlaw; *Merrick*, Anne Rice; *Masques*, Bill Pronzini.

African-American Characters • Clergy as Character • Drugs • Haiti • Human Sacrifice • Immortality • Magic • Mind Control • Music—Jazz • Musician as Character • Necromancy • New Orleans, Louisiana • Physician as Character • Police Officer as Character • Religion—Voodoo • Zombies

Recknor, Ellen.

Prophet Annie: Being the Recently Discovered Memoir of Annie Pinkerton Boone Newcastle Dearborn, Prophet and Seer. *New York: Avon, 1999. 330p.* (See chapter 16, "Comic Horror: Laughing at Our Fears.")

Rice, Anne. The Mayfair Witches Series.

The Witching Hour. *New York: Ballantine Books, 1991. 1038p.* After the death of her natural mother, Rowan Mayfair returns to New Orleans to discover her family and their legacy, the legacy of the Mayfair witches, and their relationship with the spirit Lasher. For twelve generations Lasher has allowed the family to prosper, and now Rowan, the thirteenth generation of Mayfair witches, must pay the price for that prosperity. This novel is written in Rice's usual romantic, detailed style. **Similar titles:** The Vampire Chronicles, Anne Rice; *A Game of Colors*, John Urbancik; *Wither*, J. G. Passarella; *The Rag Bone Man*, Charlotte Lawrence; *Twilight Dynasty: Courting Evil*, Barry H. Smith.

⍭ audiotape, audio download

Curry, Michael (character) • Lasher (character) • Lightener, Aaron (character) • Mayfair, Rowan (character) • New Orleans, Louisiana • Religion—Christianity—Catholicism • Talamasca, The • Witches • Witchcraft

Lasher. *New York: Alfred A. Knopf, 1993. 577p.* In this, the second novel in the Mayfair Witch Series, Rice tells of their being haunted by Lasher, a spirit. In return for a favor granted the Mayfairs, Lasher is guaranteed the possession of the body of the first strong witch born to the family. Can the women of the family survive Lasher's attempts to create a child strong enough for his spirit to inhabit? **Similar titles:** The Vampire Chronicles, Anne Rice; *A Game of Colors*, John Urbancik; *Wither*, J. G. Passarella; *The Rag Bone Man*, Charlotte Lawrence; *Twilight Dynasty: Courting Evil*, Barry H. Smith.

📀 audiotape, audio download

> *Curry, Michael (character) • Incest • History, Use of • Lasher (character) • Mayfair, Julian (character) • Mayfair, Mona (character) • Mayfair, Rowan (character) • New Orleans, Louisiana • Reincarnation • Religion—Christianity—Catholicism • Religion—Christianity—Protestantism • Religion—Paganism • Revenging Revenant • Scotland • Talamasca, The • Taltos, The • Weird Science • Witches • Witchcraft*

Taltos: Lives of the Mayfair Witches. *New York: Ballantine Books, 1995. 480p.* Continues the tale begin in *The Witching Hour* and *Lasher.* Ashlar, a member of a race of mythic, immortal giants, teams up with the Mayfair witches to battle an evil force. This is a critical success as well as a success with Rice fans, who love her ornate description and epic adventure. **Similar titles:** The Vampire Chronicles, Anne Rice; *A Game of Colors*, John Urbancik; *Wither*, J. G. Passarella; *The Rag Bone Man*, Charlotte Lawrence; *Twilight Dynasty: Courting Evil*, Barry H. Smith.

📀 audiotape, audio download

> *Curry, Michael (character) • Incest • History, Use of • Lightner, Aaron (character) • Mayfair, Mona (character) • Mayfair, Rowan (character) • New Orleans, Louisiana • Talamasca, The • Taltos, The • Witches • Witchcraft*

Rice, Anne.

Merrick. *New York: Alfred A. Knopf, 2000. 307p.* A former member of the Talamasca, David Talbot asks Merrick Mayfair, of the African-American branch of the Mayfair clan, to use her powers to raise the ghost of Claudia for the benefit of Louis, David's father in darkness. But before Merrick agrees to do so, she must tell the story of her own magical powers. This novel is the intersection between The Vampire Chronicles and The Mayfair Witch Series. **Similar titles:** The Vampire Chronicles and The Mayfair Witch Series, Anne Rice; The Silver Wolf Series, Alice Borchardt.

📀 audiotape, audio download, compact disc   📱 e-book   🔍 large print

> *Afterlife, The • African-American Characters • Claudia (character) • Dreams • Gay/Lesbian/Bisexual Characters • Guatemala • Immortality • Lestat de Lioncourt (character) • Lightner, Aaron (character) • Louis (character) • Mayfair, Merrick (character) • New Orleans, Louisiana • Religion—Mayan • Religion—Voodoo • Talamasca, The • Talbot, David (character) • Vampire's Point of View • Witches • Witchcraft*

Rickman, Phil.

Midwinter of the Spirit. *London, MacMillan- Pan Books, 2000, ©1999. 537p.* Merrily Watkins is poised to take over the Church of England's Deliverance Ministry, a kinder, gentler version of what was once called exorcism, for a church whose leaders all too often no longer believe in evil, possession, or even God. Strange things are happening in and around the Cathedral, famous shrine of St. Thomas Cantilupe, and Merrily is unprepared to deal with the powers of darkness while protecting the reputation of a faith that is becoming increasingly irrelevant in a modern world. Rickman's novel is a dense and compelling read based on the true exorcism practices of the Church of England. **Similar titles:** *The Exorcist*, William Peter Blatty, *The Wine of Angels*, Phil Rickman; *The Witching Time*, Jean Stubbs; *Stigmata* (film).

> *Cantilupe, St. Thomas • Clergy as Character • Exorcism • Ghosts • Herefordshire, England • New Age • Parapsychology • Religion—Christianity—Episcopal • Religion—Satanism • Robinson, Lol (Lawrence) (character) • Secret Sin • Watkins, Jane (character) • Watkins, Rev. Merrily (character)*

Rosen, Selina.

The Boat Man. *Alma, Ark.: Yard Dog Press, 1999. 68p.* In this novella, in the year 2060, the elderly have taken over the government, and youth have almost no rights. Police Officer Vicky Grip is punished by a superior by being given an assignment in Boiling Springs, a retirement town. There, she stumbles upon the nefarious plot of demonic creatures that use the bodies of the elderly who are comatose. Once they possess these bodies, they lobby to change even more laws to benefit themselves, and they are responsible for the disappearance of the "youngsters" of Boiling Springs. **Similar titles:** *Shadow Heart*, Bill Allen; *The Walking*, Bentley Little; *Rosemary's Baby* (film); *Ghost Story*, Peter Straub; *Insomnia* and *Dreamcatcher*, Stephen King; *Blood Crazy*, Simon Clark.

> *Demons • Police Officer as Character • Science Fiction • Senior Citizen as Character • Serial Killers*

Savile, Steve.

Secret Life of Colors. *Kansas City, Mo.: Dark Tales Publications. 2000. 192p.* (See chapter 8, "Mythological Monsters and 'The Old Ones': Invoking the Dark Gods.")

Schmidt, Dan.

The Demon Circle. *New York: Leisure, 2000. 358p.* Officer Mark Jantzen is constantly reliving in his nightmares the time he was unable to stop a group of Satanists from sacrificing his wife and daughter. Now with a new wife in Newton, Oklahoma, he finds himself being stalked by a group of maniacal killers who are mutilating the townspeople. Are the same Satanists after him again, and if so, why? Can he stop them this time? *The Demon Circle* is action oriented, with many cliff-hanger scenes. **Similar titles:** *Mecca and the Black Oracle*, Paul Masters; *Ripper*, Michael Slade; *The Scream*, Craig Spector and John Skipp; *Death's Door*, John Wooley and Ron Wolfe.

7

> *Cults • Demons • Human Sacrifice • Oklahoma • Police Officer as Character • Serial Killers • Religion—Satanism • Revenge • Stalkers*

Shirley, John.

Wetbones. *New York: Leisure, 1999, ©1993. 332p.* Ephram Pixie is a psychic vampire. a human being who lives off the life force of others while forcing them to do his bidding, until he uses them up. Now he is working on his twenty-seventh victim, a teenaged girl whom he turns into a murderous slave. Can her father, with the help of a Hollywood writer whose wife was victim number twenty-six, stop Ephram before he leaves another husk behind? **Similar titles:** *Carrion Comfort*, Dan Simmons; *The Evil Returns*, Hugh B. Cave; *Black Oak 4: Hunting Ground*, Charles Grant.

> *Clergy as Character • Hollywood, California • Los Angeles, California • Mind Control • Psychosexual Horror • Religion—Christianity • Writer as Character*

Siodmak, Curt.

Donovan's Brain. *New York: Carroll & Graf, 1942. 160p.* (See chapter 12, "Technohorror: Evil Hospitals, Military Screw-Ups, Scientific Goofs, and Alien Invasions.")

Skipp, John, and Craig Spector.

The Scream. *Lancaster, Pa.: Stealth Press, 2001, ©1998. 437p.* (See chapter 15, "Splatterpunk: The Gross-Out.")

Smith, Barry H.

Twilight Dynasty: Courting Evil. *Baltimore: Erica House, 1999. 315p.* (See chapter 8, "Mythological Monsters and 'The Old Ones': Invoking the Dark Gods.")

Somtow, S.P.

Darker Angels. *New York: Tor, 1998. 384p.* This is an extremely complex tale that weaves stories within stories, starring historical figures, shapeshifting slaves, and Voodoo shamans who want to raise the dead to form an invincible army. *Darker Angels* is clever and historically accurate and is narrated from multiple points of view. **Similar titles:** The Anno Dracula Series, Kim Newman; The Lord of the Dead Series, Tom Holland; *Other Worlds*, Barbara Michaels.

> *Alternative History • Ghosts • History, Use of • Racism • Religion—Voodoo • Shapeshifters • Slavery • United States—19th Century • War—American Civil War*

Stoker, Bram.

The Jewel of Seven Stars. *New York: Carroll & Graf, 1989, ©1903. 214p.* (See chapter 5, "Golem, Mummies, and Reaanimated Stalkers: Wake the Dead and They'll Be Cranky.")

Straub, Peter.

Floating Dragon. *New York: Putnam, 1983. 515p.* (See chapter 11, "Maniacs and Sociopaths, or the Nuclear Family Explodes: Monstrous Malcontents Bury the Hatchet.")

If You Could See Me Now. *New York: Pocket, 1977. 328p.* This early Straub chiller is about a pact made between two young lovers. When Miles returns to his hometown twenty years afterwards, he suspects that he will not be meeting the seductive Allison of his youth, but a savage demon ruled by revenge. **Similar titles:** *Ghost Story*, Peter Straub; *Hellraiser* (film); *Dawn Song*, Michael Marano.

> *Demons • Parapsychology • Revenge*

Shadowland. *New York: Berkley, 1981. 468p.* Two teenaged friends, Tom Flanagan and Del Nightingale, spend a summer as apprentices to a magician to polish up their amateur act. But then horrible events begin to occur at the boys' school, where they are picked on regularly. Is black magic at the core of these "accidents?" **Similar titles:** *If You Could See Me Now* and *Mr. X*, Peter Straub; *Carrie*, Stephen King; *The Traveling Vampire Show*, Richard Laymon; *Phantom Feast*, Diana Barron; *The Talisman*, Peter Straub and Stephen King.

> *High School • Magic*

Tomasso, Phillip, III.

Third Ring. *St. Petersburg, Fla.: Barclay Books, 2001. 325p.* When attorney Nicholas Tartaglia is called on to defend a burglar being tried for murder and armed robbery, he discovers that his client was attempting to steal a book of magic spells that could be used for the ultimate evil: allowing the devil to enter the realm of humanity. Now Tartaglia faces two challenges: to prove that his client is innocent of murder and to recover the book before innocent people are killed. **Similar titles:** *Full Moon, Bloody Moon*, Lee Driver; The Black Oak Series, Charles Grant; *Dark Detectives*, Stephen Jones (editor); *The Secret Life of Colors*, Steve Savile; *Morningstar*, Peter Atkins.

> *Clergy as Character • Lawyer as Character • Magic • Rochester, New York • Tartaglia, Nicholas (character) • Writer as Character • Witchcraft*

Urbancik, John.

A Game of Colors. *Alma, Ark.: Yard Dog Press, 2001. 54p.* In this novella, a young girl joins a coven and discovers that she must not only endure but survive a month of dangerous training if she is to accomplish what she set out to do: find her older sister who had joined a coven and then disappeared. Urbancik's novella challenges many traditional representations of witches and witchcraft. **Similar titles:** The Mayfair Witch Series, Anne Rice; *The Rag Bone Man*, Charlotte Lawrence; *Merrick*, Anne Rice; *The Silver Wolf*, Alice Borchardt.

> *Cults • Homoeroticism • Magic • Witchcraft*

Walpole, Horace.

The Castle of Otranto. *New York: Viking Penguin, 2002, ©1764. 208p.* Considered one of the first, if not the first-ever, horror work, *The Castle of Otranto* traces the fate of the cursed family of Manfred, Prince of Otranto, and their haunted castle. **Similar titles:** *Northanger Abbey*, Jane Austen; *Gothic Readings*, Rector Norton (editor); *The Monk*, Matthew Lewis; *Thirty-two Stories*, Edgar Allan Poe; *Wieland*, Charles Brockton Brown.

⌐🖱 e-book

> *Castles • Ghosts • Haunted Houses • Italy*

Wilde, Oscar.

The Picture of Dorian Gray. *New York: Tom Doherty, 1998, ©1891. 256p.* When handsome young Dorian Gray sees a portrait that has been painted of him, he bitterly regrets that he must someday grow old. He wishes that the painting would age and that he would always keep his youth. Dorian's wish comes true, and he becomes a sort of dark Peter Pan who can never grow up. Instead of getting the face he deserves through his moral excesses, Dorian's visage remains as bland as a baby's, encouraging him to live for his own pleasure alone. **Similar titles:** *Drawn to the Grave*, Mary Ann Mitchell; *The House of the Seven Gables*, Nathaniel Hawthorne; *The Hunger*, Whitney Streiber, *The Hunger* (film); *The Boat Man*, Selina Rosen.

🎵 audiotape ⌐ large print

> *Aging • London, England • Secret Sin • Victorian England • Wish Fulfillment*

Wilkins, Kim.

Grimoire. *Milsons Point, New South Wales: Random House Australia, 1999. 625p.* For centuries, magicians have compiled grimoires to call up demons. In Victorian London, one ambitious warlock, Peter Owling, designed a book of shadows to summon the Lord of the Demons, Satan himself. The plan backfired, and Owling was killed, the book ripped into four pieces and sent to the far corners of the Earth. One fragment wound up in a shipment of books destined for the Colonies. Now, at Humberstone College, a converted nineteenth-century gothic convent in Melbourne, a power-hungry group of academics is reassembling Owling's grimoire, bent on the pursuit of eternal life. Similar title: *Third Ring*, Phillip Tomasso; *Frankenstein: The Legacy*, Christopher Schildt; *The Shadow Out of Time*, H. P. Lovecraft; *The Talisman*, Jonathan Aycliffe.

> *Academia • Cursed Objects • Demons • Ghosts • Immortality • Melbourne, Australia • Revenging Revenant*

Williams, Drew.

Night Terrors. *St. Petersburg, Fla.: Barclay Books, 2001. 343p.* (See chapter 8, "Mythological Monsters and 'The Old Ones': Invoking the Dark Gods.")

Williamson, J. N.

Affinity. *New York: Leisure, 2001. 361p.* Quent Wilcox has a bright future ahead of him. He is beginning college at Indiana University, where he plays point guard for the Hoosiers. Life is treating him well until one day after practice, he goes into a trance and faints, not knowing his own identity when he comes to. His family and friends dismiss his random bouts of identity crisis as "typical teenager behavior," but as another personality begins to take over Quent's, he comes to realize that he may not be the person he has always been told he is. Sports fans will enjoy this suspenseful trek for its developed dialogue about basketball. **Similar titles:** *Paperhouse* (film); *Soul Temple*, Steven Lee Climer, *Spanky*, Christopher Fowler, *Fight Club* (film); *Dr. Jekyll and Mr. Hyde*, Robert Louis Stevenson.

> *Academia • Alter Ego • Basketball • Indiana • Parenting • Reincarnation • Telepathy*

Wohl, David. The Witchblade Series.

(See Z., Christina, and David Wohl.)

Z., Christina, and David Wohl. The Witchblade Series.

Witchblade: Origins. *Los Angeles: Top Cow Productions, 2000. 188p.* In this graphic novel series, police officer Sara Pezzini attempts to save a friend from a gangland style execution and accidentally dons the Witchblade, a centuries-old glove that morphs with the bearer's body and produces the ultimate weapon. Now Sara is the target of various crime bosses and monstrous otherwordly beings. **Similar titles:** *Spawn*, Todd McFarland, Alan Moore, and Greg Capullo; The Buffy the Vampire Slayer Series, various authors; The Crow Series, Various Authors; *Lazarus Churchyard*, Warren Ellis and D'Israeli.

🗨 graphic novels

> *Drugs • Fantasy • Graphic Novel • New York City • Organized Crime • Pezzini, Sara (character) • Police Officer as Character*

Witchblade: Revelations. *Los Angeles: Top Cow Productions, 2000. 220p.* Crime bosses are hunting down Officer Sara Pezzini, now the bearer of the Witchblade in the Big Apple, because they feel she is a real threat to their empire. But that is the least of her worries: She is seeing visions and is being pulled into alternate realities. **Similar titles:** *Spawn*, Todd McFarland, Alan Moore, and Greg Capullo; The Buffy the Vampire Slayer Series, various authors; The Crow Series, Various Authors; *Lazarus Churchyard*, Warren Ellis and D'Israeli.

🗨 graphic novels

Drugs • Fantasy • Graphic Novel • New York City • Organized Crime •
Pezzini, Sara (character) • Police Officer as Character

Witchblade: Prevailing. *Los Angeles: Top Cow Productions, 2000. 152p.* Sara Pezzini is having trouble controlling the Witchblade, that is, until it decides to allow a man to be its bearer. This man, unfortunately, is a cold-blooded killer who abuses the power. **Similar titles:** *Spawn*, Todd McFarland, Alan Moore, and Greg Capullo; The Buffy the Vampire Slayer Series, various authors; The Crow Series, Various Authors; *Lazarus Churchyard*, Warren Ellis and D'Israeli.

🗨 graphic novels

Drugs • Fantasy • Graphic Novel • New York City • Organized Crime •
Pezzini, Sara (character) • Police Officer as Character • Serial Killers

Film

Angel Heart. *Alan Parker, dir. 1987. 113 minutes.* Private investigator Harry Angel (Mickey Rourke) is hired by Louis Cyphere (Robert Di Niro) to find a missing singer, Johnny Favorite. His investigation leads him from Times Square to the French Quarter and the bayous of South Louisiana, where Christianity isn't the only religion practiced by the locals. Harry becomes the police's number one suspect when everyone he contacts ends up killed in grisly ways. Why is no one willing to say what has become of Johnny Favorite, and why does Louis Cyphere want Angel to find him? **Similar reads:** *Lovers Living, Lovers Dead*, Richard Lortz; *Rosemary's Baby*, Ira Levin.

African-American Characters • Alter Ego • Dreams • Eroticism • Human
Sacrifice • Incest • New Orleans, Louisiana • New York City • Private
Investigator as Character • Psychosexual Horror • Religion—Voodoo •
Satan (character) • Witchcraft

The Blair Witch Project. *Daniel Myrick and Eduardo Sanchez, dirs. 1999. 80 minutes. The Blair Witch Project* is a pseudo-documentary about three students who disappear while making a film about the Blair Witch legend in Burkittsville, Maryland. All that is known of their disappearance comes from their video footage found in the woods. This low-budget film made by industry unknowns mixes documentary techniques with the horror genre. People particularly prone to motion sickness may be unsettled by the directors' hand-held cameras, which give the film a jerky feel. **Similar reads:** *Demon Circle*, Dan Schmidt; *Wither*, J. G. Passarella.

Blair Witch Haunting • Burkittsville, Maryland • Documentary
Technique • Ghosts • Haunted Houses • Popular Culture • Revenging
Revenant • Wilderness • Witches • Witchcraft

Blair Witch 2: Book of Shadows. *Joe Berlinger, dir. 2000. 91 minutes.* After the success of the pseudo-documentary *The Blair Witch Project*, the small town of Burkittsville, Maryland has been overrun with tourists. Shops now hawk Blair Witch sticks and "genuine" soil from the haunted woods, and competing groups of residents offer Blair Witch camping tours retracing the steps of the ill-fated film crew. One of these tour groups discovers that the Blair Witch is no mere legend but a vengeful spirit that will not be mocked. Although there are some flaws in the script, this movie also deserves credit for its originality. **Similar reads:** *Soul Temple*, Lee Climer; *Wither*, J. G. Passarella.

> *Blair Witch Haunting • Burkittsville, Maryland • Dreams • Popular Culture •*
> *Revenging Revenant • Scholar as Character • Wilderness • Witches • Witchcraft*

Fallen. *Gregory Hoblit, dir. 1998. 123 minutes.* (See chapter 8, "Mythological Monsters and 'The Old Ones': Invoking the Dark Gods.")

The Haunting. *Richard Wise, dir. 1963.) (Black-and-white.) 112 minutes.* (See chapter 4, "Ghosts and Haunted Houses: Dealing with Presences and Absences.")

J. D.'s Revenge. *Arthur Marks, dir. 1976. 95 minutes.* The spirit of J. D., a small-time thug murdered nearly forty years in the past, requires someone to tell his tale to bring his killers to justice, so he possesses a mild-mannered law student. This is one of the few horror films with African-Americans as main characters. Joan Pringle and Lou Gossett star. **Similar reads:** *Thunderland*, Brandon Massey; *The Cleanup*, John Skipp and Craig Spector.

> *African-American Characters • Ghosts • New Orleans, Louisiana • Revenging*
> *Revenant • Secret Sin*

The Omen. *Richard Donner, dir. 1976. 111 minutes.* When the wife of the ambassador to the United States gives birth to a stillborn child, the ambassador substitutes another baby without her knowledge. The years go by, and grisly deaths befall those in close proximity to the child. Further investigation reveals that the foundling is actually the son of Satan and can be stopped only by the seven daggers of Meggado. Lee Remick and Gregory Peck star. **Similar reads:** *The Exorcist*, William Peter Blatty; The Omen Series, various authors.

> *The Antichrist (character) • Apocalypse • Religion—Christianity • Secret Sin*

Rosemary's Baby. *Roman Polanski, dir. 1968. 134 minutes.* A very faithful adaptation of Ira Levin's novel of the same name, *Rosemary's Baby* is about a man who makes a pact with the devil: His wife will bear Satan's child in exchange for his worldly success as an actor. Mia Farrow, John Cassavetes, and Ruth Gordon star. **Similar reads:** *Son of Rosemary*, Ira Levin; *Lovers Living, Lovers Dead*, Richard Lortz.

> *New York City • Pregnancy • Religion—Christianity—Catholicism •*
> *Religion—Satanism • Woodhouse, Rosemary (character)*

The Shining. *Stanley Kubrick, dir. 1980. 142 minutes.* In this film version of Stephen King's novel of the same name, Jack Nicholson stars as recovering alcoholic and abusive father and husband Jack Torrence. After losing his teaching position for assaulting one of his pupils, Torrence is given a second chance as winter caretaker of the Overlook Hotel, isolated in the Rocky Mountains. But the isolation and the hotel's ghosts push Jack over the edge and make him attempt to kill his wife and son. Shelly Duvall and Scatman Crothers also star. **Similar reads:** *Nazareth Hill*, Ramsey Campbell; *Dr. Jekyll and Mr. Hyde*, Robert Louis Stevenson.

> *Alcoholism • Colorado • Haunted House*

Sleepy Hollow. *Tim Burton, dir. 1999. 105 minutes.* In this retelling of Washington Irving's story "The Legend of Sleepy Hollow," Johnny Depp stars as criminal investigator Ichabod Crain, who has come to Sleepy Hollow to investigate some mysterious murders. Crain, for all of his scientific methods of investigating a crime scene, is not prepared for the Headless Horseman (Christopher Walken) and the supernatural means employed to bring him to life and do the bidding of Katrina van Tassel's (Christian Ricci) evil stepmother (Miranda Richardson). Burton's reinterpretation of Irving's classic story is eerie and atmospheric, incorporating elements from myth and fairy tales. Christopher Lee also stars. **Similar reads:** *Selected Tales*, Edgar Allan Poe; *Looking Glass: Ghost Stories Chosen by Edward Gorey*, Edward Gorey (editor).

Alternative Literature • Colonial America • Crain, Ichabod (character) • Fantasy • Gothicism • New York State • Private Investigator as Character • Secret Sin • Sleepy Hollow Legend, The • Witchcraft

Stigmata. *Rupert Wainwright, dir. 1999. 103 minutes.* A New York hairdresser who isn't particularly religious receives from her mother the rosary of a deceased Brazilian priest who was said to have performed miracles. Now possessed by the priest, her body manifests stigmata as it struggles to tell the story of a female apostle whose words the Catholic Church silenced. This eerie film is a sort of feminist version of *The Exorcist*. It is visually dazzling. Patricia Arquette and Gabriel Byrne star. **Similar reads:** *The Exorcist*, William Peter Blatty; *Requiem*, Graham Joyce.

Alternative History • Clergy as Character • Dreams • Feminism • Pittsburgh, Pennsylvania • Religion—Christianity—Catholicism • Stigmata

Supernatural. *Victor Halperin, dir. 1933. (Black-and-white.) 60 minutes.* A woman who is executed for murdering her lovers vows she'll return from the dead, and she does when she possesses the body of Carole Lombard, a virginal heiress, and causes her to misbehave. **Similar reads:** *Ungrateful Dead*, Gary L. Holleman; *The Influence*, Ramsey Campbell.

Parapsychology • Serial Killer

What Lies Beneath. *Robert Zemeckis, dir. 2000. 129 minutes.* (See chapter 4, "Ghosts and Haunted Houses: Dealing with Presences and Absences.")

Our Picks

June's Picks: *The 37th Mandala*, Mark Laidlaw (Leisure); *Ambrosial Flesh* and *Drawn to the Grave*, Maryann Mitchell (Leisure); *Dark Sister*, Graham Joyce (Tor); *Dorcas Good: The Diary of a Salem Witch* and *Salem's Ghosts*, Rose Earhart (Pendleton Books); *The Picture of Dorian Gray*, Oscar Wilde (Penguin); *Rosemary's Baby*, Ira Levin (Bantam); *Voodoo Child*, Michael Reaves (Tor); *Warlock: A Novel of Possession*, Perry Brass (Belhue Press); *The Witching Hour*, Anne Rice (Ballantine); *The Blair Witch Project* (film); *Sleepy Hollow* (film); *Stigmata* (film).

7

Tony's Picks: *Dead in the Water*, Nancy Holder (Bantam); *Hideaway*, Dean Koontz (Putnam); *Lovers Living, Lovers Dead*, Richard Lortz (Second Chance Press); *The Manitou*, Graham Masterton (Olmstead); *Spanky*, Christopher Fowler (Little, Brown); *Angel Heart* (film); *Stigmata* (film).

Chapter 8

Mythological Monsters and "The Old Ones": Invoking the Dark Gods

Nearly every religion and mythology has its monsters. From Kali the Destroyer in India, to the destructive Cyclops of ancient Greek legend, to Lucifer in Christianity, virtually every culture incorporates some personification of chaos and anarchy into its belief system. This being, although humanoid, is nonetheless monstrous and destructive, often threatening entire populations. In fact, these mythological destroyers are arguably the precursors for the monsters of contemporary horror literature, since "monsters" from these old stories are divine warnings about the consequences of human actions (the word "monster" derives from the Latin *monstere*, to show). Primitive humans both embraced and feared these personifications of destruction, as they acknowledged their own animal passions and their connection to and dependence on the natural world. Later religions, however, emphasized the human ability to transcend mortal desire and suffering and to perhaps control nature itself, so these later belief systems "demonized" the monster, making it totally Other, a repository of all that its adherents loathed and feared about themselves. A quick study of horror titles will indicate that the genre is generated primarily by Anglo-Saxon (English and Germanic) cultures. These two cultures are heavily influenced by strict forms of Protestantism that portray Satan, the manifestation of all that is bestial in humans, as lurking everywhere, always ready to seduce weak-willed souls from the path of righteousness.

Because of the raw power that they possess, mythological monsters make great fodder for horror fiction. They are ready-made symbols of all we fear. The Judeo-Christian *Bible* alone is an inexhaustive source of evil portents, impish monsters, ghoulish harbingers of death (think of The Four Horsemen of the Apocalypse, which Charles Grant incorporates brilliantly into his Millenium Quartet), and hellish overlords. Even human biblical characters such as the murderous Cain and the treacherous Judas have made appearances in horror, for some vampire mythologies see Cain as the father of all vampires, since it was he who first slew his brother; others see Judas as the father of all vampires because his betrayal of

Christ caused him to walk the Earth, forever damned. In Tom Holland's *Sleeper in the Sands*, all vampires can ultimately be traced back to ancient Egypt, where King Tut's father embraced monotheism under the tutelage of the biblical Joseph. Lillith, the first wife of Adam, mentioned in the *Talmud*, is the mother of all vampires.

And then there are the more recent, fictional mythologies, populated with those monsters that began as the creations of horror writers and became cultural icons afterwards. Some authors, such as H. P. Lovecraft, found set mythologies to be too constraining, so they created their own mythological monsters. One of the most famous of all these (bowing to perhaps only Godzilla, an "imported" mythological creation), Lovecraft's Cthulu mythos has become so ingrained in the American horror subconscious that later writers, and Hollywood directors, have based entire texts or films on the reawakening of Cthulu or on the accidental reading of *The Necronomicon*, which some fans argue is only half fiction. Lovecraft's Cthulhu Mythos has resurfaced at various times through the fiction of his "disciples," such as his contemporaries August Derleth and C. M. Eddy, and in the fiction of later authors like Ramsey Campbell, Victor Heck, and William Browning Spencer.

Whether a mythological monster is based on an existing religion and set of folk beliefs, or is created by a writer, readers are reminded that "the old ones," or the old deities, are ever-present and can be summoned at any time, even accidentally. Their eagerness to invade the human world when awakened by an innocent is what makes them so frightening; they remind us of the consequences of our actions, regardless of our intentions. Representative works in this subgenre include the weird tales of two of the masters of pulp horror fiction, Lovecraft and Arthur Machen. To give a good sense of the subgenre's evolution, we have also annotated in this section more recent works, novels such as Victor Heck's *A Darkness Inbred*, Dean Koontz's *Phantoms*, Elizabeth Hand's *Black Light*, and Anne Rice's *The Servant of the Bones*.

Note: Tales about mythological and dark gods can also be found in the collections and anthologies described in chapter 17. Refer to the subject/keyword index for specific titles under the keywords "mythology," "folklore," and "Cthulhu mythos."

Appeals: Familiarity with Monsters from Mythology and Religion; Believability (for Some); Learning About Other Cultures and Their Gods/Mythologies; Tendency to Be Thought-Provoking; Complexity; Intertextuality

Aczon, Kimile.

BJ: A Supernatural Horror Story. *Packland, Fla.: Universal Publishing, 1998. 260p.* Many lives were changed at the exact moment that Denise and Wesley Johnson conceived a child: namely, five people in various parts of California now find that they have been miraculously cured of various psychological and physical ills. The five start a pilgrimage to King's Mansion, the system of projects where the Johnsons live, as does a mysterious and sinister stranger with evil intentions. Here, the emphasis is on characterization over action. **Similar titles:** The Spirit Chronicles, Keith Rummel; *The Promise of Eden*, Eric Durchholz; *Dark Soul*, M. Martin Hunt; *Thunderland*, Brandon Massey

> *African-American Characters • Blindness • California • Childhood • Demons • Handicapped Characters • Religion—Christianity*

Albertson, C. E.

The Red God. *Lincoln, Neb.: iUniverse-Writer's Showcase Press, 2000. 224p.* Archeology blends with the supernatural in this political-thriller-meets-horror-novel starring agent John Ashly, a man who has lost his memory and doesn't even know his own identity. This will appeal to fans of action-oriented novels. **Similar titles:** *The Bad Place,*

Dean Koontz; *Amnesia*, Andrew Neiderman; *The Mummy Returns*, Max Allan Collins.

> *Amnesia • Archeology • Espionage • Religion—Ancient Egyptian*

Allen, Bill.

Shadow Heart. *Alma, Ark.: Yard Dog Press, 1998. 210p.* (See chapter 7, "Demonic Possession, Satanism, Black Magic, and Witches and Warlocks: The Devil Made Me Do It.")

Allred, Sam.

If Witches We Be. *San Jose, Calif.: Writer's Showcase, 2000. 218p.* (See chapter 16, "Comic Horror: Laughing at Our Fears.")

Aycliffe, Jonathan.

The Talisman. *Aschroft, B.C.: Ash-Tree Press, 1999. 209p.* An archeological dig unearths a Babylonian statue with the body of a man but a horned head and a winged torso. The statue is brought to the British Museum, where it begins to exert a mysterious influence on people. Could be the new millennium's version of *The Omen.* **Similar titles:** *Ancient Images*, Ramsey Campbell; *Darkness Demands*, Simon Clark; *The Exorcist*, William Peter Blatty; *The Shadow Out of Time*, H. P. Lovecraft.

> *Archeologist as Character • Blindness • Cursed Objects • Epistolary•*
> *Format • London, England • Magic • Museums • Satan (character)*

Bradbury, Ray.

From the Dust Returned. *London: Simon & Schuster, 2001. 256p.* A Victorian mansion in a small Illinois town is the site of a reunion for a family of immortals reminiscent of the Addams family or the Munsters. Grand Mere is a 4,000-year-old mummy, a pharaoh's daughter, who lives in the attic. Uncle Einars sports enormous wings and allows neighborhood children to use him as a kite. Other kin include vampires and ghosts, and Timothy, a mortal foundling who wishes to be special in the ways of his adoptive family. This novel is a 2001 nominee for a Bram Stoker Award. **Similar titles:** *Santa Steps Out*, Robert Devereaux; *American Gods*, Neil Gaiman; The Universal Monsters Series, various authors; *A Graveyard for Lunatics*, Ray Bradbury.

> *Fantasy • Illinois • Immortality • Mummies • Vampires*

Campbell, Ramsey.

The Hungry Moon. *New York: Tom Doherty, 1987. 360p.* An evangelical preacher from California travels to a small town near Manchester, England, where he decides that he will convert the local population, beginning by doing away with their practice of decorating a nearby cave with a rather pagan figure made of flowers. A local schoolteacher named Diana opposes him, and she soon discovers the reason behind the tribute at the cave: to appease a creature "older than Satan" that is rumored to have come from the moon. When the preacher himself is possessed by the creature, can Diana stop "the hungry moon" from devouring the life force of all humanity and lift the darkness that has suddenly enveloped the town? This is a fine novel that is a cross between dark fantasy and magical realism. **Similar titles:** *Awash In the Blood*, John Wooley; The Millenium Quartet, Charles Grant; *The Wicker Man*, Robin Hardy and Anthony Shaffer; The *Wicker Man* (film).

> *Animals Run Rampant • Clergy as Character • Dogs • England •*
> *Religion—Christianity • Religion—Paganism • Spiders • Teacher as Character*

Clark, Simon.

Darkness Demands. *New York: Leisure, 2001. 395p.* John Newton just wants to begin work on his next novel, but his plans are interrupted when he receives letters wrapped around bits of gravestones. The letters are written in a gothic script on antique paper and make quaintly spelled, mysterious demands. First he's asked to leave a bar of chocolate on the "grief stowne" of Jess Bowen, then a pint of stout and a red ball lest dire consequences befall him. But John isn't the only person in the village to receive such communiqués, nor are the letters the work of a clever prankster. Neighbors, and their grandparents decades before them, have received the same demands, and know that they ignore them at their peril. Are the letters the work of an ancient and dark force that resides in the Necropolis nearby, an ancient Victorian cemetery that holds upward of 80,000 graves? This is a well written and original work that is genuinely frightening. **Similar titles:** *The Talisman*, Jonathan Aycliffe; *Bag of Bones*, Stephen King; *Riverwatch*, Joseph M. Nassie; *The Book of the Dark*, William Meikle.

> *Afterlife, The • Alzheimer's Disease • Cemeteries • Curse • Demons • England •*
> *Human Sacrifice • Parenting • Senior Citizen as Character • Subterranean*
> *Monsters • Writer as Character*

Vampyrrhic. *London: Hoddard & Stoughton, 1998. 441p.* (See chapter 6, "Vampires and Werewolves: Children of the Night.")

Clegg, Douglas.

The Halloween Man. *New York: Leisure, 1998. 360p.* (See chapter 10, "Small Town Horror: Villages of the Damned.")

Purity. *Baltimore: Cemetery Dance Publications, 2000. 118p.* Owen Crites, teenaged son of a gardener to the rich on Outerbridge Island, pines for debutante Jenna Montgomery, a childhood sweetheart who comes to stay each summer with her parents. Devastated when Jenna arrives the summer of their eighteenth year with preppie tennis star Jimmy McTeague in tow, Owen schemes to win her back by seducing his sexually conflicted rival, then presenting himself as the victim to Jenna. He also plans to win over his love by praying to an ancient Philippine god, whose statue he found in a cave. **Similar titles:** *Gift Giver*, Jean Sapin; *Naomi*, Douglas Clegg; *Black Butterflies*, John Shirley; *Travel Many Roads*, Robert E. Wheeler.

> *Alcoholism • Homoeroticism • Marriage • New England • Obsession •*
> *Psychosexual Horror*

Climer, Steven Lee.

Soul Temple. *Grandview, Mo.: Dark Tales, 2000. 181p.* After his mother's death, a young Spencer Welles accidentally invokes Thoth, a fallen angel who now thrives on death and misery. Now a college student, Welles must discover a way to rid himself of Thoth's maniacal musings before Thoth uses him to kill his friends, his family, his fiancée, and his unborn child. This is a well written and subtle text, with a storyline bordering on both the supernatural and the psychological. **Similar titles:** *Fight Club* (film); *Spanky*, Christopher Fowler; *Frankenstein*, Mary Shelley; The Spirit Chronicles, Keith Rummel.

> *Academia • Alter Ego • Angels • Death (character) • Fairies • Michigan •*
> *Parenting • Pregnancy • Suicide • Thoth (character)*

Conley, Robert J.

Brass. *New York: Leisure, 1999. 310p.* Millennia ago, according to a Cherokee legend, the sons of Thunder defeated Untsaiyi, or Brass, an evil spirit with metallic skin and a fatal love of gambling, pinning him to the floor of the sea. In the late twentieth century, an unsuspecting Army Corps of Engineers frees Brass while cleaning up a strip of beach. Now Brass emerges in this strange new world, determined to win a fortune and kill anyone who stands in his way, and only someone who still remembers the old legends can stop him. **Similar titles:** *Riverwatch*, Joseph M. Nassie; *The Manitou*, Graham Masterton; *Ghost Dance*, Mark T. Sullivan; *Crota*, Owl Goingback.

California • Cherokees • Gambling • Immortality • Las Vegas, Nevada • Police Officer as Character • Religion—Native American • Shapeshifters

Constantine, Storm. The Grigori Trilogy.

Stalking Tender Prey. *Decatur, Ga.: Meisha Merlin, 1998, ©1995. 484p.* Jackie Collins has spent a few months living in England, reading up on Tom Stoppard and Alan Bennett. She begins to write a mystery thriller after she meets Aleister Crowley, Tanith Lee, and Joseph Campbell in the local pub. She teams up with these characters to examine both the dark and the numinous. Constantine's lush and haunting dark fantasy explores the secret nooks and crannies of our mythologies and religions, in rich language and with vivid settings. **Similar titles:** *Dark Soul*, M. Martin Hunt; *Blood Covenant*, Marilyn Lamb; *The Promise of Eden*, Eric Durchholz; *Soul Temple*, Steven Lee Climer.

Angels • England • Crowley, Aleister (character) • Fantasy • Grigori, The (characters)

Scenting Hallowed Blood. *Decatur, Ga.: Meisha Merlin, 1999, ©1996. 386p.* This sequel continues with the story of Peveral Othman, who is the fallen angel Shemyaaza, relating his adventures after leaving Little Moor with Daniel and Owen and Lily Winter. This time they move to Cornwall, but is he here to help the Grigori, or does he have plans of his own? **Similar titles:** *Dark Soul*, M. Martin Hunt; *Blood Covenant*, Marilyn Lamb; *The Promise of Eden*, Eric Durchholz; *Soul Temple*, Steven Lee Climer.

Angels • Egypt • England • Fantasy • Grigori, The (characters)

Stealing Sacred Fire. *Atlanta, Ga.: Meisha Merlin, 2000, ©1997. 356p.* Peverel Othman has come home, although not as himself. Through the old magic of the Grigori, he is now once again Shemyaza, an angel of awesome power who led the rebellion of angels to mate with and enslave humans. Now as this millennium draws to a close, Shemyaza calls his followers to him for the final battle to decide who controls the fate of humanity. Answering his call are his six Grigori brothers and sisters, who once again want to rule humanity for their own pleasure. **Similar titles:** *Dark Soul*, M. Martin Hunt; *Blood Covenant*, Marilyn Lamb; *The Promise of Eden*, Eric Durchholz; *Soul Temple*, Steven Lee Climer.

 8

Angels • Apocalypse • Egypt • England • Fantasy • Grigori, The (characters)

Devereaux, Robert.

Santa Steps Out: A Fairy Tale for Grown-ups. *New York: Leisure, 2000. 47p.* (See chapter 15, "Splatterpunk: The Gross Out.")

Due, Tananarive. The My Soul to Keep Series.

My Soul to Keep. *New York: HarperCollins, 1997. 352p.* An African immortal must deal with human feelings of love and loyalty toward his human family when his fellow immortals wish him to sever all connections to protect the secret of their existence. Due's emphasis is on characterization and psychology, but well-thought-out plots, the use of historical fact, and a suspenseful climax make this not only unique but also enjoyable. **Similar titles:** *Interview with the Vampire* and *Servant of the Bones*, Anne Rice; The Saint-Germain Chronicles, Chelsea Quinn Yarbro; The Hunger Series, Whitley Strieber.

> *African-American Characters • Immortality • Jacobs-Wolde, Jessica (character) • Journalist as Character • Magic • Marriage • Miami, Florida • Religion—Christianity • Wolde, David (character)*

The Living Blood. *New York: Pocket, 2001. 515p.* Jessica Jacobs-Wolde's life was destroyed when her husband, the immortal David Wolde, disappeared after killing both their daughter Kira and Jessica herself, then reviving Jessica to immortality with his healing blood. In this sequel to *My Soul to Keep*, Jessica, hiding with her surviving daughter in rural Botswana, attempts to make sense of her new existence as she uses her altered blood to save the incurably ill. But her daughter Fana was born with the living blood in her veins, and at the age of three can raise a storm, kill with a thought, and possess her mother's mind. Jessica's only hope of teaching Fana to control her dangerous talents is to travel to Ethiopia and find the immortals' hidden colony. Winner of the American Book Award. **Similar titles:** *Mother Julian and the Gentle Vampire*, Jack Pantaleo; *Awash in the Blood*, John Wooley; *Interview With the Vampire*, Anne Rice; *Voice of the Blood*, Jemiah Jefferson.

> *Africa • Florida • Immortality • Jacobs-Wolde, Jessica (character) • Parenting • Wolde, David (character)*

Fowler, Christopher.

Spanky. *London: Little, Brown-Warner, 1998, ©1994. 338p.* (See chapter 7, "Demonic Possession, Satanism, Black Magic, and Witches and Warlocks: The Devil Made Me Do It.")

Gaiman, Neil.

American Gods. *London: Headline, 2001. 504p.* (See chapter 16, "Comic Horror: Laughing at Our Fears.")

Giron, Sephera.

House of Pain. *New York: Leisure, 2001. 360p.* (See chapter 7, "Demonic Possession, Satanism, Black Magic, and Witches and Warlocks: The Devil Made Me Do It.")

Goingback, Owl.

Crota. *New York: Donald I. Fine, 1996. 292p.* A Missouri town is terrorized by a demonic beast with a hunger for humans and other animals. Only the famed hunter Jay Little Hawk, with the aid of the town sheriff and an old shaman, can bring down the beast. This is a suspenseful, fast read. **Similar titles:** *Ghost Dance*, Mark T. Sullivan; *Smoke Signals*, Octavio Ramos, Jr.; *The Manitou*, Graham Masterton; *Chancers*, Gerald Vizenore.

> *Demons • Missouri • Native American Characters • Religion—Native American • Subterranean Monsters*

Darker Than Night. *New York: Penguin-New American Library, 1999. 342p.* Horror novelist Michael Anthony inherits his grandmother's home, only to discover that it acts as an entrance point for shadowy creatures from the netherworld. Can he stop the "boogers" from destroying the world as we know it—beginning with his own family? Based on a real world account of a 1971 incident in Spain, during which mysterious stains resembling "faces" appeared on the floor of a cottage. Goingback's emphasis is on atmosphere. **Similar titles:** *The Lurker at the Threshold*, H. P. Lovecraft; *Five Mile House*, Karen Novack; *Bag of Bones*, Stephen King.

> *Cursed Objects • Family Curse • Haunted Houses • Missouri • Native American Characters • Religion—Native American • Writer as Character*

Golden, Christopher.

Straight on 'Til Morning. *New York: Signet, 2001. 320p.* (See chapter 14, "Psychological Horror: It's All In Your Head.")

Strangewood. *New York: Signet, 1999. 304p.* A writer of an extremely popular children's fantasy series finds himself being stalked—but not by a crazed fan. Rather, disgruntled characters from his *Strangewood* books are looking for revenge against their creator. They will stop at nothing, not even kidnapping his only child and causing him to lapse into a coma, to get what they want. Now children's writer Thomas Randall has no choice but to go into a coma himself to rescue his son. This gentle read is highly original. **Similar titles:** *The Dark Half*, Stephen King; *Phantom Feast*, Diana Barron, *Paperhouse* (film); *Thunderland*, Brandon Massey.

> *Children's Literature • Fantasy • Parenting • Stalkers • Television Industry • Writer as Character*

Grant, Charles. The Millennium Quartet.

Symphony. *New York: Tor, 1997. 332p.* The first of the Millenium Quartet novels, Grant's tale is about a group of maniacal murderers who hitchhike across country with a strange, shadowy driver, committing mass murder on the way. Their goal is to usher in the apocalypse by murdering a small town reverend on the East Coast. Grant's novel is cleverly written to correspond with the movements of a symphony, with emphasis on character and mood. **Similar titles:** *The Scream*, John Skipp and Craig Spector; *Dark Soul*, M. Martin Hunt; *Dark Resurrection*, John Karr.

> *Apocalypse • Bannock, John (character) • Chisolm, Casey (character) • Clergy as Character • Four Horsemen of the Apocalypse (characters) • Music—Classical • New England • Religion—Christianity*

In the Mood. *New York: Forge, 1998. 304p.* In this second volume of The Millennium Quartet, writer John Bannock becomes obsessed with mass murder, finding himself a target for "the Four Horsemen." Can he stop them before a worldwide famine ushers in the apocalypse? Based on music, like Grant's earlier novel *Symphony*, but on Big Band rather than classical. **Similar titles:** *The Scream*, John Skipp and Craig Spector; *Dark Soul*, M. Martin Hunt; *Dark Resurrection*, John Karr.

> *Antichrist, The (character) • Apocalypse • Bannock, John (character) • Chisolm, Casey (character) • Clergy as Character • Four Horsemen of the Apocalypse (characters) • Natural Disasters • New Orleans, Louisiana • Serial Killers • Writer as Character*

Chariot. *New York: Tor, 1998. 309p.* (See chapter 13, "Ecological Horror: Rampant Animals and Mother Nature's Revenge.")

Riders in the Sky. *New York: Forge, 1999. 304p.* This, the final book of The Millennium Quartet, follows the Four Horsemen to an isolated island off the New Jersey coast, where they gather for the fourth and final showdown with the Reverend Casey Chisholm, the only human who can defeat death. Grant's emphasis is on atmosphere and dialogue, on the eeriness of the calm before the storm. **Similar titles:** *The Scream*, John Skipp and Craig Spector; *Dark Soul*, M. Martin Hunt; *Dark Resurrection*, John Karr; *Ordinary Horror*, David Searcy.

> *Apocalypse • Bannock, John (character) • Chisolm, Casey (character) • Four Horsemen of the Apocalypse (characters) • New England • New Jersey • Religion—Christianity • Writer as Character*

Hand, Elizabeth.

Black Light. *New York: HarperPrism, 2000. 380p.* The ancient gods never really die. Instead, they are reborn again and again in an endless cycle. This time, one of the old gods is about to be reborn in Kamensic, a sleepy little village in the hills of rural New York where old television actors go to live lives of quiet decadence, and where death by misadventure and suicide is an all too common occurrence. But the old god's rebirth is dependent on the cooperation of a seventeen-year-old girl, herself the reincarnation of another ancient deity. Hand's prose is literate and compelling. **Similar titles:** *Symphony*, Charles Grant; *The Wicker Man*, Robin Hardy and Anthony Shaffer; *Midwinter of the Spirit*, Phil Rickman.

> *The Benandanti • Fantasy • Human Sacrifice • Magic • New York State • Parallel Universe • Popular Culture • Reincarnation • Religion—Paganism • Warnick, Balthazar (character)*

Hays, Clark, and Kathleen McFall.

The Cowboy and the Vampire. *St. Paul, Minn.: Llewellyn, 1999. 318p.* (See chapter 16, "Comic Horror: Laughing at Our Fears.")

Heck, Victor.

A Darkness Inbred. *Kansas City, Mo.: Dark Tales Publications, 2000. 155p.* Nate and Paige, a young couple traveling through the gothic south, find themselves stranded after a slight auto accident. The first bystanders who come by, however, are anything but innocent, and they kidnap the couple and take them back to their family farm, where the family patriarch is raising and caring for demonic creatures, which must be fed and nurtured. This is a truly creepy novel. **Similar titles:** *Correlated Contents*, James Ambuehl; *Cold Print*, Ramsey Campbell; *The Lurker at the Threshold*, H. P. Lovecraft; *Tideland*, Mitch Cullen.

> *Cthulhu Mythos • Missouri • Pregnancy • Religion—Christianity • Religion—Satanism • South, The • Torture*

Holland, Tom. The Lord of the Dead Series.

Lord of the Dead. *New York: Simon & Schuster, 1995. 342p.* (See chapter 6, "Vampires and Werewolves: Children of the Night.")

Slave of My Thirst. *New York: Simon & Schuster, 1996. 421p.* (See chapter 6, "Vampires and Werewolves: Children of the Night.")

Deliver Us from Evil. *New York: Warner, 1998. 578p.* At the close of the Interregnum, Robert Foxe's Puritan mother and father are killed by Cavaliers who have recently returned after being banished from England. But these particular Cavaliers are in possession of a mysterious being that can raise the dead. Because he has a special quality, Robert himself survives meeting this creature. Now orphaned, he is taken to London by two immortals who eventually help him discover the nature of his and the mysterious creature's existence. Holland's novel is a breathtaking, intricate tale of the world of immortals, interwoven with the history of Elizabethan and Restoration England, Jewish folklore, and colonial America. **Similar titles:** *Murcheston: The Wolf's Tale*, David Holland; *Slave of My Thirst*, Tom Holland; *Lord of the Dead*, Tom Holland; The Vampire Chronicles, Anne Rice.

> *al-Vakhel, Haroun (character)* • *Colonial New England* • *Dee, John (character)* • *Demons* • *Epic Structure* • *History, Use of* • *Immortality* • *London, England* • *Lowe, Rabbi Jehuda (character)* • *Magic* • *Marlow, Christopher (character)* • *Milton, John (character)* • *Native American characters* • *Prague, Czechoslovakia* • *Restoration England* • *Rochester, Lord (character)* • *Stonehenge* • *Vampire's Point of View*

The Sleeper in the Sands. *London, Little, Brown-Abacus, 1999, ©1998. 428p.* This last tale in the Lord of the Dead Series is a fictionalized account of Howard Carter's excursion into the Valley of the Kings in Cairo, in search of King Tut's tomb. This intricate frame tale of Carter's letters leads us back to Haroun al-Vakhel, the Pasha from *Lord of the Dead* who turns Lord Byron into an immortal. Here we discover how al-Vakhel himself became undead, how the Egyptian pharaohs maintained their immortality, and what happened to the biblical Joseph after the destruction of the house of Jacob. Holland also includes notes on characters and historical accuracy. **Similar titles:** *The Vampire Lestat*, Anne Rice; *Queen of the Damned*, Anne Rice; *Into the Mummy's Tomb*, John Richard Stevens; *The Mummy Returns*, Max Allan Collins.

> *Afterlife, The* • *al-Vakhel, Haroun (character)* • *Archeology* • *Carter, Howard (character)* • *Cursed Objects* • *Egypt* • *Epic Structure* • *Haidee (character)* • *History, Use of* • *Immortality* • *Joseph (character)* • *Lillith (character)* • *Magic* • *Monotheism* • *Mummies* • *Nefertiti (character)* • *Religion—Ancient Egyptian* • *Religion—Islam* • *Religion—Judaism* • *Tutenkamen (character)* • *Vampire's Point of View*

Hollis, Claire.

The Light. *Tampa, FL: Warfare Publications, 1999. 176p.* In this Christian fiction crossover, JJ and Lynn encounter life-threatening challenges when they uncover the secret earthly headquarters of Satan's kingdom while visiting the sleepy little town of Centerville. Rulers of the dark world retaliate by issuing a death contract against them. Can the Light save JJ and Lynn? **Similar titles:** *Soul Temple*, Steven Lee Climer; *Blood Covenant*, Marilyn Lamb; *Dark Soul*, M. Martin Hunt; *Spirit of Independence*, Keith Rummel.

8

> *Angels* • *Demons* • *Religion—Christianity* • *Satan (character)* • *Subterranean Monsters*

Hunt, M. Martin.

Dark Soul. *Baltimore: AmErica House, 2000. 416p.* Charles Simone, an evil entity disguised as a human, is using low-life criminals from the streets of Houston, Texas, to search for and destroy human beings with "blue auras" around them. Jack Wise, a police officer who can see into the future, as well as into people's hearts, is one of those humans with a blue aura, so he is gunned down in a liquor store robbery. Wise must now fight to save his own life, and he must join forces with others like himself to face Simone in the ultimate battle of good versus evil, played out among humans who are only beginning to understand their purpose in the scheme of creation. This Christian fiction crossover is complex and clever.

Similar titles: *The Blood of the Lamb*, Thomas F. Monteleone; *Soul Temple*, Steven Lee Climer; *Project Resurrection*, Karen Duval; *Blood Covenant*, Marilyn Lamb.

> *Afterlife, The • Angels • Demons • Epic Structure • Hispanic-American Characters • Houston, Texas • Police Officer as Character • Reincarnation • Religion—Christianity*

Johnstone, William W.

Cat's Cradle. *New York: Kensington-Pinnacle, 1999. 400p.* In this novel, human and cat, the latter ruled by Satan, survive on human flesh. If a victim happens to survive their attack, he or she turns into a beast. Also, Satan calls upon the cats in the town and county to attack humans. This book is full of gore and is not for the weak of stomach. **Similar titles:** The Devil's Kiss Series, William W. Johnstone; *The Battle for Barnstable*, Alan M. Brooker; *The Apostate*, Paul Lonardo.

> *Animals Run Rampant • Cats • Federal Bureau of Investigation • Police Officer as Character • Satan (character) • Shapeshifters*

Johnstone, William W. The Devil's Kiss Series.

The Devil's Kiss. *New York: Kensington-Pinnacle, 1999. 400p.* The Devil uses sex to take control of a community. Readers who enjoy action-oriented, visceral horror, including some graphic sex, will enjoy this novel. **Similar titles:** *Dark Soul*, M. Martin Hunt; *Spirit of Independence*, Keith Rummel; The Millenium Quartet, Charles Grant.

> *Apocalypse • Eroticism • Mind Control • Religion—Christianity • Satan (character)*

The Devil's Heart. *New York: Kensington-Pinnacle, 1999. 400p.* Sam Balon Sr. returns from the dead to help his son with the new burden placed on his shoulders and to help his wife through hard times to come. Johnstone will take readers as far into Satan's covens as they will ever want to go. **Similar titles:** *Dark Soul*, M. Martin Hunt; *Spirit of Independence*, Keith Rummel; The Millenium Quartet, Charles Grant.

> *Afterlife, The • Angels • Apocalypse • Demons • God (character) • Religion—Christianity • Satan (character)*

The Devil's Touch. *New York: Kensington-Pinnacle, 1999. 400p.* In the third novel of The Devil's Kiss Series, Satan is behind the rape, torture, and murder of nearly an entire community. Citizens are turned into zombies or vampires. Readers who enjoy action-oriented, visceral horror, including some graphic sex, will enjoy this novel. **Similar titles:** *Dark Soul*, M. Martin Hunt; *Spirit of Independence*, Keith Rummel; The Millenium Quartet, Charles Grant.

> *Apocalypse • God (character) • Rape • Religion—Christianity • Satan (character) • Torture • Zombies*

Joyce, Graham.

The Tooth Fairy. *New York: Tor, 1998. 320p.* As a young boy, Sam awakens one night to find an eerie presence in his room, which he believes to be the tooth fairy. The sinister being follows him throughout his childhood, causing him and his friends to get in trouble for things perpetrated by the Tooth Fairy. Sam can only go off to college when he discovers a way to force the fairy to leave him alone. This folkloric novel challenges the harmless "myths" we learn in childhood. **Similar titles:** *Santa Steps Out*, Robert Devereaux; *Soul Temple*, Steven Lee Climer; *Thunderland*, Brandon Massey.

> *Alter Ego • Childhood • Dreams • England • Eroticism • Fairies • Fantasy • Precognition • Secret Sin • Shapeshifters • The Tooth Fairy (character) • Wish Fulfillment*

Kiernan, Caitlan R.

Silk. *New York: Penguin, 1998. 353p.* (See chapter 14, "Psychological Horror: It's All In Your Head.")

Kihn, Greg.

Big Rock Beat. *New York: Forge-Doherty, 1998. 351p.* (See chapter 16, "Comic Horror: Laughing at Our Fears.")

King, Stephen.

Needful Things. *New York: Penguin, 1991. 690p.* Castle Rock, Maine, is a peaceful little town. It's not exactly Mayberry, but everyone agrees to keep certain secrets and to disagree on the fine points of theology and morality to keep the peace. Then Leland Gaunt comes to town and opens a curiosity shop in a vacant building on Main Street. Leland's store carries everyone's heart's desire, but the prices are ones they can't afford. **Similar titles:** *The Store*, Bentley Little; *Salems' Lot*, Stephen King; *Obsession*, Ramsey Campbell.

> *Castle Rock, Maine • Pangborn, Alan (character) • Police Officer as Character • Religion—Christianity—Catholicism • Religion—Christianity—Protestantism • Satan (character)*

Koontz, Dean.

Phantoms. *New York: Putnam, 1983. 352p.* This is one of Koontz's best. More than half of the residents of Snowfield, California, have either mysteriously disappeared or have died. Dr. Jennifer Paige, her fourteen-year-old sister Lisa, and Sheriff Bryce Hammond must get to the bottom of these strange occurrences, while they avoid being gruesomely killed by It, the shapeshifting creature that seems to know each person's innermost fears. **Similar titles:** *Ghost Story*, Peter Straub; *Clickers*, J. F. Gonzalez and Mark Williams; *'Salem's Lot,* Stephen King*; Old Fears*, John Wooley and Ron Wolfe.

> *Computers • History, Use of • Satan (character) • Shapeshifters • Subterranean Monsters*

Twilight Eyes. *New York: Berkley, 1985. 451p.* (See chapter 12, "Technohorror: Evil Hospitals, Military Screw-Ups, Scientific Goofs, and Alien Invasions.")

Lawrence, Charlotte.

The Rag Bone Man. *St. Paul, Minn.: Llewellyn, 1999, ©1994. 312p.* Rian McGuire owns a New Age bookstore in Maryland, where she lives an everyday existence as a believer in neo-Paganism. Enter the Rag Bone Man, a homeless wanderer who leaves a mysterious book for Rian to find, a book that awakens both powers she didn't know she possessed and the evil demon who wants to destroy her. This is an easy and enjoyable read. **Similar titles:** *Murder at Witches Bluff*, Silver Ravenwolf; *Smoke Signals*, Octavio Ramos, Jr.; *Riverwatch*, Joseph M. Nassie; *Black Light*, Elizabeth Hand; *A Game of Colors*, John Urbancik; *Project Resurrection*, Karen Duval.

8

> *Cursed Objects • Demons • Dreams • Magic • Maryland • Religion—Paganism • Tarot, The • Witchcraft*

Little, Bentley.

 The Revelation. *New York: Signet, 1999. 326p.* The quiet town of Randall, Arizona, is shattered by unexplainable occurrences: vandalism of public buildings, disappearing residents, an unnaturally high miscarriage rate. Gordon just wants to protect his pregnant wife from an ancient evil that seems drawn to the couple. **Similar titles:** *The Store*, Bentley Little; *The Town*, Bentley Little; *The Book of the Dark*, William Meikle; *Blood Crazy*, Simon Clark.

> *Arizona • Clergy as Character • Demons • Pregnancy • Religion—Native American*

Long, Jeff.

The Descent. *New York: Jove Books, 2001. 572p.* A mountaineer in Tibet falls down a hole to emerge in a subterranean world, populated by brutish and horned creatures. Is this the hell of the *Bible*? As scientists and philosophers debate, a global race gets underway to exploit its fabulous mineral deposits. An ambitious tycoon sends an expedition of scientists ever deeper into the unknown, among savage, horned tribes and the vast citadels of the civilizations that fell beneath the Earth before ours arose. A conspiracy of scholars pursues the identity of the being known as Satan, coming up with unpalatable truths about the origins of human culture and the identity of the Turin Shroud. But will they survive to relay this information back to humanity? **Similar titles:** *The Book of the Dark*, William Meikle; *A Lower Deep*, Tom Picirilli; *Dracula 2000* (film); *This Is My Blood*, David Niall Wilson.

> 𝔻 audiotape   ⌖ e-book

> *Bible, The • Clergy as Character • Economic Violence • Evolutionary Theory • Satan (character) • Subterranean Monsters • Tibet*

Lovecraft, H.P.

The Case of Charles Dexter Ward. *New York: Ballantine Books, 1995, ©1943. 127p.* Incantations of black magic unearth unspeakable horrors in a quiet town near Providence, Rhode Island. Evil spirits are being resurrected from beyond the grave, waking a supernatural force so twisted that it kills without offering the mercy of death. The scientific Charles Dexter Ward seeks the truth and discovers too much of it. He pays the price with his sanity. **Similar titles:** *The Loved Dead and Other Revisions*, H. P. Lovecraft, et al.; *More Annotated H. P. Lovecraft*, H. P. Lovecraft; *Correlated Contents*, James Ambuehl.

> *Colonial America • Cthulhu Mythos • Haunted Houses • Necronomicon, The • Providence, Rhode Island • Subterranean Monsters*

The Lurker at the Threshold. *New York: Carroll& Graf, 1999, ©1945. 186p.* Ambrose Dewart returns to his ancestral home near Dunwich, Massachusetts, where he discovers that his grandfather was involved in pseudo-witchcraft practices decades earlier. His curiosity getting the better of him, Dewart pries further and further into his family's old manuscripts, at the risk of inviting the hideous "elder gods," beings that existed before recorded time, into the modern world. **Similar titles:** *The Shadow Out of Time*, H. P. Lovecraft; *Darker Than Night*, Owl Goingback; *Five Mile House*, Karen Novack; *Bag of Bones*, Stephen King.

> *Cthulhu Mythos • Cursed Objects • Dunwich • Family Curse • Massachusetts • Miskatonic University • Native American Characters • Witchcraft*

The Shadow Out of Time. *Ed. S. T. Joshi and David E. Schultz. New York: Hippocampus Press, 2001, ©1936. 136p.* This is an impressive edition of Lovecraft's final novella, with extensive notes and introductory material by two of the finest scholars of his work, Joshi and Schultz. In the tale, a professor of political economy experiences a nervous breakdown, after which he has neither memory of his life nor any abilities to perform day-to-day functions. After five years in this state, he finally awakens to discover, after joining an archeological expedition to Australia, that his greatest fears have been realized: In those five years, his body was possessed by the soul of an ancient race of beings, and his spirit had been catapulted into the body of one of those beings. **Similar titles:** *The Tales of H. P. Lovecraft: Major Works*, H. P. Lovecraft; *Demogorgon*, Brian Lumley; *The Loved Dead and Other Revisions*, H. P. Lovecraft et al.; *Mr. X*, Peter Straub; *Lovers Living, Lovers Dead*, Richard Lortz.

> *Amnesia • Archaeology • Australia • Dramatic Monologue • Dreams • Miskatonic University • Time Travel*

Marano, Michael.

Dawn Song. *New York: Tor, 1998. 384p.* A succubus visits Boston and takes up residence in an apartment complex so she can learn about human emotions (by killing her human lovers). However, she ends up as part of a strange army of humans and demons, readied for the battle between Belial and Leviathan. This excellent work is graphic and disturbing; in short, it's downright scary. **Similar titles:** *Incubus*, Ann Arensberg; *Darklost*, Mick Farren; *Soul Temple*, Steven Lee Climer.

> *Alchemy • Boston, Massachusetts • Demons • Gay/Lesbian/Bisexual Characters • Psychosexual Horror*

Masterton, Graham.

Prey. *New York: Leisure, 1999, ©1992. 352p.* David Williams has taken on the job of restoring Fortyfoot House, an abandoned orphanage on the Isle of Wight. He moves there with his son but soon discovers that he may have placed both himself and his son in terrible danger—for the creature that inhabits the attic of Fortyfoot House is always hungry, and the house itself is alive with the ghosts of its past and present victims. Masterton is unrelenting in his use of suspense and horrific atmosphere. **Similar titles:** *Nailed by the Heart*, Simon Clark; *Five Mile House*, Karen Novack; *The Shining*, Stephen King; *The Haunting of Hill House*, Shirley Jackson.

> *Demons • England • Haunted Houses • Parenting • Pregnancy • Religion—Satanism • Time Travel • Witchcraft*

Miâeville, China.

King Rat. *New York: Tor, 2000. 318p.* Saul Garamond returns from a journey in late evening and sneaks into his bedroom to avoid a confrontation with his estranged father. He awakens to the intrusion of police and the news that his father has been murdered. Blamed for the killing, he is forgotten in a jail cell, but finally freed by a peculiar and impossibly strong stranger. The plot moves through subterranean and rooftop London, as Saul discovers his curious heritage and finds himself marked for death in an age-old secret war among frightful inhuman powers. **Similar titles:** *Santa Steps Out*, Robert Devereaux, *The Tooth Fairy*, Graham Joyce; *Tideland*, Mitch Cullen.

> *Fantasy • London, England • Pied Piper of Hamelin, The (character) • Rat King, The (character) • Subterranean Monsters*

Monteleone, Thomas F. The Blood of the Lamb Series.

The Blood of the Lamb. *New York: Tor, 1992. 421p.* The Catholic Church cloned Christ in 1968. Now, just in time for the upcoming millennium, this clone, Father Peter Carenza, is traveling across the United States in a Winnebago, performing miracles to ever- increasing crowds of adoring followers, but these miracles are both terrifying and awesome. This is a brilliant epic told through multiple points of view. It was the recipient of a Bram Stoker Award. **Similar titles:** *The Exorcist*, William Peter Blatty; The Millennium Quartet, Charles Grant; *Son of Rosemary*, Ira Levin.

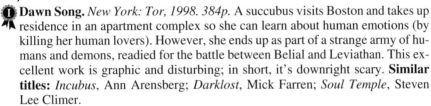

> *Carenza, Peter (character)* • *Clergy as Character* • *Cloning* • *Journalist as Character* • *Religion—Christianity—Catholicism* • *Windsor, Marion (character)*

The Reckoning. *New York: Tor, 1999. 419p.* At the beginning of the new millennium, Father Peter Carenza is elected pope after the miracles he performed in front of large crowds. But Father Carenza is no longer the gentle priest traveling the country in his Winnebago. He makes major changes to Catholic theology to win more converts, changes such as allowing priests to marry, declaring homosexuality an acceptable expression of love, and lifting the Church's ban on birth control. And stranger things than these are happening. Abnormal sunspot activity threatens to end life as we know it, as does the opening of the seven seals mentioned in the book of Revelation. Peter will stop at nothing, including murder for hire, to prevent the opening of these seals. **Similar titles:** *The Exorcist*, William Peter Blatty; The Millennium Quartet, Charles Grant; *Son of Rosemary*, Ira Levin.

> *African-American Characters* • *Apocalypse* • *Asian Characters* • *Carenza, Peter (character)* • *Clergy as Character* • *Pope, The (character)* • *Religion—Christianity—Catholicism* • *Windsor, Marion (character)*

Nassie, Joseph M.

Riverwatch. *St. Petersburg, Fla.: Barclay Books, 2001. 370p.* A construction crew drains a Vermont lake to find a tomb hidden beneath its depths. A drunken boaster makes the mistake one night of following the stairs beneath the tomb to an underground walled enclosure, where he accidentally releases the demon Moloch, which had been imprisoned there. Little do the members of the construction crew know that one of their foremen is also the descendant of the warlock who originally summoned the demon, and he now has plans for its release. Only three friends, aided by an aging "guardian" in a mental institution, can stop Moloch from destroying an entire town. Fans of traditional horror with a visceral touch will enjoy this read. **Similar titles:** *Twilight Dynasty: Courting Evil*, Barry H. Smith; *Darkness Demands*, Simon Clark; *Brass*, Robert J. Conley.

> *Angels* • *Apocalypse* • *Demons* • *Maritime Horror* • *New England* • *Police Officer as Character* • *Subterranean Monsters*

Niswander, Adam.

The Sand Dwellers. *Minneapolis, Minn.: Fedogan & Bremer, 1998. 261p.* A professor at Miskatonic University disappears in the Arizona desert, followed by a soldier stationed at a military defense post there. At the same time, an army colonel in control of the Strategic Defense Initiative begins having visions of Middle East war—and hearing voices telling him to launch missiles. Can a Miskatonic scholar investigating the occurrences piece together the evidence to discover the evil force behind them, and can he stop it before World War III begins? This is fast-paced and action-oriented. **Similar titles:** *The Tales of H. P. Lovecraft: Major Works*, H. P. Lovecraft; *The Loved Dead and Other Revisions*, H. P. Lovecraft et al.; *The Shadow Out of Time*, H. P. Lovecraft.

> *Aliens* • *Arizona* • *Cthulhu (character)* • *The Eighties* • *Fantasy* • *Military* • *Mind Control* • *Miskatonic University* • *Scholar as Character*

Rice, Anne. The Mayfair Witch Series.

(See chapter 7, "Demonic Possession, Satanism, Black Magic, and Witches and Warlocks: The Devil Made Me Do It.")

Rice, Anne.

The Servant of the Bones. *New York: Alfred A. Knopf, 1989. 387p.* In ancient Babylon, Azriel is sacrificed to become the Servant of the Bones so that his people may return to Jerusalem. But the story doesn't end for Azriel, who is condemned to an immortal life and can only relieve some of the loneliness of his condition by telling his story to Jonathan, as well as helping his chosen scribe to foil a modern-day evangelical plot. **Similar titles:** *The Mummy: Or Ramses the Damned*, Anne Rice; *The Vampire Lestat*, Anne Rice; *My Soul to Keep*, Tananarive Due; *The Last Vampire*, T. M. Wright.

 audiotape, audio download, compact disc   large print

Babylon • History, Use of • Religion—Judaism

Robinson, Frank M.

Waiting. *New York: Tom Doherty, 1999. 303p.* (See chapter 13, "Ecological Horror: Rampant Animals and Mother Nature's Revenge.")

Rummel, Keith.

Spirit of Independence. *St. Petersburg, Fla.: Barclay Books, 2001. 276p.* In this first book of the projected Spirit Chronicles, Travis Winter is murdered by his commanding officer during an American raid in World War II. He now finds himself inhabiting the spirit world and pitted against the forces of darkness, with the hopes of humanity hanging in the balance. This novel is told from multiple points of view. **Similar titles:** *Death's Door*, John Wooley and Ron Wolfe; *Soul Temple*, Steven Lee Climer; *Blood Covenant*, Marilyn Lamb; *Dark Soul*, M. Martin Hunt.

Afterlife, The • Angels • Demons • Fantasy • God (character) • Satan (character)

Savile, Steve.

Secret Life of Colors. *Kansas City, Mo.: Dark Tales Publications. 2000. 192p.* Detective Gabriel Rush discovers that his pictures can foretell tragedy when he photographs an upscale prostitute who is literally marked for death, unbeknownst to her. Soon he's on the trail of a serial killer who is phased by nothing, not even his own mortality. When his body is rendered too broken to function, a dark angel reanimates his flesh and makes him unstoppable. **Similar titles:** *The Light at the End*, John Skipp and Craig Spector; *Lifetimes of Blood*, Adam Johnson; *Tribulations*, J. Michael Straczynski; *Mr. X*, Peter Straub.

Angels • Clairvoyant as Character • Dreams • Grieving • Native American Characters • New York City • Police Officer as Character • Religion—Native American • Revenging Revenant • Serial Killers • Shapeshifters

Shirley, John.

Wetbones. *New York: Leisure, 1999, ©1993. 332p.* (See chapter 7, "Demonic Possession, Satanism, Black Magic, and Witches and Warlocks: The Devil Made Me Do It.")

8

Skipp, John, and Craig Spector.

The Cleanup. *Lancaster, Pa.: Stealth Press, 2001, ©1987. 394p.* Billy Rowe is an amateur musician living in a dirty New York apartment. In essence, he is just another loser living in a city of shattered dreams. His life is changed after he witnesses a murder that he is powerless to stop, for he is visited by Christopher, a celestial being who identifies himself as an angel who can give Billy absolute power over everything in his life, including his surroundings. Billy accepts and soon finds that with power comes responsibility and the need for temperance, both of which he often lacks. Will his nature cause him to cross the line between justice and vengeance? Can he tame his own inner demons before he tames the streets of New York? **Similar titles:** *Soul Temple*, Steven Lee Climer; *Spanky*, Christopher Fowler; *Fight Club* (film); *Thunderland*, Brandon Massey; *Shadowland*, Peter Straub.

> *Alter Ego • Angels • Demons • Music—Rock Music • New York City • Rape • Revenge • Serial Killers • Torture • Vigilantism • Wish Fulfillment*

Smith, Barry H.

Twilight Dynasty: Courting Evil. *Baltimore: Erica House, 1999. 315p.* A young journalist is thrown into a world of reincarnated demons and priests, as well as biblical spirits seeking bodies to inhabit. After her brush with a demon and his hooded followers, who try to sacrifice her on an altar in the forest, Amanda Stewart seeks the help of her uncle, a divorce lawyer who is intimately involved in an epic battle of good versus evil. Told in various voices, with narrative frame switching between the natural and supernatural characters. **Similar titles:** *Riverwatch*, Joseph M. Nassie; *Son of Rosemary*, Ira Levin; *The Millennium Quartet*, Charles Grant; *The Stand*, Stephen King; *Soul Temple*, Steven Lee Climer.

> *Canada • Demons • Human Sacrifice • Journalist as Character • Lawyer as Character • Native American Characters • Parapsychology • Reincarnation • Religion—Christianity*

Spellman, Cathy Cash.

Bless the Child. *New York: Pocket, 2000. 608p.* Maggie O'Connell's three-year-old grandson Cody is at the epicenter of a cosmic battle between good and evil. A messenger of the goddess Isis, Cody is capable of materializing the Isis Amulet, a relic that can bring about absolute good. But where's there's good, there's evil. The Stone of Sekhmet, a relic that can allow evil to reign on Earth, also awaits materialization, and Cody's drug-addicted mother is married to the person with the power to activate this stone. Needless to say, this person wants Cody dead. Now Maggie must team up with a Catholic priest, a mystic rabbi, a metaphysician, a police officer, and assorted Israeli soldiers to rescue her grandson, and the world as we know it. **Similar titles:** *Cleopatra's Needle*, Steven Siebert; *The Red God*, C. E. Albertson; *The Talisman*, Jonathan Aycliffe; *The Omen* (film).

> *Apocalypse • Demons • Egypt • Religion—Ancient Egpytian*

Spencer, William Browning.

Resume with Monsters. *Clarkston, Ga.: White Wolf, 1997. 469p.* Luckless employee Philip Kenan goes from menial job to menial job, beginning to realize that his employers, and their office machines, are in league with Cthluhian monsters who want to enslave all humanity. This clever satire was the recipient of an International Literary Guild Award for Best Novel. **Similar titles:** *The Green Man*, Kingsley Amis; *Human Resources*, Floyd Kemske; *Labor Day*, Floyd Kemske; *Irrational Fears*, William Browning Spencer; *Deadfellas*, David Whitman.

> *Austin, Texas • Corporate Horror • Cthulhu (character) • Family Curse • The Old Ones • Psychiatrist as Character • Publishing Industry • Writer as Character*

Stein, Garth.

Raven Stole the Moon. *New York: Pocket, 1999. 480p.* Two years ago, Jenna Rosen's five-year-old son drowned in Alaska near the Tlingit Indian village where her grandmother lived and died. Now Jenna is drawn back to the scene of her son's death. On impulse, she leaves a party in Seattle she's attending with her husband, driving their BMW to Bellingham, Washington, then taking the ferry to this small village. Once there, she meets a shaman who tells her of the kushtaka, shapeshifting soul stealers who inhabit the world between the living and the dead. And it is very possible that the kushtaka now have her son Bobby, taken as punishment for her wealthy husband's greed. **Similar titles:** *Brass*, Robert J. Conley; *Crota* and *Darker Than Night*, Owl Goingback; *Chancers*, Gerald Vizenor.

> *Alaska • Grieving • Native American Characters • Religion—Native American • Shapeshifters*

Straub, Peter.

Mr. X. *New York: Ballantine, 1999. 510p.* (See chapter 11, "Maniacs and Socio-paths, or the Nuclear Family Explodes: Monstrous Malcontents Bury the Hatchet.")

Tilton, Lois.

Darkspawn. *Tulsa, Okla.: Hawk Publishing, 2000. 513p.* (See chapter 6, "Vampires and Werewolves: Children of the Night.")

Vizenore, Gerald.

Chancers. *American Indian and Critical Studies Series 36. Norman: University of Oklahoma Press, 2000. 159p.* Influenced by oral narrative techniques and content, this tale tells the story of a group of Native American Solar Dancers who sacrifice the faculty of a small university one by one to resurrect mythological and historical Native figures. This is a gentle read that is more imagistic than narrative, with emphasis on characterization. **Similar titles:** *The Wicker Man*, Robin Hardy and Anthony Schaffer; *Smoke Signals*, Octavio Ramos, Jr.; *Midwinter of the Spirit*, Phil Rickman; *Brass*, Robert J. Conley.

> *Academia • Human Sacrifice • Religion—Native American*

Williams, Drew.

Night Terrors. *St. Petersburg, Fla.: Barclay Books, 2001. 343p.* In the small New England town of McKeesport, an ancient and unstoppable evil has been awakened, and it is attacking the citizens of this sleepy Connecticut enclave by infiltrating their dreams and nightmares. With a rash of suicides and brutal murders on his hands, Detective Steve Wyckoff must face his own worst fears, that his dreams will literally haunt his days. Wyckoff does have help: One man in town can stop the killing, but first he has to master his own recurring nightmares of Uncle Joe, the man who raped him when he was a boy of twelve. **Similar titles:** *Old Fears*, John Wooley and Ron Wolfe; *Darkness Demands*, Simon Clark; *Nightmare on Elm Street* (film); *The House*, Bentley Little.

> *Baseball • Child Abuse • Dreams • Drugs • New England • Police Officer as Character • Religion—Native American • Suicide • Weird Science*

Wilson, F. Paul. The Repairman Jack Series.

The Tomb. *New York: Tor, 1998, ©1984. 440p.* Much to the chagrin of his girlfriend, Gia, repairman Jack doesn't deal with electronic appliances; he fixes "situations" for people, often putting himself in deadly danger. His latest project is recovering a stolen necklace, which carries with it an ancient curse that may unleash a horde of Bengali demons. Jack is used to danger, but this time Gia's daughter Vicky is threatened. **Similar titles:** The Anita Blake, Vampire Hunter Series, Laurell K. Hamilton; The Host Series, Selena Rosen; *The Licking Valley Coon Hunters Club*, Brian A. Hopkins; *Full Moon, Bloody Moon*, Lee Driver.

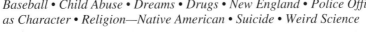

> *Cursed Objects • Demons • Repairman Jack (character)*

Conspiracies. *New York: Tor, 2000. 448p.* (See chapter 16, "Comic Horror: Laughing at Our Fears.")

Wilson, Staci Layne.

Horrors of the Holy: 13 Sinful, Sacrilegious, Supernatural Stories. *Rancho Palo Verdes, Calif.: Running Free Press, 2000. 106p.* (See chapter 17, "Collections and Anthologies.")

Film

Fallen. *Gregory Hoblit, dir. 1998. 123 minutes.* Before his execution, serial killer Edgar Reese begins mysteriously speaking to Detective John Hobbes (Denzel Washington) in biblical tongues and singing the Rolling Stone's *Time Is on My Side*. Soon after this execution, two people are murdered in a blatant imitation of Reese's style, and the fingerprints at the scene of the crime are Hobbes's. Meanwhile, Hobbes has discovered that another police officer, once a decorated hero, ended his own life after he was similarly framed. Now his daughter, a theology professor, believes that behind it all is the demon Azazel, who can switch bodies with anyone he touches. Soon Hobbes is forced to kill a man possessed by Azazel and must clear his name while protecting his family and the world from a vengeful fallen angel who would bring on the apocalypse. John Goodman and Donald Sutherland also star. **Similar reads:** *Spanky*, Christopher Fowler; *Dark Soul*, M. Martin Hunt.

> *African-American Characters • Angels • Apocalypse • Boston, Massachusetts • Demons • Mind Control • Police Officer as Character • Religion—Christianity • Revenging Revenant • Serial Killers*

Hellraiser. *Clive Barker, dir. 1987. 94 minutes.* Barker directs this film version of his novel *The Hellbound Heart*. When Frank, a playboy and thrill-seeker, decides that life holds no more pleasure for him, he experiments with Lamarchand's Box, which supposedly will summon the gods of pleasure. Instead, Frank summons demons of torture, and they want more than just Frank. **Similar reads:** *Book of the Dark*, William Meikle; *Riverwatch*, Joseph M. Nassie.

> *Demons • Eroticism • Secret Sin*

Tales from the Hood. *Rusty Cundief, dir. 1995. 98 minutes.* (See chapter 16, "Comic Horror: Laughing at Our Fears.")

Our Picks

June's Picks: *Black Light*, Elizabeth Hand (HarperPrism); *Brass*, Robert J. Conley (Leisure); *Darkness Demands*, Simon Clark (Leisure); *Dawn Song*, Michael Marano (Tor); *Deliver Us from Evil* and *The Sleeper in the Sands*, Tom Holland (Warner and Little, Brown—Abacus); *My Soul to Keep*, Tananarive Due (HarperCollins); *Needful Things*, Stephen King (Penguin); *The Store*, Bentley Little (Signet); *The Tooth Fairy*, Graham Joyce (Tor); *Hellraiser* (film).

Tony's Picks: *The Cleanup*, John Skipp and Craig Spector (Stealth); *My Soul to Keep*, Tananarive Due (HarperCollins); *Symphony*, Charles Grant (Tor); *Fallen* (film).

Chapter 9

Telekinesis and Hypnosis: Chaos from Control

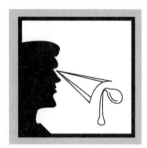

In the nineteenth century, Dr. Anton Mesmer popularized the idea of mesmerism (later known as hypnotism), whereby an individual could get others to do his or her bidding through mind control. This pseudo-science, compounded with the reality that historically, charismatic individuals have been able to exert an almost superhuman influence over the minds of others, gave rise to stories about evil people who were able to use the powers of their minds to control the actions of others. One of the first fictional examples of this type of monster was a vampire, Count Dracula. In Bram Stoker's 1897 novel, this Transylvanian nobleman used the raw power of mesmerism on his female victims, Lucy Westenra and Mina Harker. Unlike the sophisticated Count Dracula in Tod Browning's 1931 film, who was able to use charm and grace to control others, the Count as Stoker portrays him is neither handsome nor suave. He relies solely on a superhuman ability to control the thought processes of others, much like a hypnotist.

In the twentieth century, it has been widely accepted that hypnotism can be used to access an individual's unconscious mind and hopefully cure that individual of psychological problems. By extension, one can argue that if hypnotism enables the mesmerist to access another's unconscious mind, then it has the potential for great evil as well as great good. After all, in the past 100 years, we have witnessed far too many examples of "charismatic" individuals who wreak havoc by controlling followers. People such as Adolph Hitler, Jim Jones, and David Koresh, to name a few, were living proof that it is possible for one individual to *psychologically* and *emotionally* control the wills of many—with disastrous and tragic results. Robert Silverberg's short story "Passengers" illustrates the principle of mind control and the questions it raises about the nature of free will. In his story, unseen aliens come to a seemingly orderly Earth and attach themselves to individuals, causing them to behave in socially unacceptable ways. Silverberg raises the question of where the line is drawn between being controlled by an exterior force and acting on natural impulses, as his story asks whether people can be forced into doing things they are incapable of doing by an act of free will. In his tale, the characters' antisocial behaviors are more than likely manifestations of their repressed unconscious desires.

Telekinesis is another type of mind control. Whereas hypnotism requires the use of a person to accomplish the hypnotist's desires, the individual with telekinetic abilities can move objects with his or her mind. What makes this power frightening is that in horror texts, typically the person with telekinetic abilities is an angry outcast who, pushed beyond the limits of endurance, goes "postal," ushering in chaos with his or her telekinetic abilities rather than with an AK-47. Stephen King's novel *Carrie* is an excellent example of telekinesis in horror. Carrie White, the butt of all jokes in high school and the recipient of extreme abuse at the hands of her fundamentalist Christian mother, explodes when her classmates play one too many pranks on her. She abuses her telekinetic abilities, in the process destroying her hometown of Chamberlain, Maine, as well as killing half of its citizens. The average person is ill-equipped to defend himself or herself against an individual who can cause cars to swerve, make power lines break and fall to the ground, and stop a human heartbeat, simply by thinking about these things happening.

Horror tales about being controlled by others or about becoming the victim of inanimate objects that have suddenly taken on life because of an outside force serve to remind readers that the loss of free will and of control is always possible, sometimes with catastrophic results. It is a subgenre particularly geared toward American readers, for it threatens the loss of liberty, of the ability to control one's own actions and destiny. Representative works in this section include King's *Carrie*, Peter Straub's Blue Rose Trilogy, Curt Siodmak's *Donovan's Brain*, and Dean Koontz's *Strangers*.

Appeals: Fascination with, as Well as Fear of, the Human Brain's Potential; Pseudo-Scientific Appeal; Fascination with ESP, Telepathy, Hypnosis, Mind Control; Sympathetic Characters (Societal Misfits) Empowered with Telekinetic Abilities (Vicarious Empowerment); Desire to Control Others

Barker, Clive.

Galilee. New York: HarperCollins, 1998. 432p. (See chapter 14, "Psychological Horror: It's All in Your Head.")

Campbell, Ramsey.

Incarnate. London: Little, Brown, 1992, ©1983. 490p. (See chapter 14, "Psychological Horror: It's All in Your Head.")

Clark, Simon.

Darker. New York: Leisure, 2002. 410p. (See chapter 5, "Golem, Mummies, and Reanimated Stalkers: Wake the Dead and They'll Be Cranky.")

Clegg, Douglas.

Dark of the Eye. *Burton, Mich.: Subterranean Press, 2001, ©1994. 369p.* Hope Stewart, a child who unknowingly bears a mysterious, double-edged gift, can either heal or destroy. Stephen Grace kidnaps Hope, intending to remove one of her eyes, then kill her. He achieves his first aim, but a timely automobile accident lands both of them in the hospital before he can carry out his second. Hope's divorced mother then kidnaps her from the hospital and flees to Empire, a small and allegedly typical California town. There, with a group of grotesque friends, she tries to protect Hope from her would-be murderer. **Similar titles:** *Tideland*, Mitch Cullen; *Wire Mesh Mothers*, Elizabeth Massie; *Firestarter*, Stephen King; *The Halloween Man*, Douglas Clegg.

California • Childhood • Cthulhu Mythos • Werewolves

Collins, Nancy A.

Sunglasses After Dark. *New York: New American Library, 1989. 253p.* (See chapter 6, "Vampires and Werewolves: Children of the Night.")

Farris, John.

The Fury. *New York: Forge, 2000, ©1976. 334p.* This is the best-selling novel of twins and terror that became the Brian DePalma movie classic. Gillian's family is one of the wealthiest in the world, and Robin's father is a government assassin. Gillian and Robin seem to have nothing in common, but they are actually spiritual twins who possess a horrifying psychic energy. **Similar titles:** *Carrie*, Stephen King; *Firestarter*, Stephen King; *Carrie* (film).

> *Childhood • Clairvoyant as Character • Government Officials • Revenge • Twins*

Grant, Charles.

The Pet. *New York: Tor, 2001, ©1987. 343p.* Selected as one of the hundred best horror books of all time in *Horror: The Best 100 Books* (edited by Stephen Jones and Kim Newman) and nominated for a World Fantasy Award for best novel, this is the story of an unpopular teenager who takes revenge on his tormentors through a projection of his unconscious mind. **Similar titles:** *Christine* and *Carrie*, Stephen King; *Thunderland*, Brandon Massey; *Shadowland*, Peter Straub.

> *High School • Parenting • Revenge*

Halsey, W[inifred] F.

To Kill an Eidolon. *Dekalb, Ill.: Speculation Press, 1999. 243p.* Susan Danville joins an AIDS research team in Chicago, working under the tutelage of Dr. Jim Malliard. What she isn't told by Dr. Malliard is that she is one of his experiments, as he hopes to harness her inherited abilities to see and terminate Eidolon, or spirits that bring on the death of humans. Now Susan's life is no longer her own, and she has two choices: cooperate fully with the doctor's research or face extermination at the hands of the team. Halsey's novel is original, with a multilayered storyline. **Similar titles:** *The Cleanup*, John Skipp and Craig Spector; *Dogma* (film); *Stigmata* (film); *Sunglasses After Dark*, Nancy Collins.

> *Academia • AIDS • Chicago, Illinois • Epidemics • Genetics • Parapsychology • Weird Science*

Hamilton, Laurell K.

Burnt Offerings. *New York: Ace, 1998. 400p.* (See chapter 16, "Comic Horror: Laughing at Our Fears.")

Hynd, Noel.

Rage of Spirits. *New York: Pinnacle Books, 1998. 416p.* In the year 2003, a Reaganesque president of the United States slips into a coma at the will of Carl Einhorn, "a cross between the Unibomber and Hannibal Lecter." Meanwhile, the vice president, a firm believer in astrology, fears an old curse placed on him may affect his move into the White House. **Similar titles:** *The Evil Returns*, Hugh B. Cave; *Carrion Comfort*, Dan Simmons; *Black Oak 4: Hunting Ground*, Charles Grant; *University*, Bentley Little.

> *Astrology • Curse • Government Officials • Mind Control • Science Fiction • Washington, D.C.*

Hynes, James.

The Lecturer's Tale. *New York: Picador USA, 2001. 388p.* After Nelson Humboldt is dismissed from his lowly position as a composition teacher at a Midwestern university, he suffers an accident that severs his right index finger. When the finger is surgically reattached, Nelson discovers he can magically control a person's behavior by touching that person with his mysteriously burning digit. First he gets his job back, but soon his finger burns for even more power. **Similar titles:** *The Uncanny*, Andrew Klavan; *The Conjure Wife*, Fritz Leiber; *Lovers Living, Lovers Dead*, Richard Lortz.

Academia • Marriage • Midwest, The • Popular Culture • Teacher as Character

King, Stephen.

Carrie. *New York: Signet, 1972. 245p.* Carrie White is abused by her fanatically religious mother and by her peers at school. She is the perpetual foul up. But Carrie also has telekinetic powers that have lain dormant since she was five years old. Now, with the traumatic onset of her first menstruation, Carrie's telekinetic powers resurface, and she uses these powers in self-defense against her tormentors. The novel is a combination of multiple first person narratives collected in several fictional critical works that recount Carrie's amazing powers. King's classic was made into a movie of the same name by Brian DePalma. **Similar titles:** *Dragon Tears*, Dean Koontz; *The Cleanup* ; John Skipp and Craig Spector; *Carrie* (film); *Thunderland*, Brandon Massey; *Escaping Purgatory*, Gary A. Braunbeck and Alan M. Clark.

ᏸᎦ large print

Child Abuse • Documentary Techniques • High School • Maine • Menstruation • Religion—Christianity—Protestantism • Revenge

Dreamcatcher. *New York: Scribner, 2001. 620 p.* (See chapter 12, "Technohorror: Evil Hospitals, Military Screw-Ups, Scientific Goofs, and Alien Invasions.")

Firestarter. *New York: New American Library, 1981. 404p.* An English instructor and his wife volunteer for a government experiment that involves testing a classified hallucinogen. Afterwards, they find they have special telepathic powers, and later, that their daughter has telekinetic abilities. When the instructor begins to suspect that the government doctors are more dangerous than they look, all hell breaks loose. **Similar titles:** *Village of the Damned* (film); *Carrie*, Stephen King; *The Door to December*, Dean Koontz; *Thunderland*, Branden Massey.

Experiments—Military • Mind Control • Parenting • Telepathy

The Shining. *New York: Plume, 1977. 416p.* (See chapter 7, "Demonic Possession, Satanism, Black Magic, and Witches and Warlocks: The Devil Made Me Do It.")

Knight, Anne.

Death Storm. *New York: DAW, 1999. 453p.* Drew is a normal teenaged boy, except for his extraordinary psychic abilities, which he is only beginning to understand. Others would like to tap into these powers for their own sinister ends, including Russian mobsters, who already have in their possession a girl with similar powers. And these people will stop at nothing to get Drew to work for them, too. Can he escape before it's too late? **Similar titles:** *Firestarter*, Stephen King; *The Halloween Man*, Douglas Clegg; *Carrie*, Stephen King.

Adolescence • Extrasensory Perception • Organized Crime • Parenting • Russia

Koontz, Dean.

The Door to December. *New York: Penguin, 1985. 510p.* Laura answers her door one day to find police officers who tell her that her nine-year-old daughter, who was kidnapped by her father years before, has been located. As it turns out, nine-year-old Melanie has not been found, but the body of her father has been located and mutilated. When Melanie is finally located, Laura discovers that her daughter has been the guinea pig for sensory deprivation experiments, and that someone wants Melanie killed. **Similar titles:** *The Eyes of Darkness*, *Dragon Tears,* and *Mr. Murder*, Dean Koontz; *Firestarter*, Stephen King.

Parenting • Weird Science

Dragon Tears. *New York: Putnam, 1993. 377p.* A young man discovers that he can use his telekinetic/telepathic powers to become "a new God," and he takes it upon himself to "thin out the herd" of humanity by ridding it of its handicapped and destitute. **Similar titles:** *The Eyes of Darkness*, *The Door to December,* and *Mr. Murder*, Dean Koontz; *Firestarter*, Stephen King.

Drugs • Eugenics

The Eyes of Darkness. *New York: Putnam-Berkley, 1981. 369p.* This early Koontz effort tells of a grieving mother being haunted by her son's accidental death. A year after twelve-year-old Danny was horribly mangled and killed in an accident, Tina Evans sees him in a car. When strange things begin happening in Danny's old room, Tina is faced with the possibility that her son is still alive. Koontz is fast-paced and suspenseful. **Similar titles:** *Dragon Tears*, *The Door to December,* and *Mr. Murder*, Dean Koontz; *Firestarter*, Stephen King.

Experiments—Military • Las Vegas, Nevada • Telepathy

The Mask. *New York: Berkley, 1992, ©1981. 305p.* (See chapter 7, "Demonic Possession, Satanism, Black Magic, and Witches and Warlocks: The Devil Made Me Do It.")

Matheson, Richard.

Stir of Echoes. *New York: Tor, 1999, ©1958. 211p.* (See chapter 4, "Ghosts and Haunted Houses: Dealing with Presences and Absences.")

Redmond, Patrick.

Something Dangerous. *New York: Hyperion, 1999. 343p.* When Jonathan Palmer first attends Kirksten Abbey, affectionately known as "Old School," he tries desperately to fit in. However, the bullying of the older boys forces him into an uneasy alliance with the school loner, a free spirit who harbors a terrible power. This YA crossover is an easy read, yet powerful. **Similar titles:** *Shadowland*, Peter Straub; *Boy in the Water*, Stephen Dobyns; *Mischief*, Douglas Clegg; *The Traveling Vampire Show*, Richard Laymon.

Childhood • Gay/Lesbian/Bisexual Characters • High School • Homoeroticism • London, England • Mind Control • Revenge • Suicide

Siodmak, Curt.

Donovan's Brain. *New York: Caroll & Graf, 1942. 160p.* (See chapter 12, "Technohorror: Evil Hospitals, Military Screw-Ups, Scientific Goofs, and Alien Invasions.")

Williamson, J. N.

> **Affinity.** *New York: Leisure, 2001. 361 p.* (See chapter 7, "Demonic Possession, Satanism, Black Magic, and Witches and Warlocks: The Devil Made Me Do It.")

Film

> **Carrie.** *Brian DePalma, dir. 1976. 97 minutes.* This is a faithful adaptation of Stephen King's first novel of the same name. It stars Sissy Spacek, Piper Laurie, John Travolta, Amy Irving, Nancy Allen, and Betty Buckley. Carrie is made into a misfit by her fanatically fundamentalist mother and spends her young life as the butt of everyone's jokes in the small town of Chamberlain, Maine. Carrie's mother believes that sexual intercourse, even between married couples, is a sin, and that menstruation is God's sign that a woman has strayed from the path of righteousness, so she never speaks with her daughter about the facts of life. Thus when sixteen-year-old Carrie begins her period while showering with the other girls in the locker room, she believes that she is bleeding to death. When the other girls tease her about her ignorance, Carrie's telekinetic powers are reawakened, and her anger toward her peers who pick on her will culminate in their destruction by these powers. **Similar reads:** *Dorcas Good: The Diary of a Salem Witch*, Rose Earhart; *Shadowland*, Peter Straub.
>
> > *Child Abuse • High School • Maine • Menstruation • Religion—Christianity—Protestantism • Revenge*
>
> **Paperhouse.** *Bernard Rose, dir. 1988. 92 minutes.* (See chapter 14, "Psychological Horror: It's All in Your Head.")

Our Picks

> **June's Picks:** *Carrie,* Stephen King (Signet); *The Fury*, John Farris (Forge).
>
> **Tony's Picks:** *Carrie*, Stephen King (Signet); *Dragon Tears*, Dean Koontz (Putnam); *The Pet*, Charles Grant (Tor).

Chapter 10

Small Town Horror: Villages of the Damned

Our twenty-first-century world is one in which chaos, ignorance, and superstition have been replaced by scientific knowledge and enlightenment. We place a higher value on human life than ever before: We have shunned cannibalism, torture, and in most first-world nations, even capital punishment. We know that disease isn't an outward manifestation of sin but something spread by viruses and bacteria, and that antibiotics and even virus-eating drugs can control many of these things. At least this is the official story of the state of civilization. The ugly truth is that "civilized society" has not been an unqualified success. There exists, in first-world countries no less, isolated communities, and sometimes even more isolated individuals, untouched by twenty-first-century values, technology, and rationalism. The Amish and the Mennonites scorn modernity and often live without electricity, television, or cars. Members of some religious sects refuse to seek medical care for ill children, believing that God alone can cure illness. There are several towns off Southern interstates that people are advised to avoid, as they are Ku Klux Klan strongholds, and an unsuspecting traveler can fall victim to the KKK's own peculiar brand of justice.

In this chapter, we describe novels that deal with this type of horror, often referred to as small town horror. Small town horror results from the frightening realization that there are places away from home that are untouched by civilization, where any action, no matter how horrific, is possible. We have all felt this real fear at least once in our lives when we've traveled through deserted areas of highways, where the barren landscape is interrupted rarely, and then only momentarily by miniature towns. In one fictional representation of such a place, a little-known but tightly constructed film entitled *I Spit On Your Grave*, a young female novelist vacations alone in a rural upstate New York resort area, only to be savagely gang raped and left for dead by young locals who are considered fine specimens of manhood by other members of the town. The only chance the rape victim has for justice in this situation is if she is willing to dispense it herself, which she does swiftly and violently.

The relative isolation of such towns and villages makes them perfect for horrific events, which almost always occur (as slasher films teach us) when victims are alienated or separated from others. After all, the killing of wives to replace them with robots, in Ira Levin's *The Stepford Wives*, could only happen in small, insulated communities, where truly "no one can hear you scream," or more specifically, where those who hear you scream might be part of the horror. This is the realization that ultimately dawns on foolish Police Lieutenant Howie in Robin Hardy's *The Wicker Man*: that no matter how civilized *his* society (the United Kingdom proper) may be, once he is on Summers Isle, a pagan community in rural Scotland, he no longer makes the rules. There he is at the mercy of the locals and becomes part of their sacrificial ritual whether he agrees to or not. In Elizabeth Massie's novel *Sineater,* members of a rural Appalachian community punish those who would abolish their quaint custom of keeping one individual living on the fringes of their society for the purpose of taking into himself the sins of the dead.

These tales remind us of our own powerlessness within a larger community and of the dependence of the individual on others who make up society. This stands in stark contrast to the American myth of "rugged individualism," which implies that any one person can stand alone against the forces of conformity, even when those forces are evil. In addition, like antiquarian horror, small town horror serves to remind readers that sometimes it is best not to snoop around too much, lest something unspeakable be turned up. The fear of town secrets is as old as the idea of towns themselves, as the proverbial skeleton in the closet is never as dangerous as the closet's owner, when that owner desperately does not want this particular skeleton to be found.

Newer versions of small town horror are concerned with planned communities where inhabitants attempt to resurrect the feel of small town America, where children can frolic outdoors without their parents fearing they will end up on the back of a milk carton, and where residents don't have to lock their doors at night. These communities not only boast housing so expensive that the riffraff can't possibly move in, they are also located in gated, private areas and are therefore allowed the freedom to be operated as minor fiefdoms, which exist without local government interference. This is the case in Bentley Little's *The Association* and Andrew Neiderman's *Neighborhood Watch*. The trouble is, in these communities, individual liberty is the price to be paid for freedom from the social ills sometimes endured by urban dwellers. People are fined for painting their homes the wrong color, landscaping with the wrong plants, having pets, or even reproducing. And failure to pay the neighborhood association's fines can result in more serious consequences, such as being murdered or enslaved as a zombie.

Novels annotated in this chapter include Stephen King's bestseller concerned with traveling through the Nevada desert, *Desperation*.

Appeals: A Universal Fear of Being Overpowered by Society; Plays on Sense of Helplessness in New Environment; "Us Against the World" Theme; Tendency for Non-Formulaic Endings (Hero Does Not Always Win); Identifiable Settings; Universal Fear of Isolation

Africa, Chris N.

> **When Wolves Cry.** *Edmonton, Alb.: Commonwealth, 1998. 312p.* Six men go on a retreat to a remote mountain village to get some relaxation time while they hunt and fish. However, their rest is disturbed by an unseen deadly enemy that is always one step ahead. This novel will appeal to fans who like action-oriented novels. **Similar titles:** *Canyons*, P.

D. Cacek; *Black Oak 5: When the Cold Wind Blows*, Charles Grant; *A Darkness Inbred*, Victor Heck.

Hunter as Character • Shapeshifters • Werewolves

Barron, Diana.

Phantom Feast. *St. Petersburg, Fla.: Barclay Books, 2001. 269p.* (See chapter 13, "Ecological Horror: Rampant Animals and Mother Nature's Revenge.")

Bradley, Marion Zimmer.

Gravelight. *New York: Tor, 1998, ©1997. 350 p.* (See chapter 4, "Ghosts and Haunted Houses: Dealing with Presences and Absences.")

Burgess, Tony.

Caesarea. *Toronto: ECW Press, 1999. 246p.* (See chapter 13, "Ecological Horror: Rampant Animals and Mother Nature's Revenge.")

Campbell, Ramsey.

The Hungry Moon. *New York: Tom Doherty, 1987. 360p.* An evangelical preacher from California travels to a small town near Manchester, England, where he decides that he will convert the local population, beginning by doing away with their practice of decorating a nearby cave with a rather pagan figure made of flowers. A local schoolteacher named Diana opposes him, and soon she discovers the reason behind the tribute at the cave—to appease a creature "older than Satan," one that is rumored to have come from the moon. When the preacher himself is possessed by the creature, can Diana stop "the hungry moon" from devouring the life force of all humanity and lift the darkness that has suddenly enveloped the town? A fine novel that is a cross between dark fantasy and magical realism. **Similar titles:** *The Wicker Man* (film); *Awash in the Blood*, John Wooley; *Wine of Angels*, Phil Rickman. (See also chapter 7, "Demonic Possession, Satanism, Black Magic, and Witches and Warlocks: The Devil Made Me Do It.")

Citro, Joseph.

The Gore: A Novel. *Hanover, N.H.: University Press of New England, 2000. 231p.* To escape the tensions of his past, ex-newspaperman Roger Newton retreats to Vermont's fabled Northeast Kingdom, the wildest, most remote portion of the state. There he discovers a terrifying secret that turns his life upside-down, as he upsets a centuries-old balance that threatens to loose a long-buried nightmare on the people of Vermont. **Similar titles:** *Bag of Bones*, Stephen King; *Ghost Story*, Peter Straub; *The Manitou*, Graham Masterton; *The Halloween Man*, Douglas Clegg.

Secret Sin • Suicide • Vermont

Lake Monsters. *Hanover, N.H.: University Press of New England, 2001. 272p.* Downsized from his job and dumped by his girlfriend, Harrison Allen longs for a fresh start. Alone, with no prospects or plans, he relocates to a borrowed house on Friars Island in Lake Champlain to relax, contemplate, and begin redefining his life. Then he hears about the monsters; creatures similar to the famous Loch Ness monster are said to inhabit the murky waters and fog-bound marshes of his new island home. But when Allen attempts to find out about these creatures, the locals turn quiet. **Similar titles:** *Clickers*, J. F. Gonzales and Mark Williams; *The Halloween Man*, Douglas Clegg; *Welcome Back to the Night*, Elizabeth Massie.

Maritime Horror • Secret Sin • Subterranean Horror

Shadow Child. *Hanover, N.H.: University Press of New England, 1998, ©1987. 283p.* Strange disappearances, brutal murders, and animal mutilations color this tale. The Whitcome family, Pamela, Clint, and Luke, welcome Pam's cousin, Eric, who is mourning the death of his wife. Seeking comfort from the cousins to whom he was close in childhood, he finds refuge from his grief in their loving home. But soon after his arrival, strange events occur that seem to have their roots in an ancient evil. The story is related through objective narration, spiced with newspaper reports, diary entries, and other journalistic artifacts. **Similar titles:** *The House of the Seven Gables*, Nathaniel Hawthorne; *Blood Covenant*, Marilyn Lamb; *Hexes*, Tom Piccirilli; *Nazareth Hill*, Ramsey Campbell; *Carrie*, Stephen King.

Documentary Techniques • Family Curse • Grieving • Secret Sin • Vermont

Clegg, Douglas.

The Halloween Man. *New York: Leisure, 1998. 360p.* Stony Crawford returns to his hometown of Stonehaven to dispense of an evil presence that he unwittingly helped create as a young man. Clegg's strength is in writing crisp, action-oriented, and complex plots, all of which make this an enjoyable read. **Similar titles:** *Hexes*, Tom Piccirilli; *You Come When I Call You*, Douglas Clegg; *Darkness Demands*, Simon Clark; *Old Fears*, John Wooley and Ron Wolfe.

Childhood • Demons • Hispanic-American Characters • New England • Psychosexual Horror • Religion—Christianity • Secret Sin

Mischief. *New York: Leisure, 2000. 359p.* Jim Hook finally gets to attend Harrow, a mysterious prep school that both his father and older brother, now both dead, had attended. There he discovers that the least of his worries is passing classes, for he is indoctrinated by the terrifying Cadaver Society. Clegg's horror here is subtle, as his emphasis is on characterization. Similar title: *Boy in the Water*; Stephen Dobbyns; *Shadowland*, Peter Straub; *Welcome Back to the Night*, Elizabeth Massie.

Crowley, Aleister (character) • Cults • Family Curse • High School • New England • Religion—Ancient Egyptian • Religion—Satanism

Connolly, John.

Ⓑ **Every Dead Thing.** *New York: Simon & Schuster, 1999. 395p.* (See chapter 15, "Splatterpunk: The Gross-Out.")

Goingback, Owl.

Ⓑ **Crota.** *New York: Donald I. Fine, 1996. 292p.* (See chapter 8, "Mythological Monsters and 'The Old Ones': Invoking the Dark Gods.")

Evil Whispers. *New York: Signet, 2001. 340 p.* (See chapter 7, "Demonic Possession, Satanism, Black Magic, and Witches and Warlocks: The Devil Made Me Do It.")

Gonzales, J. F., and Mark Williams.

Clickers. *Grandview, MO: Dark Tales, 2000. 238p.* (See chapter 13, "Ecological Horror: Rampant Animals and Mother Nature's Revenge.")

Grant, Charles. The Black Oak Series.

Black Oak 2: The Hush of Dark Wings. *New York: Penguin-ROC, 1999. 236p.* Ethan Proctor and the Black Oak Security company have a new assignment: find the missing daughter of a multi-millionaire. To do so, they visit Hart Junction, a small Midwestern town besieged by winged creatures and a secretive cult of hooded women. As bodies are ripped to shreds, Proctor and his assistant, Vivian, try to get to the bottom of the town's secrets. **Similar titles:** *Darklost*, Mick Farren; *Lost Boys* (film); *Vampire Nation*, Thomas M. Sipos.

Black Oak Security • Chambers, Vivian (character) • Cults • Kansas •
Private Investigator as Character • Proctor, Ethan (character) •
Shapeshifters

Grant, Charles.

Symphony. *New York: Tor, 1997. 332p.* (See chapter 8, "Mythological Monsters and 'The Old Ones': Invoking the Dark Gods.")

Griffith, Kathryn Meyer.

Witches. *New York: Kensington-Pinnacle, 2000, ©1993. 383p.* (See chapter 7, "Demonic Possession, Satanism, Black Magic, and Witches and Warlocks: The Devil Made Me Do It.")

Hardy, Robin, and Anthony Shaffer.

The Wicker Man. *New York: Pocket, 1978. 239p.* Police officer Neil Howie receives an anonymous note reporting the disappearance of a young girl from the community of Summerisle, Scotland. What he discovers there are pagan fertility rituals and many deadly secrets. This brilliant text reads easily despite being a masterpiece of a story. It was adapted from a film of the same name by Robin Hardy. **Similar titles:** *The Green Man*, Kingsley Amis; *The Stepford Wives*, Ira Levin; *The Wicker Man* (film); *Man in the Moss*, Phil Rickman.

Human Sacrifice • Police Officer as Character • Religion—Christianity—
Protestantism • Religion—Paganism • Scotland

Hill, William.

The Vampire Hunters. *Doctors Inlet, FL: Otter Creek Press, 1998. 286p.* Marcus Chandler is a reclusive film producer who seems to have a rare disease that has left him with bleached skin and a heightened sensitivity to light. A cruel gang of high school kids is convinced he is a vampire, so they decide to get a picture of Chandler to make their case. But whether Chandler's vampirism is real or imagined, there are still plenty of dark forces in this small Texas hometown: Teens are disappearing and eventually turning up dead, and sometimes their corpses are drained of blood. **Similar titles:** *Morningstar*, Peter Atkins; *The Bottoms*, Joe R. Lansdale; *Southern Blood*, Lawrence Schimel and Martin H. Greenberg; *Seize the Night*, Dean Koontz.

Actor as Character • African-American Characters • Albinism • High
School • Racism • Serial Killers • Texas • Xeroderma Pigmentosum

Johnstone, William W. The Devil's Kiss Series.

(See chapter 8, "Mythological Monsters and 'The Old Ones': Invoking the Dark Gods.")

Kelly, Ronald.

Blood Kin. *New York: Pinnacle, 2001. 384p.* (See chapter 6, "Vampires and Werewolves: Children of the Night.")

Fear. *New York: Pinnacle, 2001, ©1994. 480p.* In the 1940s, a flesh-eating creature lurks in rural Beelzebub County and eats innocent children. Only ten-year-old Jeb Sweeney has the courage to hunt down this beast. **Similar titles:** *Shadow Child*, Joseph Citro; *Hexes*, Tom Piccirilli; *Desperation*, Stephen King; *The Halloween Man*, Douglas Clegg.

10

Magic • Tennessee • United States—1940s

King, Stephen.

Carrie. *New York: Signet, 1972. 245p.* (See chapter 9, "Telekinesis and Hypnosis: Chaos from Control.")

The Dead Zone. *New York: Viking, 1979. 426p.* When a small town schoolteacher emerges from a lengthy coma, he finds he is able to see into the future. Now he must stop a charismatic political candidate who will ultimately destroy the world after winning public office. This novel was made into a film of the same name, staring Christopher Walken. **Similar titles:** *The Dead Zone* (film); *Tribulations*, J. Michael Straczynski; The Host Series, Selina Rosen; *Cold Fire*, Dean Koontz.

> *Castle Rock, Maine • Government Officials • Precognition • Teacher as Character*

Desperation. *New York: Viking, 1996. 690p.* This is the companion novel to the Richard Bachman work *The Regulators* (see later in this chapter), in which burnt-out novelist John Marinville has a run-in with the law while traveling with his family to Nevada. But this is no ordinary incident of police brutality. The sheriff who lies in wait on Route 50 is actually a shapeshifting alien. **Similar titles:** *Clickers*, J. F. Gonzales and Mark Williams; *The Boat Man*, Selina Rosen; *Phantoms*, Dean Koontz; *The Apostate*, Paul Lonardo.

> 𝔇 audiotape   ᘓ large print

> *Alcoholism • God—Christian God (character) • Nevada • Police Brutality • Shapeshifters*

Needful Things. *New York: Penguin, 1991. 690p.* (See chapter 8, "Mythological Monsters and 'The Old Ones': Invoking the Dark Gods.")

'Salem's Lot. *Garden City, N.J.: Doubleday, 1975. 439p.* (See chapter 6, "Vampires and Werewolves: Children of the Night.")

King, Stephen [as Bachman, Richard].

The Regulators. *New York: Dutton, 1996. 466p.* An Ohio suburb finds itself being dragged into a twisted and murderous version of reality, thanks to the visions of an eight-year-old autistic boy and a van full of maniacs. **Similar titles:** *Thunderland*, Brandon Massey; *One Rainy Night*, Richard Laymon; *Candyman* (film); *Nightmare on Elm Street* (film).

> 𝔇 audiotape   ᘓ large print

> *Dreams • Ohio • Savant Syndrome • Suburbia*

Koontz, Dean.

Night Chills. *New York: Berkley, 1976. 367p.* (See chapter 12, "Technohorror: Evil Hospitals, Military Screw-Ups, Scientific Goofs, and Alien Invasions.")

Phantoms. *New York: G. P. Putnam, 1983. 352p.* (See chapter 8, "Mythological Monsters and 'The Old Ones': Invoking the Dark Gods.")

Laymon, Richard.

The Traveling Vampire Show. *New York: Leisure, 2001. 391p.* (See chapter 14, "Psychological Horror: It's All in Your Head.")

Levin, Ira.

The Stepford Wives. *New York: Random House, 1972. 145p.* Joanna Eberhart and her husband travel to the idyllic town of Stepford, where she notices the women are a bit too enthusiastic about homemaking and being perfect. Little does she realize that there is a dark reason for their behavior. This fine novel was made into a classic film of the same name. **Similar titles:** *The Store*, Bentley Little; *The Stepford Wives* (film); *Rosemary's Baby*, Ira Levin; *The House That Jack Built*, Graham Masterton.

Feminism • Marriage • Replicants • Suburbia

Little, Bentley.

The Association. *New York: Signet, 2001. 438p.* Barry and Maureen Welch long to escape the urban sprawl of Los Angeles, so they purchase what they believe is a dream home in Bonita Vista, a gated community in rural Utah. Since Bonita Vista is not part of any town, residents have only the homeowner's association to take care of their civic needs and keep property values high. But the homeowner's association is a little bit too protective. Soon after their arrival, the Welches receive a citation for having a garage sale. Later they're found to be in violation of other overly restrictive ordinances, and if they ignore them, there are dire consequences. Meanwhile, animals and children are being poisoned in Corbin, the town just outside of Bonita Vista. Is the homeowner's association to blame for this, too? **Similar titles:** *Neighborhood Watch*, Andrew Neiderman; *The Stepford Wives*, Ira Levin; *The Store*, Bentley Little.

Class System • Gated Communities • Neighborhood Associations •
Suburbia • Torture • Utah • Writer as Character • Zombies

The Revelation. *New York: Signet, 1999. 326p.* (See chapter 8, "Mythological Monsters and 'The Old Ones': Invoking the Dark Gods.")

The Store. *New York: Signet, 1998. 431p.* Juniper, Arizona, is a pleasant little small town, but economic life on Main Street is ruined when a retail giant, The Store, comes to town. The Store has sufficient economic muscle to undersell small business competition in Juniper, and even worse, can persuade the town council to exempt The Store from local sales taxes and to build roads at city expense. Evil lurks within The Store: Employees behave mysteriously; dead animals are found on the premises every day; townspeople who oppose The Store disappear. **Similar titles:** *Needful Things*, Stephen King; *The Stepford Wives*, Ira Levin; *The House That Jack Built*, Graham Masterton.

Arizona • Consumerism • Cults • Demons • Fantasy • Mind Control •
Zombies

The Town. *New York: Signet, 2000. 376p.* The Tomasov family returns to McGuane, Arizona, to escape big city life. But the small town isn't a quaint unspoiled place where you can raise a family without fear. Instead, McGuane is a place of provincial prejudices, haunted by past sins that have awakened an ancient evil. **Similar titles:** *The Store* and *The Revelation*, Bentley Little; *The Apostate*, Paul Lonardo.

Arizona • Demons • Human Sacrifice • Racism •
Religion—Christianity—Molokan • Religion—Native American •
Revenge • Secret Sin

Lonardo, Paul.

The Apostate. *St. Petersburg, Fla.: Barclay Books, 2001. 254p.* A teenaged runaway, a world renowned environmentalist, and a respected psychiatrist all converge on Caldera, New Mexico, a city whose inhabitants have been plagued by nightmares and hallucinations. Can it be the pollution that is poisoning the citizenry of Caldera, or is it something in the bread of the local bakery chains? Or are there even more sinister forces at work? This is an engaging and original story, rife with plot twists and fascinating characters. **Similar titles:** *One Rainy Night*, Richard Laymon; *Insomnia*, *The Tommyknockers,* and *Dreamcatcher*, Stephen King; *The Store*, Bentley Little.

> *Child Abuse • Dreams • Environmental Horror • Environmentalist as Character • New Mexico • Psychiatrist/Psychologist as Character • Rats • Satan (character) • Serial Killers*

Massie, Elizabeth.

Sineater. *New York: Leisure Books, 1998. 396p.* In Appalachia, the pious still depend on the sineater to cleanse the newly departed of sin so they can go to heaven. Traditionally, the sineater has led a solitary existence in the woods, only approaching humanity to partake of plates of food left on the chests of the dead. But the current sineater has broken with tradition and has a wife and family, and this change has brought about a spate of disappearances and murders in this small mountain town. Massie's original Southern gothic is a winner of the Bram Stoker Award. **Similar titles:** *Madeleine After the Fall of Usher*, Marie Kiraly; *The Wine of Angels*, Phil Rickman; *The Long Walk*, Stephen King; *Neighborhood Watch*, Andrew Neiderman; *The Association*, Bentley Little.

> *Childhood • Cults • Religion—Christianity—Baptist • Virginia*

Welcome Back to the Night. *New York: Leisure, 1999. 393p.* At a family reunion, three siblings connect with a woman who was briefly part of the family and learn that their family and their hometown are deeply and violently racist. **Similar titles:** *Sineater* and *Wire Mesh Mothers*, Elizabeth Massie; *The Vampire Hunters*, William Hill; *Murder at Witches' Bluff*, Silver Ravenwolf.

> *Cults • Dreams • Racism • Religion—Christianity • Secret Sin • Virginia*

Meikle, William.

The Book of the Dark. greatunpublished.com, 2001. Published on Demand. 273p. (See chapter 6, "Vampires and Werewolves: Children of the Night.")

Nassie, Joseph M.

Riverwatch. *St. Petersburg, FL: Barclay Books, 2001. 370p.* (See chapter 8, "Mythological Monsters and 'The Old Ones': Invoking the Dark Gods.")

Neiderman, Andrew.

Neighborhood Watch. *New York: Pocket Books, 2000. 326p.* Teddy and Kristen Morris need a bigger house and are thrilled to discover they can purchase a home in Emerald Lakes, an upscale gated community away from the evils of the big city, kept even more secure by an active neighborhood association, which is run by the community's developer. The problem is that the developer has a very specific idea of what a good neighborhood should be, and he doesn't care if freedom *from* various social ills also strips away the individual's freedom. Conformity is highly valued. The neighborhood association even sends out a monthly newsletter with helpful "suggestions" about hiring contractors and where to store groceries. Anyone who disagrees with the neighborhood association will receive a hefty fine, and perhaps fall victim to a horrible fate. **Similar titles:** *The Association*, Bentley Little; *The Stepford Wives*, Ira Levin; *Amnesia*, Andrew Neiderman.

> *Gated Communities • Neighborhood Associations • New York State • Suburbia*

Oliveri, Michael.

 Deadliest of the Species. *Ringgold, Ga.: VOX13, 2001. 303p.* This Bram Stoker award-winning first novel is Rush Limbaugh's version of Charlotte Perkins Gillman's *Herland*. After a nasty divorce has deprived him of nearly all of his material possessions, Tim Wilder heads west in search of a new life. On the way, he stops in the small mountain town of Rapture, a place run entirely by women. And the good ladies of Rapture must insist that Mr. Wilder accept their hospitality, relieving him of his car, his clothes, and what little money he had left in the world. And then they murder his only friend. **Similar titles:** *Black Oak 2: The Hush of Dark Wings*, Charles Grant; *The Stepford Wives*, Ira Levin; *Waking the Moon*, Elizabeth Hand.

Divorce • Matriarchy

Piccirilli, Tom.

Hexes. *New York: Leisure, 1999. 359p.* Matthew Galen returns to his hometown of Summerfell to visit a childhood friend in a mental institution. But as he suspects, the heinous murders of which his friend is accused mark the return of a terrible evil—an evil he awakened as a teen. Piccirilli uses a complex narrative structure and graphic description. **Similar titles:** *Halloween Man*, Douglas Clegg; *Viscera*, Cara Bruce (editor); *The Dead Inn*, Shane Ryan Staley (editor); *Old Fears*, John Wooley and Ron Wolfe; *Bag of Bones*, Stephen King.

Family Curse • New England • Psychiatrist/Psychologist as Character • Psychosexual Horror • Religion—Paganism • Serial Killers • Subterranean Monsters • Writer as Character

Ravenwolf, Silver.

Murder at the Witches' Bluff: A Novel of Suspense and Magick. *St. Paul, Minn.: Llewellyn, 2000. 449p.* (See chapter 7, "Demonic Possession, Satanism, Black Magic, and Witches and Warlocks: The Devil Made Me Do It.")

Rickman, Phil.

The Chalice. *London: Pan Books, 1998, ©1997. 646p.* Glastonbury, otherwise known as Avalon, lays claim to having "the holiest earthe in Englund" because of a legend that the infant Christ was carried there by his uncle Joseph of Arimathia, who returns years later with the chalice rumored to have caught the crucified Christ's blood. The cathedral and monastery later founded upon this site are ultimately seized by Henry VIII, and he hangs the reigning bishop there, thus converting this sacred spot into a place of evil. The sacred chalice is taken from the bishop's hands and given to the Ffitch family, thus founding their family fortunes while converting the vessel into the dark chalice, a conduit for evil. Glastonbury is now a haven for all sorts of New Agers looking for spiritual enlightenment, but the locals aren't thrilled at the presence of these outsiders and are desperate enough to destroy these sacred sights to evict them for good. The ensuing clash of beliefs threatens to unearth the dark chalice and destroy the town, and perhaps the entire world as we know it. **Similar titles:** *Gravelight*, Marion Zimmer Bradley; *Deathwindow*, Grace Chetwin; *Darker Than Night*, Owl Goingback.

Cursed Objects • Epic Structure • Fortune, Dion (character) • Glastonbury, England • Government Officials • History, Use of • New Age • Powys, Joe (character) • Powys, John Cowper (character) • Reincarnation • Religion—Christianity—Catholicism • Religion—Christianity—Episcopal • Religion—Paganism • Religion—Satanism • Secret Sin • Sibling Rivalry • Writer as Character

The Wine of Angels. *London: Pan Books, 1999, ©1998. 629p.* When Rev. Merrily Watkins is sent to replace the vicar of Ledwardine, she expects to live a dreary existence in this small village of black and white houses. But her first days are contentious as she's drawn into a fight about how to represent the village's history. The townies want to make the focal point of their new tourist attraction, the cider festival, a play about Ledwardine's seventeenth-century martyred vicar, but the natives are against this production since it would reveal how some of their ancestors participated in this martyring. When one of the townie's teenaged daughters goes missing and other villagers meet gruesome ends, the villagers begin to doubt the ability of a female vicar to minister their parish. **Similar titles:** *Bag of Bones* and *Needful Things*, Stephen King; *One Rainy Night*, Richard Laymon; *The Dress Lodger*, Sheri Holman.

> *Clergy as Character • Dreams • Feminism • Herefordshire, England • Incest • Orchards • Parenting • Rape • Religion—Christianity—Episcopalian • Secret Sin • Serial Killers • Sex Crimes*

Rosen, Selina.

The Boat Man. *Alma, AR: Yard Dog Press, 1999. 68p.* (See chapter 7, "Demonic Possession, Satanism, Black Magic, and Witches and Warlocks: The Devil Made Me Do It.")

Rovin, Jeff.

Return of the Wolf Man. *New York: Penguin-Putnam, 1998. 339p.* (See chapter 6, "Vampires and Werewolves: Children of the Night.")

Schmidt, Dan.

Silent Scream. *New York: Leisure, 1998. 368p.* (See chapter 11, "Maniacs and Sociopaths, or the Nuclear Family Explodes: Monstrous Malcontents Bury the Hatchet.")

White, Gillian.

Unhallowed Ground. *New York: Simon & Schuster, 1998. 286p.* A social worker leaves her London home to inhabit a rural farmhouse left to her by her brother. However, she finds anything but the escape from the everyday violence of her former life when she soon figures out that she's the target of a mysterious stalker. **Similar titles:** *In the Dark*, Richard Laymon; *Gift Giver*, Jean Sapin; *The Tormentor*, Bill Pronzini.

> *Child Abuse • Domestic Violence • England • Social Worker as Character • Stalkers*

Williams, Drew.

Night Terrors. *St. Petersburg, Fla.: Barclay Books, 2001. 343p.* (See chapter 8, "Mythological Monsters and 'The Old Ones': Invoking the Dark Gods.")

Williamson, John N.

Spree. *New York: Leisure, 1998. 384p.* (See chapter 11, "Maniacs and Sociopaths, or the Nuclear Family Explodes: Monstrous Malcontents Bury the Hatchet.")

Wooley, John.

Dark Within. *Tulsa, Okla.: Hawk Publishing, 2000. 229p.* (See chapter 12, "Technohorror: Evil Hospitals, Military Screw-Ups, Scientific Goofs, and Alien Invasions.")

Wooley, John, and Ron Wolfe.

Old Fears. *Tulsa, Okla.: Hawk Publishing, 1999, ©1982. 286p.* (See chapter 14, "Psychological Horror: It's All in Your Head.")

Film

I Spit on Your Grave. *Mark Zarchi, dir. 1978. 100 minutes.* Also known as *Day of the Woman*, *I Hate Your Guts*, and *The Rape and Revenge of Jennifer Hill*, this much written about film was banned in Austria, Germany, Finland, and the United Kingdom for its graphic representation of a brutal gang rape and a woman's equally brutal revenge. Jennifer Hill, a young writer from New York City, rents a cabin for the summer in upstate New York, only to be brutally gang raped and left for dead by a gang of local men. But Jennifer's assailants are unwilling to take responsibility for their actions, and indeed, don't even understand what they've done wrong when she confronts each man, so they must pay with their lives instead. This is not a film for the faint of heart. The lack of fancy special effects or even background music makes the rape scene especially realistic and disturbing. **Similar reads:** *Six Inch Spikes*, Edo von Belkon; *Ghost Story*, Peter Straub.

New York State • Rape • Revenge • Secret Sin • Writer as Character

The Texas Chainsaw Massacre. *Tobe Hooper, dir. 1974. 83 minutes.* (See chapter 11, "Maniacs and Sociopaths, or the Nuclear Family Explodes: Monstrous Malcontents Bury the Hatchet.")

The Wicker Man. *Robin Hardy, dir. 1973. 84 minutes.* The people of Summerisle have returned to their ancient roots and practice pagan fertility rites to ensure the success of their crops. But lately the sacrifices made to the gods haven't been sufficient, as their crops are failing. The gods demand more. Sergeant Howie is sent from the mainland to investigate a missing girl who might be the next sacrifice to the gods. However, Howie himself is tricked into participation in the yearly sacrifice, and he soon discovers that the inhabitants of Summerisle may have outsmarted him. Edward Woodward, Britt Ekland, and Christopher Lee star in this brilliant film, which was later novelized by Hardy and Anthony Shaffer. **Similar reads:** *Desperation*, Stephen King; *Midwinter of the Spirit*, Phil Rickman.

Human Sacrifice • Police Officer as Character •
Religion—Christianity—Protestantism •
Religion—Paganism • Scotland

Our Picks

June's Picks: *The Association,* Bentley Little (Penguin); *The Stepford Wives,* Ira Levin (Random House); *The Wicker Man*, Robin Hardy and Anthony Shaffer (Pocket); *The Wine of Angels,* Phil Rickman (Pan Books); *I Spit on Your Grave* (film); *The Wicker Man* (film).

Tony's Picks: *The Apostate*, Paul Lonardo (Barclay); *The Stepford Wives*, Ira Levin (Random House); *The Wicker Man*, Robin Hardy and Anthony Shaffer (Pocket); *The Wicker Man* (film).

Chapter 11

Maniacs and Sociopaths, or the Nuclear Family Explodes: Monstrous Malcontents Bury the Hatchet

The maniac tale is a relatively new subgenre of horror. Like a tale of psychological horror, the maniac narrative is not the story of a monstrous supernatural being. The maniac looks like you and me. However, the impetus of the maniac narrative is the savagery of the killer, which makes readers question whether the serial murderer is indeed human. This is the reason that many of the titles in this chapter are cross-referenced in chapter 15, "Splatterpunk."

Like the ghost story, the maniac tale often examines the mechanism that created the monster as much as it emphasizes the actions of the monster itself. Perhaps this is because the relative newness of this subgenre causes writers to use another modern tool to explain the maniac's behavior: psychoanalysis. Classic psychoanalytic theory lends itself to novels that analyze the monster human, for it cites the family as the locus for formation of the individual personality. Therefore, it is not surprising to see the creation of the maniac attributed to an overbearing mother and/or weak father. For example, in Alfred Hitchcock's film *Psycho* (based on Robert Bloch's novel of the same name), arguably the prototype for the modern slasher text, Norman Bates is warped to psychosis by an absent father and a clinging and rejecting mother. Contemporary writers of maniac fiction continue this trend, although their psychology is a bit more sophisticated, as they explore the role of all family members, of the community, and of culture in general, in the creation of sociopaths. In the words of Hillary Rodham Clinton, these writers realize that "it takes a village" to raise a child or to create a monster.

The nuclear family too is a relatively new phenomenon, seeing its halcyon days in the post-World War II forties and in the "happy days" of the 1950s. The nuclear, nonextended family, isolated within its suburban ranch house and allegedly self-sufficient, was touted by psychologists as the norm and celebrated through the new medium of television, in fifties situation comedies such as *Leave It to Beaver* and *The Donna Reed Show*. The nuclear family was the Cold War era's answer to communism. However, father doesn't always know best, and Mom isn't always content to stay home and clean dressed in pearls and her Sunday best while little monsters continually tug at her skirts and demand attention. When Mom and Pop burn out or find they don't have all the answers to run this supposedly self-sufficient family, they often have no one to turn to. The result of these instances (where the stress of everyday life becomes too much) is the production of seriously disturbed children, and perhaps maniacal parents.

In Peter Straub's novella *Blue Rose*, one of the purest examples of the subgenre, the dysfunctional Beevers family produces Harry, a charming, psychotic child able to hypnotize people into killing themselves or others. Deeply racist neighbors who share their worldviews with young Harry are also responsible for his creation. They lead him to believe, among other things, that Adolph Hitler was one of the greatest men of the twentieth century. Harry's own parents' unwillingness to parent also adds fuel to the fire. Mr. Beevers returns from World War II with a bad case of post-traumatic stress disorder and is unable to impart anything of value to his son. He is unable even to hold a steady job due to his drinking. Mrs. Beevers, Harry's shrewish mother, is the family's sole support. However, she is too self-absorbed and bitter to guide her son down a better path. As a result, Harry Beevers grows up to lead troops who gun down children in Vietnam.

Young girls are not immune to these forces, either. In Stephen King's *Carrie*, the main character's isolation in her own nuclear family (herself, her fundamentalist mother, her dead paternal father, and her Heavenly Father as invoked by her abusive mother) allows her to fester into an angry young woman who will literally cause the town to explode with her telekinetic powers. Furthermore, in this tale the townspeople's isolation in their own nuclear families prevents them from rescuing Carrie from her abusive situation. When neighbors hear first Mrs. White's screams while in childbirth and later Carrie's shouts while being abused by her mother, they choose not to intervene, explaining that they thought the noise was due to "holy rolling" on the part of the family rather than a sound made by someone in distress and in need of assistance. Like Straub's and King's exemplary texts, works in this subgenre acknowledge that every family unit has a dark side that surfaces behind closed doors, and that children from these types of families will grow up, leave home, and turn order into chaos.

The subgenre has evolved greatly in a short period of time, with a recent trend toward the creation of the abnormal personality as organic phenomenon. In other words, maniacs, like paranoid schizophrenics, are *born*, not *made*—although a dysfunctional family can exacerbate the situation. Here horror is tackling the old nature versus nurture question. In Ramsey Campbell's novel *The One Safe Place*, it isn't important *why* the Fancy family torments the innocent Travises. Perhaps class and circumstance have made them into violent criminals, but their pathology isn't the focus of the novel. Instead, the real issue here is that the British criminal justice system is incapable of protecting law-abiding citizens from dangerous deviants, in part, perhaps because it makes too great of an attempt toward understanding the criminal's pathology rather than figuring out how to effectively incarcerate this type of person. Hannibal Lecter from *The Silence of the Lambs* and *Hannibal* is another example of a monster whose deviant proclivities are organic rather than generated by his environment. True, young Hannibal survived the brutal occupation of his home during World War II by Soviet troops who killed his parents and consumed the flesh of his baby sister when their food ran out. But this glimpse into young Hannibal's psyche is a minor theme and does little to explain how he became an evil genius that no prison can hold.

A final spin on the human monster is the justifiable maniac. In Barry Hoffman's novels *Hungry Eyes* and the *Eyes of Prey*, female victims of horrific violence grow up to kill those who would harm others. They must be stopped because what they do is *legally* wrong, not *morally* wrong. Hoffman makes this even clearer in *Judas Eyes*, in which vigilante turned bounty hunter Shara Farris has to stop a vigilante killer from killing men as they are in the act of rape. Farris must distinguish between what is illegal, in this case murder, albeit for a just cause, and what is immoral.

This chapter includes benchmark slasher novels such as Robert Bloch's *American Gothic* and *Psycho*, Thomas Harris's *The Silence of the Lambs*, Stephen King's *Misery*, and various works by perhaps the master of slasher novels, Dean Koontz. In addition, more recent works in this subgenre, including Ramsey Campbell's *The Count of Eleven* and the masterful *The One Safe Place*, Bentley Little's *The Ignored*, and Joyce Carol Oates's highly disturbing *Zombie,* are also included here.

Note: Stories about maniacs, sociopaths, and dysfunctional families can also be found in the collections and anthologies described in chapter 17. Refer to the subject/keyword index for specific titles under the keywords "maniacs" and "serial killers."

Appeals: Human Curiosity Concerning the Psychology of Serial Killers; The Gore Appeal; The Monsters Are Human, Not Supernatural; Parallels the Historical American Fascination with Murderers; More in Line with "Real" Fears (Random Violence as Opposed to Vampiric Visitations)

Arnzen, Michael.

🅑 **Grave Markings**. *New York: Dell, 1994. 383p.* (See chapter 15, "Splatterpunk: 🏴 The Gross Out.")

Atkins, Peter.

Morningstar. *Lancaster, Pa.: Stealth Press, 2000, ©1992. 244p.* In this graphically violent masterpiece, a serial killer is loose on the streets of San Francisco, and only two people have any idea what he looks like: the girlfriend of one of his victims who is visited in her dreams by ghosts, and an aging reporter who is taken into confidence by the killer. But what journalist Donovan Moon is not prepared to learn is that as disturbing as the ritualistic mutilations of the victims may be, what is more unsettling is that it seems the victims were all vampires.
Similar titles: *The Light at the End*, John Skipp and Craig Spector; *The Count of Eleven*, Ramsey Campbell; *Hannibal*, Thomas Harris; *The Secret Life of Colors*, Steve Savile.

Dreams • Gay/Lesbian/Bisexual Characters • Journalist as Character • Psychosexual Horror • San Francisco, California • Serial Killers • Torture • Vampire Hunters

Aubert, Brigitte.

Death from the Woods. *David L. Karal (translator). New York: Welcome Rain Publishers, 2000, ©1996. 279p.* (See chapter 14, "Psychological Horror: It's All In Your Head.")

Ball, Donna.

Dark Angel. *New York: Signet, 1998. 368p.* Ellen Cox, a schoolteacher in Virginia, is saved from a life-threatening accident, but the notoriety it causes leads her to find out she is not who she thought she was. In the meantime, her dreams of serial murders continue to come true. **Similar titles:** *Death from the Woods*, Brigitte Aubert; *Retribution*, Elizabeth Forrest; *The Dead Zone*, Stephen King; *The Face of Fear*, Dean Koontz.

Dreams • Mistaken Identity • Serial Killers • Teacher as Character • Virginia

Banks, Ian.

The Wasp Factory. *London: Little, Brown, 2001, ©1984. 256p.* Frank Cauldhame is a weird teenager who lives on a tiny island connected to the mainland of Scotland by a bridge. He maintains grisly Sacrifice Poles to serve as his early warning system and a deterrent against anyone who might invade his territory. This novel is his tale, a deftly written first person narrative filled with dark humor, a sense of the surreal, and a serious examination of the psyche of a childhood psychopath. **Similar titles:** *The Emerald Germs of Ireland*, Patrick McCabe; *Christine*, Stephen King; *The Event*, Donald Silverman; *Portrait of the Psychopath as a Young Woman*, Lee Edward and Elizabeth Steffen.

Dramatic Monologue • High School • Schizophrenia/Multiple Personality Disorder • Scotland • Serial Killers • Torture

Barlog, J. M.

Red Hearts. *Chicago: BAK Books, 1999. 282p.* An unresolved bloody past haunts the people of Albuquerque, and after two years of silence, a serial killer has begun his killing anew. For police lieutenant Dakota Blackwood, an Apache who never quite fit in either his or the white man's world, the latest female victim rekindles images of the killer's previous M.O., which involved three deaths. Now Blackwood must stop the murderer before he can strike another victim. **Similar titles:** *Brass*, Robert J. Conley; *The Bottoms*, Joe R. Lansdale; *Storm*, Boris Starling; *Ghost Dance*, Mark T. Sullivan; *The Cell* (film).

Native American Characters • New Mexico • Police Officer as Character • Serial Killers

Billings, Andrew.

Carnage. *New York: Jove, 1999. 360p.* A young woman who takes part in a research facility raid by the League Opposed to Cruelty to Animals finds herself being stalked afterwards. As she watches her friends being killed one by one, she begins to suspect that soon her number will be up. **Similar titles:** *The Poker Club*, Ed Gorman; *Ghost Dance*, Mark T. Sullivan; *The Tormentor*, Bill Pronzini; *Storm*, Boris Starling.

Experiments—Animals • Revenge • Seattle, Washington • Stalkers • Weird Science

Bloch, Robert.

American Gothic. *New York: Simon & Schuster, 1974. 222p.* Based on historical accounts of real life serial killer Herman Mudgett, *American Gothic* tells of how Dr. Gordon G. Gregg lured victims into his castle-like home and tortured and murdered them, all during the Chicago World's Fair of 1892. **Similar titles:** *Psycho*, Robert Bloch; *Hannibal*, Thomas Harris; *Zombie*, Joyce Carol Oates.

Chicago, Illinois • History, Use of • Serial Killers • United States—19th Century

Psycho. *New York, Tor: 1989. 223p.* Norman Bates, a mentally ill loner whose condition is exacerbated by a domineering mother, kills "loose" young women who arouse him. But now Norman has made the mistake of murdering a woman who disappeared with $40,000 of her boss's money, so detectives show up at the Bates Motel to investigate. Told through several first person narratives, Bloch's novel is based on the Ed Gein murders in the 1950s. It was made into a classic film by Alfred Hitchcock. **Similar titles:** *American Gothic*, Robert Bloch; *The Face That Must Die*, Ramsey Campbell; *The Silence of the Lambs*, Thomas Harris; *Zombie*, Joyce Carol Oates.

> *Matricide/Patricide • Schizophrenia/Multiple Personality Disorder • Slasher*

Brite, Poppy Z.

The Crow: The Lazarus Heart. *New York: Harper Prism, 1998. 256p.* A serial killer murders one of a set of twins and frames his friend, a photographer, who is then executed. The second twin, Lucrece, recalls the dead photographer to seek revenge. Brite's emphasis is on description, but she does not sacrifice action. **Similar titles:** *The Crow: Quoth the Crow*, David Bishoff; *The Crow: Clash by Night*, Chet Williamson; *Spirit*, Graham Masterton.

> *The Crow (character) • Gay/Lesbian/Bisexual Characters • Gothicism • New Orleans, Louisiana • Twins*

Campbell, Ramsey.

The Count of Eleven. *New York: Tor, 1992. 310p.* Family man Jack Orchard has a run of bad luck that threatens to tear apart his life. When he finds a discarded chain letter, he decides that it must be the cause of it, so to make amends, he quickly follows the instructions on the letter—to get it out to thirteen other people without divulging the list. Whenever anyone stands between Jack and his task, however, he goes over the edge. Campbell's emphasis is on characterization and psychology. **Similar titles:** *Eyes of Prey* and *Hungry Eyes*, Barry Hoffman; *Portrait of the Psychopath As a Young Woman*, Edward Lee and Elizabeth Steffen; *Starr Bright Will Be With You Soon*, Joyce Carol Oates; *American Psycho* (film).

> *Numerology • Serial Killers*

The Doll Who Ate His Mother. *New York: Tom Doherty, 1985, ©1976. 284p.* A schoolteacher's brother is killed in a bizarre car accident, wherein his arm is sliced off, then mysteriously disappears. She begins to suspect that a strange-looking man she saw right before the accident took the arm, and eventually joins forces with three other people who also claim to have had loved ones victimized by this man, who they believe is a cannibal. The four try to track down this mysterious individual, unaware that he is the intended successor to a demonic cult leader, or that he is closer to them than they think. This novel has an excellent plot twist for an ending. **Similar titles:** *Death's Door*, John Wooley and Ron Wolfe; *Evil Whispers*, Owl Goingback; *Ambrosial Flesh*, Mary Ann Mitchell; *A Darkness Inbred*, Victor Heck.

> *Cannibalism • Cults • Liverpool, England • Parapsychology • Teacher as Character • Writer as Character*

The Face That Must Die. *New York: Tor, 1979. 351p.* A young loner named Horridge is haunted by faces, by horrifying emotional experiences as a child, and by the voice of a serial killer named Craig. Sooner or later, "Horridge the Horror," as he was called by cruel children in his youth, is going to lose his sanity. This is Campbell's subtle treatment of a psychopathic killer. **Similar titles:** *Psycho*, Robert Bloch; *Eyes of Prey* and *Hungry Eyes*, Barry Hoffman; *Portrait of the Psychopath As a Young Woman*, Edward Lee and Elizabeth Steffen.

Gay/Lesbian/Bisexual Characters • Homoeroticism • Serial Killers • Twins

The Last Voice They Hear. *New York: Forge, 1998. 384p.* Television journalist Geoff Davenport is getting mysterious phone calls from his brother, who ran away when he was eighteen. For Geoff, these calls are disturbing, because a serial killer has been murdering happily married couples in the area, and the brother claims to be the killer. This is a typical character and atmosphere tale by Campbell, the master of psychological horror. **Similar titles:** *Death from the Woods*, Brigitte Aubert; *The One Safe Place*, Ramsey Campbell; *The Poker Club* and *Shadow Games*, Ed Gorman; *Desperation*, Stephen King.

Journalist as Character • London, England • Serial Killers • Sibling Rivalry

The Nameless. *London: Little, Brown, 1992, ©1985. 278p.* The daughter of Barbara Waugh, a literary agent in London, is kidnapped, and the mother finds out that the kidnappers are the members of a cult located in Scotland. As people who try to aid her in recovering her daughter are killed, Barbara realizes that she is quickly running out of time, because this particular cult "initiates" its members at thirteen, the age of her daughter. Finally, she must travel to Scotland with a male friend of hers to rescue her daughter herself, if it is not too late. **Similar titles:** *The Parasite*, Ramsey Campbell; *Black Oak 2: The Hush of Dark Wings*, Charles Grant; *A Game of Colors*, John Urbancik; *The Demon Circle*, Dan Schmidt.

Cults • London, England • Psychiatrist/Psychologist as Character • Scotland • Violence, Theories of • Weird Science

The One Safe Place. *New York: Tor, 1996. 401p.* The Travis family immigrates to England in search of a peaceful life, only to be stalked by the Fancys, a family of petty criminals, after the father runs afoul of the Fancy patriarch during a minor traffic altercation. The Travises go to the proper authorities for help, but the police are unable to protect them in this supposedly nonviolent society that bans guns and violent films. Here, the mundane is made newly frightening. **Similar titles:** *Death from the Woods*, Brigitte Aubert; *The Last Voice They Hear*, Ramsey Campbell; *The Poker Club* and *Shadow Games*, Ed Gorman; *Desperation*, Stephen King; *Night of the Hunter* (film).

England • Parenting • Revenge • Violence, Theories of

Ⓑ 🎖 **Silent Children.** *New York: Forge, 2000. 352p.* Hector Woollie, a contractor in Jericho Close, has a taste for bringing peace to young children he feels have been abused by their parents. A pillow over the face is just fine, although a knife across the throat of a noisy kid may be called for, while Hector soothes them by singing a lullaby as he snuffs out their lives. Hector disposes of the bodies by burying them in the basements of various houses. When young Terrence sees little Harmony Duke's finger in the concrete, however, Hector decides to fake his own death by drowning, then return incognito. But when he moves next door to a troubled family, he starts to think about his old ways again. **Similar titles:** *Death from the Woods*, Brigitte Aubert; *Brotherly Love*, David Case; *Boy in the Water*, Stephen Dobyns; *Sieze the Night*, Dean Koontz.

Childhood • Child Molesters • England • Parenting • Serial Killers • Torture

Clifford, Emmett.

Night Whispers: A Story of Evil. *Nashville, Tenn.: Cumberland House, 1998. 429p.* Scanner is a man with a peculiar talent: Using his listening devices, he can eavesdrop on anyone's conversations or phone calls. And if he doesn't like what someone has to say, or if he finds out that someone stands between him and a huge real estate deal worth millions, he stalks, surprises, mutilates, and murders the offender. Can Detective Cody Rainwalker stop a maniac who knows his every move before he even makes it? **Similar titles:** *Thunderland,* Brandon Massey; *The Tormentor,* Bill Pronzini; *Neighborhood Watch,* Andrew Neiderman; *The Bottoms,* Joe R. Lansdale.

> *Nashville, Tennessee • Police Officer as Character • Rainwalker, Cody (character) • Serial Killers • Stalkers*

Connolly, John.

 Every Dead Thing. *New York: Simon & Schuster, 1999. 395p.* (See chapter 15, "Splatterpunk: The Gross Out.")

Cross, Quentin.

The Witch Rising. *Philadelphia: Xlibris, 2000. 209p.* (See chapter 7, "Demonic Possession, Satanism, Black Magic, and Witches and Warlocks: The Devil Made Me Do It.")

Deaver, Jeffery.

The Coffin Dancer. *New York: Simon & Schuster, 1998. 358p.* A millionaire arms dealer attempts to assassinate three witnesses to a murder whose testimony could put him in jail. He does succeed in killing one of them in a plane explosion. Now quadripelgic criminologist Lincoln Rhyme (from the *Bone Collector*), with the help of his able-bodied assistant Amelia Sachs, must track the killer before he can silence the remaining two witnesses. **Similar titles:** The Silence of the Lambs Series, Thomas Harris; The Headhunter Series, Michael Slade; *The Girls He Adored,* Jonathan Nasaw; *Deviant Ways,* Chris Mooney.

𝅘 audiotape

> *Federal Bureau of Investigation • Forensic Pathologist as Character • New York City • Police Officer as Character • Quadriplegic/Paraplegic as Character • Rhyme, Lincoln (character)*

Dickey, Christopher.

Innocent Blood: A Novel. *New York: Scribner Paperback, 1998. 335p.* (See chapter 14, "Psychological Horror: It's All In Your Head.")

Dobyns, Stephen.

Boy in the Water. *New York: St. Martin's Press, 1999. 436p.* After his wife and daughter die in a fire, the illustrious Dr. Jim Hawthorne takes a job as headmaster of a dying, second rate New England boarding school for troubled youth, hoping that the challenge will help bury his grief. But Hawthorne arrives to find a faculty and administration so hostile toward his attempts to turn the school around that they'll stoop to nasty tricks like staging prank phone calls from his dead wife. And then one of the school's students is found murdered and floating in the swimming pool. This is an erudite, complex, and suspenseful modern gothic novel. **Similar titles:** *The Shining,* Stephen King; *Death from the Woods,* Brigitte Aubert; *Born Bad,* Barry Hoffman.

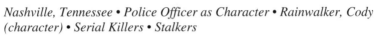

Child Abuse • Child Molester • Gothicism • Grieving • High School • New England • Secret Sin • Serial Killers • Teacher as Character

Driver, Lee.

Full Moon, Bloody Moon: A Chase Dagger Mystery. *Schereville, Ind.: Full Moon Publishing, 2000. 280p.* Private Investigator Chase Dagger and his shapeshifting sidekick Sara are called in on a police investigation after the body of a female jogger is found lodged between two branches, twenty feet off the ground. The two soon learn they are on the trail of an evil spirit, one that must appease its blood lust every Friday the 13th that has a full moon. Can they stop the 200-year-old creature before it kills again? **Similar titles:** The Black Oak Series, Charles Grant; The Host Series, Selina Rosen; *Aylmer Vance: Ghost-Seer*, Alice and Claude Askew; *The Licking Valley Coon Hunters Club*, Brian A. Hopkins.

Dagger, Chase (character) • Family Curse • Midwest, The • Religion—Native American • Serial Killers • Shapeshifters • Werewolves • Witchcraft

Fahy, Christopher.

Eternal Bliss. *New York: Kensington-Zebra, 2000, ©1988. 281p.* Fahy writes a fascinating study of a disturbed mind in this character-oriented suspense novel about the kidnapping of a famous model. Most of this claustrophobic story focuses on just two characters on a small island. **Similar titles:** *Misery*, Stephen King; *The End of It All*, Ed Gorman; *In the Dark*, Richard Laymon; *Gift Giver*, Jean Sapin.

Model as Character • Obsession • Torture

Fink, Jeri.

Virtual Terror. *Island Park, N.Y.: psychEpublishing, 2000. 348p.* Manhattan psychotherapist Melanie Wylie plunges into the uncharted world of online therapy to escape the predatory grasp of the insurance industry. Suddenly "Raven" appears on her online couch. His words lash out from the screen: "I am ready to kill. Your death will be my cure." Desperate to find Raven before he carries out his threat, Melanie enlists the help of a colleague and his cousin, an NYPD cop. They plummet into a chilling, surreal world of virtual terror, raging sexual fantasies, and dizzying psychological twists. In this explosive twilight zone between cyberspace and flesh-and-blood, Raven swoops in for the kill. **Similar titles:** *The Secret Life of Colors*, Steve Savile; The Cyber Blood Chronicles, Jonathan H. Amsbary; *Period*, Dennis Cooper.

Computers • Graphic Novel • Internet, The • New York City • Psychiatrist/Psychologist as Character

Forrest, Elizabeth.

Retribution. *New York: DAW, 1998. 464p.* A young woman who paints the images she sees in her nightmares slowly figures out that her dreams and paintings either predict the future or display a dark past, and the serial killer whose acts become a subject for her art must now hunt her down. **Similar titles:** *Dark Angel*, Donna Ball; *The Dead Zone*, Stephen King; *Shadow Games*, Ed Gorman; *The Face of Fear*, Dean Koontz; *Ghost Dance*, Mark T. Sullivan.

Artist as Character • Dreams • Serial Killers

Gibson, Jo.

Slay Bells. *New York: Kensington-Pinnacle, 2000, ©1994. 223p.* Enjoying the holiday shopping season at the new local mall, Diana Connelly is horrified when she and her friends are trapped there during a snowstorm, and a twisted killer begins checking off a list of his own. **Similar titles:** *Red Hearts*, J. M. Barlog; *Robert Bloch's Psychos*, Robert Bloch (editor); *Halloween* (film); *Spree*, John N. Williamson.

Popular Culture • Serial Killers • Shopping Malls

Giron, Sephera.

House of Pain. *New York: Leisure, 2001. 360p.* (See chapter 7, "Demonic Possession, Satanism, Black Magic, and Witches and Warlocks: The Devil Made Me Do It.")

Gonzalez, Gregg.

The Fifth Horseman: A Sleepy Hollow Legend. *Pleasantville, N.Y.: Milagro Publishing, 1999. 417p.* Has a Hessian soldier, dead for 200 years, come back to haunt present-day Sleepy Hollow, New York, or is it simply an eccentric psychopath suiting up as the Hollow's most revered legend? The death toll could reach apocalyptic proportions unless the mystery of the Headless Horseman can be solved in time. **Similar titles:** *The Guardian*, Beecher Smith; *Carmilla: The Return*, Kyle Marffin; *Sleepy Hollow* (film).

Academia • New York City • Revenging Revenant • Serial Killers • Sleepy Hollow Legend, The

Gorman, Ed.

Cold Blue Midnight. *New York: Leisure, 1998. 352p.* Photographer Jill Coffey has watched her husband's execution for several ax murders, but her terror does not end there. After his death, someone begins stalking Coffey. Is another ax murderer on the loose? **Similar titles:** *The One Safe Place*, Ramsey Campbell; *Unhallowed Ground*, Gillian White; *Whispers*, Dean Koontz.

Photographer as Character • Serial Killers • Stalkers

Daughter of Darkness. *New York: DAW, 1998. 333p.* (See chapter 12, "Technohorror: Evil Hospitals, Military Screw-Ups, Scientific Goofs, and Alien Invasions.")

The End of It All. *In Shadow Games. New York. Leisure, 2000, ©1995. 36p.* A forty-something average man, going through his mid-life crisis, becomes the object of obsession after he gets plastic surgery. This novella is a first person narrative about a stalker who will stop at nothing to get what she wants. **Similar titles:** *Whispers*, Dean Koontz; *Strangewood*, Christopher Golden; *Travel Many Roads*, Robert E. Wheeler.

Cosmetic Surgery • Obsession • Stalkers

The Poker Club. *New York: Leisure, 2000. 393p.* An ordinary poker game among four friends is interrupted one night by a burglar, and an accidental death leads to the four being stalked by a man they've never met, but who wants to kill them off one at a time—viciously. Gorman is action-oriented, but establishes solid characterization as well. **Similar titles:** *Carnage*, Andrew Billings; *Eyes of Prey* and *Hungry Eyes*, Barry Hoffman; *Ghost Story*, Peter Straub.

Accountant as Character • Police Officer as Character • Revenge • Secret Sin • Stalkers • Vigilantism

Grant, Charles.

Symphony. *New York: Tor, 1997. 332p.* (See chapter 8, "Mythological Monsters and 'The Old Ones': Invoking the Dark Gods.")

In the Mood. *New York: Forge, 1998. 304p.* (See chapter 8, "Mythological Monsters and 'The Old Ones': Invoking the Dark Gods.")

Grant, Charles. The Black Oak Series.

Black Oak 4: Hunting Ground. *New York: Penguin, ROC, 2000. 246p.* Supernatural investigator Ethan Proctor goes to Atlantic City to investigate a series of gruesome serial killings, only to discover himself pitted against an immortal as evil as he is invincible. Even knowing the creature's Achilles' heel, can Proctor and the Black Oak Society stop an ages-old shapeshifter with hypnotic powers? **Similar titles:** *Full Moon, Bloody Moon,* Lee Driver; *The Host Series,* Selina Rosen; *Aylmer Vance: Ghost-Seer,* Alice and Claude Askew; *Fallen* (film).

> *Atlantic City, New Jersey • Black Oak Security • Immortality • Mind Control • Private Investigator as Character • Proctor, Ethan (character) • Serial Killers • Vampire as New Species*

Hamilton, Laurell K.

Bloody Bones. *New York: Penguin, 1996. 370p.* (See chapter 16, "Comic Horror: Laughing at Our Fears.")

Guilty Pleasures. *New York: Penguin, 1993. 265p.* (See chapter 16, "Comic Horror: Laughing at Our Fears.")

Harris, Thomas. The Silence of the Lambs Series.

The Silence of the Lambs. *New York: St. Martin's Press, 1988. 338p.* Rookie FBI agent Clarice Starling, with the help of convicted serial killer Hannibal Lecter, must catch another serial killer, Buffalo Bill, who has kidnapped a senator's daughter. But to be an effective FBI agent, Starling must confront her own deepest fears as well. Harris's storytelling is literate and engaging in this Stoker Award Winner. This novel was made into a film by the same name. **Similar titles:** *Psycho*, Robert Bloch; *Zombie*, Joyce Carol Oates; *Hungry Eyes*, Barry Hoffman; *Hannibal*, Thomas Harris.

🎧 audiotape

> *Baltimore, Maryland • Cannibalism • Federal Bureau of Investigation • Gay/Lesbian/Bisexual Characters • Lecter, Hannibal (character) • Police Officer as Character • Police Procedural • Psychiatrist as Character • Serial Killers • Starling, Clarice (character)*

Hannibal. *New York: Delacorte Press, 1999. 484p.* This long-awaited sequel to *The Silence of the Lambs* finds the good doctor Lecter alive and well. Meanwhile, FBI agent Clarice Starling is being hung out to dry for the mistakes of a bureau that's still unable to deal with women as colleagues. This novel, which focuses more on Hannibal Lecter's past crimes than his ability to find serial killers, humanizes the enigmatic doctor by presenting us with victims who richly deserved their fates. **Similar titles:** *The Silence of the Lambs*, Thomas Harris; *Messiah*, Boris Starling; *Hannibal* (film).

🎧 audiotape, compact disc

> *Cannibalism • Childhood • Deformity • Federal Bureau of Investigation • Gay/Lesbian/Bisexual Characters • Italy • Lecter, Hannibal (character) • Pigs • Police Officer as Character • Psychiatrist/Psychologist as Character • Revenge • Serial Killers • Starling, Clarice (character) • Washington, D.C.*

Hoffman, Barry.

Born Bad. *New York: Leisure, 2000. 392p.* A young mother gives birth to a crack baby that grows up to become a young woman who has absolutely no sense of remorse. Now a young adult in college, Shanicha finds herself relieving her boredom by driving her dorm mates to suicide. She even sends poems to a local detective to hint at the possibility of murder. Can she be stopped before she claims yet another victim? **Similar titles:** *Emerald Germs of Ireland*, Patrick McCabe; *The Wasp Factory*, Ian Banks; *Butcher Boy* (film); *Portrait of the Psychopath as a Young Woman*, Lee Edward and Elizabeth Steffen.

> *Academia • African-American characters • Philadelphia, Pennsylvania • Police Officer as Character • Serial Killers • Suicide*

Hoffman, Barry. The Hungry Eyes Series.

Hungry Eyes. *New York: Leisure, 1998. 267p.* As a young girl, Renee faces one terrifying situation after another: witnessing the death of her stepfather in a botched police raid, being forced to become the family maid, being kidnapped and held in a cage for days. Now, the adult Renee is out to close the "hungry eyes" of sexual predators for good, and only her journalist friend who knows her secret can stop her before she meets a tragic end. This is an interesting psychological tale about the limits of friendship and the nature of true crime. **Similar titles:** *Eyes of Prey*, Barry Hoffman; *The Poker Club*, Ed Gorman; *Starr Bright Will Be With You Soon*, Joyce Carol Oates [as Rosamund Smith]; *Six Inch Spikes*, Edo van Belkom.

> *Farris, Shara (character) • Federal Bureau of Investigation • Journalist as Character • Revenge • Schizophrenia/Multiple Personality Disorder • Serial Killers • Vigilantism*

Eyes of Prey. *New York: Leisure, 1999. 359p.* A young girl survives a vicious attack by burglars that kills the rest of her family. Now an adult, Lysette discovers that she has the power to hunt down and kill the criminal types on the mean streets, before they can hurt innocent people. Hoffman affords excellent descriptions of the seedy underworld of exotic dancing. **Similar titles:** *Hungry Eyes*, Barry Hoffman; *The Poker Club*, Ed Gorman; *Starr Bright Will Be with You Soon*, Joyce Carol Oates [as Rosamund Smith]; *Six Inch Spikes*, Edo van Belkom.

> *Journalist as Character • Philadelphia, Pennsylvania • Police Officer as Character • Revenge • Schizophrenia/Multiple Personality Disorder • Stripper as Character • Vigilantism*

Judas Eyes. *Springfield, Pa.: Edge Books, 2001. 406p.* Shara Farris, the vigilante heroine of *Hungry Eyes*, returns as a street-smart bounty hunter who first helps acquit innocent police detective Lamar Briggs of the murder of a serial rapist, then teams up with him to hunt Mica Swann, a professional dominatrix on a monthly murder spree that leaves a trail of male victims all slaughtered in mid-rape. Shara tracks her quarry by identifying with them. **Similar titles:** The Silence of the Lambs Series, Thomas Harris; *Hungry Eyes* and *Eyes of Prey*, Barry Hoffman; *Six Inch Spikes*, Edo Van Belkom.

> *Clairvoyant as Character • Philadelphia, Pennsylvania • Rape • Revenge • Vigilantism*

Hooper, Kay.

Touching Evil. *New York: Bantam Books, 2001. 358p.* Psychic Maggie Barnes is able to walk into any abode and feel the violence that occurred within its walls. She can tell when arguments have happened in certain parts of a house, and often has a clear sense of what those arguments were about. In addition, she can sense emotions from victims when interviewing them. *Touching Evil* chronicles Barnes's first official case as part of Quentin Hayes's psychic detective team, as she searches for the Seattle serial killer who cuts out women's eyes and sexually assaults them, leaving them for dead. **Similar titles:** *Storm*, Boris Starling; *The Girls He Adored*, Jonathan Nasaw; *The Bottoms*, Joe R. Lansdale; The Black Oak Series, Charles Grant.

> *Clairvoyant as Character • Police Officer as Character • Psychosexual Horror • Reincarnation • Seattle, Washington • Serial Killers*

Houarner, Gerard.

The Beast That Was Max. *New York: Leisure, 2001. 392p.* (See chapter 15, "Splatterpunk: The Gross Out.")

Hynd, Noel.

Rage of Spirits. *New York: Pinnacle, 1998. 416p.* (See chapter 9, "Telekinesis and Hypnosis: Chaos from Control.")

Jacob, Charlee.

This Symbiotic Fascination. *New York: Leisure, 2002. 394p.* (See chapter 15, "Splatterpunk: The Gross Out.")

Kaminsky, Howard, and Susan Kaminsky.

The Twelve. *New York: St. Martin's Press, 1999. 306p.* Five years after the immolation of a cult compound by federal agents, a dozen of the surviving children disappear—and then a murderous rampage against the agents begins. Can anyone stop the survivors of the Cult of the Patriots' Redeemer from exacting their revenge? **Similar titles:** *The Parasite*, Ramsey Campbell; *Mischief*, Douglas Clegg; *The Servants of Twilight*, Dean Koontz.

> *Cults • Federal Bureau of Investigation • Religion—Christianity • Revenge • Serial Killers*

Ketchum, Jack.

Cover. *Springfield, Pa.: Gauntlet, 2000. 282p.* A psychotic Vietnam veteran hunts down a group of people on a weekend outing in the woods. Can any of them survive? **Similar titles:** *The Lost*, Jack Ketchum; The *Tormentor*, Bill Pronzini; *Among the Missing*, Richard Laymon; *Mine*, Robert McCammon.

> *Post Traumatic Stress Disorder • Soldier as Character • Stalker*

The Lost. *New York: Leisure, 2001. 394p.* At five foot three inches, Ray Pye suffers from little man syndrome. So he stuffs his cowboy boots with crushed beer cans and carries himself in such a way that no one can ignore him or fail to demonstrate the proper respect for him. And anyone, especially any woman, he even perceives as slighting him will be made to pay. Officer Ed Schilling has his own regrets. He had long suspected Pye of killing two women, but was unable to prove anything. And now, he must make that connection before others dear to him are in danger. This novel is loosely based on the life of serial killer Charles Schmid, The Pied Piper of Tucson, who was the inspiration for Joyce Carol Oates's "Where Are You Going, Where Have You Been?" **Similar titles:** *From Hell*, Alan Moore and Eddie Campbell; *American Gothic*, Robert Bloch; *From Hell* (film).

> *Drugs • Manson, Charles—Murders • New Jersey • Police Officer as Character • Popular Culture • Psychosexual Horror • Revenge • Secret Sin • Serial Killers • The Sixties*

King, Stephen.

Carrie. *New York: Signet, 1988. 245p.* (See chapter 9, "Telekinesis and Hypnosis: Chaos from Control.")

The Green Mile. *New York: Signet, 1996. 592p.* (See chapter 14: Psychological Horror: It's All In Your Head)

Misery. *New York, New American Library: 1988. 338p.* Best-selling bodice ripper novelist Paul Sheldon meets his biggest fan, a nurse tending his body after an automobile accident. But she is also his captor, keeping him prisoner in her isolated house. Now she wants Paul to write his greatest work—just for her. This claustrophobic novel, recipient of a Bram Stoker Award, was made into a film of the same name. **Similar titles:** *The End of It All*, Ed Gorman; *Travel Many Roads*, Robert E. Wheeler; *Gift Giver*, Jean Sapin.

　audiotape, audio download

> *Colorado • Nurse as Character • Obsession • Writer as Character*

Rose Madder. *New York: Viking, 1995. 420p.* An abused woman who's endured all she can becomes "Rose Madder," an angry woman bent on revenge. Will her need for vengeance change her into a monster? **Similar titles:** *Dolores Claiborne*, Stephen King; *Emerald Germs of Ireland*, Patrick McCabe; *The Funhouse*, Dean Koontz.

　large print

> *Alter Ego • Domestic Violence • New England • Revenge*

The Shining. *New York: Plume, 1977. 416p.* (See chapter 7, "Demonic Possession, Satanism, Black Magic, and Witches and Warlocks: The Devil Made Me Do It.")

King, Stephen, and Peter Straub. The Talisman Series.

Black House. *New York: Random House, 2001. 625p.* In this sequel to *The Talisman*, Travelin' Jack is now a man who has convinced himself that his experiences in the Territories were all a boyish fantasy, and that his mother's imminent death is mere histrionics on the part of an aging actress. At the age of thirty-one, he's retired as a police detective after solving a particularly gruesome murder. All he wants to do is settle down in tiny Tamarack, Wisconsin, and live life as a private citizen. But the children of Tamarack are mysteriously disappearing, their dismembered bodies turning up days later. Jack must remember how to travel once again and venture into the Territories to catch the killer. **Similar titles:** *Mr. X*, Peter Straub; *Stangewood*, Christopher Golden; *Thunderland*, Brandon Massey.

　audiotape　　 e-book　　 large print

> *Blindness • Cannibalism • Child Molester • Disc Jockey as Character •*
> *Epic Structure • Fantasy • Nursing Homes • Parallel Universe •*
> *Parenting • Police Officer as Character • Sawyer, Jack (character) •*
> *Senior Citizen as Character • Serial Killers • Shapeshifters • Territories,*
> *The • Wisconsin*

Koontz, Dean.

The Bad Place. *New York: Berkley, 1990. 417p.* Frank Pollard awakens one day to find himself on a deserted street, with no memories of how he got there. Soon his destiny will be tied to that of a computer hacker and a maniacal killer who believes he is a vampire. This is a suspenseful tale that is related from multiple points of view. **Similar titles:** *Dark Side: The Haunting*, J. M. Barlog; *Amnesia*, Andrew Neiderman; *Morningstar*, Peter Atkins.

> *Amnesia • Computer Hackers • Serial Killers*

Dragon Tears. *New York: Putnam, 1993. 377p.* (See chapter 9, "Telekinesis and Hypnosis: Chaos from Control.")

The Face of Fear. *New York: Berkley, 1985. 306p.* A clairvoyant in New York has visions of the killings executed by a deranged killer called "the butcher." His latest vision, that of his own death at the hands of the butcher, may come true if he cannot overcome his own fears. This is one of Koontz's early novels; it culminates spectacularly in a high rise chase scene. **Similar titles:** *Dead Zone*, Stephen King; *Retribution*, Elizabeth Forest, *Tribulations*, J. Michael Straczynski; *From Hell*, Alan Moore and Eddie Campbell.

New York City • Parapsychology • Police Officer as Character • Serial Killers

The Funhouse: A Novel. *New York: Berkley, 1980. 333p.* In this thriller, a woman is hunted by her ex-husband, a handsome carnival barker who is out for revenge for her killing their son, whom she was convinced was evil. Although he had to wait twenty-five years, her ex now has his chance, so he sets out to take her children away the way she took his. **Similar titles:** *Rose Madder*, Stephen King; *Gift Giver*, Jean Sapin; *The Stepfather* (film); *The Caretaker*, William Thomas Simpson.

Domestic Violence • Revenge

Hideaway. *New York: Putnam, 1992. 384p.* (See chapter 7, "Demonic Possession, Satanism, Black Magic, and Witches and Warlocks: The Devil Made Me Do It.")

Intensity. *New York: Ballantine Books, 1995. 436p.* Chyna Shepherd witnesses the brutal murders of a friend and his entire family and decides to follow the killer to his isolated home to exact revenge. There's only one problem: The killer knows he's being followed. This is a suspenseful novel that's a fan favorite. **Similar titles:** *The Poker Club* and *Shadow Games*, Ed Gorman; *The Lost*, Jack Ketchum; *Hannibal*, Thomas Harris; *The One Safe Place*, Ramsey Campbell.

𝔇 audiotape

Childhood • Revenge • Serial Killers

Lightning. *New York: Berkley, 1989. 355p.* A mysterious, tall blond man continually shows up at events of life and death in Laura Shane's life—usually to save her. Unfortunately, so does a tall dark-haired man with a facial scar, who tries to kill her. What secrets does she hold, and what is Laura Shane's destiny? This is a marvelous study of time travel and alternative realities. **Similar titles:** The Talisman Series, Stephen King and Peter Straub; *Mr. X*, Peter Straub; *Dark Soul*, Martin M. Hunt; *Twilight Dynasty: Courting Evil*, Barry H. Smith.

𝔇 audiotape

Alternative History • Nazism • Time Travel

Seize the Night. *New York: Bantam Books, 1999. 443p.* (See chapter 12, "Technohorror: Evil Hospitals, Military Screw-Ups, Scientific Goofs, and Alien Invasions.")

The Servants of Twilight. *Arlington Heights, Ill.: Dark Harvest, 1988. 327p.* A mother and her six-year-old son are getting in their car in a store parking lot when an old woman approaches them and insists the boy is evil and must die. Thus begins this action/suspense novel about a religious cult whose leader has marked a child for death. **Similar titles:** *The Halloween Man*, Douglas Clegg; *The Doll Who Ate His Mother*, Ramsey Campbell; *Ghost Story*, Peter Straub.

Cults • Religion—Christianity

Shattered. *New York: Berkley, 1985. 289p.* Alex Doyle and his nephew-in-law Colin travel across country, from Philadelphia to San Francisco. On their way there, they find themselves being followed by a white Automover van. It seems the van's owner has murderous intentions. **Similar titles:** *The Demon Circle*, Dan Schmidt; *Thunderland*, Brandon Massey; *Another Side of Evil*, Jax Laffer; *The Tormentor*, Bill Pronzini; *The Regulators*, Stephen King.

> *Philadelphia, Pennsylvania • San Francisco, California • Stalkers*

The Vision. *New York: Berkley, 1977. 353p.* A young woman is having visions of serial killings that actually happen. Can these visions be somehow connected to her childhood, which she cannot remember, and to her fear of sex? This one is a roller coaster ride of suspense. **Similar titles:** *The Dead Zone*, Stephen King; *Tribulations*, J. Michael Straczynski; *The Face of Fear*, Dean Koontz; *Secret Life of Colors*, Steve Savile.

> *Clairvoyant as Character • Genetics • Religion—Satanism*

The Voice of the Night. *New York: Berkley, 1980. 339p.* Colin and Roy are best friends, but they are complete opposites: Colin is introspective, compassionate, and sympathetic; Roy is extroverted, detached—and a sociopath. When Roy begins threatening Colin, and some of their mutual acquaintances are murdered, it becomes apparent that the friendship must be severed. **Similar titles:** *Spanky*, Christopher Fowler; *Dr. Jekyll and Mr. Hyde*, Robert Louis Stevenson; *The Tooth Fairy*, Graham Joyce; *Thunderland*, Brandon Massey.

> *Alter Ego • Psychosexual Horror*

Watchers. *New York: Berkley, 1996. 464p.* (See chapter 12, "Technohorror: Evil Hospitals, Military Screw-Ups, Scientific Goofs, and Alien Invasions.")

Whispers. *New York: Berkley, 1980. 509p.* Hollywood writer Hillary Thomas returns to her home one night to find a male acquaintance hiding in her closet, prepared to rape and knife her. She manages to chase him away with a gun, but he returns, again and again—even after she stabs him to death during one of his attacks. Now her "undead" assailant not only wants to kill her, he wants to brutally mutilate her for what she did to him. Can she escape the stalker who will not die? **Similar titles:** *The Tormentor*, Bill Pronzini; *Unhallowed Ground*, Gillian White; *Cold Blue Midnight*, Ed Gorman; *I Spit on Your Grave* (film).

> *Hollywood, California • Police Officer as Character • Rape • Stalkers •*
> *Twins • Writer as Character*

Laffer, Jax.

> **Another Side of Evil.** *Alma, Ark.: Yard Dog Press, 1999. 343p.* (See chapter 14, "Psychological Horror: It's All In Your Head.")

Lansdale, Joe R.

> **The Bottoms.** *New York: Warner Books-Mysterious Press, 2000. 328p.* A teen-aged boy and his sister find a mutilated body in the Sabine River, and clues point to the possibility that the murderer is "the Goat Man," a half-man, half-demon creature that resides in the woods. This is an insightful character study that chronicles the problems with race relations during the Great Depression. **Similar titles:** *The Girls He Adored*, Jonathan Nasaw, *The Cell* (film); *The Silence of the Lambs*, Thomas Harris; *The Lost,* Jack Ketchum; *The Vampire Hunters*, William Hill.

> > *African-American Characters • Childhood • Demons • Police Officer as Character • Psychosexual Horror • Race Relations • Racism • Rape • Serial Killers • Texas*

Laymon, Richard.

Among the Missing. *New York: Leisure, 2000. 393p.* In a small California mountain town, someone is murdering women, beheading them, and ravishing their corpses. Can the local police stop him before he kills again? This thriller is told from multiple points of view. **Similar titles:** *Storm*, Boris Starling; *Headhunter*, Michael Slade; *The Bottoms*, Joe R. Lansdale; *Stealing Faces*, Michael Prescott.

> *California • Necrophilia • Police Officer as Character • Psychosexual Horror • Serial Killers • Sex Crimes*

Come Out Tonight. *Baltimore: Cemetery Dance, 1999. 436p.* The Santa Ana winds are blowing fire toward L.A., and teenaged Toby Bones, who with his brother murdered his wealthy parents, is on the loose. Teacher Sherry Gates and her boyfriend Duane are involved in a secret rendezvous, when she is kidnapped by Toby, a student from a recent class. He beats and tries to rape her, and kills anyone who comes to her aid. **Similar titles:** *Meh'Yam*, Gloria Evans; *Whispers*, Dean Koontz; *The Girls He Adored*, Jonathan Nasaw; *Cuts*, Richard Laymon.

> *High School • Los Angeles, California • Rape • Serial Killers • Teacher as Character • Torture*

Cuts. *Baltimore: Cemetery Dance, 1999. 327p.* A teenager in Illinois goes on a killing spree, raping and mutilating women. One of the women takes pity on him when he is critically wounded. This graphic read contains scenes of sexual violence that are intimately detailed. **Similar titles:** *Another Side of Evil*, Jax Laffer; *The Girls He Adored*, Jonathan Nasaw; *The Bottoms*, Joe R. Lansdale; *In The Dark*, Richard Laymon.

> *Academia • Marriage • Rape • Sado-Masochism • Serial Killers*

In the Dark. *New York, Leisure, 2001, ©1994. 503p.* While closing the library, Jane finds an envelope with name on it. Inside is a $50 bill and a note, along with instructions to "look homeward angel," signed by the Master of Games. Jane soon pulls from the shelves a Thomas Wolfe novel of the same name, only to find a $100 bill and another clue. Thus begins the game that Jane willingly plays to receive amounts of cash that double with each new round. But as the money awarded increases, so do the stakes. **Similar titles:** *The Girls He Adored*, Jonathan Nasaw; *Another Side of Evil*, Jax Laffer; *Gerald's Game*, Stephen King; *The People Under the Stairs* (film).

> *Librarian as Character • Obsession • Psychosexual Horror • Stalkers • Torture*

One Rainy Night. *New York: Leisure, 2000. 410p.* An unexplainable black rain falls on the rural town of Bixby the night that a Jamaican high school student is killed. Once the rain touches a person, that individual becomes a sociopathic murderer, brutally killing the next person he or she sees. Laymon's emphasis is on plot and graphic description. **Similar titles:** *Supernatural* (film); *Ghost Story*, Peter Straub; *J. D.'s Revenge* (film); *Green Light Cemetery*, David Kosciolek.

> *Cursed Objects • High School • Police Officer as Character • Racism • Revenge*

Lee, Edward, and Elizabeth Steffen.

Dahmer's Not Dead. *Baltimore: Cemetery Dance, 1999. 288p.* Mere days after Jeffrey Dahmer's burial, Columbus County, Wisconsin, is terrorized by a new cannibal killer whose fingerprints, handwriting, and phone voice all match those of the supposedly deceased Dahmer. The press and police are convinced that Dahmer has either faked his death or been resurrected. But Helen Cross, a captain of the Wisconsin State Police Violent Crimes Unit, detects nuances in the crimes that suggest that a copycat with a different M.O. has made a diabolical change in his model's methods. **Similar titles:** *Ambrosial Flesh*, Mary Ann Mitchell; *Hannibal*, Thomas Harris; *Whispers*, Dean Koontz.

> *Cannibalism • Dahmer, Jeffrey (character) • Police Officer as Character •*
> *Police Procedural • Serial Killers*

Portrait of the Psychopath As a Young Woman. *Orlando, Fla.: Necro Publications, 1998. 292p.* This is a gory, thought-provoking tale of two women who suffered sexual abuse as children, one a feminist advice columnist, the other a sociopath who tortures her victims. This unique read is filled with irony, witty dialogue, and stomach-churning violence. **Similar titles:** *Starr Brite Will Be with You Soon*, Joyce Carol Oates [as Rosamund Smith]; *Morningstar*, Peter Atkins; The Silence of the Lambs Series, Thomas Harris.

> *Child Abuse • Child Molester • Feminism • Gay/Lesbian/Bisexual*
> *Characters • Journalist as Character • Police Officer as Character •*
> *Serial Killers*

LeRoux, Gaston.

The Phantom of the Opera. *New York: NAL-Signet, 1998, ©1911. 288p.* The Opera Ghost in Paris, a man ill treated since childhood because of his deformed face, who is schooled in the arts of murder and torture, becomes obsessed with the singer Christine Daae and takes her to his subterranean lair, where he tries to force her to become his bride. This is the original story that inspired four Hollywood films and Andrew Lloyd Weber's musical *Phantom of the Opera.* **Similar titles:** *Wuthering Heights*, Emily Brontë; *Dracula*, Bram Stoker; *Frankenstein*, Mary Shelley.

🎧 audiotape   ᏺᐩ large print

> *Daae, Christine (character) • France—19th Century • Music—Opera •*
> *Paris, France • Phantom of the Opera (character)*

Lewton, J. V.

Just Pretend. *New York: Pinnacle, 2000. 256p.* Teenage clairvoyant Clay Brannon races against time to protect a little girl from the lethal madman who is after her, after the child calls into a radio show about the killer and the police dismiss the call as a prank. **Similar titles:** *The Secret Life of Colors*, Steve Savile; *Tribulations*, J. Michael Stracynzski; *The Infinite*, Douglas Clegg; *Visions*, Dean Koontz.

> *Adolescence • Clairvoyant as Character • Disc Jockey as Character •*
> *Serial Killers*

Lord, David Thomas.

Bound in Blood. *New York: Kensington, 2001. 346p.* (See chapter 6, "Vampires and Werewolves: Children of the Night.")

Massey, Brandon.

Thunderland. *Atlanta, Ga.: Dark Corner Press, 2001, ©1998. 280p.* (See chapter 14, "Psychological Horror: It's All In Your Head.")

Massie, Elizabeth.

Ⓑ **Sineater.** *New York: Leisure, 1998. 396p.* (See chapter 10, "Small Town Horror: 🏅 Villages of the Damned.")

Welcome Back to the Night. *New York: Leisure Books, 1999. 393p.* (See chapter 10, "Small Town Horror: Villages of the Damned.")

Wire Mesh Mothers. *New York: Leisure, 2001. 393p.* Kate McDolan just wants to experience the joy of doing good, which is why she resumed her teaching career after her only child left home. One day, she seizes the opportunity to protect one of her charges from an abusive family. She flees with the girl, Mistie, hoping to shelter her with do-gooding college friends in Canada. On the way out of town, Kate is kidnapped by a fifteen-year-old girl trying to escape a botched convenience store robbery. The three make their way toward Texas, where Kate and her kidnapper learn what each is capable of. **Similar titles:** *Sineater* and *Welcome Back to the Night*, Elizabeth Massie; *Tideland*, Mitch Cullen; *The Way the Family Got Away*, Michael Kimball.

> *Child Abuse • Childhood • Domestic Violence • Incest • Parenting • Rape • Teacher as Character*

Masters, Paul.

Meca and the Black Oracle. *New York: Leisure, 1999. 327p.* (See chapter 15, "Splatterpunk: The Gross Out.")

McCabe, Patrick.

Emerald Germs of Ireland. *New York: HarperCollins, 2001. 306p.* McCabe's Irish homage to Robert Bloch's *Psycho* tells the story of Pat McNab, a small town boy who loves his mother, even when she makes him so angry sometimes he could just kill her. Pat grows up in a dysfunctional family with a violent, implacable father who is a career military officer, and a clinging, shrewish mother who refuses to let her little boy grow up. Young Pat is abused by all in town, but when he's finally had enough and kills his mother with a saucepan, there's no turning back his murderous rampage. **Similar titles:** *Butcher Boy* (film); *The Wasp Factory*, Ian Banks; *Portrait of the Psychopath as a Young Woman*, Edward Lee and Elizabeth Steffan; *Psycho*, Robert Bloch.

> *Child Abuse • Childhood • Domestic Violence • Incest • Ireland • Matricide/Patricide • Obsession • Parenting • Revenge • Secret Sin • Serial Killers*

McCammon, Robert R.

Mine. *New York: Pocket, 1990. 487p.* Mary Terror is an ex- freedom fighter from the 1960s who carries a grudge and lots of weapons. She also steals infants and brutally murders them when they do not please her. But now she has kidnapped Laura Clayborne's child, and Laura will stop at nothing to get him back. This nonstop thriller was the winner of a Bram Stoker Award. **Similar titles:** *Wire Mesh Mothers*, Elizabeth Massie; *The Stepfather* (film); *Strangewood*, Christopher Golden; The Poltergeist Series, James Kahn.

> *Federal Bureau of Investigation • Journalist as Character • Serial Killers*

Moline, Karen.

Belladonna. *New York: Warner Books, 1998. 480p.* A young woman is locked away and used as a sex slave by the rich in the early twentieth century. But she breaks free after a decade, and now is obsessed with revenge. This erotic novel is one of terror and adventure, narrated by a eunuch twin. **Similar titles:** *Ghoul*, Michael Slade; *Portrait of the Psychopath as a Young Woman*, Edward Lee and Elizabeth Steffan; *Eyes of Prey* and *Hungry Eyes*, Barry Hoffman; *Starr Bright Will Be with You Soon*, Joyce Carol Oates [as Rosamund Smith].

> *Class System • Eroticism • Italy • New York City • Revenge • Sex Crimes*

Mooney, Chris.

Deviant Ways. *New York: Pocket, 2000. 370p.* FBI Profiler Jack Casey is faced with the greatest challenge of his life. He must find the torturer/murderer who calls himself The Sandman, all the while protecting his loved ones from this vicious killer. Unfortunately,

The Sandman knows Jack's every move, for as Jack soon figures out, The Sandman is a surveillance expert. Jack must therefore tread lightly to avoid subjecting his daughter to the same fate that his wife met with years before—that of being murdered by one of Jack's suspects. **Similar titles:** *The Girls He Adored*, Jonathan Nasaw; The Silence of the Lambs Series, Thomas Harris; The Headhunter Series, Michael Slade; *The Extremes*, Christopher Priest.

> *Boston, Massachusetts • Federal Bureau of Investigation • New England • Police Procedural • Profiler as Character • Psychosexual Horror • Serial Killers • Torture*

Moore, Alan, and Eddie Campbell.

From Hell. *Paddington, Australia: Eddie Campbell Comics, 2000. 531p.* In his quest to find Jack the Ripper, Inspector Frederick Abberline is led through a vast conspiracy involving the royal family, Scotland Yard, and the Freemasons. Moore and Campbell's graphic novel does a fine job of incorporating all known theories about Jack the Ripper's identity, motivations, and victims. This incredible text includes an appendix with historical notes. **Similar titles:** *From Hell* (film); The Anno Dracula Series, Kim Newman; *Dr. Jekyll and Mr. Hyde* (film); *Ripper*, Michael Slade.

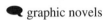 graphic novels

> *Clairvoyant as Character • Drugs • Freemasons, The • Graphic Novel • History, Use of • Jack the Ripper (character) • Jack the Ripper Murders • Kelley, Mary (character) • London, England • Physician as Character • Police Officer as Character • Prostitute as Character • Scotland Yard • Victorian England*

Moore, Joseph, and Brett A. Savory.

Filthy Death, The Leering Clown. *Kansas City, Mo.: Dark Tales, 2000. 44p.* (See chapter 15, "Splatterpunk: The Gross Out.")

Nasaw, Jonathan.

The Girls He Adored. *Pocket: New York, 2001. 325p.* A serial killer with multiple personality disorder breaks out of jail and kidnaps Irene Cogan, his state-appointed psychiatrist, in part because she is the type of woman he feels compelled to kill, and in part because he would like to ultimately fuse his feuding alters into one coherent whole. Meanwhile, only FBI Agent E. L. Pender fully realizes how many victims can be linked to this killer and how dangerous he is. Can Irene survive the ordeal without setting off one of his homicidal personalities? **Similar titles:** *The Silence of the Lambs*, Thomas Harris; *Psycho*, Robert Bloch; *The Bottoms*, Joe R. Lansdale; *Storm*, Boris Starling.

🔊 audio download

> *California • Child Abuse • Deformity • Federal Bureau of Investigation • Incest • Obsession • Oregon • Police Officer as Character • Police Procedural • Psychiatrist/Psychologist as Character • Psychosexual Horror • Rape • Schizophrenia/Multiple Personality Disorder • Serial Killers*

Newman, J[ames].

Holy Rollers. *Kansas City, Mo.: Dark Tales, 2001. 29p.* This short but suspenseful novella begins when an average middle class husband and wife open their front door to two door-to-door evangelists—only to discover that the two are actually crazed maniacal twin brothers who torture and kill in the name of Jesus. This text is original, with emphasis on quick-paced dialogue and action-oriented prose. **Similar titles:** *Awash in the Blood*, John Wooley; *Hungry Moon*, Ramsey Campbell; The Blood of the Lamb Series, Thomas F. Monteleone; *Horrors of the Holy*, Staci Layne Wilson.

Dramatic Monologue • Psychosexual Horror • Religion—Christianity • Torture

Oates, Joyce Carol [as Rosamund Smith].

Starr Bright Will Be with You Soon. *New York: Penguin-Dutton, 1999. 264p.* A thirty-seven year old stripper who has taken it upon herself to become "God's instrument" for cleaning up the world—by luring business men into secluded areas where she can slash their throats—returns home to visit her sister. Will the family be safe when Starr Bright tries to insinuate herself into a normal family unit? **Similar titles:** *Hungry Eyes* and *Eyes of Prey*, Barry Hoffman; *Portrait of the Psychopath as a Young Woman*, Edward Lee and Elizabeth Steffan; *I Spit on Your Grave* (film); *Belladonna*, Karen Moline.

Las Vegas, Nevada • New York City • Revenge • Serial Killers • Sibling Rivalry • Stripper as Character • Twins

Oates, Joyce Carol.

Zombie. *New York: Dutton, 1995. 181p.* Perhaps the candidate for the most disturbing analysis of a serial killer ever written, this engrossing tale, told in journal form by the killer himself, known only as Quentin P., chronicles the meetings of killer and victim, the killer's motives, and the gory methods used. What sets Oates's novel apart from others is her ability to allow the serial murderer to speak for himself, without the author's interjecting subtle hints of condemnation or aggrandizement. Once you pick it up, you will not be able to put down this winner of a Bram Stoker Award. **Similar titles:** *Psycho*, Robert Bloch; The Silence of the Lambs Series, Thomas Harris; *The Wasp Factory*, Ian Banks; *Emerald Germs of Ireland*, Patrick McCabe.

Diary Format • Gay/Lesbian/Bisexual Characters • Necrophilia • Serial Killers

Prescott, Michael.

Stealing Faces. *New York: Signet, 1999. 424p.* A young woman finds herself marked for extinction by an old acquaintance; she is his next victim in a game of cat and mouse in which he kidnaps women, takes them out into the wilderness, and hunts them down, cutting off their faces after he catches them. Can even a sympathetic police officer help her survive, considering that she is a former mental institution ward, and the murderer a prominent psychiatrist? This is an evenly paced novel that concentrates on character interaction instead of body counts. **Similar titles:** *Afterimage. Aftershock*, Kristine Kathryn Rusch and Kevin J. Anderson; *In the Dark*, Richard Laymon; *Storm*, Boris Starling; *The Girls He Adored*, Jonathan Nasaw.

large print

Arizona • Mental Institutions • Police Officer as Character • Psychiatrist/Psychologist as Character • Serial Killers • Torture

Preston, Richard.

The Cobra Event. *New York: Ballantine, 1998. 448p.* (See chapter 12, "Technohorror: Evil Hospitals, Military Screw-Ups, Scientific Goofs, and Alien Invasions.")

Pronzini, Bill.

The Tormentor. *New York: Leisure, 2000, ©1994. 394p.* Dix Mallory is being plagued by phone calls from a man who claims to be his dead wife's lover. As he investigates the possibility of her infidelity, he begins to suspect that her death may not have been an accident and begins to realize that his stalker may be out to harm his friends as well. This novel is energetic and fun to read, with emphasis on character interaction. **Similar titles:** *Night Whispers: A Story of Evil*, Emmett Clifford; *Whispers*, Dean Koontz; *Unhallowed Ground*, Gillian White; *Thunderland*, Brandon Massey.

California • Grieving • Oregon • Parenting • Pyromania • Stalkers

Randisi, Robert J. The Shadow of the Arch Series.

In the Shadow of the Arch. *New York: Leisure, 2000. 355p.* Detective Joe Keough moves to the Midwest to escape the murderous streets of New York City but finds himself confronted with orphaned children, missing parents, and blood-covered crime scenes. Randisi's emphasis is on detection, with Keough as the main character. **Similar titles:** *The Lost*, Jack Ketchum; *The Bottoms*, Joe R. Lansdale; *Black House*, Stephen King and Peter Straub; *Mecca and the Black Oracle*, Paul Masters.

Keough, Joe (character) • Police Officer as Character • Psychosexual Horror • Serial Killers • St. Louis, Missouri

Blood on the Arch. *New York: Leisure, 2001. 394p.* Detective Joe Keough had left New York City to get away from the violence and death, but what he finds in St. Louis is more of the same. This time he is on the trail of a small time political assassin who not only kills his victims but kills them in the most horrible way possible, by using heavy duty axes and other gardening tools. And he always leaves clues for Keough. This novel packs many surprises, and the question of who is working for whom is not answered until the very end. **Similar titles:** *Messiah* and *Storm*, Boris Starling; The Headhunter Series, Michael Slade; *Meca and the Black Oracle*, Paul Masters.

Assassinations • Keough, Joe (character) • Police Officer as Character • Serial Killers • St. Louis, Missouri

Rickman, Phil.

The Wine of Angels. *London: Pan Books, 1999, ©1998. 629p.* (See chapter 10, "Small Town Horror: Villages of the Damned.")

Rosen, Selina.

Fright Eater. *Alma, Ark.: Yard Dog Press, 1998. 175p.* (See chapter 6, "Vampires and Werewolves: Children of the Night.")

Rusch, Kristine Kathryn, and Kevin J. Anderson.

Afterimage. Aftershock. *Decatur, Ga.: Meisha Merlin, 1998. 446p.* In this omnibus edition, previously published novella *Afterimage* is combined with its previously unpublished sequel *Aftershock*. The Joan of Arc killer, a sadistic rapist who burns his victims before he murders them, has captured Rebecca Tamerlane, and is ready to burn her, when suddenly her body becomes completely whole and surprisingly strong. It turns out she is one of the darklings, or shapeshifters, who have always lived in peace with the land. But as the landscape is injured by humans and nature, the darklings begin to change and die. **Similar titles:** *Morningstar*, Peter Atkins; *Boy in the Water*, Stephen Dobyns; *Stealing Faces*, Michael Prescott.

Fantasy • Rape • Serial Killers • Science Fiction • Shapeshifters • Torture

Sapin, Jean.

Gift Giver. *Berkeley, Calif.: Creative Arts Book, 2000. 239p.* Ellen Cates makes the mistake of leaving her headlights on one night, thus draining her car battery, which results in her acceptance of an act of kindness from a local restaurant owner. Soon, his acts of kindness become more numerous, and he becomes obsessed with the young widow—to the point where he begins following her around town and spying on her dates with a young teacher at the local community college. When Cates confronts him, he begins to show his true colors as a murderous maniac. This is a gentle read that takes a close look at how the court system fails female victims of male stalkers. **Similar titles:** *Travel Many Roads*, Robert E. Wheeler; *The End of It All*, Ed Gorman; *In the Dark*, Richard Laymon; *Whispers*, Dean Koontz.

> *California • Greek-American Characters • Obsession • Revenge • Stalkers • Teacher as Character*

Savile, Steve.

Secret Life of Colors. *Kansas City, Mo.: Dark Tales Publications. 2000. 192p.* (See chapter 8, Mythological Monsters and 'The Old Ones': Invoking the Dark Gods.")

Saylor, Steven.

A Twist at the End. *New York: St. Martin's Press, 2001. 576p.* (See chapter 14, "Psychological Horror: It's All In Your Head.")

Schmidt, Dan.

The Demon Circle. *New York: Leisure, 2000. 358p.* (See chapter 7, "Demonic Possession, Satanism, Black Magic, and Witches and Warlocks: The Devil Made Me Do It.")

Silent Scream. *New York: Leisure, 1998. 368p.* When John Wilkins gets a letter from his brother Mike, he is unaware of the hatred that Mike has for him—and of the special powers his brother now possesses. It is only a matter of time before the two face off, at the family reunion. **Similar titles:** *Spirit*, Graham Masterton; *Mr. X*, Peter Straub; *The Last Voice They Hear*, Ramsey Campbell.

> *Cursed Objects • Mind Control • Revenge • Sibling Rivalry*

Sharp, Roger.

Psyclone. *St. Petersburg, Fla.: Barclay Books, 2001. 237p.* (See chapter 12, "Technohorror: Evil Hospitals, Military Screw-Ups, Scientific Goofs, and Alien Invasions.")

Silverman, Donald.

The Event. *Berkeley, Calif.: Creative Arts Book, 1999. 206p.* A meek, middle-aged women's clothing salesman harbors a deep, dark secret: While a teenager at an all boys private school, he murdered his roommate out of sheer anger at being picked on constantly. Now, with his marriage on the rocks and his livelihood threatened, will he resort to the same solution a second time? This first person narrative is fast-paced and well-written, told through time frame shifts between the main character's past and present lives. **Similar titles:** *Emerald Germs of Ireland*, Patrick McCabe; *The Wasp Factory*, Ian Banks; *Portrait of the Psychopath as a Young Woman*, Edward Lee and Elizabeth Steffan; *Dolores Claiborne*, Stephen King.

> *Dramatic Monologue • High School • Marriage • New England • Revenge • Secret Sin*

Simpson, William Thomas.

The Caretaker. *New York: Bantam, 1999, ©1998. 561p.* Gunn Henderson was born to be a salesman, so it's no surprise when he's recruited by Arthur James Reilly of Creative Marketing Enterprises. Neither Gunn nor his wife, Sam, can believe their good fortune, especially after Reilly shows them the rent-free company mansion that will be theirs and promises to make Gunn a millionaire within a year. However, working for Reilly puts Gunn under terrific pressure, on the road seven days a week, leaving Samantha at home with the two bratty Henderson kids and Brady, the handsome, sensitive, thoughtful, intelligent caretaker. But Brady may be a wolf in sheep's clothing, and all is not as it seems at Creative Marketing Enterprises. **Similar titles:** *Tormentor*, Bill Pronzini; *The One Safe Place*, Ramsey Campbell; *Storm*, Boris Starling.

> *Economic Violence • Marriage • Revenge*

Slade, Michael. The Headhunter Series.

(See chapter 15, "Splatterpunk: The Gross Out.")

Starling, Boris.

Messiah. *New York: Penguin-Onyx, 1999. 457p.* Detective Red Metcalfe is on the trail of a serial killer in London, who is always one step ahead of Red's investigations. To understand his adversary, Red must delve into that part of his mind that empathizes with the killer and his motives. Can Red stop the killer before he finishes "his mission," and if he does, will he be able to save his own psyche? **Similar titles:** *Storm*, Boris Starling; *The Cell* (film); *The Extremes*, Christopher Priest; The Silence of the Lambs Series, Thomas Harris.

> *Alter Ego • London, England • Marriage • Police Officer as Character • Police Procedural • Religion—Christianity • Scotland Yard • Serial Killers*

Storm. *London: Signet, 2000. 454p.* In this very graphic police procedural, detective Kate Beauchamp finds herself on the trail of a serial killer who tortures and mutilates women in Aberdeen, Scotland, and chasing a terrorist organization that has claimed responsibility for sinking a local ferry while she was on it, killing 352 people and permanently scarring her emotionally. Beauchamp soon discovers that the two cases may actually be related, and that the killer may even be someone she knows and trusts. More worrisome for her is the fact that his trail of victims seems to lead to her doorstep. Starling may well be the next Thomas Harris. **Similar titles:** *Messiah*, Boris Starling; *The Cell* (film); *The Extremes*, Christopher Priest; The Silence of the Lambs Series, Thomas Harris; *Stealing Faces*, Michael Prescott.

> *Journalist as Character • Police Procedural • Scotland • Serial Killers • Terrorism • Torture*

Stevenson, Robert Louis.

Dr. Jekyll and Mr. Hyde. *New York: Viking Penguin, 2002, ©1886. 224p.* Dr. Jekyll, a proper Victorian gentleman, creates a magic potion that transforms him into Mr. Hyde, who is not a Victorian gentleman, and who, instead, delights in trampling children and beating to death old men. **Similar titles:** *Mr. Murder*, Dean Koontz; *The Return*, Walter de la Mare; *Dr. Jekyll and Mr. Hyde* (film).

> 🎧 audiotape, audio download, compact disc   👓 large print   💾 e-book

> *Alter Ego • Hyde, Edward (Character) • Jekyll, Dr. Henry (Character) • Mad Scientist • Victorian England*

Straczynski, J. Michael.

Tribulations. *Kansas City, Mo.: Dark Tales, 2000. 236p. Tribune* crime reporter Susan Randall is assigned the story of Los Angeles's most recent serial killer: a man who mutilates victims with an exacto knife before killing them. During her investigations, she meets an old man who claims to be a psychic and who knows details of the murders. When Susan's colleagues and friends find themselves at the mercy of the killer, she begins to wonder if her newfound information source isn't who he claims to be, but is in fact the killer. **Similar titles:** *Secret Life of Colors*, Steve Savile; *From Hell*, Alan Moore and Eddie Campbell; *Morningstar*, Peter Atkins; *Project Resurrection*, Karen Duval.

> *Clairvoyant as Character • Journalist as Character • Los Angeles, California • Police Officer as Character • Religion—Christianity • Schizophrenia/Multiple Personality Disorder • Serial Killers*

Straub, Peter.

Blue Rose *(novella).* (See Straub, Peter. The Blue Rose Trilogy.)

Straub, Peter. The Blue Rose Trilogy.

KoKo. *New York: Dutton, 1988. 562p.* Members of Harry Beevers Vietnam platoon are being systematically murdered by a crazed killer. Is the killer one of the platoon members? Is the killer even human? Straub readers will enjoy this detective horror follow up to the Blue Rose stories about Beevers' childhood. *Note:* The Blue Rose stories continue with the detective novels *Mystery* and *The Throat*. **Similar titles:** *Carrion Comfort*, Dan Simmons; *One Rainy Night*, Richard Laymon; *Shadowland*, Peter Straub.

🎧 audiotape

> *Serial Killers • Underhill, Tim (character) • War—Vietnam*

Blue Rose *(novella). In Houses Without Doors. New York: Signet, 1991. 100p.* Young Harry Beevers, the fourth child in a family of five boys, is neglected by his alcoholic father and abused physically and verbally by his mother, a woman left embittered by a spouse who is incapable of supporting the family. In the Beevers household, the older boys traditionally subject their younger siblings to cruel torments while their parents turn a blind eye, and Harry is no exception to this rule. Bullied by his siblings, Harry turns his fury on his little brother Eddie. And when Harry discovers hypnosis, his torture of Eddie can be taken to new extremes. Straub's novella is a graphic and disturbing picture of a dysfunctional family who are not the Cleavers. **Similar titles:** *The Wasp Factory*, Ian Banks; *Emerald Germs of Ireland*, Patrick McCabe; *The Butcher Boy* (film); *The Voice of the Night*, Dean Koontz.

> *Beevers, Harry (character) • Childhood • Dysfunctional Families • Hypnotism • Mind Control • New York State • Torture • United States—1950s*

Mystery. Although part of Straub's Blue Rose Trilogy, *Mystery* is not annotated in *Hooked on Horror* because this work is actually a mystery and does not fit into any broad definition of horror.

Straub, Peter.

Floating Dragon. *New York: Putnam, 1983. 515p.* A small New England town is menaced by both a poisonous gas that eats away flesh and a maniacal killer who mutilates his victims. No one is safe in this Straub tour de force of reincarnation, occultism, technohorror, and splatterpunk. Similar title: The Talisman Series, Stephen King and Peter Straub; *Mr. X*, Peter Straub; *It*, Stephen King; The Millennium Quartet, Charles Grant.

> *New England • Reincarnation • Serial Killers • Slasher*

The Hellfire Club. *New York: Random House, 1996. 463p.* (See chapter 14, "Psychological Horror: It's All In Your Head.")

Mr. X. *New York: Ballantine Books, 1999. 510p.* Ned Dunstan has always felt an unseen presence following him, and when he comes home for his mother's funeral, he finally learns the mysterious secrets of his family and his hometown. He also discovers his own paranormal abilities. This novel of parallel realities is complex and original. **Similar titles:** *The Dark Half*, Stephen King; The Talisman Series, Stephen King and Peter Straub; *Thunderland*, Brandon Massey.

𝄢 audiotape, audio download

> *Deformity • Fantasy • Illinois • Lovecraft, H. P. (the works of) • Mistaken Identity • Parallel Universe • Parapsychology • Secret Sin • Sibling Rivalry • Time Travel • Twins • Writer as Character*

The Throat. *New York: Dutton, 1993. 689p.* Private investigator Tim Underhill enlists the aid of a reclusive genius in trying to clear a childhood friend of murder charges. This is the third book in the Blue Rose trilogy, and the winner of a Bram Stoker Award. **Similar titles:** *Carrion Comfort*, Dan Simmons; *One Rainy Night*, Richard Laymon; *Shadowland*, Peter Straub.

> *Blue Rose Murders • Serial Killers • Underhill, Tim (character)*

Sullivan, Mark T.

Ghost Dance. *New York: HarperCollins-HarperTorch, 1999. 342p.* A documentary writer/director teams up with an ex-alcoholic police officer in Vermont to try and stop a killer who rapes and mutilates his victims, all in the name of revenge for the genocide of the Sioux tribe. To further complicate the issue, the female officer comes to realize that she too is on the killer's list because she is the keeper of one-sixth of a journal given to her by her mother, and the killer is systematically murdering those who have parts of this work. **Similar titles:** *The Manitou*, Graham Masterton; *Crota*, Owl Goingback, *Brass*, Richard J. Conley; *Smoke Signals*, Octavio Ramos Jr.

> *Alcoholism • Director as Character • New England • Police Officer as Character • Rape • Religion—Christianity • Religion—Native American • Revenge • Serial Killers*

Tessier, Thomas.

Fog Heart. *New York: St. Martin's Press, 1998. 320p.* (See chapter 14, "Psychological Horror: It's All In Your Head.")

Truong, Chau Van.

Killing Star. *In For the Love of the Kill. Miami, Fla.: Minerva Publishing, 2001. 47p.* In this novella, a Vietnamese-American would-be actor becomes a serial killer after he accidentally discovers the pleasures of taking a life. As he gets bolder and begins stalking high-profile victims, such as models and rock stars, the police begin closing in on him. But can they stop him from pursuing the only pleasure he has in his life? **Similar titles:** *The Wasp Factory*, Ian Banks; *Eyes of Prey* and *Hungry Eyes*, Barry Hoffman; *Zombie*, Joyce Carol Oates; *Ticktock*, Dean Koontz.

> *Actor as Characters • Asian-American Characters • Hispanic-American Characters • Miami, Florida • Police Officer as Character • Serial Killers*

Wheeler, Robert E.

Travel Many Roads. *Miami, Fla.: Minerva Publishing, 2001. 191p.* (See chapter 14, "Psychological Horror: It's All In Your Head.")

White, Gillian.

Unhallowed Ground. *New York: Simon & Schuster, 1998. 286p.* (See chapter 10, "Small Town Horror: Villages of the Damned.")

Williams, Ron.

Deliver Us from Evil. *Philadelphia: Xlibris, 1999. 232p.* On the workroom floor in a large U.S. postal facility, the tension between workers and managers is not just about job performance but about personal relationships. A confused and disturbed letter carrier, his estranged wife, and an overbearing supervisor are the main characters in this tale about how ordinary workers with seemingly small problems can be driven over the brink and "go postal." **Similar titles:** *The Count of Eleven*, Ramsey Campbell; *Spree*, John N. Williamson; *Emerald Germs of Ireland*, Patrick McCabe.

Marriage • Serial Killers • U. S. Postal Service

Williamson, John N.

Spree. *New York: Leisure, 1998. 384p.* A disturbed forty-year-old misfit and his teenaged girlfriend want to escape small town life, so they go on a killing spree, beginning with her parents. This novel is action-oriented. **Similar titles:** *Killing Star*, Chau Van Truong; *Tideland*, Mitch Cullen; *Deviant Ways*, Chris Mooney.

Matricide/Patricide • Serial Killers

Yeager, Drew.

Bitten by Evil. *Victoria, B.C.: Trafford, 2000. 247p.* After witnessing the death of his mother at the hands of his abusive father, young Derrick Vaughn developed a case of multiple personality disorder. Now women suffer at the hands of the adult Vaughn's "evil" side; he beats and abuses them when in an altered state. Only a beautiful and unconventional psychiatrist can save him, but to do so she must become one of his victims. **Similar titles:** *This Symbiotic Fascination*, Charlee Jacob; *Gift Giver*, Jean Sapin; *The Beast That Was Max*, Gerard Houarner.

California • Domestic Violence • Psychiatrist/Psychologist as Character • Schizophrenia/Multiple Personality Disorder

Film

The Butcher Boy. *Neil Jordan, dir. 1997. 109 minutes.* Twelve-year-old Francie Brady is disturbingly angry for one so young, but he has had much to deal with at his tender age: a mother who commits suicide, an alcoholic father who drinks himself to death, and a town that has nothing but scorn for the boy. Francie tries to maintain some semblance of family life after his father dies, even keeping his father's corpse and cleaning the house. But the neighbors ultimately notice Mr. Brady's absence and force their way in, sending Francie to an orphanage. Little wonder that he begins to have visions of the Virgin Mary (played by Sinead O' Connor), who understands his compulsion to kill anyone who has slighted him. **Similar reads:** *The Wasp Factory*, Ian Banks; *Emerald Germs of Ireland*, Patrick McCabe.

Alcoholism • Alter Ego • Childhood • Dreams • Ireland • Obsession • Orphans • Pigs • Religion—Christianity—Catholicism • Revenge

Dr. Jekyll and Mr. Hyde. *Victor Flemming, dir. 1941. (Black-and-white.)114 minutes.* This is a faithful adaptation of Robert Louis Stevenson's story, stressing psychological horror. Excellent make-up and special effects for the time transform Spencer Tracy from the handsome Dr. Henry Jekyll into the hideous, cruel Mr. Hyde. Lana Turner and Ingrid Bergman also star. **Similar reads:** *Dr. Jekyll and Mr. Hyde*, Robert Louis Stevenson; *Spanky*, Christopher Fowler.

Alter Ego • Hyde, Edward (character) • Jekyll, Dr. Henry (character) • London, England • Victorian England • Weird Science

Freaks. *Tod Browning, dir. 1932. (Black-and-white.) 64 minutes.* A troupe of sideshow freaks demonstrate their camaraderie in a deadly way when one of their own is ill used by a "normal" person. Browning, who used actual side-show freaks for this film, gives dignity to people the world would often rather not see as human. **Similar reads:** *Phantom Feast*, Diana Barron; *A Graveyard for Lunatics*, Ray Bradbury.

Circuses • Deformity • Revenge

From Hell. *Albert and Allen Hughes, dir. 2001. 137 minutes.* In his quest to find Jack the Ripper, Inspector Frederick Abberline (Johnny Depp) is led through a vast conspiracy involving the royal family, Scotland Yard, and the Freemasons. The film does a fine job of incorporating all known theories about Jack the Ripper's identity, motivations, and victims. Heather Graham and Ian Holm also star. The Hughes brothers' interpretation of Alan Moore and Eddie Campbell's graphic novel of the same name isn't as dark as the original but remains reasonably faithful to their story. **Similar reads:** *Anno Dracula*, Kim Newman; *From Hell*, Alan Moore and Eddie Campbell.

Clairvoyant as Character • Drugs • Freemasons, The • History, Use of • Jack the Ripper (character) • Jack the Ripper Murders • Kelley, Mary (character) • London, England • Physician as Character • Police Officer as Character • Prostitute as Character • Scotland Yard • Victorian England

The Green Mile. *Frank Darabont, dir. 1999. 188 minutes.* (See chapter 14, "Psychological Horror: It's All In Your Head.")

Halloween. *John Carpenter, dir. 1978. 93 minutes.* Young Michael Meyers murdered his sister on Halloween night, 1963, and was promptly sent to a mental institution. Now, fifteen years later, Michael has escaped and come home to kill again. This is a well-made example of the slasher film, and it has inspired several sequels, as well as the copy cat film series *Friday the 13th* and *Nightmare on Elm Street.* Jamie Lee Curtis (her mother Janet Leigh was murdered by Norman Bates in *Psycho*) stars. **Similar reads:** *Whispers*, Dean Koontz; *The Girls He Adored*, Jonathan Nasaw.

Serial Killers • Slasher

Hannibal. *Ridley Scott, dir. 2001. 131 minutes.* This is a faithful adaptation of Thomas Harris's novel of the same name, starring Anthony Hopkins as the infamous Dr. Hannibal Lecter, who is lured out of hiding by the evil Mason Verger (Gary Oldman), the only one of his victims to survive. Juliette Moore does an excellent job of filling Jodi Foster's shoes as FBI agent Clarice Starling in her thirties. She must attempt to capture America's most-wanted serial killer. Ray Liotta also stars. Thomas Harris collaborated with David Mamet to write the script of this atmospheric and gory film. **Similar reads:** *Hannibal*, Thomas Harris; *Messiah*, Boris Starling.

*Cannibalism • Deformity • Federal Bureau of Investigation •
Gay/Lesbian/Bisexual Characters • Italy • Lecter, Hannibal (character) • Pigs •
Psychiatrist/Psychologist as Character • Revenge • Serial Killers • Starling,
Clarice (character) • Washington, D.C.*

I Spit on Your Grave. *Mark Zarchi, dir. 1978. 100 minutes*. (See chapter 10, "Small Town Horror: Villages of the Damned.")

M. *Fritz Lang, dir. 1931. (Black-and-white.) 99 minutes. (German with subtitles)*. Early talkie about a psychotic child murderer who is hunted down and brought to justice by the Berlin underworld. Dazzling cinematography and fine acting by Peter Lorre make this film a classic. **Similar reads:** *Death from the Woods*, Brigitte Aubert; *Seize the Night*, Dean Koontz.

Berlin, Germany • Child Molesters • Serial Killers

Night of the Hunter. *Charles Laughton, dir. 1955. (Black-and-white.) 93 minutes*. A psychotic traveling evangelist marries the widow of a recently executed bank robber in the hopes of finding the stolen money that was never recovered. When he can't find the whereabouts of the money from his new bride, he kills her and tries to pry the information out of her young stepchildren, who travel across the country to elude him. Robert Mitchum, Shelley Winters, and Lillian Gish star. **Similar reads:** *Tormentor*, Bill Pronzini; *Shattered*, Dean Koontz.

Clergy as Character • The Great Depression • Religion—Christianity • Serial Killers

Peeping Tom. *Michael Powell, dir. 1960. (Black-and-white.) 109 minutes*. A photographer by day and a serial killer by night photographs his nubile female victims before he kills them. This is a cult classic that doesn't end with a pat psychological analysis of the killer as does its more famous and obvious comparison, Alfred Hitchcock's *Psycho*. **Similar reads:** *Psycho*, Robert Bloch; *The Bottoms*, Joe R. Lansdale.

*England • Photographer as Character • Psychosexual Horror • Serial Killers •
Voyeurism*

People Under the Stairs, The. *Wes Craven, dir. 1992. 102 minutes*. On his thirteenth birthday, Fool and his family are being evicted from their tenement home by their money-hungry landlords, a brother and sister couple who pose as man and wife. The only way Fool can save his family is to brave the landlords' house and steal the gold that is kept there. But during his sojourn into the foreboding house, Fool discovers a secret greater than the hoard of gold kept by these people. **Similar reads:** *In the Dark*, Richard Laymon; *A Darkness Inbred*, Victor Heck.

African-American Characters • Cannibalism • Child Abuse • Incest • Racism

Psycho. *Alfred Hitchcock, dir. 1960. (Black-and-white.) 108 minutes*. Alfred Hitchcock's classic film rendition of Robert Bloch's slasher novel of the same name is about a boy's love for his mother, and to what lengths he will go to prove that love. Based on the Ed Gein murders of the 1950s, this classic stars Anthony Perkins and Janet Leigh. Perkins went on to star in *Psycho II* and *Psycho III*, a sequel and a prequel to Hitchcock's 1960 masterpiece. **Similar reads:** *Psycho*, Robert Bloch; *Portrait of the Psychopath as a Young Woman*, Edward Lee and Elizabeth Steffen.

*Arizona • California • Matricide/Patricide • Schizophrenia/Multiple Personality
Disorder • Slasher*

Scream. *Wes Craven, dir. 1996. 111 minutes*. It's Halloween 1996, and exactly one year before to the day, Sidney's mother was raped and murdered. Now a killer cognizant of the conventions of horror film is stalking her. *Scream* has spawned two sequels of the same name: *Scream II* (1998) and *Scream III* (2000). Drew Barrymore, Neve Campbell, and Courtney Cox star. **Similar reads:** *The Uncanny*, Andrew Clavan; *Deadfellas*, David Whitman.

Journalist as Character • Police Officer as Character • Popular Culture •
Revenge • Secret Sin • Serial Killers • Slasher

The Silence of the Lambs. *Jonathan Demme, dir. 1991. 118 minutes.* Young
FBI agent Clarice Starling is assigned to help find the kidnapped daughter of a
U.S. senator before she becomes the next victim of a psychopathic serial killer
who skins women. Clarice attempts to gain a better insight into the twisted mind
of the killer by talking to another psychopath, ex-psychiatrist Hannibal Lecter, a
man now in a maximum security prison because of his cannibalistic habits.
Clarice must first try to gain Lecter's confidence before he is to give away any
information, if she can survive the ordeal emotionally intact. Demme's masterpiece of atmosphere was one of the first modern horror films to win an Oscar.
Anthony Hopkins and Jodi Foster star. **Similar reads:** The Silence of the Lambs
Series, Thomas Harris; *Storm*, Boris Starling.

Cannibalism • Federal Bureau of Investigation • Lecter, Hannibal
(character) • Psychiatrist/Psychologist as Character • Serial Killers •
Starling, Clarisse (character)

The Stepfather. *Joseph Ruben, dir. 1987. 89 minutes.* Jerry Blake is a cheer-
leader for the traditional American family; as a matter of fact, he'd kill for it, and
he has, when his family disappointed him. Now he has assumed a new identity,
has married a widow with a teenaged daughter, and is settling into his role as *pa-
ter familias*. The only problem is that his standards are too high, and now this
family is also beginning to disappoint him. This sleeper hit stars Terry O'Quinn
in one of the most masterful portrayals of a serial killer ever filmed. **Similar
reads:** *Unhallowed Ground*, Gillian White; *Gift Giver*, Jean Sapin.

Domestic Violence • Marriage • Parenting • Serial Killers

The Texas Chainsaw Massacre. *Tobe Hooper, dir. 1974. 83 minutes.* This is a
drive-in theater classic about a group of five teens who fall victim to a family of
unemployed meat-packers turned cannibals. This campy horror flick is historically important in that the last person to survive the maniac's wrath is a female
and rescues herself rather than depending on a man to do so. After *The Texas
Chainsaw Massacre*, all other slasher films would follow the pattern of a vulnerable woman having to rely on herself rather than a stronger male to survive.
Hooper's cult classic also features what's arguably the longest scream in the history of horror cinema. John Larroquette narrates. **Similar reads:** *A Darkness Inbred*, Victor Heck; *Sineater*, Elizabeth Massie.

Cannibalism • Serial Killers • Slasher • Texas

Our Picks

June's Picks: *The One Safe Place,* Ramsey Campbell (Tor); *Sineater*, Elizabeth
Massie (Leisure); *Boy in the Water*, Stephen Dobyns (St. Martin's Press);
Hannibal, Thomas Harris (Delacorte Press); *The Lost*, Jack Ketchum (Leisure);
Misery, Stephen King (New American Library); *Emerald Germs of Ireland*, Pat-
rick McCabe (HarperCollins); *Mr. X*, Peter Straub (Ballantine Books); *Freaks*
(film); *From Hell* (film); *Hannibal* (film).

Tony's Picks: *Zombie*, Joyce Carol Oates (Dutton); *The Wasp Factory*, Ian
Banks (Little, Brown); *Storm*, Boris Starling (Signet); *Stealing Faces*, Michael
Prescott (Signet); *Psycho* (film); *Hannibal* (film).

Chapter 12

Technohorror: Evil Hospitals, Military Screw-Ups, Scientific Goofs, and Alien Invasions

Technohorror exists at the polar opposite of utopian science fiction: Whereas what is often called "futurism" implies that science will, with time, cure all diseases, find ways to feed and clothe all humanity, and allow us to travel to the stars to meet intelligent cultures on other planets, technohorror warns us that science cannot possibly be all goodness and light. Scientists can make horrible mistakes. Worse yet, scientific discoveries and new inventions can be used for the benefit of the few against the many. This can be the product of an overtly evil scientific mind or, as in various novels by mainstream authors Mark Twain and Kurt Vonnegut Jr., it may simply be the by-product of the amoral practice of scientific experimentation for experimentation's sake. Where futurism is eternally optimistic, technohorror is pessimistic. In technohorror, the elderly can (and therefore will) be made into food for the young, organs can (and therefore will) be stolen from live patients to replenish failing body parts of the highest bidders, and clones can (and therefore will) be produced illegally, even without the consent or knowledge of the human being who is cloned.

To the futurist, the glass is always half full; to the technohorror writer, not only is the glass always half empty, it is also likely to severely cut the person drinking from it, who should have seen it coming when he or she decided to use it. In general, all horror involves an acknowledgment of the fact that things can go horribly wrong if given the chance, but technohorror takes this negative outlook one step further and implies that technology *will* be the downfall of humanity. Made more and more intelligent, computers will rebel against their makers, as in Dean Koontz's *Demon Seed* or in the extremely popular *Terminator* films. If we travel to the stars, we will attract the attention of aliens that will pose immediate physical threats to the human race, as in Gloria Evans's *Meh'Yam* or Stephen King's *Dreamcatcher*. On a less fantastic level, medical horror reminds readers that although their family doctors may not be stealing organs, they will withhold cures if it means their own financial benefit or bigger HMO profits.

These types of fictions reflect the all-too-real fears of placing our lives in the hands of people we may barely know, like scientists and doctors, who work for organizations that we rarely trust, such as biotechnology corporations, military organizations, and hospitals. Next to vampire fiction, technohorror has seen the largest rise in popularity in the past decade. There are of course various reasons for this, which are enumerated in the *Appeals* list of this chapter. However, in essence, what makes technohorror so compelling is that the subgenre challenges science, the "religion" of the modern world. It questions the medical profession, the government, and the military by exposing the dark sides of these typically unquestioned facets of society.

Mary Shelley's *Frankenstein* is one of the first examples of the subgenre. In this novel that reads like a philosophical treatise, Victor Frankenstein attempts to play god and creates life in the form of a man or golem (a golem is loosely defined as a man of clay), but because he is *not* god, and also *not* female and *naturally* capable of creating offspring, he is incapable of nurturing his "experiment." Frankenstein's creation invariably turns into a monster. How could the creature not? He becomes what is tantamount to an angry young man who is bent on destroying his entire family because of an unhappy childhood. James Whales's 1931 movie version of *Frankenstein* forever changed the romantic elements and argument for nurturing our creations of the original text into a treatise against "weird science" or experimentation, which, no matter how good its intentions, will undoubtedly lead to undesired results. But even the movie version touches on the necessity of compassion and understanding: Frankenstein's "monster" would have been benign if Fritz had supplied his master with a normal brain and had not taunted his master's creation. What these diverse versions of the same story emphasize is moral complicity: the belief that scientists, who are only human after all, must consider all the implications, both positive and negative, of their experiments.

Since the Universal Studios *Frankenstein*, there has been a proliferation of scientific and medical horror texts to satiate the public's appetite for weird science, medical horror, military experimentation horror, and technology-gone-awry horror. More than any horror subgenre, technohorror taps into Americans' everyday fears, as readers are faced with the modern age's realization that any seemingly benevolent discovery, such as Einstein's Theory of Relativity, can easily find itself being transformed, Jekyll and Hyde fashion, into an element of destruction, such as the nuclear bombs dropped on Hiroshima and Nagasaki (Japan ironically became the birthing ground for one of the greatest film contributions to horror, the radioactive Godzilla). Although there may be lulls in the technohorror publishing frenzy, the subgenre is so successful at pinpointing the insecurities of humans that, like Arnold Schwartzenegger's character in *The Terminator*, it will always be back.

Representative works in this section include Dean Koontz's *Demon Seed* and *Watchers*, as well as Richard Matheson's *The Incredible Shrinking Man*. Benchmark texts in this subgenre include Stephen King's *Firestarter*, Ira Levin's *The Stepford Wives*, and Curt Siodmak's *Donovan's Brain*.

Note: Stories about the horrors of technology can also be found in the collections and anthologies described in chapter 17. Refer to the subject/keyword index for specific titles under the keywords "aliens," "experiments—military," "experiments—scientific/medical," "medical horror," "science fiction," and "weird science."

Appeals: Universal Fear of Technology; Realism of Medical Horror; Pseudo-Scientific Appeal; These Are Warning Texts–They Show the Perils of Scientific Experimentation; Stories Closely Parallel Concerns of Real Life; Higher Sense of "Possibility" (Believability); Play on Fear of Technological Takeover/Dehumanization of the World

Amos, Beth.

Second Sight. *New York: Harper, 1998. 449p.* An investigative reporter submits to a cutting-edge eye surgery after being left blind by an explosion. Although her sight never becomes 20/20 again, she begins to see "auras"—one of which could point to the murderer of a colleague. **Similar titles:** *The Secret Life of Colors*, Steve Savile; *Dark Soul*, M. Martin Hunt; *Project Resurrection*, Karen Duval; *To Kill an Eidolon*, Winifred F. Hausey.

> *Blindness • Extrasensory Perception • Journalist as Character • Medical Horror*

Anderson, Kevin J.

Resurrection, Inc. *Woodstock, Ga.: Overlook Connection Press, 1999. 263p.* Resurrection, Inc. is a futuristic company that has found a way to profit from raising the dead. All it takes is a microprocessor brain, a synthetic heart, and synthetic blood, and anyone wealthy enough can buy a trainable servant with no mind of his or her own. But for every Servant created, a live human is laid off, and soon Resurrection, Inc.'s profits are society's loss. Only one individual can challenge the power of Resurrection, Inc., and that person is not a living human but a resurrected servant. **Similar titles:** *Project Resurrection*, Karen Duval; *The Boat Man*, Selena Rosen; *The Stepford Wives*, Ira Levin; *Regeneration*, Max Allan Collins and Barbara Collins.

> *Economic Violence • Replicants • Science Fiction • Zombies*

Bakis, Kirsten.

B Lives of the Monster Dogs. *New York: Farrar, Straus & Giroux, 1997. 291p.* In the New York of 2009, 150 "monster" dogs arrive by helicopter and chartered plane, dressed in the clothing of nineteenth-century Prussian burghers, speaking through surgically implanted voice boxes, able to perform the tasks of humans by virtue of prosthetic hands and enhanced intelligence. The dogs come from a remote village in Canada where German followers of a mad visionary, Augustus Rank, have worked since 1882 to create a superior race of canine soldiers that will possess the intelligence of men but the courage and loyalty of dogs. Eventually, the dogs rebel against their masters and, in need of a place to go, choose New York, the quintessential melting pot. **Similar titles:** *Resurrection, Inc.*, Kevin J. Anderson; *Phantom Feast*, Dianna Barron; *William F. Nolan's Dark Universe*, William F. Nolan; *King Rat*, China Miâeville.

> *Dogs • Experiments—Military • Fantasy • New York City • Science Fiction*

Baugh, Bruce, and Richard Dansky.

Darkness Revealed: Descent Into Darkness. *Clarkston, Ga.: White Wolf, 1998. 118p.* (See chapter 6, "Vampires and Werewolves: Children of the Night.")

Cave, Hugh B.

The Dawning. *New York: Leisure, 2000. 359p.* (See chapter 13, "Ecological Horror: Rampant Animals and Mother Nature's Revenge.")

Clifford, Emmett.

Night Whispers: A Story of Evil. *Nashville, Tenn.: Cumberland House, 1998. 429p.* (See chapter 11, "Maniacs and Sociopaths, or the Nuclear Family Explodes: Monstrous Malcontents Bury the Hatchet.")

Collins, Max Allan, and Barbara Collins.

Regeneration. *New York: Leisure, 1999. 311p.* An aging advertising executive, recently fired for not being sufficiently young and fresh, turns to the X-Gen Agency, a group of doctors who regenerate humans into younger, more marketable employees. However, a contract with X-Gen means giving up all rights and freedoms to its doctors, including the right to continue living once one is past one's prime. The authors produce a scathing and tragic commentary on ageism, especially regarding women. **Similar titles:** *Resurrection, Inc.*, Kevin J. Anderson; *Navigating the Terror*, John Hyatt; *Fountain Society*, Wes Craven; *Mutation*, Robin Cook.

> Aging • Cosmetic Surgery • Los Angeles, California • Medical Horror • Midwest, The • Private Investigator as Character • Weird Science

Cook, Robin.

Toxin. *New York: Putnam, 1998. 357p.* The father of a child skater who dies from e-coli exposure decides to take revenge against any and all whom he holds responsible. **Similar titles:** *Escaping Purgatory*, Gary A. Braunbeck and Alan M. Clark; *Spirit*, Graham Masterton; *Blackrose Avenue*, Mark Shepherd.

> Epidemics • Grieving • Medical Horror • Revenge

Craven, Wes.

Fountain Society: A Novel. *New York: Simon & Schuster, 1999. 350p.* Dying scientist Peter Jance has one chance to save his life, but it involves undergoing a controversial experiment, with the aid of his wife, a geneticist. The procedure: implant his brain into a young, fresh corpse. But are Jance and his colleagues prepared for the results? This is the first novel by famed director Wes Craven, who emphasizes technological detail and characterization. **Similar titles:** *Regeneration*, Max Allan Collins and Barbara Collins; *Frankenstein*, Mary Shelley; *The Picture of Dorian Grey*, Oscar Wilde; *The Experiment*, John Darnton; *Elixir*, Gary Goshgarian [as Gary Braver].

🎧 audiotape

> Eugenics • Immortality • Medical Horror • Replicants • Weird Science

Darnton, John.

The Experiment. *New York: Signet, 2000. 481p.* A young man named Skyler escapes from a scientific compound off the Carolina coast when he discovers that his friends who have been disappearing actually turn up dead, and then suspects that he is next in line for extermination. He ultimately drifts to New York City, where he meets a journalist named Jude Harley, who is working on a murder case that leads to an investigation of missing twins. As it turns out, Jude and Skyler are indeed identical twins, yet Skyler is five years Jude's junior. Jude and Skyler now must trace their pasts to find out how this is possible, and as they come closer to the truth, they are both marked for extermination. **Similar titles:** *Mr. Murder*, Dean Koontz; The Blood of the Lamb Series, Thomas F. Montelene; *Blackrose Avenue*, Mark Shepherd.

🎧 audio download   🔍 large print

Cloning • Genetics • Immortality • Journalist as Character •
New York City • North Carolina • Twins • Weird Science

Duval, Karen.

Project Resurrection. *Dekalb, Ill.: Speculation Press, 2000. 288p.* In 2013, Dr. Terrance Labriola discovers a method of resurrecting cryogenically frozen corpses. However, in his haste to "play god" he has miscalculated what happens to the spirit after death, and he ends up reanimating amoral beings that exist in the realm between life and death. Unfortunately, one of these beings is his wife, who had been diagnosed with breast cancer years before, and she has brought back an evil spirit with her to the land of the living. Only LaNaya Seville, an Inuit physical therapist with psychic abilities, can save humanity now. **Similar titles:** *Resurrection, Inc.*, Kevin J. Anderson, *To Kill an Eidolon*, Winifred F. Halsey; *Frankenstein,* Mary Shelley; *Sleepeasy*, T. M. Wright.

Clairvoyant as Character • Demons • Medical Horror • Native American
Characters • Religion—Christianity • Religion—Native American •
Weird Science • Zombies

Ellis, Warren, and D'Israeli.

Lazarus Churchyard: The Final Cut. *Fullerton, Calif.: Image Comics, 2001. 126p.* Image Comics collects, in this graphic novel, the complete adventures of Lazarus Chruchyard, the man of plastic who cannot die. Churchyard, now 400 years old, was used as an experiment by an evil corporation, and is now 90 percent adaptable plastic. All he wants is to end his miserable existence. **Similar titles:** *Spawn*, Todd McFarland, Alan Moore, and Greg Capullo; The Witchblade Series, Christina Z. and David Wohl; Buffy the Vampire Slayer Series, various authors; The Crow Series, various authors.

Ꙭ graphic novels

Economic Violence • Gothicism • Graphic Novel • Immortality • Science
Fiction • Weird Science

Gear, W. Michael, and Kathleen O'Neal Gear.

Dark Inheritance. *New York: Warner Books, 2001. 528p.* A Colorado State University anthropologist finds himself in possession of an extremely intelligent bonobo ape. Soon he begins to suspect, and is proven correct, that the ape was a subject of genetic experimentation, and that she is not one of a kind. When the company that commissioned the experimentation finds out that its secret may be revealed, it transports the ape and the anthropologist to Africa, where they discover that other intelligent apes are at war with humans. **Similar titles:** *The Claw*, Ramsey Campbell; *Cujo*, Stephen King; *Planet of the Apes* (film).

Academia • Africa • Anthropologist as Character • Colorado • Genetics •
Weird Science

Glyde, Tania.

Junk DNA. *Hove: Codex Books, 2000. 192p.* Junk DNA begins as the Human Genome Project is drawing to a close. The Britain of the future is menaced by marauding gangs of armed children, and most people are employed by the heritage industries in reenactments of historical events. Glyde's heroines, Regina, a sex therapist, and Lucy, a dyslexic ten-year-old who paints pictures with blood and feces, provide an accurate commentary on the consequences of early twenty-first-century excesses in this dystopic satire. **Similar titles:** *William F.*

Nolan's Dark Universe, William F. Nolan; *Resurrection, Inc.*, Kevin J. Anderson; *Blackrose Avenue*, Mark Shepherd; *The Experiment*, John Darnton; *The Bachman Books*, Stephen King.

> *Childhood • Computers • England • Genetics • Parenting • Psychiatrist/Psychologist as Character • Science Fiction*

Gorman, Ed.

Daughter of Darkness. *New York: DAW, 1998. 333p.* When twenty-year-old socialite Jenny Stafford is found one night outside a homeless shelter, she has no recollection of who she is or what she has been doing in the past week. Ex-police officer Michael Coffey offers to help her, and the two discover that Ms. Stafford is somehow involved in the brutal murder of a man she doesn't know. As Coffey further investigates the murder and Ms. Stafford's condition, he finds that she has been unwittingly used in mind control experiments and is at the mercy of some of the people closest to her and whom she most trusts. Gorman's prose is full of plot twists and surprises. **Similar titles:** *Carrion Comfort*, Dan Simmons; *Blue Rose*, Peter Straub; *Amnesia*, Andrew Neiderman.

> *Central Intelligence Agency • Chicago, Illinois • Mental Institutions • Mind Control • Police Officer as Character • Schizophrenia/Multiple Personality Disorder • Violence, Theories of • Weird Science*

Goshgarian, Gary [as Gary Braver].

Elixir. *New York: Forge, 2000. 352p.* Chemist/scientist Christopher Baen has discovered the fountain of youth in an elixir made from a rare New Zealand orchid. Can he keep his discovery from being abused by an evil CEO with mob debts, or better yet, by himself in his desperation to avoid the Alzheimer's fate of his father? This novel is suspenseful, with emphasis on plot twists and psychological dilemma. **Similar titles:** *Fountain Society*, Wes Craven; *The Experiment*, John Darnton; *Regeneration*, Max Allan Collins and Barbara Collins; *My Soul to Keep*, Tananarive Due.

> *Aging • Biologist as Character • Boston, Massachusetts • Drugs • Immortality • New Zealand • Organized Crime • Weird Science*

Hemingway, Hilary. The Dreamchild Series.

Dreamland: A Novel of the UFO Cover-Up. *New York: Forge, 1995. 319p.* Annie Katz and her engineer husband, Stanley, live in the Southwest, where Stanley is working on a top-secret government project. Annie, who is happily pregnant after a series of painful miscarriages, suffers from horrible nightmares that become reality when she discovers that her baby is missing from her womb despite the fact that she hasn't miscarried. Annie's friend Carol is a therapist who hypnotizes Annie to try to discover the truth about Annie's dreams and the missing child. **Similar titles:** *Firestarter*, Stephen King; *The Fury*, John Farris; *Shadow Fires*, Dean Koontz; *Dreamcatcher*, Stephen King; *Rosemary's Baby*, Ira Levin.

> *Aliens • Experiments—Military • Government Officials • Pregnancy • Roswell, New Mexico • Weird Science*

Dreamchild. *New York: Tor-Forge, 2000, ©1998. 288p.* The fate of the Earth rests on the frail shoulders of Max Carol Kat, a five-year-old alien-human hybrid, in this action-packed sequel to *Dreamland*. Evidence of alien presence is sighted throughout the world, as UFOs are tracked from an underground center in New Mexico. While scientists scramble to chart the rising evidence of global warming and stop an alien takeover, Max's parents try to break through to their unresponsive child and save their doomed marriage. **Similar titles:** *Firestarter*, Stephen King; *The Fury*, John Farris; *Shadow Fires*, Dean Koontz; *Dreamcatcher*, Stephen King; *Son of Rosemary*, Ira Levin.

Aliens • Apocalypse • Experiments—Military • Marriage • Parenting • Weird Science

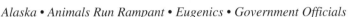

Huggins, James Byron.

Hunter. *New York: Simon & Schuster, 1999. 428p.* In Alaska, an ape-like beast is created during illegal secret government experiments with DNA. When the ape escapes, a famous hunter is hired to eliminate the evidence, but he is not told that the ape has been genetically engineered to be virtually indestructible. He gets a shock when the beast corners him—and speaks. **Similar titles:** *The Nature of Balance*, Tim Lebbon; *Dark Inheritance*, George W. Gear and Kathleen O'Neal Gear; *Shadows and Dark Rivers of the Heart*, Dean Koontz.

Alaska • Animals Run Rampant • Eugenics • Government Officials

Keller, Norman Erik.

Geometries of the Mind. *Lincoln, Neb.: iUniverse.com 2000. 292p.* An electrical engineer who has spent years struggling to make his secret dream a reality unwittingly releases on the world a beast that humans can't understand or survive. Can he stop it before it destroys humanity? **Similar titles:** *Frankenstein* (film); *Terminator* (film) and *Terminator II* (film); *Mr. Murder*, Dean Koontz; *The Virtual Boss*, Floyd Kemske.

Engineer as Character • Science Fiction

Kemske, Floyd. The Corporate Nightmare Series.

The Virtual Boss. *North Haven, Conn.: Catbird Press, 1993. 237p.* The second in Kemske's corporate horror series, *The Virtual Boss* follows the lives of three employees at Information Accuracy, Inc., as each of the three attempts to deal with his or her life being taken over by Chuck, the software system that literally manages the company. As Chuck asserts itself into even their private lives, Arthur, Linda, and Jones must reconsider their decisions to give up freedom and privacy for security and financial gain. Or will Chuck even allow them the freedom to make that decision? Kemske is clever and original. **Similar titles:** *Resume with Monsters*, William Browning Spencer; *The Association*, Bentley Little; *Neighborhood Watch*, Andrew Neiderman; *Dark Within*, John Wooley.

Computers • Corporate Horror • Programmer as Character

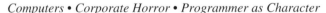

Ketchum, Jack.

Ladies' Night. *Springfield, Pa.: Gauntlet Pub., 2000, ©1997. 166p.* (See chapter 13, "Ecological Horror: Rampant Animals and Mother Nature's Revenge.")

King, Stephen.

Christine. *New York: Viking, 1983. 526p.* (See chapter 7, "Demonic Possession, Satanism, Black Magic, and Witches and Warlocks: The Devil Made Me Do It.")

Dreamcatcher. *New York: Scribner, 2001. 620p.* Four boyhood friends on their annual hunting trip in rural Maine discover dazed people wandering around the woods in freezing weather. These mysterious strangers are all permeated by a faintly sweet smell, harbinger of the alien life force inside of them waiting to be born. Anyone in the presence of these creatures begins receiving telepathic communications. Meanwhile, the U.S. military knows about this dangerous state of affairs, and has quarantined the entire area, willing to sacrifice the unaffected to save the rest of the world from contamination. **Similar titles:** *The Tommyknockers*, Stephen King; *Blood Crazy*, Simon Clark; *Winter Moon*, Dean Koontz.

🔊 audiotape, audio download, compact disc   🖱 e-book   👁 large print

> *Alcoholism • Aliens • Epidemics • Government Officials • Maine • Mind Control • Pregnancy • Psychiatrist/Psychologist as Character • Teacher as Character • Wilderness*

Firestarter. *New York: New American Library, 1981. 404p.* (See chapter 9, "Telekinesis and Hypnosis: Chaos from Control.")

The Stand. *New York: Signet, 1991, ©1978. 1141p.* A nanosecond of computer error in a Defense Department laboratory ends the world as we know it. The next day, 99 percent of the Earth's population is dead, and the survivors choose to be allied with the good Mother Abigail, a frail 108-year-old woman, or the evil Randall Flagg, a man with a lethal smile and unspeakable powers. **Similar titles:** The Millenium Quartet, Charles Grant; *The Nature of Balance*, Tim Lebbon; The Bewdley Series, Tony Burgess.

> *Apocalypse • Computers • Magic*

Koontz, Dean.

Dark Rivers of the Heart. *New York: Alfred A. Knopf, 1994. 487p.* Spencer Grant just wants to get to know the waitress named Valerie who served him on the previous night. When he follows her home, he finds himself caught up in the middle of a conspiracy that involves computers, blackmail, and murder. Do two individuals stand a chance against the strength of a government conspiracy? **Similar titles:** *Firestarter*, Stephen King; *Carrion Comfort*, Dan Simmons; *Blackrose Avenue*, Mark Shepherd; *The Virtual Boss*, Floyd Kemske.

🔊 audiotape

> *Computers • Eugenics • Secret Sin*

Demon Seed. *New York: Berkley, 1997. 301p.* Dr. Susan Harris lives a secluded but safe life, guarded round the clock by a computer that runs every aspect of her daily life. But when this artificial intelligence decides it wants to better understand the ways of the flesh, it turns against Dr. Harris and attempts to impregnate her with a cyborg-like fetus. This brilliant novel is narrated mainly by the computer, and this updated re-release adds considerably to the original 1973 novel. **Similar titles:** *The Virtual Boss*, Floyd Kemske; *Rosemary's Baby*, Ira Levin; *Navigating the Terror*, John Hyatt; *Village of the Damned* (film).

> *Computers • Pregnancy • Rape • Science Fiction • Zombies*

Dragon Tears. *New York: Putnam, 1993. 377p.* (See chapter 9, "Telekinesis and Hypnosis: Chaos from Control.")

Fear Nothing. *New York: Bantam Books, 1998. 400p.* A twenty-eight-year-old suspects that he is the product of military experimentation. His investigation into exactly what happened, and who is responsible, will test his limitations (he is hypersensitive to sunlight) and teach him his strengths. **Similar titles:** *Mr. Murder* and *Seize the Night*, Dean Koontz; *The Experiment*, John Darnton.

🔊 audiotape

> *Experiments—Military • Xeroderma Pigmentosum*

Midnight. *New York: Putnam, 1989. 383p.* A mad computer genius is terrorizing the inhabitants of Moonlight Cove. Can two of the Cove's natives and a couple of outsiders stop him before it is too late? **Similar titles:** *Pandora's Game*, Christopher Andrews; *Dark Within*, John Wooley; *Geometries of the Mind*, Norman Erik Keller.

> *Computers • Federal Bureau of Investigation • Religion—Native American • Replicants • Werewolves*

Night Chills. *New York: Berkley, 1983, ©1976. 308p.* The inhabitants of Black River are plagued by "night chills," a virus-like scientifically engineered condition that causes them to become violent. What can save these innocent men and women who are being used as a government testing ground? As always, Koontz is filled with action, suspense, erotic language, and danger. **Similar titles:** *Insomnia*, Stephen King; *The Apostate*, Paul Lonardo; *Old Fears*, John Wooley and Ron Gardner.

𝒢𝒢 large print

> *Biological Warfare • Mind control • Rape • Violence, Theories of • Weird Science*

Seize the Night. *New York: Bantam Books, 1999. 443p.* Five-year-old Jimmy Wing goes missing in the quiet town of Moonlight Bay, California, and only one person, Christopher Snow, has any hope of finding him before something terrible happens. For Snow, the dark of night and of the underground passages where Wing may have been taken are not unusual, as his rare genetic disorder, xeroderma pigmentosum, forces him to live in the darkness rather than the light of day. However, Snow must battle the conspiratorial forces of the U.S. government and the local police force, as they attempt to keep secret the genetic experiments that have gotten out of control and may be responsible for what is happening to the children in Moonlight Bay. **Similar titles:** *Fear Nothing*, Dean Koontz; *Death From the Woods*, Brigitte Aubert; *Silent Children*, Ramsey Campbell.

> *Animals Run Rampant • California • Child Molesters • Genetics • Snow, Christopher (character) • Subterranean Monsters • Weird Science • Xeroderma Pigmentosum*

Shadow Fires. *New York: Berkley, 1990. 509p.* Rachael Leben wants nothing more than a divorce from her multi-millionaire husband, Eric. Unfortunately, he is so embittered that he comes back from the dead to get even. And he isn't the only one trying to kill Rachael. This novel is suspenseful and action-oriented, with lots of plot twists. **Similar titles:** *Rose Madder*, Stephen King; *The Funhouse*, Dean Koontz; *The Stepfather* (film); *The Tormentor*, Bill Pronzini.

> *Domestic Violence • Genetics • Government Officials • Revenge*

Twilight Eyes. *New York: Berkley, 1985. 451p.* A man sought for murder is actually humanity's best defense against the "others," demons that were genetically engineered and belong to an ancient civilization. Koontz is suspenseful, and this novel is an excellent gentle read. **Similar titles:** *Phantoms* and *Midnight*, Dean Koontz; *Crota*, Owl Goingback; *The 37th Mandala*, Mark Laidlaw.

> *Demons • Genetics • Weird Science*

The Vision. *New York: Berkley, 1977. 353p.* (See chapter 11, "Maniacs and Sociopaths, or the Nuclear Family Explodes: Monstrous Malcontents Bury the Hatchet.")

Watchers. *New York: Berkley, 1996. 464p.* Two altered life forms escape from a top-secret lab, and only one of them is benign. A super-intelligent dog; a murderous, grotesque beast; and a hit man who takes too much pleasure in his work populate this novel about science gone wrong. The novel is action-oriented, but characterization is solid as well. **Similar titles:** *Mr. Murder*, Dean Koontz; *The Beast That Was Max*, Gerard Houarner; *Cujo*, Stephen King; *Chelydra Serpentina*, Dan Sanders.

California • Dogs • Genetics • Serial Killers • Weird Science

Korn, M. F.

Aliens and Minibikes. *In Aliens, Minibikes, and Other Staples of Suburbia. Morton, Pa.: Silver Lake, 2001. 71p.* A couple of young boys in Baton Rouge, Louisiana, find an alien creature in the woods. Despite its potential dangers, they decide to keep it as a pet, and have to deal with the attention, from both friends and strangers, that their decision brings. This novella is more nostalgic than unsettling and is a wonderful gentle read. **Similar titles:** *The Illustrated Man*, Ray Bradbury; *Escaping Purgatory*, Gary A. Braunbeck and Alan M. Clark; *Zom Bee Moo Vee*, Mark McLaughlin; *Thank You for the Flowers*, Scott Nicholson.

Aliens • Baton Rouge, Louisiana • Childhood • Suburbia

Skimming the Gumbo Nuclear. *Fountain Hills, Ariz.: Eraserhead Press, 2001. 287p.* (See chapter 13, "Ecological Horror: Rampant Animals and Mother Nature's Revenge.")

Levin, Ira.

The Stepford Wives. *New York: Random House, 1972. 145p.* (See chapter 10, "Small Town Horror: Villages of the Damned.")

Matheson, Richard.

I Am Legend. *(novella). In Matheson, Richard. I Am Legend. New York: Tor, 1995, ©1954. 312p.* (See chapter 6, "Vampires and Werewolves: Children of the Night.")

The Incredible Shrinking Man. *(novella). In Matheson, Richard. The Incredible Shrinking Man. New York: Tor, 1994, ©1956. 207p.* This well-known novella, the basis for the movie of the same name, follows Scott Carey as he shrinks due to his exposure to a potent combination of radiation and insecticide. Carey's diminutive stature represents the feelings of many post-World War II men that after the war they too were shrinking in status in their homes and communities. **Similar titles:** *The Incredible Shrinking Man* (film); *Flowers from the Moon and Other Lunacies*, Robert Bloch; *The Illustrated Man*, Ray Bradbury.

⌂ e-book

Isolation • Parallel Universe • Radiation • Science Fiction • Weird Science

Mezrich, Ben.

Reaper. *New York: HarperCollins, 1998. 342p.* A virologist and a paramedic have seventy-two hours to find the cause of a virus that twists the spines of its victims. Can they find the billionaire whose plan it is to "bring down the barriers" through computers, who is at the center of the epidemic, or will death spread too quickly on the information superhighway? **Similar titles:** The Bewdley Series, Tony Burgess; *The Stand*, Stephen King; The Millenium Quartet, Charles Grant.

🎧 audiotape

Boston, Massachusetts • Computer Hackers • Computers • Epidemics • The Internet • Medical Horror • Paramedic as Character • Weird Science

Odom, Mel, and David S. Goyer.

Blade. *New York: Harper Mass Market Paperbacks, 1998. 343p.* (See chapter 6, "Vampires and Werewolves: Children of the Night.")

Perry, S. D.

Virus. *New York: Tor, 1998. 224p.* (See chapter 5, Golem, Mummies, and Reanimated Stalkers: Wake the Dead and They'll Be Cranky.")

Priest, Christopher.

The Extremes. *New York: St. Martin's Press, 1998. 393p.* FBI agent Teresa Simons travels to Bulverton, England, the small town where she was born, to investigate a spree killing that occurred the same day that her husband was killed by a spree killer in Texas. To fully understand the minds of the killer and his victims, Teresa undergoes EX/EX virtual reality training, in which one can "experience" the reality of death. This title is original and extremely eerie. **Similar titles:** *The Cell* (film); *The Prestige*, Christopher Priest; *Pandora's Game*, Christopher Andrews; The Silence of the Lambs Series, Thomas Harris.

England • Federal Bureau of Investigation • Grieving • History, Use of • Science Fiction • Serial Killers • Virtual Reality • Weird Science

Sanders, Dan.

Chelydra Serpentina: Terror in the Adirondacks. *Santa Barbara, Calif.: Astral Publishing, 2000. 332p.* Two scientists at a Harvard research facility, trying to study a case of "time lapse" evolution, create a reptilian creature that evolves in a matter of months into a humanoid. During that time, however, people begin disappearing from a nearby lake, and women are attacked by a serial rapist. Biology professor Matt Goddard suspects that the experimental creature is responsible, but he is mysteriously fired just as he begins investigating. Can anyone stop the killing before the experiment goes too far? This intriguing read is written from both the human and reptile point of view. **Similar titles:** The Meg Series, Steve Alten; *Clickers*, J. F. Gonzales and Mark Williams; *Lake Monsters*, Joseph Citro.

Academia • Evolutionary Theory • Genetics • Maritime Horror • Police Officer as Character • Rape • Teacher as Character • Weird Science

Searcy, David.

Ordinary Horror. *New York: Penguin-Viking, 2001. 230p.* (See chapter 13, "Ecological Horror: Rampant Animals and Mother Nature's Revenge.")

Sharp, Roger.

Psyclone. *St. Petersburg, Fla.: Barclay Books, 2001. 237p.* As a young boy, Darryl Brooks lost his father and twin brother. Now as an adult and one of the top scientific minds in the United States, Brooks has mastered the science of cloning adult humans. When he decides to clone himself to reproduce the family he lost as a child, he overlooks the possibility that his clone will not have a conscience. When people near his Arizona lab are murdered, Brooks must face the fact that his own double may be a killer. **Similar titles:** *Mr. Murder*, Dean Koontz; *Mr. X*, Peter Straub; The Blood of the Lamb Series, Thomas F. Monteleone; *The Experiment*, John Darnton.

Alter Ego • Cloning • Dallas, Texas • Phoenix, Arizona • Serial Killers • Twins • Weird Science

Shelley, Mary.

Frankenstein. *Oxford: Oxford University Press, 1998, ©1817. 322p.* (See chapter 5, "Golem, Mummies, and Reanimated Stalkers: Wake the Dead and They'll Be Cranky.")

Shepherd, Mark.

Blackrose Avenue. *Alma, Ark.: Yard Dog Press, 2001. 336p.* In the near future, the Christian right convinces Americans that an internment camp for AIDS sufferers is a good idea. The Good Law, as it is called, leads to the imprisonment and escape of a young man who begins a trek across country toward not only freedom but also the discovery of an insidious government plot to ostracize AIDS carriers and gay men in general, to keep them away from an already discovered cure. **Similar titles:** *The Experiment*, John Darnton; *The Hungry Moon*, Ramsey Campbell; *Holy Rollers*, J. Newman.

> *AIDS • Epidemics • Gay/Lesbian/Bisexual Characters • Medical Horror • Religion—Christianity • Science Fiction*

Shirley, John.

The View from Hell. *Burton, Mich.: Subterranean Press, 2001. 190p.* (See chapter 14, "Psychological Horror: It's All in Your Head.")

Siodmak, Curt. The Patrick Cory Novels.

Hauser's Memory. *New York: Putnam, 1968. 184p.* Dr. Patrick Cory is approached by the CIA and is asked to transfer the memory of a dying German scientist to another body. He succeeds, but his experiment gets out of hand when the subject escapes. **Similar titles:** *Donovan's Brain*, Kurt Siodmak; *Frankenstein*, Mary Shelley; *Fountain Society*, Wes Craven.

> *Central Intelligence Agency • Cory, Patrick (character) • Espionage • Genetics • Weird Science*

Donovan's Brain. *Cutchogue, N.Y.: Buccaneer Books, 1993, ©1942. 160p.* Told in the form of scientific diary entries, this classic chronicles the experiments of Dr. Patrick Cory. Cory allows a millionaire, Warren Howard Donovan, to die, so that he can keep Donovan's brain alive in his laboratory. The only problem is that the brain develops telepathic powers. This classic is not for the faint of heart; Siodmak is raw and uncompromising. **Similar titles:** *Hauser's Memory*, Curt Siodmak; *Frankenstein*, Mary Shelley; *Fountain Society*, Wes Craven.

> 𝔇 audiotape

> *Cory, Patrick (character) • Diary Format • Eugenics • Telepathy • Weird Science*

Spencer, William Browning.

Resume with Monsters. *Sag Harbor, NY: Permanent Press, 1997, ©1995. 212p.* (See chapter 8, "Mythological Monsters and 'The Old Ones': Invoking the Dark Gods.")

Stone, Del, Jr.

Dead Heat. *Mojo Press, 1996. 188p.* (See chapter 16, "Comic Horror: Laughing at Our Fears.")

Straub, Peter.

Floating Dragon. *New York: Putnam, 1983. 515p.* (See chapter 11, "Maniacs and Sociopaths, or the Nuclear Family Explodes: Monstrous Malcontents Bury the Hatchet.")

Wells, H. G.

The Invisible Man. *New York: Dover, 1992, ©1897. 110p.* This is Wells's classic tale of a "scientific investigator" fascinated with the properties of light who accidentally renders himself invisible and wreaks havoc on an English village. Wells is action-oriented and has fun with science. **Similar titles:** *Frankenstein*, Mary Shelley; *Dr. Jekyll and Mr. Hyde*, Robert Louis Stevenson; *The Invisible Man* (film); *The Incredible Shrinking Man*, Richard Matheson.

👂 audiotape, compact disc

Albinism • England • Science Fiction • Weird Science

Wilson, F. Paul.

Conspiracies. *New York: Tor, 2000. 448p.* (See chapter 16, "Comic Horror: Laughing at Our Fears.")

Wooley, John.

Dark Within. *Tulsa, Okla.: Hawk Publishing, 2000. 229p.* The citizens of a small, sleepy Midwestern town are awakened one night to find that they have a new visitor in their midst, a man who calls himself Kard and who lives inside a silver, coffin-shaped box. At first, everyone is pleased with Kard's generosity; he pays farmers and blue collar workers $100 a month just to keep his "home" on their property, and good fortune comes to whomever allows Kard to set up house. However, soon residents discover that Kard has been placing boxes all over the town, and that they are part of his "experiment." **Similar titles:** *Obsession*, Ramsey Campbell; *Careful What You Wish*, June Hubbard; *Needful Things*, Stephen King; *Spanky*, Christopher Fowler.

Computers • Midwest, The • Senior Citizen as Character • Weird Science • Wish Fulfillment

Wooley, John, and Ron Wolfe.

Death's Door. *Tulsa, Okla.: Hawk Publishing, 2000, ©1992. 388p.* (See chapter 14, "Psychological Horror: It's All in Your Head.")

Film

Alien. *Ridley Scott, dir. 1979. 117 minutes.* A commercial exploration spacecraft unwittingly takes on an alien life form that stalks the crew in deep space, where no one can hear them scream. The monster special effects are stunning, even twenty years later. Sigourney Weaver, Tom Skerritt, John Hurt, Veronica Cartwright, and Harry Dean Stanton star. **Similar reads:** *Meh'Yam*, Gloria Evans; *Phantoms*, Dean Koontz.

Aliens • Outer Space • Science Fiction

Attack of the 50-Foot Woman. *Nathan Juran, dir. 1958. (Black-and-white.) 66 minutes.* A wealthy woman marries a gold-digging playboy and finds her only solace in alcohol and shrewishness after she discovers his inability to remain faithful. An encounter with an alien makes her literally larger than life. As her size grows proportionate to her wrath, the fifty-foot woman wreaks vengeance on her faithless spouse and his paramour before being destroyed by the military. The story is a metaphor for post-World War II male fears of women. **Similar reads:** *The Incredible Shrinking Man*, Richard Matheson; The Witchblade Series, Christina Z. and David Wohl.

Aliens • Radiation • Science Fiction • Weird Science

Bride of Frankenstein. *James Whale, dir. 1935. (Black-and-white.) 75 minutes.* (See chapter 5, "Golem, Mummies, and Reanimated Stalkers: Wake the Dead and They'll Be Cranky.")

The Cell. *Tarsem Singh, dir. 2000. 107 minutes.* This gorgeous art film tells an extremely disturbing story about a child psychologist who uses virtual reality technology to communicate with comatose, emotionally disturbed children. After a serial killer is caught but goes into a coma, she must go into his deranged mind to find the whereabouts of his latest kidnap victim—before it is too late. The only problem is that no one is sure if it is possible to survive in the physical world after dying in virtual reality. **Similar reads:** *The Extremes*, Christopher Priest; *Project Resurrection*, Karen Duval.

> *Child Abuse • Childhood • Dreams • Federal Bureau of Investigation • Psychiatrist/Psychologist as Character • Psychosexual Horror • Serial Killers • Virtual Reality • Weird Science*

Frankenstein. *James Whale, dir. 1931. (Black-and-white.) 71 minutes.* (See chapter 5, "Golem, Mummies, and Reanimated Stalkers: Wake the Dead and They'll Be Cranky.")

Incredible Shrinking Man, The. *Jack Arnold, dir. 1957. (Black-and-white.) 81 minutes.* This classic movie is based on the novella by Richard Matheson, who also wrote the script. After he is sprayed by radioactive mist, Scott Carey begins to shrink until he is so small he can no longer be seen by his family, and is forced to battle a spider to survive. The story is often seen as a metaphor for the position of men in post-World War II American society. The special effects are excellent. **Similar reads:** *The Incredible Shrinking Man*, Richard Matheson; The Corporate Nightmare Series, Floyd Kemske.

> *Radiation • Science Fiction • Weird Science*

Invasion of the Body Snatchers. *Don Siegel, dir. 1956. (Black-and-white.) 80 minutes.* Small town residents are being replaced by mindless replicants that are hatched by pods. This is a classic science fiction/horror film with a McCarthy era subtext. **Similar reads:** *Carrion Comfort*, Dan Simmons; *The Tommyknockers*, Stephen King.

> *Aliens • Replicants • Science Fiction*

The Invisible Man. *James Whale, dir. 1933. (Black-and-white.) 71 minutes.* This movie is James Whale's relatively faithful adaptation of H. G. Wells's novel of the same name. Claude Raines stars as a mad scientist who makes himself invisible and wreaks havoc on small English villages. **Similar reads:** *The Invisible Man*, H. G. Wells; *William F. Nolan's Dark Universe*, William F. Nolan.

> *England • Science Fiction • Weird Science*

Night of the Living Dead. *George Romero, dir. 1968. (Black-and-white.) 108 minutes.* Radiation fallout from a recently launched satellite causes the newly dead to reanimate, and they're hungry for human flesh. Once the dead bite the living, the living are similarly turned into zombies. Seven strangers are thrust together in a remote farmhouse next to a cemetery, and all are trying to keep the ravenous dead at bay, while working out their generational and ethnic differences. **Similar reads:** *I Am Legend*, Richard Matheson; *The Walking*, Bentley Little.

> *African-American Characters • Apocalypse • Cannibalism • Zombies*

Night of the Living Dead. *Tom Savini, dir. 1990. 96 minutes.* This is a remake of George Romero's classic film, with Tony Todd (who would later go on to play Candyman in Bernard Rose's film of the same name) as Ben. It also features a Barbara who picks up a gun and quickly turns into Savini's version of Sigourney Weaver's Ripley from the *Alien* films, instead of merely playing the shrieking, hysterical Barbara of the earlier version.

This version is both a faithful remake of and improvement on the original. George Romero, as producer, had considerably more money to pour into this production than he did his original film, so the zombie special effects are much more graphic. This version also gives the viewer a peek at the post-zombie world that necessarily must follow the night of the living dead. Fans of the original *Night* and of the other films in the series will enjoy this remake. **Similar reads:** *Carrion*, Gary Brandner; *Bubbas of the Apocalypse*, Selina Rosen.

African-American Characters • Apocalypse • Cannibalism • Zombies

The Stepford Wives. *Bryan Forbes, dir. 1975. 111 minutes.* This is a faithful adaptation of Ira Levin's novel of the same name. In Stepford, every woman acts like every man's dream of the perfect wife and has no desire beyond pleasing her husband, caring for her children, and cleaning her house, and certainly has no time to help start a local feminist consciousness raising group. One newcomer watches this dream become a nightmare and sees this nightmare engulf her best friend. This excellent film stars Katharine Ross, Paula Prentiss, and Tina Louise, with a screenplay by William Goldman. **Similar reads:** *The Stepford Wives*, Ira Levin; *Regeneration*, Max Allan Collins and Barbara Collins.

Feminism • Replicants • Suburbia

The Terminator. *James Cameron, dir. 1984. 108 minutes.* A cyborg is sent from the future to kill a woman pregnant with a future revolutionary leader. Arnold Schwarzenegger, Linda Hamilton, Paul Winfield, and Bill Paxton star. **Similar reads:** *Mr. X*, Peter Straub; *Revelations*, Douglas E. Winter (editor).

Apocalypse • Cyborgs • Shapeshifters • Time Travel

Terminator 2: Judgment Day. *James Cameron, dir. 1991. 136 minutes.* The cyborg from the future returns, this time to protect the soon-to-be savior of humanity from destruction by a rival terminator. Arnold Schwarzenegger and Linda Hamilton star. **Similar reads:** *Lightning*, Dean Koontz; *Don't Dream*, Donald E. Wandrei.

Apocalypse • Cyborgs • Shapeshifters • Time Travel

Village of the Damned. *Wolf Rilla, dir. 1960. (Black-and-white.) 78 minutes.* Nine months after a bus accident, all the fertile women in an English village are suddenly pregnant. The resulting progeny are all eerily similar in appearance, and can fix people with their mesmerizing stare. **Similar reads:** *Blood Crazy*, Simon Clark; *Phantom Feast*, Diana Barron.

Aliens • Pregnancy

Our Picks

June's Picks: *The Incredible Shrinking Man* (novella), Richard Matheson (Tor); *The Invisible Man*, H. G. Wells (Dover); *Alien* (film); *Night of the Living Dead* (film); *The Stepford Wives* (film).

Tony's Picks: *Demon Seed*, Dean Koontz (Berkley); *Regeneration*, Max Allan Collins and Barbara Collins (Leisure); *The Cell* (film); *Night of the Living Dead* (film—1968 version).

Chapter 13

Ecological Horror: Rampant Animals and Mother Nature's Revenge

Human arrogance has led us to believe that we are at the top of the food chain, that we outrank all other species. The prevalent mindset is that we are somehow special and therefore can dispose of the Earth and its non-human creatures as we see fit. We chop down acres of the rain forest so that we can use the land to raise cattle for the fast food industry. We blind rabbits to make sure that yet another shade of eye shadow is safe for consumers. We drill holes in the Earth to suck out fossil fuels that run sport utility vehicles that take us through the drive-in windows of the bank and fast food establishments, where we idle our cars and further destroy the ozone. And we wrap everything in layers of disposable yet nonbiodegradable plastic and Styrofoam. Ecological scientists constantly remind us that this sort of wasteful behavior has its consequences: It has made several species of animals extinct, has depleted the ozone layer, and has created new super-bacteria resistant to our drugs. Now our horror writers are reminding us that there is always a price to pay when we waste our natural resources.

Ecological horror, which is a relatively recent subgenre, reflects, through metaphor and dark imagery, these frightening and very real results of humanity's thoughtless "mastery" of nature. Authors like Steve Alten in *Meg* argue that humans never have been and are still not at the top of the food chain. Although this novel deals with fictional creatures with prehistoric ties, nonetheless it reminds us that "lions and tigers and bears" are the ultimate supreme hunters. Other horror texts emphasize the revenge of the downtrodden, smaller animals in nature. Alfred Hitchcock's *The Birds* is a not-so-lighthearted view of our feathered friends, and several Stephen King short stories shed light on the reason some cultures fear our feline friends.

It should come as no surprise that various entries in this chapter are crossovers from the technohorror subgenre. These texts demonstrate why it is not nice to fool with Mother Nature. In Hugh B. Cave's novel *The Dawning*, Mother Nature herself, or her creatures, rebel. Civilization as we know it is utterly destroyed by humans, and the survivors who would not learn from their mistakes are literally consumed by the Earth. Sometimes natural monstrosities aren't even the fault of humans; nature itself can be completely unpredictable and chaotic, and thus scary. A loving pet like Cujo can become a monster and rip his master limb from limb when an uncontrollable variable like rabies is introduced into the animal-human relationship. In Daphne DuMaurier's *The Birds*, these creatures, emblems of romantic love, unleash their fury on a licentious sexpot who would tear asunder the sort of love that's the basis for the traditional home.

The horror of Mother Nature's revenge serves as a reminder that we must face the repercussions of our actions when we mine the land and pollute the air and waterways or violate laws that are at least perceived as being "natural laws." Due to the relative newness of this subgenre of horror, this chapter is much briefer than the others in *Hooked on Horror*. However, some benchmark texts do exist in ecological horror, such Stephen King's *Cujo* and Alfred Hitchcock's film *The Birds*.

Appeals: Universal Fear of Animals; Appeals to Human's Sense of Guilt Concerning Nature; "Warning" Horror–Enlightens on Ecological Problems While Entertaining

Alten, Steve. The Meg Series.

Meg. *New York: Dell, 1997. 278p.* Paleontologist Jonas Taylor has just discovered that the fiercest predator ever to live on Earth, the giant shark-like *Carchardon megalodon*, is not extinct as was believed. But now that its waters have been disturbed, the meg has discovered a new prey: humans. This is a fast-paced, easy read. **Similar titles:** *Clickers*, J. F. Gonzales and Mark Williams; *Chelydra Serpentina: Terror in the Adirondacks*, Dan Sanders; *Lake Monsters*, Joseph Citro.

> *Asian-American Characters • Marine Biologist as Character • Maritime Horror • Paleontology • Prehistoric Monsters • Taylor, Jonas (character)*

The Trench. *New York: Kensington, 1999. 296p.* Follow-up to *Meg*, in which paleontologist Jonas Taylor is forced to face his biggest fear when Angel, the baby megalodon shark he once captured, escapes from a Monterey marina. Alten writes fast-paced, plot driven prose, with Taylor battling prehistoric creatures and evil businessmen. **Similar titles:** *Clickers*, J. F. Gonzales and Mark Williams; *Chelydra Serpentina*, Dan Sanders; *Lake Monsters*, Joseph Citro.

🎧 audiotape

> *California • Environmental Horror • Marine Biologist as Character • Maritime Horror • Prehistoric Monsters • Taylor, Jonas (character)*

Barron, Diana.

Phantom Feast. *St. Petersburg, Fla.: Barclay Books, 2001. 269p.* This dark fantasy is about a small New York town that is besieged by the ghosts of captive animals that died when P. T. Barnum's warehouse burned down decades earlier. Two dwarves, twin midgets, and a morbidly obese phone sex operator living in the twins' parents' mansion possess a dark secret: They can animate the animals in their paintings to take revenge on the people who insult them. When two members of the motley crew also discover how to leave their human bodies and shapeshift into phantom animals, no one is safe from being gored, trampled, or eaten alive. **Similar titles:** *The Illustrated Man*, Ray Bradbury; *Freaks* (film); *Phantoms*, Dean Koontz; *Strangewood*, Christopher Golden.

> *Animals Run Rampant • Deformity • Dwarves • Fantasy • Magic • Matricide/Patricide • Midgets • New York State • Revenging Revenant • Shapeshifters • Twins*

Burgess, Tony. The Bewdley Series.

Pontypool Changes Everything. *Toronto: ECW Press, 1998. 276p.* This imagistic novel begins when drama instructor Les Reardon surprises a poacher on his land and chases the man down, only to find him dead, with half his face missing. A domino effect of madness and cannibalism then grips the town and eventually sweeps over the entire Canadian landscape, leaving millions dead. Crisp prose imagery adorns this work, which reads more like a dream vision than a plot-oriented novel. Burgess is excellent for patrons who enjoy a challenging read in the genre. **Similar titles:** *Zom Bee Moo Vee*, Mark McLaughlin; The Headhunter Series, Michael Slade; *Cold Comfort*, Nancy Kilpatrick; *The Cipher*, Kathe Koja.

Apocalypse • Canada • Cannibalism • Epidemics • Zombies

Caesarea. *Toronto: ECW Press, 1999. 246p.* This sequel to *Pontypool Changes Everything* switches from a national scene to the small town of Caesarea, where Mayor Robert Forbes helplessly watches his fellow citizens begin to act strangely, refusing to enter their own homes. Ultimately, an unknown force begins killing people, and a young boy disappears from a local trailer park, causing Forbes to realize that the world may be falling apart. Like *Pontypool Changes Everything*, the emphasis here is on atmosphere and characterization rather than linear narrative, and the writing style is imagistic, at times poetic. **Similar titles:** *Period*, Dennis Cooper; *Filthy Death: The Leering Clown*, Joseph Moore and Brett A. Savory; *The Book of the Dark*, William Meikle; *Ordinary Horror*, David Searcy; *Old Fears*, John Wooley and Ron Wolfe.

Child Molesters • Computers • Dreams • Epidemics • Hunter as Character • Internet, The • Writer as Character

Campbell, Ramsey.

The Hungry Moon. *New York: Tom Doherty, 1987. 360p.* (See chapter 10, "Small Town Horror: Villages of the Damned.")

Midnight Sun. *New York: Tor, 1991. 336p.* (See chapter 14, "Psychological Horror: It's All in Your Head.")

Cave, Hugh B.

The Dawning. *New York: Leisure, 2000. 359p.* In the not so distant future, the Earth is polluted, and civilization is destroyed by hoards of druggies, crazed by a new, super-addictive substance that makes the users ultra-violent. A band of ten people escape to the wilderness to hopefully create civilization anew. But people raised to believe that everything on the planet is theirs for the taking have little understanding of, let alone respect for, nature, and the Earth is not amused. The modern-day Robinson Crusoes must learn to treat the planet with care if they are to survive. **Similar titles:** *Blood Crazy*, Simon Clark; *Gang Approval*, Selina Rosen; *The Stand*, Stephen King; *Godzilla* (film).

Animals Run Rampant • Apocalypse • Canada • Drugs • Native American Characters

Citro, Joseph.

The Gore: A Novel. *Hanover, N.H.: University Press of New England, 2000. 231p.* (See chapter 10, "Small Town Horror: Villages of the Damned.")

Lake Monsters. *Hanover, N.H.: University Press of New England, 2001. 272p.* (See chapter 10, "Small Town Horror: Villages of the Damned.")

Dvorkin, David.

Ursus. *Holicong, Pa.: Wildside Press, 2000, ©1989. 379p.* North Hill, once the commercial center of a growing city in the Rocky Mountains, is now a place of boarded-up stores and roaming gangs. And now even-deadlier predators have arrived. City officials blame wild dogs for the mysterious disappearances of locals, but a zoologist knows better. **Similar titles:** *Clickers*, J. F. Gonzales and Mark Williams; *Vespers*, Jack Rovin; *Ginger Snaps* (film); *Jaws* (film).

Animals Run Rampant • Bears • Biologist as Character • Rocky Mountains, The

Gear, W. Michael, and Kathleen O'Neal Gear.

Dark Inheritance. *New York: Warner Books, 2001. 528p.* (See chapter 12. "Technohorror: Evil Hospitals, Military Screw-Ups, Scientific Goofs, and Alien Invasions.")

Gonzales, J. F., and Mark Williams.

Clickers. *Grandview, Mo.: Dark Tales, 2000. 238p.* The small town of Phillisport, Maine, is invaded by giant crab-like creatures that possess not only voracious appetites for human flesh but also foot-long claws and poisonous stingers that immobilize. Having been asleep for centuries, they are ready to strike again, and aided by the Dark Ones, semi-intelligent reptilian humanoids that coexisted with primitive Homo sapiens, they threaten to destroy the entire town. Unfortunately for horror novelist Rick Sychek, he has chosen to vacation in Phillisport, and he must pit his survival skills against monsters that rival anything ever created by his own imagination. **Similar titles:** *Chelydra Serpentina*, Dan Sanders; *Waiting*, Frank M. Robinson; *Phantoms*, Dean Koontz; *The Birds* (film).

Dinosaurs • Evolutionary Theory • History, Use of • Maine • Maritime Horror • Police Officer as Character • Writer as Character

Grant, Charles. The Millennium Quartet.

Chariot. *New York: Tor, 2000. 309p.* Trey Falkirk lives in a virtually abandoned subdivision outside Las Vegas with a small group of outcast neighbors. It alone has escaped the ravages of a mutant strain of smallpox, and Falkirk, living inside its limits, cannot be killed. He lives a reclusive life until Eula, an old psalm-singing choralist, and Sir John Harp, a mysterious Englishman who has tracked Falkirk from the far side of the planet, invade his little community. These two, and the four horsemen, know that Falkirk's destiny lies beyond his small world and is tied to the destiny of all humanity. **Similar titles:** The Bewdley Series, Tony Burgess; *Blood Crazy*, Simon Clark; *The Stand*, Stephen King; *Revelations*, Douglas E. Winter (editor).

Apocalypse • Epidemic • Las Vegas, Nevada • Popular Culture

Grant, Charles.

Genesis [Black Oak I]. *New York: ROC, 1998. 271p.* (See chapter 6, "Vampires and Werewolves: Children of the Night.")

Holland, David.

Murcheston: The Wolf's Tale. *New York: Tor, 2000. 349 p.* (See chapter 6, "Vampires and Werewolves: Children of the Night.")

Johnstone, William W.

Cat's Cradle. *New York: Kensington-Pinnacle, 1999. 400 p.* (See chapter 8, "Mythological Monsters and 'The Old Ones': Invoking the Dark Gods.")

Ketchum, Jack.

Ladies' Night. *Springfield, Pa.: Gauntlet Publishing, 2000, ©1997. 166p.* A tanker truck overturns, its mysterious contents spilling in the middle of New York City. The substance has a sweet, cherry scent, and causes most of the female population to become sexually aroused, and later, be filled with the desire to kill all the men in the city. **Similar titles:** *Night Chills*, Dean Koontz; *Night of the Living Dead* (film); *Dreamcatcher*, Stephen King.

> *Environmental Horror • Epidemic • Mind Control • New York City • Psychosexual Horror*

King, Stephen.

Cujo. *New York: Plume, 1981. 277p.* Murderer Frank Dodd has figured out a way to come back after death: He has managed to possess the body of Cujo, beloved family pet of the Camber family. Once Dodd's spirit and intelligence inhabit the body of the 200-pound St. Bernard, the dog goes on a rampage (attributed to rabies), dismembering and killing anyone who crosses his path. *Cujo* is another of King's masterpieces of suspense. You will never look at your pets the same again. This popular read was made into a movie of the same name. **Similar titles:** *The Birds* (film); *Vespers*, Jeff Rovin; *Phantom Feast*, Diana Barron.

> ᏶ large print

> *Animals Run Rampant • Castle Rock, Maine • Dogs*

Korn, M. F.

Skimming the Gumbo Nuclear. *Fountain Hills, Ariz.: Eraserhead Press, 2001. 287p.* Twenty-year-old college student Ricky Harrison begins having strange, visionary dreams about a plague sweeping the state of Louisiana. The only problem is that his dreams are a portent of reality, as the industrial pollution in the state begins to take its toll, producing fearsome mutant reptiles and fish in its waterways and a virulent strain of a virus that causes people to become insane and violent. With the realization that very few will escape the new plague, Ricky knows that the end is near. Korn's apocalyptic novel alternates between dark comedy and tragedy, and is very well written. **Similar titles:** *The Apostate*, Paul Lonardo; The Bewdley Series, Tony Burgess; *Ordinary Horror*, David Searcy; *Revelations*, Douglas E. Winter (editor).

> *Academia • Baton Rouge, Louisiana • Dreams • Environmental Horror • Epidemic • Maritime Horror*

Lebbon, Tim.

The Nature of Balance. *New York: Leisure, 2001. 395p.* In her nightmares, Peer sees her own death, and then she awakens to a world gone mad, where humans are no longer the dominant species. In fact, most of the world's humans have been killed and mutilated by an unseen natural force. In the face of so much death, Peer joins forces with two other teenagers, Blane and Mary, who have both mysteriously survived as well, and the three travel in search of answers. This is a nightmarish and imagistic text, but one that uses graphic description to create and sustain an atmosphere of danger. **Similar titles:** *Phantom Feast*, Diana Barron; *Clickers*, J. F. Gonzales and Mark Williams; *The Birds* (film); *Cujo*, Stephen King.

> *Animals Run Rampant • Apocalypse • Dreams • England • Fantasy*

Lonardo, Paul.

The Apostate. *St. Petersburg, Fla.: Barclay Books, 2001. 254 p.* (See chapter 10, "Small Town Horror: Villages of the Damned.")

Ravenwolf, Silver.

Murder at the Witches' Bluff: A Novel of Suspense and Magick. *St. Paul, Minn.: Llewellyn, 2000. 449p.* (See chapter 7, "Demonic Possession, Satanism, Black Magic, and Witches and Warlocks: The Devil Made Me Do It.")

Robinson, Frank M.

Waiting. *New York: Tom Doherty, 1999. 303p.* A respected doctor who is investigating the death of a seemingly superhuman John Doe is murdered, as are his friends who investigate the murder. When a conspiracy involving The Old People, another species of human that evolved parallel to Homo sapiens, is discovered, the survival of humanity as we know it is called into question. **Similar titles:** *Lurker at the Threshold*, H. P. Lovecraft; *The Loved Dead*, H. P. Lovecraft et. al.; *The Sand Dwellers*, Adam Niswander; *Chelydra Serpentina*, Dan Sanders; *Clickers*, J. F. Gonzales and Mark Williams.

> *California • Evolutionary Theory • Journalist as Character • Mind Control • Psychiatrist/Psychologist as Character • Violence, Theories of*

Rovin, Jeff.

Vespers. *New York: St. Martin's Press, 1998. 320p.* Bats are attacking and killing people in New York City. Can a detective and a bat expert from the Bronx Zoo figure out why, and stop them? This novel was made into a movie called *Bats*. **Similar titles:** *The Birds* (film); *Clickers*, J. F. Gonzales and Mark Williams; *The Nature of Balance*, Tim Lebbon.

> 𝔻 audiotape

> *Animals Run Rampant • Bats • New York City • Police Officer as Character*

Sanders, Dan.

Chelydra Serpentina: Terror in the Adirondacks. *Santa Barbara, Calif.: Astral Publishing, 2000. 332p.* (See chapter 12, "Technohorror: Evil Hospitals, Military Screw-Ups, Scientific Goofs, and Alien Invasions,")

Searcy, David.

Ordinary Horror. *New York: Penguin-Viking, 2001. 230p.* When gophers invade his prized rose garden, Frank Delabano, retired science teacher living alone in a tract housing neighborhood, sends away for four exotic plants that are advertised to control gophers without harming pets. However, soon all the pets and animals in the neighborhood disappear, and Delabano's neighbor begins to suspect that the plants growing next door could spell the end of the world as we know it. Searcy's text is a gentle read with emphasis on characterization and personal philosophy. **Similar titles:** *Ghost Stories of Henry James*, Henry James; *Our Lady of Darkness*, Fritz Leiber; *The Return*, Walter de la Mare; *Don't Dream*, Donald Wandrei; *The Apostate*, Paul Lonardo.

> *Apocalypse • Gardens • Senior Citizen as Character • Suburbia • Teacher as Character*

Film

The Birds. *Alfred Hitchcock, dir. 1963. 120 minutes.* A promiscuous blonde bombshell pursues a staid widower to the island home he shares with his mother and daughter, and her presence in the community, and in the family unit, provokes an attack on all by the birds. The script for this film was loosely based on a Daphne DuMaurier story. Tippi Hedron, Jessica Tandy, Suzanne Pleshette, and Rod Taylor star. **Similar reads:** *Vespers*, Jeff Rovin; *Cujo*, Stephen King.

>   *Animals Run Rampant • Birds • California*

Ginger Snaps. *John Fawcett, dir. 2000. 108 minutes.* (See chapter 6, "Vampires and Werewolves: Children of the Night.")

13

Godzilla, King of the Monsters. *Terry Morse, dir. 1956. (Black-and-white.) 80 minutes.* A giant, fire-breathing lizard threatens Japan and terrifies a young reporter, played by Raymond Burr. This is the original classic that has spawned several sequels that transformed Godzilla from a monster to the protector of Japan. It has inspired several remakes, most notably, and most expensively, in 1998. **Similar reads:** *The Dawning*, Hugh B. Cave; *The Meg Series*, Steve Alten.

>   *Animals Run Rampant • Japan*

The Wolf Man. *George Waggner, dir. 1941. (Black-and-white.) 70 minutes.* (See chapter 6, "Vampires and Werewolves: Children of the Night.")

Our Picks

June's Picks: *Phantom Feast*, Diana Barron (Barclay Books); *Cujo*, Stephen King (Plume); *The Birds* (film).

Tony's Picks: *Phantom Feast*, Diana Barron (Barclay Books); *Clickers*, J. F. Gonzales and Mark Williams (Dark Tales); *The Birds* (film).

Chapter 14

Psychological Horror: It's All In Your Head

Although stories of psychological horror are for the most part devoid of supernatural monsters and bloodthirsty psychopaths, they are no less frightening. They deal with torment stemming from mental illness, child abuse, guilt, and countless other types of human suffering and emotional instability. These novels question the very nature of our world, as do horror texts in general, but they take that inquiry one step further. Often they challenge the fictional reality that the writer creates. Perhaps the best way to define psychological horror is by citing one of the better examples of the subgenre, Ramsey Campbell's *Obsession.* Campbell's novel about being haunted by our childhoods suggests that the characters' obsession with their own guilt due to youthful indiscretions to which they attribute their adult fears is more horrific than any ghost or phantom sent from a supernatural realm to mete out justice. After all, we know that monsters are not real.

Many of the entries in this category are indexed under the keyword "gothicism," a word that we chose to indicate characters that view the world from a gothic or horrific perspective, for they suffer in hells of their own making. These characters may be the type who wear black clothing daily and listen to the often depressing or frustration-filled lyrics of gothic industrial music, or they may be the boy-next-door type, with one twist: They see the world as frightening, ominous, or even dangerous. For example, in the gothic world of Campbell or of Caitlin R. Kiernan, adult heroes and heroines suffer not only because they are un*able* to break away from a harmful situation, but because they are un*willing* to challenge the cultural expectations that created the harmful situation. In this sense, they *participate* in their own victimization. For example, in Daphne DuMaurier's *Rebecca,* the nameless second Mrs. Maxim de Winter finds that she will forever be commanded by her husband, because the far more interesting but dead Rebecca (who refused to be commanded by Maxim de Winter) will always cast a shadow over her.

Aside from examining how we build dungeons in our own minds, psychological horror can also give voice to those darkest desires that we are foolish enough to believe will remain eternally buried in the murky waters of the unconscious mind. In other words, when we repress desires in real life, they may come to life in nightmares or in other more dysfunctional ways. Similarly, when fictional characters repress their darkest desires, those desires actually come to life, resulting in the surreal fictional worlds that define the psychological horror tale. Edgar Allan Poe's main character Roderick in "The Fall of the House of Usher" is dying because of his stubborn refusal to acknowledge his unspeakable, incestuous longings for his now-deceased twin sister Madeline and his inability to desire anyone outside of the family. Madeline's demise and subsequent entombment within the walls of the house are representative of the degree to which Roderick has repressed this desire. The house itself, which reflects the psychological state of its owner, begins to crumble, and eventually dies—at least in the mind of the narrator (Roderick's friend). Finally, because Roderick's desires cannot be continually repressed, ultimately Madeline claims him; she returns from the grave and drags him and the house down with her.

Our point here is not that horror is *either* psychological or supernatural. Those two categories are useful in compartmentalizing or organizing horror texts (as we have done here in *Hooked on Horror*), but the truth is, all horror contains elements of both, albeit in different quantities. The novels that we have included in this chapter stand apart in that they leave the "reality" of the monster's existence up to the reader, who is left wondering what really happened. Was it all in the characters' heads, all along?

Titles in this chapter include Clive Barker's dark fantasy *Galilee,* Ramsey Campbell's *Obsession,* and Dean Koontz's *Key to Midnight*. Benchmark titles in this category include Jane Austen's *Northanger Abbey*, Daphne DuMaurier's *Rebecca*, and Caitlin R. Kiernan's critically acclaimed goth rock best-seller, *Silk.*

Note: Stories of psychological horror can also be found in the collections and anthologies described in chapter 17. Refer to the subject/keyword index for specific titles under the keyword "gothicism."

Appeal: Psychological Appeal; More Realistic Fears; Tendency to Be Thought-Provoking; Character Driven Texts; Open-Ended Rather Than Explained Endings; Universality of Psychologically Horrifying Experience; More "Domestic" Than Other Subgenres

Alonso, Juan.

Killing the Mandarin. *Lincoln, Neb.: iUniverse, 2000. 320p.* An American scholar teaching in the Argentinean city of Montevideo becomes involved in a violent love triangle with a revolutionary student and his childhood love. To avoid bloodshed and political turmoil in a country whose politics are unstable, he has only one chance to make the right decisions. This stream-of-consciousness narrative emphasizes the psychological portrait of its characters more than it does the terrifying consequences of their actions, yet it is effective in its shock value. **Similar titles:** *Fight Club* (film); *Soul Temple*, Steven Lee Climer; *Travel Many Roads*, Robert E. Wheeler.

Academia • Argentina • Gay/Lesbian/Bisexual Characters • History, Use of •
Teacher as Character • Violence, Theories of

Andrews, Christopher.

Pandora's Game. *Philadelphia: Xlibris, 1999. 248p.* Neil Carpenter, a college junior working toward a theater degree at the University of Oklahoma, has been writing comic books for his own pleasure since grade school. While working on a play, he meets Mark Hudson, and they hit it off. After Neil reads that hypnotism can help bring out the creative side of the subconscious, Mark hypnotizes Neil so that he will now think that he is Alistair, one of their monstrous characters. Mark then proceeds to interview Alistair about his past and present, gathering data for the comic book. When people start showing up dead, with their bodies shredded as if by an animal, Neil begins to suspect that their grand little experiment may have somehow gone awry. **Similar titles:** *Dark Within*, John Wooley; *Period*, Dennis Cooper; The Cyber Blood Chronicles, Jonathan H. Amsbary; *Soul Temple*, Steven Lee Climer.

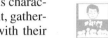

Academia • Comic Books • Hypnotism • Oklahoma • Werewolves • Zombies

Arensberg, Ann.

Incubus. *New York: Alfred A. Knopf, 1999. 322p.* (See chapter 7, "Demonic Possession, Satanism, Black Magic, and Witches and Warlocks: The Devil Made Me Do It.")

Atkins, Peter.

Morningstar. *Lancaster, Pa.: Stealth Press, 2000, ©1992. 244p.* (See chapter 11, "Maniacs and Sociopaths, or the Nuclear Family Explodes: Monstrous Malcontents Bury the Hatchet.")

Aubert, Brigitte.

Death from the Woods. *David L. Karal (translator). New York: Welcome Rain Publishers, 2000, ©1996. 279p.* Elise Andreioli suffers a terrible accident that leaves her without the use of her legs, arms, eyes, and voice. So when a young girl in her small French village tells her that she saw death come from the woods to kill her little brother, Elsie must figure out how to signal this to the police. Her task becomes even more crucial when she realizes that "death" will strike again, and when someone tries to kill her for knowing too much. Aubert emphasizes characterization as well as suspense in this novel that was voted France's best thriller of 1997. **Similar titles:** *Seize the Night*, Dean Koontz; *Norton Vyse, Psychic*, Rose Champion de Crespigny; *M.* (film).

Child Molesters • France • Police Officer as Character • Quadriplegic/Paraplegics as Character • Serial Killers

Austen, Jane.

Northanger Abbey. *Oxford: Oxford University Press, 2000, ©1818. 221p.* (See chapter 16, "Comic Horror: Laughing at Our Fears.")

Aycliffe, Jonathan.

A Shadow on the Wall. *Sutton, England: Severn House, 2000. 217p.* (See chapter 4, "Ghosts and Haunted Houses: Dealing with Presences and Absences.")

Bachman, Richard.

Roadwork. (See King, Stephen [as Richard Bachman]. *Roadwork*. New York: Signet, 1999, ©1981. 307p.)

Barker, Clive.

Galilee. *New York: HarperCollins, 1998. 432p.* Departure novel for Barker that contains no demons or gore but is instead a dark fantasy about two families, interracial sex, and the American Civil War. Galilee is the son of Cesaria, for whom Thomas Jefferson erected a mansion, and he plays the central role in bringing tensions between the Barbarossa and Geory families to a head. **Similar titles:** *Merrick,* Anne Rice; *Historical Hauntings,* Martin H. Greenberg and Jean Rabe (editors); *Ghosts and Haunts of the Civil War,* Christopher K. Coleman (editor); The My Soul to Keep Series, Tananarive Due.

African-American Characters • Diary Format • Eroticism • History, Use of • North Carolina • Slavery • War—American Civil War

Barlog, J. M.

Dark Side: The Haunting. *Chicago: BAK Books, 1999. 293p.* (See chapter 4, "Ghosts and Haunted Houses: Dealing with Presences and Absences.")

Beman, Donald.

Avatar. *New York: Leisure, 1998. 366p.* A young man enamored of a famous female sculptor, known for her grotesque and horrific works, finally gets a chance to meet, and become involved with, his idol. Will he survive the encounter with her dark vision of reality? **Similar titles:** *Silk,* Caitlin R. Keirnan; *Drawn to the Grave,* Mary Ann Mitchell; The Love in Vein Series, Poppy Z. Brite (editor); *Embraces,* Paula Guran (editor).

Artist as Character • Eroticism

Bergstrom, Elaine.

The Door Through Washington Square. *New York: Ace, 1998. 360p.* Deirdre MacCallum leaves her tranquil life to visit a dying grandmother in New York City. At her grandmother's house, she finds a portal to the past, where she meets her grandmother in youth and learns about her family's dark secrets. **Similar titles:** The Talisman Series, Stephen King and Peter Straub; *Neverwhere,* Neil Gaiman; *Salem's Ghosts,* Rose Earhart; *Mr. X,* Peter Straub.

Crowley, Aleister (character) • Fantasy • Gothic Romance • Magic • New York City • Religion—Satanism • Roaring Twenties, The • Time Travel

Berliner, Janet, and George Guthridge. The Madagascar Manifesto.

Child of the Light. *Clarkston, Ga.: White Wolf, 1996. 438p.* This acclaimed novel is part one of The Madagascar Manifesto, an alternative history that asks, "what if the Nazis had expelled the Jews to Madagascar," as one of them had planned. **Similar titles:** *Requiem,* Graham Joyce; The Anno Dracula Series, Kim Newman; *Carrion Comfort,* Dan Simmons; *From Hell,* Alan Moore and Eddie Campbell; *Killing the Mandarin,* Juan Alonso.

Africa • Alternative History • Nazism • Religion—Judaism • War—World War II

Child of the Journey. *Clarkston, Ga.: White Wolf, 1996. 471p.* This is part two of The Madagascar Manifesto, an alternative history that questions the Nazi idea of exiling all the Jews to Madagascar. **Similar titles:** *Requiem,* Graham Joyce; The Anno Dracula Series, Kim Newman; *Carrion Comfort,* Dan Simmons; *From Hell,* Alan Moore and Eddie Campbell; *Killing the Mandarin,* Juan Alonso.

Africa • Alternative History • Nazism • Religion—Judaism • War—World War II

Children of the Dusk. *Clarkston, Ga.: White Wolf, 1997. 447p.* The third part of The Madagascar Manifesto, this alternative history takes up with the arrival of the Jews in Madagascar. Berliner and Guthridge are winners of a Bram Stoker Award. **Similar titles:** *Requiem*, Graham Joyce; The Anno Dracula Series, Kim Newman; *Carrion Comfort*, Dan Simmons; *From Hell*, Alan Moore and Eddie Campbell; *Killing the Mandarin*, Juan Alonso.

> *Africa • Alternative History • Nazism • Religion—Judaism • War—World War II*

Billings, Andrew.

Carnage. *New York: Jove, 1999. 360p.* (See chapter 11, "Maniacs and Socio-paths, or the Nuclear Family Explodes: Monstrous Malcontents Bury the Hatchet.")

Bonansigna, Jay.

Head Case. *New York: Simon & Schuster, 1998. 318p.* John McNally wakes up in a mental hospital with amnesia and is told that he is a suspected serial killer. With the help of a private investigator, he escapes and begins to track down his own identity. *Head Case* is more action-oriented than the typical psychological horror novel. **Similar titles:** *Amnesia*, Andrew Neiderman; *The Bad Place*, Dean Koontz; *The Red God*, C. E. Albertson; *The Dark Side*, J. M. Barlog.

> *Amnesia • Mental Institutions • Serial Killers*

Bradbury, Ray.

A Graveyard for Lunatics: Another Tale of Two Cities. *New York: Perennial, 2001. 307p.* It is Halloween Night, 1954, and a young, film-obsessed script-writer has just been hired at Maximus Studios. An anonymous investigation leads him from the giant Maximus Films back lot to an eerie graveyard separated from the studio by a single wall. There he makes a terrifying discovery that thrusts him into a maelstrom of intrigue and mystery and into the dizzy exhilaration of the movie industry at the height of its glittering power. **Similar titles:** *Death From the Woods*, Brigitte Aubert; *Green Light Cemetery*, David Cosciolek; The Universal Monsters Series, various authors; *Whispers*, Dean Koontz.

> *Cemeteries • Hollywood, California • Writer as Character*

Bradley, Marion Zimmer.

Gravelight. *New York: Tor, 1998, ©1997. 350p.* (See chapter 4, "Ghosts and Haunted Houses: Dealing with Presences and Absences.")

Burgess, Tony. The Bewdley Series.

(See chapter 13, "Ecological Horror: Rampant Animals and Mother Nature's Revenge.")

Cady, Jack.

The Haunting of Hood Canal. *New York: St. Martin's Press, 2001. 306p.* (See chapter 4, "Ghosts and Haunted Houses: Dealing with Presences and Absences.")

Campbell, Ramsey.

Incarnate. *London: Little, Brown, 1992, ©1983. 490p.* Five individuals who have each had strange experiences with dreams so realistic that they mistake them for reality agree to undergo a scientific experiment into the nature of their dreams. They discover, however, that one of the individuals involved in the experiment is indeed the strange creature that has appeared to each of them in different guises, and which seems to control their dreams and their realities. Now they must join forces to resist the mysterious being, using their collective dream ability to change the face of London. **Similar titles:** *Dreamside*, Graham Joyce; *Mr. X*, Peter Straub; *Nightmare on Elm Street* (film).

> *Dreams • England • Fantasy • Journalist as Character • Police Brutality • Revenging Revenant • Shapeshifters • Weird Science*

The Last Voice They Hear. *New York: Forge, 1998. 384p.* (See chapter 11, "Maniacs and Sociopaths, or the Nuclear Family Explodes: Monstrous Malcontents Bury the Hatchet.")

The Long Lost. *New York: Tor, 1996. 375p.* The Owains invite a long-lost relative to the family picnic, but then she begins manipulating them with her knowledge of the darkest secrets—and her ability to deliver their darkest desires. **Similar titles:** *Needful Things*, Stephen King; *Welcome Back to the Night*, Elizabeth Massie; *Obsession*, Ramsey Campbell.

> *Family Curse • Secret Sin • Wales • Wish Fulfillment • Witchcraft*

Midnight Sun. *New York: Tor, 1991. 336p.* As a young boy, Ben Sterling finds himself being strangely attracted to the magical yet eerie powers that seem to inhabit Sterling Forest. Twenty years later, Sterling, now a successful writer of children's books and a family man, has inherited his aunt's house, which sits on the edge of the forest—and he is even more attracted to the dark forces there than ever. As the forest's shadow approaches his house, can he break its hypnotic hold before it takes him and his family? **Similar titles:** *House of Pain*, Sephera Giron; *The Town*, Bentley Little; *Darkness Demands*, Simon Clark; *Strangewood*, Christopher Golden.

> *Natural Disasters • Wilderness • Writer as Character*

The Nameless. *London: Little, Brown, 1992, ©1985. 278p.* (See chapter 11, "Maniacs and Sociopaths, or the Nuclear Family Explodes: Monstrous Malcontents Bury the Hatchet.")

Needing Ghosts. *London: Century, 1990. 80p.* (See chapter 16, "Comic Horror: Laughing at Our Fears.")

Obsession. *New York: Macmillan, 1985. 247p.* Four teenagers receive an ad in the mail that says simply, "Whatever you want most, I do." When the four decide to try their luck with the ad, their wishes are fulfilled, to disastrous ends. Twenty-five years later, the four suddenly find themselves under siege by a power that wants payment for granting their wishes. Campbell pens erudite prose; subtlety and psychological horror pervade this chiller. **Similar titles:** *The Store*, Bentley Little; *Needful Things*, Stephen King; *The Cleanup*, John Skipp and Craig Spector; *Careful What You Wish*, June Hubbard.

> *Childhood • Obsession • Wish Fulfillment*

Case, David.

Brotherly Love and Other Tales of Trust and Knowledge. *Nottingham, England: Pumpkin, 1999. 276p.* A young girl runs away from an abusive father, only to get caught in an old bear trap in the forest. Instead of release, her screams bring someone with rape on his mind. The local sheriff is of no help, even though the girl's story fits a pattern of crimes in the area. For a brother, already alarmed at the disappearance of his sister, there can be nothing more disturbing than finding evidence that she may not have been the only victim of the man who lives at Lavender Hall, and realizing that he may have to take the law into his own hands. **Similar titles:** *Escaping Purgatory*, Gary A. Braunbeck and Alan M. Clark; *The Bottoms*, Joe R. Lansdale; *The One Safe Place*, Ramsey Campbell; *Storm*, Boris Starling.

> *Child Molester • Police Officer as Character • Rape • Revenge •*
> *Vigilantism*

Cave, Hugh B.

Isle of the Whisperers. *Nottingham, England: Pumpkin Books, 1999. 265p.* (See chapter 7, "Demonic Possession, Satanism, Black Magic, and Witches and Warlocks: The Devil Made Me Do It.")

Cisco, Michael.

🎗 **The Divinity Student.** *Tallahassee, Fla.: Buzzcity Press, 1999. 149p.* The Divinity Student, a "word finder" extraordinaire, travels through a nightmarish world of the dead to find the secret meanings of "lost words." Atmospheric and poetic, written in dream-like stream-of-consciousness prose, this novel is a winner of the International Horror Guild Award for Best First Novel, 1999. **Similar titles:** The Bewdley Series, Tony Burgess; *Period*, Dennis Cooper; *Cold Comfort*, Nancy Kilpatrick.

> *Clergy as Character • Dreams • Prognostication •*
> *Religion—Christianity—Catholicism*

Clegg, Douglas.

Purity. *Baltimore: Cemetery Dance Publications, 2000. 118p.* (See chapter 8, "Mythological Monsters and 'The Old Ones': Invoking the Dark Gods.")

Climer, Steven Lee.

Soul Temple. *Grandview, Mo.: Dark Tales, 2000. 181p.* (See chapter 8, "Mythological Monsters and 'The Old Ones': Invoking the Dark Gods.")

Conley, Brian.

The Killer of Love: A Novel. *Atlanta, Ga.: Buckhead Press, 1999. 207p.* Jimmy Love, a very intelligent yet confused nineteen-year-old drug addict and alcoholic, struggles to overcome his inner and outer demons in this contemporary horror story in the tradition of Stephen King. The evil in Conley's novel is real, earthbound, historical, and lives in the frightening characters that take on the status of myth. This novel is about what happens when we give control of our lives to others. **Similar titles:** *Tideland*, Mitch Cullen; *The Way the Family Got Away*, Michael Kimball; *Obsession*, Ramsey Campbell; *Dial Your Dreams*, Robert Weinberg.

> *Alcoholism • Drugs • Mind Control*

Constantine, Storm. The Grigori Trilogy.

(See chapter 8, "Mythological Monsters and 'The Old Ones': Invoking the Dark Gods.")

Cooper, Dennis.

Period. *New York: Grove Press, 2000. 109p.* This experimental novel is a story of sexual and artistic obsessions, set in a world of drugs, pornography, Satanism, and mysterious Internet chat rooms. Its nonlinear narrative will appeal to readers who prefer more nontraditional prose. **Similar titles:** The Bewdley Series, Tony Burgess; *The Divinity Student*, Michael Cisco; *Cold Comfort*, Nancy Kilpatrick; *Natural Selection*, Westen Ochse.

> *Diary Format • Gay/Lesbian/Bisexual characters • Internet,*
> *The—Chatrooms • Miles, George (character) • Music—Rock Music •*
> *Obsession • Religion—Satanism • Writer as Character*

Cullen, Mitch.

Tideland. *Chester Springs, Pa.: Dufour Editions, 2000. 192p.* Jeliza-Rose's elderly father takes her to live on his mother's property in rural Texas after a drug overdose kills her morbidly obese mother. Upon arrival, he too dies, leaving Jeliza-Rose to survive as best as she can with nothing but four Barbie heads for company. *Tideland* is gothic, eerie, and compelling. **Similar titles:** *The Dress Lodger*, Sheri Holman; *The Bottoms*, Joe R. Lansdale; *The Way the Family Got Away*, Michael Kimball; *The Vampire Hunters*, William Hill.

Childhood • Deformities • Gothicism • Musician as Character • Obsession • Texas

Danielewski, Mark Z.

House of Leaves. *2d ed. London, England: Anchor, 2000. 709p.* Tattoo-shop apprentice Johnny Truant discovers a monograph written by an insane, blind professor about a non-existent documentary film, itself about a photojournalist who finds a house with supernatural qualities. The house itself is disturbing. The last family who tried to live there discovered it was larger on the inside than on the outside. But then Johnny is driven to near insanity trying to corroborate the old professor's story, for which a scrap of evidence doesn't seem to exist. **Similar titles:** *The House*, Bentley Little, *The Blair Witch Project* (film); *The Haunting of Hill House*, Shirley Jackson; *Black House*, Stephen King and Peter Straub.

Documentary Technique • Haunted Houses • Parallel Universe

Dann, Jack.

The Silent. *New York: Bantam Books, 1998. 301p.* This is the horrific tale of thirteen-year-old Mundy McDowell, who is left to wander in a nightmare landscape between haunting dreams and reality after witnessing the murder of his parents. This historical fiction is set during the American Civil War. **Similar titles:** *Galilee*, Clive Barker; *Dead Promises*, June Hubbard; *Beloved*, Toni Morrison; *Darker Angels*, S. P. Somtow.

Dreams • History, Use of • War—American Civil War

Davis, Kathryn.

Hell: A Novel. *Hopewell, N.J.: Ecco Press, 1998. 179p.* Three tales of death and despair are interwoven in this unique novel—all centered around an evil dollhouse. This is an erudite and clever novel, with emphasis on style and atmosphere. **Similar titles:** *The 37th Mandala*, Mark Laidlaw; *The House*, Bentley Little; *Ancient Images*, Ramsey Campbell.

Cursed Objects • Parenting • Writer as Character

de la Mare, Walter.

The Return. *Mineola, N.Y.: Dover, 1997, ©1922. 224p.* (See chapter 7, "Demonic Possession, Satanism, Black Magic, and Witches and Warlocks: The Devil Made Me Do It.")

Desmond, Sean.

Adam's Fall. *New York: Thomas Dunne Books, 2000. 245p.* (See chapter 4, "Ghosts and Haunted Houses: Dealing with Presences and Absences.")

Dickey, Christopher.

Innocent Blood: A Novel. *New York: Scribner Paperback, 1998. 335p.* Journalist Christopher Dickey takes that stock figure of fiction on the page and screen, the Muslim terrorist, and turns him into an understandable human being. Kurt Kurtovic could be the boy next door, but he goes from Kansas schoolboy, to Army Ranger hero, to World Trade

Center bomber. In his mind, America's actions in Panama and the Persian Gulf deservedly bring terrorism to its own shores, so the blond-haired, blue-eyed boy decides to take matters into his own hands. The author, Christopher Dickey, states: "*Innocent Blood* was always meant to be a warning about the very real dangers, very close at hand, that threaten America." **Similar titles:** *The Wasp Factory*, Ian Banks; *The Emerald Germs of Ireland*, Patrick McCabe; *Storm*, Boris Starling.

> *Domestic Terrorism • Kansas • New York City • Soldier as Character • Revenge • War—Gulf War*

DuMaurier, Daphne.

Rebecca. *New York: Avon, 1971, ©1938. 380p.* In this ghost story without a ghost, the second Mrs. de Winter is haunted by the presence of the first, Rebecca. Rebecca is dead but not forgotten at Manderly, where the decor of the house is a monument to her taste, and the housekeeper, the malign Mrs. Danvers, continually compares the second Mrs. De Winter unfavorably to Rebecca, whom she adored. And while Maxim De Winter would like to forget his first wife and settle down to a nice quiet life with his second spouse, a discovery in the bay off of Manderly won't let Rebecca, or him, rest. This classic was made into a film by Alfred Hitchcock. **Similar titles:** *The Return*, Walter de la Mare; *A Bottomless Grave*, Hugh B. Lamb; *Nightshade: Gothic Tales by Women*, Victoria A. Brownworth (editor).

> *England • Gothicism • Incest • Secret Sin • Marriage • Obsession*

Dungan, Marilyn.

Field of Stones. *Paris, Ky.: Arcane Books, 2001. 245p.* Parker Webb University is conducting an archeological dig in Laney McVey's own front yard. While daily watching level after level of dirt disappear, Laney can hardly contain her excitement and anticipation. But suddenly the absorbing dig goes horribly wrong, so wrong that Laney wishes that the first trowel of dirt had never been removed. Something is waiting under the stones, and when she attempts to solve the puzzle of how the horror got into her field of stones, she uncovers secrets that are twisted, raw, and deadly. **Similar titles:** *The Sleeper in the Sands*, Tom Holland; *Isle of the Whisperers*, Hugh B. Cave; *Riverwatch*, Joseph M. Nassie; *Into the Mummy's Tomb*, John Richard Stevens (editor).

> *Academia • Archeology • Secret Sin • Subterranean Monsters*

Earhart, Rose.

Dorcas Good: The Diary of a Salem Witch. *New York: Pendleton Books, 2000. 375p.* (See chapter 10, "Small Town Horror: Villages of the Damned.")

Fahy, Christopher.

Eternal Bliss. *New York: Kensington-Zebra, 2000, ©1988. 281p.* (See chapter 11, "Maniacs and Sociopaths, or the Nuclear Family Explodes: Monstrous Malcontents Bury the Hatchet.")

Fowler, Christopher.

Spanky. *London: Little, Brown-Warner, 1998, ©1994. 338p.* (See chapter 7, "Demonic Possession, Satanism, Black Magic, and Witches and Warlocks: The Devil Made Me Do It.")

Gaiman, Neil.

The Sandman: The Dream Hunters. *New York: Vertigo-DC Comics, 1999. 126p.* The product of Gaiman's immersion in Japanese art, culture, and history, this is a classic Japanese tale that he has subtly morphed into his Sandman universe. Like most fables, the story begins with a wager between two jealous animals, a fox and a badger. Meanwhile, in faraway Kyoto, the wealthy Master of Yin-Yang, the onmyoji, is plagued by his fears and seeks tranquillity in his command of sorcery. He dispatches demons to plague the monk in his dreams and eventually kill him to bring his peace. **Similar titles:** *Spawn*, Todd McFarland, Alan Moore, and Greg Capullo; The Witchblade Series, Christina Z. and David Wohl; Buffy the Vampire Slayer Series, Various Authors; *Lazarus Churchyard*, Warren Ellis and D'Israeli.

🔊 graphic novels

Clergy as Character • Demons • Dreams • Graphic Novel • Japan • Sandman, The (character) • Shapeshifters

Garton, Ray.

The Folks. *Baltimore: Cemetery Dance, 2001. 136p.* A young man, an outcast in his rural town because of his fire-scarred face and his problem with the area's fundamentalist Christian ambience, encounters an incestuous family of grotesques: a pinhead, Siamese twins, a massive man-boy with a tail, and many other misshapen creatures. The young man learns that he, because of his scars, has been chosen to lead the family into the future. Garton has storytelling talent; the pacing here is brisk. **Similar titles:** *Freaks* (film); *Tideland*, Mitch Cullen; *Phantom Feast*, Dianna Barron; *A Darkness Inbred*, Victor Heck.

Deformity • Psychosexual Horror • Religion—Christianity • Serial Killers

Gebhard, Patricia.

Motives for Murder. *Berkeley, Calif.: Creative Arts Book, 2000. 260p.* Lucy Metzger, whose popular professor husband is poisoned during a solo business trip to New York, faces accusations not only from police but also from her own father. Now she must find out who has framed her. As the narrator, Lucy devotes most of the book to detailing her early obsession with her husband and why she could not have killed him, although she provides many reasons to the contrary. **Similar titles:** *The Event*, Donald Silverman; *Selected Tales*, Edgar Allan Poe; *Travel Many Roads*, Robert E. Wheeler; *The Emerald Germs of Ireland*, Patrick McCabe.

Academia • Dramatic Monologue • Marriage • Teacher as Character

Golden, Christopher.

Straight on 'Til Morning. *New York: Signet, 2001. 320p.* Thirteen-year-old Kevin is in love with Nikki, a girl two years his senior, and actually has a chance to date her. That is, he does until a mysterious older boy comes into the picture and carts her away. Kevin and his friends see evidence that makes them begin to suspect that this older boy, Pete, isn't exactly human, so they venture out to save Nikki. What they find in their travels is that Nikki has been taken to a dark fantasyland filled with grotesque, troll-like creatures. Can Kevin and his friends save Nikki? **Similar titles:** *Ginger Snaps* (film); *Christine*, Stephen King; *The Lost*, Jack Ketchum.

Childhood • Fantasy • High School • Psychosexual Horror

Strangewood. *New York: Signet, 1999. 304p.* (See chapter 8, "Mythological Monsters and 'The Old Ones': Invoking the Dark Gods.")

Gorman, Ed.

The Poker Club. *New York: Leisure, 2000. 393 p.* (See chapter 11, "Maniacs and Sociopaths, or the Nuclear Family Explodes: Monstrous Malcontents Bury the Hatchet.")

Shadow Games. *New York: Leisure, 2000, ©1993. 296p.* A has-been child star makes a comeback after three years in a mental institution, a sentence he received for statutory rape. But then a gruesome murder leads him to question his sanity as well as the motives of his friends. Is he unwittingly killing young women, or is he being framed? This novel is written from various points of view, with interview transcripts, articles, and police reports adding variety to the narration. **Similar titles:** *Blue Rose*, Peter Straub; *Pandora's Game*, Christopher Andrews; *Fight Club* (film).

> *Actor as Character • Chicago, Illinois • Police Officer as Character • Private Detective as Character • Revenge • Secret Sin*

Hawthorne, Nathaniel.

The House of the Seven Gables. *New York: Oxford University Press, 1991, ©1851. 328p.* Young Phoebe cannot escape the family curse that is somehow linked to a grotesque daguerreotype of the family patriarch. Hawthorne's emphasis is on atmosphere and characterization. **Similar titles:** *The Picture of Dorian Gray*, Oscar Wilde; *Thirty-Two Stories*, Edgar Allan Poe; *Green Tea and Other Stories*, Joseph Sheridan Le Fanu; *Gothic Readings: The First Wave*, Rictor Norton (editor).

> 𝄞 audiotape

> *Family Curse • Haunted Houses • New England*

Holland, David.

Murcheston: The Wolf's Tale. *New York: Tor, 2000. 349p.* (See chapter 6, "Vampires and Werewolves: Children of the Night.")

Holman, Sheri.

The Dress Lodger. *New York: Ballantine Books, 2000. 291p.* Holman's novel is an erudite and gruesome gothic tale of an early nineteenth-century English city besieged by cholera, ignorance, and superstition. Dr. Henry Chiver has recently arrived in this godforsaken town to resume his practice of medicine after being compelled to flee Edinburgh because he was involved in a scandal concerning his profession's means of procuring bodies necessary to further medical research. Hoping to begin anew in a different location, Chiver enlists Gustine, a factory worker/prostitute in his search for corpses. But the townspeople aren't supportive of medical science, and they will ultimately exact their terrible revenge on those they believe have wronged them and their loved ones. **Similar titles:** *Tideland*, Mitch Cullen; *The Way the Family Got Away*, Michael Kimball; *Dead in the Water*, Nancy Holder.

> *Actor as Character • Cholera • England • Epidemic • Gothicism • History, Use of • Medical Horror • Physician as Character • Prostitute as Character • Secret Sin • Writer as Character*

Hynd, Noel.

The Prodigy. *New York: Kensington, 1999. 352p.* Rolf Geiger lives a charmed life. He has seen his awesome talents as a virtuoso pianist rewarded with worldwide fame, fabulous wealth, and passionate love from the beautiful woman he adores. But Rolf is about to learn that genius has its price. Poised to embark on a stunning world tour, he is slowly, savagely tormented by the vengeful spirit of his dead mentor, the famous maestro Rabinowitz. **Similar titles:** *Spanky*, Christopher Fowler; *The Cleanup*, John Skipp and Craig Spector; *Violin*, Anne Rice.

> *Music—Classical • Musician as Character • Revenging Revenant*

Jackson, Shirley.

The Haunting of Hill House. *Cutchogue, N.Y.: Buccaneer Books-Lightyear, 1993, ©1949. 306p.* (See chapter 4, "Ghosts and Haunted Houses: Dealing with Presences and Absences.")

Jak, Alister.

Tainted Lake: A Ghost Story for Grownups. *Greenfield, Ind.: Horror House Publishing, 1999. 331p.* Financial analyst Marie Dericci-Rath, her husband, and two of their friends are excited about their SCUBA diving adventure: Joined by their loyal canine buddy, Angus, they trek to a remote country lake nestled in the secluded hills and forests of southern Indiana. Their weekend adventure soon becomes a bizarre and malevolent mystery, however, when they find the body of a small child that had seemingly been sacrificed on an inverted crucifix. Will their diving expedition submerge them deep in the bowels of absolute evil? **Similar titles:** *Meca and the Black Oracle*, Paul Masters; *The Demon Cirle*, Dan Schmidt; *Masques*, Bill Pronzini.

> *Dogs • Indiana • Maritime Horror • Religion—Satanism*

Jones, Melissa.

Cold in Earth. *New York: St. Martin's Press, 1998. 247p.* When the infant daughter of British TV hostess Zoë Warren is found dead in her crib, Zoë abruptly quits her job and stays at home with her two remaining children. Zoë's decision only brings turmoil. She begins favoring one child over the other and quarreling with her spouse. Then Zoë is found murdered in her bed, and her husband Paul is arrested for a crime he claims he didn't commit. **Similar titles:** *Indigo*, Graham Joyce; *The Witching Time*, Jean Stubbs; *Bereavements*, Richard Lortz; *Now You See It*, Richard Matheson.

> *Diary Format • England • Grieving • Parenting*

Joyce, Graham.

Dark Sister. *New York: Tor, 2000. 304p.* (See chapter 7, "Demonic Possession, Satanism, Black Magic, and Witches and Warlocks: The Devil Made Me Do It.")

Dreamside. *New York, Tor, 2001, ©1991. 254p.* In the 1970s, four university students participate in a psychology experiment with lucid dreaming, or a type of dreaming in which the sleeper is *aware* that he or she is dreaming and can actively shape the dream. Soon the four begin to physically meet one another in their dreams. When the professor conducting the experiment dies in the middle of the term, the dreamers opt to continue their interactive dreaming unsupervised, with disastrous results. **Similar titles:** *The House*, Bentley Little; *Needing Ghosts*, Ramsey Campbell; *The Cell* (film).

> *Alter Ego • Dreams • England • Fantasy • Parapsychology • Rape • Secret Sin • Teacher as Character • Weird Science*

Indigo. *New York: Pocket, 1999. 258p.* When Jack's father dies in Chicago, he must fly over from England to settle the estate of the mysterious and charismatic man that he never really liked very much. But to do that, mysterious heirs must be found, and a bizarre manuscript about invisibility and the elusive color indigo. This is a literate and original blend of dark fantasy and suspense fiction. **Similar titles:** *Black Light*, Elizabeth Hand; *Dark Sister*, Graham Joyce; *The Door Through Washington Square*, Elaine Bergstrom.

> *Alchemy • Artist as Character • Chicago, Illinois • Fantasy • Parenting • Rome, Italy*

Kemske, Floyd.

Human Resources. *North Haven, Conn.: Catbird Press, 1995. 223p.* (See chapter 6, "Vampires and Werewolves: Children of the Night.")

Labor Day. *North Haven, Conn.: Catbird Press, 2000. 203p.* When union organizer Harvey Lathrop finds that employees of his own organization, the Federation of Office Workers, are at risk of being organized by the International Brotherhood of Labor, he calls upon his old union-busting nemesis Stillman Colby for help. Lathrop now finds himself disoriented when he's on the other end of the organizing process, and Stillman too is disoriented when he discovers his wife is now working for union organizers. In the end, both men are utterly transformed by the experience. This, the fourth novel in Kemske's Corporate Nightmare Series, is another witty and original look at corporate America. **Similar titles:** *Resurrection, Inc.*, Kevin J. Anderson; *Fight Club* (film); *The Incredible Shrinking Man*, Richard Matheson.

> *Asian-American Characters • Economic Violence • Espionage •*
> *Marriage • New York City • Secret Sin • Union Buster as Character •*
> *Union Organizer as Character • Unions*

Kessler, Gabriel Devlin.

Landscape of Demons and The Book of Sarah. *Boston: Millennium Press, 1998. 233p.* A young man from an abusive family grows up unable to distinguish reality from fantasy. Will his acting out the personalities of his real and imaginary friends lead to evil? **Similar titles:** *The House*, Bentley Little; *Needing Ghosts*, Ramsey Campbell; *Thunderland*, Brandon Massey.

> *Child Abuse • Schizophrenia/Multiple Personality Disorder*

Kiernan, Caitlin R.

Silk. *New York: Penguin, 1998. 353p.* Members of a struggling Birmingham, Alabama, underground band take up with Spyder, an ex-mental institution ward who was abused as a child. During a strange ritual in Spyder's childhood home, the group awakens to what its members believe to be demonic forces. Or is it all in their minds? This was a well-received debut novel by this goth-noire horror novelist. **Similar titles:** *Avatar*, Donald Beman; *The Scream*, John Skipp and Craig Spector; *Queen of the Damned* (film).

> *Alabama • Asian-American Characters • Child Abuse • Drugs •*
> *Gay/Lesbian/Bisexual Characters • Gothicism • Music—Rock Music*

Threshold: A Novel of Deep Time. *New York: Onyx, 2001. 272p.* Set in Birmingham, Alabama, Kiernan's novel follows the life of Chance Matthews, a young paleontologist. The novel begins with a flashback to a drunken expedition into the waterworks tunnels set deep in the Alabama mountains. Chance and her friends, Deacon and Elise, fueled by alcohol and pot, explore the tunnels and find that something is not quite right. All three can never quite remember what exactly happened within those tunnels, only that it was evil. Now Chance, with the help of a stranger, must discover what the creatures they found there are. **Similar titles:** *Riverwatch*, Joseph M. Nassie; *Book of the Dark*, William Meikle; *The Cipher*, Kathe Koja.

> *Alabama • Albinism • Gothicism • Grieving • Paleontologist as*
> *Character • Subterranean Monsters*

Kimball, Michael.

The Way the Family Got Away. *New York: Four Walls, Eight Windows, 2000. 143p.* Two young children narrate this grotesque tale: They tell of their infant brother's demise and their parents' inability to balance life and death, resulting in a road trip across America with the dead child in a trunk. The stream-of-consciousness narrative makes this disturbing and darkly comic, reminiscent of William Faulkner's classic *As I Lay Dying.* **Similar titles:** *Tideland,* Mitch Cullen; *Wire Mesh Mothers,* Elizabeth Massie; *The Vampire Hunters,* William Hill; *Escaping Purgatory,* Gary A. Braunbeck and Alan M. Clark.

> *Childhood • Grieving • The Midwest • Parenting • Texas*

King, Stephen.

Dolores Claiborne. *New York: Signet, 1993. 372p.* Dolores Claiborne stands accused of murdering the wealthy old woman she has cared for over the past thirty years. And although she's innocent of this crime, she does confess to the 1963 killing of her husband, Joe St. George. Dolores's confession, related in extended monologue format, reveals a plucky, capable woman who has been harrowed like a gothic heroine. **Similar titles:** *Rose Madder,* Stephen King; *Gift Giver,* Jean Sapien; *Motives for Murder,* Patricia Gebhard; *The Event,* Donald Silverman.

> 𝔖 audiotape   ✍ large print
>
> *Aging • Child Molester • Domestic Violence • Dramatic Monologue • Gothicism • Maine • Marriage • Secret Sin • Senior Citizen as Character*

Gerald's Game. *New York: Viking, 1992. 332p.* Jessie Burlingame and her husband Gerald vacation at a secluded cottage in the woods. When one of Gerald's "sex games" goes awry, Jessie finds herself hand cuffed to a bed with no one around to save her. *Gerald's Game* is an excellent study of the effects of dysfunctional families. **Similar titles:** *Ambrosial Flesh,* Mary Ann Mitchell; *In the Dark,* Richard Laymon; *Thirteen Stories,* Ed Cain; *Scared Stiff,* Ramsey Campbell.

> 𝔖 audiotape
>
> *Animals Run Rampant • Dysfunctional Families • Psychosexual Horror • Sado-Masochism*

The Girl Who Loved Tom Gordon. *New York: Scribner, 1999. 224p.* Nine-year-old Tricia McFarland wanders off the trail during a hike with her mother and older brother to escape their constant bickering, only to become lost in the woods for days. During her ordeal, as she grapples with her own mortality, her Walkman provides her only link to civilization. **Similar titles:** *The Blair Witch Project* (film); *Tideland,* Mitch Cullen; *Thunderland,* Brandon Massey; *Dracula's Children,* Richard Lortz.

> 𝔖 audiotape, audio download, compact disc   ✍ large print   ⏻ e-book
>
> *Baseball • Childhood • Maine • Swamps • Wilderness*

Ⓑ🏅 **The Green Mile.** *New York: Signet, 1996. 592p.* Prison guard Paul Edgecombe is beginning to suspect that John Coffey, a death row inmate at Cold Mountain Penitentiary, has special powers—almost god-like powers over living creatures. This heartbreaking tale is narrated by Edgecombe in a pseudo-journalistic format. It was the winner of a Bram Stoker Award, and was originally published serially, in six parts: *The Two Dead Girls, The Mouse on the Mile, Coffey's Hands, The Bad Death of Edward Delacroix, Night Journey,* and *Coffey on the Mile.* **Similar titles:** *Bag of Bones,* Stephen King; *Cronos* (film); *Dreamside,* Graham Joyce; *Smoke Signals,* Octavio Ramos Jr.

> 𝔖 audiotape, audio download

Capital Punishment • Diary Format • Fantasy • Immortality •
Inmates—Death Row • Maine • Racism • Prison Guard as Character

Insomnia. *New York: Penguin-Signet, 1995. 663p.* After his wife's death, Ralph Roberts begins seeing things: auras around people, and three small, bald-headed men in doctors' uniforms. Do these men have anything to do with the sudden violent tendencies of some of Ralph's friends? King's writing is steadily paced and conversational. **Similar titles:** *Strangewood*, Christopher Golden; The Talisman Series, Stephen King and Peter Straub; *Mr. X*, Peter Straub.

 audiotape    large print

Domestic Terrorism • Domestic Violence • Insomnia •
Violence—Theories of

It. *New York: Viking, 1986. 1138p.* Pennywise the Clown, a monstrous personification of all that is scary and evil, has returned to a small New England town to claim the souls of a handful of adults whom he terrorized as children. This novel was made into a television miniseries staring Tim Curry of *The Rocky Horror Picture Show* fame. **Similar titles:** *Ghost Story* and *Floating Dragon*, Peter Straub; *The Town*, Bentley Little.

Childhood • Clowns • New England • Shapeshifters

King, Stephen [as Richard Bachman].

Roadwork. *New York: Signet, 1999, ©1981. 307p.* Originally written under the Richard Bachman pseudonym, this narrative is the tale of a lone man who takes on progress. When a highway project puts him out of work and threatens to destroy his home, he has more than enough time on his hands to plot his revenge. He pushes the powers-that-be to the limit, taking a stand against what he sees as a criminal act in progress, but in doing so he drives his wife and friends away. Will his obsession ultimately lead to chaos? **Similar titles:** *The Count of Eleven*, Ramsey Campbell; *Fight Club* (film); *The Virtual Boss*, Floyd Kemske; *The Lecturer's Tale*, James Hynes.

Obsession • Revenge

King, Stephen, and Peter Straub. The Talisman Series.

The Talisman. *New York: Ballantine Books, 2001, ©1984. 735p.* Twelve-year-old Jack Sawyer has come to the East Coast with his dying mother, B-movie actress Lily Cavanaugh. Lily just wants to die in peace and escape the machinations of her deceased husband's business partner, Morgan Sloat. Soon Jack meets Speedy Parker, who hails him as "Travelin' Jack" and introduces him to a parallel universe, The Terrorities, a world similar to our own universe, except that it's ruled by magic instead of science. Now Jack must travel to The Terrorities and bring back the Talisman to save his mother's life. **Similar titles:** *Mr. X*, Peter Straub; *Insomnia*, Stephen King; *Thunderland*, Brandon Massey.

Actor as Character • African-American Characters • Alter Ego •
Childhood • Clergy as Character • Epic Structure • Fantasy •
Hollywood, California • Indiana • Lawyer as Character • Magic •
Music—Jazz • New Hampshire • Parallel Universe • Sawyer, Jack
(character) • Shapeshifters • Terrorities, The • Twins • Werewolves

Knight, Tracy.

The Astonished Eye. *Leeds: PS Publishing, 2001. 192p.* Two visitors and an alien arrive in the rural town of Elderton in downstate Illinois. Jeffrey Sprague is a runaway, a reject of the foster care system. Seemingly accepted without question by the community, his hope is that he has finally found a home. Ben Savitch, on the other hand, is a cynical, wise-to-the-world reporter working for the tabloid *The Astonished Eye*. But Elderton, for all its rustic, Mayberry-like charm, turns out to be a rather odd town, with some truly peculiar traditions and residents. **Similar titles:** *Thank You for the Flowers*, Scott Nicholson; *Galilee*, Clive Barker; *From the Dust Returned*, Ray Bradbury.

Aliens • Fantasy • Ghosts • Illinois • Journalist as Character • Midwest, The

Koja, Kathe.

The Cipher. *New York: Bantam Books, 1991. 356p.* Nicholas and Nakota, two gen-X nonconformists, discover a mysterious black hole, which devours and/or changes anything that ventures into it. When an adventurous Nakota tries to stick her head through, Nicholas tries to stop her, and sticks his hand in instead. After that, life is never the same, as his hand becomes a weeping sore, and he begins hearing voices. This graphic page turner was the winner of a Bram Stoker Award. **Similar titles:** *Silk*, Caitlin R. Kiernan; *Extremities*, Kathe Koja; *Viscera*, Cara Bruce (editor); *Hexes*, Tom Piccirilli.

Eroticism • Gothicism • Obsession

Koontz, Dean.

The Face of Fear. *New York: Berkley, 1985. 306p.* (See chapter 11, "Maniacs and Sociopaths, or the Nuclear Family Explodes: Monstrous Malcontents Bury the Hatchet.")

The House of Thunder. *New York: Berkley, 1992. 253p.* In Koontz's version of "Sometimes They Come Back," Susan Thornton awakens from an accident-induced coma to find herself in the same hospital with the four men who murdered her boyfriend twelve years earlier. The only problem is that these four men supposedly died violent deaths years before. Now it seems their ghosts want to finish off the witness who got away the first time, namely Susan. **Similar titles:** *The Key to Midnight,* Dean Koontz; *Bag of Bones*, Stephen King; *Wither*, J. G. Passarella; *Whispers*, Dean Koontz.

large print

Amnesia • Revenging Revenants • Espionage

The Key to Midnight. *New York: Berkley, 1979. 416p.* When Alex Hunter spots Joanna Rand singing in a Kyoto nightclub, she seems vaguely familiar. After the two begin seeing one another, he realizes that she is the daughter of a famous U.S. senator; however, she cannot remember her past or the reason she has recurring nightmares about a man with metallic fingers. **Similar titles:** *The House of Thunder* and *Mr. Murder*, Dean Koontz; *Amnesia*, Andrew Neiderman; *Dark Side*, J. M. Barlog.

Amnesia • Dreams • Espionage • Japan • Mistaken Identity • Rape

Strangers. *New York: Putnam, 1986. 681p.* Across the country, a handful of people who don't know one another begin having similar nightmares and sharing a sense of paranoia. Soon, their paths will cross, and they will have to face their greatest fears. Koontz is heavy on suspense. **Similar titles:** *The House*, Bentley Little; *Dreamside*, Graham Joyce; *Paperhouse* (film); *Blair Witch II: Book of Shadows* (film); *Caesarea*, Tony Burgess.

Aliens • Clergy as Character • Dreams • Experiments—Military

Whispers. *New York: Berkley, 1980. 509p.* (See chapter 11, "Maniacs and Sociopaths, or the Nuclear Family Explodes: Monstrous Malcontents Bury the Hatchet.")

Kosciolek, David.

Green Light Cemetery. *Hazlet, N.J.: Green Light Ventures, 1999, ©1993. 183p.* Thirty-year-old David Kane returns to his hometown to face his greatest fear: the Green Light Cemetery. It is the place where he and his high school buddies visited one night, the night David met the ghost of Bucky Billy. Now David is afraid of what the spirit of the most picked on kid in school has in store for him. **Similar titles:** *Carrie*, Stephen King; *Dead Love*, Donald Beman; *Darkness Demands*, Simon Clark, *Cemetery Sonata* and *Cemetery Sonata II*, June Hubbard (editor).

> *Cemeteries • Dreams • High School • Music—Rock Music • Psychosexual Horror • Revenging Revenant • Writer as Character*

Laffer, Jax.

Another Side of Evil. *Alma, Ark.: Yard Dog Press, 1999. 343p.* Joe E. Green and his dad have a father-and-son business: Dad is hired by desperate people who desire to ruin the lives of female enemies, and Joe is a serial rapist who is so good at his job that he never leaves a trace of evidence. Joe's new assignment is to psychologically destroy a talk radio host whose father is emotionally abusing her by withholding her inheritance until she gives him a grandson. **Similar titles:** *The Caretaker*, William Thomas Simpson; *In the Dark*, Richard Laymon; *Scared Stiff*, Ramsey Campbell; *The Voice of the Night*, Dean Koontz.

> *Artist as Character • California • Disc Jockey as Character • Pregnancy • Psychosexual Horror • Rape • Stalkers*

Laymon, Richard.

The Midnight Tour. *London: Headline Feature, 1999, ©1998. 536p.* The town of Malcasa Point has changed a lot in a few years, and so has the Beast House tour. Due to several popular books and movies about the infamous house of death, the tour is bigger and better than ever. The self-guided daytime tour, safe for the whole family, gives the sanitized version of the attacks and murders. If you want the real story, however, you have to get it on the Midnight Tour. **Similar titles:** *The Nightmare Factory*, Douglas Clegg; *Hell House*, Richard Matheson; *Black Butterflies*, John Shirley; *Viscera*, Cara Bruce (editor).

> *Dysfunctional Families • Haunted Houses • Serial Killers • Torture*

The Traveling Vampire Show. *New York: Leisure, 2001. 391p.* The traveling vampire show comes to town one summer during the adolescence of three childhood friends, and their lives are changed utterly when they plot to see what is forbidden to everyone under eighteen. Events unfold during the course of one day, and emphasis is on characterization. This is very similar to horror novelist Robert McCammon's non-horror work, *A Boy's Life.* **Similar titles:** *The Book of the Dark*, William Meikle; *Straight on 'Til Morning*, Christopher Golden; *Thunderland*, Brandon Massey.

> *Adolescence • Eroticism • Popular Culture*

Le Fanu, Joseph Sheridan.

Uncle Silas: A Tale of Bartram-Haugh. *Victor Sage (editor). London; New York: Penguin, 2000, ©1864. 476p.* In Uncle Silas, Joseph Sheridan Le Fanu's most celebrated novel, Maud Ruthyn, the young, naïve heroine, is plagued by Madame de la Rougierre from the moment the enigmatic older woman is hired as her governess. A liar, bully, and spy, when Madame leaves the house, she takes her dark secret with her. When Maud is orphaned, she is sent to live with her Uncle Silas, her father's mysterious brother, a man with a scandalous, perhaps even a murderous, past. Once again she encounters Madame, whose sinister role in Maud's destiny becomes all too clear. **Similar titles:** *The House of the Seven Gables*, Nathaniel Hawthorne; *Wieland*, Charles Brockden Brown; *De Lore's Confession*, Paulette Crain; *In a Glass Darkly*, Joseph Sheridan Le Fanu.

Adolescence • England • Family Curse • Gothicism • Secret Sin

Leiber, Fritz.

Our Lady of Darkness. *In The Conjure Wife. New York, Tor, 1991, ©1978. 162p*. A horror writer living in San Francisco finds himself becoming obsessed with a little-known occult text that chronicles paranormal activity stemming from the city itself. Will his obsession devour him, or can he be saved by a "white witch?" **Similar titles:** *Dark Sister*, Graham Joyce; *The Lurker at the Threshold*, H. P. Lovecraft; *The 37th Mandala*, Mark Laidlaw; *The Third Ring*, Phillip Tomasso.

Obsession • Parapsychology • San Francisco, California • Witches • Witchcraft

Little, Bentley.

The House. *New York: Signet, 1999. 360p*. (See chapter 4, "Ghosts and Haunted Houses: Dealing with Presences and Absences.")

The Store. *New York: Signet, 1998. 431p*. (See chapter 10, "Small Town Horror: Villages of the Damned.")

Lonardo, Paul.

The Apostate. *St. Petersburg, Fla.: Barclay Books, 2001. 254p*. (See chapter 10, "Small-Town Horror: Villages of the Damned.")

Lortz, Richard.

Bereavements. *Sagaponack, N.Y.: The Permanent Press, 1980. 215p*. An heiress who has lost her only child, a son, puts an ad in *The Village Voice* for "son who has lost mother." Three young men answer her ad, and what ensues leads to murder, suicide, and borderline necrophilia. Lortz pens an original and erudite story that explores the depths of grief and love, even their darker manifestations. **Similar titles:** *Tideland*, Mitch Cullen; *The Way the Family Got Away*, Michael Kimball; *Dracula's Children*, Richard Lortz; *Beloved,* Toni Morrison.

Grieving • Hispanic-American Characters • Necrophilia • New York City • Obsession • Parenting

Lovers Living, Lovers Dead. *Sagaponak, NY: Second Chance Press, 1981, ©1977. 222p*. (See chapter 7, "Demonic Possession, Satanism, Black Magic, and Witches and Warlocks: The Devil Made Me Do It.")

Massey, Brandon.

Thunderland. *Atlanta: Dark Corner Press, 2001, ©1998. 280p*. Thirteen-year-old Jason Brooks falls out of a tree while trying to escape the wrath of his alcoholic mother, and he ends up in a coma for three days. When he comes out, he finds himself stalked by "The Stranger," a murderous, mysterious entity that knows all his secrets and desires. Along with his two friends Brains and Shorty, Jason must travel to Thunderland to face The Stranger before the evil being can cross over into Jason's reality and terminate his family problems. Similar titles: *Mr. X*, Peter Straub; *Strangewood*, Christopher Golden; *Soul Temple*, Lee Climer; *Spanky*, Christopher Fowler.

African-American Characters • Alcoholism • Alter Ego • Childhood • Dreams • Magic • Marriage • Midwest, The • Parallel Universe • Stalkers • Wish Fulfillment

Massie, Elizabeth.

 Sineater. *New York: Leisure, 1998. 396p.* (See chapter 10, "Small Town Horror: Villages of the Damned.")

Welcome Back to the Night. *New York: Leisure, 1999. 393p.* (See chapter 10, "Small Town Horror: Villages of the Damned.")

Wire Mesh Mothers. *New York: Leisure, 2001. 393p.* (See chapter 11, "Maniacs and Sociopaths, or the Nuclear Family Explodes: Monstrous Malcontents Bury the Hatchet.")

Matheson, Richard.

The Incredible Shrinking Man. *New York: Tor, 1994, ©1956. 373p.* (See chapter 17, "Collections and Anthologies.")

Now You See It. *New York: Tor, 1996, ©1995. 220p.* A paralyzed magician must use the darkest of tricks to prevent his ungrateful son and nefarious daughter-in-law from pirating his act. Matheson's novel is filled with plot twists, word play, visual tricks, and suspense. **Similar titles:** *Shadowland*, Peter Straub; *Death from the Woods*, Brigitte Aubert; *Cycle of the Werewolf* and *Thinner*, Stephen King.

> *Magic • Mistaken Identity • Quadriplegic as Character • Revenge*

Stir of Echoes. *New York: Tor, 1999, ©1958. 211p.* (See chapter 4, "Ghosts and Haunted Houses: Dealing with Presences and Absences.")

Maturin, Charles Robert.

Melmoth the Wanderer. *Victor Sage (editor). London, England; New York: Penguin Books, 2000, ©1820. 659p.* (See chapter 10, "Small Town Horror: Villages of the Damned.")

McCabe, Patrick.

Emerald Germs of Ireland. *New York: HarperCollins, 2001. 306p.* (See chapter 11, "Maniacs and Sociopaths, or the Nuclear Family Explodes: Monstrous Malcontents Bury the Hatchet.")

McFarland, Dennis.

A Face at the Window. *New York: Bantam, 1998. 309p.* (See chapter 4, "Ghosts and Haunted Houses: Dealing with Presences and Absences.")

Moorcraft, Paul.

Anchoress of Shere. *Scottsdale, Ariz.: Poisoned Pen Press, 2002. 320p.* Father Michael Duval is obsessed with the history of Christine Carpenter, a fourteenth-century woman who volunteered to be the Anchoress of Shere, a woman who was walled up in a small room next to the church to spend the rest of her life in religious contemplation. Father Michael has attempted to bring the anchoress to life by penning her biography, but ultimately this proves unsatisfactory, and he must resort to other means to recreate history. He kidnaps a young woman and keeps her locked in a cell in his basement so that she might be persuaded to become a modern day anchoress and relive Christine's life. Moorcroft's novel is an eerie and original tale of obsession. **Similar titles:** *A Twist at the End*, Steven Saylor; *The Chalice*, Phil Rickman, *Wine of Angels*, Phil Rickman.

> *Clergy as Character • England • Gothicism • History, Use of • Obsession • Religion—Christianity*

Mullen, Laura.

The Tales of Horror: A Flip Book. *Berkeley, Calif.: Kelsey St. Press, 1999. 107p.* A haunted room, a presence that is there and not quite there, nightmares, and an eerie atmosphere populate this experimental piece that is part poem, part prose poem, and part epistolary. The emphasis isn't so much on frightening the reader as on leading the reader to think about reality and relationships. **Similar titles:** *The Divinity Student*, Michael Cisco; *Zom Bee Moo Vee*, Mark McLaughlin; The Bewdley Series, Tony Burgess; *Halloween Candy*, Thomas M. Sipos.

Dreams • Epistolary Format • Gothicism • Haunted Houses

Neiderman, Andrew.

Amnesia. *New York: Pocket, 2001. 341p.* One day, standing in the middle of Grand Central Station during rush hour, businessman Aaron Clifford suddenly forgets who he is, where he lives, and what his wife and child look like. His only hope lies with his doctors, who cannot figure out whether he is suffering from a severe form of Alzheimer's or some kind of dementia that has caused him to lose all long-term memory. In addition, Clifford sees grotesque parodies of humanity in his everyday interactions with people, and he finds he has no control over when such visions occur. This is a well-written character study that emphasizes atmosphere over action. Similar titles: *The Red God*, C. E. Albertson; *Dark Side*, J. M. Barlog; *Head Case*, Jay Bonansigna; *The Bad Place*, Dean Koontz.

Amnesia • Marriage • Medical Horror • New England • Parenting

Curse: A Novel. *New York: Pocket, 2000. 357p.* No one will miss Henry Deutch, the miserly landlord who died of a heart attack after evicting Anna Young's mother from their tenement. But did Anna have something to do with his death? She is the proprietor of a shop selling love charms and protective amulets, and some of her clients attest that Anna is a master of black magic. Even more damning, Anna swore a blood oath of vengeance against Henry just before he died. And now a politically ambitious prosecutor has decided to file first degree murder charges against Anna, alleging that she frightened him to death with her curse. **Similar titles:** *Thinner*, Stephen King; *The Walking*, Bentley Little; *Darkness Demands*, Simon Clark; *The Witching Time*, Jean Stubbs.

Curse • Magic • Revenge • Witches • Witchcraft

Oates, Joyce Carol.

Beasts. *New York: Carroll & Graff, 2002. 128p.* During her first years of college, Gillian Brauer becomes obsessed with her charismatic poetry teacher, Andre Harrow, who encourages his students to write erotic prose, and his sculptor wife Dorcas, who carves wooden totems that express a bestial sexuality. Gillian falls under the Harrows' spell, as have others before her. Meanwhile, there is a disturbing rash of suicides at the college, and strange fires are breaking out all over campus. **Similar titles:** *Incubus*, Ann Arensberg; *Black Light*, Elizabeth Hand; *The Collector of Hearts: New Tales of the Grotesque*, Joyce Carol Oates.

Academia • Drugs • New England • Psychosexual Horror • Teacher as Character • United States—1970s

Zombie. *New York: Dutton, 1995. 181p.* (See chapter 11, "Maniacs and Sociopaths, or the Nuclear Family Explodes: Monstrous Malcontents Bury the Hatchet.")

Ochse, Weston.

Natural Selection. *Kansas City, Mo.: Dark Tales, 2001. 33p.* Jaded ex-veteran turned bar bouncer Kimo takes up with a masochistic woman and a mysterious stranger who preaches the philosophy of violence in this short novella set in a world of bar fights and accidental killings. Ochse's emphasis is on characterization, as Kimo is faced with the greatest challenge of his life: trying to save the woman he loves from a life of torture, pain, and certain death. **Similar titles:** *Cold Heart Canyon*, Clive Barker; *The Asylum*, Victor Heck (editor); *The Beast That Was Max*, Gerard Houarner; *Holy Rollers*, J. Newman.

> *Aliens • Bouncer as Character • Florida • Sado-Masochism • Soldier as Character • Torture*

O'Nan, Stewart.

A Prayer for the Dying. *New York: Henry Holt, 1999. 208p.* Jacob Hansen, a Civil War veteran who thought his military experience had inured him to everything terrible, is stricken with guilt when a diphtheria epidemic claims the lives of many in his town, and he must live with the knowledge that he may have infected his wife and child, who now lay dying. The experience causes Hansen to question his faith and ponder the nature of evil. **Similar titles:** *Skimming the Gumbo Nuclear*, M. F. Korn; *The Dress Lodger*, Sheri Holman; *Blackrose Avenue*, Mark Shepard; *I Am Legend*, Richard Matheson.

> *Clergy as Character • Diphtheria • Epidemics • History, Use of • Religion—Christianity • Secret Sin • War—American Civil War • Wisconsin*

Pronzini, Bill.

Masques. *New York: Leisure, 1999, ©1981. 269p.* Steve Giroux visits New Orleans for his first Mardi Gras, where he is terrorized by members of a Voodoo cult. A stranger comes to his aid, but she harbors even more dangerous secrets than the cult members who kidnap and psychologically torture him. Pronzini's emphasis is on setting and description. **Similar titles:** *Welcome Back to the Night*, Elizabeth Massie; *The Twelve*, Howard Kaminsky and Susan Kaminsky; *The Demon Circle*, Dan Schmidt; *Death's Door*, John Wooley and Ron Wolfe.

> *Cults • Mardi Gras • Music—Jazz • New Orleans, Louisiana • Religion—Voodoo*

Redmond, Patrick.

Something Dangerous. *New York: Hyperion, 1999. 343p.* (See chapter 9, "Telekinesis and Hypnosis: Chaos from Control.")

Salamanca, J. R.

Lilith: A Novel of One Woman's Electrifying Obsession. *New York: Welcome Rain Publishers, 2000, ©1961. 381p.* In the late 1940s, Vincent Bruce is an orderly in a private mental institution for schizophrenics, and it is here that he becomes obsessed with a patient whose own particular brand of madness challenges the very ideas about human sexuality that organize our society. Lilith believes herself to be a deity to a people who express their spirituality through their sexuality. **Similar titles:** *Daughter of Darkness*, Ed Gorman; *Daughters of Darkness*, Pam Keesey (editor); *Night Shade*, Victoria A. Brownworth (editor); *Bending the Landscape*, Nicola Griffith and Stephen Pagel (editors).

> *Eroticism • Gay/Lesbian/Bisexual Characters • Gothicism • Maryland • Mental Institutions • Obsession • Psychosexual Horror*

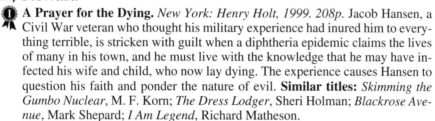

Saylor, Steven.

A Twist at the End. *New York: St. Martin's Press, 2001. 576p.* In 1906, Will Porter, a.k.a. the famous writer O. Henry, receives a mysterious letter summoning him back to Austin, Texas, regarding a series of murders committed in 1885 by the "Servant Girl Annihilator" who was never caught. The letter's writer claims to know the killer's identity. **Similar titles:** *Ghost Story*, Peter Straub; *Salem's Ghosts*, Rose Earhart; *The Bottoms*, Joe R. Lansdale; *Resume with Monsters*, William Spencer Browning.

> *Austin, Texas • History, Use of • O. Henry (character) • Secret Sin • Serial Killers • Writer as Character*

Searcy, David.

Ordinary Horror. *New York: Penguin-Viking, 2001. 230p.* (See chapter 13, "Ecological Horror: Rampant Animals and Mother Nature's Revenge.")

Shirley, John.

The View from Hell. *Burton, Mich.: Subterranean Press, 2001. 190p.* Interdimensional beings who lack corporeal form are studying our species' relationship to suffering. First, they are merely content to observe patients in hospitals, abused and violent children, etc., but then they introduce a new element into their experiment by causing members of the upper class to commit acts of homicide and mayhem. The subjects of their experiments then awaken in a sort of bland purgatory, a building about as big as a stadium with side rooms containing different sorts of environments. The only escape from this place occurs when a subject dies. **Similar titles:** *Meh'yam*, Gloria Evans; *Dark Within*, John Wooley; *Dreamcatcher* and *The Tommyknockers*, Stephen King.

> *Aliens • Experiments—Scientific/Medical • Los Angeles, California • Science Fiction • Parallel Universe*

Simpson, William Thomas.

The Caretaker. *New York: Bantam, 1999, ©1998. 561p.* (See chapter 11, "Maniacs and Sociopaths, or the Nuclear Family Explodes: Monstrous Malcontents Bury the Hatchet.")

Skipp, John, and Craig Spector.

The Cleanup. *Lancaster, Pa.: Stealth Press, 2001, ©1987. 394p.* (See chapter 8, "Mythological Monsters and 'The Old Ones': Invoking the Dark Gods.")

Spencer, William Browning.

Resume with Monsters. *Clarkston, Ga.: White Wolf, 1997.* (See chapter 8, "Mythological Monsters and 'The Old Ones': Invoking the Dark Gods.")

Starling, Boris.

Messiah. *New York: Penguin-Onyx, 1999. 457p.* (See chapter 11, "Maniacs and Sociopaths, or the Nuclear Family Explodes: Monstrous Malcontents Bury the Hatchet.")

Straub, Peter.

The Hellfire Club. *New York: Random House, 1996. 463p.* This meta-fictionalized narrative traces the fall of a wealthy New England family whose male heir belongs to a club that inspires shameless self-indulgence. Straub's narrative style is complex but clever, with elements of mystery fiction interwoven. **Similar titles:** *Hell House*, Richard Matheson; *Ghost Story*, Peter Straub; *From Hell* (film).

> *Family Curse • New England • Secret Sin • Writer as Character*

Straub, Peter, and Stephen King. The Talisman Series.

(See King, Stephen, and Peter Straub. The Talisman Series.)

Stubbs, Jean.

The Witching Time. *New York: St. Martin's Press, 1998. 383p.* Recently widowed, Imogen leaves London for a small English village, where she tries to make a new life for herself. She finds her place in a community of craftspeople who also practice the old religion among the stone circle on the hill, but not everyone in this idyllic village respects the witches' religious freedom. The local church is desecrated in such a way that the witches are blamed. When the body of a retarded villager is found in the stone circle, people believe the witches are practicing human sacrifice and call for their blood. **Similar titles:** *Dark Sister*, Graham Joyce; *Wither*, J. G. Passarella; *Murder at Witch's Bluff*, Silver Ravenwolf; *Salem's Ghosts*, Rose Earhart.

> *Clergy as Character • England • Grieving • Religion—Paganism • Revenge • Secret Sin • Witches • Witchcraft*

Taylor, Lucy.

🅘 🅑 **The Safety of Unknown Cities.** *Woodstock, Ga.: Overlook Connection Press,* 🏹 🏹 *1999. 284p.* Val and Breen have a desperate need for human connection. Val attempts to achieve this connection by frequently changing sexual partners. Breen, on the other hand, achieves the same ends by burglarizing people's houses and going through their possessions, and later, through perusing the actual contents of their bodies. This graphic and disturbing novel is a winner of a Bram Stoker Award. **Similar titles:** *Scared Stiff*, Ramsey Campbell; *Lilith*, J. R. Salamanca; *This Symbiotic Fascination*, Charlee Jacob.

> *Kleptomania • Psychosexual Horror*

Tem, Melanie.

The Tides. *New York: Leisure, 1999. 308p.* (See chapter 4, "Ghosts and Haunted Houses: Dealing with Presences and Absences.")

Tessier, Thomas.

Father Panic's Opera MacAbre. *Burton, Mich.: Subterranean, 2001. 162p.* When Neil O'Netty's car breaks down while he's sightseeing in rural Italy, he must accept Marisa Panic's offer for overnight shelter in her dilapidated mansion. As the night wears on, Neil's increasing sexual obsession with the beautiful Marisa dulls his fear of the eerie dwelling she shares with her eccentric, elderly relatives, all part of a retired troupe of traveling puppeteers. And after a night of disembodied voices, dead bodies that seem to appear and disappear, and some really over-the-top sex, Neil awakens in a Concentration Camp, running for his life from guards who torture him for sport. **Similar titles:** *The Folks*, Ray Garton; *Head Injuries*, Conrad Williams; *Demons By Daylight*, Ramsey Campbell.

> *Italy • Psychosexual Horror • Torture*

Fog Heart. *New York: St. Martin's Press, 1998. 320p.* The ghosts of dead relatives visit two couples, so together they approach a famous medium to contact the dead. However, doing so means revealing the secrets of each person's past—including murder. Tessier's novel is a nice mixture of the psychological and supernatural. **Similar titles:** *What Lies Beneath* (film); *The Long Lost*, Ramsey Campbell; *Stir of Echoes*, Richard Matheson; *Beloved*, Toni Morrison.

Marriage • Parapsychology • Secret Sin

Wheeler, Robert E.

Travel Many Roads. *Miami, Fla.: Minerva Publishing, 2001. 191p.* The emphasis is on characterization in this subtly horrific story about a womanizing liberal arts professor who gets involved with one of his star pupils, only to find that their relationship begins to become an obsession for both himself and the young girl, who begins stalking him. As acquaintances and friends begin to disappear, their bodies later found mutilated, it becomes apparent that the pressure of the teacher-student relationship is pushing someone over the edge. **Similar titles:** *Ordinary Horror*, David Searcy; *Chancers*, Gerald Vizenore; *Lovers Living, Lovers Dead*, Richard Lortz; *The Lecturer's Tale*, James Hynes.

Academia • Obsession • Serial Killers • Stalkers • Teacher as Character

Wilde, Oscar.

The Picture of Dorian Gray. *New York: Tom Doherty, 1998, ©1891. 256p.* (See chapter 7, "Demonic Possession, Satanism, Black Magic, and Witches and Warlocks: The Devil Made Me Do It.")

Williams, Conrad.

Head Injuries. *London: The Do-Not Press, 1998. 206p.* David Munro answers a summons from his friends Helen and Seamus to return to the seaside town of Morecombe. There he is forced to face his past, a past that is so traumatic it has remained buried in his unconscious mind. This work is disturbing and graphic, with gory scenes, yet it is compelling and haunting. **Similar titles:** *Nailed by the Heart*, Simon Clark; *Fog Heart*, Thomas Tessier; *Shadow Games*, Ed Gorman; *Dolores Claiborne*, Stephen King.

Childhood • Dreams • England • Music—Rock Music • Psychosexual Horror • Secret Sin

Williams, Drew.

Night Terrors. *St. Petersburg, Fla.: Barclay Books, 2001. 343p.* (See chapter 8, "Mythological Monsters and 'The Old Ones': Invoking the Dark Gods.")

Wooley, John, and Ron Wolfe.

Death's Door. *Tulsa, Okla.: Hawk Publishing, 2000, ©1992. 388p.* In this thoughtful and intelligent character study, security guard Case Hamilton faces his innermost demons and fears of death after being given a second chance at life. While a cop on the beat, Hamilton was fatally wounded but was resuscitated after ten minutes of death. Hamilton becomes a security guard at a famous surgeon's lab, where he discovers questionable practices. Mindful of the fact that he is himself one of the "experiments," he struggles on until a second brush with death leads to visitations by The Grey Man, Death itself, who wants more from Hamilton than just his own life. **Similar titles:** *Sleepeasy*, T. M. Wright; *Strangewood*, Christopher Golden; *Nazareth Hill*, Ramsey Campbell; *The Devil's Heart*, William W. Johnstone.

Cults • Death (character) • Experiments—Animals • Gang Violence • Parenting • Police Officer as Character • Weird Science

Wooley, John, and Ron Wolfe.

Old Fears. *Tulsa, Okla.: Hawk Publishing, 1999, ©1982. 286p.* Mick Winters returns to his hometown in Oklahoma, and after meeting up with his childhood friend Jerry at a local bar, decides to revisit an old culvert on the edge of town that the two desperately feared as youngsters. Jerry, in a an effort to face his childhood fears, forces Mick to "dare" him to crawl into the culvert to prove that nothing is there, only to discover that something does indeed inhabit that culvert. Jerry's hideous murder sets off a chain of events in which each of the citizens of Tanapah, Oklahoma, is individually visited by his or her worst childhood fear. Mick now must clear his own name of a murder charge and must discover what is causing the mass hallucinations. **Similar titles:** *Dreamside*, Graham Joyce; *Caesarea*, Tony Burgess; *Night Terrors*, Drew Williams.

Childhood • Demons • Oklahoma • Spiders

Film

The Blair Witch Project. *Daniel Myrick and Eduardo Sanchez, dir. 1999 80 minutes.* (See chapter 7, "Demonic Possession, Satanism, Black Magic, and Witches and Warlocks: The Devil Made Me Do It.")

The Butcher Boy. *Neil Jordan, dir. 1997. 109 minutes.* (See chapter 11, "Maniacs and Sociopaths, or the Nuclear Family Explodes: Monstrous Malcontents Bury the Hatchet.")

Carnival of Souls. *Herk Harvey, dir. 1962. (Black-and-white.) 80 minutes.* A young church organist has a near-death experience when her car veers off a bridge and she nearly drowns. Months later, she leaves home to pursue her musical career in another city but is inexplicably drawn to a now-defunct carnival haunted by beings only she can see. This is a low budget film shot mostly on location in Kansas, but it has rightfully developed quite a cult following. What *Carnival of Souls* lacks in plot it makes up for with its eerie atmosphere. **Similar reads:** *Death's Door*, John Wooley and Ron Wolfe; *Strangewood*, Christopher Golden.

Gothicism • Kansas

The Cell. *Tarsem Singh, dir. 2000. 107 minutes.* (See chapter 12, "Technohorror: Evil Hospitals, Military Screw-Ups, Scientific Goofs, and Alien Invasions.")

Dr. Jekyll and Mr. Hyde. *Victor Flemming, dir. 1941. (Black-and-white.) 114 minutes.* (See chapter 11, "Maniacs and Sociopaths, or the Nuclear Family Explodes: Monstrous Malcontents Bury the Hatchet.")

Fight Club. *David Fincher, dir. 1999. 139 minutes.* A darkly comic rendition of Chuck Palahniuk's novel of the same name in which an average, run-of-the-mill claims investigator for an automobile manufacturer becomes friends with an antisocial monomaniac. Together, the two form "Fight Club," a support group for men based on the idea that a little violence helps us get through the day and reconnect to our essential selves. But when things get out of hand and Project Mayhem is born, the unnamed narrator has to try to stop his new "friend" from committing the ultimate act of terrorism: the oblivion of Free Enterprise. **Similar reads:** *Spanky*, Christopher Fowler; *Soul Temple*, Lee Climer.

Alter Ego • Consumerism • Domestic Terrorism • Insomnia • New York City • Support Groups • Violence, Theories of

The Green Mile. *Frank Darabont, dir. 1999. 188 minutes.* Film version of Steven King's novel of the same name, in which prison guard Paul Edgecombe discovers that John Coffey, a death row inmate at Cold Mountain Penitentiary, has special powers—almost god-like powers over living creatures. Tom Hanks stars. **Similar reads:** *The Green Mile*, Stephen King; *Smoke Signals*, Octavio Ramos Jr.

> *African-American Characters • Capital Punishment • Immortality •*
> *Inmates—Death Row • Louisiana • Prison Guards as Character*

The Haunting. *Richard Wise, dir. 1963. (Black-and-white.) 112 minutes.* (See chapter 4, "Ghosts and Haunted Houses: Dealing with Presences and Absences.")

I Spit on Your Grave. *Mark Zarchi, dir. 1978. 100 minutes.* (See chapter 10, "Small Town Horror: Villages of the Damned.")

The Others. *Alejandro Amenabar, dir. 2001. 101 minutes.* (See chapter 4, "Ghosts and Haunted Houses: Dealing with Presences and Absences.")

Paperhouse. *Bernard Rose, dir. 1988. 92 minutes.* This early film by the director of *Candyman* is the tale of a young teenaged girl named Anna, who is becoming lost in the loneliness of her own world. She discovers that she can visit another one based on a house she has drawn herself, but which is mysteriously occupied by a young disabled boy. As she discovers more of the links between her fantasy world, the mundane present, and the world of a dying boy she has never met but who lives across the city, she is drawn deeper into her dream, which turns into a nightmare when a mysterious adult stalker begins invading it. Truly eerie, with brilliant cinematography. Stars Charlotte Burke, Jane Bertish, and Ben Cross. **Similar reads:** *Affinity*, J. N. Williamson; *The House*, Bentley Little.

> *Childhood • Dreams • Parallel Universe • Parenting • Stalkers • Telepathy*

The Sixth Sense. *M. Night Shyamalan, dir. 1999. 106 minutes.* (See chapter 4, "Ghosts and Haunted Houses: Dealing with Presences and Absences.")

Rebecca. *Alfred Hitchcock, dir. 1940. (Black-and-white.) 130 minutes.* Hitchcock's first American film is a faithful adaptation of Daphne DuMaurier's novel of the same name about a young woman who marries a widowed nobleman. Both fight the "ghost" of his former wife. Joan Fontaine and Lawrence Olivier star. This film was the winner of Academy Awards for Best Picture and Cinematography. **Similar reads:** *Rebecca*, Daphne DuMaurier; *The Caretaker*, William Thomas Simpson.

> *England • Gothic Romance • Incest • Marriage • Obsession • Secret Sin*

Our Picks

June's Picks: *The Dress Lodger*, Sheri Holman (Ballantine); *Tideland*, Mitch Cullen (Dufour); *The Witching Time*, Jean Stubbs (St. Martin's Press); *Fight Club* (film).

Tony's Picks: *Death's Door*, John Wooley and Ron Wolfe (Hawk Publishing); *Innocent Blood*, Christopher Dickey (Scribner); *Midnight Sun*, Ramsey Campbell (Tor); *Thunderland*, Brandon Massey (Dark Corner Press); *Tideland*, Mitch Cullen (Dufour); *Fight Club* (film); *The Green Mile* (film); *Paperhouse* (film).

Chapter 15

Splatterpunk: The Gross Out

Splatterpunk, a subgenre that emerged sometime in the late 1980s, is a *style* of writing more than it is a *theme* with any particular type of monster (which explains why so many of the works in this chapter are actually cross-references from other chapters). What separates the monster in this subgenre from any other "ordinary" maniac, vampire, werewolf, or alien is that it revels in torturing and mutilating ordinary humans. For example, Gloria Evans's alien creature Meh'Yam is a true connoisseur of both the hunting and massacre of victims. He/it rapes women out of a need to feed off of their melanin but also delights in how much he can make them cry out in pain. Equally important in defining the subgenre is how such characters relate their depravity in loving, almost sensuous, detail, without apology. For these reasons, splatterpunk is also known by the name "extreme horror."

Typical splatterpunk fiction is also characterized by a grotesque decadence. These are not the shocking excesses of monsters that kill because they must. Instead, graphic sex and violence abound for their own sake, and heinous acts of torture are routinely perpetrated by bored mortals and immortals. Similarly, these monsters often have similar extreme tastes in music, so punk, hardcore alternative, and heavy metal music are often part of the backdrop of their stories. Here are no reluctant vampires or antiheroes, à la Anne Rice; in splatterpunk, monsters revel in their monstrosity. In addition, there are no taboos in splatterpunk. In *Santa Steps Out*, Santa Claus, the Tooth Fairy, and the Easter Bunny suddenly remember their old lives as pagan deities before they were housebroken by the new monotheistic regime, and woe befalls anyone who would prevent these three from gratifying their physical desires. Likewise, nothing is taboo in the fiction of author John Shirley, who challenges all boundaries of sexual decadence in *Black Butterflies*. In this brilliant collection of short stories, characters take drugs and sexual depravity to extremes, simply for the pleasure of doing so.

So why do many fans of horror gravitate toward this extreme version of the genre? Fans are generally people who are quite literate within the genre itself and seek a type of fiction that will shock as well as challenge their ideas about horror. For example, splatterpunk's excesses often explore the nature of violence itself. Why, in a world full of technology and knowledge of the human psyche, do we have people who will harm others? Past explanations offered by earlier texts are insufficient. According to Robert Bloch's *Psycho*, Norman Bates is a serial killer because his mother was a nagging shrew. But this explanation is inadequate. Many of us are badly parented, yet we do not become serial killers. Splatterpunk in general scorns such neat psychological diagnoses and perhaps hearkens back to an earlier era of horror, when monsters were monsters because they were wicked, or because they simply enjoyed doing bad things. According to splatterpunk, violence and deviant behavior aren't phenomena we can easily explain, let alone control. Unlike other subgenres of horror, splatterpunk deals with material that is truly horrifying to readers who have read and seen it all.

Writers represented in this section include Simon Clark, Robert Devereaux, Gloria Evans, John Shirley, John Skipp, Michael Slade, and Craig Spector.

Note: Stories with splatterpunk elements can also be found in the collections and anthologies described in chapter 17. Refer to the subject/keyword index for specific titles under the keyword "splatterpunk."

Appeals: Gore Appeal; Shock Appeal; Punk Appeal; Youthful, Often Beautiful Characters; Curiosity and Fascination with Amorality; Breaking the Rules and Conventions of Society; Truly Evil Monsters; "Hard-Boiled" Narrative Techniques; Appeal of Raw Power; Horror That Deconstructs the Conventions of the Genre

Arnzen, Michael.

Ⓑ Grave Markings. *New York: Dell, 1994. 383p.* Living in pain, an insane, egomaniacal tattoo artist is obsessed with the mad images in his mind and the need for recognition, so he seeks new flesh to fulfill his ambition. Nothing, not even death, will stop him in his art. This is an excellent read for those who enjoy clever fiction, particularly if they can stomach grotesquerie and violence. **Similar titles:** *Extremities*, Kathe Koja; *The Scream*, John Skipp and Craig Spector; *Ambrosial Flesh*, Mary Ann Mitchell; *Wetbones*, John Shirley.

> *Artist as Character • Necrophilia • Tattoos • Torture*

Baker, Trisha.

Crimson Kiss. *New York: Pinnacle, 2001. 432p.* Meghann had a good life, until she met Simon, a cruel vampire who changed her life forever. Then one day, Megahnn had had enough abuse and put a stake through his heart, leaving him on a roof as the sun was coming up. She thought she killed him. She was wrong. Now Simon is going to have Meghann again, and kill everyone and anyone who gets in his way. **Similar titles:** *Interview with the Vampire*, Anne Rice; *Bound in Blood*, David Thomas Lord; The Midnight Series, Nancy Gideon; *De Lore's Confession*, Paulette Crain.

> *New York City • Psychiatrist/Psychologist as Character • Revenge • Sado-Masochism*

Barron, Diana.

Phantom Feast. *St. Petersburg, FL: Barclay Books, 2001. 269p.* (See chapter 13, "Ecological Horror: Rampant Animals and Mother Nature's Revenge.")

Bischoff, David.

The Crow: Quoth the Crow. *New York: HarperPrism, 1998. 256p.* (See chapter 4, "Ghosts and Haunted Houses: Dealing with Presences and Absences.")

Blake, Dan L.

Killing Frost. *Catskill, N.Y.: Press-Tige Pub., 1998. 300p.* Being eaten alive must be a horrible way to die, and Raymond Frost's fiancée could attest to this, if she weren't dead. A lot of people are dead in Farmington, Indiana, all disemboweled and half-eaten. Blake is both suspenseful and thought provoking, as he puts a new spin on the werewolf in this gory tale. **Similar titles:** *Canyons*, P. D. Cacek; *When Wolves Cry*, Chris N. Africa; *Black Oak 5: When the Cold Wind Blows*, Charles Grant.

> *Indiana • Shapeshifters • Werewolves*

Brite, Poppy Z.

The Crow: The Lazarus Heart. *New York: HarperPrism, 1998. 256p.* (See chapter 11, "Maniacs and Sociopaths, or the Nuclear Family Explodes: Monstrous Malcontents Bury the Hatchet.")

Clark, Simon.

Blood Crazy. *New York: Leisure, 2001. 394p.* One Sunday morning, everyone on the planet over the age of nineteen is suddenly stricken with the inexplicable desire to kill the young, especially their children. Now the surviving youngsters must band together to survive and recreate civilization. This is a terrifying and graphic, but original and engrossing read. **Similar titles:** *The Stand*, Stephen King; Millennium Quartet, Charles Grant; *Night of the Living Dead* (film) (1968 and 1990 versions); *The Dawning*, Hugh B. Cave; *Revelations*, Douglas E. Winter (editor).

> *Apocalypse • Childhood • England • Epidemics*

Connolly, John.

Every Dead Thing. *New York: Simon & Schuster, 1999. 395p.* NYPD detective Charlie "Bird" Parker was busy boozing at Tom's Oak Tavern when his wife Susan and young daughter Jennifer were mutilated by a killer called the Traveling Man. Consumed by guilt and alcoholism, Charlie soon loses his job, and almost his sanity. Several months later he is sober and ready to get his life back in order, so he takes up private investigating. One of his first cases involves the disappearance of a woman called Catherine Demeter. At first this puzzle seems unrelated to the Traveling Man—but Charlie has a gut feeling that the slayer is pulling the strings. Similar title: *Deviant Ways*, Chris Mooney; *The Demon Circle*, Dan Schmidt; *Death's Door*, John Wooley and Ron Wolfe; *From Hell*, Alan Moore and Eddie Campbell.

> *Alcoholism • Louisiana • New York City • Private Investigator as Character • Serial Killers • Torture • Virginia*

Devereaux, Robert.

Santa Steps Out: A Fairy Tale for Grown-ups. *New York: Leisure, 2000. 347p.* One Christmas in 1969, the Almighty is on vacation, and his minions allow Santa Claus and the Tooth Fairy to begin a torrid adulterous affair, which allows them to remember their natures before the current ruler of creation was the Judeo-Christian god. Then, humans and supernatural beings had different ideas about sexuality and the flesh. But much has changed in nearly 5,000 years, and allowing these two icons of childhood innocence to satiate their fleshly desires has the potential to change the world as we know it. Devereaux's novel is erudite, transgressive, and full of graphic sex. **Similar titles:** *The Tooth Fairy*, Graham Joyce; *The Beast That Was Max*, Gerard Houarner; *Viscera*, Cara Bruce (editor); *Are You Loathsome Tonight*, Poppy Z. Brite.

> *Clause, Mrs. Santa [Anya] character • Claus, Santa (character) • The Easter Bunny (character) • Eroticism • Fairy Tales • Fantasy • Gaia (character) • God—Christian God (character) • Immortality • Magic • Marriage • The North Pole • Pan (character) • Revenge • Tooth Fairy (character) • Zeus (character)*

Evans, Gloria.

Meh'Yam. *Gainesville, Fla.: T. Bo Publishing, 2000. 257p.* In the year 2017, an alien from an ancient interplanetary tribe that has coexisted with humans since the era of the Egyptian Empire is combing the streets of Orlando and nearby Eatonville, searching for unsuspecting young women whom he can seduce, rape, and then feed from. The FBI and the CDC both know that they have a monster on their hands, but both agencies are powerless to stop the vampiric rapist from leaving the desiccated bodies of even more young black women in his wake. Only a young female journalist and a seasoned television reporter are able to piece together the puzzle of the Meh'Yam, and only they have hopes of stopping it—if the creature doesn't find them first. Evans's rookie tale is easily one of the most inventive novels in print. Fans of grisly horror will find this an excellent read. **Similar titles:** *The Last Vampire*, T. M. Wright; The My Soul to Keep Series, Tananarive Due; *Wetbones*, John Shirley; *Voice of the Blood*, Jemiah Jefferson.

> *African-American Characters • Aliens • Center for Disease Control, The • Federal Bureau of Investigation, The • Florida • Journalist as Character • Psychosexual Horror • Racism • Rape • Serial Killers*

Houarner, Gerard.

The Beast That Was Max. *New York: Leisure, 2001. 392p.* Max is your typical government hit man—a ruthless psychopath who really enjoys his work—so he's quite upset when his employers don't want to take full advantage of his skills and instead force him to protect a special woman, someone physically adept at getting into the minds of others. But this special woman he must protect allows Max to think about the beast within himself who is a connoisseur of the art of killing. Houraner's narrative defies neat categorization in that he manages to incorporate many types of monsters and belief systems in his tale, which is best described as a graphic and disturbing depiction of the mind of a societally sanctioned psychopath. **Similar titles:** *Santa Steps Out*, Robert Devereaux; *My Brain Escapes Me*, Robert Steven Rhine; *Full Moon, Bloody Moon*, Lee Driver.

> *Alter Ego • Asian Characters • Demons • Eroticism • Mind Control • Organized Crime • Parapsychology • Psychosexual Horror • Sado-Masochism • Serial Killers • Sex Crimes • Torture • Twins • Zombies*

Jacob, Charlee.

This Symbiotic Fascination. *New York: Leisure, 2002. 394p.* Thirty-seven-year-old Tawne Delaney isn't the kind of woman that men see as beautiful. Large and plain looking, she remains a virgin despite her age. Only one man shows any interest in her, co-worker and serial rapist Arcan Tyler, a man who is controlled by a triumvirate of animal spirits. Against the backdrop of a city haunted by a brutal serial killer, the two pursue a relationship in this imagistic narrative. **Similar titles:** *House of Pain*, Sephera Giron; *Natural Selection*, Weston Ochse; *Ambrosial Flesh*, Mary Ann Mitchell; *Phantom Feast*, Diana Barron.

> *Rape • Serial Killers • Shapeshifters • Vampire as New Species*

Koja, Kathe.

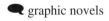 **The Cipher.** *New York: Bantam, 1991. 356p.* (See chapter 14, "Psychological Horror: It's All in Your Head.")

Lee, Edward, and Elizabeth Steffen.

Portrait of the Psychopath As a Young Woman. Orlando, Fla.: Necro Publications, 1998. 292p. (See chapter 11, "Maniacs and Sociopaths, or the Nuclear Family Explodes: Monstrous Malcontents Bury the Hatchet.")

Masters, Paul.

Meca and the Black Oracle. *New York: Leisure, 1999. 327p.* Newly promoted police Lieutenant Steve Tanner takes over a case involved with a serial killer of young women. This killer first murders them and then dissects their bodies, removing all internal organs. Tanner soon figures out that a well-organized Satanic cult is behind the murders. But to stop the Black Oracle cult, he will first have to infiltrate their ranks. This is a graphic and gory pseudo-police procedural. **Similar titles:** *Demon Circle*, Dan Schmidt; *Ripper*, Michael Slade; *The Bottoms*, Joe R. Lansdale; *Morningstar*, Peter Atkins.

Cults • Police Officer as Character • Police Procedural • Religion—Satanism • Serial Killers

McFarlane, Todd, Alan Moore, and Greg Capullo.

Spawn, Book 8: Betrayal of Blood. *Fullerton, Calif.: Image Comics, 1999,* ©1995. 96p. Al Simmons, now known as the mutant Spawn, must defend himself against crooked cops who attempt to frame him for murder. The real kicker is that one of those who is engineering his frame-up is also the current husband of Spawn's wife, who thinks he is dead. **Similar titles:** The Witchblade Series, Christina Z. and David Wohl; The Buffy the Vampire Slayer Series, Various Authors; The Crow Series, Various Authors; *Lazarus Churchyard*, Warren Ellis and D'Israeli.

 graphic novels

African-American Characters • Graphic Novel • Police Officer as Character • Shapeshifters

Mitchell, Mary Ann.

Ambrosial Flesh. *New York: Leisure, 2001. 391p.* (See chapter 7, "Demonic Possession, Satanism, Black Magic, and Witches and Warlocks: The Devil Made Me Do It.")

Moore, Joseph, and Brett A. Savory.

Filthy Death, The Leering Clown. *Kansas City, Mo.: Dark Tales, 2000. 44p.* Strange imagistic novella that begins when a serial killer is himself terminated immediately after committing a murder. The story then follows maniac Justin Maynard into the afterlife, where he meets the spirits of some of his victims and ultimately runs into his mother and his abusive father. Well written, with emphasis on style and characterization/motivation, rather than linear plot line. **Similar titles:** *The Secret Life of Colors*, Steve Savile; *The Cell* (film); *Robert Bloch's Psychos*, Robert Bloch (editor); *The Asylum*, Victor Heck (editor).

Afterlife, The • Cannibalism • Child Abuse • Clergy as Character • Religion—Christianity—Catholicism • Serial Killers

Skipp, John, and Craig Spector.

The Scream. *Lancaster, Pa.: Stealth Press, 2001, ©1998. 437p.* Sex, drugs, and rock and roll lead to the horrifying mutilations of a group of teenagers at a party in California. Soon televangelists and parenting groups are blaming the deaths on rock music itself, especially on the sounds of a Goth metal band called The Scream. Is music influencing American youth toward evil, driving twelve-year-olds to stab classmates, or is there a more sinister force at work? The authors create a fast-paced and thoughtful treatment of a popular subject. **Similar titles:** *Big Rock Beat*, Greg Kihn; *The Cleanup*, John Skipp and Craig Spector; *Queen of the Damned* (film); *Morningstar*, Peter Atkins.

> *California • Cults • Drugs • Music—Rock Music • New York City • Parenting • Religion—Christianity • Religion—Satanism • Televangelism • Zombies*

Slade, Michael. The Headhunter Series.

Headhunter. *New York: Onyx Books, 1984. 422p.* Royal Canadian Mountie Robert DeClerq is persuaded to come out of retirement to help catch the Headhunter, a serial killer who decapitates his female victims and taunts the police by sending them pictures of the women's' severed heads. Clever plot, surprise ending, and a wealth of details about criminology, as practiced in both Canada and the lower forty-eight, make this novel a page-turner. It is told from multiple points of view, including the murderer's. Similar works: *Carrion Comfort*, Dan Simmons; *Messiah*, Boris Starling; *Tribulations*, J. Michael Straczynski.

> *DeClerq, Robert (character) • Federal Bureau of Investigation • Headhunter, The (character) • Police Officer as Character • Police Procedural • Psychosexual Horror • Royal Canadian Mounties • Schizophrenia/Multiple Personality Disorder • Serial Killers • Vancouver, British Columbia*

Ghoul. *New York: New American Library, 1989. 386p.* Horror fiction fuels the already twisted imagination of a schizophrenic, an ingenious serial murderer obsessed with H. P. Lovecraft's Cthulu mythos. It's up to Mountie Zinc Chandler to track the killer through Canada, the United States, and England and stop him before he kills again. Michael Slade's (the pen name of three who write collaboratively) writing is gory and gripping and full of the intricate details of modern police work. **Similar titles:** All of Slade's other titles; *Carrion Comfort*, Dan Simmons; *Messiah*, Boris Starling; *Tribulations*, J. Michael Straczynski; *Fallen* (film).

> *Canada • Chandler, Zinc (character) • Cthulhu (character) • Incest • London, England • Lovecraft, H. P. (the works of) • Pittsburgh, Pennsylvania • Police Officer as Character • Police Procedural • Royal Canadian Mounties • Serial Killers*

Cut Throat. *New York: Signet, 1992. 397p.* A ruthless pharmaceutical corporation based in Hong Kong and run by an ancient family of warlords routinely engages in brutal human experimentation and harvests organs of Chinese peasants for sale to the highest bidder. The CEO of this corporation is skilled in the arts of torture and murder to ensure the success of the family business, and he brutally slays anyone who gets in his way. Royal Canadian Mounties Zinc Chandler and Robert DeClerq collaborate with FBI agent Carol Tate to solve the murders in this gory and well-written police procedural. Similar works: *Death's Door*, John Wooley and Ron Wolfe; *Meca and the Black Oracle*, Paul Masters; *Coma*, Robin Cook; *Messiah*, Boris Starling.

> *Asian Characters • Chandler, Zinc (character) • DeClerq, Robert (character) • Drugs • Police Officer as Character • Police Procedural • Royal Canadian Mounties • Vancouver, British Columbia*

Ripper. *New York: Penguin, 1994. 416p.* The militant feminists are ultimately to blame for a group of Satanic serial killers, who slash to shreds the body of America's foremost feminist, rip off her face, and display her corpse under a bridge. The Royal Canadian Mounted Police track the killers in this literate, well-researched novel of detection and horror. **Similar titles:** *Exquisite Corpse*, Poppy Z. Brite; *Carrion Comfort*, Dan Simmons; *Demon Circle*, Dan Schmidt; *Meca and the Black Oracle*, Paul Masters.

> *Chandler, Zinc (character) • Craven, Nick (character) • Jack the Ripper Murders • Police Officer as Character • Police Procedural • Religion— Satanism • Revenge • Royal Canadian Mounties • Serial Killers • Tarot, The*

Evil Eye. *New York: Signet, 1997. 417p.* Royal Canadian Mounties Zinc Chandler and Robert DeClerq work together to stop a killer who bashes in the skulls of his victims and then disembowels them. This novel features minor characters Alex Hunt and Katt Dark from Slade's previous novel *Ripper,* and as with all of Slade's work, is full of meticulous details of Canadian history and police work. Details of the Canadian legal system are particularly fascinating for American readers. **Similar titles:** *Silence of the Lambs*, Thomas Harris; *Death from the Woods*, Bridget Aubert; *Eyes of Prey*, Barry Hoffman; *The Bottoms*, Joe R. Lansdale.

> *African-American Characters • Asian Characters • Chandler, Zinc (character) • DeClerq, Robert (character) • Police Officer as Character • Police Procedural • Royal Canadian Mounties • Serial Killers • Vancouver, British Columbia*

Primal Scream. *New York: Signet, 1998. 432p.* Inspector Robert DeClercq is being stalked by a killer from his past, the Headhunter. Can DeClercq save a young child, and himself, or will the Headhunter finally have his revenge? **Similar titles:** *The Silence of the Lambs* and *Hannibal*, Thomas Harris; *The Bottoms*, Joe R. Lansdale; *Mr. X.*, Peter Straub; *Portrait of the Psychopath as a Young Woman*, Edward Lee and Elizabeth Stephen.

> *DeClerq, Robert (character) • Headhunter, The (character) • Police Officer as Character • Police Procedural • Revenge • Royal Canadian Mounties • Vancouver, British Columbia*

Burnt Bones. *New York: Signet, 2000. 408p.* Mephisto, a collecter of Scottish artifacts who fancies himself an ancient Highland warrior, is searching for the Hoard, the silver skull of Antogonis Severus, who was killed by the Picts in a.d. 297. Possession of this skull will make his deal with the devil complete and allow him to release a deadly plague on the world and decimate its population. Mephisto especially enjoys using bizarre forms of torture and sacrifice to extract information from the unwilling while appeasing his dark gods. Can Robert DeClerq stop Mephisto before he kills one of his old friends? **Similar titles:** *The Wicker Man*, Robin Hardy and Anthony Schaffer; *The Silence of the Lambs*, Thomas Harris.

> *Craven, Nick (character) • DeClerq, Robert (character) • History, Use of • Human Sacrifice • Obsession • Police Officer as Character • Police Procedural • Rape • Religion—Druidism • Royal Canadian Mounties • Scotland • Seattle, Washington • Stonehenge • Torture • Vancouver, British Columbia*

Film

American Psycho. *Mary Harron, dir. 2000. 101 minutes.* Harron's second film is a faithful adaptation of the novel of the same name by Brent Easton Ellis, and is as much a parody of the "greed is good" eighties as it is a portrait of a serial killer. Christian Bale, Willem Dafoe, Jared Leto, and Reese Witherspoon star in this brilliant character study. The script is by Brent Easton Ellis. **Similar reads:** *Zombie*, Joyce Carol Oates; *Ripper*, Michael Slade.

> *The Eighties • New York City • Serial Killers • Slasher*

I Spit on Your Grave. *Mark Zarchi, dir. 1978. 100 minutes.* (See chapter 10, Small Town Horror: Villages of the Damned.")

Our Picks

June's Picks: *Blood Crazy*, Simon Clark (Leisure); *Headhunter*, Michael Slade (Onyx Books); *Ripper,* Michael Slade (Signet); *Santa Steps Out*, Robert Devereaux (Leisure); *American Psycho* (film).

Tony's Picks: *Meh'Yam*, Gloria Evans (T. Bo); *The Scream*, John Skipp and Craig Spector (Stealth Press); *American Psycho* (film).

Chapter 16

Comic Horror: Laughing at Our Fears

Many fans of horror do not realize that the genre has *always* had an element of the comic in it. Freddy Kreuger and the mysterious Crypt Keeper may have been the first high-profile monsters to crack jokes before disposing of victims or when introducing a tale of horror, but lines such as "she has a nice neck," were "spoken" by Max Von Schrek's vampire character when he first saw a picture of Mina in the 1922 film *Nosferatu*. Schrek's observation is nothing less than a comic threat that predates Freddy's and the Crypt Keeper's by more than fifty years. The old gypsy woman in Tod Browning's *Dracula*, or the aging busybody in James Whale's *Frankenstein*, are both excellent examples of comic relief in early Universal Studios horror films, and these works helped define the genre for decades to come. When it comes to literary horror, laughing at our fears goes back to the earliest of horror texts. Humor in horror can be found in the understated reactions of Hrothgar's warriors to the monster Grendel in the Old English epic *Beowulf*, in the ridiculousness of the messengers' repeating "The helmet! The helmet!" in Horace Walpole's *The Castle of Otranto*, and in the melodrama and irony of a good Poe tale.

This relationship between humor and horror should come as no surprise, for psychologically speaking, the two go hand in hand—in the reactions of both the characters in texts as well as in the reactions of the readers or viewers. Characters in these texts, especially in film, will invariably, in their hurry to escape the monster, run into posts and walls, trip over small rocks, or fall victim to their own footwear. In more recent, self-reflective horror, it is not even unusual to find an intended victim making highly ironic comments foreshadowing his or her own certain demise. As for the reader or viewer, he or she will laugh nervously at those moments when terrifying expectations are built up—and the monster is surely about to appear—but the mysterious noise turns out to be only a cat or raccoon rummaging in a trash can.

Sometimes the humor in horror is not as subtle as the instances cited above, as recent films by Kevin Smith (*Dogma*) and Rusty Cundieff (*Tales From the Hood*) exemplify. Like any other genre, horror has writers and directors who choose parody as their method. These masters of comic horror realize how important it is that we laugh at our fears when we see them satirized. Of a less absurd type are novels such as Jane Austen's *Northanger Abbey*, which shows that often horror is just a product of an overactive imagination, or even Kingsley Amis's *The Green Man*, which leaves the reader comically suspended between the world of the supernatural and that of an alcoholic innkeeper in considering the possible existence of a ghost. Obviously, the relationship between horror and comedy has not been lost on either the publication or the film industry. In film, it has resulted in lines dripping with dramatic irony, such as when the serial killer stepfather in Joseph Ruben's film *The Stepfather* tells his stepdaughter, and soon to be intended victim, "let's just bury the hatchet." It is also apparent in brilliant comic scenes such as the opening frame tale of Cundieff's *Tales from the Hood*, when three gangbangers try to put on a brave front while paying a midnight visit to a strange-looking funeral home run by a crazed mortician. Their false bravado is easily overcome when the mortician looks through a sliding window on his door, and one of the three turns to flee, running into a pole and knocking himself unconscious.

To those horror texts that teach us that we can indeed laugh at our fears, we devote this chapter. Listed in this category are works that revolve around comic characters, off-the-wall situations, and downright silly manifestations of monsters (as in William Browning Spencer's *Resume with Monsters*, which includes possessed office machines). Also included are parodies of serious works and dark comedies. Benchmark works of fiction in this category include Kingsley Amis's *The Green Man* and Jane Austen's *Northanger Abbey*. More recent gems such as Laurell K. Hamilton's Anita Blake Series, Greg Kihn's *Big Rock Beat*, Dean Koontz's *Ticktock*, and newcomer David Whitman's absolutely hilarious novella *Deadfellas* are also annotated in this chapter.

Note: Stories with comic elements can also be found in the collections and anthologies described in chapter 17. Refer to the subject/keyword index for specific titles listed under the keyword "humor."

Appeals: Humor; The Sense of Familiarity Achieved with Parody (Inside Joke Appeal); Identification with Complex Character Emotions of Humor/Horror; Enjoyment of Works That Stretch the Formulas of the Genre to Absurdity

Allred, Sam.

> **If Witches We Be.** *San Jose, Calif.: Writer's Showcase, 2000. 218p.* A Valkyrie is sent to Earth to counter the threat posed by a Scottish woman who has the ancient codes necessary to summon the legions of hell. Sigrun Morgrun infiltrates the household of Alella Aboyne and marries her son, producing four daughters. These daughters are half-mortal and can help Sigrun lead the fight to save Earth. They flee and attempt to hide to give the heroes of Valhalla time to organize a defense against the hordes of the netherworld. The pitched showdown combines the heroes, the Valkyrie, the Atlanta Braves baseball team, and Sigrun and the children against an infinite number of fiends. **Similar titles:** *Black Light*, Elizabeth Hand; *The Ten Ounce Siesta*, Norman Patridge; *Salem's Ghost*, Rose Earhart.
>
> *Apocalypse • Demons • Religion—Paganism • Scotland*

Amis, Kingsley.

The Green Man. *New York: Harcourt Brace, 1969. 252p.* Alcoholic innkeeper Maurice Allington is seeing ghosts at The Green Man Inn. Is his mind playing tricks on him, or are they real and dangerous? Amis is subtle in his humorous approach, so this masterful piece of British satire is quite enjoyable. **Similar titles:** *Northanger Abbey*, Jane Austen; *The Shining*, Stephen King; *The Canterville Ghost*, Oscar Wilde; *In a Glass Darkly*, Joseph Sheridan Le Fanu.

Alcoholism • Haunted Houses

Austen, Jane.

Northanger Abbey. *Oxford: Oxford University Press, 2000, ©1818. 221 p.* When Catherine Morland comes to Northanger Abbey, she meets all the trappings of gothic horror and imagines the worst. Fortunately, she has at hand her own fundamental good sense and the irresistible but unsentimental Henry Tilney. Disaster does eventually strike, in the real world as distinct from the romantic one of her imagination, but without spoiling for too long the gay, good-humored atmosphere of this most delightful of books. **Similar titles:** *The Green Man*, Kingsley Amis; *The Canterville Ghost*, Oscar Wilde; *The Castle of Otranto*, Horace Walpole.

England • Gothic Romance

Banks, Ian.

The Wasp Factory. *London: Little, Brown, 2001, ©1984. 256p.* (See chapter 11, "Maniacs and Sociopaths, or the Nuclear Family Explodes: Monstrous Malcontents Bury the Hatchet.")

Brezsny, Rob.

The Televisionary Oracle. *Berkeley, Calif.: Frog Ltd.-North America Books, 2000. 483p.* A practical joking goddess worshipper and fellow members of the Menstrual Temple of the Funky Grail kidnap an aging rock star. If he can survive an indoctrination into the holy order, as well as his own foolish chauvinism, he may just end up a happy man. **Similar titles:** *The Bubba Chronicles*, Selina Rosen (editor); *Big Rock Beat*, Greg Kihn; *The Licking Valley Coon Hunters Club*, Brian A. Hopkins; *Deadfellas*, David Whitman.

Astrology • California • Feminism • Music—Rock Music • Prognostication • Religion—Paganism

Cacek, P. D.

Night Prayers. *Darien, Ill.: Design Image, 1998. 219p.* (See chapter 6, "Vampires and Werewolves: Children of the Night.")

Campbell, Ramsey.

Needing Ghosts. *London: Century, 1990. 80p.* This is Campbell's strange dark fantasy about a horror writer named Simon Mottershead, told in stream of consciousness technique. Mottershead finds himself trapped in alternate states of reality where he forgets who he is. Upon realizing that he is a writer of horror fiction and that he has a family, he returns home to find his wife and children murdered. Is Mottershead trapped in his own nightmare, or in one of his fictional works? Campbell's novella is a challenging, tongue-in-cheek text that will be appreciated by readers who enjoy experimental prose. **Similar titles:** *Strangewood*, Christopher Golden; *The Nightmare Factory*, Thomas Ligotti; *The Uncanny*, Andrew Klavan.

Dreams • England • Fantasy • Writer as Character

Collins, Max Allan.

The Mummy Returns. *New York: Berkley Boulevard, 2001. 290p.* (See chapter 5, "Golem, Mummies, and Re-animated Stalkers: Wake the Dead and They'll Be Cranky.")

Ellis, Warren, and D Israeli.

Lazarus Churchyard: The Final Cut. *Fullerton, Calif.: Image Comics, 2001. 126p.* (See chapter 12, "Technohorror: Evil Hospitals, Military Screw-Ups, Scientific Goofs, and Alien Invasions.")

Elrod, P. N.

Chill in the Blood. *New York: Ace, 1998. 288p.* (See chapter 6, "Vampires and Werewolves: Children of the Night.")

Gaiman, Neil.

American Gods. *London: Headline, 2001. 504p.* This scary, strange, and hallucinogenic road-trip story wrapped around a deep examination of the American spirit tackles everything from the onslaught of the information age to the meaning of death. Shadow gets out of prison early when his wife is killed in a car crash. At a loss, he takes up with a mysterious character called Wednesday, who is actually the god Odin. Odin is roaming America, rounding up his forgotten fellows in preparation for an epic battle against the upstart deities of the Internet, credit cards, television, and all that is wired. **Similar titles:** *Big Rock Beat*, Greg Kihn; *The Ten Ounce Siesta*, Norman Partridge; *The Televisionary Oracle*, Rob Brezsny.

Ⓑ audiotape   e-book

Computers • Epic Structure • Grieving • Internet, The • Odin (character) • Popular Culture

Garton, Ray.

Sex and Violence in Hollywood. *Burton, Mich.: Subterranean Press, 2001. 505p.* Adam Julian, son of a Hollywood screenwriter, has a life many would kill for, and some would kill to keep. He's tangled in a web of forced sex and coerced into robbery, where killing becomes the only free choice he can make. Garton's characters are quirky and unique. **Similar titles:** *California Ghosting*, William Hill; *Big Rock Beat*, Greg Kihn; *American Gods*, Neil Gaiman.

Hollywood, California • Los Angeles, California • Writer as Character

Goldberg, D.G.K.

Skating on the Edge. *New York: iPublishing.com, 2002. 279p.* A collection of misfit creatures who could be guests on the *Jerry Springer Show* discussing their disorders instead embark on a journey to answer the great riddles of the universe, drink lots of coffee, chain smoke, and annoy bystanders. This group, which includes a vampire with a feeding disorder, a surfer Viking, an incompetent shapeshifter, and a warrior saint, will travel through space and time, encountering famous dead people, mythical creatures and bad jokes, only to discover that no one will help them. **Similar titles:** *American Gods*, Neil Gaiman; *Big Rock Beat*, Greg Kihn; *From the Dust Returned*, Ray Bradbury.

Fantasy • Magic • Popular Culture • Vampires • Vikings

Hamilton, Laurell K. The Anita Blake, Vampire Hunter Series.

Guilty Pleasures. *New York: Penguin, 1993. 265p.* In a futuristic world where the Supreme Court protects vampires' rights, someone is still managing to kill them. Can vampire hunter extraordinaire Anita Blake stop the murders? Hamilton's prose is quirky, with emphasis on character and action. She uses hard-boiled first person narration. **Similar titles:** Eyes of the Daemon Series, Camille Bacon-Smith; The Vampire Files Series, P. N. Elrod; *Full Moon, Bloody Moon*, Lee Driver; The Host Series, Selina Rosen; *Sunglasses After Dark*, Nancy A. Collins.

> *Blake, Anita (character) • Private Investigator as Character • Serial Killers • St. Louis, Missouri • Vampire Hunters*

The Laughing Corpse. *New York: Penguin, 1994. 293p.* A mercenary "animator" is raising the dead and causing problems for Anita Blake. This novel chronicles the further adventures of Hamilton's sassy and tough vampire killer, complete with the wry humor and hard-boiled edge that defines the series. **Similar titles:** Eyes of the Daemon Series, Camille Bacon-Smith; The Vampire Files Series, P. N. Elrod; *Full Moon, Bloody Moon*, Lee Driver; The Host Series, Selina Rosen; *Sunglasses After Dark*, Nancy A. Collins.

> *Blake, Anita (character) • Private Investigator as Character • St. Louis, Missouri • Vampire Hunters*

Circus of the Damned. *New York: Berkley-Ace, 1995. 329p.* The third book in the Anita Blake Series, this one tells about Blake being fought over by two rival vampires who both want her as their human servant/lover. Can she survive being caught in the middle of a feud between the undead? Hamilton's emphasis is on dark fantasy and detection in this first person narration. **Similar titles:** Eyes of the Daemon Series, Camille Bacon-Smith; The Vampire Files Series, P. N. Elrod; *Full Moon, Bloody Moon*, Lee Driver; The Host Series, Selina Rosen; *Sunglasses After Dark*, Nancy A. Collins.

> *Blake, Anita (character) • Private Investigator as Character • St. Louis, Missouri • Vampire Clans • Vampire Hunters*

Bloody Bones. *New York: Penguin, 1996. 370p.* The misadventures of vampire hunter/animator Anita Blake as she must juggle a request to raise the dead to gain information and a need to solve a series of killings in and around Branson, Missouri. Hamilton uses hard-boiled first person narration for humorous ends. **Similar titles:** Eyes of the Daemon Series, Camille Bacon-Smith; The Vampire Files Series, P. N. Elrod; *Full Moon, Bloody Moon*, Lee Driver; The Host Series, Selina Rosen; *Sunglasses After Dark*, Nancy A. Collins.

> *Blake, Anita (character) • St. Louis, Missouri • Serial Killers • Vampire Hunters*

The Lunatic Cafe. *New York: Penguin-Ace, 1996. 369p.* In this tongue-in-cheek first person narrative adventure, Anita Blake must determine who or what is killing werewolves. The only problem is that this time she is personally involved in her work; she is in love with one of them. **Similar titles:** Eyes of the Daemon Series, Camille Bacon-Smith; The Vampire Files Series, P. N. Elrod; *Full Moon, Bloody Moon*, Lee Driver; The Host Series, Selina Rosen; *Sunglasses After Dark*, Nancy A. Collins.

> *Blake, Anita (character) • Private Investigator as Character • St. Louis, Missouri • Vampire Hunters • Werewolves*

The Killing Dance. *New York: Ace, 1997. 387p.* Anita Blake is caught between warring werewolves and the master vampire Jean-Claude, and one of them has put a price on her head. Will she have to form an uneasy alliance to survive? **Similar titles:** Eyes of the Daemon Series, Camille Bacon-Smith; The Vampire Files Series, P. N. Elrod; *Full Moon, Bloody Moon*, Lee Driver; The Host Series, Selina Rosen; *Sunglasses After Dark*, Nancy A. Collins.

Blake, Anita (character) • Private Investigator as Character • St. Louis, Missouri •
Vampire Hunters • Werewolves

Burnt Offerings. *New York: Berkley-Ace, 1998. 400p.* The sixth book in The Anita Blake
Series continues the love triangle among Anita, her werewolf/lover, and the vampire
Jean-Claude. Interspersed with the romance is Anita's attempt to catch a telekinetic fire
starter. **Similar titles:** Eyes of the Daemon Series, Camille Bacon-Smith; The Vampire
Files Series, P. N. Elrod; *Full Moon, Bloody Moon*, Lee Driver; The Host Series, Selina
Rosen; *Sunglasses After Dark*, Nancy A. Collins.

Blake, Anita (character) • St. Louis, Missouri • Vampire Hunters

Blue Moon. *New York: Penguin, 1998. 342p.* The eighth book in Hamilton's series has
Blake attempting to save a friend from corrupt police and werewolf clans. **Similar titles:**
Eyes of the Daemon Series, Camille Bacon-Smith; *Shattered Glass,* Elaine Bergstrom;
The Vampire Files Series, P. N. Elrod; *Full Moon, Bloody Moon*, Lee Driver; The Host
Series, Selina Rosen; *Sunglasses After Dark*, Nancy A. Collins.

Blake, Anita (character) • Private Investigator as Character • Tennessee •
Vampire Clans • Werewolves

Obsidian Butterfly. *New York: Ace, 2000. 386p.* Anita Blake gets a call from bounty
hunter Ted Forrester, which leads her to Santa Fe to investigate serial slayings and mutilations. Not only does Anita have to deal with a centuries-old vampire with powers of
magic, but she must also contend with Ted's bounty hunter friends, many of whom resent
her. **Similar titles:** Eyes of the Daemon Series, Camille Bacon-Smith; The Vampire Files
Series, P. N. Elrod; *Full Moon, Bloody Moon*, Lee Driver; The Host Series, Selina Rosen;
Sunglasses After Dark, Nancy A. Collins.

Blake, Anita (character) • Forrester, Ted (character) • Private Investigator as
Character • Santa Fe, New Mexico • Serial Killers • Torture • Vampire Hunters

Narcissus in Chains. *New York: Berkley, 2001. 424p.* Six months after Anita Blake had
faced down her most powerful foe ever (in *Obsidian Butterfly*), she is again called upon to
save the day, as a serial kidnapper is targeting the people she was sworn to protect. To defeat this new foe, however, Blake will have to join forces with the vampire Jean-Claude
and Richard the werewolf. But when she does, the kidnapper is not her only enemy; now
she must fight the beast within herself before it gets out of control. **Similar titles:** Eyes of
the Daemon Series, Camille Bacon-Smith; The Vampire Files Series, P. N. Elrod; *Full
Moon, Bloody Moon*, Lee Driver; The Host Series, Selina Rosen; *Sunglasses After Dark*,
Nancy A. Collins.

Blake, Anita (character) • Private Investigator as Character • Shapeshifters • St.
Louis, Missouri • Vampire Hunters • Werewolves

Hays, Clark, and Kathleen McFall.

The Cowboy and the Vampire. *St. Paul, Minn.: Llewellyn, 1999. 318p.* Unwilling vampire
Lizzie Vaughan and Tucker, her cowboy lover, find themselves at the middle of a vampire
war that could exterminate the human race. Pitted against the powerful vampire Julius and
his consort Elita, as well as the biblical Lazarus (now a vampire), the unlikely lovers must
save each other and (hopefully) the human race. This popular novel is full of clever and
energetic writing, with likable comic characters. **Similar titles:** The Silver Wolf Series,
Alice Borchardt; The Midnight Series, Nancy Gideon; *Dracul: An Eternal Love Story*,
Nancy Kilpatrick; *DeLore's Confession*, Paulette Crain; *Prophet Annie*, Ellen Recknor.

Apocalypse • Cowboy as Character • History, Use of • Journalist as Character •
New Mexico • New York City • Vampire Clans • Vampire's Point of View

Hill, William.

California Ghosting. *Middleburg, Fla.: Otter Creek Press, 1998. 523p.* The nephew of a resort hotel owner and manager travels to Ghostal Shores, located near San Francisco, to take over the family business after his uncle's murder. There he meets his uncle's attorney and executor, who introduces him to the hotel staff, a group of amiable ghosts. Together, the spirits of Ghostal Shores and its new manager try to piece together clues to the identity of the murderer, all the while battling a new group of "troublemaker" ghosts who have suddenly taken up residence at the resort. **Similar titles:** *The Canterville Ghost*, Oscar Wilde; *The Green Man*, Kinsley Amis; *The Uncanny*, Andrew Klavan.

> *Clairvoyant as Character • Haunted Houses • Lawyer as Character • San Francisco, California*

Hopkins, Brian A.

 The Licking Valley Coon Hunters Club. *Alma, Ark.: Yard Dog Press, 2000. 173p.* Private Investigator Martin Zolotow is kidnapped at an airport and taken out into the desert, where he is physically coerced into working for a mobster who needs him to help save his daughter from a man who thinks he is a vampire. Zolotow must now travel to Oklahoma City to visit a vampire nightclub, if he can survive long enough to get there. This is a fun read, half hard-boiled detective novel, half vampire wannabe B-flick. **Similar titles:** *Big Rock Beat*, Greg Kihn; The Anita Blake Vampire Hunter Series, Laurell K. Hamilton; *Full Moon, Bloody Moon*, Lee Driver; The Black Oak Series, Charles Grant.

> *Oklahoma City, Oklahoma • Organized Crime • Private Investigator as Character • Psychiatrist/Psychologist as Character • Zolotow, Martin (character)*

Hynes, James.

The Lecturer's Tale. *New York: Picador USA, 2001. 388p.* (See chapter 9, "Telekinesis and Hypnosis: Chaos from Control.")

 16

Kihn, Greg.

Big Rock Beat. *New York: Forge, 1998. 351p.* Hollywood B-movie director Landis Woodley finds himself in a pickle: He needs more money for his new film. Enter El Diablo, a rich Latino aristocrat with money to burn. He saves the film, but at what price? Kihn's second novel is quirky and fast-paced. **Similar titles:** *California Ghosting*, William Hill; *The Uncanny*, Andrew Klavan; *The Scream*, John Skipp and Craig Spector; *The Bubba Chronicles*, Selina Rosen.

> *Clairvoyant as Character • Drugs • Hollywood, California • Horror Movie Industry • Los Angeles, California • Music—Rock Music • Satan (character) • Woodley, Landis (character)*

Klavan, Andrew.

The Uncanny. *New York: Crown, 1998. 343p.* Hollywood producer Richard Storm travels to England to find the real ghosts that have inspired his horror flicks. Instead, he finds a strange array of weird characters and an alternate reality that follows the plot of one of his films. The emphasis is on character, dialog, and description. **Similar titles:** *California Ghosting*, William Hill; *Big Rock Beat*, Greg Kihn; *Strangewood*, Christopher Golden; *Zom Bee Moo Vee*, Mark McLaughlin.

 audiotape

> *England • Horror Movie Industry*

Koontz, Dean.

Ticktock. *New York: Ballantine Books, 1996. 335p.* Koontz's novel is a subtly humorous tale of a young Vietnamese-American man who is "brought back" into his family in a most extreme way. A cursed rag doll turned reptilian demon pursues him. He has from nightfall until dawn to escape it, and to find love. **Similar titles:** *Tales from the Hood* (film); *The Mummy* (film) and *The Mummy Returns* (film); *Prophet Annie*, Ellen Recknor; *The Ten Ounce Siesta*, Norman Partridge.

👂 audiotape

Asian-American Characters • Demons • Writer as Character

Laymon, Richard.

Bite. *New York: Leisure, 1999, ©1996. 378p.* (See chapter 6, "Vampires and Werewolves: Children of the Night.")

Friday Night in Beast House. *Baltimore: Cemetery Dance, 2001, ©1979. 161p.* (See chapter 4, "Ghosts and Haunted Houses: Dealing with Presences and Absences.")

Once Upon a Halloween. *Baltimore: Cemetery Dance, 2000. 252p.* Laymon blends horror and humor in this novel: A boy arrives at a house on Halloween screaming that something is after him. Will his parents and his friends believe him? **Similar titles:** *Thunderland*, Brandon Massey; *The Traveling Vampire Show*, Richard Laymon; *It*, Stephen King.

Childhood • Halloween • Parenting

Partridge, Norman.

The Ten Ounce Siesta. *New York: Berkley, 1998. 254p.* Jack Baddalach, ex-boxing champion and current mob runner, is given a strange assignment: He must escort a sick chihuahua across the Nevada desert. But to do so, he will have to face gun-toting maniacs, Satanists, and dragons, in this clever and original satire. **Similar titles:** *Ticktock*, Dean Koontz; *Big Rock Beat*, Greg Kihn; *Deadfellas*, David Whitman; *Northanger Abbey*, Jane Austen.

Fantasy • Las Vegas, Nevada • Organized Crime • Religion—Satanism

Recknor, Ellen.

Prophet Annie: Being the Recently Discovered Memoir of Annie Pinkerton Boone Newcastle Dearborn, Prophet and Seer. *New York: Avon, 1999. 330p.* This first person narrative frame tale chronicles the years after Annie Pinkerton Boone Newcastle Dearborne's husband dies on their wedding night. She fearfully begins to hear his voice, but once he inhabits her body, her life becomes a comic romp as she becomes a respected seer in the turn-of-the-century West. **Similar titles:** *The Green Man*, Kingsley Amis; *Irrational Fears*, William Browning Spencer; *California Ghosting*, William Hill; *The Cowboy and the Vampire*, Clark Hays and Kathleen McFall.

Arizona • Clairvoyant as Character • Feminism • Marriage • Native American Characters • United States—19th Century

Spencer, William Browning.

Irrational Fears. *Clarkston, Ga.: White Wolf, 1998. 233p.* An alcoholic literature professor and his alcoholic love interest cross paths with a group of "twelve steppers" and their extremist rivals. A kidnapping leads them to a realization of the true causes of alcoholism: Lovecraftian monsters. **Similar titles:** *Resume with Monsters*, William Browning Spencer; *Dead Heat*, Del Stone Jr.; *The Ten Ounce Siesta*, Norman Partridge; *Big Rock Beat*, Greg Kihn.

Academia • Alcoholism • Cthulhu (character) • Cults • Virginia

Resume with Monsters. Sag Harbor, New York: Permanent Press, 1995. 212p. (See chapter 8, "Mythological Monsters and 'The Old Ones': Invoking the Dark Gods.")

Stone, Del, Jr.

Dead Heat. *Austin, Tex.: Mojo Press, 1996. 188p.* A loner and Harley rider becomes a zombie following a biological apocalypse. But he is different from other zombies because he can think and control the dead masses. Stone's modern classic is darkly humorous. It was the recipient of an International Literary Guild Award for Best First Novel. **Similar titles:** *Irrational Fears*, William Browning Spencer, *Deadfellas*, David Whitman; *Bubbas of the Apocalypse*, Selina Rosen; *Bite*, Richard Laymon.

Apocalypse • Biological Warfare • Cyberpunk • Texas • Zombies

Whitman, David.

Deadfellas. *Kansas City, Mo.: Dark Tales, 2001. 54p.* Whitman pens this brilliantly funny, darkly comic novella of hit men who find themselves face to face with zombies, mischievous aliens, Cthulhonic gods, and alternate realities. The story is extremely clever and intriguing, with emphasis being placed on witty "wiseguy" dialogue and character interaction. This chapbook is a must read for anyone who is a fan of the horror genre or of comic novels. **Similar titles:** *Dead Heat*, Del Stone Jr.; *Obsidian Butterfly*, Laurell K. Hamilton; *Tales from the Hood* (film); *Scary Movie* (film).

Aliens • Demons • Irish-American Characters • Necronomicon, The • Organized Crime • Replicants • Science Fiction • Zombies

Wilde, Oscar.

The Canterville Ghost. *Cambridge, Mass.: Candlewick Press, 1997, ©1887. 126p.* This classic is a tale about an American family that moves into a haunted English manor, then refuses to believe in its resident ghost. The teenaged daughter begins to witness strange occurrences, but can she convince her parents? This work is exemplary of Wilde's comic wit and flair for language. **Similar titles:** *The Green Man*, Kingsley Amis; *Northanger Abbey*, Jane Austen; *California Ghosting*, William Hill; *The Canterville Ghost* (film).

audiotape

England • Haunted Houses

Wilson, F. Paul. The Repairman Jack Series.

The Tomb. *New York: Tor, 1998, ©1984. 440p.* (See chapter 8, "Mythological Monsters and 'The Old Ones': Invoking the Dark Gods.")

Conspiracies. *New York: Tor, 2000. 448p.* Repairman Jack is a home care technician of a different nature: He investigates crimes that go beyond the norms of traditional law. "I don't do missing wives," Jack protests at first, but the bizarre circumstances surrounding Melanie Ehler's disappearance convince him to help out the woman's distraught husband. Melanie is a leading voice in the conspiracy-theory movement, a true believer that crop circles, UFOs, and even El Niño are all part of the same vast plot against humankind. Jack is plunged deep into her weird world as he attends the conference where Melanie was due to speak. **Similar titles:** The Anita Blake, Vampire Hunter Series, Laurell K. Hamilton;

The Host Series, Selena Rosen; *The Licking Valley Coon Hunters Club*, Brian A. Hopkins; *Full Moon, Bloody Moon*, Lee Driver.

> *Aliens • Demons • Parapsychology • Private Investigator as Character • Repairman Jack (character)*

Film

Dogma. *Kevin Smith, dir. 1999. 130 minutes.* Two fallen angels (Matt Damon and Ben Affleck) attempt to reenter heaven while God (Alanis Morrisette) is occupied playing a game of bocci ball with mortals. The last living descendant of Jesus Christ, along with Jay and Silent Bob and the 13th Apostle (Chris Rock), must stop the duo, whose reentry will destroy the fabric of the universe and end the world as we know it. This is more than a satire; it is a funny and thoughtful film. **Similar reads:** *Soul Temple*, Steven Lee Climer; *The Spirit of Independence*, Keith Rummel.

> *African-American Characters • Angels • Apocalypse • God—Christian God (character) • Religion—Christianity • Revenge*

Fight Club. *David Fincher, dir. 1999. 139 minutes.* (See chapter 14, "Psychological Horror: It's All In Your Head.")

The Mummy. *Stephen Sommers, dir. 1999. 124 minutes.* Sommers's film is a parody of Karl Freund's classic film of the same name. This version, with its emphasis on action adventure, is more a cross between *Bram Stoker's Dracula* and *Raiders of the Lost Ark*. The Mummy, former high priest Imhotep, is executed for falling in love with Pharaoh's favorite concubine. Imhotep is spending eternity quietly in the Underworld when librarian and Egyptologist Evelyn Carnahan accidentally raises him from the dead by the reading of a book. Now he must be stopped before he manages to reincarnate his former love and looses his armies on the world. Brendan Fraser and Rachael Weisz star. **Similar reads:** *Into the Mummy's Tomb*, John Richard Stevens (editor); *The Mummy Returns*, Max Allan Collins.

> *Archeology • Carnahan, Evelyn (character) • Curse • Egypt • Imhotep (character) • Immortality • Librarian as Character • Mummies • O'Connell, Rick (character) • Revenging Revenant*

The Mummy Returns. *Stephen Sommers, dir. 2001. 120 minutes.* Sommers's sequel to the parody of Karl Freund's classic film begins ten years after Rick O'Connell and Evelyn Carnahan (now O'Connell's wife) sent Imhotep back to the underworld. He is raised from the dead once more and bent on destroying the world as we know it. Now Rick and Evelyn must remember their own past lives and relationships with Imhotep to thwart his plan. Brendan Fraser, Rachael Weisz, and The Rock star. The film's emphasis is on action adventure and special effects. **Similar reads:** *The Mummy Returns*, Max Allan Collins; *Into the Mummy's Tomb*, John Richard Stevens (editor).

> *Archeology • Carnahan, Evelyn (character) • Cursed Objects • Egypt • Imhotep (character) • Immortality • Mummies • Nefertiti (character) • O'Connell, Rick (character) • Revenging Revenant*

Scary Movie. *Keenan Ivory Wayans, dir. 2000. 88 minutes.* This is Wayans's parody of the *Scream* series and *I Know What You Did Last Summer*. The film is chock full of references to all horror flicks ever made, as well as to parodies of many well-known commercials and some of the Wayans brothers' own comedy, as well as many bawdy jokes. Shawn and Marlon Wayans, Cheri Oteri, Carmen Electra, and David L. Lander (of *Lenny* *and Squiggy* fame) star. **Similar reads:** *The Ten Ounce Siesta*, Norman Partridge; *Deadfellas*, David Whitman.

> *African-American Characters • High School • Journalist as Character • Police Officer as Character • Popular Culture • Revenge • Secret Sin • Serial Killer • Slasher*

Tales from the Hood. *Rusty Cundief, dir. 1995. 98 minutes.* Four gangsters come to a funeral home just before midnight to make a drug deal with the proprietor, who insists on regaling them with tales of each of his clients before agreeing to make the deal. The frame tale and the tales themselves parody the classic style of the Universal Studios horror pics of the 1930s, as well as B-movie horror from the 1950s and 1960s, but the content of these tales is deadly serious. The creatures viewers would normally identify as monsters are monsters in the original meaning of the word: They're divine warnings. The true monsters are humans who refuse to heed these warnings. The film stars Corbin Bernsen, David Allen Grier, and Clarence Williams III. **Similar reads:** *The Nightmare Chronicles*, Douglas Clegg; *More Monsters from Memphis*, Beecher Smith (editor).

> *African-American Characters • Domestic Violence • Gang Violence • Haunted Houses • Police Brutality • Racism • Revenging Revenant • Satan (character)*

Young Frankenstein. *Mel Brooks, dir. 1974 (Black-and-white.) 98 minutes.* Mel Brooks's parody of James Whale's 1931 film *Frankenstein* has the good doctor's grandson inheriting the family castle and resuming his ancestor's experiments in reanimating the dead. Gene Wilder, Marty Feldman, Madeline Kahn, Teri Garr, and Cloris Leachman star. **Similar reads:** *Frankenstein: The Legacy*, Christopher Schildt; *Bubbas of the Apocalypse*, Selina Rosen.

> *Alternative Literature • Frankenstein, Dr. (character) • Frankenstein, Monster (character) • Mad Scientist • Popular Culture • Weird Science*

Comic Films Related to the Horror Industry

Ed Wood. *Tim Burton, dir. 1994. 127 minutes.* Biography of cross-dressing B-horror director Ed Wood (Johnny Depp), known for making some of the worst horror films ever, including *Plan 9 from Outer Space*. Martin Landau plays one of the stars of *Plan 9*, an aging Bela Lugosi who is addicted to heroin. Bill Murray also stars. **Similar reads:** *Big Rock Beat*, Greg Kihn; The Universal Monsters Series, various authors.

> *Hollywood, California • Horror Film Industry • Lugosi, Bela (character) • Popular Culture • Wood, Ed (character)*

Matinee. *Joe Dante, dir. 1993. 99 minutes.* In small town America in the 1960s, a theater showman who specializes in 1950s-style B-flicks introduces a coastal town to a unique movie experience, capitalizing on the Cuban Missile Crisis hysteria with a kitschy horror extravaganza combining film effects, stage props, and actors in rubber suits. John Goodman puts in one of his best performances as producer Lawrence Woolsey in this story about facing the real horrors of nuclear annihilation. Cathy Moriarty also stars. **Similar reads:** *The Uncanny*, Andrew Klavan; *Big Rock Beat*, Greg Kihn.

> *Horror Film Industry • Popular Culture • United States—1960s • Woolsey, Lawrence (character)*

Our Picks

June's Picks: *Big Rock Beat*, Greg Kihn (Forge-Doherty); *The Canterville Ghost*, Oscar Wilde (Candlewick Press); *Dogma* (film); *The Mummy* (film); *Tales from the Hood* (film).

Tony's Picks: The Anita Blake Series, Laurell K. Hamilton (Penguin, Berkley); *Deadfellas*, David Whitman (Dark Tales); *Northanger Abbey*, Jane Austen (Oxford University Press); *Tales from the Hood* (film).

Part 3

An Annotated Bibliography of Horror Short Story Collections

Chapter 17

Collections and Anthologies

To many scholars and fans of the genre, it is common knowledge that horror first took literary form as the full-length novel, with publications such as Horace Walpole's *The Castle of Otranto,* Anne Radcliffe's *The Mysteries of Udolpho,* and Matthew Lewis's *The Monk,* all of which appeared in England in the late 1700s. However, it can be argued that those texts are the ancestors of dark fantasy and magical realism, rather than horror as we know it today. The first examples of the simultaneous use of the psychological and the supernatural in horror, a trait that informs modern horror, appeared in America in short story form. In the mid-nineteenth century, two American literary mainstays, Nathaniel Hawthorne and Edgar Allan Poe, made their marks in the horrific allegorical tale (which is perhaps the ancestor of the weird tale), as well as in maniacal musings of murderous madmen (the prototype of both the maniac horror novel and the true crime text).

Despite the importance of the short story to the genre, very few collections of tales by a single author take their places on the shelves of local bookstores, as these collections are usually not big sellers. Nonetheless, the short tale has proven marketable to publishers in the horror business in the form of countless numbers of short story anthologies, collections of tales by diverse hands. Anthologies can be found on the genre's best-seller lists at any given time. Perhaps this is because—and the format of *Hooked on Horror* is based on this supposition—fans of the genre tend to prefer tales that have quite a bit in common *thematically,* whether they be in the same subgenre or are simply concerned with the same type of monster. For this reason, in this chapter we acknowledge the importance of anthologies intended for readers of particular subgenre horror fiction. Such anthologies are not only preferable to many horror readers but are integral to the thriving of authors in the genre as well. They allow readers both to sample works by different authors with whom they may have been unfamiliar and to gain an increased understanding of the expanding parameters of any given subgenre. In the long run, short story anthologies encourage readers to pick up novels by up-and-coming writers.

Anthologies are also important to the marketability of the genre because they allow writers who normally do not write horror fiction, and who may never have considered producing a novel in the genre, a chance to dabble in the supernatural and the psychotic. Glancing through the annotations in this chapter, readers will notice William Faulkner, Isabel Allende, Angela Carter, Jorge Luis Borges, Eudora Welty, Joyce Carol Oates, Isak Dinesen, Thomas Hardy, Charlotte Perkins Gillman, Fay Weldon, F. Scott Fitzgerald, Sir Walter Scott, Honoré de Balzac, Guy de Maupassant, Franz Kafka, Robert Graves, Roald Dahl, Muriel Spark, and Patricia Highsmith listed as authors of horror tales. In a best case scenario, the result of these "dabblings" could be a renewed interest in horror by a writer who has much to offer the genre, such as was the case with Joyce Carol Oates, who wrote only short stories in the genre until recently. Her 1997 publication of the disturbing diary of a psychopath, entitled *Zombie*, is one of the finest novel-length first person narratives about a maniac ever published, and will help give the genre more legitimacy in the eyes of its detractors. In other cases, the results of these dabblings could simply be the production of a fine horror text, in the form of a short story. Works such as Robert Aickman's "Pages from a Young Girl's Journal," Oliver Onions's "The Beckoning Fair One," and Angela Carter's "The Company of Wolves" rival *any* vampire, ghost, or dark erotic novel published before or since their conception (for these titles, see the first edition of *Hooked on Horror*).

The bottom line is that, for whatever reason, there is a huge market for short story anthologies, and fans of the genre cannot seem to get enough of them. Horror publishers, of course, have chosen to more than meet the reader demand for these collections. The result is a list of horror anthologies on almost any subject possible, from vampires, to werewolves, to cats and dogs, to eroticism, to Lovecraftian mythologies, to horrors populated by gay and lesbian protagonists. In this chapter, we annotate as many of these anthologies as possible, concentrating mainly on those published since 1998. We have improved our annotations over those of the first edition, attempting to more fully annotate and keyword these anthologies, as well as to assign more similar titles.

Anthologies in this chapter include such perpetually popular titles as *Love in Vein* and *Love in Vein II*, *The Best of Cemetery Dance*, and *The Year's Best Science Fiction, Fantasy, and Horror*. In addition, readers will find in this chapter various others of interest, including *The Horror Writers Association Presents Robert Bloch's Psychos* and *Queer Fear*. Moreover, we list here recent and notable anthologies that do not have a thematic bent but that are nonetheless important because of the collector or editor or the publisher. This list includes anthologies edited by Chris Baldick, Robert Bloch, Michael Cox, Ellen Datlow, Terry Windling, Charles Grant, Martin H. Greenberg, and Stephen Jones. Our goal here is to raise awareness of the short story's place in the genre and to encourage collection development officers in libraries that have a strong horror readership to add these thematic anthologies to their collections.

We have also included in this guide collections of short stories by individual authors. Collections are particularly important for two reasons: They identify for readers' advisors those writers who excel in the horror genre but who write exclusively, or almost exclusively, in the short story format; and they complete the bibliographies of those writers who are essentially novelists but who have produced a few collections of short fiction in their careers. After all, the horror genre was born of the short tale format, so in many ways these writers of short fiction are the keepers of tradition. Yet the most important reason to include collections in *Hooked on Horror* is the fact that many of these authors—namely Edgar

Allan Poe, Nathaniel Hawthorne, Edith Wharton, Joseph Sheridan Le Fanu, H. P. Lovecraft, Angela Carter, Robert Aickman, and Thomas Ligotti—create nothing short of masterpieces using this brief literary form. Tales such as "The Tell-Tale Heart" and "The Black Cat," by Poe; "Young Goodman Brown," by Hawthorne; "Afterwards," by Wharton; *Carmilla,* by Le Fanu; "The Dunwich Horror" and "The Rats in the Walls," by Lovecraft; "In the Company of Wolves," by Carter; and "No Stronger Than a Flower" and "Pages from a Young Girl's Journal," by Aickman, as well as the Grimscribe stories by Ligotti, have seldom been matched for their eloquence, atmosphere, and chilling effect. Horror fans have responded to these works with avid appreciation of the format.

In this chapter we annotate classic collections such as those by Le Fanu, Bram Stoker, Hawthorne, Poe, and Ambrose Bierce, as well as more recent additions to the genre by twentieth-century authors of science fiction and horror's "Golden Age," like Lovecraft and Arthur Machen. In addition, we include texts by diverse masters of the short tale, such as Aickman, Elizabeth Bowen, Oliver Onions, and Donald Wandrei. We also identify short story collections by novelists, both genre oriented horror novelists and mainstream canonical authors, who dabble in the short horror tale on occasion, such as Clive Barker, Poppy Z. Brite, Isak Dinesen, Stephen King, Joyce Carol Oates, and Peter Straub.

Appeals: Brevity in the Reading Experience; Introduction to New Authors; Similar Thematic Concerns; Similar Monsters; Variety in the Reading Experience; Having Access to the "Classics"; Enjoyment of Writers Who Write Only Short Fiction in the Genre; Writer Loyalty

Collections by Individual Authors

Ambuehl, James.

Correlated Contents. *Poplar Bluffs, Mo.: Mythos Books, 1998. 96p.* These six tales continue H. P. Lovecraft's Cthulhu Mythos. Ambuehl pens horrifying tales of artists, tourist traps, and southern swamplands, each one effective in its grotesque descriptions and atmospheric narrative. **Similar titles:** *Alone with the Horrors,* Ramsey Campbell; *More Annotated H. P. Lovecraft,* H. P. Lovecraft; *The Loved Dead and Other Revisions,* H. P. Lovecraft et al.; *A Darkness Inbred,* Victor Heck.

Artist as Character • Cthulhu Mythos • South, The • Werewolves

17

Askew, Alice, and Claude Askew.

Aylmer Vance: Ghost-Seer. *Jack Adrian (editor). Ashcroft, B.C.: Ash-Tree Press, 1998. 131p.* Among the popular husband-and-wife writing teams in the years before the First World War were Alice and Claude Askew. Like A. M. Burrage, another prolific contributor to the many newspapers and magazines that flourished in the first three decades of the century, the Askews turned their hands to many different types of tales, only once applying their talents to a purely supernatural theme; the result was the creation of *Aylmer Vance: Ghost-Seer.* In these eight stories, we see Vance and his companion Dexter probing various mysteries involving vampires and unidentifiable fears. **Similar titles:** The Black Oak Series, Charles Grant; *Full Moon, Bloody Moon,* Lee Driver; *Don't Dream,* Donald Wandrei; *Tales of Unease,* Arthur Conan Doyle.

Dreams • Parapsychology • Private Investigator as Character • Vampire Hunters

Bachman, Richard.

The Bachman Books: Four Early Novels. *New York: Penguin, 1996. 692p.* (See Steven King, *The Bachman Books.*)

Barker, Clive.

The Essential Clive Barker: Selected Fictions. *New York: HarperCollins, 1999. 752p.* This lengthy text is a collection of some seventy passages from novels and plays, four complete stories, and excerpts of interviews. It includes excerpts from Barker's most famous novels and most popular short stories. **Similar titles:** *Black Butterflies*, John Shirley; *Santa Steps Out*, Robert Devereaux; *13 Stories*, Ed Cain; *Are You Loathsome Tonight*, Poppy Z. Brite.

Demons • Fantasy • Gay/Lesbian/Bisexual Characters • Psychosexual Horror

Benson, E. F. Collected Spook Stories of E. F. Benson.

The Terror by Night. *Jack Adrian (editor). Ashcroft, B.C.: Ash-Tree Press, 1998. 161p.* Although E. F. Benson's four volumes of short weird tales are acknowledged classics of their kind, original hardback editions are now difficult to obtain, and when copies are offered for sale the price is often prohibitive. The Ash-Tree Press now brings together all of E. F. Benson's known tales of the strange and the supernatural into an extended five-volume set. *The Terror by Night* is the first volume in the series and covers the period between 1899 and 1911. **Similar titles:** *Tales of Unease*, Arthur Conan Doyle; *The Haunted Looking Glass*, Edward Gorey (editor); *Green Tea and Other Stories*, Joseph Sheridan Le Fanu.

Ghosts • Haunted Houses • Revenging Revenant

The Passenger. *Jack Adrian (editor). Ashcroft, B.C.: Ash-Tree Press, 1999. 153p. The Passenger* is the second volume in the series and covers the period between 1912 and 1921, including the famous "The Room in the Tower." **Similar titles:** *Tales of Unease*, Arthur Conan Doyle; *The Haunted Looking Glass*, Edward Gorey (editor); *Green Tea and Other Stories*, Joseph Sheridan Le Fanu.

Animals Run Rampant • Haunted Houses • Revenging Revenant

Berglund, E[dward]. P[aul].

Shards of Darkness. *Fan Mythos 2. Poplar Bluffs, Mo.: Mythos Books, 2000. 158p.* Berglund presents eleven stories, published between 1977 and 1998, involved with the Cthulhu Mythos. The collection includes "The Feaster from the Stars," a cautionary tale concerned with the search for immortality; "Vision of Madness," a story in which a painting causes insanity; and "The Sand Castle," about a man trapped in a labyrinth-like structure. **Similar titles:** *Tales of H. P. Lovecraft: Major Works*, H. P. Lovecraft; *The Loved Dead and Other Revisions*, H. P. Lovecraft et al.; *Exit Into Eternity*, C. M. Eddy.

Cthulhu Mythos • Fantasy • Immortality • Oregon

Bierce, Ambrose.

The Moonlit Road and Other Ghost and Horror Stories. *Mineola, N.Y.: Dover Publications, 1998. 91p.* These twelve weird tales by America's other "master of the macabre" are intelligently written. Narrated from various points of view, this collection will appeal to fans of the classic ghost story as well as those who like to delve into the darker realms of the human mind. **Similar titles:** *Classic Ghost Stories*, John Grafton (editor); *Ghosts and Haunts of the Civil War*, Christopher K. Coleman (editor); *Tales of H. P. Lovecraft: Major Works*, H. P. Lovecraft; *Tales of Unease*, Arthur Conan Doyle; *The Haunted*

Looking Glass, Edward Gorey (editor); *Civil War Ghosts*, Martin Harry Greenberg, Frank McSherry Jr. and Charles G. Waugh.

> *Dreams • Ghosts • Gothicism • Haunted Houses • Maritime Horror • Shapeshifters • Weird Science*

Blackwood, Algernon.

The Complete John Silence Stories. *S. T. Joshi (editor). Mineola, N.Y.: Dover Publications, 1997. 246p.* Inspired by the Sherlock Holmes tales of Arthur Conan Doyle, Blackwood created John Silence just after the turn of the century. The complete set of John Silence stories has not been in print for at least three decades. Joshi collects these, including for the first time ever the story "Victim of Higher Spaces," which was not included in the previous prints. This is a great read for all horror fans who enjoy erudite prose and psychic detective fiction. **Similar titles:** *Dark Detectives*, Stephen Jones (editor); The Black Oak Series, Charles Grant; *Full Moon, Bloody Moon*, Lee Driver; *Don't Dream*, Donald Wandrei.

> *England • Magic • Parapsychology • Silence, John (character)*

Bloch, Robert.

Flowers from the Moon and Other Lunacies. *Robert Price (editor). Sauk City, Wisc.: Arkham House Publishers, 1998. 296p.* Arkham House has assembled, for the first time, a variety of Robert Bloch's early stories from *Weird Tales* and *Strange Stories*. Tales range from the whimsical or darkly humorous to the straightforward. Editor Price includes "The Druidic Doom," "Fangs of Vengeance," "Death Is an Elephant," "A Question of Identity," "Death Has Five Guesses," and others. Many of these stories are unknown and/or rarely anthologized tales. **Similar titles:** *Alone with the Horrors*, Ramsey Campbell; *The Moonlit Road and Other Ghost and Horror Stories*, Ambrose Bierce; *Don't Dream*, Donald Wandrei; *I Am Legend*, Richard Matheson.

> *Cthulhu Mythos • Magic • Maritime Horror • Religion—Paganism • Revenge • Satan (character)*

Braddon, M[ary] E[lizabeth].

The Cold Embrace and Other Ghost Stories. *Richard Dalby (editor). Ashcroft, B.C.: Ash-Tree Press, 2000. 285p.* In the latter years of the nineteenth century, Mary Elizabeth Braddon was one of the best known, and best-selling, authors of the day. Her best-known work was undoubtedly "Lady Audley's Secret" (1862), a melodramatic tale of bigamy, madness, desertion, and murder that catapulted its author to the forefront of the literary world. In the years that followed she turned out dozens of novels and scores of short stories. Among Braddon's prodigious output were many tales of the supernatural and the weird. Richard Dalby has now collected eighteen of Braddon's finest tales of the uncanny, all of which demonstrate her mastery of the form and show why she was one of the best-selling authors of her time. **Similar titles:** *A Bottomless Grave and Other Victorian Tales of Terror*, Hugh Lamb; *In a Glass Darkly*, Joseph Sheridan Le Fanu; *The Mammoth Book of Victorian and Edwardian Ghost Stories*, Richard Dalby.

> *Dreams • England • Ghosts • Haunted Houses • Marriage*

Bradbury, Ray.

The Illustrated Man. *New York: Avon, 1997, ©1951. 275p.* Eighteen of Bradbury's dark futuristic tales, including "The Illustrated Man," "The Veldt," and "Kaleidoscope," are interwoven into this frame tale about a tattooed storyteller of horror and fantasy. This collection is one of the classics of sci-fi horror and fantasy, with stories set on Mars, Venus, and in space. **Similar titles:** *Escaping Purgatory*, Gary A. Braunbeck and Alan M. Clark; *Thank You for the Flowers*, Scott Nicholson; *Don't Dream*, Donald Wandrei.

*African-American characters • Fantasy • Holograms • Racism • Replicants •
Science Fiction • Space Exploration*

Braunbeck, Gary A., and Alan M. Clark.

Escaping Purgatory: Fables in Words and Pictures. *Eugene, Oreg.: IFD Publishing, 2001. 304p.* Writer Gary Braunbeck collaborates with illustrator Alan Clark to produce seven tales of people who build personal hells or find themselves trapped in them. This collection includes the unique modern classics "Mr. Hands," about a woman who avenges her daughter's death at the hands of a child molester by evoking a giant demon that rips his body to shreds; "A Host of Shadows," a tale of the final days of eighty-year- old Jack the Ripper, now a world renowned doctor who has spent his entire post-serial killer existence doing good for his fellow man, only to find that his fame and respect have alienated him from his son; and "The Big Hollow" (a darker version of the third act of *Our Town*), which chronicles the day to day "life" in purgatory of the newly dead in a small country grave-yard. The collection is nothing short of brilliant in its creativity and writing style, and is a must read for any fan of modern horror short stories. **Similar titles:** *The Illustrated Man*, Ray Bradbury; *Don't Dream*, Donald Wandrei; *Whispers in the Night*, Basil Copper; *Dial Your Dreams*, Robert Weinberg.

*Afterlife, The • Child Molesters • Demons • Jack the Ripper (character) •
Native American Characters • Obsession • Revenge • Zombies*

Brite, Poppy Z.

Are You Loathsome Tonight? *Springfield, Pa.: Gauntlet, 1998. 193p.* One of the most popular goth scene writers in the genre pens a dozen weird tales and horrible visions. Ti-tles include "In Vermis Veritas," "Mussolini and the Axeman's Jazz," and "Entertaining Mr. Orton" and show her flair for morbid humor and clever self-referentiality. It also in-cludes photos and illustrations by J. K. Potter, as well as an introduction by Peter Straub. **Similar titles:** *Viscera*, Cara Bruce (editor); *Bending the Landscape*, Nicola Griffith and Stephen Pagel (editors); *Extremities*, Kathe Koja; *Bubbas of the Apocalpyse*, Selina Rosen (editor).

Eroticism • History, Use of • Necrophilia • Serial Killers • Splatterpunk

Bryant, Edward.

The Baku: Tales of the Nuclear Age. *Burton, Mich.: Subterranean Press, 2001. 111p.* This collection of four fictional works concerned with the aftermath of Hiorshima in-cludes an unfilmed *Twilight Zone* script. In the title story, nightmares and ghosts of Naga-saki victims haunt a former World War II bomber pilot and current head of a nuclear power consortium. **Similar titles:** *Killing the Mandarin*, Juan Alonso; *Ghosts and Haunts of the Civil War*, Christopher K. Coleman; *Historical Hauntings*, Jean Rabe and Martin H. Greenberg.

*Dreams • Hiroshima, Japan • History, Use of • Nagasaki, Japan • Revenging
Revenant • War—World War II*

Burk, James K.

Strange Twists of Fate. *Alma, Ark.: Yard Dog Press, 2001. 51p.* These four darkly comic short stories have subjects as diverse as witchcraft, vampires, and werewolves. Burk's prose is subtly tongue-in-cheek, and his tales are brief and to the point, with emphasis on character development and interaction. **Similar titles:** *Vampire Slayers*, Martin H. Greenberg and Elizabeth Ann Scarborough (editors); *Zom Bee Moo Vee*, Mark McLaughlin; *The Bubba Chronicles*, Selina Rosen; The American Vampire Series, various authors.

Humor • Vampires • Vampire's Point of View • Werewolves • Witchcraft • Writer as Character

Burke, John.

We've Been Waiting for You, and Other Tales of Unease. *Ashcroft, B.C.: Ash-Tree Press, 2000. 260p.* Many of Burke's stories concern the dead and the power that they continue to wield over the living. This power is, almost without exception, cold, malevolent, and without pity. Not all of John Burke's stories concern ghosts, however. The author prefers the term "tales of unease" to describe his writings, and in all his stories a sense of unease is effortlessly conjured up, whether concerned with beings from beyond the grave or with the powerful forces for violence and evil contained in human beings. **Similar titles:** *Ghosts and Grisly Things*, Ramsey Campbell; *The House*, Bentley Little; *Boy in the Water*, Stephen Dobyns.

Demons • Dreams • Grieving • Revenging Revenant

Cain, Ed.

13 Stories. *Chesapeake, Va.: Maximilian Press, 2000. 170p.* This volume of thirteen highly original horror stories and dark fantasy tales by a Bram Stoker Award nominee would be an excellent addition to any library. Stories include "The Travelers," about a New York doctor in Appalachia who discovers the dark secret that explains why the town has few children; "Glory Hole," a tale of sexual decadence and one man's realization that he has been used as a pawn by an ancient Asian evil; and "Dear Diary," which chronicles the loneliness of a woman who is betrayed by her husband, as well as her revenge. Cain is consistently brilliant, emphasizing characterization and psychological accuracy. **Similar titles:** *Thanks for the Flowers*, Scott Nicholson; *Escaping Purgatory*, Gary A. Braunbeck and Alan M. Clark; *Whispers in the Night*, Basil Copper; *Dial Your Dreams*, Robert Weinberg.

Alcoholism • Appalachia • Cursed Objects • Drugs • Ghosts • Gothicism • Parapsychology • Pregnancy • Psychosexual Horror • Revenge • Revenging Revenant

17

Campbell, Ramsey.

Alone with the Horrors: The Great Short Fiction of Ramsey Campbell, 1961–1991. *London: Headline Book Publishing, 1993. 493p.* This omnibus collection, the largest to date of Campbell's stories, contains thirty-nine of his tales written in the thirty years between 1961 and 1991. Stories include something for almost everyone: the Lovecraftian "The Room in the Castle," the award-winning tales "Mackintosh Willy" and "The Chimney," the erotic stories "The Man in the Underpass" and "Loveman's Comeback," and the traditional ghost stories "Out of Copyright" and "Where the Heart Is." This impressive work will appeal to fans of gentle reads and subtle horror. If you add one collection of a single writer's short stories to your library, it would be difficult to find a better one than *Alone with the Horrors*, which also includes sixteen marvelous black-and-white illustrations by J. K. Potter (as a photomontage interior). **Similar titles:** *Thank

You for the Flowers, Scott Nicholson; *Whispers in the Night*, Basil Copper; *Don't Dream*, Donald Wandrei; *Cold Print*, Ramsey Campbell.

> *Childhood • Cthulhu Mythos • England • Eroticism • Gothicism • Liverpool, England • Psychosexual Horror • Revenging Revenant • Subterranean Monsters • Writer as Character*

Cold Print. *New York: Tor, 1987. 331p.* These fifteen Lovecraftian tales are from Campbell's early period of publishing, in which he incorporates the Cthulhu Mythos into his own visions of gothic English rural landscapes. Campbell create stories of eerie, grotesque creatures that reside under bridges, in lakes, and in haunted dwellings, and these creatures are always waiting for the right moment to claw their way across the threshold that separates their world from ours. An excellent read for fans of H. P. Lovecraft and August Derleth. **Similar titles:** *More Annotated H. P. Lovecraft*, H. P. Lovecraft; *The Loved Dead and Other Revisions*, H. P. Lovecraft et al.; *Alone With the Horrors*, Ramsey Campbell.

> *Cthulhu Mythos • Dramatic Monologue • England • Gothicism • Haunted Houses • Maritime Horror • Necronomicon, The • Subterranean Monsters • Witchcraft*

Dark Companions. *New York: Tor, 1982. 318p.* Perhaps Ramsey's best collection of traditional ghost stories in the vein of M. R. James and Joseph Sheridan Le Fanu, *Dark Companions* contains twenty-one of his most subtly horrific tales of haunted houses and vengeful ghosts. It includes the hugely popular, award-winning "Mackintosh Willy," as well as lesser-known gems like "Out of Copyright" and "The Chimney." Fans of gentle reads and traditional ghost stories will find this extremely enjoyable. **Similar titles:** *Green Tea and Other Ghost Stories*, Joseph Sheridan Le Fanu; *In a Glass Darkly*, Joseph Sheridan Le Fanu; *Ghost Stories of Henry James*, Henry James; *Whispers in the Night*, Basil Copper.

> *Childhood • England • Gothicism • Haunted Houses • Revenging Revenants • Subterranean Monsters • Witchcraft • Writer as Character*

Demons by Daylight. *London: W. H. Allen-Star, 1975. 192p.* Fourteen of Campbell's early stories are subdivided into three sections: "Nightmares," "Errol Undercliffe," and "Relationships." The emphasis is on atmosphere and psychological realism, with stories about drug-induced visions, pseudo-demonic lovers, and alternative realities. Readers who enjoy subtle horror mixed with magical realism, and those who like the horrors of everyday life, will find this collection excellent. **Similar titles:** *Darkness Divided*, John Shirley; *Escaping Purgatory*, Gary A. Braunbeck and Alan M. Clark; *Smoke Signals*, Octavio Ramos *Jr.; Dial Your Dreams*, Robert A. Weinberg.

> *Demons • Drugs • Fantasy • Marriage • Psychosexual Horror • Time Travel • Undercliffe, Errol (character)*

Ghosts and Grisly Things. *New York: Tom Doherty, 2000, ©1998. 300p.* These twenty tales will appeal to readers who enjoy the classic tale of terror. Stories range from supernatural terror to psychological studies of characters forced to confront the phantoms of their minds. **Similar titles:** *Whispers in the Night*, Basil Copper; *Talking in the Dark*, Dennis Etchison; *Don't Dream*, Donald Wandrei; *The Haunted Looking Glass*, Edward Gorey (editor); *Ghost Stories of Edith Wharton*, Edith Wharton.

> *Revenge*

The Height of the Scream. *London: W. H. Allen-Star, 1976. 208p.* This collection contains sixteen lesser known stories by Campbell, including "The Scar," about a man who meets his doppelgänger; "Jack's Little Friend," a second person narrative in which the reader is made into a serial killer who has found the box believed to have been where Jack the Ripper kept his victims' organs; and "Cellars," wherein a couple in Liverpool discovers and explores an eerie underground series of catacombs. As with most of Campbell's fiction, this book will appeal to fans of traditional horror and British subtlety. **Similar titles:** *13 Stories*, Ed Cain; *Don't Dream*, Donald Wandrei; *Escaping Purgatory*, Gary A. Braunbeck and Alan M. Clark.

> *Alter Ego • Cursed Objects • England • Jack the Ripper Murders •*
> *Liverpool, England • Religion—Voodoo • Serial Killers • Subterranean*
> *Monsters*

Scared Stiff. *New York: Warner Books, 1987. 173p.* These seven stories are not typical of Campbell's usual proper British style, yet they show that he can excel in many subgenres, including erotic horror. Bordering on the weird tale or "strange story," tales like "The Other Woman" and "Lilith's" present readers with characters who visit the darkest recesses of the human mind, discovering the connection between death and sex. Perhaps the finest collection of erotic horror stories published to date, *Scared Stiff* challenges the reader, as Campbell does not offer tidy or happy endings. **Similar titles:** *Love in Vein*, Poppy Z. Brite (editor); *Six Inch Spikes*, Edo von Belkom; *Embraces*, Paula Guran (editor).

> *Drugs • Eroticism • Fantasy • Gothicism • Necrophilia • Psychosexual*
> *Horror • Revenge • Sado-Masochism • Witchcraft*

Strange Things and Stranger Places. *New York: Tor, 1993. 256p.* Tor presents ten tales of dark fantasy, horror, and dystopian science fiction by Campbell, arguably the best writer in the genre. The collection is unique in that it includes his juvenilia, pieces like "Cat and Mouse" and "Medusa," as well as the more polished and experimental piece from mid-career, "Needing Ghosts." This text also includes an introduction by Campbell, in which he gives brief background material on the stories. **Similar titles:** *13 Stories*, Ed Cain; *Don't Dream*, Donald Wandrei; *Escaping Purgatory*, Gary A. Braunbeck and Alan M. Clark.

> *England • Fantasy • Haunted Houses • Science Fiction • Zombies*

Waking Nightmares. *New York: Tor, 1991. 273p.* These nineteen tales, published between 1980 and 1989, emphasize childhood and the fears associated with it. In addition, this collection includes some extremely clever self-referential tales about horror writers, omnibus editors, and professional booksellers. As Campbell states in his introduction to *Waking Nightmares*, these stories are for the most part traditional ghost stories, in the vein of M. R. James and Joseph Sheridan Le Fanu, so they will appeal to fans of gentle reads and subtle horror. **Similar titles:** *Whispers in the Night*, Basil Copper; *Talking in the Dark*, Dennis Etchison; *Don't Dream*, Donald Wandrei; *The Haunted Looking Glass*, Edward Gorey (editor); *Ghost Stories of Edith Wharton*, Edith Wharton.

> *Childhood • Cursed Objects • England • Gothicism • Liverpool, England •*
> *Revenge • Witchcraft • Writer as Character • Zombies*

Capes, Bernard Edward Joseph.

The Black Reaper. *Hugh Lamb (editor). Ashcroft, B.C.: Ash-Tree Press, 1998, ©1989. 227p.* Until his death in 1918, Bernard Capes was a prolific, talented, and highly regarded author of short stories, reviews, articles, and more than forty novels. Among his short stories were some of the most imaginative tales of terror of his era: stories of werewolves and the Wandering Jew, of lost souls and vengeful suicides, of horrors from beyond the grave that enfold the unsuspecting. This new edition is augmented tales that have not been seen since their original book publication more than eighty years ago. **Similar titles:** *The Cold Embrace and*

Other Ghost Stories, Mary Elizabeth Braddon; *Correlated Contents*, James Ambuehl; *The Terror By Night*, E. F. Benson; *More Binscombe Tales*, John Whitbourn.

Haunted Houses • Revenge • Revenging Revenants

Castle, Mort.

In Memoriam: Papa, Blake, and HPL. *Kansas City, Mo.: Dark Tales, 1999. 32p.* Ernest Hemingway as a cranky old man in purgatory and Robert Bloch as a writing student are featured in this chapbook collection of two tales, "The Old Man and the Dead" and "Teachers." Castle's emphasis is on the cleverness of the story rather than on horrific images or plot. **Similar titles:** *Dystopia*, Richard Christian Matheson; *Zom Bee Moo Vee*, Mark McLaughlin; *Filthy Death: The Leering Clown*, Joseph Moore and Brett A. Savory; *Tales of Love and Death*, W. H. Pugmire.

Afterlife, The • Bloch, Robert (character) • Hemingway, Ernest (character) • Humor • Lovercraft, H. P. (character) • Miskatonic University • Writer as Character

Chambers, Robert W.

Out of the Dark. *Hugh Lamb (editor). Ashroft, B.C.: Ash-Tree Press, 1998. 200p.* Robert William Chambers (1865–1933) was one of America's most popular authors of his time. An early interest in art was eventually turned into a writing career, and his first book, *In the Quarter*, was based on his experiences in France as an art student. Its success was sufficient to encourage him to try a second book, *The King in Yellow* (1895), which turned out to be an instant success and started Chambers on a writing career that lasted forty years. For this volume, the first of a two-volume collection of supernatural tales from Ash-Tree Press, Hugh Lamb has selected the finest of the stories written in the period prior to 1900. **Similar titles:** *Correlated Contents*, James Ambuehl; *More Binscombe Tales*, John Whitbourn; *The Passenger*, E. F. Benson; *Alone with the Horrors*, Ramsey Campbell.

Artist as Character • France

Out of the Dark, Volume 2. *Hugh Lamb (editor). Ashroft, B.C.: Ash-Tree Press, 1998. 206p.* In this volume Hugh Lamb has selected the best of the author's weird fiction from the post-1900 period. There is an introduction by Lamb, which provides further information about the author, who was, in his heyday, called "the most popular writer in America." **Similar titles:** *Correlated Contents*, James Ambuehl; *More Binscombe Tales*, John Whitbourn; *The Passenger*, E. F. Benson; *Alone with the Horrors*, Ramsey Campbell.

Paleobiologist as Character • Maritime Horror • Magic

Champion de Crespigny, Rose.

Norton Vyse, Psychic. *Jack Adrian (editor). Ashcroft, B.C.: Ash-Tree Press, 1999. 97p.* Adrian has collected stories written by Champion de Crespigny in 1919 for David Whitelaw's *Premier Magazine*. These tales about Norton Vyse, a psychic investigator, exhibit her plotting and writing skills. **Similar titles:** *Aylmer Vance, Ghost-Seer*, Alice Askew and Claude Askew; *The Complete John Silence Stories*, Algernon Blackwood; The Black Oak Series, Charles Grant; *Death from the Woods*, Brigitte Aubert.

Clairvoyant as Character • Parapsychology

Christensen, Jo-Anne.

Ghosts, Werewolves, Witches and Vampires. *Edmonton, Alb.: Lone Pine Publishing, 2001. 224p.* Seventeen oral tales concerned with the supernatural in Canada and the United States are divided into four sections based on the type of creature in the tale: witches, werewolves, vampires, and ghosts. Cristensen's emphasis in this collection is on transcribing or transforming these narratives into horror tales, and she does so admirably.

As she states in her introduction, these are all stories "grounded in fact" but written with a flair for dramatics. **Similar titles:** *Haunted Houses*, Nancy Roberts; *San Diego Specters*, John J. Lamb; *Ghosts and Haunts of the Civil War*, Christopher K. Coleman (editor).

> *Folklore • Ghosts • Haunted Houses • Shapeshifters • Vampires • Werewolves • Witches*

Clegg, Douglas.

 **The Nightmare Chronicles.** *New York: Leisure, 1999. 360p.* This collection of thirteen stories related in a unique frame tale technique tells of the young victim of a kidnapping who forces his captors to listen to tales of violence and horror. Clegg crosses lines and treats various taboo subjects in this collection. **Similar titles:** *Are You Loathsome Tonight?* Poppy Z. Brite; *Frights of Fancy*, J. N. Williamson; *Tales from the Hood* (film); *The Asylum*, Victor Heck (editor).

> *Alternative Literature • Cannibalism • Human Sacrifice • India • Mind Control • Mythology • Psychosexual Horror • Religion—Christianity • Religion—Paganism • Shapeshifters • Witchcraft*

Cole, Alonzo Deen.

The Witch's Tale. *Yorktown Heights, N.Y.: Dunwich Press, 1998. 253p.* Dunwich Press has collected thirteen radio dramas by Cole, with subject matter ranging from demons, to werewolves, to vampires. It includes photos of the original *Witch's Tale* radio program, as well as program notes and an introduction and epilogue by Miriam Wolfe, one of Cole's radio actors, making it different than the usual horror fare but enjoyable nonetheless, especially to fans of radio and of easy reads. **Similar titles:** *Edgar Allan Poe: Thirty-two Stories*, Edgar Allan Poe; *Into the Mummy's Tomb*, John Richard Stephens (editor); *The Haunted Looking Glass*, Edward Gorey (editor).

> *Demons • Fantasy • Radio • Shapeshifters • Vampire Hunters • Vampires • Weird Science • Werewolves • Witches*

Coleman, Christopher K.

Ghosts and Haunts of the Civil War. *Nashville, Tenn.: Rutledge Press, 2000. 178p.* Coleman rewrites thirty-six tales of Civil War related ghost material, including stories about Nat Turner, John Brown, and Abraham Lincoln. Stories are brief and to the point, and are excellent for fans of gentle reads. Coleman also includes two appendices listing Civil War related ghost tours. **Similar titles:** *Civil War Ghosts*, Martin Harry Greenberg, Frank McSherry Jr. and Charles G. Waugh; *The Moonlight Road and Other Ghost and Horror Stories*, Ambrose Bierce; *Classic Ghost Stories*, John Grafton (editor); *Southern Blood*, Lawrence Schmiel and Martin H. Greenberg.

> *African-American Characters • Ghosts • Haunted Houses • History, Use of • Lincoln, Abraham (character) • Racism • South, The • War—American Civil War*

Collins, Nancy A.

Avenue X, and Other Dark Streets. *Philadelphia: Xlibris, 2000. 290p.* Collins presents thirteen short stories, including "The Sign of the ASP," "Billy Fearless," "Furies in Black Leather," and "Avenue X." In one tale, Cleopatra attempts to obtain and keep power with the help of a vampire, while in others Robin Hood discovers he has an evil twin, and Sonya Blue comes for vampire wannabees. **Similar titles:** *13 Stories*, Ed Cain; *Historical Hauntings*, Jean Rabe and Martin H. Greenberg; *The Bubba Chronicles*, Selena Rosen; *Strange Twists of Fate*, James K. Burk.

> *Blue, Sonya (character)* • *Cleopatra (character)* • *Haunted Houses* • *Magic* • *New York City* • *Private Investigator as Character* • *Robin Hood (character)* • *Twins* • *Vampires* • *Vampire's Point of View*

Collins, Wilkie.

Wilkie Collins: The Complete Shorter Fiction. *Julian Thompson (editor). New York: Carroll & Graff, 1995. 925p.* This collection of Collins's short fiction includes approximately a dozen of his ghost stories and tales of the occult. These tales will appeal to readers who enjoy British subtlety and the traditional horror tale, particularly those who are fond of Edgar Allan Poe and Henry James. Similar title: *Best Ghost and Horror Stories*, Bram Stoker; *The Ghost Stories of Edith Wharton*, Edith Wharton; *Tales of Unease*, Arthur Conan Doyle; *Whispers in the Night*, Basil Copper.

> *Dreams* • *Ghosts* • *Gothicism* • *Mind Control* • *Obsession* • *Revenging Revenant* • *Twins* • *Victorian England*

Copper, Basil.

Whispers in the Night: Stories of the Mysterious and the Macabre. *Minneapolis, Minn.: Fedogan & Bremer, 1999. 271p.* Copper's writing is elegant yet straightforward in these eleven stories that range from the weird tale, to the Poe-esque twisted plot story, to the traditional ghost story. Emphasis is on suspense. Stephen Jones adds an introduction to the little known writer, who will appeal to those who like traditional horror. **Similar titles:** *Wilkie Collins: The Complete Shorter Fiction*, Wilkie Collins; *Ghosts and Grisly Things*, Ramsey Campbell; *Don't Dream*, Donald Wandrei; *Selected Tales*, Edgar Allan Poe; *Thank You for the Flowers*, Scott Nicholson.

> *Artist as Character* • *Cursed Objects* • *Haunted Houses* • *Gothicism* • *London, England* • *Obsession* • *Religion—Satanism* • *Weird Science*

Cowles, Frederick Ignatius.

The Night Wind Howls: Complete Supernatural Stories. *Hugh Lamb (editor). Ashcroft, B.C.: Ash-Tree Press, 1999. 391p.* When Frederick Cowles died in 1948, he left behind two collections of supernatural fiction: *The Horror of Abbot's Grange* and *The Night Wind Howls*, which rank among the rarest books in the genre. Cowles, an admirer of M. R. James, Bram Stoker, Joseph Sheridan Le Fanu, and Edgar Allan Poe, drew on all of these influences for his tales, which range from the horrific to the gently sentimental. *The Night Wind Howls* includes all sixty-one of Frederick Cowles's supernatural stories, as well as an account of true hauntings written by Cowles and never before reprinted. **Similar titles:** *Casting the Runes*, M. R. James; *Selected Tales*, Edgar Allan Poe; *In a Glass Darkly*, Joseph Sheridan Le Fanu; *The Jewel of the Seven Stars*, Bram Stoker.

> *Cursed Objects* • *Haunted Houses* • *Maritime Horror* • *Religion—Voodoo* • *Revenge* • *Revenging Revenant*

Doyle, Arthur Conan.

Tales of Unease. *Hertfordshire, England: Wordsworth Editions, 2000. 208p.* Fifteen horror tales from the legendary creator of Sherlock Holmes range from gratuitously gruesome revenge stories, to traditional ghost stories, to tales of aliens and underground monsters. This is a rare find for most fans of the genre, who know Doyle only as a detective story writer. **Similar titles:** *Edgar Allan Poe: Selected Tales*, Edgar Allan Poe; *A Bottomless Grave and Other Victorian Tales of Terror*, Hugh Lamb (editor); *Classic Ghost Stories*, John Grafton (editor); *Ghost Stories of Henry James*, Henry James.

*Academia • Aliens • Mummies • Parapsychology • Revenge •
Subterranean Monsters • Torture*

Duffy, Steve.

The Night Comes On. *Ashcroft, B.C.: Ash-Tree Press, 1998. 278p.* In sixteen
stories, Steve Duffy evokes the Golden Age of the ghost story with practiced
ease. Set mainly in the period between the world wars, the stories are con-
sciously Jamesian in style and setting. They feature libraries and academics and
great old country houses, colleges and branch railway stations and cathedrals;
and, of course, any number of things less easily defined, which lie in wait for the
foolish, the unwary, or the unlucky. **Similar titles:** *Casting the Runes*, M. R.
James; *In a Glass Darkly*, Joseph Sheridan Le Fanu; *The Complete John Silence
Stories*, Algernon Blackwood; *Don't Dream*, Donald Wandrei.

> *Academia • Clergy as Character • Cursed Objects • Haunted Houses •
> Revenging Revenant*

Eddy, C[lifford]. M[artin], Jr.

Exit into Eternity: Tales of the Bizarre and Supernatural. *Narragansett,
R.I.: Fenham Publishing, 2000, ©1973. 194p.* Fenham Publishing resurrects
four short stories and a fragment of a novella by Eddy, who was a friend and
co-author of H. P. Lovecraft in the 1920s. Tales include "Pilgrimage of Peril," in
which a scientist crosses the realm between the human world and the netherworld; "The Vengeful Vision," wherein a miserly businessman is visited by the
ghost of a young girl he'd killed out of jealousy twenty-five years before; and
"Miscreant from Murania," about a vampire who is hunted down and trapped.
Being similar to the fiction of Lovecraft and that of M. R. James, *Exit into Eternity* will appeal to fans of traditional fiction, especially those who like surprise
endings. **Similar titles:** *The Shadow Out of Time*, H. P. Lovecraft; *Tales of H. P.
Lovecraft: Major Works*, H. P. Lovecraft; *Cold Print*, Ramsey Campbell; *The
Loved Dead*, H. P. Lovecraft et al.

> *Mind Control—Self-Hypnosis • Parapsychology • Revenging Revenant •
> Vampire Hunters • Weird Science • Writer as Character*

Etchison, Dennis.

The Death Artist. *New York: Leisure, 2002. 282p.* Leisure Books has collected
twelve of Etchison's previously published stories in one volume here, which will
appeal to fans of "the horror of the ordinary." Etchison is a master of the eerie.
The collection includes "The Dog Park," "On Call," "No One You know," and
"The Scar." **Similar titles:** *Don't Dream*, Donald Wandrei; *Alone with the
Horrors*, Ramsey Campbell; *Scared Stiff*, Ramsey Campbell; *Ordinary Horror*,
David Searcy.

> *Ghosts • Parallel Universe • Revenging Revenant*

Talking in the Dark: Selected Stories of Dennis Etchison. *Lancaster, Pa.:
Stealth Press, 2001. 355p.* Ramsey Campbell calls Etchison the best short story
writer in the horror genre today. In these twenty-four stories, Etchinson's main
characters are ordinary humans who suddenly find themselves thrust into *Twilight Zone*-type unreality, where dark and sinister forces have taken over and
control their every move. The tales are well written, with emphasis on characterization and dialogue over action or atmosphere. **Similar titles:** *Ghosts and*

Grisly Things, Ramsey Campbell; *The House*, Bentley Little; *Boy in the Water*, Stephen Dobyns, *Ordinary Horror*, David Searcy.

> *California • Clairvoyant as Character • Gothicism • Hispanic-American Characters • Native-American Characters • Serial Killers • Writer as Character • Zombies*

Gorman, Ed.

The Dark Fantastic. *New York: Leisure, 2001. 391p.* These seventeen short stories range from tales of serial killers, to the chronicles of a time-traveling professor, to the story of a battered wife who takes revenge on her husband. Gorman writes with a flair for dialogue and action. The stories were originally published between 1989 and 2000. **Similar titles:** *Robert Bloch's Psychos*, Robert Bloch (editor); *The Poker Club*, Ed Gorman; *The Cleanup*, John Skipp and Craig Spector; *The Event*, Donald Silverman.

> *Chicago, Illinois • Domestic Violence • Medical Horror • Midwest, The • Police Officer as Character • Psychosexual Horror • Revenge • Science Fiction • Serial Killers • Time Travel*

Grimm, Jacob, (editor).

Grimm's Grimmest. *San Francisco: Chronicle Books, 1997. 144p.* These twenty-two fairy tales are based on the Grimm Brothers' 1822 edition (the contemporary horror literature of its day), before the stories became white-washed Disney productions. Maria Tatar, a scholar of fairy tales who writes the book's introduction, says that the stories in the genre are "the ancestors of our urban legends about vanishing hitchhikers and cats accidentally caught in the dryer or as the preliterate equivalents of tabloid tales describing headless bodies found in topless bars." **Similar titles:** *The Tooth Fairy*, Graham Joyce; *Strangewood*, Christopher Golden; *Sleepy Hollow* (film).

> *Fairy Tales*

Hand, Elizabeth.

Last Summer at Mars Hill. *New York: HarperPrism, 1998. 325p.* As always, Hand's work is an eerie blend of new age beliefs, popular culture, and classical mythology. In this collection, Hand continues to skillfully blend old and new, and her writing is reminiscent of the works of Joseph Sheridan Le Fanu. **Similar titles:** *Through a Glass Darkly* and *Green Tea and Other Stories*, Joseph Sheridan Le Fanu; *Black Light*, Elizabeth Hand; *The 37th Mandala*, Mark Laidlaw.

> *Fantasy • New Age • Parapsychology • Weird Science*

Hautala, Rick.

Bedbugs. *Baltimore: Cemetery Dance Publications, 1999. 393p.* Hautala presents twenty-six tales of supernatural and psychological horror, including "The Back of My Hands," "The Voodoo Queen," "Rubies and Pearls," and "Breakfast at Earl's." **Similar titles:** *Flowers from the Moon and Other Lunacies*, Robert Bloch; *The Dark Fantastic*, Ed Gorman; *Dial Your Dreams*, Robert Weinberg.

> *Religion—Voodoo • Revenge • Revenging Revenant • Shapeshifters*

Hivert-Carthew, Annick. The Ghostly Lights Series.

Ghostly Lights: Great Lakes Lighthouse Tales of Terror. *Chelsea, Mich.: Wilderness Adventure Books, 1998. 162p.* Hivert-Carthew penned twenty-two tales based on folklore of twenty-one different lighthouses in the Great Lakes area. Each tale is a fictionalized version of the folk tale and is followed by a brief note on the history of the tale and lighthouse. Hivert-Carthew also includes a map illustrating the locations of each lighthouse.

Similar titles: *Ghostly Lights Return*, Annick Carthew-Hivert; *San Diego Specters*, John J. Lamb; *Haunted Houses*, Nancy Roberts; *Ghost and Haunts of the Civil War*, Christopher K. Coleman.

> *Canada • Ghosts • Great Lakes, The • Haunted Houses • Lighthouses •*
> *Maritime Horror • Revenging Revenant • Secret Sin*

Ghostly Lights Return: More Great Lakes Lighthouse Fiends and Phantoms. *Manchester, Mich.: Wilderness Adventure Books, 1999. 184p.* Sixteen tales continue the folkloric chronicling of the lighthouses in the Great Lakes area. Each story is followed by a discussion of the lighthouse's history, as well as the source of the story. This collection is a good gentle read for fans with eclectic tastes. **Similar titles:** *Ghostly Lights*, Annick Carthew-Hivert; *Civil War Ghosts*, Martin Harry Greenberg (editor) et al; The Lone Pine Ghost Stories Series, various authors.

> *Folklore • Ghosts • Great Lakes, The • Isolation • Lighthouses •*
> *Maritime Horror • Revenge • Vampires*

Hodgson, William Hope.

Gothic Horror: The Ghost Pirates and Carnacki the Ghost Finder. *Philadelphia: Xlibris, 2000. 335p.* Dreadful forces lurk just beneath the veneer of reality and may surface at any moment to drag humans to destruction. The second of these novellas, *Carnacki, the Ghost Finder*, is about a Victorian psychic detective. **Similar titles:** *The Complete John Silence Stories*, Algernon Blackwood; *Aylmer Vance, Ghost-Seer*, Alice Askew and Claude Askew; *Full Moon, Bloody Moon*, Lee Driver; The Black Oak Series, Charles Grant.

> *Ghosts • Maritime Horror • Pirates • Private Investigator as Character •*
> *Revenging Revenant • Victorian England*

Hoogson, Sheila.

The Fellow Travellers. *Ashcroft, B.C.: Ash-Tree Press, 1998. 198p.* When M. R. James penned his essay "Stories I Have Tried to Write," he left several plot ideas for, as he wrote, "the benefit of somebody else." One writer who appreciated James's generosity was Sheila Hoogson, who determined to bring some of his ideas to fruition. Thus in this collection we find James involved in a witch hunt in southwest England, searching for the missing pages of a mediaeval text in Scotland, puzzling over mysterious happenings in the ruins of Medborough Abbey, and piecing together the strange events behind the account of a centuries-old trial. **Similar titles:** *Casting the Runes*, M. R. James; *The Complete John Silence Stories*, Algernon Blackwood; *Aylmer Vance, Ghost-Seer*, Alice Askew and Claude Askew; *More Annotated H. P. Lovecraft*, H. P. Lovecraft.

> *Clergy as Character • England • Haunted Houses • James, Montague*
> *Rhodes (character) • Revenging Revenant • Scotland*

Hubbard, June.

Careful What You Wish. *Rochester Hills, Mich.: Chameleon Publishing, 1998. 93p.* In the tradition of W. W. Jacobs, June Hubbard's nine original tales explore what happens when we actually get what we wish for. **Similar titles:** *Night Voices*, June Hubbard; *Confessions of a Ghoul*, M. F. Korn.

> *Wish Fulfillment*

Night Voices. *Atlanta, Ga.: Chameleon Publishing, 1998. 157p.* In *Night Voices*, June Hubbard retells stories from Appalachia she heard as a girl, tales that shouldn't be allowed to die. **Similar titles:** *Careful What You Wish*, June Hubbard; *Confessions of a Ghoul*, M. F. Korn.

Appalachia • Gothicism • The South

Jackson, Shirley.

The Lottery and Other Stories. *New York: Farrar, Straus & Giroux: 1982. 306p.* Twenty-five stories by the author of *The Haunting of Hill House* expose the elitism and racism of the self-satisfied and make the familiar uncanny. The collection includes "The Lottery," "The Daemon Lover," "Come Dance with Me in Ireland," and "A Fine Old Firm." **Similar titles:** *Collector of Hearts*, Joyce Carol Oates; *I Am Legend* and *The Incredible Shrinking Man*, Richard Matheson; *Skeleton Crew*, Stephen King.

🎧 audio download

Afterlife • Gothicism • Human Sacrifice

Jackson, Thomas Graham.

Six Ghost Stories. *Richard Dalby (editor). Ashcroft, B.C.: Ash-Tree Press, 1999, ©1919. 243p.* Sir Thomas Graham Jackson (1835–1924) was celebrated in his day as one of the foremost architects in England. Jackson was also a keen traveler and antiquarian, whose journeys took him throughout Britain and Europe. His wide-ranging interests were to stand him in good stead when, later in his life, he wrote several traditional ghost stories for the amusement of family and friends. These tales were collected in book form in 1919; and, with one exception, none of the stories has been reprinted since, until now. **Similar titles:** *Casting the Runes* and *Ghost Stories of an Antiquary*, M. R. James; *The Fellow Travellers*, Sheila Hoogson; *In a Glass Darkly*, Joseph Sheridan Le Fanu.

Cursed Objects • Ghosts • Haunted Houses • Italy • London, England • Revenging Revenant • Subterranean Monsters

James, Henry.

Ghost Stories of Henry James. *Hertfordshire, England: Wordsworth Classics, 2001. 344p.* This edition of Henry James's supernatural tales contains an excellent introduction and very helpful endnotes, both contributed by Martin Scofield of the University of Kent at Canterbury. Wordsworth Classics collects ten of James's ghost stories, including his two most famous pieces, "The Turn of the Screw" and "The Jolly Corner." This is a gentle read that will appeal to academic fans of the genre, as well as fans of James's erudite writing style and subtle sensibility. His ghosts are neither wholly supernatural nor metaphorical, but a combination of both. **Similar titles:** *Ghost Stories of Edith Wharton*, Edith Wharton; *Best Ghost and Horror Stories*, Bram Stoker; *Green Tea and Other Stories* and *In a Glass Darkly*, Joseph Sheridan Le Fanu; *Ordinary Horror*, David Searcy.

Alter Ego • Cursed Objects • Family Curse • Ghosts • Gothicism • Haunted Houses • Psychosexual Horror • Secret Sin • War

James, M. R.

Casting the Runes, and Other Ghost Stories. *New York: Oxford University Press, 1998. 352p.* James was a professor and antiquarian who set most of his stories in the contemporary (early 1900s) ruins of England's medieval past. The title story is a marvelous tale of a vicious crank whose occult revenge is turned against him. Other stories included are "Canon Alberic's Scrap-Book," "Number 13," "Count Magnus," and " 'Oh, Whistle, and I'll Come to You, My Lad'." This is probably one of the most comprehensive collections of James's work. **Similar titles:** *In a Glass Darkly* and *Green Tea and Other Stories*, Joseph Sheridan Le Fanu; *The Terror by Night*, E. F. Benson; *Fellow Travellers*, Sheila Hoogson.

    Cursed Objects • Demons • Ghosts • Haunted Houses • Magic •
    Parapsychology • Revenging Revenant

Ghost Stories of an Antiquary. *Baltimore: Penguin Books, 1974, ©1911. 303p.* M. R. James's strength is his subtle way of incorporating horror into a tale, since it is what we do not see or what we think we hear that is truly frightening. This particular work is the single most influential and most sold collection of ghost stories in history, and it includes the classics "The Ash-Tree," "Count Magnus," and "O Whistle and I'll Come to You My Lad." **Similar titles:** *In a Glass Darkly* and *Green Tea and Other Stories*, Joseph Sheridan Le Fanu; *The Terror by Night*, E. F. Benson; *Fellow Travelers*, Sheila Hoogson.

    Cursed Objects • Demons • Ghosts • Haunted Houses • Magic •
    Parapsychology • Revenging Revenant • Spiders

Jewett, Sarah Orne.

Lady Ferry, and Other Uncanny People. *Ashcroft, B.C.: Ash-Tree Press, 1998. 146p.* The supernatural plays a pivotal role in many of the works of Sarah Orne Jewett, reflecting her fascination with worlds both seen and unseen. Ghosts, the afterlife, and telepathy all play their part in many of Jewett's stories. In these stories, we meet the (possibly) immortal Lady Ferry; travel back to dark New England days for a tale of witchcraft; journey beyond the toll-gate with a little girl searching for unearthly delights; watch as Death himself comes to live in a haunted house; and encounter other uncanny people and places, all rooted firmly in the New England of a century ago. **Similar titles:** *Green Tea and Other Stories*, Joseph Sheridan Le Fanu; *The Moonlit Road and Other Ghost and Horror Stories*, Ambrose Bierce; *Fellow Travellers*, Sheila Hoogson; *Selected Tales*, Edgar Allan Poe.

    Death (character) • Gothicism • Haunted Houses • Immortality • New
    England • United States—19th Century • Witchcraft

Kilpatrick, Nancy.

Cold Comfort. *Grand View, Mo.: Dark Tales, 2001. 183p.* Kilpatrick presents twenty-seven weird tales that range from the dark fantastic to the horrific. Her prose is imagistic and poetic, with emphasis on suspense and surprise. The collection includes stories of ghosts, aliens, serial killers, cannibals, and outright demented human beings. **Similar titles:** *Extremities*, Kathe Koja; *The Tides*, Melanie Tem; *The Dress Lodger*, Sheri Holman.

    Cannibalism • Eroticism • Gothicism • Irish-American Characters •
    Obsession • Revenge • Serial Killers

The Vampire Stories of Nancy Kilpatrick. *Oakville, Ont.: Mosaic Press Canada, 2000. 192p.* In this collection of nineteen stories, Canada's Queen of the Undead, Nancy Kilpatrick, reflects on the dark side of humanity, including our desires for passion, longevity, power, creativity, and control. **Similar titles:** *Daughters of Darkness: Lesbian Vampire Stories*, Pam Keesey (editor); *Cold Comfort*, Nancy Kilpatrick; The American Vampire Series; Lawrence Schmiel and Martin H. Greenberg (editors).

    Immortality • Vampire's Point of View

King, Steven [as Richard Bachman].

The Bachman Books: Four Early Novels. *New York: Penguin, 1996. 692p.* Penguin collects four Richard Bachman novellas in a single volume: *Rage*, *The Long Walk*, *Roadwork*, and *The Running Man*. King includes the introduction "The Importance of Being Bachman." **Similar titles:** *Desperation*, Stephen King; *The Last Voice They Hear*, Ramsey Campbell; *The Illustrated Man*, Ray Bradbury; *William F. Nolan's Dark Universe*, William F. Nolan.

Animals Run Rampant • High School • Maine • Obsession

King, Stephen.

Six Stories. *Bangor, Maine: Philtrum Press, 1997. 197p.* This short collection of dark fantasy by King includes two previously unpublished tales. Selections include "Lunch at the Gotham Cafe," "Autopsy Room Four," and "The Man in the Black Suit." **Similar titles:** *Houses Without Doors*, Peter Straub; *Frights of Fancy*, J. N. Williamson; *The Nightmare Chronicles*, Douglas Clegg.

Fantasy

Skeleton Crew. *New York: Putnam, 1985. 512 p.* King's collection of psychological horror and campy weird tales is reminiscent of B-movie horror flicks from the 1950s and 1960s. In the book-length story "The Mist," a supermarket becomes the last bastion of humanity as a sort of acid fog menaces humanity. And in "Word Processor of the Gods," one can change reality with the stroke of a key. **Similar titles:** *The Illustrated Man*, Ray Bradbury; *The Incredible Shrinking Man*, Richard Matheson; *Attack of the 50 Foot Woman* (film); *Bubbas of the Apocalypse*, Selina Rosen.

🎧 audiotape

Fantasy • Maine

Kipling, Rudyard.

The Mark of the Beast and Other Horror Tales. *Mineola, N.Y.: Dover Publications, 2000. 188p.* Seventeen tales by Kipling, gathered in one volume for the first time, range from comic ghost stories to tales of psychological terror and the returning dead. **Similar titles:** *The Moonlit Road and Other Ghost and Horror Stories*, Ambrose Bierce; *The Complete John Silence Stories*, Algernon Blackwood; *The Black Reaper*, Bernard Edward Joseph Capes; *Edgar Allan Poe: Selected Tales*, Edgar Allan Poe.

England • Gothicism • Haunted Houses

Koja, Kathe.

Extremities. *New York: Four Walls, Eight Windows, 1998. 200p.* These sixteen stories explore the darker side of desire, love, and creativity. They are reminiscent of Poe's rambles of madmen, in which the horror comes from putting the everyday under a microscope, and will appeal to readers who like atmosphere, subtlety, and poetic language, rather than gore and action. **Similar titles:** *Embraces*, Paula Guran; *Viscera*, Cara Bruce (editor); The Love in Vein Series, Poppy Z. Brite; *Silk*, Caitlan R. Kiernan.

Artist as Character • Eroticism • Fantasy • Gothicism • Mythology • Obsession • Psychosexual Horror • Wish Fulfillment

Koontz, Dean.

Strange Highways. *New York: Warner Books, 1995. 561p.* Koontz's collection includes a novella about a young man who lives the same nightmare over and over again, as well as "The Black Pumpkin," "Miss Atilla the Hun," "Down in the Darkness," "Ollie's Hands," "Snatcher," "Trapped," "Bruno," "We Three," "Hardshell," "Kittens," "The Night of the

Storm," "Twilight of the Dawn," and "Chase." **Similar titles:** *Six Stories*, Stephen King; *The Nightmare Chronicles*, Douglas Clegg; *The Dark Fantastic*, Ed Gorman; *Night Freight*, Bill Pronzini.

🎧 audiotape

Alcoholism • Time Travel

Korn, M. F.

Aliens, Minibikes, and Other Staples of Suburbia. *Morton, Pa.: Silver Lake, 2001. 110p.* Korn's dark musings populate the pages of this thought-provoking collection, which includes tales of antique stores that sell anachronistic historical artifacts, carnivals that kidnap children to make mutants for future shows, and fishermen who catch 150-million-year-old fish. **Similar titles:** *The Illustrated Man*, Ray Bradbury; *Escaping Purgatory*, Gary A. Braunbeck and Alan M. Clark; *Zom Bee Moo Vee*, Mark McLaughlin; *Thank You for the Flowers*, Scott Nicholson.

Aliens • Alternative Literature • Baton Rouge, Louisiana • Childhood • Evolutionary Theory • Fantasy • Suburbia

Confessions of a Ghoul and Other Stories. *Morton, Pa.: Silver Lake Publishing, 2001. 118p.* This collection of several very short tales and a novella concerns itself with recluses and curmudgeons meeting people even stranger than themselves. During an all-nighter in the International House of Pancakes, a perpetual student speaks with several social misfits with varying predictions for the fate of humanity, an educated misanthrope corresponds with some barely literate, homicidal metal musicians, and a graduate student writes his thesis on the ghoul haunting the local cemetery. This is a humorous and witty collection of gentle southern gothic stories. **Similar titles:** *Collector of Hearts*, Joyce Carol Oates; *The Illustrated Man*, Ray Bradbury; *Dial Your Dreams*, Robert Weinberg; *Selected Tales*, Edgar Allan Poe.

🖱 CD rom, e-book

Academia • Baton Rouge, Louisiana • Cemeteries • Ghouls • Gothicism • Louisiana • New Orleans, Louisiana • Popular Culture

Lawrence, Margery H.

The Terraces of Night: Being the Further Chronicles of the "Club of the Round Table." *Richard Dalby (editor). Ashcroft, B.C.: Ash-Tree Press, 1999, ©1932. 199p.* Ash-Tree Press has reprinted yet another undeservedly forgotten volume of ghost stories with this collection. Lawrence favors traditional, subtle horror, as can be seen in many of her tales: An Englishman stationed on an island off Zanzibar learns too late the secret of "The Dogs of Pemba," while an antiquarian's new purchase proves even more morbid than he thinks in "The Death Strap." **Similar titles:** *The Cold Embrace*, Mary Elizabeth Braddon; *We've Been Waiting for You*, John Burke; *Out of the Dark*, Robert W. Chambers; *Norton Vyse, Psychic*, Rose Champion de Crespigny.

Africa • Cursed Objects • France • Ghosts • Revenge

Lebbon, Tim.

As the Sun Goes Down: Stories. *San Francisco: Night Shade Books, 2000. 248p.* Lebbon's collection of sixteen short stories is about unpleasant people doing disgusting things, including a mother who wishes to feed her child to lions and one boy leaving another in the clutches of a monster while bargaining with the other child for his possessions. *As the Sun Goes Down* is a 2001 Bram Stoker Award nominee. **Similar titles:** *13 Stories*, Ed Cain; *The Dark Fantastic*, Ed Gorman; *My Brain Escapes Me*, Robert Steven Rhine.

> *Fantasy*

Le Fanu, Joseph Sheridan.

Green Tea and Other Ghost Stories. *Mineola, N.Y.: Dover Publications, 1993, ©1945. 92p.* These four classic short stories by one of the nineteenth century's masters of the genre will appeal to the more sophisticated reader, and Le Fanu's British subtlety will be enjoyed by fans of gentle reads. Subject matter ranges from possession, to demonic manifestations, to murder. **Similar titles:** *A Bottomless Grave and Other Victorian Tales of Terror*, Hugh Lamb (editor); *Whispers in the Night*, Basil Copper; *Ghost Stories of Edith Wharton*, Edith Wharton; *Midnight Tales*, Bram Stoker.

> *Clergy as Character • Demons • Dogs • Dreams • England • Ghosts • Hesselius, Dr. Martin (character) • Ireland • Possession • Satan (character) • Scholar as Character • Sibling Rivalry*

In a Glass Darkly. *New York: Oxford University Press, 1999, ©1872. 347p.* These five stories were supposedly collected by Le Fanu's character Dr. Hesselius, a "metaphysical doctor" who is a sort of precursor of Bram Stoker's Abraham Van Helsing. Stories include "Green Tea," "The Familiar," "Mr. Justice Harbottle," "The Room in the Dragon Volant," and the classic novella *Carmilla*. **Similar titles:** *Best Ghost and Horror Stories*, Bram Stoker; *Ghosts and Grisly Things*, Ramsey Campbell; *Dial Your Dreams*, Robert Weinberg; *Classic Ghost Stories*, John Grafton (editor).

> *England • Ghosts • Gothicism • Hesselius, Dr. Martin (character)*

Ligotti, Thomas.

The Nightmare Factory. *New York: Carroll & Graf, 1996. 551p.* This selection of works from four Ligotti collections (*Songs of a Dead Dreamer*, *Grimscribe*, *Noctuary*, and *Teatro Grottesco and Other Tales*) includes a foreword by Poppy Z. Brite and is the winner of a Bram Stoker Award. **Similar titles:** *Cold Comfort*, Nancy Kilpatrick; *Zom Bee Moo Vee*, Mark McLaughlin; *Houses Without Doors*, Peter Straub; *In Memoriam Papa, Blake, and HPO*, Mort Castle.

> *Dreams • Fantasy*

Longyear, Barry B.

The Enemy Papers. *Clarkston, Ga.: White Wolf Publishing, 1998. 655p.* This collection contains a newly edited and expanded-by-the-author version of *Enemy Mine* and its two sequels, "The Last Enemy" and "The Tomorrow Testament," published together for the first time. A battle between the Dracs and humans becomes personal when a fighter pilot from each side crashes on a distant planet. Survival means overcoming their greatest enemy: their own rage. **Similar titles:** *I Am Legend*, Richard Matheson; *The Illustrated Man*, Ray Bradbury; *William F. Nolan's Dark Universe*, William F. Nolan.

> *Aliens • Dracs, The (characters) • Science Fiction • Talman, The • War*

Lovecraft, H. P.

More Annotated H. P. Lovecraft. *New York: Dell, 1999. 312p.* This illustrated volume of Lovecraft's popular tales, with annotations by S. T. Joshi and an introduction by Peter Cannon, includes "Herbert West—Reanimator," "Pickman's Model," "The Call of Cthulhu," "The Thing on the Doorstep," and "The Horror at Red Hook." **Similar titles:** *The Loved Dead and Other Revisons*, H. P. Lovecraft; *Ghoul*, Michael Slade; *Irrational Fears* and *Resume with Monsters*, William Spenser Browning.

Arkham Horrors, The • *Bloch, Robert (character)* • *Cthulhu Mythos* • *Dramatic Monologue* • *Epistolary Format* • *Haunted Houses* • *History, Use of* • *Miskatonic University* • *Necronomicon, The* • *New England* • *Parapsychology* • *Weird Science* • *West, Herbert (character)* • *Zombies*

Tales of H. P. Lovecraft: Major Works. *Joyce Carol Oates (editor). Hopewell, N.J.: Ecco Press, 1997. 328p.* Ten stories by Lovecraft show why he is the master of weird tales who influenced modern-day masters of the genre such as Stephen King and Ramsey Campbell. The book's introduction by editor Joyce Carol Oates explains how "Lovecraft initiated the fusion of the gothic tale and what would come to be defined as science fiction." Stories in this collection include "The Call of Cthluhu," "At the Mountains of Madness," and "The Music of Erich Zann." **Similar titles:** *Darklost*, Mick Farren; *The Lurker at the Threshold* and *More Annotated H. P. Lovecraft*, H. P. Lovecraft; *The Sand Dwellers*, Adam Niswander.

Cthulhu Mythos • *Science Fiction*

Lumley, Brian.

A Coven of Vampires. *Minneapolis, Minn.: Fedogan & Bremer, 1998. 228p.* Thirteen tales about various types of vampires by the author of The Necroscope Series range from first person narratives to fragmented experimental pieces, with emphasis always on suspense and plot twists. **Similar titles:** The American Vampire Series, Lawrence Schmiel and Martin W. Greenberg (editors); *Vampire Slayers*, Martin H. Greenberg and Elizabeth Ann Scarborough (editors); *Love in Vein*, Poppy Z. Brite (editor); *Dark Universe*, William F. Nolan.

Alternative Literature • *Fantasy* • *Museums* • *Science Fiction* • *Shapeshifters* • *Vampire as New Species* • *Vampires* • *Werewolves*

The Whisperer and Other Voices. *New York: Tor, 2001. 333p.* Lumley's latest collection of nine short stories concerns everyday people who, when confronted by extraordinary circumstances, are reduced to their more primitive desires. **Similar titles:** *Escaping Purgatory*, Gary A. Braunbeck and Alan M. Clark; *Careful What You Wish For*, June Hubbard; *The Lottery and Other Stories*, Shirley Jackson.

Fantasy • *Science Fiction*

Matheson, Richard.

I Am Legend. *New York: Tor, 1995. 312p.* This is a reissue of a collection of weird tales by Richard Matheson, including his well-known vampire novella, *I Am Legend*, a tale of a post-apocalyptic world overrun by vampires, which was later made into the film *The Omega Man.* Other stories included are "Dance of the Dead," "The Funeral," and "Dress of White Silk." **Similar titles:** *The Queen of Darkness*, Miguel Connor; *The Illustrated Man*, Ray Bradbury; *The Lottery and Other Stories*, Shirley Jackson; *Dark Universe*, William F. Nolan.

Apocalypse • *Epidemics* • *Los Angeles, California* • *Science Fiction* • *Vampire Hunters*

The Incredible Shrinking Man. *New York: Tor, 2001. 352p.* Matheson's classic novella, *The Incredible Shrinking Man*, tells the tale of a post-World War II world in which an unsuspecting man begins shrinking after being sprayed by a mysterious radioactive mist. The story was made into a film by Jack Arnold in 1957. Also included in this collection are nine other stories, including "Duel" (later made into a film in 1971 by Stephen Spielberg) and "Nightmare at 20,000 Feet" (which was made into an episode of *The Twilight Zone*). **Similar titles:** *The Incredible Shrinking Man* (film); *Dystopia*, Richard Christian Matheson; *Dial Your Dreams*, Robert Weinberg.

⌐ e-book

Science Fiction

Matheson, Richard Christian.

Dystopia: Collected Stories. *Springfield, PA: Gauntlet, 2000. 412p.* Sixty short stories by the screenwriter, producer, director and novelist, include one tale co-authored with his father, Richard Matheson. Readers who enjoy brief, to-the-point prose will enjoy Matheson's style. **Similar titles:** *Cold Comfort*, Nancy Kilpatrick; *Frights of Fancy*, J. N. Williamson; *Haunted Houses*, Nancy Roberts; *The Asylum*, Victor Heck (editor).

Alcoholism • Psychosexual Horror • Science Fiction • Serial Killers

McLaughlin, Mark.

Zom Bee Moo Vee and Other Freaky Shows. *Auburn, Wash.: Fairwood Press, 1999. 57p.* McLaughlin, in nine stories, poem series, and prose poems, effectively straddles the fence between experimental "art" literature and comic horror fiction. He assimilates images from film and pop culture to produce tales of gay men who are enchanted by female porn star werewolves, of actresses whose careers and lives are haunted by children's movie typecasting, and of film critics who find themselves in film festival hell. It will be extremely enjoyable for fans of academic style literature, and for those who are very familiar with the genre. **Similar titles:** *Deadfellas*, David Whitman; *Period*, Dennis Cooper; *In Memoriam: Papa, Blake, and HPL*, Mort Castle; *The Divinity Student*, Michael Cisco.

Actor as Character • Gay/Lesbian/Bisexual Characters • Humor • Journalist as Character • Werewolves

Mignola, Mike.

Hellboy: The Chained Coffin and Others. *Milwauke, Oreg.: Dark Horse Comics, 1998. 168p.* Hellboy's graphic novel adventures take him through a series of traditional European folk tales concerning monsters. Tales include "Almost Colossus," which incorporates parts of Mary Shelley's *Frankenstein*, "The Wolves of St. Augustus," and "The Iron Shoes." **Similar titles:** *Spawn, Book 8: Betrayal of Blood*, Todd McFarlane, Alan Moore, and Greg Capullo; The Witchblade Series, Christina Z. and David Wohl; *The Beast That Was Max*, Gerard Houarner.

✎ graphic novels

Afterlife, The • Bureau for Paranormal Research and Defense • Clergy as Character • Demons • England • Fantasy • Folklore • Graphic Novel • Hellboy (character) • Ireland • Parapsychology • Religion—Christianity • Romania • Shapeshifters • Werewolves

Nicholson, Scott.

Thank You for the Flowers: Stories of Suspense and Imagination. *Boone, N.C.: Parkway Publishers, 2000. 190p.* Thirteen weird tales range from a gripping tale of haunted ghosts, to a darkly comic story about a vampire Little Leaguer and his quest for acceptance, to an atmospheric dream vision about donor corpses that haunt the recipient of their organs, to a dramatic monologue by a paranoid schizophrenic inmate who claims that his mind is being read by famous horror novelists, who then steal his story ideas. Fans of Rod

Serling and Robert Aickman will enjoy Nicholson. **Similar titles:** *Dial Your Dreams*, Robert Weinberg; *The Others* (film); *The Sixth Sense* (film); *Escaping Purgatory*, Gary A. Braunbeck and Alan M. Clark; *The Illustrated Man*, Ray Bradbury.

> *Afterlife, The • Baseball • Dramatic Monologue • Dreams • Haunted Houses • High School • Medical Horror • Serial Killers • Vampires*

Nolan, William F.

William F. Nolan's Dark Universe: A Grandmaster of Suspense Collects His Best Stories. *Lancaster, Pa.: Stealth Press, 2001. 470p.* Nolan offers forty-one of his dark fantasy, horror, and dark science fiction tales published between 1956 and 1999. Readers with various interests, such as alternate realities, serial killer stories, and zombie fare, will find something to their liking here, all served up with a healthy dose of dark humor. Nolan's writing style will appeal to fans of traditional horror and of the weird tale, associated with the Golden Age of science fiction. **Similar titles:** *I Am Legend* and *The Incredible Shrinking Man*, Richard Matheson; *The Illustrated Man*, Ray Bradbury; *Don't Dream*, Donald Wandrei.

> *Afterlife, The • Alter Ego • Apocalypse • Science Fiction • Serial Killers • Zombies*

Oates, Joyce Carol.

The Collector of Hearts: New Tales of the Grotesque. *New York: Dutton, 1998. 321p.* Twenty-six modern gothic tales by Oates focus on the horrors of everyday life, such as surviving childhood intact. The book includes the frequently anthologized story "■■■■ (black rectangle)." **Similar titles:** *The Lottery and Other Stories*, Shirley Jackson; *A Bottomless Grave*, Hugh Lamb (editor); *The Ghost Stories of Edith Wharton*, Edith Wharton; *The Haunted Looking Glass*, Edward Gory (editor).

⏎ large print

> *Childhood • Gothicism • Grieving • Secret Sin*

Poe, Edgar Allan.

Edgar Allan Poe: Selected Tales. *David Van Leer (editor). New York: Oxford University Press, 1998. 338p.* Oxford University Press offers these twenty-four tales of terror by the father of modern psychological horror, including "The Fall of the House of Usher," "The Murders in the Rue Morgue," "The Masque of the Red Death," "The Pit and the Pendulum," "The Tell-Tale Heart," "The Black Cat," "The Purloined Letter," and "The Cask of Amontillado." The collection also includes bibliographical information, a selected bibliography of Poe collections, a biographical chronology, and endnotes. The introduction is by David Van Leer, professor of English at the University of California. **Similar titles:** *Tales of Unease*, Arthur Conan Doyle; *The Shadow Out of Time*, H. P. Lovecraft; *Talking in the Dark*, Dennis Etchison; *The Asylum*, Victor Heck (editor).

> *Dupin, C. Auguste (character) • Gothicism • Haunted Houses • New England • Obsession • Police Officer as Character • Revenge • Secret Sin • Twins • Usher, Madeleine (character) • Usher, Roderick (character)*

Selected Tales. *New York: Vintage, 1991. 436p.* Vintage collects stories by the father of American psychological horror and the detective story, including "The Tell-Tale Heart," "The Masque of the Red Death," "The Pit and the Pendulum,"

"The Fall of the House of Usher," "The Black Cat," and "The Cask of Amontillado." **Similar titles:** *The Moonlit Road and Other Ghost and Horror Stories*, Ambrose Bierce; *The Dark Fantastic*, Ed Gorman; *Naomi*, Douglas Clegg; *The Lurker at the Threshold*, H. P. Lovecraft.

> *Gothicism • New England • Revenge • Secret Sin • Twins • Usher, Madeleine (character) • Usher, Roderick (character)*

Thirty-two Stories. *Stuart Levine and Susan F. Levine (editors). Indianapolis, Ind.: Hackett Publishing, 2000. 385p.* One of the most well-crafted collections by the man considered to be the father of the modern horror tale, with explanatory notes describing each selected work. Levine and Levine include classics like "The Black Cat," "The Cask of Amontillado," and "The Fall of the House of Usher," as well as lesser known early works, such as "Metzengerstein" (Poe's first published story). This edition will prove useful to both Poe fans and Poe scholars. **Similar titles:** *Green Tea and Other Stories*, Joseph Sheridan Le Fanu; *Great Ghost Stories*, John Grafton (editor); *Tales of Love and Death*, W. H. Pugmire; *Strange Twists of Fate*, James K. Burk.

> *Death (character) • Demons • Diary Format • Gothicism • Grieving • Incest • Obsession • Revenge • Torture • Twins*

Pronzini, Bill.

Night Freight. *New York: Leisure, 2000. 343p.* Twenty-six short stories, some previously anthologized, span much of Pronzini's career from 1967 to the present day. Although the subject matter ranges from serial killers, to the mentally unstable, to werewolves, Pronzini's brand of horror never depends on supernatural explanations, and is a bit reminiscent of the *Night Gallery* television series in this regard. Pronzini is a master of dark suspense, in the vein of Robert Bloch. **Similar titles:** *Frights of Fancy*, J. N. Williamson; *The Nightmare Chronicles*, Douglas Clegg; *Six Stories*, Stephen King; *The Tormentor*, Bill Pronzini; *Shadow Games*, Ed Gorman.

> *Domestic Violence • Marriage • Obsession • Psychosis • Werewolves*

Pugmire, W. H.

Tales of Love and Death. *North Webster, Ind.: Delirium Books, 2001. 72p.* In the tradition of Lovecraft, Poe, and Henry James, these sixteen stories chronicle the relationship between the living and the dead, the real world and the supernatural. The collection includes the masterfully written tale, "Pale Trembling Youth," about a sixteen-year-old ghost that haunts an abandoned industriaplex. Stories tend to be brief, with emphasis on atmosphere, emotion, and language. **Similar titles:** *Selected Tales*, Edgar Allan Poe; *The Dead Inn*, Shane Ryan Staley; *Embraces*, Paula Guran (editor); *Cold Comfort*, Nancy Kilpatrick; *Extremities*, Kathe Koja.

> *Demons • Gay/Lesbian/Bisexual Characters • Ghosts • Homoeroticism • Miskatonic University • Necronomicon, The • Necrophilia • Sequa Valley • Splatterpunk • Suicide*

Ramos, Octavio, Jr.

Smoke Signals. *North Webster, Ind.: Delirium Books, 2001. 72p.* Eight stories that revolve around Native American characters emphasize times they are faced with the reality of the modern world and therefore face crises of faith. Tales range from traditional shamans coming of age stories to narratives set in prisons and on mean inner city streets, and the emphasis is on characterization. **Similar titles:** *Crota*, Owl Goingback, *Brass*, Robert J. Conley; *Skeleton Crew* and *The Green Mile*, Stephen King.

> *Demons • Magic • Native American Characters • Religion—Native American*

Rhine, Robert Steven.

My Brain Escapes Me. *Northville, Mich.: Sun Dog Press, 1999. 352p.* Rhine's eclectic collection of stories is about the horrors of consciousness while encased in mortal flesh. The title story concerns a rebellious cerebellum that longs to escape the bony confines of the cranium. "Fast Acting Xilotripimene" explores the possibilities of a drug that can prolong any one sensation for several weeks. A series of tales about Raoul, a low-life ex-cop, follow the exploits of an all-too-human protagonist whose downfall is the pleasures of the flesh. Rhine's hard-boiled and often humorous writing style makes for an original and disturbing collection. **Similar titles:** *Are You Loathsome Tonight?*, Poppy Z. Brite; *Viscera*, Cara Bruce (editor); *Six Inch Spikes*, Edo van Belkom; *Black Butterflies* and *Darkness Divided*, John Shirley.

Alter Ego • Drugs • Fantasy • Science Fiction • Splatterpunk

Roberts, Nancy.

Haunted Houses: Chilling Tales from American Homes. *3d ed. Guilford, Conn.: Globe Pequot, 1998, ©1995. 184p.* Roberts has ghost-written twenty-four short tales of haunted American dwellings, each one based on interviews with the local populace and with the curators of the homes. Stories include the Lizzie Borden House, Andrew Johnson's Home, and The Whaley House/Museum, which has been authenticated as "haunted" by the U. S. Chamber of Commerce. This quirky collection is a fun read for aficionados of haunted houses, and it includes photos of each home. **Similar titles:** *Ghosts and Haunts of the Civil War*, Christopher K. Coleman; *Ghostly Lights* and *Ghostly Lights Return*, Annick Hivert-Carthew.

California • Ghosts • Haunted Houses • History, Use of • New England • South, The

Rosen, Selina.

The Bubba Chronicles. *Alma, Ark.: Yard Dog Press, 2000. 126p.* Rosen collaborated on eleven tales with various other authors, including Bill Allen, Beverly Hale, and Brand Whitlock, producing stories about zombie prom dates, aliens that grow out of people's noses, men who are pushed to gruesome murder, and ghosts of high school football stars who plot revenge for their deaths. Stories are quirky and humorous, with emphasis on character and regional flavor. **Similar titles:** *Deadfellas*, David Whitman; *Bubbas of the Apocalypse*, Selina Rosen (editor); *The Televisionary Oracle*, Rob Brezsny; *The Licking Valley Coon Hunters Club*, Brian A. Hopkins.

Aliens • Demons • High School • Humor • Revenge • Revenging Revenant • Writer as Character • Zombies

Schow, David J.

Eye. *Burton, Mich.: Subterranean Press, 2000. 256p. Eye,* featuring thirteen tales of trap doors, keyholes and cover ups, will delight and scare readers. Schow presents the world's most scatalogical crime boss, spooky guys from outer space, monsters disguised as people, humans with powers no less monstrous, and Mexican wrestlers. This collection contains several rare stories, such as "2¢ Worth," plus several more appearing here for the first time, like "Watcher of the Skies." **Similar titles:** *Twelve Tales of Murder*, Jack Adrian; *The Evil Returns*, Hugh B. Cave; *Tales of Unease*, Arthur Conan Doyle.

Aliens • Organized Crime • Private Investigator as Character • Revenge

Seignolle, Claude.

The Nightcharmer and Other Tales of Claude Seignolle. *Eric Hollingsworth Deudon (translator). Boulder, Colo.: NetLibrary, 2000, ©1983. 115p.* Deudon translates eight gothic stories by Seignolle in this chapbook collection, which was originally published by the University of Texas A&M Press. **Similar titles:** *Death from the Woods*, Brigitte Aubert; *Norton Vyse, Psychic*, Rose Champion de Crespigny; *Thirty-Two Stories* and *Selected Tales*, Edgar Allan Poe.

⌐🖱 e-book

France • Gothicism

Shirley, John.

Black Butterflies. *New York: Leisure, 2001. 350p.* These sixteen tales of murder, addiction, obsession, and revenge emphasize plot twists and imagery. Shirley will appeal to readers who like graphic sexual and physiological description, and his stories range from tales of mind control and revenge, to tales of sexual decadence and torture, to tales of evil tattooists. **Similar titles:** *The Illustrated Man*, Ray Bradbury; *My Brain Escapes Me*, Robert Steven Rhine; *Viscera*, Cara Bruce (editor); *Embraces*, Paula Guran (editor); The Love in Vein Series, Poppy Z. Brite.

Alcoholism • Drugs • Eroticism • Fantasy • Revenge • Sado-Masochism • Splatterpunk

Darkness Divided. *Lancaster, Pa.: Stealth Press, 2001. 337p.* Twenty-two short stories about characters trapped in their own psychological hells take place in contemporary times and the not-so-distant future. These stories were originally published in various magazines and anthologies between 1976 and 2000, although the bulk of them were published after 1991. Even though the tales in this collection deal with similar themes to Shirley's other collections, they are much more traditional and subtle than the rest of his oeuvre, and will appeal to readers who enjoy his skilled narratives but are squeamish about his typical visceral decadence. **Similar titles:** *Alone with the Horrors*, Ramsey Campbell; *William F. Nolan's Dark Universe*, William F. Nolan; *Don't Dream*, Donald Wandrei; *Dial Your Dreams*, Robert Weinberg.

Alter Ego • Childhood • Computers • Fantasy • Psychosexual Horror • Sado-Masochism • Satan (character) • Science Fiction • Serial Killers

Silva, David B.

Through Shattered Glass. *Springfield, Pa.: Gauntlet, 2001. 280p.* In this long-overdue story collection, which chills rather than terrifies, Silva displays a talent not unlike that of Ray Bradbury, delving into thought-provoking sentimentality, with leisurely pacing and strong character development rather than action and gore. His lead story, the Stoker Award-winning "The Calling," poignantly examines the pain caregivers endure watching a loved one die. Other standouts in this cohesive collection include "Slipping," a chronicle of an ad executive's mental disintegration as he begins to experience missing time in rapid acceleration; "Dwindling," a tribute to unwanted children who disappear as parents will them away and a probing comment on sexual abuse; and "Empty Vessels," an enlightening twist on the traditional vampire story. **Similar titles:** *Thank You for the Flowers*, Scott Nicholson; *Dial Your Dreams*, Robert Weinberg; *Escaping Purgatory*, Gary A. Braunbeck and Alan M. Clark.

Alcoholism • Childhood • Grieving • Vampire as New Species

Sipos, Thomas M.

Halloween Candy. *Santa Monica, Calif.: 1st Books Library, 2001. 250p.* In this "Jack O' Lantern of a book," Sipos collects his screenplay *Halloween Candy*, about a witch who gives mean children candy that causes them to have nightmares, along with a couple of the stories (including the highly original and gory "The Lady Who Ate Dolls") that chronicle the nightmares. Originally intended as a script for a film, *Halloween Candy* is a cornucopia of drama, short fiction, book reviews, and essays on the genre; it also contains an interview with *Dark Shadows* star Jonathan Frid. **Similar titles:** *Zeppelins West*, Joe R. Lansdale; *Zom Bee Moo Vee*, Mark McLaughlin; *The Witch's Tale*, Alonzo Deen Cole.

California • Dreams • Horror Movie Industry • Replicants • Splatterpunk • Torture • Vampires • Witches

Stoker, Bram.

Best Ghost and Horror Stories. *Mineola, N.Y.: Dover Books, 1997. 242p.* Fourteen of Stoker's stories from various earlier editions are compiled here. Although not all the selections deal with the ghostly and supernatural, they are always bizarre, and some are equal to Poe at his best. The collection includes "The Dualists," "A Dream of Red Hands," "The Secret of the Growing Gold," and "Dracula's Guest," which was omitted from Stoker's 1897 novel *Dracula*. Richard Dalby contributes the introduction. **Similar titles:** *In a Glass Darkly*, Joseph Sheridan Le Fanu; *Tales of Unease*, Arthur Conan Doyle; *A Bottomless Grave*, Hugh Lamb (editor); *Classic Ghost Stories*, John Grafton (editor).

Dracula (character) • Fantasy • Ghosts • Gothicism

Midnight Tales. *Chester Springs, Pa.: Dufour Editions, 1995. 182p.* A collection of Stoker's lesser works edited by Peter Haining, with a foreword by Christopher Lee, includes "Midnight Tales," "Bridal of Dead," The Man from Shorrox," and "The Spectre of Doom." **Similar titles:** *The Haunted Looking Glass*, Edward Gorey; *Great Ghost Stories*, John Grafton (editor); *Gothic Readings*, Rictor Norton (editor); *Green Tea and Others*, Joseph Sheridan Le Fanu.

Gothicism • Revenge

Straub, Peter.

Houses Without Doors. *New York: Signet, 1991. 454p.* Straub's first collection of short fiction reflects his elegant, hard-edged approach to horror, both psychological and occult oriented. It includes the novella *Blue Rose*. **Similar titles:** *Bending the Landscape*, Nicola Griffith and Stephen Pagel (editors); *The Loved Dead*, H. P. Lovecraft; *Nightmare Chronicles*, Douglas Clegg; *One Rainy Night*, Richard Laymon.

🎧 audiotape

Beevers, Harry (character) • Childhood • Dysfunctional Families

🅱🔺 **Magic Terror: Seven Tales.** *New York: Random House, 2000. 335p.* Straub presents seven stories of subtle horror about diverse subjects, ranging from the psychological profile of a desperate overweight kindergarten teacher; to the story of the Vietnam military commander who killed thirty innocent civilians; to the tale of a child who suffers from night terrors, which he translates into grotesque and eerie drawings that have a strange power all their own. This collection is more in the vein of traditional horror and gentle reads than Straub's usual fare, with more emphasis on characterization and psychology. **Similar titles:** The Blue Rose Trilogy, Peter Straub; *Dial Your Dreams*, Robert Weinberg; *Demons By Daylight*, Ramsey Campbell; *Escaping Purgatory*, Gary A. Braunbeck and Alan M. Clark.

⑨ audio download

> *Beevers, Harry (character) • Dreams • Gothicism • Grieving • Music—Jazz • Teacher as Character • War—Vietnam War*

Tem, Steve Rasnic.

City Fishing. *Seattle, Wash.: Silver Salamander Press, 2000. 340p*. This retrospective of Tem's short fiction covers two decades of writing and features three dozen stories. **Similar titles:** *The Nightmare Chronicles*, Douglas Clegg; *Scared Stiff*, Ramsey Campbell; *The Dark Fantastic*, Ed Gorman; *Extremities*, Kathe Koja.

> *Fantasy • Psychosexual Horror*

Tessier, Thomas.

Ghost Music and Other Tales. *Baltimore: Cemetery Dance Publications, 2000. 296p*. Thomas Tessier's first collection of short fiction consists of twenty tales ranging from science fiction, to Lovecraftian horror, to weird tales. In this collection, a woman's obsession with food causes her to morph into something that proves unfortunate for her neighbor, a travel writer's curiosity causes him to run afoul of a small town custom, in the future a virus will destroy everyone's memory, and a man out for an evening stroll witnesses what is either a suicide or a bizarre piece of performance art. **Similar titles:** *The Illustrated Man*, Ray Bradbury; *The Incredible Shrinking Man* and *I Am Legend*, Richard Matheson; *My Brain Escapes Me*, Robert Steven Rhine.

> *Gothicism • Science Fiction*

van Belkom, Edo.

Six Inch Spikes. *Kansas City, Mo.: Dark Tales, 2001. 170p*. Van Belkom collects sixteen tales of no-holds-barred, extremely graphic sexual horror, ranging from tales about strippers who get revenge on cruel clients, to stories of sexual torture, to chronicles of erotic encounters with alien beings and mythological creatures. His emphasis is on building suspense and working toward horrific final images, but his characterization is excellent as well. This is not a text for squeamish readers. **Similar titles:** *Black Butterflies*, John Shirley; *Viscera*, Cara Bruce (editor); *Embraces*, Paula Guran (editor); *My Brain Escapes Me*, Robert Steven Rhine.

> *Aliens • Eroticism • Magic • Mind Control • Psychosexual Horror • Shapeshifters • Splatterpunk • Stripper as Character • Torture*

Wandrei, Donald.

Don't Dream: The Collected Horror and Fantasy of Donald Wandrei. *Minneapolis, Minn.: Fedogan & Bremer, 1997. 394p*. Twenty-six short stories by one of the "greatest of the pulp visionaries" and one of the founding members of Arkham House include "The Green Flame," When the Fire Creatures Came," "The Fire Vampires," "The Lady in Grey," "A Scientist Divides," and "The Destroying Hoard." It also includes some prose poems, essays, and marginalia, and is illustrated by Rodger Gerberding. **Similar titles:** *Whispers in the Night*, Basil Copper; *Dark Universe*, William F. Nolan; *Ghosts and Grisly Things*, Ramsey Campbell; *Ghost Stories of Henry James*, Henry James.

> *Aliens • Dreams • Fantasy • Gardens • Gothic Romance • Maritime Horror • Weird Science*

Weinberg, Robert.

Dial Your Dreams and Other Nightmares. *Kansas City, Mo.: Dark Tales Publications, 2001. 191p.* This collection of fourteen stories is divided into four sections: "Nightmares," "Sidney Taine," "Riverworld," and "A Touch of Humor." Weinberg is a master of psychological horror and the weird tale, writing tales of phobias and recurring nightmares, much in the vein of Rod Serling's *Twilight Zone* tales. His stories collected here range from thoughtful tales of fear of the dark and post traumatic stress syndrome (of a Vietnam War prison camp survivor) to outrageously clever stories of the dead being animated to vote in an election. Weinberg would appeal to an eclectic audience, even those who love gentle reads and subtle horror. **Similar titles:** *Thank You for the Flowers*, Scott Nicholson; *Nazareth Hill*, Ramsey Campbell; The Black Oak Series, Charles Grant; *Full Moon, Bloody Moon*, Lee Driver.

Chicago, Illinois • Dreams • Gothicism • History, Use of • Humor • Riverworld • Taine, Sidney (character) • Writer as Character

Wharton, Edith.

The Ghost Stories of Edith Wharton. *New York: Scribner, 1997, ©1937. 288p.* Eleven of Wharton's chilling tales are collected here by Scribner with illustrations by Laszlo Kubinyi. The book also includes her 1937 preface. **Similar titles:** *Ghost Stories of Henry James*, Henry James; *Classic Ghost Stories*, John Grafton (editor); *Tales of Unease*, Arthur Conan Doyle; *The Others* (film).

Ghosts • New England • United States—19th Century

Whitbourn, John.

More Binscombe Tales: Sinister Sutangli Stories. *Ashcroft, B.C.: Ash-Tree Press, 1999. 225p.* Binscombe is the most English of English towns in the south of the country, one that has had a long and well-documented past. John Whitbourn's stories, however, concern another Binscombe, a place that is a slightly sinister, far less reassuring place than its real counterpart. In this Binscombe, things are seldom what they seem, and people should not be taken at face value. No one has learned this lesson more thoroughly than Mr. Oakley, a relative newcomer to the area whose family has long had roots there. **Similar titles:** *The Apostate*, Paul Lonardo; *Midwinter of the Spirit*, Phil Rickman; *Wine of Angels*, Phil Rickman.

Anglo-Saxon England • Cromwell, Oliver (character) • History, Use of • Maritime Horror • Secret Sin

Williamson, J. N.

Frights of Fancy. *New York: Leisure, 2000. 361p.* Williamson, who began his lengthy career as a novelist, has published a collection of sixteen short stories that demonstrate the breadth of his writing abilities. It includes an author's preface for each tale. **Similar titles:** *Night Freight*, Bill Pronzini, *The Nightmare Chronicle*, Douglas Clegg; *The Dark Fantastic*, Ed Gorman; *The Asylum*, Victor Heck (editor).

Apocalypse • Science Fiction

Wilson, F. Paul. The Repairman Jack Series.

The Barrens and Others. *New York: Forge, 1998. 379p.* Wilson's collection of thirteen tales runs the gamut from gory horror stories to bizarre supernatural tales, and in each piece, one thing is glaringly obvious: Wilson knows how to write people. From the sociopath in "Tenants" to the vigilante, Repairman Jack, in "A Day in the Life," Wilson's characters are painfully accurate and believable. **Similar titles:** The Anita Blake, Vampire Hunter Series, Laurell K. Hamilton; The Host Series, Selena Rosen; *The Licking Valley Coon Hunters Club*, Brian A. Hopkins; *Full Moon, Bloody Moon*, Lee Driver.

> *Family Curse • Humor • Joker, The (character) • Lawyer as Character • Psychiatrist/Psychologist as Character • Repairman Jack (character) • Secret Sin • Serial Killers*

Wilson, Gahan.

The Cleft and Other Odd Tales. *New York: Doherty, 1998. 333p.* This illustrated collection of twenty-four weird tales that were originally published in various magazines from 1972 to 1995 by the *New Yorker* and *Playboy* cartoonist will serve as an easy read that blends wit, surprise, and fright. **Similar titles:** *The Selected Tales of Edgar Allan Poe*, Edgar Allan Poe; *The Loved Dead*, H. P. Lovecraft; *The Moonlit Road*, Ambrose Bierce.

> *Alternative Literature • Fantasy • Science Fiction • Suicide*

Wilson, Staci Layne.

Horrors of the Holy: 13 Sinful, Sacrilegious, Supernatural Stories. *Rancho Palo Verdes, Calif.: Running Free Press, 2000. 106p.* These thirteen tongue-in-cheek tales, in which vampires, hard-boiled detectives, demons, fairies, and historical villains cross paths with unwitting humans, are straightforward and simple. Wilson's excursions into the imagination are clever and complex, with subtle humor at their core. **Similar titles:** The Blood of the Lamb Series, Thomas F. Monteleone; *Messiah*, Boris Starling; *Awash in the Blood*, John Wooley; The Host Series, Selina Rosen.

> *Clergy as Character • Cults • Demons • Humor • Music—Rock Music • Revenge • Vampire's Point of View • Zombies*

Anthologies of Stories by Multiple Authors

Adrian, Jack (editor).

Twelve Tales of Murder. *Oxford: Oxford Univesrity Press, 1998. 256p.* Adrian has collected twelve short stories starring ingenuous and captivating murderers. The stories are at times gruesome, at times tragic, and yet always imaginative. Writers include Richard Marsh, Edgar Wallace, and Vincent Cornier. Fans of Poe and of Victorian ghost stories will enjoy these macabre tales. **Similar titles:** *Edgar Allan Poe, Selected Tales*, Edgar Allan Poe; *The Mammoth Book of Victorian and Edwardian Ghost Stories*, Richard Dalby (editor); *Monsters in Our Midst*, Robert Bloch (editor); *Tales of Unease*, Arthur Conan Doyle.

> *England • Maniacs • Police Officer as Character • Revenge • Torture*

Ashley, Mike (editor).

Phantom Perfumes and Other Shades: Memories of *Ghost Stories Magazine*. *Ashcroft, B.C.: Ash-Tree Press, 2000. 244p. Ghost Stories* is, perhaps, the least remembered of the many pulp magazines that flourished during the golden age of the 1920s and 1930s. Yet the magazine managed to survive for more than five years. Ashley has selected seventeen of the very best tales to appear in *Ghost Stories* between 1926 and 1931. **Similar titles:** *Tales of Terror from Blackwood's Magazine*, Robert Morrison and Chris

Baldick (editors); *The Best of Cemetery Dance, Volumes I and II*, Richard Chizmar (editor); *Casting the Runes*, M. R. James.

> *Afterlife, The • Ghosts • Haunted Houses • Maritime Horror • Revenging Revenant • Zombies*

Badger, Scott (editor).

The Peddler and the Cloud. *Redding, Calif.A: Fivebadgers, 2000. 141p.* This anthology of science fiction, dark fantasy, and horror includes only four horror tales, which range from stories of time travel gone awry to weird tales of alien creatures who find themselves in danger when faced with human fear and misunderstanding. **Similar titles:** *Zom Bee Moo Vee*, Mark McLaughlin; *Escaping Purgatory*, Gary A. Braunbeck and Alan M. Clark; *Cold Comfort*, Nancy Kilpatrick; *Strange Twists of Fate*, James K. Burke.

> *Academia • Aliens • Fantasy • Gothicism • Religion—African • Time Travel*

Baker, Mike, and Martin H. Greenberg (editors).

My Favorite Horror Story. *New York: DAW, 2000. 303p.* Ramsey Campbell, Peter Straub, Poppy Z. Brite, Joyce Carol Oates, and Steven King are some of the writers asked to select their favorite horror stories for this diverse and unusual collection. Represented are the science fiction horror of Richard Matheson and Philip K. Dick; the subtle horror of M. R. James, Robert Aickman, and Ramsey Campbell; the classic horror of Robert Bloch, Ambrose Bierce, Nathaniel Hawthorne, and Edgar Allan Poe; and the weird horror of H. P. Lovecraft. This is a good collection for anyone interested in sampling some works truly representative of the breadth of the genre. **Similar titles:** *The Haunted Looking Glass*, Edward Gorey (editor); *The Mammoth Book of 20th Century Ghost Stories*, Peter Haining (editor); The Year's Best Fantasy and Horror Series, Ellen Datlow and Terri Windling.

> *Childhood • Gothicism • Science Fiction*

Birch, A. G., et al. (editors).

The Moon Terror. *Indianapolis, Ind.: Popular Fiction, 1999, ©1927. 192p.* Four stories are reprinted from early issues of the magazine *Weird Tales*. The collection contains two stories from 1927: A.G. Birch's "The Moon Terror" and Anthony M. Rud's "Ooze." Both stories are dark science fantasy by little known writers. Although they are dated, they give readers a glimpse into the mindset of Americans in the 1920s, and they will appeal to fans of dark fantasy. **Similar titles:** *My Favorite Horror Story*, Mike Baker and Martin H. Greenberg (editors); *Tales of Terror From Blackwood's Magazine*, Chris Baldick and Robert Morrison (editors); *Tales of H. P. Lovecraft*, H. P. Lovecraft.

> *Asian-American Characters • Genetics • Magic • Racism • Science Fiction*

Blease, Kathleen (editor).

One Dark Night: 13 Masterpieces of the Macabre. *New York: Ballantine Books, 2000. 206p.* Fans of old-fashioned ghost stories and chilling tales will enjoy this collection, which includes works from such masters of supernatural storytelling as Bram Stoker, Edgar Allan Poe, H.G. Wells, Washington Irving, and Ambrose Bierce. **Similar titles:** *The Mammoth Book of 20th Century Ghost*

Stories, Peter Haining (editor); *My Favorite Horror Story*, Mike Baker and Martin H. Greenberg (editors); *20th Century Ghost Stories*, Robert Phillips (editor).

Gothicism • Obsession • Revenge • Revenging Revenant • War—American Civil War

Bloch, Robert (editor).

The Horror Writers Association Presents Robert Bloch's Psychos. *New York: Pocket, 1998. 373p.* Diverse horror writers pay homage to Robert Bloch, the master of the subgenre of maniac fiction. Contributors include Stephen King, Charles Grant, Ed Gorman, Richard Matheson, Yvonne Navarro, Billie Sue Mosiman, and Jane Yolen. **Similar titles:** *Monsters in Our Midst*, Robert Bloch (editor); *The Best of Cemetery Dance, Volumes I and II,* Richard Chizmar (editor); *The Asylum*, Victor Heck (editor); *The Height of the Scream*, Ramsey Campbell.

Popular Culture • Psychological Thriller • Serial Killers

Monsters in Our Midst. *New York: Tor, 2000, ©1993. 303p.* Bloch has pieced together an original anthology of seventeen horror stories, and penned the introduction himself. This unique anthology includes such favorites as Ramsey Campbell, Richard Christian Matheson, Chet Williamson, Charles L. Grant, S. P. Somtow, and Billie Sue Mosiman. **Similar titles:** *Robert Bloch's Psychos*, Robert Bloch (editor); *The Best of Cemetery Dance, Volumes I and II,* Richard Chizmar (editor); *Are You Loathsome Tonight*, Poppy Z. Brite.

Child Molester • Fantasy • Music • Revenge • Serial Killers

Bovberg, Jason, and Kirk Whitman (editors).

Skull Full of Spurs: A Roundup of Weird Westerns. *Fort Collins, Colo.: Dark Highway Press, 2000. 245p.* Readers will find here cutting-edge fiction from Richard Laymon, Brian Hodge, Rick Hautala, Jack Ketchum, Edward Lee, Nancy A. Collins, Robert Devereaux, Richard Lee Byers, Yvonne Navarro, Adam-Troy Castro, Lawrence Walsh, and Michael Heck. Following each story is a complete bibliography of the author, including books and short stories, making this an indispensable reference for the genre collector. **Similar titles:** *Bubbas of the Apocalypse*, Selena Rosen (editor); *The Cowboy and the Vampire*, Clark Hays and Kathleen McFall; *The Last Vampire*, T. M. Wright; *Rare*, Brian Knight (editor).

Cowboy as Character • Humor • Native American Characters • Popular Culture • West, The

Brite, Poppy Z. The Love in Vein Series.

Love in Vein: Twenty Original Tales of Vampire Erotica. *New York: Harper Paperbacks, 1995, ©1994. 396p.* Brite has brought together this genre's most powerful and seductive authors in an original collection of vampiric erotica. This classic anthology includes contributions by well-known horror writers such as Melanie Tem and Kathe Koja. It was the winner of an International Horror Guild Award for Best Anthology. **Similar titles:** *Dark Seductions*, Alice Alfonsi and John Scognamiglio (editors); *Scared Stiff*, Ramsey Campbell; *Embraces*, Paula Guran (editor); *Extremities*, Kathe Koja.

Eroticism • Gay/Lesbian/Bisexual Characters • Homoeroticism • Splatterpunk • Vampire as New Species • Vampires • Vampire's Point of View

Love in Vein II: Eighteen More Original Tales of Vampire Erotica. *New York: Book Sales, Inc., 2000, ©1997. 375p.* Brite's second anthology of vampire erotica continues the tradition begun with *Love in Vein*. If you enjoyed *Love in Vein*, you'll love *Love in Vein II*. Contributors include Christopher Fowler, David J. Schow, Lucy Taylor, and Richard

Laymon. **Similar titles:** *Scared Stiff*, Ramsey Campbell; *Embraces*, Paula Guran (editor); *Extremities*, Kathe Koja.

> *Eroticism • Gay/Lesbian/Bisexual Characters • Homoeroticism •*
> *Splatterpunk • Vampire as New Species • Vampires • Vampire's Point of View*

Brownworth, Victoria A. (editor).

Night Shade: Gothic Tales by Women. *Seattle, Wash.: Seal, 1999. 256p.* Brownworth has collected seventeen short stories that take place in everyday settings: contemporary houses, a bar, and a veterinary hospital. Yet in this collection, the familiar is subverted. Characters include bored housewives, teen-aged girls with parapsychological talents, and various shapeshifters. **Similar titles:** *Love in Vein*, Poppy Z. Brite (editor); *The Dead Inn*, Shane Ryan Staley (editor); *Embraces*, Paula Guran (editor); *Viscera*, Cara Bruce (editor).

> *Eroticism • Gothicism • Marriage • Parapsychology • Replicants •*
> *Shapeshifters*

Bruce, Cara (editor).

Viscera. *San Francisco: Venus or Vixen Press, 2000. 194p.* Twenty-five tales of "bizarre erotica" include darkly comic escapades of necrophiliacs, serial killers, and average people who have just gone over the edge. This anthology is extremely graphic and often gratuitously pornographic, but effective in its ability to shock. **Similar titles:** *Black Butterflies*, John Shirley; *Embraces*, Paula Guran (editor); *Ambrosial Flesh*, Mary Ann Mitchell.

> *Eroticism • Gay/Lesbian/Bisexual Characters • Necrophilia •*
> *Psychosexual Horror • Revenge • Splatterpunk*

Cacek, P.D. (editor).

Bell, Book and Beyond: An Anthology of Witchy Tales. *Darien, Ill.: Design Image, 2000. 287p.* P. D. Cacek and The Horror Writers Association, the global professional organization of horror and dark fiction writers, proudly present these new voices in terror: twenty-one exciting new talents weaving their own spells with new tales of witchcraft. **Similar titles:** *The Witching Hour*, Anne Rice; *Deathwindow*, Grace Chetwin; *The Rag Bone Man*, Charlotte Lawrence; *A Game of Colors*, John Urbancik.

> *Childhood • Magic • Witches*

Chizmar, Richard (editor).

The Best of *Cemetery Dance,* **Volumes I and II.** *New York: Roc, 2000. 401p.* The best short fiction to appear in the first twenty-five issues of *Cemetery Dance,* these are truly impressive samplers of contemporary writings in the genre. In volume I novelty toys come to life and protect their owners, parents attempt to protect humanity by making preemptive strikes against their disturbed children, people are confronted by their pasts, and everyday individuals must engage in ritual murder to forestall the end of the world. Contributors include Stephen King, Lucy Taylor, Nancy Holder, Ramsey Campbell, Jack Ketchum, Gary A. Braunbeck, Ed Gorman, Douglas Clegg, Brian Hodge, Graham Masterton, Norman Partridge, Bentley Little, and David Niall Wilson. In volume II spree killers suffer from cruel irony and disturbed young loners attempt to recreate the imitation of life from the silver screen. Contributors include Peter Crowther, Norman Partridge, Poppy Z. Brite, Joe R. Lansdale, Richard Laymon, William F. Nolan; Hugh B. Cave, Melanie Tem, Bill Pronzini, Thomas F.

Monteleone, Steven Spruill, Rick Hautala, Nancy Collins, and James Dorr. **Similar titles:** *Robert Bloch's Psychos,* Robert Bloch (editor); *Night Visions 10,* Richard Chizmar (editor); The Year's Best Fantasy and Horror Series, Ellen Datlow and Terri Windling (editors)

> *Secret Sin • Serial Killers*

Night Visions 10. *Burton, Mich.: Subterranean Press, 2001. 293p.* Nearly twenty years ago, the legendary *Night Visions* series was conceived by Dark Harvest Press as a showcase for the outstanding short fiction being produced by the best of the established authors and the most talented of the new writers in the fields of horror and dark fantasy. *Night Visions* returns with original novellas by Jack Ketchum and John Shirley, and five new stories from David B. Silva. **Similar titles:** *The Lost,* Jack Ketchum; *Darkness Divided,* John Shirley; *Black Butterflies,* John Shirley; *Blue Rose,* Peter Straub.

> *Childhood • Demons • Maniacs • Possession • Psychosexual Horror • Revenging Revenant • Secret Sin*

Trick or Treat: A Collection of Halloween Novellas. *Baltimore: Cemetery Dance, 2001. 385p.* This collection of novellas by five well-known contemporary horror writers is a 2001 Bram Stoker Award nominee for best collection. Contributors include Gary A. Braunbeck, Nancy A. Collins, Rick Hautala, Al Sarrantonio, and Thomas Tessier. All five novellas are set during Halloween. **Similar titles:** *Skull Full of Spurs*, Jason Bovberg and Kirk Whitman (editors); The Cemetery Sonata Series, June Hubbard (editor); *Hideous Progeny*, Brian Willis (editor).

> *Adolescence • Animals Run Rampant • Halloween*

Dalby, Richard (editor).

12 Gothic Tales. *Oxford; New York: Oxford University Press, 1998. 221p.* These twelve tales are by some of the most famous writers of gothic and horror fiction, including Charles R. Maturin, Mary Shelley, Edgar Allan Poe, Joseph Sheridan Le Fanu, Bram Stoker, and F. Marion Crawford. Dalby's anthology is good for a change of pace. It does not include the usual collection of titles, which is refreshing. **Similar titles:** *Night Shade: Gothic Tales by Women*, Victoria A. Brownworth (editor); *Selected Tales*, Edgar Allan Poe; *In a Glass Darkly,* Joseph Sheridan Le Fanu.

> *Castles • Demons • England • Germany • Ireland • Nobility • Revenging Revenant • Witchcraft*

The Mammoth Book of Victorian and Edwardian Ghost Stories. *New York: Carroll & Graf, 1995. 573p.* Dalby has collected forty ghost stories from the genre's golden age, 1839 to 1910. Representative writers of the period include Charles Dickens, Joseph Sheridan Le Fanu, Henry James, Bram Stoker, M. R. James, F. Marion Crawford, and Ambrose Bierce. **Similar titles:** *The Ghost Stories of Henry James*, Henry James; *The Moonlit Road and Other Ghost and Horror Stories*, Ambrose Bierce; *A Bottomless Grave and Other Victorian Tales of Terror*, Hugh Lamb (editor).

> *Gothicism • Haunted Houses • Revenging Revenant*

Datlow, Ellen, and Terri Windling (editors). The Year's Best Fantasy and Horror Series.

The Year's Best Fantasy and Horror: Ninth through Fourteenth Annual Collections (1995–2000). *New York: St. Martin's Press, 1996–2001. 534p.* These large (most volumes fall within the 500–600-page range) collections are impressive and thorough compilations of forty-six poems and short stories. The editors' comprehensive year-end summations of the genres and long list of honorable mentions make these valuable reference sources as well as must-have collections of current horror and fantasy fiction. Contributors include (ninth annual) Joyce Carol Oates, Nina Kiriki Hoffman, Charles de Lint, Peter Crowther, Stephen King, Ursula K. LeGuin, Tanith Lee, and S. P. Somtow; (tenth annual) Tanith Lee, Angela Carter, Robert Silverberg, Thomas Ligotti, Gabriel Garcia Marquez, Charles de Lint, Dennis Etchison, Robert Olen Butler, and Jane Yolen; (eleventh annual) Ray Bradbury, Charles deLint, Jane Yolen, Joyce Carol Oates, Caitlin R. Kiernan, Douglas Clegg, Norman Partridge, and Vickram Chandra; (twelfth annual) Stephen King, Dennis Etchison, Neil Gaiman, Jane Yolen, Norman Partridge, Delia Sherman, Jorge Luis Borges, Peter Straub, Michael Blumlein, Ellen Kushner, Charles de Lint, and Terry Dowling; (thirteenth annual) Ursula K. Le Guin, Delia Sherman, Neil Gaiman, Steve Rasnic Tem, Kim Newman, Michael Marshall Smith, Douglas E. Winter, Peter Crowther, Elizabeth Engstrom, Tim Lebbon, Gary A. Braunbeck, and Charles de Lint; and (fourteenth annual) Harlan Ellison, Louise Erdrich, Charles de Lint, Ramsey Campbell, Jack Dann, Elizabeth Engstrom, Kathe Koja, Terry Dowlin, Steve Rasnic Tem and Melanie Tem, Jack Cady, Tanith Lee, Jonathan Carroll, Jack Ketchum, and Esther M. Friesner. Each volume includes two essays providing summations of the previous year's fantasy and horror, as well as obituaries of notable authors in the genre who have passed away during the previous year. This handsome anthology is a must-have for any library with a serious horror collection. **Similar titles:** The Mammoth Book of Best New Horror Series, Stephen Jones (editor); *The Best of Cemetery Dance, Volumes I and II*, Richard Chizmar (editor).

Fantasy • Magic • Science Fiction

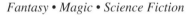

Ellis, Monique, Sara Blayne, and Janice Bennett (editors).

Lords of the Night. *New York: Zebra Books, 2001, ©1997. 320p.* These three previously published tales of supernatural romance in Regency London allow the writers to give their views on vampirism, the special powers of the undead, and how a person joins the ranks of nosferatu. This is a wonderful read for the Regency or vampire romance fan looking for something different. **Similar titles:** The Midnight Series, Nancy Gideon; The Saint-Germain Chronicles, Chelsea Quinn Yarbro; *De Lore's Confession*, Paulette Crain; *The Red Witch*, Serena Devlin.

London, England • Eroticism • Vampires • Vampire's Point of View

Elrod, P. N. (editor).

Dracula in London. *New York: Ace, 2001. 263p.* The sixteen original stories in this collection attempt to answer the question "What else was Dracula doing in London when he was not being chased by Van Helsing et al.?" Contributors include Chelsea Quinn Yarbro, Fred Saberhagen, Tanya Huff, Judith Proctor, Gary A. Braunbeck and Elaine Bergstrom. **Similar titles:** The Anno Dracula Series, Kim Newman; (editor); *Bram Stoker's Dracula* (film); *The Secret Life of Laszlo, Count Dracula*, Patrick Anscombe; The I, Vampire Series, Michael Romkey.

Alternative Literature • Dracula (character) • England • Vampire Hunters • Vampires • Victorian England

Etchison, Dennis (editor).

The Museum of Horrors. *New York: Dorchester-Leisure, 2001. 384p. The Museum of Horrors* is a treasure trove of eighteen great offerings from some of the best horror writers today. Writers such as Peter Straub, Joyce Carol Oates,

Ramsey Campbell, and Tom Piccirilli make this a superb collection, which also includes "Hammerhead" by the late Richard Layman, a dark comedy that gets inside the head of a serial killer; Tom Piccirilli's "Those Vanished I Recognize," about a man on a journey to nowhere, and "Whose Ghosts These Are," by veteran author Charles L. Grant. **Similar titles:** *The Dead Inn*, Shane Ryan Staley (editor); *Darkness Divided*, John Shirley; *Darkness Rising 2*, L. H. Maynard and M. P. N. Sims (editors).

> *Child Molesters • Ghosts • Psychosexual Horror • Serial Killers*

Golden, Christopher (editor).

Hellboy: Odd Jobs. *Milwaukie, Oreg.: Dark Horse Comics, 1999. 216p.* Golden has collected fourteen original stories about Hellboy, preternatural spawn and investigator of the paranormal. Contributors include Yvonne Navarro, Nancy Holder, Nancy Collins, Rick Hautala, Chet Williamson, Max Allan Collins, Christopher Golden, Mike Mignola, Poppy Z. Brite, and Brian Hodge, with illustrations by Mike Mignola. **Similar titles:** *From Hell*, Alan Moore and Eddie Campbell; The Witchblade Series, Christina Z. and David Wohl; *Lazarus Churchyard: The Final Cut*; Warren Ellis and D'Israeli; The Buffy the Vampire Slayer Series, various authors.

🔎 graphic novels

> *Bureau for Paranormal Research and Defense • Demons • Hellboy (character) • Parapsychology • Religion—Christianity • Weird Science*

Gorey, Edward (editor).

The Haunted Looking Glass: Ghost Stories Chosen by Edward Gorey. *New York: New York Review of Books, 2001. 251p.* Before his death in 2000, Edward Gorey collected and illustrated these twelve tales, with his preference being the "classics" by many of the genre's masters. Selected authors include M. R. James, L. P. Hartley, Charles Dickens, Wilkie Collins, Bram Stoker, and Algernon Blackwood. Gorey's anthology is excellent for fans of traditional horror and gentle reads. **Similar titles:** *20th Century Ghost Stories*, Robert Phillips (editor); *Phantom Perfumes and Other Shades*, Mike Ashley (editor); *My Favorite Horror Story*, Mike Baker and Martin H. Greenberg (editors).

> *Cursed Objects • Demons • Dreams • England • Ghosts • Haunted Houses • Revenging Revenant • Weird Science*

Grafton, John (editor).

Classic Ghost and Horror Stories by Wilkie Collins, M. R. James, Charles Dickens, and Others. *Mineola, N.Y.: Dover Publications, 1998. 164p.* This impressive collection of classics is a Dover Thrift edition containing eleven tales of horror and the supernatural, with emphasis on ghosts and haunted houses. The stories are by such masters as Joseph Sheridan Le Fanu, Robert Louis Stevenson, and Henry James, as well as Wilkie Collins, M. R. James, and Dickens. The anthology includes one of the most popular cursed object/ghost tales of all time, M. R. James's "Oh Whistle and I'll Come to You My Lad." Grafton's collection is excellent as a gentle read and as an introduction to the ghost story subgenre. **Similar titles:** *The Haunted Looking Glass*, Edward Gorey (editor); *The Cold Embrace and Other Ghost Stories*, Mary Elizabeth Braddon; *The Mammoth Book of Ghost Stories*, Peter Haining (editor); *The Mammoth Book of Haunted Houses*, Peter Haining (editor).

> *Cursed Objects • England • Germany • Ghosts • Haunted Houses • Parenting • Suicide • Switzerland*

Greenberg, Martin H. (editor).

Children of the Night: Stories of Ghosts, Vampires, Werewolves, and "Lost Children." *Children of the Night Series. Nashville, Tenn.: Cumberland House, 1999. 224p.* This anthology is an eclectic collection of eleven tales about growing up and dealing with the horrors of the world—some natural, some supernatural. It includes an early version of Orson Scott Card's novel *Lost Boys*, with his commentary afterwards, as well as tales by Suzy McKee Charnas, Joseph Sheridan Le Fanu, Nikki Kiriki Hoffman, Charles deLint, and Fritz Leiber. **Similar titles:** *Ghosts, Werewolves, Witches and Vampires*, Joe-Anne Christensen; *Dark Companions*, Ramsey Campbell; The Universal Monster Series, various authors; *The Sixth Sense* (film).

> *Child Molesters • Childhood • Ghosts • Magic • Shapeshifters • Revenge • Revenging Revenant • Vampires • Werewolves • Wish Fulfillment*

Greenberg, Martin H., and Elizabeth Ann Scarborough (editors).

Vampire Slayers: Stories of Those Who Dare to Take Back the Night. *Nashville, Tenn.: Cumberland House, 1999. 239p.* With its eleven tales of the men and women who dedicate their lives to hunting and killing the undead, this anthology contains an excellent range of stories, set in the U. S. West, Canada, the Indian Ocean, and a futuristic America. The writing is crisp and energetic, with more emphasis on plot development and characterization than on action and gore. The editors include selections by Manly Wade Wellman, Brian Hodge, August Derleth, Richard Laymon, Hugh B. Cave, Charles deLint, Tanya Huff, Ed Gorman, and F. Paul Wilson. **Similar titles:** The American Vampire Series, Lawrence Schmiel and Martin H. Greenberg (editors); The Anita Blake, Vampire Hunter Series, Laurell K. Hamilton; *Dracula in London*, P. N. Elrod (editor).

> *Clergy as Character • Eroticism • Shapeshifters • Vampire as New Species • Vampire Hunters • Vampires • Vampire's Point of View • Werewolves*

Griffith, Nicola, and Stephen Pagel (editors).

Bending the Landscape: Original Gay and Lesbian Writing: Horror. *New York: Overlook Press, 2001. 332p.* Griffith and Pagel present eighteen original modern tales with gay or lesbian protagonists. This anthology is only one of three volumes in this series, the others focusing on science fiction and fantasy. Some stories express horrifically the difficulties of being gay or lesbian in a heterosexist society, while others are about everyday people who just happen to not be heterosexual. Themes range from domestic violence, to "passing" as heterosexual, to the Holocaust, to persecution of gays and lesbians. The horror in this collection is generally subtle, and writers seldom rely too heavily on supernatural agency to achieve their effects. **Similar titles:** *Queer Fear*, Michael Rowe (editor); *The Essential Clive Barker*, Clive Barker; *Bound in Blood*, David Thomas Lord; *Warlock*, Perry Brass.

> *Eroticism • Fantasy • Gay/Lesbian/Bisexual Characters • Homoeroticism • Psychosexual Horror • Science Fiction*

Guran, Paula (editor).

Embraces: Dark Erotica. *San Francisco: Venus or Vixen Press, 2000. 220p.* Demon lovers, vampires, maniacs, and just plain kinky people populate this original and disturbing collection of tales that push the definition of the erotic. Contributors include Poppy Z. Brite, Robert Devereaux, Nancy Holder, Steve Rasnic Tem, Charlee Jacob, John Shirley, and David J. Schow. **Similar titles:**

The Love in Vein Series, Poppy Z. Brite (editor); *Black Butterflies*, John Shirley; *Viscera*, Cara Bruce (editor).

> *Eroticism • Gay/Lesbian/Bisexual Characters • Homoeroticism • Obsession •*
> *Psychosexual Horror • Sado-Masochism • Splatterpunk • Wish Fulfillment*

Haining, Peter (editor).

The Mammoth Book of Haunted House Stories. *New York: Carroll & Graf, 2000. 576p.* This anthology contains thirty-five haunted house stories by well-known authors of the genre. Contributors include Joseph Sheridan Le Fanu, Algernon Blackwood, Virginia Woolf, Mary Eleanor Freeman, W. W. Jacobs, Basil Copper, Fay Weldon, A. E. Coppard, Robert Bloch, Ramsey Campbell, M. R. James, Hugh Walpole, Sir Arthur Conan Doyle, William Hope Hodgson, E. F. Benson, Joan Aiken, James Herbert, and Ruth Rendell. Haining's collection also includes a selected bibliography of haunted house novels. **Similar titles:** *The Mammoth Book of 20th Century Ghost Stories*, Peter Haining (editor); *The Haunted Looking Glass*, Edward Gorey (editor); *Tales of Unease*, Arthur Conan Doyle; *Cemetery Sonata* and *Cemetery Sonata II*, June Hubbard (editor); *Whispers in the Night*, Basil Copper.

> *Afterlife, The • England • Ghosts • Gothicism • Haunted Houses • Secret Sin*

The Mammoth Book of 20th Century Ghost Stories. *New York: Carroll & Graf, 1998. 482p.* This anthology contains thirty-one stories, mainly by well-known contemporary authors of the genre, as well as respected, more canonical authors. These are not the same stories that are generally anthologized in books purporting to represent a genre, subgenre, or historical period. Authors include Henry James, H. G. Wells, Sir Arthur Conan Doyle, Jack London, Theodore Dreiser, P. G. Wodehouse, Agatha Christie, Arthur Machen, A. Merritt, Algernon Blackwood, Daphne du Maurier, John Steinbeck, Muriel Spark, Ruth Rendel, Mary Higgins Clark, and Fay Weldon. **Similar titles:** *Ghost Stories of Henry James*, Henry James; *The Ghost Stories of Edith Wharton*, Edith Wharton; *Classic American Ghost Stories*, Deborah L. Downer (editor).

> *Afterlife, The • Ghosts • Gothicism • Haunted Houses • Secret Sin*

Heck, Victor (editor).

The Asylum, Volume I: The Psycho Ward. *Kansas City, Mo.: Dark Tales, 1999. 165p.* Heck puts together a collection of thirteen short stories by diverse hands, including Douglas Clegg, Scott Nicholson, Sephera Giron, and J. F. Gonzalez. *The Asylum's* tales are all concerned with the limits of sanity, and range from a clever monologue by an inmate who believes that Stephen King, Peter Straub, William Peter Blatty, and Ira Levin are all stealing his story ideas, which come to him as horrific visions, to the very disturbing psychosexual monologue by a matricidal maniac with an insect fetish. **Similar titles:** *The Nightmare Chronicles*: Douglas Clegg; *Thank You for the Flowers*, Scott Nicholson; *Careful What You Wish*, June Hubbard; *Darkness Divided*, John Shirley.

> *Dramatic Monologue • Matricide/Patricide • Mental Institutions • Psychosexual*
> *Horror • Sado-Masochism • Schizophrenia/Multiple Personality Disorder •*
> *Serial Killers • Splatterpunk • Torture*

Hubbard, June (editor). The Cemetery Sonata Series.

Cemetery Sonata. *Rochester, Mich.: Chameleon Publishing, 1999. 460p.* Hubbard has compiled forty-three short stories about cemeteries and ghosts. This collection is unusual in its emphasis on burial places. Contributors include Steven Lee Climer, Edo van Belkom, Robert Devereaux, Tina L. Jens, and John Urbancik. **Similar titles:** The Lone Pine Publishing Ghost Stories Series, various authors; *Ghost and Grisly Things*, Ramsey Campbell; *Dead Promises*, June Hubbard (editor).

> *Cemeteries • Ghosts • Gothicism • Grieving • Haunted Houses*

Cemetery Sonata II. *Rochester, Mich.: Chameleon Publishing, 2000. 203p.* Here are twenty-four more stories about cemeteries and ghosts, death and grieving. Contributors include Tina L. Jens, John Urbancik, and Denise M. Bruchman. **Similar titles**: The Lone Pine Publishing Ghost Stories Series, various authors; *Ghost and Grisly Things*, Ramsey Campbell; *Dead Promises*, June Hubbard (editor).

Cemeteries • Ghosts • Gothicism • Grieving • Haunted Houses

Hubbard, June (editor).

Dead Promises: A Treasury of Civil War Ghost Stories. *Rochester, Mich.: Chameleon Publishing, 1999. 220p.* Hubbard has collected eighteen stories about the war between the states. Contributors include Owl Goingback, Wendy Webb, and Stephen Lee Climer. **Similar titles:** *Ghosts and Haunted Houses of the Civil War*, Christopher K. Coleman (editor); *Civil War Ghosts*, Martin H. Greenberg et al. (editors); The Cemetery Sonata Series, June Hubbard (editor); *Ghosts and Haunts of the Civil War*, Christopher K. Coleman (editor).

Ghosts • Haunted Houses • History, Use of • War—American Civil War

Jones, Stephen (editor).

Dark Detectives: Adventures of the Supernatural Sleuths. *Minneapolis, Minn.: Fedogan & Bremer-F and B Mystery, 1999. 395p.* This collection of eighteen short stories about famous "psychic detectives" contains tales by Kim Newman, William Hope Hodgson, Manly Wade Wellman, Brian Lumley, Clive Barker, and Neil Gaiman, among others. Edited by award winner Stephen Jones, who also writes an excellent introduction, this collection chronicles the history of horror detection. Randy Broecher illustrates the tales. **Similar titles:** *Alymer Vance: Ghost Seer*, Alice Askew and Claude Askew; *The Complete John Silence Stories*, Algernon Blackwood; The Black Oak Series, Charles Grant; *Full Moon, Bloody Moon*, Lee Driver.

Alternative Literature • Egypt • Fantasy • History, Use of • New York City • Parapsychology • Weird Science

White of the Moon: New Tales of Madness and Dread. *Nottingham, England: Pumpkin Books, 1999. 339p.* In this original collection of all-new stories concerning psychological and supernatural dread, a Web page predicts the death of everyone on Earth, an imaginary friend turns out to be a killer, a woman obsessed with fire is consumed by her terror, and an author enters a strangely familiar parallel world. Contributors include Ramsey Campbell, Christopher Fowler, Graham Masterton, Kim Newman, David J. Schow, Michael Marshall Smith, and Brian Stableford. **Similar titles:** *The Best of Cemetery Dance, Volumes I and II*, Richard Chizmar (editor); *Bending the Landscape*, Nicola Griffith and Stephen Pagel (editors); *The Asylum*, Victor Heck (editor); *Careful What You Wish*, June Hubbard.

Obsession • Parallel Universe

Jones, Stephen (editor). The Mammoth Book of Best New Horror Series.

The Mammoth Book of Best New Horror, Volumes 8–12. *New York: Carroll & Graf, 1997–2001. 512p.* These annual collections of horror, terror, and dark fantasy showcase major and up-and-coming authors of the genre. Contributors include (vol. 8) Poppy Z. Brite, Norman Partridge, Steve Rasnic Tem, Douglas Clegg, Thomas Ligotti, Thomas Tessier, Christopher Fowler, Karl Edward Wagner, and Terry Lamsley; (vol. 9) Ramsey Campbell, Christopher Fowler,

Neil Gaiman, Tanith Lee, Peter Straub, Dennis Etchison, Kathe Koja, Kim Newman, and Caitlin R. Kiernan; (vol. 10) Christopher Fowler, Neil Gaiman, Kathe Koja, Kim Newman, Ramsey Campbell, Caitlin R. Kiernan, Tanith Lee, Dennis Etchison, Harlan Ellison, and Peter Straub; (vol. 11) Steve Rasnic Tem, James Herbert, T. E. D. Klein, David J. Schow, Ramsey Campbell, Neil Gaiman, Kim Newman, Caitlin R. Kiernan, Thomas Tessier, Graham Masterton, F. Paul Wilson and Peter Straub; and (vol. 12) Kim Newman, Christopher Fowler, Caitlin R. Kiernan, Ramsey Campbell, Dennis Etchison, Graham Joyce, Kathe Koja, and Thomas Ligotti. **Similar titles:** *The Best of Cemetery Dance, Volumes I and II*, Richard Chizmar (editor); The Year's Best Fantasy and Horror Series, Ellen Datlow and Terri Windling (editors); *Night Visions 10*, Richard Chizmar (editor).

Fantasy • Gothicism

The Mammoth Book of Vampire Stories by Women. *New York: Carroll& Graf, 2001. 624p.* Jones has compiled a nice mix of vampire tales by older and well-known contemporary female authors. The tales included span two centuries. Contributors include well-known vampire novelists Anne Rice, Nancy A. Collins, Tanya Huff, and Chelsea Quinn Yarbro. Also included are stories by women who write mainly horror, science fiction, and dark fantasy, such as Poppy Z. Brite, Wendy Webb, Caitlin R. Kiernan, Elizabeth Hand, Elizabeth Massie, and Jane Yolen. Older authors include Mary Elizabeth Braddon and Mary E. Wilkins-Freeman. **Similar titles:** *Daughters of Darkness*, Pam Keesey (editor); *Dracula in London*, P. N. Elrod (editor); *The Voice of the Blood*, Jemiah Jefferson.

Eroticism • Gay/Lesbian/Bisexual Characters • Immortality • Vampire as New Species • Vampire Clans • Vampire Hunters • Vampires • Vampire's Point of View

Joshi, S. T. (editor).

Great Weird Tales: 14 Stories by Lovecraft, Blackwood, Machen and Others. *Mineola, N.Y.: Dover Publications, 1999. 239p.* Joshi puts together a collection of various "weird tales" published during the "Golden Age" of science fiction and horror, roughly between 1880 and 1940. In addition to the masters noted in the title, this anthology includes works by William Hope Hodgeson, Ambrose Bierce, and Fitz-James O'Brien, with an introduction by noted literary critic Joshi. **Similar titles:** *The Loved Dead and Others*, H. P. Lovecraft et al.; *More Annotated H. P. Lovecraft*, H. P. Lovecraft; *The Moonlit Road and Others*, Ambrose Bierce; *The House on the Borderland*, William Hope Hodgeson.

England • Fantasy • Religion—Christianity • Wales • Weird Science • Wilderness

Keesey, Pam (editor).

Daughters of Darkness: Lesbian Vampire Stories. *2d ed. San Francisco: Cleis Press, 1998. 253p.* These ten tales examine the role of women, especially lesbians, in vampire lore. Selections include Joseph Sheridan Le Fanu's *Carmilla* and nine much more contemporary stories set in leather and S and M bars and in a distant future in space. All selections are followed by a brief annotated filmography and unannotated bibliography. **Similar titles:** *Bending the Landscape*, Nicola Griffith and Stephen Pagel (editors); *Queer Fear*, Michael Rowe (editor); The Love in Vein Series, Poppy Z. Brite (editor).

Gay/Lesbian/Bisexual Characters • Psychosexual Horror • Vampire Hunters • Vampires • Vampire's Point of View

Knight, Brian (editor).

Rare: An Anthology of Rare Horror. *Santa Fe, N.Mex.: Disc-Us Books, 2001. 221p.* Here are seventeen original stories created by members of an online horror writer's community. Contributors vary from novice to professional writers, as do the extremes of the tales they spin. Stories range from the subtle to the gory. **Similar titles:** *Revelations*, Douglas E. Winter (editor); *The Dead Inn*, Shane Stanley Ryan (editor); *Bubbas of the Apocalypse*, Selina Rosen (editor); *The Asylum*, Victor Heck (editor).

Gothicism • Psychosexual Horror

Lamb, Hugh (editor).

A Bottomless Grave and Other Victorian Tales of Terror. *Mineola, N.Y.: Dover Publications, 2001. 224p.* Lamb has unearthed twenty-one little-known tales by well-known American and British authors and put them together in this one collection. Many of the stories are humorous. The editor's commentary at the beginning of each story provides important historical information. Contributors include Ambrose Bierce, Joseph Sheridan Le Fanu, Frank Norris, and Guy de Maupassant. This collection is not just another book of the usual anthologized tales of terror but is truly unique. **Similar titles:** *The Mammoth Book of Victorian and Edwardian Ghost Stories*, Richard Dalby (editor); *Tales of Terror from Blackwood's Magazine*, Robert Morrison and Chris Baldick (editors); *The Mammoth Book of Haunted House Stories*, Peter Haining (editor).

Dreams • England • Gothicism • Haunted Houses • Revenging Revenant • Victorian England

Lassen, Jeremy (editor).

After Shocks: An Anthology of So-Cal Horror. *San Diego: Freak Press, 2000. 221p.* The twelve contributors to this collection inform their tales with California settings and situations. Lisa Morton's "El Cazador" and Stephen Woodworth's "Street Runes" both decode dark truths encrypted in the tags of Los Angeles graffiti artists. In Dana Vander Els's "A Flock of Drunk Witches," a stalker menaces a runaway Valley Girl. Christa Faust's "Bodywork" finds a bizarre intersection between the California car culture and the cosmetic makeover industry, and James van Pelt's "Parallel Highways" is about a Flying Dutchman of the freeway. **Similar titles:** *Dark Soul*, M. Martin Hunt; *Dracula's Children*, Richard Lortz; *Regeneration*, Max Allan Collins and Barbara Collins; The Lone Pine Publishing Ghost Story Series, various authors.

California • Graffiti • Hispanic-American Characters • Revenging Revenant • Stalkers

Lovecraft, H. P., et al.

The Loved Dead and Other Revisions. *August Derleth (editor). New York: Carroll& Graf, 1999, ©1970. 243p.* August Derleth serves up fourteen tales of cosmic horror by diverse hands, each author working with H. P. Lovecraft on his or her tale. Most of the stories involve Lovecraft's Cthulhu Mythos, incorporating it into modern urban horror, haunted house tales, and science fiction stories about alternative dimensions or realities. This is excellent for fans of traditional horror and gentle reads. **Similar titles:** *Tales of H. P. Lovecraft*, *The Shadow Out of Time*, and *More Annotated H. P. Lovecraft*, H. P. Lovecraft; *Eternal Lovecraft*, Jim Turner (editor); *Great Weird Tales*, S. T. Joshi (editor).

Cthulhu Mythos • Epidemics • Ghosts • Haunted Houses • Louisiana • Maritime Horror • Museums • New England • Religion—African • Religion—Voodoo • San Francisco, California • Science Fiction

Maynard, L. H., and M. P. N. Sims.

Darkness Rising 2: Hideous Dreams. *Holicong, Pa.: Wildside Press, 2001. 180p.* This is the second volume of a collection of stories that seem to include anything that might be even remotely termed supernatural, and hence it has a refreshing range and variety. Rhys Hughes's "The Century Just Gone" examines the most evil people in the twentieth century, while Steve Lockley and Paul Jones introduce the chairman of all angels in their story, "Gabriel Restrained." Iain Darby has a most original story of human sacrifice in "Phylotas' Tomb," and William Simmons's "The Wind, When It Comes" is baffling, haunting, and beautifully written. **Similar titles:** *The Year's Best Fantasy and Horror*, Ellen Datlow and Terri Windling (editors); *The Peddler and the Cloud*, Scott Badger (editor); *The Best of Cemetery Dance*, Richard Chizmar (editor).

Angels • Fantasy • History, Use of • Human Sacrifice • Mythology

Morrison, Robert, and Chris Baldick (editors).

Tales of Terror from Blackwood's Magazine. *New York: Oxford University Press, 1995. 298p.* This is a rare collection of gothic tales published in *Blackwood's Edinburgh Magazine* between 1817 and 1832. *Blackwood's,* one of the most important and influential literary-political journals of its time, was notorious for its shocking literary offerings. Many of these tales are reminiscent of the works of Edgar Allan Poe. Contributors include Sir Walter Scott, John Galt, and William Godwin, half brother of Mary Shelley. **Similar titles:** *Great Weird Tales*, S. T. Joshi (editor); *A Bottomless Grave and Other Victorian Tales of Terror*, Hugh Lamb (editor); *Phantom Perfumes and Other Shades*, Mike Ashley (editor); *The Vampyre and Other Tales of the Macabre*, Robert Morrison and Chris Baldick (editors).

England • Gothicism • Parapsychology • Vampires

The Vampyre and Other Tales of the Macabre. *New York: Oxford University Press, 2001, ©1997. 278p.* Morrison and Baldick present fourteen nineteenth-century gothic tales previously published in Dublin and London magazines that were rivals of the immensely popular *Blackwood's Magazine*. This anthology includes John Polidori's tale "The Vampyre," as well as stories by Joseph Sheridan Le Fanu, Edward Bulwer Lytton (writing as Edward Bulwer), Catherine Gore, Leticia Landon, and James Hogg. On the whole, it is valuable to those interested in the early history of vampire literature and in Lord Byron's influence on John Polidori's famous story. Appendices include the original editorial comments from the *New Monthly Magazine* that preceded "The Vampyre"; Polidori's introductory notes to his one published novel, which include comments about "The Vampyre"; and Lord Byron's short story "Augustus Darvell," his contribution to the famous ghost story writing contest that spawned Mary Shelley's *Frankenstein*. **Similar titles:** *The Mammoth Book of Victorian and Edwardian Ghost Stories*, Richard Dalby (editor); *The Mammoth Book of Haunted House Stories*, Peter Haining (editor); *Gothic Readings*, Rictor Norton (editor).

England • Gothicism • Ireland

Phillips, Robert (editor).

20th Century Ghost Stories. *New York: Carroll & Graf, 1999. 470p.* These twenty-seven ghost stories, originally published from 1911 to 1999, include tales by such masters as Elizabeth Bowen, L. P. Hartley, Shirley Jackson, Henry James, Joyce Carol Oates, and Edith Wharton. This text also includes an introduction by Robert Phillips. **Similar titles:** *The Lottery and Other Stories*, Shirley Jackson; *The Ghost Stories of Edith Wharton*, Edith Wharton; *Ghost of Stories of Henry James*, Henry James.

Ghosts • Gothic Romance • Haunted Houses • Maritime Horror • Revenging Revenant

Rabe, Jean, and Martin H. Greenberg (editors).

Historical Hauntings. *New York: DAW-Penguin, 2001. 320p.* These eighteen tales borrow historical figures as either ghosts or protagonists. Stories range from modern-day tales of visitations by Harry Houdini and Vincent Van Gogh to period pieces set during the American Civil War. This anthology is an excellent gentle read. Similar titles: *Dead Promises*, June Hubbard (editor); *Dark Detectives*, Steven Jones (editor); *More Monsters from Memphis*, Beecher Smith (editor).

> *Artist as Character • Demons • Ghosts • History, Use of • Revenging Revenant • Writer as Character*

Rosen, Selina (editor).

Bubbas of the Apocalypse. *Alma, Ark.: Yard Dog Press, 2001. 210p.* In the year 2025, a strange virus lays waste to civilization as we know it, turning almost everyone into a zombie cannibal. But the working classes, who consume vast quantities of low-priced barbecue sauce laden with preservatives, have been rendered immune to this virus. Now they must survive in a world where Yuppies would turn poor white people into the new white meat. This collection of stories by different authors functions as a loosely jointed novel that explores this theme. Rosen's editorial contribution is as unusual and witty as her own fiction. **Similar titles:** *The Bubba Chronicles*, Selina Rosen; *Confessions of a Ghoul*, M. F. Korn; *Strange Twists of Fate*, James K. Burk; *The Licking Valley Coon Hunters Club*, Brian A. Hopkins.

> *Apocalypse • Cannibalism • Class System • Epidemics • Humor • Science Fiction • Weird Science • Zombies*

Rowe, Michael (editor).

Queer Fear. *Vancouver, B.C.: Arsenal Pulp Press, 2000. 252p.* Rowe offers a collection of eighteen short stories with gay protagonists. Themes in these tales range from problems peculiar to male/male relationships, to gay bashing, to AIDS. Contributors include Douglas Clegg, Caitlin R. Kiernan, Brian Hodge, Michael Marano, Edo Van Belkom, and Nancy Kilpatrick. Rowe's text is literate and original. **Similar titles:** *Queer Fear*, Michael Rowe (editor); *The Essential Clive Barker*, Clive Barker; *Bound in Blood*, David Thomas Lord; *Warlock*, Perry Brass.

17

> *Eroticism • Fantasy • Gay/Lesbian/Bisexual Characters • Homoeroticism • Psychosexual Horror*

Sarrantonio, Al (editor).

⑧ **999: New Stories of Horror and Suspense.** *New York: Avon Books, 1999. 666p.* In this award-winning and popular anthology, Al Sarrantonio presents twenty-nine tales ranging from the Satanic to the psychological, by such benchmark authors as William Peter Blatty, Ramsey Campbell, Nancy A. Collins, Ed Gorman, Stephen King, T. E. D. Klein, Thomas Ligotti, Bentley Little, Kim Newman, Joyce Carol Oates, and Tim Powers. This volume has a little something for everyone's taste. **Similar titles:** *Revelations*, Douglas E. Winter (editor); The Year's Best Fantasy and Horror Series, Ellen Datlow and Terri Windling (editors); The Mammoth Book of Best New Horror Series, Stephen Jones (editor).

> *Apocalypse • Demons • Fantasy • Gothicism • Science Fiction • Serial Killers*

Schimel, Lawrence, and Martin H. Greenberg (editors). The American Vampire Series.

Blood Lines: Vampire Stories from New England. *Nashville, Tenn.: Cumberland House, 1997. 224p.* In New England, vampires are like anyone else. People who can date their lineage back to the *Mayflower* are accepted as insiders. Everyone else is an interloper to be regarded with suspicion. In this collection of vampire tales set in New England, a small town protects its own against a snooping IRS agent, and proprietors of a quaint old inn who make their money off of city dwelling "leaf peepers" struggle to keep the secret of family longevity when one of the inn's guests wants to share their immortality. **Similar titles:** *Vampire Slayers*, Elizabeth Ann Scarborough and Martin H. Greenberg (editors); *Dracula in London*, P. N. Elrod (editor); *'Salem's Lot*, Stephen King.

> *Connecticut • Gothicism • Immortality • Maine • Massachusetts • New England • New Hampshire • Rhode Island • Vampires • Vampire's Point of View • Vermont*

Southern Blood: Vampire Stories from the American South. *Nashville, Tenn.: Cumberland House, 1997. 203p.* In these vampire stories, the South really *does* rise again. A disaffected Confederate soldier turns a twentieth-century Yankee tourist during Mardi Gras. A Southern belle marries old money while trying to keep secret both her nature and her humble parentage. A young vampire tough fights his way through working-class Florida bars in search of Dracula, his ultimate opponent, who is currently in retirement in St. Augustine, the city with the largest per capita prune consumption. And Elvis isn't dead—he's undead. Contributors include Fred Chappell, Esther Friesner, Billie Sue Mosiman, Manly Wade Welman, and Brian Hodge. This quirky collection also includes the first chapter of Dan Simmons's epic vampire novel, *Carrion Comfort*. **Similar titles:** *Vampire Slayers*, Elizabeth Ann Scarborough and Martin H. Greenberg (editors); *Dracula in London*, P. N. Elrod (editor); *Red Moon Rising*, Billie Sue Mosiman.

> *Alabama • Eroticism • Florida • Georgia • Gothicism • Immortality • Louisiana • North Carolina • Presley, Elvis (Impersonator/Character) • Shapeshifters • South, The • South Carolina • Tennessee • Texas • Vampires • Vampire's Point of View • Virginia • West Virginia*

Fields of Blood: Vampire Stories of the American Heartland. *Nashville, Tenn.: Cumberland House, 1998. 208p.* Life in America's heartland is anything but bland. Pumpkins bleed in North Dakota, while in Ohio, vampires congregate in the privacy of a twelve-step program. Contributors include August Derleth, P. N. Elrod, Hugh B. Cave, Nancy Holder, and Peter Crowther. **Similar titles:** *Vampire Slayers*, Elizabeth Ann Scarborough and Martin H. Greenberg (editors); *Dracula in London*, P. N. Elrod (editor); *The Vampire Stories of Nancy Kilpatrick*, Nancy Kilpatrick.

> *Gothicism • Illinois • Immortality • Indiana • Iowa • Kansas • Midwest, The • Minnesota • Missouri • Nebraska • North Dakota • Ohio • Shapeshifters • South Dakota • Vampires • Vampire's Point of View • Wisconsin*

Streets of Blood: Vampire Stories from New York City. *Nashville, Tenn.: Cumberland House, 1998. 232p.* Thirteen literate, atmospheric tales set in Gotham explore the various and more subtle manifestations of the vampire. Contributors include Julian Hawthorne, son of Nathaniel Hawthorne; Chelsea Quinn Yarbro; and Suzy McKee Charnas, with an excerpt from her novel *The Vampire Tapestry*. **Similar titles:** *Vampire Slayers*, Elizabeth Ann Scarborough and Martin H. Greenberg (editors); *Dracula in London*, P. N. Elrod (editor); The Time of Feasting Series, Mick Farren.

> *Eroticism • Gothicism • Immortality • Monroe, Marilyn (character) • New York City • Saint-Germain, Count Ragoczy de (character) • Shapeshifters • Vampires • Vampire's Point of View • Weyland, Dr. Edward Lewis (character)*

Smith, Beecher (editor).

More Monsters from Memphis. *Palo Alto, Calif.: Zapizdat Productions, 1998. 315p.* Smith offers thirty-two diverse tales of horror and the macabre, with subjects varying from aliens, to ghosts, to "shadow monsters" that spread terminal disease, to sea-creatures, to Satan's reclaiming human souls. Contributors include Brent Monahan, Steve Rasnic Tem, Tom Piccirilli, Janet Berliner, and Smith himself. **Similar titles:** *The Guardian*, Beecher Smith; *Night Voices*, June Hubbard; *Southern Blood*, Lawrence Schimel and Martin H. Greenberg (editors).

> *African-American Characters • Demons • Folklore • Haunted Houses • History, Use of • King, Dr. Martin Luther (character) • Maritime Horror • Memphis, Tennessee • Mythology • Presley, Elvis (impersonator/character) • Race Relations • Religion—African • Religion—Ancient Egyptian • Religion—Voodoo • Satan (character)*

Staley, Shane Ryan.

The Dead Inn: Gross Oddities, Erotic Perversities, and Supernatural Entities. *North Webster, Ind.: Delirium Books, 2001. 232p.* Staley has collected twenty-five stories by as many writers, and subdivides these weird tales and escapades into erotic horror into three classes: those dealing with revulsion and the human body, those dealing with grotesque eroticism, and those dealing with supernatural psychosexual horror. Staley includes some notable contributions such as Charlee Jacob's "Baby," about a freak show barker whose "owl-girl" find not only shows clients their most depraved desires, but allows them to live them; Michael Laimo's "Snuff's Enough," which chronicle's the final days of a Mafioso porn king; John Everson's "Sacrificing Virgins," a tale of a rock star's final hour, when he must pay for having sold his soul; and Scott Thomas's poetic yet disturbing "Summer Gargoyles," a story of dark sexual fantasies. Not for the weak of stomach, this anthology is graphic and often gory. **Similar titles:** *Viscera*, Cara Bruce (editor); *Embraces*, Paula Guran (editor); *Black Butterflies* and *Wetbones*, John Shirley.

> *Demons • Eroticism • Gay/Lesbian/Bisexual Characters • Homoeroticism • Music—Rock Music • Psychosexual Horror*

Stevens, John Richard. (editor).

Into the Mummy's Tomb. *New York: Berkley, 2001. 352p.* This is an unusual collection of fiction and nonfiction about mummies by well-known writers and Egyptologists. Fiction contributors include Bram Stoker, Anne Rice, Louisa May Alcott, H. P. Lovecraft, Tennessee Williams, Agatha Christie, Edgar Allan Poe, Ray Bradbury, Sir Arthur Conan Doyle, and Mark Twain. Nonfiction contributors include Howard Carter, Victorian Egyptologist and discoverer of Tutankhamen's tomb. **Similar titles:** *The Jewel of Seven Stars*, Bram Stoker; *The Sleeper in the Sands*, Tom Holland; *The Mummy, or Ramses the Damned*, Anne Rice; *Tales of Unease*, Sir Arthur Conan Doyle.

> *Afterlife, The • Archeologist as Character • Cursed Objects • Egypt • History, Use of • Houdini, Harry (character) • Immortality • Mummies • Religion—Ancient Egyptian • Revenging Revenant • Victorian England*

Turner, Jim (editor).

Eternal Lovecraft. *Collinsville, Ill.: Golden Gryphon Press, 1998. 410p.* Turner presents eighteen "Lovecraftian" tales by various writers, including Nancy Collins, Thomas Ligotti, Harlan Ellison, Stephen King, T. E. D. Klein,

and Fritz Leiber. A bio-bibliographic preface by Jim Turner serves as an introduction to H. P. Lovecraft's style. **Similar titles:** *The Loved Dead and Others*, H. P. Lovecraft et al.; *More Annotated H. P. Lovecraft*, H. P. Lovecraft; *Tales of H. P. Lovecraft*, H. P. Lovecraft.

> *Arkham, Massachusetts • London, England • Necronomicon, The • Police Officer as Character • Science Fiction • Subterranean Monsters • Roman Empire*

Willis, Brian (editor).

Hideous Progeny. *Cardiff, Scotland: RazorBlade Press, 2000. 293p.* Willis has collected nineteen tales based on the proposition that Victor Frankenstein's creation didn't go hideously wrong. Contributors include James Lovegrove, Steve Rasnic Tem, and Peter Crowther. The anthology includes an introduction by *Anno Dracula* author Kim Newman. **Similar titles:** *Frankenstein*, Mary Shelley; *Frankenstein: The Legacy*, Christopher Schildt; *Dracula in London*, P. N. Elrod (editor).

> *Afterlife, The • Alternative Literature • Fantasy • Frankenstein, Dr. (character) • Golem • Medical Horror • Science Fiction • Weird Science*

Winter, Douglas E. (editor).

Revelations. *New York: HarperPrism, 1998. 650p.* Winter's collection of science-fiction/dark-fantasy/horror tales by contemporary writers well known for their contributions to the horror genre includes works by Poppy Z. Brite, F. Paul Wilson, Charles Grant, Whitley Streiber, Elizabeth Massie, Richard Matheson, David J. Schow, Ramsey Campbell, Clive Barker, and Joe R. Lansdale. This collection is a winner of an International Horror Guild Award for Best Anthology. **Similar titles:** The Millennium Quartet, Charles Grant; *Bubbas of the Apocalypse*, Selina Rosen (editor); *The Stand*, Stephen King.

> *Apocalypse • Fantasy • Science Fiction*

Our Picks of Collections

June's Picks: *Houses Without Doors*, Peter Straub (Signet); *I Am Legend*, Richard Matheson (Tor); *The Incredible Shrinking Man*, Richard Matheson (Tor); *In a Glass Darkly,* Joseph Sheridan Le Fanu (Oxford University Press).

Tony's Picks: *13 Stories*, Ed Cain (Maximilian); *Alone with the Horrors*, Ramsey Campbell (Headline Book Publishing); *Escaping Purgatory*, Gary Braunbeck and Alan M. Clark (IFD); *Ghostly Lights: Great Lakes Lighthouse Tales of Terror*, Annick Hivert-Carthew (Wilderness Adventure Books); *The Illustrated Man*, Ray Bradbury (Avon); *Thank You for the Flowers*, Scott Nicholson (Parkway); *Whispers in the Night*, Basil Copper (Fedogan & Bremer).

Our Picks of Anthologies

June's Picks: *Bending the Landscape: Original Gay and Lesbian Writing: Horror*, Nicola Griffith and Stephen Pagel (editors) (Overlook Press); *The Best of Cemetery Dance, Volume I*, Richard Chizmar (editor) (ROC); *Embraces: Dark Erotica*, Paula Guran (editor) (Venus or Vixen Press); *Into the Mummy's Tomb*, John Richard Stephens (editor) (Berkley); *Love in Vein*, Poppy Z. Brite (editor) (Harper); *My Favorite Horror Story*, Mike Baker and Martin H. Greenberg (editors) (DAW); *Queer Fear*, Michael Rowe (editor) (Arsenal Pulp Press); *Southern Blood: Vampire Stories from the American South*, Lawrence Schimel and Martin H. Greenberg (editors) (Cumberland House); *The*

Year's Best Fantasy and Horror Series, Ellen Datlow and Terri Windling (editors) (St. Martin's Press).

Tony's Picks: *Love in Vein*, Poppy Z. Brite (editor) (Harper); *Revelations*, Douglas E. Winter (editor) (HarperPrism); *Tales of Terror from Blackwood's Magazine*, Robert Morrison and Chris Baldick (editors) (Oxford University Press); The Year's Best Fantasy and Horror Series, Ellen Datlow and Terri Windling (editors) (St. Martin's Press).

Part 4

Further Reading on the Genre

Chapter 18

Resources

Ready Reference

Although there are a limited number of reference works in the horror genre, they are important to readers because they make available important information that sheds light on many a horror writer and his or her literary oeuvre, and because they often offer other information of interest to horror fans. These reference works remind horror fans and scholars that the monsters populating the works of Ramsey Campbell, Stephen King, Dean Koontz, Bentley Little, H. P. Lovecraft, Kim Newman, Joyce Carol Oates, Edgar Allan Poe, Phil Rickman, Bram Stoker, Peter Straub, and countless other writers of the grotesque and the horrific are often descendants of folklore and fairy tale creatures that once were invoked by adults to teach young and old alike tough lessons about the dangers of the world and of giving in to base human desires.

In this chapter, we list and briefly describe encyclopedias, dictionaries, and bibliographies that deal with the horror genre, including representative titles such as Mike Ashley's *Who's Who in Horror and Fantasy Fiction*, which, although dated, makes accessible biographical and bibliographical information on some benchmark writers in the genre. Ashley's groundbreaking bio-bibliography and other older titles may not be in print, but they are readily available through other means, such as ILL and through World Wide Web services that find out-of-print texts, and librarians will find that acquiring them is well worth the trouble. Also included in this section is Neil Barron's *Horror Literature*, perhaps the single most important reference work that deals with the genres of science fiction, horror, and fantasy as a whole. Other works, lesser known but just as important to horror fans, such as Thomas C. Clarke's *Occult Bibliography*, Peter Haining's *A Dictionary of Ghost Lore* and *Terror: A History of Horror Illustrations*, Jack Sullivan's *The Penguin Encyclopedia of Horror*, and Everett F. Bleiler's *Supernatural Fiction Writers*, are also included in this reference chapter.

Our mission here is to draw attention to the usefulness of these sources in answering readers' advisory questions, as many of them contain bibliographies and/or brief discussions of horror literature in general. In addition, we hope to remind librarians and readers alike that these works are valuable in and of themselves, as secondary sources that offer valuable information that is not accessible elsewhere. For the purposes of creating a practical categorization for these works, we have subdivided this chapter into three sections, one listing reference works that deal with readers' advisory in general, a second dealing with works that examine horror as a genre, and one listing works that deal with specific aspects of the genre, such as a particular writer or a specific type of monster. This latter category may not have as broad an appeal as the former, but readers enjoy them nonetheless.

Horror Readers' Advisory

Barron, Neil (editor).

What Fantastic Fiction Do I Read Next? A Reader's Guide to Recent Fantasy, Horror, & Science Fiction. *Farmington Hills, Mich.: Gale, 1999. 1954p.* Barron et al. briefly annotate some 5,000 books in the fantasy, horror, and science fiction genres. Approximately one-fourth of Barron's selective bibliography is dedicated to horror.

Barron, Neil.

Fantasy and Horror. *Lanham, Md.: Scarecrow Press, 1999. 832p.* This guide directs readers and viewers to the historically important works of the fantastic imagination, as well as to the scholarship that helps us understand their nature and appeal. Arranged chronologically, narrative introductions provide historical and analytical perspectives on the period or subjects covered, while annotated bibliographies describe and evaluate the books and other materials judged most significant for literary or historical reasons. More than 2,300 works of fiction and poetry are discussed, each cross-referenced to other works with similar or contrasting themes.

Horror Literature: A Reader's Guide. *Garland Reference Library of the Humanties 1220. New York; London: Garland, 1990.* Barron pens this bibliography and critical introduction to the horror genre, which is a good basic source, though somewhat dated. **Appeal:** Popular.

CARL Corporation

NoveList. *CD-ROM/Online. CARL Corporation. 1994– .* Based on *Genreflecting*, NoveList helps students and teachers find fiction based on books they have read or topics in which they are interested. Utilizing the EBSCOhost search engine, it features expanded searching, such as Boolean, Natural Language searching, and full-text searching of reviews. Readers can search for books by title or author or by simply describing a book that would be interesting to read. NoveList now offers the ability to search for books based on readability (Lexile) scores. It provides access to more than 100,000 searchable fiction titles and more than 36,000 individual subject headings based on Hennepin County Public Library's renowned cataloging system.

What Do I Read Next? *CD-ROM/Online. Gale Research, 1996– .* This CD-ROM product contains brief descriptions of more than 63,000 adult, young adult, and children's titles. Gale gives libraries and their users 96,000 titles, more than 52,000 plot summaries, 553 award titles, several recommended reading lists, and biographical information. To be included in *What Do I Read Next?,* a book must be an award winner, a best seller, or have appeared on a recommended reading list. Genres include inspirational, mystery, romance, science fiction, fantasy, horror, Western and historical novels, general fiction, classic fiction, and nonfiction. The user-friendly software includes custom, in-depth search options by title, author, subject, genre, locale and more.

Herald, Diana.

Genreflecting. *5th ed. Littleton, Colo.: Libraries Unlimited, 2000. 553p.* Covering nearly 6,000 titles in such popular genres as crime, adventure, romance, Western, science fiction, fantasy, and horror, Herald's indispensable reference defines each, describes its characteristics and subgenres, and groups authors and books according to type or subject. Readers will find everything they need to know about traditional genre literature, and they will learn about some of the latest subgenres to emerge.

Horror Reference

Bush, Lawrence C.

Asian Horror Encyclopedia: Asian Horror Culture in Literature, Manga, and Folklore. *San Jose, Calif.: Writers Club Press, 2001.* Bush, a long-time reviewer of horror texts, collects information dealing with supernatural horror literature in Japan and China. **Appeal:** Academic, Popular.

Clute, John, and John Grant.

The Encyclopedia of Fantasy. *New York: St. Martin's Press, 1997.* A benchmark work in the genre, Clute and Grant's encyclopedia contains over 1,000 pages of entries on science fiction, horror, and fantasy. **Appeal:** Popular, Academic.

Jones, Stephen (editor).

Clive Barker's A-Z of Horror. *New York: HarperPrism, 1997.* One of the masters of horror, Clive Barker, takes readers on an encyclopedic tour of the genre. This book is based on a BBC television series that inspired an Arts and Entertainment series. **Appeal:** Popular.

Jones, Stephen, and Kim Newman (editors).

Horror: The Best 100 Books. *New York: Carroll & Graf, 1998.* This is the reissue of a Bram Stoker Award-winning survey of horror scholarship. **Appeal:** Popular, Academic.

Lofficier, Jean-Marc, and Randy Lofficier.

French Science Fiction, Fantasy, Horror and Pulp Fiction: A Guide to Cinema, Television, Radio, Animation, Comic Books and Literature from the Middle Ages to the Present. *Jefferson, N.C.: McFarland Publishing, 2000.* This is a two-part work that gives a historical overview, complete lists, descriptions, and summaries for works in film, television, radio, animation, comic books, and graphic novels, and examines major authors and literary trends of French science fiction, fantasy, and horror from the Middle Ages to the present day. **Appeal:** Academic.

Mulvey-Roberts, Marie (editor).

The Handbook to Gothic Literature. *Washington Square, N.Y.: New York University Press, 1998.* Mulvey-Roberts writes an encyclopedia-like treatment of gothic literature, from Brontë to Melville. **Appeal:** Academic.

Weinberg, Robert.

Horror of the Twentieth Century: An Illustrated History. *Portland, Oreg.: Collector's Press, 2000.* This oversized collection of movie poster prints, original art renderings, and book covers would make a nice addition to any library's collection of horror paraphernalia, and would be useful to both the casual horror fan and the serious academic scholar of the genre. Contains literally hundreds of color plates and illustrations dating from the late 1800s to the 1990s. **Appeal:** Popular, Academic.

References and Resources for Horror Subgenres

Maniacs

Evans, Stewart P., and Keith Skinner (editors).

The Ultimate Jack the Ripper Companion: An Illustrated Encyclopedia. *New York: Carroll & Graf, 2001. 758p.* The next best thing to squatting amid Scotland Yard's dusty files yourself, this collection of police and autopsy reports, witness statements, letters, newspaper stories, and sometimes gory photos presents the primary sources, including thirty-two plates of illustrations, without interpretation. **Appeal:** Popular, Academic.

Newton, Michael.

The Encyclopedia of Serial Killers. *New York: Checkmark Books, 1999.* Newton's encyclopedia is a fairly comprehensive reference source about hundreds of nineteenth- and twentieth-century serial killers. It includes appendices of solo killers, team killers, and unsolved serial killer homocides. **Appeal:** Popular, Academic.

Vampires

Bowen, Phyllis, et al.

Kindred of the East Companion. *Clarkston, Ga.: White Wolf, 1998. 140p.* Bowen and others composed this guide to the role-playing game Kindred of the East. **Appeal:** Popular.

Bunson, Matthew.

The Vampire Encyclopedia. *New York: Crown Trade Paperbacks, 1993.* Bunson is an excellent source of vampire lore and beliefs. **Appeal:** Popular.

Dakan, Richard.

Clanbook: Ventrue. *Clarkston, Ga.: White Wolf, 2000. 100p.* This book covers disciplines, the feeding restriction, example characters, Sabbat material, and history. More than half of this book looks at the history of the clan. **Appeal:** Popular.

Davis, Graeme (editor).

The Art of Vampire: The Masquerade. *Clarkston, Ga.: White Wolf Game Studio, 1998. 98p.* In this lavishly illustrated art book readers will be able to see the creatures of the night in all their glory, not to mention the stories behind the very look and imagery of Vampire. **Appeal:** Popular.

Melton, J. Gordon.

The Vampire Book: The Encyclopedia of the Undead. *2d ed. Detroit: Visible Ink, 1998.* Gordon produces this artistic encyclopedia of literary and historical vampires, including notes on history, folklore, and societies. **Appeal:** Popular.

Vampire Gallery: A Who's Who of the Undead. *Detroit: Visible Ink, 1998.* Melton covers the spectrum of vampirism, from terminology, to geography, to organizations, to literary characters. **Appeal:** Popular, Academic.

Horror Authors

General Author Reference

Ashley, Mike.

> **Who's Who in Horror and Fantasy Fiction.** *New York: Taplinger, 1977.* Ashley collects an impressive list of important horror writers, with a brief biography and bibliography of each. **Appeal:** Popular, Academic.

Bloom, Clive (editor).

> **Gothic Horror: A Reader's Guide from Poe to King and the Beyond.** *New York: St. Martin's Press, 1998.* This guide contains excerpts of writings by psychologists and well-known horror critics. **Appeal:** Academic.

Etchison, Dennis (editor).

> **St. James Guide to Horror, Ghost and Gothic Writers.** *Detroit: St. James-Gale, 1998.* Etchison collects bio-bibliographic information on ghost stories, gothic literature, and horror. **Appeal:** Popular.

Wiater, Stanley.

> Ⓑ **Dark Thoughts on Writing.** *Grass Valley, Calif.: Underwood Books, 1997.* Based on interviews with fifty horror writers, Wiater preents a text that examines why writers of horror enjoy the genre, where they get their ideas, and how they deal with censorship. This is the winner of a Bram Stoker Award. **Appeal:** Popular, Academic.

Reference Works on Individual Authors

Neil Gaiman

Bender, Hy.

> **The Sandman Companion.** *London: Titan, 2000. 273p.* Bender composes a highly readable companion/encyclopedia to Neil Gaiman's *Sandman* comics, and includes interviews with Gaiman himself. **Appeal:** Popular.

Dean Koontz

Greenberg, Martin (editor).

> **The Dean Koontz Companion.** *London: Headline, 1994. 406p.* This first-ever look at Koontz and his career includes an exclusive interview, his first published short story, a complete annotated guide to his work, and more. **Appeal:** Popular, Academic.

H. P. Lovecraft

Joshi, S. T. (editor).

> **Sixty Years of Arkham House.** *Sauk City, Wis.: Arkham House, 1999.* Joshi's bibliography continues August Derleth's *Thirty Years of Arkham House* (1970), by cataloging Arkham House's publications. Joshi includes brief notes and indexes of authors and titles. **Appeal:** Popular, Academic.

Edgar Allan Poe

Smith, Don G.

The Poe Cinema: A Critical Filmography. *Jefferson, N.C.: McFarland Publishing, 1999.* Smith collects these lists of credits, casts, story summaries, and production and marketing techniques for films based on the works of Edgar Allan Poe and made from 1908 to 1992. The text includes films from various countries, and each entry contains a brief critique section. **Appeal:** Academic.

Sova, Dawn B.

Edgar Allan Poe, A to Z. *New York: Facts on File-Checkmark Books, 2001.* Sova collects information on Poe's life and literary works and categorizes them as encyclopedia entries. She also includes a Poe timeline, a chronology of his works, and a listing of Poe research collections. **Appeal:** Academic.

Peter Straub

Collings, Michael R.

Hauntings: The Official Peter Straub Bibliography. *Woodstock, Ga.: Overlook Connection Press, 1999. 193p.* This is the first volume documenting and collecting Peter Straub's work for the last thirty years. It includes an interview with Straub. **Appeal:** Academic.

Bram Stoker

Joslin, Lyndon W.

Count Dracula Goes to the Movies: Stoker's Novel Adapted, 1922–1995. *Jefferson, N.C.: McFarland Publishing, 1999.* Joslin pens this complete guide to eleven films based on Stoker's classic tale of horror. **Appeal:** Academic.

Horror Film Reference and Resources

Atkins, Rick.

Let's Scare 'Em: Grand Interviews and a Filmography of Horrific Proportions, 1930–1961. *Jefferson, N.C.: McFarland Publishing, 1997.* Atkins documents and illustrates the suspension of disbelief and audience manipulation employed over these three decades of horror, fantasy, and monster movies. He includes photographs, interviews, and a filmography of 251 of the best-known (and some not so well-known) releases. **Appeal:** Popular, Academic.

Brunas, Michael, John Brunas, and Tom Weaver.

Universal Horrors: The Studio's Classic Films, 1931–1946. *Jefferson, N.C.: McFarland Publishing, 1990.* Brunas's work is the definitive study of the eighty-five films produced by Universal Studios between 1931 and 1946. It is generously illustrated and includes complete cast lists, credits, storylines, behind-the-scenes information, production history, commentary from the cast and crew, and in-depth critical analysis. **Appeal:** Popular, Academic.

Dendle, Peter.

The Zombie Movie Encyclopedia. *Jefferson, N.C.: McFarland Publishing, 2001.* Dendle's publication is an exhaustive overview of over 200 zombie movies from sixteen countries, spanning approximately sixty-five years. **Appeal:** Popular, Academic.

Fischer, Dennis.

Horror Film Directors, 1931–1990. *Jefferson, N.C.: McFarland Publishing, 1991.* Fischer's text is a lengthy and exhaustive study of the major directors of horror films in the past six decades. Each entry includes a complete filmography, including television work, a career summary, critical assessment, and behind-the-scenes production information. **Appeal:** Popular, Academic.

Flynn, John L.

Cinematic Vampires: The Living Dead on Film and Television, from *The Devil's Castle* (1896) to *Bram Stoker's Dracula* (1992). *Jefferson, N.C.: McFarland Publishing, 1992.* Flynn pens a complete look at 372 vampire films, and he includes alternate titles and original titles of non-English films. **Appeal:** Popular, Academic.

Holston, Kim R., and Tom Winchester.

Science Fiction, Fantasy and Horror Film Sequels, Series and Remakes: An Illustrated Filmography, with Plot Synopses and Critical Commentary. *Jefferson, N.C.: McFarland Publishing, 1997.* Holston and Winchester analyze more than 400 horror, science fiction, and fantasy films in this comprehensive reference to the genre's sequels, series, and remakes. **Appeal:** Popular, Academic.

Joslin, Lyndon W.

Count Dracula Goes to the Movies: Stoker's Novel Adapted, 1922–1995. *Jefferson, N.C.: McFarland Publishing, 1999.* Joslin pens this complete guide to eleven films based on Stoker's classic tale of horror. **Appeal:** Academic.

Kinnard, Roy.

Horror in Silent Films: A Filmography, 1896–1929. *Jefferson, N.C.: McFarland Publishing, 1999.* This filmography includes all silent films that were horrific in nature or contained one or more of the stock horror movie elements. Annotations include release date, running time, cast and credit information, and in the case of foreign films, the original title and country of origin. **Appeal:** Academic.

Mayo, Mike.

Videohound's Horror Show: 999 Hair-Raising, Hellish, and Humorous Movies. *Detroit: Gale-Visible Ink, 1998.* Mayo's lengthy tome is a large catalog of horror and suspense films, with a brief annotation of each. **Appeal:** Popular.

Senn, Bryan, and John Johnson.

Fantastic Cinema Subject Guide: A Topical Index to 2,500 Horror, Science Fiction, and Fantasy Films. *Jefferson, N.C.: McFarland Publishing, 1992.* Senn and Johnson annotate over 2,500 genre films,providing year of release, distribution company, country of origin, director, producer, screenwriter, cinematographer, cast credits, plot synopsis, and critical commentary. **Appeal:** Academic.

Smith, Don G.

The Poe Cinema: A Critical Filmography. *Jefferson, N.C.: McFarland Publishing, 1999.* Smith collects these lists of credits, casts, story summaries, and production and marketing techniques for films based on the works of Edgar Allan Poe and made from 1908 to 1992. The text includes films from various countries, and each entry contains a brief critique section. **Appeal:** Academic.

Writing Guides

Castle, Mort.

Writing Horror. *Cincinnati, Ohio: Digest Books, 1997.* A published writer himself, Castle creates a "how-to" book on horror, including example tales and interviews with writers. **Appeal:** Popular, Academic.

Nolan, William F.

How to Write Horror Fiction. Genre Writing Series. *Cincinnati, Ohio: Writer's Digest, 1990.* Nolan discusses writing horror, from the idea stage to the production stage. **Appeal:** Popular.

Williamson, J. N. (editor).

How to Write Tales of Horror, Fantasy, and Science Fiction. *Cincinnati, Ohio: Writer's Digest, 1987.* Williamson reprints excerpts from essays by Robert Bloch, Ray Bradbury, Dean Koontz, Charles Grant, Robert McCammon, Ramsey Campbell, Richard Christian Matheson, Douglas Winter, and himself. **Appeal:** Popular.

History and Criticism

Certainly one of the most noticeable trends in the horror genre has been its gradual acceptance into the university curriculum, which indicates that more and more readers are beginning to realize how important the genre is as a cultural barometer. More professors and instructors of literature, gender studies, and sociology are beginning to understand how Stephen King's *Carrie* chronicles the sexual revolution of the 1960s, how Dan Simmons's *Carrion Comfort* examines the "greed is good" mindset of the 1980s, and how William Browning Spencer's *Resume with Monsters* pokes fun at the technology-crazed 1990s. Literary scholars find themselves becoming interested in the evolution of particular thematic concerns in horror. For example, one could trace the evolving manifestations of the vampire through texts such as Stoker's *Dracula*, Richard Matheson's *I Am Legend*, Anne Rice's *Interview with the Vampire*, and T. M. Wright's *The Last Vampire,* finding that the changing face of the vampire reveals something about American and Western society, particularly of the era contemporary to each writer.

Moreover, university students are flocking to the horror classes of these professors and instructors as quickly as they are offered. At Louisiana State University, where we team taught courses in horror fiction/film and vampire fiction/film, classes would fill up in two hours or less (which is record time), and we often ended up with standing room only. Honors students especially enjoyed the chance to seriously study works they had previously read for pure pleasure, or, in a sense, to look at the familiar world anew.

The reserve reading materials for these classes always consisted of works concerned with the history of the genre and with critical interpretations of its most historically famous texts. We include these secondary sources in this edition of *Hooked on Horror* for the same reasons that we included them in our course descriptions: They help readers to better understand and appreciate horror. In general, the works in this chapter reflect the differing interests we noted among the critics of the genre. Various studies examine the nature of horror itself, or why it appeals to the human emotions, as do Stephen King's *Danse Macabre,* James Twitchell's *Dreadful Pleasures*, William Patrick Day's *In the Circle of Fear and Desire*, and Terry Heller's *The Delights of Terror: An Aesthetics of the Tale of Terror.* Other texts seem more concerned with what horror fiction has to say about the societies in which we live or in which our ancestors had lived. Such studies as David Punter's *The Literature of Terror*, Nina Auerbach's *Woman and the Demon* and *Our Vampires, Ourselves*, Carol J. Clover's *Men, Women, and Chainsaws*, Teresa Goddu's *Gothic America*, and Kelly Hurley's *The Gothic Body* speak to us of our cultural fears and desires.

However, to view horror scholars as merely social or historical critics would be a great oversimplification. Many writers who are, for want of a better term, aficionados of horror literature, publish simply to share their love of the genre and to impart their individual insights concerning its value as an excellent storytelling device. Jack Sullivan's *Elegant Nightmares*, S. T. Joshi's *The Weird Tale*, and Tony Magistrale and Michael Morrison's *A Dark Night's Dreaming* are excellent examples of texts that not only analyze what horror literature has to say but show an appreciation for how horror literature delights its fans in saying it.

This chapter lists some of the better older secondary sources, and most of the recently published criticism in the horror genre, including both histories of the genre and focused analyses of specific themes and trends in the genre and its various subgenres, as well as individual studies of benchmark writers. Aside from those texts discussed in the previous paragraphs, it includes such benchmark publications as Julia Briggs's *Night Visitors*, Les Daniels' *Living in Fear*, H. P. Lovecraft's *Supernatural Horror in Literature*, Elizabeth MacAndrew's *The Gothic Tradition in Literature*, Ray McNally and Radu Florescu's *In Search of Dracula*, and S. S. Prawer's *Caligari's Children*. Because the focus of this book is not criticism but fiction, our annotations in this section are extremely brief, but we append an appeal note to each entry to help the readers' advisory librarian identify publications in which patrons may be interested. In addition, the appeal note will aid collection development officers in suggesting and collecting these sources to meet user demographics.

General History and Criticism

Aguirre, Manuel.

> **The Closed Space: Horror Literature and Western Symbolism.** *Manchester, England: Manchester University Press, 1990.* Aguirre is known for his psychological/sociological theories of horror and horror symbolism, as seen in this monograph. **Appeal:** Academic.

18

Andriano, Joseph.

> **Our Ladies of Darkness: Feminine Daemonology in Male Gothic Fiction.** *University Park, Pa.: Pennsylvania State University Press, 1993.* Andriano presents psychological theories on Otherness and the Feminine in gothic/horror fiction. **Appeal:** Academic.

Botting, Fred.

> **The Gothic.** *New Critical Idiom Series. New York: Routledge, 1996.* Botting explains the fundamental premises of gothic literature and defines the parameters. **Appeal:** Academic.

Clemons, Valdine.

> **The Return of the Repressed: Gothic Horror from *The Castle of Otranto* to *Alien*.** *SUNY Series in Psychoanalysis and Culture. Albany: State University of*

New York Press, 1999. In psychological analyses, Clemons studies various horror texts, including *The Monk, Frankenstein, Dr. Jekyll and Mr. Hyde, Dracula,* and *The Shining.* **Appeal:** Academic.

Day, William Patrick.

In the Circles of Fear and Desire: A Study of Gothic Fantasy. *Chicago: University of Chicago Press, 1985.* In this benchmark work, Day analyzes the attraction/repulsion reaction to horror. **Appeal:** Academic, Popular.

Goddu, Teresa A.

Gothic America: Narrative, History, and Nation. *New York: Columbia University Press, 1997.* Goddu examines the roles of women and African Americans in American gothic fiction. **Appeal:** Academic.

Halberstam, Judith.

Skin Shows: Gothic Horror and the Technology of Monsters. *Durham, N.C.: Duke University Press, 1995.* Halberstam presents a comprehensive view of the gothic revival in England, chronicling the roles of monsters in British film and literature. **Appeal:** Academic.

Heller, Terry.

The Delights of Terror: An Aesthetics of the Tale of Terror. *Urbana, Ill.: University of Chicago Press, 1987.* In this excellent study, Heller analyzes the appeal of horror to the reader or viewer. **Appeal:** Academic, Popular.

Ingebresten, Ed.

Maps of Heaven, Maps of Hell: Religious Terror as Memory from the Puritans to Stephen King. *Armonk, N.Y.: M. E. Sharpe, 1996.* Ingebresten studies the role of Christianity in American gothic and horror literature. **Appeal:** Academic.

Jancovich, Mark.

Horror. *Batsford Cultural Studies. London: Batsford, 1992.* Jancovich produces an informative and brief beginner's guide to the study of horror. **Appeal:** Academic, Popular.

Joshi, S. T.

The Modern Weird Tale. *Jefferson, N.C.: McFarland Publishing, 2001.* Joshi presents this critical study of many of the leading writers of horror and supernatural fiction since World War II. **Appeal:** Academic, Popular.

Kendrick, Walter M.

The Thrill of Fear: 250 Years of Scary Entertainment. *New York: Grove-Weidenfeld, 1991.* Kendrick pens this popular study of English and American horror tales and film. **Appeal:** Academic, Popular.

Kilgour, Maggie.

The Rise of the Gothic Novel. *New York: Routledge, 1995.* Kilgour defines gothic fiction and its movements, from its beginnings in England to the present day. **Appeal:** Academic.

King, Stephen.

Danse Macabre. *New York: Everest House, 1981.* King theorizes on the psychology of the horror writer and the appeal of horror, with emphasis on sociological theories. **Appeal:** Academic, Popular.

Leonard, Elizabeth Anne (editor).

Into Darkness Peering: Race and Color in the Fantastic. *Westport, CT: Greenwood, 1997.* Leonard collects essays about race in horror, science fiction, and fantasy. **Appeal:** Academic.

Lovecraft, H. P.

The Annotated Supernatural Horror in Literature. *Ed. S. T. Joshi. New York: Hippocampus Press, 2000.* Joshi edits the definitive edition of H. P. Lovecraft's extended essay that traces horror fiction from its earliest (biblical) manifestations to the modern masters of the 1930s. Lovecraft's discussions of specific works are fairly extensive, and Joshi's notes make this an indispensable tool for any scholar of the genre. **Appeal:** Popular, Academic.

Magistrale, Tony, and Michael A. Morrison.

A Dark Night's Dreaming: Contemporary American Horror Fiction. *Columbia, S.C.: University of South Carolina Press, 1996.* This is part of the Understanding Contemporary American Literature series dealing with history and criticism in the genre. **Appeal:** Academic, Popular.

Malchow, Howard L.

Gothic Images of Race in Nineteenth-Century Britain. *Stanford, Calif.: Stanford University Press, 1996.* Malchow discusses the role of race and racial representations in nineteenth-century English fiction, with emphasis on vampirism and cannibalism. **Appeal:** Academic.

Punter, David.

Gothic Pathologies: The Text, The Body and the Law. *London: Macmillan, 1998.* Punter writes this new psychoanalytic study on gender in gothic literature. **Appeal:** Academic.

Skal, David J.

The Monster Show: A Cultural History of Horror. *New York: Norton, 1993.* Skal studies horror film and fiction, from the early Universal Studio flicks to Stephen King and beyond. **Appeal:** Academic, Popular.

Screams of Reason: Mad Science in Modern Culture. *New York: Norton, 1998.* Skal concentrates on the mad scientist character in science fiction and horror film, from the 1920s to the 1990s, and includes a list of mad scientists and the films in which they appear as an appendix. **Appeal:** Academic, Popular.

Sullivan, Jack.

Elegant Nightmares. *Athens, Ohio: Ohio University Press, 1978.* Sullivan takes a general look at horror in this nice basic text for the uninitiated fan interested in horror criticism. **Appeal:** Academic, Popular.

Tropp, Martin.

Images of Fear: How Horror Stories Helped Shape Modern Culture (1818–1918). *Jefferson, N.C.: McFarland Publishing, 1999, ©1990.* Tropp examines how before the actual horrors of World War I, many of the fears we still face came from the pages of popular fiction, such as *Frankenstein* and *Dr. Jekyll and Mr. Hyde*. **Appeal:** Academic.

Twitchell, James B.

Dreadful Pleasures: An Anatomy of Modern Horror. *Oxford: Oxford University Press, 1985.* Twitchell analyzes the appeal of horror fiction and film. **Appeal:** Academic.

Ursini, James.

More Things Than Are Dreamt of: Masterpieces of Supernatural Horror, From Mary Shelley to Stephen King, in Literature and Film. *New York: Limelight, 1994.* Ursini collects notes on horror tales, both in literature and film. **Appeal:** Academic, Popular.

Criticism of Horror Classics

Auerbach, Nina.

Woman and the Demon: The Life of a Victorian Myth. *Cambridge, Mass.: Harvard University Press, 1982.* Aurebach studies the relationship between women and monsters in Victorian gothic/horror fiction. **Appeal:** Academic.

Bayer-Berenbaum, Linda.

The Gothic Imagination: Expansion in Gothic Literature and Art. *London: Associated University Press, 1982.* In this classic, Bayer-Berenbaum writes about the psychology behind gothic literature and about writer motivation. **Appeal:** Academic.

Briggs, Julia.

Night Visitors: The Rise and Fall of the English Ghost Story. *London: Faber, 1977.* Brigg's emphasis is on the traditional ghost tale à la M. R. James, with an argument that the subgenre is dead. **Appeal:** Academic.

DeLamotte, Eugenia C.

Perils of the Night: A Feminist Study of Nineteenth-Century Gothic. *Oxford: Oxford University Press, 1990.* DeLamotte presents a feminist study of Victorian gothicism. **Appeal:** Academic.

Norton, Rictor (editor).

Gothic Readings: The First Wave, 1764-1840. *London: Leicester University Press, 2000.* (See the ready reference sources in this chapter.)

Punter, David.

The Literature of Terror: A History of Gothic Fictions from 1765 to the Present Day. *New York: Longman, 1980.* This is one of the benchmark studies of horror fiction; it elaborates on English and American horror. **Appeal:** Academic.

Schmitt, Cannon.

Alien Nation: Nineteenth-Century Gothic Fictions and English Nationality. *Philadelphia: University of Pennsylvania Press, 1997.* Scmitt analyzes nineteenth-century English gothic fiction and its relationship to national identity. **Appeal:** Academic.

Horror Themes/Motifs and Subgenres

Golem (Mummies)

Cowie, Susan D., and Tom Johnson.

The Mummy in Fact, Fiction and Film. *Jefferson, N.C.: McFarland Publishing, 2001.* This text compares the religious, social, and scientific aspects of mummies to how they are portrayed in fiction and movies. **Appeal:** Popular.

Maniacs

Coville, Gary, and Patrick Lucanio.

Jack the Ripper: His Life and Crimes in Popular Entertainment. *Jefferson, N.C.: McFarland Publishing, 1999.* Coville and Lucanio survey the literary, film, television, and radio treatments of Jack the Ripper and his crimes. **Appeal:** Popular, Academic.

Gordon, R. Michael.

Alias Jack the Ripper: Beyond the Usual Whitechapel Suspects. *Jefferson, N.C.: McFarland, 2001.* Gordon takes a comprehensive look at the crimes and the case evidence, with a discussion of the life of the man Gordon believes was the actual killer. **Appeal:** Popular, Academic.

Vampires

Auerbach, Nina.

Our Vampires, Ourselves. *Chicago: University of Chicago Press, 1995.* Aurebach notes the cultural significance of vampires, from Dracula to Lestat. **Appeal:** Academic, Popular.

Barber, Paul.

Vampires, Burial and Death. *New Haven, Conn.: Yale University Press, 1988.* Barber writes an ethnographic/folkloric examination of mainly Eastern European vampire mythology. This monograph is a favorite among vampire fans. **Appeal:** Popular, Academic.

Gordon, Joan, and Veronica Hollinger (editors).

Blood Read: The Vampire as Metaphor in Contemporary Culture. *Philadelphia: University of Pennsylvania Press, 1997.* The editors collect very readable essays on post-1970s horror fiction and film. **Appeal:** Academic, Popular.

Heldreth, Leonard G., and Mary Pharr.

The Blood Is the Life: Vampires in Literature. *Bowling Green, Ohio: Bowling Green State University Popular Press, 1999.* Heldreth and Pharr collect nineteen essays concerned with literary vampires, from Polidori's "The Vampyre" to Nancy A. Collins's Sonja Blue series. **Appeal:** Academic.

McNally, Raymond T., and Radu Florescu.

In Search of Dracula: The History of Dracula and Vampires. *Boston: Houghton Mifflin, 1994. 297p.* This is one of the first books to examine the history and folklore of fifteenth-century Romanian beserker Vlad Tepes, thought to be the historical basis for Dracula, and the folklore of vampires in general. It includes a filmography, an appendix of folk stories about Tepes, a bibliography of vampire fiction and nonfiction sources about Tepes and vampires, and a travel guide to Dracula-related places in Romania and the United Kingdom. **Appeal:** Popular, Academic.

Werewolves

Duclos, Denis.

Le Complexe du loup-garou (The Werewolf Complex: America's Fascination with Violence). *Trans Amanda Pingree. Paris: Berg, 1994; Oxford: Oxford International, 1998.* Duclos, the director of the CNRS in Paris, studies werewolves in literature, film, and popular culture. **Appeal:** Academic, Popular.

Witches

Fitzhugh, Pat.

The Bell Witch Haunting: An Historical and Modern-Day Account of the Most Terrifying Legend in American History. *Nashville, Tenn.: Armand Press, 1999.* (See chapter 7, "Demonic Possession, Satanism, Black Magic, and Witches and Warlocks: The Devil Made Me Do It.")

Kovacs, Lee.

The Haunted Screen: Ghosts in Literature and Film. *Jefferson, N.C.: McFarland Publishing, 1999.* The literature-based ghost films of the 1930s and 1940s provide the underpinnings for many of the gentle supernatural films of the 1990s The following are examined in this monograph: *Wuthering Heights, The Ghost and Mrs. Muir, Portrait of Jennie, Letter from an Unknown Woman, The Uninvited, Liliom, Our Town, Ghost,* and *Truly, Madly, Deeply.* **Appeal:** Academic.

Summers, Montague.

The History of Witchcraft and Demonology. *Secaucus, N.J.: Castle Books, 1992, ©1926.* This reissue is one of the most important analyses of the development, spread, persecution, and survival of witchcraft, by the Catholic priest who is considered one of the leading scholars of witchcraft, vampirism, and Satanism. The text is extremely important historically, and fairly well-written in reasoned, erudite language. **Appeal:** Academic.

Criticism on Horror Authors

General

Schweitzer, Darrell.

Speaking of Horror: Interviews with Writers of the Supernatural. *The Millford Series Popular Writers of Today 48. San Bernardino, CA: Borgo Press, 1994.* Schweitzer interviews Robert Bloch, Ramsey Campbell, Dennis Etchinson, Charles L. Grant, Tanith Lee, Thomas Ligotti, Brian Lumley, William F. Nolan, Manly Wade Wellman, Chet Williamson, and F. Paul Wilson. **Appeal:** Popular, Academic.

Clive Barker

Hoppenstand, Gary.

Clive Barker's Short Stories: Imagination as Metaphor in *The Books of Blood* **and Other Works.** *Jefferson, N.C.: McFarland Publishing, 1994.* Hoppenstand pens a detailed study of significant themes in Barker's writing, placing him in the British gothic tradition of Marlowe, Saki, and others. **Appeal:** Academic.

William Peter Blatty

Blatty, William Peter.

If There Were Demons Then Perhaps There Were Angels: William Peter Blatty's Own Story of *The Exorcist. Southwold, Suffolk: Screen Press Books, 1998.* Screen Press reprints this popular transcript of a 1974 interview with Blatty, the author of *The Exorcist.* **Appeal:** Popular.

Ramsey Campbell

Joshi, S. T.

Ramsey Campbell and Modern Horror Fiction. *Liverpool, England: Liverpool University Press, 2001.* One of the premier scholars in the genre traces the career of arguably the best writer in horror today, Ramsey Campbell, from his early Lovecraftian stories to his novels of modern psychological horror. **Appeal:** Academic, Popular.

Stephen King

Bloom, Harold (editor).

Stephen King. *Philadelphia: Chelsea House, 1998.* Bloom writes on the history and criticism of American horror, with emphasis on placing the fiction of Stephen King. **Appeal:** Academic, Popular.

Collings, Michael R.

Scaring Us to Death: The Impact of Stephen King on Popular Culture. *2d ed. Popular Writers of Today No. 63. San Bernardino, Calif.: Borgo Press, 1997.* Collings discusses the role of Stephen King in American horror. **Appeal:** Academic, Popular.

Russell, Sharon A.

Stephen King: A Critical Companion. *Westport, Conn.: Greenwood, 1996.* Russsell discusses the history and criticism of American horror, with emphasis on Stephen King. **Appeal:** Academic.

Spignesi, Stephen J.

Lost Work of Stephen King: A Guide to Unpublished Manuscripts, Story Fragments, Alternative Versions and Oddities. *Secausus, N.J.: Birch Lane Press, 1998.* Spignesi guides readers through Stephen King's unpublished works. **Appeal:** Academic, Popular.

Underwood, Tim, and Chuck Miller (editors).

Fear Itself: The Early Works of Stephen King. *San Francisco: Underwood Miller, 1993. 239p.* Underwood and Miller examine Stephen King's early novels. This critical work includes an introduction by Peter Straub and an afterword by George Romero. **Appeal:** Popular, Academic.

Dean Koontz

Kotker, Joan G.

Dean Koontz: A Critical Companion. *Westport, Conn.: Greenwood, 1996.* Kotker discusses American horror, with emphasis on Dean Koontz. **Appeal:** Academic.

Ramsland, Katherine.

Dean Koontz: A Writer's Biography. *New York: HarperCollins, 1997.* Ramsland pens this illustrated biography of one of America's most famous horror writers. **Appeal:** Academic, Popular.

Richard Laymon

Laymon, Richard.

A Writer's Tale. *Apache Junction, Ariz.: Deadline Press, 1998. 348p.* This autobiographical chronicle takes readers behind the scenes in the life of a dedicated artist, one who despite often sizable odds persisted to become one of the best-selling horror writers in England and around the world. **Appeal:** Popular, Academic.

H. P. Lovecraft

Carter, Lin.

Lovecraft: A Look Behind the Cthulhu Mythos. *San Bernadino, Calif.: Borgo Press, 1997.* Carter pens this biographical study of Lovecraft, with emphasis on the history of the mythos itself. **Appeal:** Popular, Academic.

Joshi, S. T. (editor).

The Annotated H. P. Lovecraft. *New York: Dell, 1997.* Joshi, a Lovecraft scholar and co-editor of *Necrofile: The Review of Horror Fiction*, annotates the works of Lovecraft. **Appeal:** Academic, Popular.

Lovecraft, H. P.

Selected Letters, 1911-1924. August Derleth and Donald Wandrei (editors). *Sauk City: Wis.: Arkham House, 1965.* This collection contains correspondence from 1911 to 1924 to and from the creator of the Cthulhu Mythos, edited by his foremost disciple, August Derleth. **Appeal:** Popular, Academic.

Schweitzer, Darrell.

Discovering H. P. Lovecraft. *Mercer Island, Wash.: Starmont House, 1987.* Schweitzer collects essays concerned with the fiction of H. P. Lovecraft. **Appeal:** Academic, Popular.

Edgar Allan Poe

Carlson, Eric W. (editor).

A Companion to Poe Studies. *Westport, Conn.: Greenwood, 1996.* This is Carlson's lengthy study of Poe's detective and horror fiction, including bibliographical references. **Appeal:** Academic, Popular.

Kennedy, J. Gerald and Liliane Weissberg (editors).

Romancing the Shadow: Poe and Race. *Oxford: Oxford University Press, 2001. 292p.* Collection of essays about Poe and race. **Appeal:** Academic.

Anne Radcliffe

Rogers, Deborah D.

Anne Radcliffe: A Bio-Bibliography. *Westport, Conn.: Greenwood, 1996.* Rogers presents biographical facts about Anne Radcliffe, concentrating on how her life and her writing were interrelated. **Appeal:** Academic.

Anne Rice

Hoppenstand, Gary, and Ray B. Browne (editors).

The Gothic World of Anne Rice. *Bowling Green, Ohio: Popular Press, 1996.* The editors collect fifteen essays on Anne Rice's novels, including an essay by Katherine Ramsland, one of Rice's biographers. **Appeal:** Academic.

Keller, James R. (editor).

Anne Rice and Sexual Politics: The Early Novels. *Jefferson, N.C.: McFarland Publishing, 2000.* Keller collects diverse essays about Rice's *Interview with the Vampire*, *The Feast of All Saints*, *Cry to Heaven*, The Sleeping Beauty Series, *Exit to Eden*, and the Mayfair Witch Series. **Appeal:** Popular.

Ramsland, Katherine.

The Anne Rice Reader. *New York: Ballantine Books, 1997.* Ramsland writes this very popular biographical criticism and interpretation of America's top vampire fiction writer. **Appeal:** Academic, Popular.

Smith, Jennifer.

Anne Rice: A Critical Companion. *Westport, Conn.: Greenwood, 1996.* Smith writes criticism and interpretation on Rice, with emphasis on her use of witchcraft, mummies, women, and vampires. **Appeal:** Academic.

Riley, Michael.

Conversations with Anne Rice. *New York: Ballantine Books, 1996.* Riley, a long-time friend of Rice, collects interviews wherein she discusses her now cult-status Vampire Chronicles, along with various minor novels. **Appeal:** Popular, Academic.

Robert Louis Stevenson

Nollen, Scott Allen.

Robert Louis Stevenson: Life, Literature and the Silver Screen. *Jefferson, N.C.: McFarland Publishing, 1994.* Nollen examines the film adaptations of Stevenson's works. **Appeal:** Academic.

Bram Stoker

Belford, Barbara.

Bram Stoker: A Biography of the Author of *Dracula.* *New York: Alfred A. Knopf, 1996.* Belford collects biographical information about and criticism on Bram Stoker, with emphasis on his theatrical ties. **Appeal:** Academic, Popular.

Glover, David.

Vampires, Mummies, and Liberals: Bram Stoker and the Politics of Popular Fiction. *Durham, N.C.: Duke University Press, 1996.* Glover analyzes what vampires, mummies, and eroticism reflected about the popular culture of nineteenth- and twentieth-century England. **Appeal:** Academic.

Hughes, William.

Beyond *Dracula*: **Bram Stoker's Fiction and Its Cultural Context.** *New York: St. Martin's Press, 2000.* Hughes uses cultural and sociological theories to analyze Bram Stoker's fiction other than *Dracula*, with emphasis on his treatment of race, religion, and society. **Appeal:** Academic.

Leatherdale, Clive (editor).

Bram Stoker's *Dracula* Unearthed [Annotated edition of *Dracula*]. *Westcliff-on-Sea, Essex: Desert Island Books, 1998, ©1897.* This annotated edition of Bram Stoker's *Dracula* contains hundreds of footnotes by Leatherdale, one of the foremost Stoker critics/scholars. **Appeal:** Academic, Popular.

McNally, Raymond T.

Dracula: Truth and Terror. *(CD-ROM). South Burlington, Vt.: Voyager Sotfware, 1996.* This impressive CD-ROM contains a searchable text of Dracula, movie clips of various vampire films, and a searchable vampire folklore (worldwide) index. **Appeal:** Popular, Academic.

Miller, Elizabeth (editor).

Dracula: The Shade and the Shadow. *Westcliff-on-Sea, Essex: Desert Island Books, 1998.* Miller, one of the top *Dracula* scholars in the field today, collects twenty essays presented at the "Dracula '97" centennial celebration, including contributions by Nina Auerbach and Radu Florescu. **Appeal:** Academic.

Wolf, Leonard.

Dracula: The Connoisseur's Guide. *New York: Broadway Books, 1997.* Wolf explains the role of vampires, especially the famous Dracula, in horror literature and film. **Appeal:** Academic, Popular.

Criticism on Horror Film

Blatty, William Peter.

If There Were Demons Then Perhaps There Were Angels: William Peter Blatty's Own Story of *The Exorcist*. *Southwold, Suffolk: Screen Press Books, 1998.* Screen Press reprints this popular transcript of a 1974 interview with Blatty, the author of *The Exorcist*. **Appeal:** Popular.

Clover, Carol J.

Men, Women and Chain Saws: Gender in the Modern Horror Film. *Princeton, N.J.: Princeton University Press, 1992.* This is Clover's critically acclaimed and very popular study of women's roles in slasher films, from *Psycho* to *Silence of the Lambs*. **Appeal:** Academic, Popular.

Freeland, Cynthia A.

The Naked and the Undead: Evil and the Appeal of Horror. *Boulder, Colo.: Westview, 2000.* This is Freeland's cognitive and feminist study of how horror films work and why they appeal to their audiences. Illustrated with scenes from films, 1930 to the present. **Appeal:** Academic.

Jancovich, Mark.

Rational Fears: American Horror in the 1950's. *Manchester, England, Manchester University Press, 1996.* Jancovich collects historical and critical accounts of horror films of the 1950s. **Appeal:** Academic.

Jensen, Paul M.

The Men Who Made the Monsters. *Twayne's Filmmaker Series. New York: Twayne, 1996.* Jensen collects biographical and critical notes on horror producers and directors in the United States and Britain. **Appeal:** Academic, Popular.

McCarty, John.

The Fearmakers. *New York: St. Martin's Press, 1994.* McCarty discusses detective, mystery, and horror films. **Appeal:** Academic, Popular.

Muir, John Kenneth.

Terror Television: American Series, 1970–1999. *Jefferson, N.C.: McFarland, 2001.* Muir documents the genre, from the dawn of modern horror television through more than thirty programs, including those of the 1998–1999 season. Includes complete histories, critical reception, episode guides, cast, crew and guest star information, as well as series reviews. **Appeal:** Popular, Academic.

Paul, William.

Laughing, Screaming: Modern Hollywood Horror and Comedy. *New York: Columbia University Press, 1994.* Paul examines the roles of comedy, sensationalism, sex, and violence in horror film. **Appeal:** Academic.

Prawer, S. S.

Caligari's Children: The Film as Tale of Terror. *New York: Oxford University Press, 1980.* Prawer pens this important study of horror film, with emphasis on early Universal Studios productions. **Appeal:** Academic.

Presnell, Don, and Marty McGee.

A Critical History of Television's *The Twilight Zone*, 1959–1964. *Jefferson, N.C.: McFarland Publishing, 1998.* Presnell and McGee collect a complete history of the show, including incisive analyses of all 156 episodes. Also included are biographical profiles of writers and contributors. **Appeal:** Popular, Academic.

Skal, David J.

Dark Carnival: The Secret World of Tod Browning—Hollywood's Master of the Macabre. *New York: Doubleday, 1995.* In this wonderful study, Skal chronicles the life and filmmaking career of Tod Browning. **Appeal:** Academic, Popular.

Periodicals: Journals, Magazines, and E-Zines

Recent trends in horror account for the variety of journals, fan magazines, and electronic magazines that can be found at the local newsstand or on the World Wide Web. For example, the move toward dark erotica in the genre has spawned such e-zines as *Blue Blood* (www.blueblood.com), an adults-only soft porn celebration of S and M, while the less erotic, more politicized gothic alternative movement has found its voice in the online fan mag *Carpe Noctem* (www.carpenoctem.com), which exhibits the same macabre and self-effacing sense of humor characteristic of the movement itself. In addition, the trend toward incorporating horror into the literary canon in colleges and universities across the nation, where ivory-towered Conradians must be running through the halls screaming "the horror! the horror!" at the prospect of Stephen King in the classroom, has led to the surging popularity of scholarly studies of horror, as seen in *The Journal of the International Association for the Fantastic in the Arts*, as well as in the recently defunct *Necrofile: The Review of Horror Fiction* and its current sister e-zine, *Necropsy: The Review of Horror Fiction* (www.lsu.edu/necrofile). Of course, fan-oriented magazines that exist to entertain hard-core horror fans, such as *Fangoria* and *Cemetery Dance*, continue to thrive.

The popularity of the Internet has also left its mark on horror periodicals, as there are now more e-zines and small press magazines with Web sites, making it possible for amateur and rookie writers of dark fiction to publish. This opening of the doors for publication will ultimately help publishers and fans alike discover new voices in horror, some of which may produce quality fiction. To make publishing even more interesting for the writer and reader, some e-zines allow for interactive storytelling, whereby writers can add to stories in progress or even sell their characters (if their characters are marketable) to be used by other writers for future tales.

In short, horror periodicals, like periodicals in all fields, range from the sublime to the ridiculous, from the strictly informational to the graphically erotic. In this chapter, we have listed and annotated most of these periodicals, from the benchmark horror journals and magazines, such as *Necrofile/Necropsy* and *Cemetery Dance*, to the lesser-known small press journals, such as *Crimson* and *Hellnotes*. Although we do not assume libraries will rush to purchase these journals, we hope to impress upon librarians and patrons that much good horror short fiction, as well as many excellent reviews and interviews, are published by these periodicals. Therefore, horror readers will want to at least be cognizant of their existence.

Note: Librarians should be aware that many "fanzines" in the genre go in and out of print, and may, at a moment's notice, cease altogether, be incorporated into another zine, or die and be resurrected as a totally new zine. Information for each journal and e-zine was obtained from Ulrich's online. Circulation, price, and ISSN are given if that information was noted in Ulrich's. Web sites in this chapter were verified as of October 28, 2002.

> **Aberrations**, a product of Sirius Fiction, publishes a broad range of fiction in the sister genres of science fiction, adult horror, and dark fantasy, from the pulp style of storytelling of the 1930s and 1940s to the more experimental and literary fiction of today. It promises "a wild literary ride going where most fiction does not go." *Aberrations* is edited by Richard W. Blair and published monthly by Sirius Fiction of San Francisco. It includes book reviews. Circulation: 1,000 paid; price $31/year; ISSN 1058-2509.

> **Bibliographies and Indexes in Science Fiction, Fantasy, and Horror**, published by Greenwood Press, has been around since 1987 and is released irregularly. It is a monographic series that produces bibliographies of science fiction, fantasy, and horror. Price varies; ISSN 1053-4636.

> **Carpe Noctem** is a bimonthly online alternative magazine located at http://www.carpenoctem.com. It includes artwork, exclusive interviews, and short stories. It is now in its seventh year of publication, and past issues of the print version are still available via special order. Price $20/year; ISSN 1083-5334.

Cemetery Dance is the genre's most revered popular magazine, and in 2001 it was in its eleventh year of publication. This quarterly, which is edited and published by Richard T. Chizmar, is out of Baltimore, Maryland, and has won the World Fantasy Award. *Cemetery Dance* uses regular columnists and has published works by King, Barker, Rice, Straub, Campbell, Simmons, Bloch, Ellison, and Matheson, as well as by hundreds of others. It includes both original fiction and reviews. It includes book and film reviews. *Cemetery Dance* can be found online at www.horrornet.com/dance.htm. Price $15/year; ISSN 1047-7675.

Champagne Horror is a print journal published by Champagne Productions out of Canada. It was begun in 1990 and is published annually. Its editor is Cathy Buburuz, and it includes horror fiction, poetry, and art. Price $6/year; ISSN 0847-1711.

Chiaruscuro, also known as *Chizine*, is found at www.thechiaroscuro.com, and it is an e-zine that features new fiction and poetry, editorial columns, and book reviews. It is partnered with Leisure Books, one of the largest horror publishers in the field, and is produced by The Chiaroscuro, "a society of dark art appreciators . . . nearly 1,300 members strong . . . drawing on 40 countries for its membership." Members of this organization include published writers and scholars. Not found in Ulrich's.

Chills is published by the British Fantasy Society (see Horror-Related Organizations) and has been active since. It is a print and online journal and is free to members of the BFS. It covers literary works in science fiction, fantasy, and horror, and is edited by Peter Coleborn.

Crimson is a quarterly newsletter of stories, case studies, and news and reviews on vampires. A referred serial, it is published quarterly by the Vampire Guild in Dorset, England, and is edited by Phill White. Circulation 1000. Price £12/year domestic, £18/year foreign; ISSN not supplied.

Crypt of Cthulhu is a pulp thriller and theological journal that publishes general critical articles on the fiction of H. P. Lovecraft and his literary disciples. It regularly includes fiction and poetry by fans and major writers. It is published irregularly by Necronomicon Press out of West Warwick, Rhode Island and is edited by Robert M. Price. Circulation: 650; price $5.95/issue; ISSN 1077-8179.

The Dark Planet Webzine (located at http://www.sfsite.com/darkplanet/) is edited by Lucy A. Snyder and publishes science fiction, fantasy, and horror, as well as *book reviews*. Price per issue; ISSN not supplied.

Dead of Night is an annual referred serial containing horror fiction, fantasy, mystery, and science fiction, and is published by Dead of Night Publications in Longmeadow, Massachusetts. It is edited by Lynn Stein. Circulation: 3,200; price $9/year; ISSN 1049-0892.

Fangoria is one of the all-time most popular horror zines, and one of the oldest. Published ten times a year out of New York by Starlog Group and edited by Anthony Timpone, this visually appealing fan mag covers horror in film, on television, in literature, in comics, in videos, and on video games and laser discs. Circulation: 214,500; price $37.97/year; ISSN 0164-2111.

Horror: The Newsmagazine of the Horror and Dark Fantasy Field is published quarterly by Wildside Press, which is located in Berkeley Heights, New Jersey. Wildside specializes in horror, science fiction, and fantasy, and publishes anthologies and collections as well. The journal is edited by John G. Betancourt and includes book reviews, illustrations, and information on the horror publishing and book trade industries in the United States and Canada. Price $36/year; ISSN not supplied.

Haunts publishes tales of unexpected horror and the supernatural tri-annually by Night Shade publications of Cranston, Rhode Island. Circulation: 2,500; price $16/year; ISSN 1043-3503.

Hellnotes, formerly titled *Horror Show,* is "your weekly insider's guide to the horror field." It includes nonfiction, interviews, best-seller lists, publicity trends, and other horror-related information, and is self-published. Its home page can be found at www.hellnotes.com, and its editor is David B. Silva. Circulation: 1,000; price $40/year; ISSN not supplied.

The Journal of the Fantastic in the Arts is published quarterly by The International Association for the Fantastic in the Arts (see Horror-Related Organizations). This organization is a collection of academics, scholars, researchers, writers, and fans of science fiction, fantasy, and horror. The journal is edited by Carl Yoke and produced by Florida Atlantic University (Jade Seas Publishing). *JFA* includes some original work by big name writers, such as Dan Simmons, but is composed mainly of articles and studies in horror, science fiction, and fantasy. The journal also publishes, on occasion, guest speeches delivered at the annual International Conference on the Fantastic in the Arts. Circulation: 500; price $20/year; ISSN 0897-0521.

Lovecraft Studies is a scholarly journal that is published twice a year by Necronomicon Press of West Warwick, Rhode Island. It is concerned with the writings of H. P. Lovecraft. The editor is Lovecraft scholar S. T. Joshi. Price $12/year; ISSN 0899-8361.

Necrofile: The Review of Horror Fiction is now defunct, but back issues of this quarterly are an indispensable publication for librarians in horror collection development, as the journal published the most comprehensive listing of all new horror titles in the United States and Britain up until the year 2000. The bulk of this small journal (produced by Necronomicon Press of West Warwick, Rhode Island, and edited by horror experts Stefan Dziemianowicz, S. T. Joshi, and Michael A. Morrison) was made up of authoritative, extended book reviews of both current fiction and newly released older fiction. Although not very visually appealing, this scholarly publication is packed with information. Back issues can be purchased at www.necropress.com. Price $12/year. Ulrich's information is outdated.

Necropsy: The Review of Horror Fiction, located at www.lsu.edu/necrofile, is an e-zine in the vein of the now defunct print journal *Necrofile: The Review of Horror Fiction*. Necropsy is housed at Louisiana State University, Department of English. Begun in 2001, it features professional book reviews (extended reviews of novels, collections of short fiction, poetry, graphic novels, and films in the genre). It is unaffiliated with any publisher, and its staff consists primarily of academics and librarians. The editors are June Pulliam and Tony Fonseca, two former *Necrofile* reviewers. Price free. Not found in Ulrich's.

Sinister Element Online is located at www.darktales.com/sinister/current/current.htm and is edited by Butch Miller. It features new fiction, editorials, interviews, book reviews, video reviews, and horoscopes. Not found in Ulrich's.

Terminal Fright, published by Charles McKee Books, is a forum for writers in the genre, and is edited by Ken Abner. This quarterly is a magazine of traditional horror literature. Circulation: 3,000; price $20; ISSN 1080-6873.

Horror-Related Organizations

In this section we list those sources that are the most difficult to find: human beings who are experts in the genre. Horror fans often join societies and attend conventions, such as The World Horror Convention, The International Association for the Fantastic in the Arts Convention, The Popular Culture Association's Conference, and NECON (The Northeast Writers' Conference). These conventions are excellent places to hear readings of early drafts of both primary and secondary works in the genre, to meet writers and critics, and to exchange ideas and e-mail addresses with other readers and fans. We will also list here various smaller societies, such as The Lord Ruthven Assembly (an International Vampire Society). We briefly describe each and give enough information for interested patrons and librarians to contact these societies when desired.

Note: URLs for these organizations were verified on October 29, 2002.

The British Fantasy Society (www.britishfantasysociety.org.uk) promotes the enjoyment of fantasy, science fiction, and horror in all its forms, and hosts Fantasy Con (a conference for fantasy, science fiction, and horror) annually. Members receive a newsletter six times per year (*Prism UK*) and a free copy of *Dark Horizons*. Members also receive a preferential rate at Fantasy Con. The current president is horror writer Ramsey Campbell. Its mailing address is 201 Reddish Road, South Reddish, STOCKPORT, SK5 7HR, England.

18

The Edgar Allan Poe Society of Baltimore (www.eapoe.org) was officially established following a commemorative celebration of Poe's birthday on January 19, 1923. It offers information about Poe including, but not limited to, general topics, his works, his life, his home, his death, and his burial site. Prospective members should visit the society's home page.

The Horror Writers' Association (www.horror.org) brings together writers and others with a professional interest in horror. Members receive a newsletter, e-mail bulletins, and access to private online services. Its current president is David Niall Wilson. This organization votes on and awards the most prestigious honor in the genre, The Bram Stoker Awards for fiction and nonfiction. Interested parties can contact the HWA through e-mail (hwa@horror.org) or through mail at Horror Writers' Association, P.O. Box 50577, Palo Alto, CA 94303.

The International Association for the Fantastic in the Arts (www.iafa.org) is an organization of scholars and fans of horror, science fiction, and fantasy that meets at an annual conference in Ft. Lauderdale, Florida. Writer/critic Joe Andriano heads the division for horror literature. Readers seeking further information should contact William A. Senior at Broward Community College. The IAFA's mailing address is Prof. Martha Bartter (mbartter@truman.edu), IAFA Treasurer, Dept. of Languages and Literature, Truman State University, Kirksville, MO 63501, and its home page is found at http://ebbs.english.vt.edu/iafa/ iafa.home.html

The Lord Ruthven Assembly (www.wiz.cath.vt.edu/LRA)is a scholarly organization recognized as a special interest group within the International Association for the Fantastic in the Arts. Its objectives include the serious pursuit of scholarship and research, focusing on the vampire/revenant figure in a variety of disciplines. The current president is Stephanie Moss. Prospective members should e-mail the Lord Ruthven Assembly (cmrusse@ruby.indstate.edu).

The Popular Culture Association (www2.h-net.msu.edu/~pcaaca/pop.html) is dedicated to the study of popular culture in all forms, including horror. Phil Simpson is the current area chair for the horror section of PCA. For further information about PCA, readers should contact Ray Browne at Bowling Green State University, Bowling Green, Ohio. Prospective members should visit the PCA's home page for membership applications.

The Transylvanian Society of Dracula, Canadian Chapter (www.chebucto.ns.ca/Recreation/TSD/tsdhompg.html) is a nonprofit cultural/historical organization that provides a clearing house of information pertaining to the serious study of Dracula and related topics. Its members include historians, folklorists, literary critics, researchers, students, and film enthusiasts. Its current president is Dr. Elizabeth Miller (emiller@mun.ca), who can be contacted by prospective members through her e-mail address.

The UK Chapter of The Horror Writers Association (www.horror.org/uk) is a subset of the American-based Horror Writers Association. Membership in the HWA allows membership in the UK chapter, and one does not have to live in the United Kingdom to join the UK chapter. The organization offers a monthly newsletter and various publications.

Horror on the World Wide Web

The World Wide Web is quickly becoming one of the best resources for information. As a whole, the Web offers the strength of comprehensiveness; one of its best (and worst) attributes is that it offers choices of information on every subject imaginable, no matter how trivial. All a researcher need know is how to take advantage of Internet search engines, such as the popular Yahoo! or AltaVista, or the less popular but often better engines such as Profusion (www.profusion.com), Highway 61 (www.highway61.com), Metacrawler (www. metacrawler.com), Mamma (www.mamma.com), Google (www.google.com), and Infoseek (www.infoseek.com). For horror fans, these search engines hold the key to information on subjects ranging from vampire folklore, to vampire music, to vampire clans.

Another strength of the World Wide Web is its ability to offer the most current information available; that is, when the author of a Web site makes a conscientious effort to keep that site as current as possible. Those of us who have built and maintained Web pages, either for our personal use or for the libraries and institutions for which we work, know that a Web page can be changed within minutes of information receipt. This means that on a well-maintained site, the "What's New" section can contain information that is mere minutes old. Of course, the great advantage of this to horror readers and fans is that a site like *Fiona's Fear and Loathing* (annotated in this chapter) will list horror titles that were released that same week, or that a site like *Dark Echo Horror* can contain an interview with Poppy Z. Brite that was conducted just a day before it was posted to the Web page.

Of course, there are drawbacks to finding information on the Web. Because the Web is an international and unedited collection of ideas, notes, musings, and personal theories, it will by its nature contain lots of relevant information for the horror fan. However, it will also contain lots of incorrect information. If researchers are not careful, they might be duped into thinking that just because information is on the Web, it is current; this is not necessarily so (in fact, it is more often *not so*). The careful researcher looks for a copyright date at the bottom of the index page (the opening or main page) of a Web site, and pays attention to this date.

It is the objective of this chapter to help librarians and horror readers avoid some of these pitfalls by listing some of the better horror Web sites we have encountered in our research, both as instructors of horror film and fiction courses and as bibliographers collecting hard-to-find information for *Hooked on Horror*. Site entries give the site name first, then site address, and finally date last accessed. To facilitate the production of a list containing sites that were still actually available, we waited until the last possible second to run a final check on these sites, even though we had been using many of them habitually for three to four years. We avoided sites about specific authors and works, as this chapter is intended to list horror Web sites with a general emphasis. The annotations in this chapter, like the other annotations in this guide, are not evaluative. The discussion on how to evaluate Web sites is a voluminous part of the library and information science literature, and we leave it to librarians and readers to educate themselves on this subject and then to try evaluating sites for themselves.

These URLs were verified on October 29, 2002.

Darkecho Horror

http://www.darkecho.com/darkecho/index.html. This site incorporates all of the content of DarkEcho OMNI Horror (1996–1998), originally produced professionally under editors Ellen Datlow and Pam Weintraub for OMNI Online, as well as most of the original DarkEcho's Horror Web. Since October 1998, DarkEcho's writer/editor has been the literature editor for Universal Studios' Horror Online, so readers will find an extensive section of author features, book reviews, and essays produced monthly for that site. The woman behind DarkEcho is Paula Guran. An active member of the Horror Writers Association, she chaired the Bram Stoker Awards Jury for two terms and is a former member of the Board of Trustees. Guran also serves as Facilitator for the International Horror Guild Awards.

Fiona's Fear and Loathing

http://www.oceanstar.com/horror. Subtitled "A Space Devoted to Horror Literature," this independently run Web page includes ninety-five short book reviews of true crime books, a gallery of grotesque art from the sixteenth to the twentieth centuries, a list of recent book reviews, and various mini-reviews. Aside from excellent reviews that are unaffiliated with any publisher, *Fiona's Fear and Loathing* boasts a list of the best horror books since 1980 and a list of horror publishes and booksellers. It also includes a section for writers of original fiction.

Horror at Indiana Discussion List

http://php.indiana.edu/~mlperkin/horror.html. Horror at Indiana is an e-mail discussion list based at Indiana University in Bloomington. The topic is horror (natural, supernatural, and preternatural) in film and literature. There are currently almost 500 members spread out over five continents, and with that many diverse people the discussion wanders quite a bit. On any given day talk can cover current or classic horror films and stories, reviews, requests for information on a favorite novel, reminiscences of a film seen long ago, friendly debates, and in-depth critical analyses. Group activities also occur, such as the biweekly Group View, where group members take turns choosing a film for weekend viewing, followed by on-list discussions of that film.

Horror World

www.horrorworld.cjb.net. Previously known as Masters of Terror, Horror World is a wonderfully designed site that features new books reviews, lists of the top 100 horror novels and short stories of all time, and valuable pre-release information from various publishers, especially Leisure Press. Aside from reviews and collection-related information, Horror World offers interviews, links to author pages, links to comics pages, links to live chat rooms, and a link to the Masters of Terror anthology. At its peak MOT/Horror World was clocking more than 30,000 visitors a week. Its Web master is Andy Fairclough.

Literature of the Fantastic

http://www.sff.net/people/doylemacdonald/lit.htp. This very simply designed site offers easy-to-find links to selected online horror and gothic texts that are in the public domain, so it is especially useful for finding eighteenth-and nineteenth-century titles online. In addition, it has links to discussion lists and to various Web sites having to do with early gothicism and horror.

Chapter 19

Major Awards

This chapter lists and briefly describes the major awards given annually in horror fiction, from the prestigious Bram Stoker Awards for best horror to the smaller but just as meaningful International Horror Guild Awards.

The Bram Stoker Awards, Winners, and Nominees

The Horror Writers' Association (HWA) gives the Bram Stoker Awards for Superior Achievement in fiction annually. The winners are determined by vote of the active members of HWA, and the awards themselves are presented at HWA's Annual Meeting and Awards Banquet.

Winners are denoted in boldface. The other items listed are nominees.

2001

Novels

Bradbury, Ray. *From the Dust Returned*
Gaiman, Neil. *American Gods*
Ketchum, Jack. *The Lost*
King, Stephen and Peter Straub. *Black House*

First Novels

Barron, Diana. *Phantom Feast*
goldberg, d. g. k. *Skating on the Edge*
Naassise, Joe. *Riverwatch*
Oliveri, Michael. *Deadliest of the Species*

Nonfiction

Campbell, Bruce. *If Chins Could Kill: Confessions of a B Movie Actor*
Hopkins, Brian A., and Garrett Peck. *Personal Demons*
Keene, Brian. *Jobs in Hell*
Silva, David B. and Paul F. Olson. *Hellnotes*

Illustrated Narratives

Azzarello, Brian. *Freezes Over*
Kiernan, Caitlin R. *The First Adventures of Miss Catterina Poe*
Mariotte, Jeff. *Desperados: Quiet of the Grave*
Smith, Kevin. *Quiver*
Various Authors. *Weird Western Tales*
No winner indicated.

Lifetime Achievement: No award given

2000

Novels

Braunbeck, Gary A. *The Indifference of Heaven*
Campbell, Ramsey. *Silent Children*
Hopkins, Brian A. *The Licking Valley Coon Hunters*
Laymon, Richard. *The Traveling Vampire Show*
Piccirilli, Tom. *The Deceased*

First Novels

Clark, Simon. *Nailed by the Heart*
Danielewski, Mark Z. *House of Leaves*
Hopkins, Brian A. *The Licking Valley Coon Hunters Club*
Winter, Douglas E. *Run*

Fiction Collections

Jacob, Charlee. *Up, Out of Cities That Blow Hot and Cold*
Rogers, Bruce Holland. *Wind Over Heaven and Other Dark Tales*
Straub, Peter. *Magic Terror*
Tem, Steve Rasnic. *City Fishing*

Anthologies

Datlow, Ellen, and Terri Windling (editors). *The Year's Best Fantasy & Horror*, 13th Annual Collection

Eller, Steve. *Brainbox: The Real Horror*

Hopkins, Brian A. (editor). *Extremes: Fantasy & Horror from the Ends of the Earth*

Laymon, Richard. *Bad News*

Nonfiction

King, Stephen. *On Writing*

Sheehan, Bill. *At the Foot of the Story Tree*

Silva, David B., and Paul F. Olson. *Hellnotes*

Weinberg, Robert. *Horror of the 20th Century*

Illustrated Narratives

Moore, Alan. *The League of Extraordinary Gentlemen* (miniseries)

Weinberg, Robert. *Cable 79-84*

Wrightson, Bernie. "Spuds" (*Night Terrors #1*)

Lifetime Achievement: Nigel Kneale

Trustees' Award for Specialty Press Excellence: Subterranean Press, William K. Schafer

1999

Novels

Goingback, Owl. *Darker than Night*

Harris, Thomas. *Hannibal*

King, Stephen. *Low Men in Yellow Coats*

Piccirilli, Tom. *Hexes*

Straub, Peter. *Mr. X*

First Novels

Beai, Steve. *Widow's Walk*

Connolly, John. *Every Dead Thing*

Miéville, China. *King Rat*

Passarella, J. G. *Wither*

Fiction Collections

Clegg, Douglas. *The Nightmare Chronicles*

King, Stephen. *Hearts in Atlantis*

Piccirilli, Tom. *Deep into that Darkness Peering*

Van Belkom, Edo. *Death Drives a Semi*

Anthologies

Datlow, Ellen, and Terri Windling (editors). *The Year's Best Fantasy & Horror, Twelfth Annual Collection*

Jones, Stephen (editor). *The Mammoth Book of Best New Horror 10*

Pelan, John (editor). *The Last Continent: New Tales of Zothique*

Sarrantonio, Al (editor). *999: New Stories of Horror and Suspense*

Illustrated Narratives

Gaiman, Neil. *Sandman: The Dream Hunters*

Lansdale, Joe R. *Jonah Hex: Shadows West #1*

Mignola, Mike. *Hellboy: Box Full of Evil*

Quinn, David. *Faust: Book of M*

Nonfiction

Guran, Paula. *DarkEcho*

Jones, Stephen. *The Essential Monster Movie Guide*

Price, Victoria. *Vincent Price: A Daughter's Biography*

Silva, David B., and Paul F. Olson (editors). *Hellnotes*

Lifetime Achievement: Edward Gorey, Charles L. Grant

Trustees' Award for Specialty Press: Excellence Ash-Tree Press, Christopher and Barbara Roden

1998

Novels

King, Stephen. *Bag of Bones*

Koontz, Dean. *Fear Nothing*

Somtow, S. P. *Darker Angels*

Tessier, Thomas. *Fog Heart*

First Novels

Cacek, P. D. *Night Prayers*

Jacob, Charlee. *This Symbiotic Fascination*

Kiernan, Caitlin R. *Silk*

Marano, Michael. *Dawn Song*

Fiction Collections

Cacek, P. D. *Leavings*

Gaiman, Neil. *Smoke and Mirrors*

Shirley, John. *Black Butterflies*

Wilson, Gahan. *The Cleft and Other Odd Tales*

Anthologies

Bloch, Robert (editor). *Robert Bloch's Psychos*

Chizmar, Richard (editor). *Best of Cemetery Dance*

Datlow, Ellen, and Terri Windling (editors). *The Year's Best Fantasy and Horror, 11th Annual Collection*

Dziemianowicz, Stefan, Martin H. Greenberg, and Robert Weinberg (editors). *Horrors! 365 Scary Stories*

Comic Books, Graphic Novels, or Other Illustrated Narratives

Aragones, Sergio, and Mark Evanier. *Sergio Aragones' Dia de las Muertos (Day of the Dead)*

Ennis, Garth. *Preacher*

Ennis, Garth. *The Son of Man* (*Hellblazer* #129–133)

Wein, Len. *The Dreaming: Trial and Error*

No winner indicated.

Lifetime Achievement: Ramsey Campbell, Roger Corman

1997

Novel

Berliner, Janet, and George Guthridge. *Children of the Dusk*

Dobyns, Stephen. *The Church of Dead Girls*

Due, Tananarive. *My Soul to Keep*

Powers, Tim. *Earthquake Weather*

First Novel

Bakis, Kirsten. *Lives of the Monster Dogs*

Dedman, Stephen. *The Art of Arrow Cutting*

Hoffman, Barry. *Hungry Eyes*

Mitchell, Mary Ann. *Drawn to the Grave*

Murrey, Mary. *The Inquisitor*

Collection

Braunbeck, Gary A. *Things Left Behind*
McNaughton, Brian. *The Throne of Bones*
Taylor, Lucy. *Painted in Blood*
Wagner, Karl Edward. *Exorcisms and Ecstasies*

Nonfiction

Clute, John, and John Grant. *The Encyclopedia of Fantasy*
Hearn, Marcus, and Alan Barnes. *The Hammer Story*
Jones, Stephen. *Clive Barker's A-Z of Horror*
Lucas, Tim. *Video Watchdog*
Ramsland, Katherine. *Dean Koontz: A Writer's Biography*
Wiater, Stanley. *Dark Thoughts: On Writing*

Lifetime Achievement: William Peter Blatty, Jack Williamson

1996

Novels

Brite, Poppy Z. *Exquisite Corpse*
Goingback, Owl. *Crota*
King, Stephen. *The Green Mile*
Straub, Peter. *The Hellfire Club*

First Novels

Burleson, Donald. *Flute Song*
Goingback, Owl. *Crota*
Kihn, Greg. *Horror Show*
Stone, Del. *Dead Heat*

Fiction Collections

Hodge, Brian. *The Convulsion Factory*
Ligotti, Thomas. *The Nightmare Factory*
Massie, Elizabeth. *Shadow Dreams*
Sallee, Wayne Allen. *With Wounds Still Wet*
Somtow, S. P. *The Pavilion of Frozen Women*

Nonfiction

Belford, Barbara. *Bram Stoker: A Biography of the Author of Dracula*
Hutchison, Don. *The Great Pulp Heroes*
Jones, Stephen. *The Illustrated Werewolf Movie Guide*

Joshi, S. T. *H.P. Lovecraft: A Life*
Skal, David. *V is for Vampire*

Lifetime Achievement: Ira Levin, Forrest J. Ackerman

1995

Novels

Mosiman, Billie Sue. *Widow*
Navarro, Yvonne. *Deadrush*
Oates, Joyve Carol. *Zombie*
Rodgers, Alan. *Bone Music*

First Novels

Bowen, Gary. *Diary of a Vampire*
Due, Tananarive. *The Between*
Girardi, Robert. *Madeleine's Ghost*
Taylor, Lucy. *The Safety of Unknown Cities*
Van Belkom, Edo. *Wyrm Wolf*

Fiction Collections

Carroll, Jonathan. *The Panic Hand*
Gorman, Ed. *Cages*
Grant, Charles. *The Black Carousel*
Koontz, Dean. *Strange Highways*

Nonfiction

Ashley, Michael, and William Contento. *The Supernatural Index*
Leigh, Janet, and Christopher Nickens. *Psycho: Behind the Scenes of the Classic Thriller*
Randi, James. *An Encyclopedia of Claims, Frauds, and Hoaxes of the Occult and Supernatural*
Tohill, Cathal, and Pete Tombs. *Immoral Tales: European Sex & Horror Movies 1956–1984*

Lifetime Achievement: Harlan Ellison

1994

Novels

Carr, Caleb. *The Alienist*
Carroll, Jonathan. *From the Teeth of Angels*
Holder, Nancy. *Dead in the Water*

King, Stephen. *Insomnia*

McCabe, Patrick. *The Butcher Boy*

First Novels

Arnzen, Michael. *Grave Markings*

Bonansinga, Jay R. *The Black Mariah*

Devereaux, Robert. *Deadweight*

Kilpatrick, Nancy. *Near Death*

Collections

Bloch, Robert. *The Early Fears*

Lansdale, Joe R. *Writer of the Purple Rage*

Taylor, Lucy. *The Flesh Artist*

Vachs, Andrew. *Born Bad*

Lifetime Achievement: Christopher Lee

1993

Novels

Denton, Bradley. *Blackburn*

Brite, Poppy Z. *Drawing Blood*

Little, Bentley. *The Summoning*

Newman, Kim. *Anno Dracula*

Straub, Peter. *The Throat*

First Novels

Billson, Anne. *Suckers*

Hoffman, Nina Kiriki. *The Thread That Binds the Bones*

Matheson, Richard Christian. *Created By*

Navarro, Yvonne. *Afterage*

Nutman, Philip. *Wet Work*

Collections

Campbell, Ramsey. *Alone with the Horrors*

King, Stephen. *Nightmares and Dreamscapes*

Laymon, Richard. *A Good and Secret Place*

Simmons, Dan. *Lovedeath*

Taylor, Lucy. *Close to the Bone*

Nonfiction

Bloch, Robert. *Once Around the Bloch*
Harrison, Shirley, and Michael Barrett. *The Diary of Jack the Ripper*
Skal, David J. *The Monster Show*

Lifetime Achievement: Joyce Carol Oates

Special Trustees Award: Vincent Price

1992

Novels

Costello, Matthew. *Homecoming*
Hodge, Brian. *Deathgrip*
Koontz, Dean. *Hideaway*
Monteleone, Thomas. *Blood of the Lamb*
Simmons, Dan. *Children of the Night*

First Novels

Brite Poppy Z. *Lost Souls*
D'Amato, Brian. *Beauty*
Massie, Elizabeth. *Sineater*
Raisor, Gary. *Less Than Human*
Sallee, Wayne Allen. *The Holy Terror*

Collections

Engstrom, Elizabeth. *Nightmare Flower*
Partridge, Norman. *Mr. Fox and Other Feral Tales*
Tarchetti, I. U. *Fantastic Tales*

Nonfiction

Clover, Carol J. *Men, Women and Chainsaws*
Golden, Christopher. *Cut! Horror Writers On Horror Film*
Kies, Cosette. *Young Adult Horror Fiction*
Russo, John. *Scare Tactics*
Wiater, Stanley. *Dark Visions*

Lifetime Achievement: Ray Russell

1991

Novels

Disch, Thomas M. *The M. D.*

King, Stephen. *Needful Things*

King, Stephen. *Dark Tower III: The Waste Lands*

McCammon, Robert R. *Boy's Life*

Simmons, Dan. *Summer of Night*

First Novels

Curry, Chris, and L. Dean James. *Winter Scream*

Danvers, Dennis. *Wilderness*

Koja, Kathe. *The Cipher* (tie)

McConnell, Ashley. *Unearthed*

Tem, Melanie. *Prodigal* (tie)

Collections

Campbell, Ramsey. *Waking Nightmares*

Simmons, Dan. *Prayers to Broken Stones*

Sutphin, Richard. *Sex Punks & Savage Sagas*

Williamson, J. N. *Naked Flesh of Feeling*

Nonfiction

Guillen, Ellen. *Vampires Among Us Rosemary*

Jones, Stephen. *Clive Barker's Shadows of Eden*

Ramsland, Katherine. *Prism of the Night: A Biography of Anne Rice*

Spignesi, Stephen J. *The Shape Under the Sheet: The Complete Stephen King Encyclopedia*

Lifetime Achievement: Gahan Wilson

1990

Novels

Lansdale, Joe R. *Savage Season*

Laymon, Richard. *Funland*

McCammon, Robert R. *Mine*

Williamson, Chet. *Reign*

First Novels

Little, Bentley. *The Revelation*
Martindale, T. Chris. *Nightblood*
Piccirilli, Tom. *Dark Father*
Rodgers, Alan. *Blood Of The Children*

Collections

Blumlein, Michael. *The Brains of Rats*
King, Stephen. *Four Past Midnight*
Straub, Peter. *Houses Without Doors*
Simmons, Dan. *Prayers to Broken Stones*

Nonfiction

Barron, Neil. *Horror Literature: A Reader's Guide*
Briggs, Joe Bob. *Joe Bob Goes Back to the Drive-In*
Joshi, S. T. *The Weird Tale*
Skal, David J. *Hollywood Gothic*
Wiater, Stanley. *Dark Dreamers*

Lifetime Achievement: Hugh B. Cave, Richard Matheson

1989

Novels

Dunn, Katherine. *Geek Love*
Grant, Charles L. *In a Dark Dream*
Koontz, Dean. *Midnight*
McCammon, Robert R. *The Wolf's Hour*
Simmons, Dan. *Carrion Comfort*

First Novels

Clegg, Douglas. *Goat Dance*
Collins, Nancy A. *Sunglasses After Dark*
Elliot, Tom. *The Dwelling*
Paiva, Jean. *The Lilith Factor*
Smith, Dean Wesley. *Laying the Music to Rest*

Collections

Cadigan, Pat. *Patterns*
Lansdale, Joe R. *By Bizarre Hands*

Matheson, Richard. *Collected Stories*
McCammon, Robert R. *Blue World*
Wilson, F. Paul. *Soft and Others*

Nonfiction

Cannon, Peter. *H.P. Lovecraft*
Dresser, Norine. *American Vampires: Fans, Victims, Practitioners*
Ellison, Harlan. *Harlan Ellison's Watching* **(tie)**
Jones, Stephen, and Kim Newman. *Horror: The 100 Best Books* **(tie)**
Wolf, Leonard. *Horror: A Connoisseur's Guide to Literature and Film*

Lifetime Achievement: No award given

1988

Novels

Harris, Thomas. *The Silence of the Lambs*
Lansdale, Joe R. *The Drive-In*
Laymon, Richard. *Flesh*
McCammon, Robert R. *Stinger*
Rice, Anne. *Queen of the Damned*
Wilson, F. Paul. *Black Wind*

First Novels

Anderson, Kevin J. *Ressurection, Inc.*
Byrne, John L. *Fear Book*
Harris, Alan Lee. *Deliver Us From Evil*
Paine, Michael. *Cities of the Dead*
Straczynski, J. Michael. *Demon Night*
Wilde, Kelley. *The Suiting*

Collections

Beaumont, Charles. *Selected Stories*
Bradbury, Ray. *The Toynbee Convector*
Ellison, Harlan. *Angry Candy*
Etchison, Dennis. *The Blood Kiss*
Farris, John. *Scare Tactics*
McGrath, Patrick. *Blood and Water and Other Tales*

Nonfiction: No award given

Lifetime Achievement: Ray Bradbury, Ronald Chetwynd-Hayes

1987

Novels

Garton, Ray. *Live Girls*
King, Stephen. *Misery* (tie)
McCammon, Robert R. *Swan Song* (tie)
Nunn, Kem. *Unassigned Territory*
Williamson, Chet. *Ash Wednesday*

First Novels

Barker, Clive. *The Damnation Game*
Cantrell, Lisa. *The Manse*
Miller, Rex. *Slob*
Rasnic Tem, Steve. *Excavation*
Richards, Tony. *The Harvest Bride*

Collections

Bloch, Robert. *Midnight Pleasures*
Campbell, Ramsey. *Scared Stiff*
Ellison, Harlan. *The Essential Ellison*
Wagner, Karl Edward. *Why Not You And Bit I?*
Waldrop, Howard. *All About Strange Monsters of the Recent Past*

Nonfiction

Briggs, Joe Bob. *Joe Bob Goes to the Drive-In*
Gagne, Paul A. *The Zombies That Ate Pittsburgh*
Spark, Muriel. *Mary Shelley*

Lifetime Achievement: Fritz Leiber, Frank Belknap Long, Clifford D. Simak

The International Horror Guild Awards

The International Horror Critics Guild was created in 1995 as a way to recognize the achievements of those who toil in the horror field. Before that date, only the Bram Stoker Award, which is presented by the Horror Writers Association, was considered a mark of distinction, but voting on it is limited to HWA members. The International Horror Guild Award represents a large, unaffiliated group of writers who are recognized for excellence by their peers.

Best Novel

2001—*Threshold*, Caitlin R. Kiernan

2000—*Declare*, Tim Powers

1999—*A Prayer for the Dying*, Stewart O'Nan

1998—*Fogheart*, Thomas Tessier

1997—*Nazareth Hill*, Ramsey Campbell

1996—*The 37th Mandala*, Marc Laidlaw

1995—*Resume with Monsters*, William Spencer

1994—*Anno Dracula*, Kim Newman

Best First Novel

2001—*Ordinary Horror*, David Searcy

2000—*Adam's Fall*, Sean Desmond

1999—*The Divinity Student*, Michael Cisco

1998—*Dawn Song*, Michael Marano

1997—*Drawn to the Grave*, Mary Ann Mitchell

1996—*Dead Heat*, Del Stone Jr.

1995—*The Safety of Unknown Cities*, Lucy Taylor

1994—*Grave Markings*, Michael Arnzen

Best Collection

2001—*Through Shattered Glass*, David B. Silva

2000—*City Fishing*, Steve Rasnic Tem (TIE)

2000—*Ghost Music and Other Tales*, Thomas Tessier (TIE)

1999—*The Nightmare Chronicles*, Douglas Clegg

1998—*Black Butterflies*, John Shirley

1997—*The Throne of Bones*, Brian McNaughton

1996—*Conference with the Dead*, Terry Lamsley

1995—*Cages*, Edward Gorman

1994—*Angels and Visitations*, Neil Gaiman

Best Anthology

2001—*Night Visions 10*, Richard Chizmar (editor)

2000—*October Dreams: A Celebration of Halloween*, Richard Chizmar and Robert Morrish (editors)

1999—*Subterranean Gallery*, Richard Chizmar and William Schafer (editors)

1998—*Dark Terrors 4*, Stephen Jones and David Sutton (editors)

1997—*Revelations*, Douglas E. Winter (editor)

1996—*Darkside: Horror for the Next Millennium*, John Pelan (editor)

1995—*Best New Horror #6,* Stephen Jones (editor)

1994—*Love in Vein*, Poppy Z. Brite (editor)

Best Publication (Award Given for Best Periodicals Devoted to Horror)

2001—*The Spook*

2000—*Horror Garage*

1999—*DarkEcho*

1998—*Hellnotes*

1997—*Necrofile*

1996—*Cemetary Dance*

1995—*Death Realm*

1994—*Answer Me!*

Living Legend Award

2001—William F. Nolan

2000—No award available for this year.

1999—Richard Matheson

1998—No award available for this year.

1997—No award available for this year.

1996—Edward W. Bryant

1995—Clive Barker

1994—Harlan Ellison

Chapter 20

Publishers and Publishers' Series

Included at the end of this chapter is a list of many publishers and publishers series mentioned in the annotations of chapters 4 through 18. Included are publishers whose catalogs offer some or a great deal of horror, or whose wares include science fiction, fantasy, or even romance that often straddle the horror genre. When we first set out to write this chapter, we intended to mention *only* those publishers who either specialized in horror or were responsible for *much* of the horror currently on the market. However, we soon realized this task was impossible. A quick glance at this list of publishers and publishers' series will show the reader one thing: There are very few publishing companies, or even imprints, dedicated *exclusively* to the horror genre. In fact, according to their listings in *Writer's Market*, many publishers actively discourage genre fiction, especially anything from the "degraded" genre of horror. According to Stephen Jones in his introduction to *The Mammoth Book of Best New Horror, Volume 9,* "the number of horror titles published in 1997 was down slightly on previous years on both sides of the Atlantic."

Furthermore, "Zebra cancelled its horror line, the oldest in mass-market publishing" and in the United Kingdom, Random House has decided to "pull out of the SF/fantasy/horror market entirely (except for the occasional blockbuster)." Thus, librarians wishing to begin horror collections or to augment previously existing ones can't simply order catalogs from a few major publishers and expect to do one-stop shopping. True, much horror still comes from Tor and Forge, owned by Thomas Doherty, but these publishers also produce science fiction and fantasy. Today, the biggest single publisher of horror is Leisure, an imprint of Dorchester publishing. Leisure generally puts out about twenty-four horror titles per year, and their offerings range from some well-known authors of the genre such as Simon Clark, Richard Laymon, J. N. Williamson, Elizabeth Massie, and Maryann Mitchell, to authors publishing their first novels in the genre. Leisure also has a horror book club, which sends selections to members every six weeks. Smaller, independently owned houses such as Necro Press and Arkham House are single-genre publishers, but their offerings aren't sufficient to furnish a representative collection. Librarians seeking to build their collections will have to look through the catalogs of large publishers such as HarperCollins, St. Martin's, Berkley, Penguin, and White Wolf to find individual horror offerings. However, they should by no means limit their browsing to these publishers' wares. They should also look through the catalogs of some of the more quirky publishers, who have horror titles among their many non-mainstream books.

Alyson Books, Los Angeles, CA

Medium-sized press specializing in lesbian- and gay-related material. Their horror offerings feature gay or lesbian characters.

Arkham House, Sauk City, WI

A small press originally created to publish the works of H. P. Lovecraft. Now continues that tradition by publishing reprints of his work, as well as Lovecraftian-type horror.

Ash-Tree Press, Ashcroft, BC (http://www.ash-tree.bc.ca/ashtreecurrent.html)

Publishers of high-quality volumes of the finest in supernatural fiction in limited editions.

August House, Little Rock, AK

Small independent publisher of storytelling resources.. Their offerings also include story collections of, for example, scary tales and ghost stories, as well as audiotapes and how-to books about storytelling.

Avon, New York

Large publisher of paperback and hardback originals and reprints. One of their imprints, Avon EOS, specializes in fantasy and science fiction, while another, Avon Science Fiction, publishes that genre exclusively.

Bantam (Bantam Doubleday Dell Publishing Group), New York

Publishes the gauntlet of fiction from mystery to science to fantasy to romance.

Berkley/Ace Science Fiction (G. P. Putnam), New York

An imprint of Berkley Publishing offering science fiction, as well as some science fiction to horror cross-overs.

Carroll & Graf, New York

One of the few remaining independent trade publishers, Carroll & Graff works with first-time as well as established authors. Publications include science fiction, fantasy, and erotica.

Catbird Press, North Haven, CT

Small, independent trade publisher specializing in quality, imaginative prose humor and Central European literature in translation.

CD Publications (or Cemetery Dance Publications), Baltimore, MD

A small press publishing *Cemetery Dance Magazine* as well as hardback horror novels by well-known authors in the genre. Cemetery Dance often reissues modern classics of the genre that have temporarily gone out of print.

Circlet Press, Cambridge, MA

Small, independent publisher specializing in science fiction and dark fantasy of an erotic nature.

Crown Publishing Group, New York

Large publisher whose fiction offerings include horror.

DarkTales Publications, Grand View, MO (www.darktales.com)

Small publisher of horror and dark fantasy.

Daw (Penguin Putnam), New York

Publishes science fiction, fantasy, and mainstream thrillers.

Fine Publications, or Donald I. Fine (Penguin Putnam), New York (http://www.booksnbytes.com/authors/fine_donaldi.htm)

This imprint of Penguin Putnam publishes dark fantasy and psychological horror, as well as mystery and suspense.

Forge (Thomas Doherty Associates), New York

Mid-sized company publishing mostly genre fiction, including horror, thrillers, mystery, and suspense.

Full Moon Publishing, Schereville, IN (http://www.fullmoonpub.com)

Publisher of mostly nontraditional mysteries and books that combine mystery with an element of paranormal, fantasy, and horror. Books are published at every full moon.

Gauntlet Press, Springfield, PA

Small press offering science fiction and horror.

Golden Gryphon Press, Collinsville, IL (http://www.goldengryphon.com)

Founded by the long-time editor of Arkham House, with the mission to publish handsome, quality books of short story collections by today's master writers and tomorrow's rising stars.

Headline, London

Mainstream publisher of popular fiction and nonfiction in hardcover and mass-market paperback.

Hippocampus Press, New York (http://www.hippocampuspress.com)

Founded in 1999, Hippocampus Press specializes in classic horror and science fiction with an emphasis on the works of H. P. Lovecraft and other pulp writers of the 1920s and 1930s. They offer unique, high-quality, affordable editions of important works.

Hyperion (Walt Disney Co.), New York (http://www.hyperionbooks.com)

Mainstream commercial publisher whose offerings include mystery/suspense, thriller/espionage, and general literary fiction.

ImaJinn Books, Hickory Corners, MI (http://www.imajinnbooks.com)

Publisher of supernatural, paranormal, fantasy, futuristic, and time travel romances, as well as science fiction and fantasy for children and young adults.

Alfred A. Knopf (Random House), New York (http://www.randomhouse.com/knopf)

Publishes hardcover literary, contemporary, suspense, and spy fiction.

Leisure, New York

An imprint of Dorchester Publishing; offerings include horror and technothrillers.

Llewellyn Publications, St. Paul, MN

Mid-sized publisher of New Age and occult fiction and nonfiction.

William Morrow & Co., New York

Large publisher whose offerings include science fiction and horror.

Mysterious Press (Warner Books), New York

An imprint of Warner Books offering crime and mystery fiction.

Necro Press, Orlando, FL

Small independent publisher of horror and fantasy.

New American Library (Penguin Putnam), New York

An imprint of Penguin that publishes works by American authors who are either part of the literary canon or have achieved their own immortality by remaining on the best-seller list. Currently publishes almost everything ever written by Stephen King.

Onyx (Dutton Signet), New York

An imprint of Dutton offering horror and romance.

Otter Creek Press, Middleburg, FL (http://www.otterpress.com)

A small independent publisher of fine imaginative fiction, which includes mysteries, intrigue, supernatural thrillers, and fantasy novels for both young adults and mature readers.

Penguin Books (Penguin Putnam), New York

Generally offers editions of the classics such as *Frankenstein* and *Dracula*.

Philtrum Press, Bangor, ME

Very small press run by Stephen King and his assistant to publish his work. Lately publishes his newest e-text, which is marketed from his official Web site.

Pinnacle Books (Kensington Publishing), New York (http://www.kensingtonbooks.com)

An imprint of Kensington Publishing, Pinnacle offerings include some horror.

Plume (Dutton Plume), New York

An imprint of Dutton whose offerings include some horror.

Pocket Books (Simon & Schuster), New York

Large publisher of paperback and hardback originals and reprints. Their offerings include horror and science fiction.

G. P. Putnam & Sons (Penguin Putnam), New York

An imprint of Penguin Putnam specializing in hardcover originals. Offerings include science fiction and mystery/suspense.

Random House, New York

Large publisher of quality hardback and paperback originals, including mystery/suspense and short story collections.

Roc (Penguin Putnam), New York

An imprint of Penguin Putnam devoted to horror, fantasy, and science fiction.

Severn House Publishers, Surrey, England, and New York

Medium to large publisher whose offerings include fantasy, science fiction, and horror.

Silver Lake Publishing, Morton, PA (www.silverlakepublishing.com)

Small publisher of horror, fantasy, and science fiction in both traditional and electronic formats.

Speculation Press, Dekalb, IL (http://www.speculationpress.com)

Publisher of cross-genre fiction that combines elements of science fiction, fantasy, mystery, and paranormal.

Stealth Press, Lancaster, PA (http://www.stealthpress.com)

Publisher of horror, science fiction, thrillers, and historical fiction, as well as first editions of books that have been out of print.

St. Martin's Press, New York

Large press whose offerings include gothic, psychic/supernatural, fantasy, and horror fiction.

Story Line Press, Brownsville, OR (http://www.storylinepress.com)

Small, nonprofit literary press publishing works in various genres.

Tor (Thomas Doherty Associates), New York

Publishes fantasy, science fiction, and horror.

Twayne, New York

An imprint of the Gale Group (http://www.galegroup.com), Twayne has been a leading source of concise, introductory books on literary criticism, American history, film studies, women's studies, and sociology for high school, college, and general interest readers.

Venus or Vixen Press, San Francisco (venusorvixen.com)

Offers the finest in erotic fiction and dark fantasy.

White Wolf, Clarkston, GA (http://www.white-wolf.com)

Small publisher of horror and dark fantasy.

Word Books, Dallas, TX

Small publisher of Christian fiction. A few of their fiction titles fall into the horror/dark fantasy genre.

Yard Dog Press, Alma, AK (yarddogpress.com)

Small publisher of horror, science fiction, fantasy, and children's fiction, often with a Southern flair.

Zebra (Kensington Publishing), New York

An imprint of Kensington Publishing offering mostly romance, as well as some romance to horror cross-overs.

Appendix A

Stretching the Boundaries: Cross-Genre Horror Fiction

Many readers come to the horror genre from other genre fiction. For example, readers who love action and adventure will find Dean Koontz much to their liking, and the current spate of vampire romance novels has inspired some fans of romance novels to pick up an Anne Rice or Chelsea Quinn Yarbro vampire series. In this appendix we list those horror works that "cross over" into other genres, such as action-adventure, classic fiction, Christian fiction, detective fiction, gentle reads, romance, and Westerns. We strongly suspect that by the third edition of *Hooked on Horror*, this list will include much more Western horror, plus more inspirational horror, as these seem to be increasing in popularity.

Fans of fantasy and science fiction might notice that the horror texts that contain elements of their favored genres are not in this list. Rather, we chose to establish the subject keyword terms "fantasy" and "science fiction"; these can be found in each applicable annotated entry, and works in which they appear can be found in the subject index. Our reasoning was that there are so many titles that overlap these two genres that the lists of titles would be unwieldy. Therefore, readers who enjoy horror fiction with elements of science fiction and fantasy are advised to consult the subject/keyword index for titles. Our reasoning was the same for historical fiction; it can be accessed through a keyword search under the term *history, use of,* or under specific names of historical figures and events. We sincerely hope that this has not made our guide less accessible for fans of those two genres. In essence, they can get the same information; they simply have to follow a different route to retrieve it.

Action Adventure

The following titles contain high levels of action and adventure, which will appeal to readers of those genres as well as to horror fans who enjoy a fast-paced, action-oriented read.

> Adams, Scott Charles. *Never Dream.*
>
> Africa, Chris N. *When Wolves Cry.*
>
> Albertson, C. E. *The Red God.*
>
> Allen, Bill. *Shadow Heart.*

Alten, Steve. The Meg Series.

Amos, Beth *Second Sight*.

Amsbery, Jonathan H. The Cyber Blood Chronicles.

Bacon-Smith, Camille. *Eyes of the Daemon*.

Ball, Donna. *Dark Angel*.

Cave, Hugh B. *The Evil Returns*.

Clifford, Emmett. *Night Whispers: A Story of Evil*.

Collins, Max Allan. *The Mummy Returns*.

Darnton, John. *The Experiment*.

Goingback, Owl. *Crota*.

Golden, Christopher. *Hellboy: The Lost Army*; *Strangewood*; *Spike and Dru: Pretty Maids All in a Row*.

Goshgarian, Gary [as Gary Braver]. *Elixir*.

Grant, Charles. *Black Oak 4: Hunting Ground*.

Hamilton, Laurell K. The Anita Blake, Vampire Hunter Series.

Heck, Victor. *A Darkness Inbred*.

Holland, Tom. *The Sleeper in the Sands*.

Hopkins, Brian A. *The Licking Valley Coon Hunters Club*.

Huggins, James Byron. *Hunter*.

Kaminsky, Howard and Susan Kaminsky. *The Twelve*.

King, Stephen. *Desperation*.

Koontz, Dean. *The Bad Place*, *Dark Fall*, *The Eyes of Darkness*, *The Face of Fear*, *Fear Nothing*, *Intensity*, *The Mask*, *Mr. Murder*, *Night Chills*, *The Servants of Twilight*, *Twilight Eyes*, *Watchers*.

Matheson, Richard. *The Incredible Shrinking Man*.

McCammon, Robert. *Mine*.

Mezrich, Ben. *Reaper*.

Moline, Karen. *Belladonna*.

Monahan, Brent. *The Blood of the Covenant: A Novel of the Vampire*.

Newman, J[ames]. *Holy Rollers*.

Niswander, Adam. *The Sand Dwellers*.

Romkey, Michael. *The Vampire Virus*.

Rosen, Selina. *The Boat Man*.

Sharp, Roger. *Psyclone*.

Shepherd, Mark. *Blackrose Avenue*.

Siebert, Steven. *Cleopatra's Needle*.

Simmons, Dan. *Carrion Comfort*.

Slade, Michael. The Headhunter Series.

Sipos, Thomas. M. *Vampire Nation*.

Stone, Del Jr. *Dead Heat.*

Tilton, Lois. *Darkspawn.*

Williams, Drew. *Night Terrors.*

Williamson, John N. *Spree.*

Christian Fiction

The following titles contain inspirational Christian plot lines, which will appeal to readers of that genre as well as to horror fans who enjoy a faith-affirming read.

Aczon, Kimile. *BJ: A Supernatural Horror Story.*

Cisco, Michael. *The Divinity Student.*

Climer, Steven Lee. *Soul Temple.*

Durchholz, Eric. *The Promise of Eden.*

Duval, Karen. *Project Resurrection.*

Hollis Claire. *The Light.*

Hunt, M. Martin. *Dark Soul.*

Johnstone, William W. *The Devil's Kiss, The Devil's Heart, The Devil's Touch.*

Lamb, Marilyn. *Blood Covenant.*

Long, Jeff. *The Descent.*

Rummel, Keith. *Spirit of Independence.*

Smith, Barry H. *Twilight Dynasty: Courting Evil.*

Classic Fiction

The following titles are considered classics in the genre, and they will appeal to readers who enjoy classic and canonical literature.

Ashley, Mike (editor). *Phantom Perfumes and Other Shades: Memories of Ghost Stories Magazine.*

Austen, Jane. *Northanger Abbey.*

Benson, E. F. *The Terror By Night.*

Benson, E. F. *The Passenger.*

Bierce, Ambrose. *The Moonlit Road and Other Ghost and Horror Stories.*

Blackwood, Algernon. *The Complete John Silence Stories.*

Dalby, Richard (editor). *12 Gothic Tales (The Mammoth Book of Victorian and Edwardian Ghost Stories).*

de la Mare, Walter. *The Return.*

DuMaurier, Daphne. *Rebecca*

Gorey, Edward (editor). *The Haunted Looking Glass: Ghost Stories Chosen by Edward Gorey.*

Grafton, John (editor). *Classic Ghost and Horror Stories by Wilkie Collins, M. R. James, Charles Dickens, and Others.*

Hawthorne, Nathaniel. *The House of the Seven Gables.*

Hodgson, William Hope. *The House on the Borderland.*

James, Henry. *Ghost Stories of Henry James.*

James, M. R. *Casting the Runes, and Other Ghost Stories, Ghost Stories of An Antiquary.*

Joshi, S. T. (editor). *Great Weird Tales: 14 Stories by Lovecraft, Blackwood, Machen and Others.*

Le Fanu, Joseph Sheridan. *Carmilla, Green Tea and Other Ghost Stories, In a Glass Darkly.*

Lewis, Matthew. *The Monk.*

Lovecraft, H. P. *The Case of Charles Dexter Ward, The Loved Dead and Other Revisions, The Lurker at the Threshold, Tales of H. P. Lovecraft: Major Works, More Annotated H. P. Lovecraft, The Shadow Out of Time.*

Maturin, Charles Robert. *Melmoth the Wanderer.*

Morrison, Robert, and Chris Baldick (editors). *The Vampyre and Other Tales of the Macabre.*

Poe, Edgar Allan. *Edgar Allan Poe: Selected Tales, Selected Tales, Thirty-two Stories.*

Polidori, John. *The Vampyre.*

Shelley, Mary. *Frankenstein.*

Stevenson, Robert Louis. *Dr. Jekyll and Mr. Hyde.*

Stoker, Bram. *Best Ghost and Horror Stories.*

Stoker, Bram. *Dracula, Midnight Tales, The Jewel of Seven Stars.*

Walpole, Horace. *The Castle of Otranto.*

Wells, H. G. *The Invisible Man.*

Wharton, Edith. *The Ghost Stories of Edith Wharton.*

Wilde, Oscar. *The Picture of Dorian Gray.*

Detective Fiction

The following titles feature detectives, police officers on criminal investigations, private investigators, and plot lines that emphasize the discovery of a crime. These will appeal to readers of detective fiction, as well as to horror fans who enjoy a good mystery being solved.

Adrian, Jack (editor). *Twelve Tales of Murder.*

Askew, Alice, and Claude Askew. *Aylmer Vance: Ghost-Seer.*

Aubert, Brigitte. *Death from the Woods* [*La mort des bois*].

Bacon-Smith, Camille. *Eyes of the Daemon, Eyes of the Empress, The Face of Time.*

Barlog, J. M. *Dark Side: The Haunting, Red Hearts.*

Blackwood, Algernon. *The Complete John Silence Stories.*

Bloch, Robert. *Psycho, Psycho House.*

Bonansinga, Jay R. *Head Case.*

Bradbury, Ray *A Graveyard for Lunatics: Another Tale of Two Cities.*

Campbell, Ramsey *Ancient Images II, The Doll Who Ate His Mother.*

Clifford, Emmett. *Night Whispers: A Story of Evil.*

Collins, Max Allan, and Barbara Collins. *Regeneration.*

Collins, Wilkie. *Wilkie Collins: The Complete Shorter Fiction.*

Connolly, John. *Every Dead Thing.*

Cross, Quentin. *The Witch Rising.*

Darnton, John. *The Experiment.*

Deaver, Jeffrey *The Coffin Dancer.*

Driver, Lee. *Full Moon, Bloody Moon: A Chase Dagger Mystery.*

Elrod, P. N. The Vampire Files Series.

Gorman, Ed. *Cold Blue Midnight, Daughter of Darkness.*

Grant, Charles. The Black Oak Series.

Hamilton, Laurell K. *Bloody Bones, Burnt Offerings, Guilty Pleasures.*

Hardy, Robin and Anthony Shaffer. *The Wickerman.*

Harris, Thomas. *The Silence of the Lambs.*

Hill, William. *California Ghosting.*

Hodgson, William Hope. *Gothic Horror: The Ghost Pirates and Carnacki the Ghost Finder.*

Hoffman, Barry. *Born Bad*, The Hungry Eyes Series.

Hopkins, Brian A. *The Licking Valley Coon Hunters Club.*

Jones, Stephen (editor) *Dark Detectives: Adventures of the Supernatural Sleuths.*

Ketchum, Jack. *The Lost.*

King, Stephen. *Bag of Bones , The Tommyknockers, The Dark Half.*

Koontz, Dean *The Bad Place, Dark Fall, The Face of Fear, Fear Nothing, Hide-away, Lightning, Shattered, The Voice of the Night.*

Lauria, Frank. *Raga Six.*

Le Fanu, Joseph Sheridan. *Carmilla.*

Levin, Ira. *The Stepford Wives.*

LeRoux, Gaston. *The Phantom of the Opera.*

Masters, Paul. *Meca and the Black Oracle.*

Matheson, Richard. *Now You See It.*

Mooney, Chris. *Deviant Ways.*

Prescott, Michael. *Stealing Faces.*

Pronzini, Bill. *The Tormentor.*

Randisi, Robert J. The In the Shadow of the Arch Series.

Rickman, Phil. *The Chalice, The Wine of Angels.*

Robinson, Frank M. *Waiting.*

Slade, Michael. The Headhunter Series.

Starling, Boris. *Messiah, Storm.*

Stephens, John Richard (editor). *Into the Mummy's Tomb.*

Stevenson, Robert Louis. *Dr. Jeykll and Mr. Hyde.*

Straczynski, J. Michael. *Tribulations.*

Straub, Peter. *KoKo, The Hellfire Club, The Throat.*

Sullivan, Mark T. *Ghost Dance.*

Swiniarski, S. A. *The Flesh, the Blood, and the Fire.*

Taylor, Karen E. *Blood Secrets.*

Tomasso, Phillip III. *Third Ring.*

Weinberg, Robert. *Dial Your Dreams.*

Wooley, John, and Ron Wolfe. *Old Fears.*

Wright, T. M. *Sleepeasy.*

Gentle Reads

The following titles refer to books that emphasize the subtler features of horror, rather than violence and gore, and they will appeal to readers with those preferences, as well as to fans of gentle reads.

Amis, Kingsley. *The Green Man.*

Aubert, Brigitte. *Death from the Woods.*

Austen, Jane. *Northanger Abbey.*

Benson, E. F. *The Terror By Night, The Passenger.*

Bergstrom, Elaine. *The Door Through Washington Square.*

Bierce, Ambrose. *The Moonlight Road and Other Ghost and Horror Stories.*

Blackwood, Algernon. *The Complete John Silence Stories.*

Braddon, M[ary] E[lizabeth]. *The Cold Embrace and Other Ghost Stories.*

Campbell, Ramsey. *Ghosts and Grisly Things, The One Safe Place.*

Chetwin, Grace. *Deathwindow.*

Cole, Alonzo Deen. *The Witch's Tale.*

Coleman, Christopher K. *Ghosts and Haunts of the Civil War.*

Collins, Wilkie. *Wilkie Collins: The Complete Shorter Fiction.*

Copper, Basil. *Whispers in the Night: Stories of the Mysterious and the Macabre.*

Crain, Paulette. *De Lore's Confession.*

Doyle, Arthur Conan. *Tales of Unease.*

Earhart, Rose. *Dorcas Good: The Diary of a Salem Witch, Salem's Ghosts.*

Fitzhugh, Pat. *The Bell Witch Haunting: An Historical and Modern-Day Account of the Most Terrifying Legend in American History.*

Fowler, Christopher. *Spanky.*

Gioia, Dana. *Nosferatu: An Opera Libretto.*

Golden, Christopher. *Strangewood.*

Haining, Peter (editor). *The Mammoth Book of Haunted House Stories, The Mammoth Book of 20th Century Ghost Stories.*

Hardy, Robin and Anthony Shaffer. *The Wicker Man.*

Hawkes, Judith. *The Heart of a Witch.*

Hays, Clark and Kathleen McFall. *The Cowboy and the Vampire.*

Hoogson, Sheila. *The Fellow Travellers.*

Hill, William. *California Ghosting.*

Hivert-Carthew, Annick. *Ghostly Lights: Great Lakes Lighthouse Tales of Terror, Ghostly Lights Return: More Great Lakes Lighthouse Fiends and Phantoms.*

James, Henry. *Ghost Stories of Henry James.*

James, M. R. *Casting the Runes, and Other Ghost Stories, Ghost Stories of An Antiquary.*

Jewett, Sarah Orne. *Lady Ferry, and Other Uncanny People.*

Kemske, Floyd. *Labor Day, The Virtual Boss.*

King, Stephen. *Bag of Bones, Dolores Claiborne, The Girl Who Loved Tom Gordon, The Green Mile.*

Kipling, Rudyard. *The Mark of the Beast and Other Horror Tales.*

Klavan, Andrew. *The Uncanny.*

Koontz, Dean. *Ticktock.*

Lamb, Hugh (editor). *A Bottomless Grave and Other Victorian Tales of Terror.*

Le Fanu, Joseph Sheridan. *Green Tea and Other Ghost Stories, In a Glass Darkly.*

Lortz, Richard. *Bereavements.*

Matheson, Richard. *The Incredible Shrinking Man, Stir of Echoes.*

McFarland, Dennis. *A Face at the Window.*

Nicholson, Scott. *Thank You for the Flowers: Stories of Suspense and Imagination.*

Polidori, John. *The Vampyre.*

Recknor, Ellen. *Prophet Annie: Being the Recently Discovered Memoir of Annie Pinkerton Boone Newcastle Dearborn, Prophet and Seer.*

Roberts, Nancy. *Haunted Houses: Chilling Tales From American Homes.*

Salamanca. J. R. *Lilith: A Novel of One Woman's Electrifying Obsession.*

Sapin, Jean. *Gift Giver.*

Searcy, David. *Ordinary Horror.*

Stoker, Bram. *Best Ghost and Horror Stories, Midnight Tales.*

Vizenore, Gerald. *Chancers.*

Wharton, Edith. *The Ghost Stories of Edith Wharton.*

Wheeler, Robert E. *Travel Many Roads.*

Williamson, J. N. *Affinity.*

Romance

The following titles contain love stories and romantic heroes and heroines. They will appeal to readers of romance fiction, particularly fans of bodice rippers, as well as to horror fans who enjoy eroticism and a love story.

Arthur, Keri. *Dancing with the Devil.*

Borchardt, Alice. *The Silver Wolf* ; *Night of the Wolf.*

Boyd, Donna. *The Passion* ; *The Promise.*

Crain, Paulette. *De Lore's Confession.*

Devlin, Serena. *The Red Witch.*

DuMaurier, Daphne. *Rebecca.*

Ellis, Monique, Sara Blayne, and Janice Bennett (editors). *Lords of the Night.*

Gideon, Nancy. *Midnight Enchantment, Midnight Gamble.*

Hays, Clark and Kathleen McFall. *The Cowboy and the Vampire.*

Kilpatrick, Nancy. *Child of the Night, Dracul: An Eternal Love Story.*

Lord, David Thomas. *Bound in Blood.*

Moore, Elaine. *Madonna of the Dark.*

Parker, Lara. *Dark Shadows: Angélique's Descent.*

Roycraft, Jaye. *Double Image.*

Taylor, Karen E. *Blood Secrets, Bitter Blood, Blood Ties.*

Thorne, Tamara. *Candle Bay.*

Western

The following titles feature Western settings and cowboys or Western pioneers, and they will appeal to readers of Westerns, as well as to horror fans who enjoy Westerns.

Bovberg, Jason, and Kirk Whitman (editors). *Skull Full of Spurs: A Roundup of Weird Westerns.*

Hill, William. *California Ghosting.*

Recknor, Ellen. *Prophet Annie: Being the Recently Discovered Memoir of Annie Pinkerson Boone Newcastle Dearborn, Prophet and Seer.*

Appendix B

Collection Development: A Core List

Of course, the first step in building any horror fiction collection in any library, be it a public, academic, or even a school library, is collection development. Although it is the goal of collection development to meet the information needs of every user of the community, this is not usually realized due to financial constraints and the diversity of user information needs, especially when we are speaking of a user community as small as horror fiction fans. Yet conscientious collection development officers must strive to provide the greatest number of resources to meet recreational needs of the user community. To this end, we hope that the second edition of *Hooked on Horror: A Guide to Reading Interests in the Genre* can live up to the praise bestowed upon it in Joyce G. Saricks's *The Readers' Advisory Guide to Genre Fiction* (Chicago: ALA, 2001): "If I had to choose just one [reference source for horror], it would be *Hooked on Horror*, . . . a valuable resource that covers the history, subgenres, and themes, as well as core lists, award winners, and references to other genres with which Horror crosses over." To this end, we have attempted to make this edition of *Hooked on Horror* a work that will serve well as a primary resource for collection development or collection management officers when they seek to identify, evaluate, select, and ultimately acquire the library resources (e.g., print materials, audiovisual materials, electronic resources) for a community of horror fans.

Selection is at the heart of the collection development process. This core function builds the library's collection for any user community. Skill, knowledge, and the right tools are required to select appropriate library materials that meet the needs of patrons who are interested in horror fiction and nonfiction. The challenge is to select core works by benchmark authors, so that a balanced collection that meets the needs of the largest portion of the horror user community can be created. In this appendix we limit the material format to print materials, namely books, and by extension, audiovisual materials, as periodicals and electronic and online resources are enumerated in various chapters of *Hooked on Horror*. Despite the popularity and easy access of online information, books remain the cornerstone of any public, academic, and school library.

Considering that there are so many well-written works of horror fiction being published yearly by both large and independent presses, and that each library's patrons will have their own set of wants when it comes to the horror genre, we cannot help but be hesitant to publish a core list of horror titles for libraries. Nonetheless, we felt it might be helpful to collection development officers if we were to include in this appendix a list of important titles and authors that no library developing a horror fiction section should be without. Of course the classics, such as Bram Stoker's *Dracula*, Mary Shelley' s *Frankenstein*, Poe's collected works, and Nathaniel Hawthorne's *The House of the Seven Gables,* are included here, but so are works by important modern writers, such as Ramsey Campbell, Stephen King, Ira Levin, Joyce Carol Oates, Kim Newman, and Anne Rice. In addition, high-quality works that are destined to become new classics, by little known writers such as Tananarive Due, Bentley Little, and Richard Lortz, are also identified here. In essence, the lists in this appendix combine those items that are absolutely necessary to any good horror collection with those works that we thought deserved special praise because of their quality.

In short, readers will find in this core list mostly classics and critically acclaimed works, along with some "modern" classics (works chosen based on a combination of critical acclaim and our own opinions). The writers and series lists are informed almost solely by the classics, works that virtually all people knowledgeable in the genre would suggest. Finally, the nonfiction list contains all benchmark texts.

The category "Individual Works" covers important fictional monographs by writers who are known for possibly one or two works, and also contains scholarship and reference. The second category, "Authors," lists those writers whose contributions to the genre are so extensive that it would have been impractical to list all their important works. Virtually everything written by these writers belongs on any good horror fiction core list, because patrons will ask for them. Finally, the category "Series" lists those series in the genre that belong in any core collection. In a few cases, such as with Anne Rice, there was some overlap between single works and series, and we avoided reproducing titles in such cases. These writers have produced not only genre defining series works but also an admirable body of horror fiction.

Individual Works

Classics

1. Benson, E. F. *The Passenger*
2. Benson, E. F. *The Terror by Night*
3. Bierce, Ambrose. *The Moonlit Road, and Other Ghost and Horror Stories*
4. Blackwood, Algernon. *The Complete John Silence Stories*
5. Bronte, Emily. *Wuthering Heights*
6. Collins, Wilkie. *Wilkie Collins: The Complete Shorter Fiction*
7. DuMaurier, Daphne. *Rebecca*
8. Hawthorne, Nathaniel. *The House of the Seven Gables*
9. Hodgson, William Hope. *The House on the Borderland*
10. James, Henry. *Ghost Stories of Henry James*
11. James, M. R. *Casting the Runes*

12. James, M. R. *Ghost Stories of an Antiquary*
13. Le Fanu, Joseph Sheridan. *In a Glass Darkly*
14. Le Fanu, Joseph Sheridan. *Carmilla*
15. Lewis, Matthew. *The Monk*
16. Maturin, Charles Robert. *Melmoth the Wanderer*
17. Poe, Edgar Allan. *Thirty-Two Stories*
18. Shelley, Mary. *Frankenstein*
19. Stoker, Bram. *Dracula*
20. Walpole, Horace. *The Castle of Otranto*
21. Wilde, Oscar. *The Picture of Dorian Gray*

Modern Classics

22. Amis, Kingsley. *The Green Man*
23. Blatty, William Peter. *The Exorcist*
24. Bloch, Robert. *American Gothic*
25. Bloch, Robert. *Psycho*
26. Bradbury, Ray. *The Illustrated Man*
27. Campbell, Ramsey. *Alone With the Horrors*
28. Campbell, Ramsey. *The Face That Must Die*
29. Campbell, Ramsey. *Nazareth Hill*
30. Campbell, Ramsey. *The One Safe Place*
31. Copper, Basil. *Whispers in the Night*
32. Etchison, Dennis. *Talking in the Dark*
33. Hardy, Robin, and Anthony Shaffer. *The Wicker Man*
34. Harris, Thomas. *The Silence of the Lambs*
35. Jackson, Shirley. *The Haunting of Hill House*
36. Jackson, Shirley. *The Lottery and Other Stories*
37. King, Stephen. *Bag of Bones*
38. King, Stephen. *Carrie*
39. King, Stephen. *The Shining*
40. King, Stephen. *The Stand*
41. Koontz, Dean. *Demon Seed*
42. Koontz, Dean. *Dragon's Tears*
43. Koontz, Dean. *Hideaway*
44. Leiber, Fritz, *The Conjure Wife*
45. Leiber, Fritz. *Our Lady of Darkness*
46. Levin, Ira. *Rosemary's Baby*
47. Levin, Ira. *The Stepford Wives*
48. Ligotti, Thomas. *The Nightmare Factory*
49. Lortz, Richard. *Dracula's Children*
50. Lortz, Richard. *Lovers Living, Lovers Dead*

51. Lovecraft, H. P. *The Shadow Out of Time*
52. Lovecraft, H. P. *Tales of H. P. Lovecraft: Major Works*
53. Masterton, Graham. *The Manitou*
54. Matheson, Richard. *I Am Legend*
55. Matheson, Richard. *The Incredible Shrinking Man*
56. Morrison, Toni. *Beloved*
57. Nolan, William F. *William F. Nolan's Dark Universe*
58. Simmons, Dan. *Carrion Comfort*
59. Siodmak, Curt. *Donovan's Brain*
60. Straub, Peter. *Ghost Story*
61. Straub, Peter, and Stephen King. *The Talisman*
62. Strieber, Whitley. *The Hunger*
63. Wandrei, Donald. *Don't Dream*
64. Wells, H. G. *The Invisible Man*
65. Wooley, John, and Ron Wolfe. *Old Fears*

Our Picks

66. Braunbeck, Gary A., and Alan M. Clark. *Escaping Purgatory*
67. Brite, Poppy Z., ed. *Love in Vein*
68. Clark, Simon. *Blood Crazy*
69. Clark, Simon. *Darkness Demands*
70. Collins, Nancy A. *Sunglasses After Dark*
71. Cullen, Mitch. *Tideland*
72. Dobyns, Stephen. *Boy in the Water*
73. Due, Tananarive. *The Living Blood*
74. Due, Tananarive. *My Soul to Keep*
75. Elrod, P. N., ed. *Dracula in London*
76. Evans, Gloria. *Meh'yam*
77. Fowler, Christopher. *Spanky*
78. Goingback, Owl. *Crota*
79. Harris, Thomas. *Hannibal*
80. Hays, Clark, and Kathleen McFall. *The Cowboy and the Vampire*
81. Holder, Nancy. *Dead in the Water*
82. Hopkins, Brian A. *The Licking Valley Coon Hunters' Club*
83. Jefferson, Jemiah. *Voice of the Blood*
84. Kemske, Floyd. *Human Resources*
85. Klavan, Andrew. *The Uncanny*
86. Koja, Kathe. *The Cypher*
87. Laidlaw, Marc. *The 37ᵗʰ Mandala*
88. Lebbon, Tim. *The Nature of Balance*
89. Little, Bentley. *The Association*

90. Little, Bentley. *The Store*
91. Nicholson, Scott. *Thank You for the Flowers*
92. Oates, Joyce Carol. *Zombie*
93. Rice, Anne. *Violin*
94. Searcy, David. *Ordinary Horror*
95. Shirley, John. *Black Butterflies*
96. Shirley, John. *Darkness Divided*
97. Starling, Boris. *The Storm*
98. Straub, Peter. *Mr. X*
99. Wooley, John. *Awash in the Blood*

Authors

1. Ambrose Bierce
2. Ramsey Campbell
3. M. R. James
4. Stephen King
5. Dean Koontz
6. Ira Levin
7. Bentley Little
8. H. P. Lovecraft
9. Arthur Machen
10. Barbara Michaels
11. Edgar Allan Poe
12. Anne Rice
13. Phil Rickman
14. Dan Simmons
15. Peter Straub

Series

1. Nancy A. Collins, The Sonja Blue novels
2. Ellen Datlow and Terri Windling, eds., *The Year's Best Fantasy and Horror* (Annual)
3. Charles Grant, The Millenium Quartet
4. Laurell K. Hamilton, The Anita Blake, Vampire Hunter Series
5. Tom Holland, The Lord of the Dead Series
6. Kim Newman, The Anno Dracula Series
7. Anne Rice, The Mayfair Witch Series
8. Anne Rice, The Vampire Chronicles
9. Michael Romkey, The I, Vampire Series

10. Chelsea Quinn Yarbro, The Saint-Germaine Chronicles

Nonfiction

1. Ashley, Mike. *Who's Who in Horror and Fantasy*
2. Barron, Neil. *Horror Literature: A Reader's Guide*
3. Barron, Neil. *What Fantastic Fiction Do I Read Next?*
4. Day, William Patrick. *In the Circles of Fear and Desire*
5. Heller, Terry. *The Delights of Terror*
6. Jancovich, Mark. *Horror*
7. King, Stephen. *Danse Macabre*
8. Lovecraft, H. P. *The Annotated Supernatural Horror in Literature*
9. Sullivan, Jack. *Elegant Nightmares*
10. Skal, David J. *The Monster Show*

Appendix C

True Ghost Tales

In this appendix, we include books that do not belong comfortably elsewhere in this guide: collections, retellings, and critical interpretations of true ghost stories from around the United States. We include them in this edition because they exemplify the range of the genre, and because they resemble the campfire tales told on hiking excursions and campouts and will therefore greatly appeal to readers who enjoy gentle reads and traditional ghost fictions.

Carroll, Rick. Hawaii's Best Spooky Tales Series.

Hawaii's Best Spooky Tales: More True Local Spine-Tinglers. *Honolulu: Bess Press, 1996.* Author and travel writer Rick Carroll is the collector of *Hawaii's Best Spooky Tales*, one of Hawaii's most popular book series. The original is Carroll's first of five collections of true accounts of inexplicable encounters in the Hawaiian Islands.

Hawaii's Best Spooky Tales 2: More True Local Spine-Tinglers. *Honolulu: Bess Press, 1998.* In this second of five volumes, Rick Carroll collects more familiar Hawaiian ghost stories. Carroll includes "The Guide to Spooky Places." **Appeal:** Popular.

Hawaii's Best Spooky Tales 3: More True Local Spine-Tinglers. *Honolulu: Bess Press, 1999.* In this third of five volumes, Rick Carroll collects more familiar Hawaiian ghost stories. **Appeal:** Popular.

Hawaii's Best Spooky Tales 4: More True Local Spine-Tinglers. *Honolulu: Bess Press, 2000.* In this fourth of five volumes, Rick Carroll collects more familiar Hawaiian ghost stories. **Appeal:** Popular.

Lamb, John J.

San Diego Specters. *San Diego: Sunbelt Publication, 1999.* Lamb notes briefly his findings from his investigations of seventeen haunted dwellings in San Diego county. The text includes photos. **Appeal:** Popular.

The Lone Pine Publishing Ghost Story Series. Various Authors.

Christensen, Jo-Anne.

Ghost Stories of Illinois. *Edmonton, Alb.: Lone Pine Publishing, 2000*. Christensen collects information and snippets of interviews pertaining to ghost and poltergeist sightings in Illinois. Stories include that of Al Capone being haunted by his victims, as well as tales of Abe Lincoln's ghost. Cities from which stories are taken include Chicago, Decatur, Joliet, and Normal. **Appeal:** Popular.

Ghost Stories of Texas. *Edmonton, Alb.: Lone Pine Publishing, 2001*. Christensen collects information and snippets of interviews pertaining to ghost and poltergeist sightings in Texas, including a tale of spirits that defend The Alamo in San Antonio. Cities from which stories are taken include San Antonio, Houston, Austin, and Killeen. **Appeal:** Popular.

Smith, Barbara.

Ghost Stories of Manitoba. *Edmonton, Alb.: Lone Pine Publishing, 1998*. Smith collects information and snippets of interviews pertaining to ghost and poltergeist sightings in and around the Manitoba area. **Appeal:** Popular.

Ghost Stories of British Columbia. *Edmonton, Alb.: Lone Pine Publishing, 1999*. Smith collects information and snippets of interviews pertaining to ghost and poltergeist sightings, as well as UFO sightings and diverse paranormal occurrences, in and around Victoria and other towns in British Columbia. **Appeal:** Popular.

Ghost Stories of the Rocky Mountains. *Edmonton, Alb.: Lone Pine Publishing, 1999*. Smith collects information and snippets of interviews pertaining to ghost and poltergeist sightings, including those in and around the cities of Denver, Butte, and Santa Fe. **Appeal:** Popular.

Ghost Stories of Hollywood. *Edmonton, Alb.: Lone Pine Publishing, 2000*. Smith collects information and snippets of interviews pertaining to ghost and poltergeist sightings in and around the Hollywood, California, area, including Marilyn Monroe sightings and tales of the revenant that haunts the giant Hollywood sign. **Appeal:** Popular.

Ghost Stories of Washington. *Edmonton, Alb.: Lone Pine Publishing, 2000*. Smith collects information and snippets of interviews pertaining to ghost and poltergeist sightings in and around the Seattle area, including the Underground Seattle tour. **Appeal:** Popular.

Norman, Michael, and Beth Scott.

Haunted America. *New York: St. Martin's Press, 2000*. Arranged by state and province, Norman and Scott chronicle over seventy tales of documented hauntings, from tales of battlefield specters at Little Big Horn to reports of a ghostly projectionist in a Florida movie palace. These ghost histories are based on the authors' interviews with witnesses, and accounts from archives and newspapers will appeal to the ghost story aficionado of any age range. **Appeal:** Popular.

Historic Haunted America. *New York: Tor, 2000*. Norman and Scott collect some of the most compelling true ghost stories from North America. These tales are fascinating, and they are all documented, based on eyewitness testimony. **Appeal:** Popular.

Taylor, Troy.

Haunted New Orleans. *Alton, Ill.: Whitechapel Production Press, 2000*. Taylor collects various information about the supernatural in the Big Easy, including stories about Marie Laveau, Jackson Square, and the St. Louis Cathedral. **Appeal:** Popular.

Subject Index

Index of Authors and Titles

Short Story Index